085199
19.10.70

# DAVID GARRICK

By the same author

# GARRICK with the Bust of Shakespeare.

## By *Thomas Gainsborough* ($91\frac{1}{2}'' \times 59\frac{1}{2}''$)

Painted for Stratford-upon-Avon new Town Hall, 1769. Gainsborough was paid, by the Corporation, £63 for this portrait, which was considered by Mrs Garrick the best likeness of her husband. Horace Walpole identified the temple and bridge in the background as that at Prior Park, near Bath, the residence until 1769 of Garrick's friend William Warburton, Bishop of Gloucester. The original picture was destroyed by fire at Stratford-upon-Avon, 1946.

Engraved by Valentine Green, April 2, 1769.

*Reproduced by kind permission of the Governors, the Shakespeare Memorial Theatre, Picture Gallery and Museum, Stratford-upon-Avon.*

# DAVID GARRICK

CAROLA OMAN

HODDER AND STOUGHTON

WESTFIELD
UNW.
LONDON
COLLEGE

Copyright © 1958 by Carola Oman

*Printed in Great Britain
for Hodder & Stoughton, Limited,
by Richard Clay and Company, Ltd.,
Bungay, Suffolk*

# CONTENTS

# GARRICK PEDIGREE

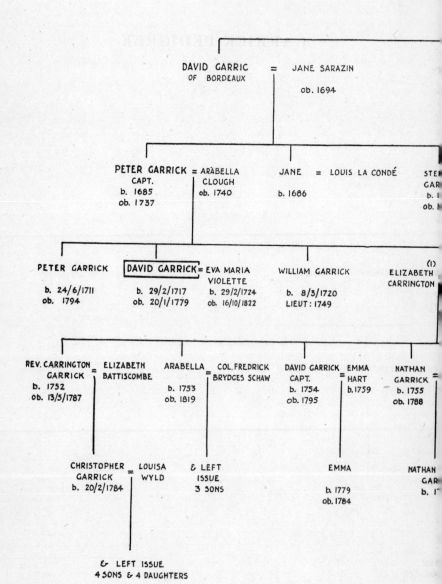

DAVID GARRIC = JANE SARAZIN
OF BORDEAUX
                    ob. 1694

PETER GARRICK = ARÀBELLA      JANE = LOUIS LA CONDÉ      STE
CAPT.           CLOUGH                                   GAR
b. 1685         ob. 1740       b. 1686                   b. I
ob. 1737                                                 ob. I

PETER GARRICK   DAVID GARRICK = EVA MARIA    WILLIAM GARRICK      (1)
                                VIOLETTE                     ELIZABETH
b. 24/6/1711    b. 29/2/1717    b. 29/2/1724  b. 8/3/1720    CARRINGTON
ob. 1794        ob. 20/1/1779   ob. 16/10/1822 LIEUT: 1749

REV. CARRINGTON = ELIZABETH    ARABELLA _ COL.FREDRICK   DAVID GARRICK EMMA    NATHAN
GARRICK        BATTISCOMBE            BRYDGES SCHAW      CAPT.    = HART   GARRICK =
b. 1752                         b. 1753                 b. 1754    b.1759  b. 1755
ob. 13/5/1787                   ob. 1819                ob. 1795           ob. 1788

CHRISTOPHER _ LOUISA    & LEFT                           EMMA            NATHAN
GARRICK       WYLD      ISSUE                                            GAR
b. 20/2/1784            3 SONS                           b. 1779         b. I
                                                        ob. 1784

& LEFT ISSUE
4 SONS & 4 DAUGHTERS

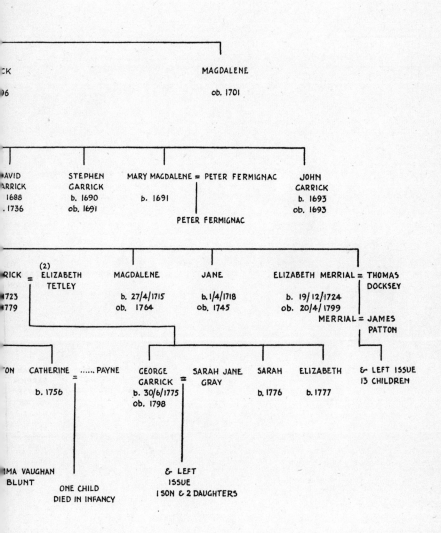

MAGDALENE

ob. 1701

| ːK | | | | |
|---|---|---|---|---|
| ʻ6 | | | | |

| ʻAVID ːARRICK 1688 . 1736 | STEPHEN GARRICK b. 1690 ob. 1691 | MARY MAGDALENE = PETER FERMIGNAC b. 1691 | | JOHN GARRICK b. 1693 ob. 1693 |

PETER FERMIGNAC

| ːRICK = ʻ723 ʻ779 | (2) ELIZABETH TETLEY | MAGDALENE b. 27/4/1715 ob. 1764 | JANE b. 1/4/1718 ob. 1745 | ELIZABETH MERRIAL = THOMAS DOCKSEY b. 19/12/1724 ob. 20/4/1799 |

MERRIAL = JAMES PATTON

| ʻON | CATHERINE b. 1756 | ...... PAYNE | GEORGE GARRICK b. 30/6/1775 ob. 1798 | SARAH JANE GRAY | SARAH b. 1776 | ELIZABETH b. 1777 | & LEFT ISSUE 13 CHILDREN |
|---|---|---|---|---|---|---|---|

| ʻMA VAUGHAN BLUNT | ONE CHILD DIED IN INFANCY | | & LEFT ISSUE 1 SON & 2 DAUGHTERS | | | | |

ʻSSUE
ʻAUGHTER

# ILLUSTRATIONS

IV. Garrick as Ranger in " The Suspicious Husband ".
   $(27\frac{3}{4}'' \times 35\frac{1}{2}''.)$                     *Facing page* 96
   *By Francis Hayman.*

Hayman was the principal scene-painter at Drury Lane, in the
early days of Garrick's career there.   Garrick created the part
of Ranger, in Benjamin Hoadly's comedy, on December 4, 1747,
and appeared in it last on May 23, 1773.   Another version of this
conversation piece, of which this reproduction is a detail, is the
property of the Garrick Club.
*Reproduced by kind permission of the Trustees, the London Museum.*

V. David Garrick and His Wife.            *Facing page* 154
   *By William Hogarth.*

This picture, begun in 1752, was sold on the death of Mrs Garrick
seventy-one years later, for £75 11s. to Mr Locker of Greenwich
Hospital.   It has changed hands only twice, as on Locker's death
it was bought by George IV and added to the Royal collection at
Windsor.   Hogarth evidently kept it unfinished in his studio
until 1757, when Dr John Hoadly wrote to Dr Thomas Warton,
on April 21, " Hogarth has got into portraits, and has his hands
full of business, and at a high price.   He has just finished a most
noble one of our sprightly friend David Garrick and his wife;
they are a fine contrast.   David is sitting at a table, smiling
thoughtfully; Madam is, archly enough, stealing away his pen."
The picture appeared in Christie's catalogue, June 23, 1823 as
" Portrait of Mr Garrick, seated at his writing table, composing
the prologue to ' Taste '; and of Mrs Garrick behind, interrupting his reverie; painted with great truth and spirit ".   " Taste ",
by Samuel Foote, was produced on January 11, 1752, and was
performed only seven times.
*Reproduced by gracious permission of Her Majesty the Queen.*

VI. Garrick Between Tragedy and Comedy.   (58" ×
   72".)                                    *Facing page* 222
   *By Sir Joshua Reynolds.*
   *Exhibited Society of Artists, 1762.*
   *Engraved by Edward Fisher, 1762.*

In January 1765, Garrick wrote to his brother George, to ask him to
send " prints " of every available picture of him by Reynolds,
Zoffany, Benjamin Wilson, and Liotard which had been
" scraped ".   He needed them for farewell gifts in Paris after his
Tour of Europe.   The sequel was unexpected.   In the following
year, George Colman was in Paris, and wrote to him, " There hang

out here, in every street, pirated prints of Reynolds' picture of
you, which are underwritten, ' L'Homme entre le Vice et la
Vertu '."
*Reproduced by kind permission of the Lord Rothschild.*

VII. Shakespeare's Temple and Portraits of Mr and Mrs
Garrick Resting in the Steps of the Portico, with
a Favourite Dog in the Front Ground, and a View
of a Reach of the River.          *Facing page* 260

*By Johann Zoffany.*

Garrick first made the acquaintance of Zoffany when he was engaged
in the studio of Benjamin Wilson, painting draperies etc., about
1759. Wilson was exceedingly jealous of Garrick's patronage of
his employee, and wrote in complaint: " On coming to town this
morning, I could not resist the temptation to inquire after my
very worthy brother artist, Zoffani. But, alas! how unlucky, he
had left his work and was gone to breakfast, loaded with his
pencils etc. in an invisible conveyance. As you will chance to
see him before I shall, you will oblige him by desiring him to
fulfill his engagements, and act, if he can, like an honest man."
Garrick replied that Mr Wilson " need not employ his runners and
spies to discover what Zoffani is doing at my house; it will save
some expense in feeing them, and save themselves from a ducking
if they should be caught near our part of the river ". This
picture was bought at the sale at Christie's on the death of Mrs
Garrick, for £28 7s. by Mr Lambton, and descended by inheritance to the present owner.
*Reproduced by kind permission of the Earl of Durham.*

VIII. Mr and Mrs Garrick taking Tea upon the Lawn of
their Villa at Hampton.          *Facing page* 310

*By Johann Zoffany.*

This picture was bought at the sale at Christie's in 1823, by Mr
Lambton, for £49 7s. and has descended by inheritance to the
present owner. The catalogue indentifies the figure to whom
Garrick is offering a cup of tea as " Mr George Garrick, angling "
and the large clergyman as " Mr Bowden ".
*Reproduced by kind permission of the Earl of Durham.*

IX. Garrick as Abel Drugger in Act 2, Scene VI of
Ben Jonson's " The Alchymist ".          *Facing page* 345

*By Johann Zoffany.*

Garrick first appeared in this part on March 21, 1743, and played it
for the last time on April 11, 1776, in his farewell season. " Last
night I played Abel Drugger for the last time. I thought the

audience were cracked, and they almost turned my brain." Dr
Johnson related that a Lichfield tradesman, who was urged by
Peter Garrick to witness a performance by his famous brother,
when in London, reported on his return: " Well, by God!  Mr
Garrick, though he is your brother, he is one of the shabbiest,
meanest, most pitiful hounds I ever saw in the whole course of
my life."

Detail, engraved from a conversation piece, which includes the
figures of Burton as Subtle and Palmer as Face, by John Dixon,
1771.

There are versions of the picture in the Garrick Club and Lord
Durham's collection.

*Reproduced by kind permission of the Trustees, the Victoria and Albert
Museum, from the engraving in the Enthoven Theatre Collection.*

# PROLOGUE

The news that Garrick was going to retire startled Europe in the spring of 1776. People who had never seen him, and still more people who had, hurried from all over the British Isles, and in parties from Paris, to attend at least one of his farewell performances. Only those who had failed to obtain admittance were disappointed. He was sixty, and his powers appeared unimpaired. For another two and a half years he was a familiar figure of the English social scene. His death, after a very short final illness, took all but a small circle by surprise.

He had been far more than Britain's first actor. Until six months before he ceased to perform, he had been also manager of Drury Lane Theatre. He had written twenty successful plays, re-written or adapted many more (including nine by Shakespeare); he had never ceased to produce poems, songs, prologues and epilogues. A biographer of large stature was required. The obvious choice was Samuel Johnson, who had instructed him in his schooldays, and had never lost touch with him. But after a year there appeared a two volume publication, Memoirs of the Life of David Garrick Esq, by Thomas Davies. It was dedicated to Sheridan, and made acknowledgements for encouragement and information to Johnson. Davies stated that Johnson had accepted the suggestion of many friends that he should write the life of Garrick but had said that Mrs Garrick must invite him. His message had been carried to the widow by Garrick's favourite nephew and namesake, but she had given no invitation or sign of approval. She had at this date a most possessive friend in close attendance. Miss Hannah More perfectly recollected the answer Garrick had made when she had asked him, hardly tactfully, " Why Johnson was so often harsh and unkind in his speeches, both to and of him? " Garrick, who was accused of vanity, had mildly replied, " It is very natural. Is it not to be *expected he should be angry, that I, who have so much less merit than he, should have had so much greater success?"* Johnson, decided Miss More, *"with all his genius had no taste for Garrick's acting; and with all his virtues, was envious of his riches"*.

Tom Davies, who was destined to descend to history primarily as the bookseller in whose shop Boswell first met Johnson, possessed as a biographer all the disadvantages which Mrs Garrick may have attributed to Johnson, and nothing like the prestige and power. But he had been a member of Drury Lane Company and an intimate friend, and until his life of Garrick was given to a hungry public, nothing had appeared beyond a flood of elegiac verse, and expanded obituary notices in leading magazines. Davies's work passed into four editions, and brought him solvency and reputation. In the final chapter, he had dealt firmly with the persistent rumour that Garrick had been avaricious. He had produced many instances of his humanity, benevolence and charity. It was done in vain.

In *1785*, The Poetical Works of David Garrick Esq, in two volumes, was prefaced by an anonymous *"short account"* of his career. Dramatic Works, *similarly introduced,* followed, in three volumes, in *1798*. Both were incomplete. The world, both of the theatre and letters, was still thronged by chagrined persons whose acting or plays had not been appreciated by the greatest of actor-managers. Arthur Murphy, the next two-volume biographer, thought he had suffered in both capacities. Davies, who had been a sober Scotsman, had produced a readable narrative, rather racy in style. Some of Garrick's traditional gaiety seemed to have been bestowed upon him. Murphy, who was an ebullient Irishman, author of some spirited comedies, produced something pompous and lifeless. There was an ironical circumstance in that he had unblushingly *"lifted"* material from Davies, who had been notorious as a literary pirate. In his biography, Murphy had conformed perfunctorily to Davies's sketch of Garrick's character. It was in conversation, reported by Samuel Rogers, in his Table Talk that he undid, in a single sentence, Davies's efforts to correct one mistaken belief. *"Off the*

*stage," said Murphy, " he was a mean sneaking little fellow ".*
*He threw up his eyes, and hands, as he added, " But, on the*
*stage! Oh! my great God!" It confirmed previous com-*
*plaints; it was witty; it stuck.*

*After Murphy's publication in 1801, no biography of*
*Garrick was attempted for over thirty years. Until 1822, a*
*guardian angel with a flaming sword barred the doors of an*
*Eden. The widow of the Adelphi and Hampton still lived, in*
*two houses which were veritable Garrick Museums. She had*
*kept them unchanged, in furniture and decoration; she had*
*his books, his clothes, his silver, his pictures and, most valuable*
*of all to a biographer, his vast and characteristic correspond-*
*ence. Murphy's and Davies's works had, of necessity, been*
*almost entirely devoted to Garrick as actor, author and manager.*
*By the time that Mrs Garrick died, in her ninety-ninth year,*
*all persons who had known her husband in his prime were no*
*longer available. The Keeper of a department in the British*
*Museum could electrify the inhabitants of a stage-coach by*
*announcing that he had once seen Garrick. So he had, but he*
*had been nine years old. A few ladies, well-stricken in years,*
*cherished nursery-day memories of a Richard, or a Lear, who*
*had reduced them to strong hysterics. To convey horror had*
*been his* forte. *Nobody lived who had seen him as Romeo, or*
*Ranger; and he had himself instructed an actor who begged*
*to be allowed to play comedy, " No, no! You may humbug*
*the town some time longer as a tragedian, but comedy is a*
*serious thing."*

*Mrs Garrick died, and the floodgates opened, but slowly.*
*Garrick had ranked very high in his own day, as an author.*
*Johnson had said that " in the lighter kinds of poetry, in the*
*appendages of the drama, he was,* if not the first, in the very
first class ". *But his farces and comedies had been topical;*
*they were now neither quite period pieces nor suited to the taste*
*of the day. The catalogue of Garrick's library, sold by order*
*of his widow's executors, in April and May 1823, was im-*
*posing. It displayed him as a serious student of his pro-*
*fession and gave him an honourable place amongst bibliophiles.*

*John Forster, historian, playwright and biographer, bought*
*Garrick's private papers, and in 1831-1832 a selection was*

B

*published with a memoir by James Boaden, who had drawn some information from Mrs Garrick. His two quartos weigh thirteen pounds, they are without an index, and his few notes offer moralizations but no explanations. Some of the letters are placed in incorrect sequence, and misdated, and in the middle of the second volume, he blandly produces a bunch, some of importance, all undated, but mostly containing internal evidence as to date. For no discoverable reason, he chose to reproduce, mainly, letters to Garrick, and he eschewed almost every family and domestic letter. But his task had been hard. Forster's collection, which he left to the Victoria and Albert Museum, occupies about forty volumes. It has never been indexed, apart from a list of correspondents. It is the delight and despair of the Garrick biographer. Garrick was a torrential letter-writer, to his last days, and he kept drafts. The Theatrical Department of Harvard College has been assembling and editing for some twenty-eight years the collected letters of David Garrick. These include over thirteen hundred from about seventy-five manuscript sources, of which more than half have never been published. Of these only about two hundred and fifty were printed by Boaden.*

*The Forster Collection was not used by a biographer until* 1868, *when Percy Fitzgerald's* Life of David Garrick, *from* original family papers and numerous published and unpublished sources, *became at once a standard work. It was divided into two volumes and seven books, and chapters headed* The Playwrights, Hampton and its Circle, The Great Actors, Friends and Acquaintances *and* In the Green-Room, *indicate that no very strict attempt had been made to present events in chronological order. Even the revised 1899 edition has the most pitiful attempt at an index, and no references are offered. Fitzgerald's talent for research was far superior to his powers of deduction, but he was enthusiastic and supplied a long-felt want. Nothing on the same scale was ever afterwards attempted. Joseph Knight, author of the article on Garrick in the* Dictionary of National Biography, *published in 1894 a monograph which is strong on Garrick as actor and author, but often deteriorates into a mere catalogue of Drury Lane performances. Miss Margaret Barton, in 1948, stated*

*in the preface to her* Garrick *that her comparatively brief
survey was intended for the general reader. She referred
students to Knight, her bibliography, and two valuable works
dealing with separate aspects of Garrick's career.* These
were Garrick and his Circle, *produced in 1906 by Mrs Clement
Parsons, who had seen Sir Henry Irving's four grangerized
folios,* David Garrick, a memorial *and* David Garrick and
his French Friends, *by Frank Hedgcock, 1911.*

*From America have come four works of true scholarship, of
varying scope. In 1905, Professor George Pierce Baker
edited sixty-six unpublished Garrick letters, bought at Sotheby's
in 1899 by Mr J. H. Leigh. Professor David Mason Little
followed this, in 1930, with a further forty-four. Professor
R. C. Alexander in 1928 had edited the Paris 1751 Diary of*
David Garrick, *unknown to Knight and dismissed by Fitzgerald as lost. Until Professor Dougal MacMillan in 1938
produced* Drury Lane Calendar, 1747–1776, *students had
been dependent for details of the years of Garrick's management
on the third and fourth volumes of Genest's ten-volume* Account
of the English Stage from the Restoration to 1830, *published
in 1832. Professor MacMillan's compilation includes
glorious excerpts from the diaries of William Hopkins,
prompter at Drury Lane, and father-in-law of Kemble. This
book of reference is invaluable to the Garrick biographer, who
can work out from it where Garrick was, and why, on significant
dates.*

*The very small supply of lives of Garrick by no means
indicates lack of material. Anecdotes abound to an embarrassing degree. He met almost everyone prominent in his day in
the artistic, literary and social world. Many of his friends,
acquaintances and critics recorded their experiences vividly,
generally in memoirs remarkably vague as to dates. His name
never ceased to have magic, particularly for members of his
profession. Other giants arose in it, none, it was whispered,
superior to him in every respect. Two plays were written about
him. Three theatres and a London street were called after him.
In 1831, an uncle of Queen Victoria became patron of a Club
bearing his name which has numbered amongst its members
almost every great man connected with the English stage. He*

*had raised the status of the actor. He was a national monument. As years passed, the features of the idol became more and more indistinct. Some of the pictures of him were ludicrous. Some of the stories were not endearing. But he had been a man of extraordinary vitality. His legend survived.*

*The authorities, published and unpublished, on which the following text is founded, are stated in notes grouped at the end of the book, under reference numerals which correspond to those in the margins of the text.*

*The author wishes to record her gratitude to Lieut.-Colonel Rex Solly (great-great-grandson of Thomas Rackett, executor to Mrs. Garrick); to Mr Levi Fox, Director of Shakespeare's Birthplace Trust, Stratford-upon-Avon, and to Major H. B. Martindale, Curator, the Shakespeare Memorial Theatre Picture Gallery and Museum, Stratford-upon-Avon; to Sir Bronson Albery and to Commander Satterthwaite, Secretary of The Garrick Club; to Mr Arthur Wheen, Keeper of the Library, and Mr G. W. Nash, Keeper of the Enthoven Theatre Collection, Victoria and Albert Museum; to Mr Edward Croft Murray, Keeper of the Department of Prints and Drawings, British Museum; to Mr C. K. Adams, Director, The National Portrait Gallery, and to Miss Sybil Rosenfeld, Honorary Secretary, The Society for Theatre Research.*

*Acknowledgements to the many other people who have kindly shown her individual Garrick relics, or provided local information, have been made in the apposite notes.*

*C. O.*
*1954–1958*

# "FIRST, THE INFANT"

## 1717–1737

### I

HIS MAJESTY'S speech, upon opening Parliament in the third week of February 1717, dwelt with satisfaction upon the Treaty of Utrecht, " the happy consequences of which have already very sensibly appeared by the flourishing condition of our trade and credit ". George I had hoped that the putting down of the late Rebellion in Scotland (" the Pretender is actually Removed beyond the Alps ") might have so far secured the tranquillity of his kingdom as to justify him in a considerable reduction of the Forces. But the safety of his people was not as yet certain. Invasion still threatened. Soldiers and war-like supplies were still absolutely necessary for the defence 1 of the realm.

Home Defence and Invasion were always good cards in the hand of a recruiting officer, and a Lieutenant in Colonel James Tyrrell's Regiment of Dragoons, ordered from Lichfield to Hereford on this duty, took up his quarters in the Angel Inn quite cheerfully. Hereford boasted a romantic ruined castle, a stately cathedral, and town walls pierced by six old gates. Its streets were well paved, and handsome as to breadth and length; the river Wye was pronounced by Londoners as wide as the Thames—at least at Maidenhead. It was in flood now, and thick and yellow, but said to contain very fine salmon. The surrounding district was a promising recruiting ground, particularly in the dark months of winter. It was pre-eminently agricultural, rich in fields of wheat and barley, hop-gardens and cider orchards. It had always been of strategic importance, owing to its proximity to the Welsh marches. It produced a strong, solid type of young man.

Sergeants and men of a recruiting party were chosen, understandably, by reason of their *savoir-faire* and military bearing, and the officer in charge of Tyrrell's dragoons was undoubtedly a gentleman, and with very pleasing manners. Given a few more inches, he must have been the *beau idéal* of a dashing cavalryman, and fatal to the peace of mind of the spinsters of a cathedral city. But he was not quite tall enough, and he was very much married. His party included his lady, his Arabella. At first sight it seemed something inhuman to have brought her right across England in such weather,

but a second glance might have revealed the reason. The young ₂
couple were poor and much in love. They had been married ten
years, and the child to be born in the Angel Inn would not be their
first. They had already one at heel and one in arms—little Peter
and Magdalene.

The Angel was central. It stood on the corner of Maylord Street
and Widemarsh Street, the main road to Leominster and the North,
to Shrewsbury and Chester. It was a timber-framed, black-and-
white house, with big red-brick chimney-stacks, two steeply pitched
gables, three storeys and attics. Its casement windows were stone-
mullioned and in the centre of its façade on the main street there was
a cavernous entry, large enough for a coach to pass through. On the
side facing the lesser thoroughfare there were massive oak doors to
admit stores, shutters to the ground-floor windows which could be
let down to form drinking counters, and an attached outbuilding.
The Angel looked comfortable, as the better inns in a county town
usually were, since they were employed, not only by travellers, but
as courts by coroners and churchwardens, as an informal club by the
local gentry and, where their galleried courtyards were of sufficient
size, by strolling players. The new century had brought a great
increase of coach travel, and many of the new inns had been originally private houses. They had been modernized and given a lick of
paint, but they were picturesque and rambling. The best bedroom
on the first floor of the Angel had linen-fold panelling. Outside its
long windows of winking, diamond-paned, greenish glass, swinging
in every breeze, hung the inn sign, a rather worldly-looking depic-
tion of the Angel of the Salutation or Annunciation, descending from
heaven rapidly. Underneath, all day, traffic was continual, and in- ₃
side there was a warm hum of perpetual motion. A popular inn,
like one of His Majesty's ships, was never at peace in the twenty-four
hours. The kitchen fire was never let out. There were always fresh
arrivals. Dragoons, coachmen, postboys, grooms, drawers and
ostlers, scullions and barbers, went about their duty, or lounged and
laughed, and drank and ate, awaiting their calls. Chambermaids,
old and young, thin and fat, broke off their conversations to run to
answer bells.

On Tuesday, February 19, 1717, there was additional excuse for a
glass. The Lieutenant's lady, poor, delicate-looking young thing,
had done her duty, had given His Majesty another recruit. The
busy scene to which the young gentleman in the oak-chamber had
arrived, was a world in miniature, as good as a play. Nine days later
a small procession went to the nearby church of All Saints, a very
short journey, and after a grave and simple service, the Reverend H.

Lewis entered in his register of baptisms—

*4*          DAVID, son of Mr Peter and Arabella GARRICK.

A lively, dark-skinned, dark-eyed infant was no novelty in a town so near the marches, but this one did not look Welsh. He looked French. For this there was an excellent reason.

2

The Journal of the first David Garric (as he spelt himself) to settle in England has come to rest, somewhat appropriately, in the Heralds' College, only a few hundred yards from many of the places in the City of London mentioned by him.

*5*    He was a Huguenot refugee, obliged to fly his country upon the Revocation of the Edict of Nantes. His Journal is outstandingly Spartan. It abounds in expressions of gratitude to the Almighty for preservation from destruction, in various forms, and resigned catalogues of deaths and burials. The copy in the Pulman collection in the College of Arms is a translation from the original French by a great-nephew, Peter Fermignac, a contemporary of David Garrick

*6*    III. Fermignac added explanatory marginal notes up to 1737.

The story told by David Garric is quite clear. It opens dramatically. "*The 5th October 1685.* I, Garric, arrived at London, having come from Bourdeaux the 31st August of the same year, running away from the persecution of our Holy Religion. I passed on to Xaintonge, Poitou and Brittany. I embarked at St Malo for Guernsey."

Garric was united with his wife, Jane (née Sarazin), in London, on December 5 of the same year. (He is strong on dates.) She also had escaped from Bordeaux, but had a more terrible journey. She was a month at sea, " with strong tempests ", below hatches in a fourteen-ton bark. (" The Master of the Bark ", adds Peter Fermignac, " is called Peter Cock of Guernsey.") Jane Garric evidently told her husband that she had been " hid in a Hole ". No doubt Peter Cock had prudently desired cargo which might be difficult to explain to descend to the hold for the passage. Jane, having escaped the double perils of being lost at sea or martyred (" by our persecutors, who were then very inveterate. Pray God convert them "), was received by her husband as a gift from God for the second time. The first occasion had been on their marriage, on an April day, three years earlier. The Garric family in England began to swell in numbers.

*The 6th Sept: 1686.* God gave us a girl, who was baptized at our English Parish Church, St Andrew's, Mary-Hill, in our street, Philpot Lane. The godfather was Mr John Sarazin, proxy for his father; the godmothers were Miss Forrester, and Fermignac, who gave her the name of my wife, Jane, whom God bless.   Amen.

*The 5th Sept: 1687.*   God gave us a boy, who was baptized the 14th of the same month at the Walloon Church.   His godfather was Mr Stephen Pigou, marchand, native of the city of Amiens, in Picardy; his godmother was Madame Mary Perin of Paris, wife of Mr Stephen Soulhard of London, merchant, who gave him the name of Stephen, whom God bless.   Amen.

God took him away, Sunday evening, the 28th April, at 7 o'clock 1689, and was buried at the Post House, Monday evening, at ½ an hour of six. He lived 19 months and 24 days.   [" Dead " comments Peter Fermignac laconically in the margin.]

The next entry is more cheerful.   The Garrics had been forced to leave behind, out at nurse, at La Bastide, a suburb of the great Gascon port of Bordeaux, their first born, " a Little Boy four months old, called Peter Garric ".

The 22nd May, 1687, Little Peter arrived at London, by the grace of God, in the ship John White with a servant, Mary Mougnier, and I paid for their passage 22 guineas.

This French-born boy became Captain Peter Garrick, the father of England's most famous actor.

David Garric's Journal continues until 1701.   Four more children were born, a daughter, Mary Magdalene; a son, David, a John, and one more Stephen, who shared the fate of the first of that name. John was hopefully described by his father as a fine boy, at birth. Peter Fermignac noted his funeral expenses.

| | |
|---|---|
| Coffin | 10 sh: |
| Gloves | 3 |
| Coach | 8 |
| 3 Bottles | 4 |
| Minister | 17 |
| Sexton | 10 |
| | 52 sh: |

The last two sons were buried at Putney and Wandsworth respectively, but may have been sent to these places for country air, for when the worst blow fell, on December 2, 1694, " my poor wife " was buried in Bartholomew's Lane, behind the Royal Exchange. " God hath afflicted me."

After eighteen months two more Garrics arrived in England, but both elderly, and invalids.   " My poor brother, Mr Peter Garric from Rotterdam " with the stone (" God preserve us from the like distemper ") lasted three weeks only. " My sister Magdalene, the eldest daughter of all, being 63 years old," succumbed to dropsy after five years. Both were buried beside Jane, " behind the Change ". This ends David Garric's narrative. It presents some interesting features. The picture of the unbending middle-aged Huguenot refugee is quite true to type. He had courage, devout belief, a business head and no sense of humour. He was a good family man and knew how to make a home and a happy marriage, traits which were to descend. As a species, the French Protestant refugees tended to marry within their own ranks. They formed an *émigré* society and kept to trades in which they excelled, bringing French realism and French elegance. They took a firm root in England, and produced many olive branches; but they were French, and the French notoriously are home-keeping.

David Garric, naturalized together with his Jane, in the year following their arrival in England, is described in his marriage certificate as " *bourgeois et marchand* " and his wife as the daughter of a " *marchand* ". The surname Garrick, in the forms of Garric, Garrigues, Garriques, Garricques, Jarrige, is familiar in the history of civic Bordeaux, and a Pierre Garric, mentioned in the registers of the Parish of St André, in 1530 and 1635, who might by date be the father of David, is described as " *marchand mangonnier* ", general broker. There are letters to Lord Hatton from David, eight years after his arrival in London, dealing with business matters. " M. Isaac Cazalis is my good friend at Amsterdam. I know vere well Mr Gervais of that City, Frenchman, and my good friend." Gervais is another well-known Huguenot name. The Cazalets were cousins who appear later in Chelsea. David evidently never mastered the English aspirate. " Ye Exchange is now vere eigh."

His son David II went into the wine trade in Portugal and prospered. Of his daughters, Mary Magdalene, married a Fermignac cousin, and Jane, one Louis La Condé, settled at Carshalton. Little Peter entered the army in 1706. At the age of twenty-three he was a Lieutenant in Sir Roger Bradshaigh's Regiment of Foot, changed next year to Colonel James Tyrrell's Regiment, and disbanded in 1713. He was on half-pay from 1713 to 1715, when Tyrrell raised a Regiment of Dragoons to repel the Invasion of the Old Pretender, and he rose to the rank of Captain-Lieutenant in the Dragoons; but when the Invasion scare blew over they too were disbanded. He was thirty-three. This was the more serious, as, at the age of twenty-one, when an Ensign, he had married the daughter of a Vicar-choral of Lichfield Cathedral, called Clough, of Irish descent. No fortune had come with the bride, and she was no *belle*, but she was sprightly and engaging, and the Cloughs had a house in Beacon Street, conveniently close to the west gate of the cathedral, in which she and her bridegroom were always welcome. This house became the home of the Garrick family. It was pulled down in 1825.

### 3

The youth of David Garrick, the second son born so inconveniently in the Angel at Hereford, was very happy. Only two things clouded it, poverty and, as a result of poverty, the absence of his father. Since he was always good at making the best of things, he saw the humorous side of dunning tradesmen and patched clothes, and he enjoyed writing duty letters. Twelve letters from him addressed " To Captain Garrick, at Brigadier Kirk's Regiment, at Gibraltar " performed their long journey safely, were treasured and brought home, and were eventually preserved amongst his own manuscripts. Their handwriting does credit to Lichfield Grammar School, though he spells badly. They bear seals, generally with the design of a heraldic lion. He sometimes encloses notes from other *9* people, and is apt to drop into verse for tedious periods. The picture presented is of a small cheerful society. He knew security.

In July 1732, Captain Garrick, who had been on Captain's half-pay in a regiment of foot for six years, accepted the offer of an officer at Gibraltar to come out and take his place. The decision was made *10* with anguish, but on active service he would be on full pay, and he was by now the parent of seven children. (Three more had died in infancy.) David, turned fifteen, would be the head of the family while his father was abroad, for his elder brother Peter had gone to sea. David's first letter is dated Lichfield, January 20, 1732–33.

Hond. Sir,
    It is not to be expresst ye Joy that the family was in at ye Receipt of Dear Pappa's Letter which we receiv'd the 7th of this Month. My poor Mamma was in very good Spirits two or three Days after she receiv'd your Letter but now begins to grow maloncolly again, and has little ugly fainting fits. She is in great hopes of ye Transports going for you every Day, for we Please ourselves with ye hopes of your spending this Summer with yr Family.
    My Mamma rec'd ye thirty Pounds you was so good to send her. She has Paid ten Pounds to Mr Rider for one Year's Rent, and ten Pounds to the Baker, and if you can spare a little more, as you tell her you will, she is in hopes of paying all ye Debts that you may have nothing to fret you when you come home.
    My Mamma staid six weeks in London after you left her at Mr Bronker's for she was very much out of order when she was there, and they would not part with Her before and was very good to her. Mr Adair came twice to see my Mamma at Mr Bronker's, and was prodigiously civil and obliging,

and beg'd her to send him some Ale which she designs to do very soon. My Mamma paid for your Stockings and Holland as soon as you left her, and as soon as She came down to us, not to her great Joy, she found us very shabby in Cloaths and in all our accoutrements, that we was rather like so many beggars than Gentlemen Soldiers, but with much ado at last she equipt us out a little better, and now with a great deal of Mending and Patching we are in Stato Quo.

We receiv'd a letter from Brother Peter which was directed to you and we thought it would be too troublesome to send it inclos'd so have sent you a Coppy of it on ye other side.

At present we have but little News. Doctor Hector is married to Miss Pop Smith, and Mr Lawrence who is at London is married to ye Lady who you saw at Captn. Goddard's, a very pretty Woman only she squints a little (as Captn. Brazen says in *Ye Recruiting Officer*). Captn. Weldon has parted wth: his Commission, and has half Pay as Lieutenant of a Man of War. Every Body loves and likes Mrs Weldon, but he had quarell'd with most of ye People in this Place, which gives ye poor Woman a great deal of uneasyness, but they are both highly Civil to our family. Mr and Mrs Hervey came to see my Mamma as soon as she came to Town. She is a very fine Lady and has return'd but few of her visits. I am a great favourite of both of them and am with them every Day. Mr Walmesley has had a very great quarrel with Captn: [Name blacked out in the MS.] and I think (considering his being always so civil to ye Officers) us'd him very ill. But at Present all is over, but they dont visit one another.

I have been to Mr Ofleys, who sent a Man and horse for me, with Mr and Mrs Hervey and Mr Walmesley, where I got acquainted with his two Sons, who are fine young Gentlemen. Mr Walmesley gave me slyly half a crown for ye Butler and another for ye Groom, for myself, which made me look very grand. All yr friends are very well. We had a letter from my Uncle Day who says that Mr Lowe preach't a Sermon which was thought by every body one of ye Best they had heard for a long Time. Mrs Lowndes send love and Service, but has not yet conquer'd her fever. My Grandmother is very poorly and sends her blessing and would fain live to see you once more. My Brothers and Sisters their Duty and am, in a particular manner,

Dear Sr,

Yr ever Dutifull Son

David Garrick.

P.S. Dr Sir if you could possibly send Mr Walmesley a little Wine I am sure he would take it as a Particular Favour.

11

David Garrick's first letter to his absent sire mentions (and misspells) nearly every Lichfield worthy prominent in his little world. Only one family never appears, in any letter; but this is not surprising, for although everyone knew the Johnsons, they could hardly be said to mingle in the gay society of the cathedral city which was also a market and garrison town.

Lichfield, dominated by its superb red cathedral with flying buttresses, lay mainly on a hill rising from the river Witham, at the north east point of a remarkably flat district. It was over a hundred and twenty miles from London, and strangers found the surrounding country featureless and depressing, but natives of Staffordshire knew that the atmospheric effects over their fens were often of surpassing beauty, and when the picture included the city of Lichfield, one of the most ancient and famous in the realm, silhouetted against a lowering sky full of autumn clouds, drowsing in midsummer blue, or shot with spring sunshine, it was something of which to be proud.

On a closer view Lichfield displayed further charms. There were green lawns and lime-walks near the cathedral, glassy streams, flowing through rich water-meadows, and on the outskirts several good bathing-pools, relics of the days when the place aspired to rank as a spa. The gardens of its brick-and-timber houses, and white thatched cottages, contained loaded fruit trees, and also picturesque groups of old masonry. The Civil War had brought destruction. The town had been taken, re-taken and taken again. The cathedral had now been re-roofed, re-floored and provided with new windows, and the Bishop's Palace had been entirely rebuilt. The Market Cross had not been replaced, but the square in which it stood was still the hub of the town. The house of Michael Johnson, the bookseller (who also sold writing-paper, patent medicines, almanacs and engravings), was a new one, four storeys high and rather grim-looking, on the corner of Market, or Sadler Street. He had built it himself on a promising site for his business, had he been businesslike. The sad large old man was a familiar figure in the town, and he had an extraordinary son, Samuel, even larger than himself, and a younger son, Nathaniel, and a wife; but their home, unlike the Garricks', was not a happy one. Mrs Johnson, whose children, like those of most people in Lichfield, had been brought into the world by Dr Hector, had not married until she was six and thirty, or become a mother until she was past forty. She might have thought herself lucky, but she adored her first-born in a dreadful possessive way, and despised her husband. Samuel Johnson had had Dr Samuel Swinfen for godfather. That well-born young gentleman had happened to be staying as a paying-guest in the Johnsons' house at the time of the christening. Samuel Johnson had left the Grammar School by the time that David Garrick went there, for he was nearly nine years older, but he kept on turning up at Lichfield, like a bad penny, and he was quite unforgettable, for he was very pallid, and had, when he was an infant, had something wrong with his eyes, and his skin, so was short-sighted and scarred. He was shockingly uncouth, and spoke broad Stafford- 12 shire, yet once was heard to announce that the people of his native town were " the most sober, decent people in England, the genteelest in proportion to their wealth, and spoke the purest English ". But although he was so extraordinary, it was impossible not to like him, and even after his quiet old father had died, fine gentlemen, like Mr Walmesley, who possessed a library, and had often had the bookseller up in the way of business, continued to see his son. It was at the Palace that David Garrick generally met Samuel Johnson. Mr Walmesley was the most important character in David's world. He was Registrar of the Ecclesiastical Court of Lichfield, and lived in the Bishop's Palace, the most beautiful house in the city. No Bishop had ever lived there since it had been rebuilt—in 1687, the date incised on either side of a mitre, on the pediment high above the entrance. The Bishops preferred Eccleshall Castle, twenty-six miles from their cathedral. When Mr Walmesley was in residence hardly a day passed without David Garrick running across to the Close, and in at the fine wrought-iron gates, between brick pillars topped by classical vases, and up a curved flight of stone steps to a double front door. Inside his palace, as might have been expected, Mr Walmesley had everything handsome about him—lofty, sun-filled panelled rooms, with fine plaster-work, a service staircase almost as substantial as the great oak staircase, and a north withdrawing room large enough to contain a great company. Behind the house there were gardens, and a terrace which seemed designed for after-dinner conversation. But Mr Walmesley was not always at home, for in his youth he had been, if not a rake, at least a *beau* (" Gill Walmesley "), and he still went for long stays to Town, London. He was forty-seven when David Garrick was ten, and a bachelor. Already he had gout, and David made him laugh. He liked a clever boy. David was very quick, and he had a gift for imitating all sorts of people which was uncanny, and argued good powers of observation; but he did not excel at school. At the old four-gabled Grammar School, in St John Street—an easy run from Beacon Street, and without a single turning—he learned Latin and Greek. The headmaster, Dr John Hunter, was a flogger. He never appeared except in full panoply of flowing wig, rustling black gown and snowy-white bands. As he belaboured his boys, he said, " And this I do to save you from the gallows." Johnson said, " He was not severe, sir. A master ought to be severe. Sir, he was cruel." Johnson thought that Hunter beat a boy equally for not knowing a thing as for neglecting to know it. This terrible pedagogue had his Achilles heel—field sports, shooting. Boys soon learned that they could distract his attention by telling him where they had seen a covey of partridges. But David Garrick did not go directly under Hunter's tuition. Little boys were taken by Humphrey Hawkins,

usher, who was of saint-like gentleness.  Hawkins got £10 a year,
as salary, and was glad to make 11s. 6d. for washing surplices, as he
himself noted in his copper-plate hand in the churchwarden's accounts
of the parish of St John.

When he had been at school a year, David, seeing so much
promising material around him, organized some of his school-fellows
to perform a play.  He had seen several plays when strolling companies visited the town, and some ladies of Lichfield had once put on
*The Distressed Mother*, for which Sam Johnson had written an epilogue.  The piece chosen by David Garrick for his own first appearance, as actor-manager, was *The Recruiting Officer*, quoted by him in
his first letter to his father.  It was particularly appropriate, for the
scene in which it was laid—except that it was called Shrewsbury, not
Hereford—was that in which he had been born, when his own parent
had been a recruiting officer.  It was not a new play, and it could
not honestly be called a very good play, but it had been a favourite
since 1705.  It had life.  The wars mentioned in it were those of
Marlborough, and the soldiers bribed females with bits of Mechlin
lace from the Low Countries.  David allotted to himself the part of
Sergeant Kite, which was unselfish of him, though when Kite, that
old soldier in the worst sense, disguises himself as a fortune-teller, he
holds the stage, for a scene.  In later years he was to play the principal officer, Captain Plume, the clown, Costar Pearmain, a glorious
country half-wit, and Captain Brazen, who was an officer, but not
nearly a gentleman, a type which always had existed in the army
and always would, a " thruster " who kept on calling strangers " My
dear ", and could not hear a name without having known someone of
that family very well.  " Is he anything related to Frank Plume, in
Northamptonshire?  Honest Frank! many, many a dry bottle have
we cracked, hand to fist.  You must have known his brother Charles
that was concerned in the India Company;  he married the daughter
of old Tonguepad, the Master of Chancery, a very pretty woman,
only she squinted a little.  She died in childbed of her first child, but
the child survived.  'Twas a daughter, but whether 'twas called
Margaret or Margery, upon my soul, I can't remember."

The dialogue and action went at a rattling pace, and none of the
characters could be called lay figures, although many of them came
out of the property box.  They could not be said to be high-minded.
Justice Ballance, the heavy father, and Silvia, the heroine (who added
to the turgidity of the plot by disguising herself as a third recruiting
officer), heard of the deaths of their nearest relatives with the utmost
calm, their only and immediate concern being what they would inherit.  Captain Plume, who was supposed to be a gallant hero, when

he had won the hand of his heiress, announced his intention of re-
signing his commission forthwith, whereupon the curtain rang down
amongst approving cheers.

The eldest Garrick daughter, Magdalene, " Lennie ", played the
*soubrette*, Lucy, a small part, but with some sophisticated lines. She
was eleven, one year older than David. Samuel Johnson had been
applied to for a prologue, but none was forthcoming. Mr Walmesley,
however, who had promised to lend the Palace, was as good as his
word. The piece was applauded by a " select audience " who found
the performance much above their expectation, and David Garrick's
ease, vivacity and humour, as Kite, were long remembered in Lichfield. He, and several of his contemporaries, had to appear roaring
drunk, and some of what they spoke was remarkably coarse, but in
1727 it was generally accepted that plays were of that sort. *The
Recruiting Officer* was comparatively innocent, moreover the story of
its author, Mr George Farquhar, afforded a grand moral lesson, and a
perfect awful warning against having anything to do with the stage.
He had been the son of a poor clergyman, but a gentleman (there was
a shadowy baronet on his mother's side), and he had been at Trinity
College, Dublin, for a year at least, but had drifted down to Smock
Alley Theatre, Dublin, and in and out of the army. No less than six
of his plays had been produced in London, some of which had made
managers rich, but he had died, at the age of twenty-nine, in a back
garret, in miserable anxiety about the future of two infant daughters.
One of them had married a tradesman, and sunk into an early grave,
but the other was said to be still alive, somewhere, in the capacity of
a domestic servant.

Soon after his success with *The Recruiting Officer*, the young
actor-manager left home. The wolf was at the door in Beacon
Street. His parents knew that they could not afford to reject the
offer of Mr David Garrick, vintner, of Lisbon, who had an opening for
a smart lad. The boy David was back under Mr Hunter's tuition in
Lichfield in an uncommonly short time. " Uncle Day " had, apparently, been diverted by the antics of his namesake, but decided very
soon that he was too volatile for the business in hand. Only four
anecdotes of this venture survive. The English merchants of the
port, who often had the boy to dine, had enjoyed placing him upon
the table after the meal, and calling upon him to repeat verses and
speeches from plays, which he did with great readiness. Some
Portuguese young gentlemen, of his own age, of the highest rank, had
always been delighted with his conversation. He was heard, in
later life, to recall with a suddenly tragic mien, that he had often
been in company with the Duque d'Aveiro, who, for a conspiracy

against the King of Portugal, had been broken on the wheel and then burned alive. But he also remembered, and could imitate strikingly, humbler figures of the Portuguese scene, " characters met on the road ".

Judging by his letters to his father, no sooner had the unfortunate Captain announced his arrival in Gibraltar than his family began to plan for his return, on leave. It must be admitted that letters appear to have taken not less than four months in transit, except on one outstanding occasion, when the surgeon's mate of a ship that had called at the Rock presented himself at Beacon Street. It was accepted that Mr Walmesley was the person who could help " about your coming for England ". Unfortunately, a situation which even Mr Walmesley could not avert, seemed threatening. There were rumours that the country might be going to war again. When she had been a grass-widow for two and a half years, Mrs Garrick enclosed in one of her son's letters a little note indicative of strong emotion.

> I must tell my Dear Life and Soul that I am not able to live easy longer with out him for I grow very jealous—but in the midst of all this I do not blame my dear. I have very sad dreams for you etc: but I have the pleasure when I am up, to think were I with you how tender my Dear Soul would be to me, nay was when I was with you last. O that I had you in my armes, I would tell my Dear Life how much I am his.
>
> A.G.

David's accompanying epistle was colourful. Like many in Lich-field, he was much interested in the Royal Family, and secretly longed for them to be more glamorous. The Stuart Pretenders, who would—aided by France—bring back Popery, were hereditarily anathema to the Huguenot refugees, but they were undeniably romantic. At last there was a prospect of romance in the House of Hanover. The Prince of Orange had arrived in England to woo the Princess Anne, Princess Royal. She was rising five and twenty, much marked by the small-pox, pasty, stout and low-statured, but no fool. She told her father that she would accept the Prince were he a baboon. " Well then," replied George II, " there is baboon enough for you." The Prince was deformed. David wrote that he heard he was a very good scholar and " mighty liked by the ladies ". Mr Walmesley and Mr Hervey returned from London in time to take a prominent part in Lichfield rejoicings on the royal wedding day.

> Mr Walmesley treated ye Ladies and Gentlemen at ye Assembly with Rack Punch, and presented ye Gentlemen with Cockades and ye Ladies with Favours. His House was illuminated from top to bottom. All ye Town came up to see it. Most of ye Gentlemen of ye Town met at ye " Swan ".

In the Garricks' kitchen a faithful servitor who never failed to send her duty to her absent master was in less happy case.

> Poor Mrs Lowndes too is almost constantly rowling about ye flower with ye Cholick, or has her Head tide about with a Napkin with ye head-Ach —like one that is a Victim for a Sacrifice.

Dr Hector was also attending Jane, "Jenny", who had not been out of the house for six months. Mama was getting Mr Hervey to compose a pretty letter for her to "the Brigadier" asking for leave for her husband.

> The Dragoons are removed to Boston thro' the Interest of Mr Plummer, but Mr Hervey and his Lady remain at Lichfield. She has lately lain in, and ye Child has been Baptized, and my Mamma was invited to it. He has lately come from London and has brought me two Pairs of large Silver Buckles, one Pair for my Shoes and ye other for my Breeches, and Mr Walmesley a fine Snuff Box. He wishes every Day to see you at Lichfield, and always drinks in a Bumper "Our friends at Gibraltar".

Mr Walmesley's grand design was now unfolded. If Captain Garrick could be made a Burgess, which seemed simple, he could apply for leave to come over to vote (for the influential Mr Plummer). Not only Mr Walmesley raised his glass in memory of the absent Captain.

> My Grandmother sends her Blessing, Mrs Lowndes her Love and Service, together with Aunt Kinaston and Couzen Bailye's family. Mrs ——— one Night got tipsy by Drinking "Here is to all our Friends by Land and by Sea".

Good news had come of Peter, the sailor of the family, but the Captain was beginning to worry about the future of his second son.

> You was pleased to write in one of your Letters, when should I be fit for the University? I fancy in about two Years. I should have been ready now, only my going to Lisbon backened me a great deal.

Mr Walmesley had now thought of another ingenious method of getting the Captain home—"King's Leave", something special. Lady Biddulph, at his request, was approaching her brother. Hopes rose. The family began to look to every post for the good news. The only drawback was that "at Lichfield they talk of War and very little else". Not only his mother sent messages by David. Young Dr James was disgusted by the adulteration of the Peruvian Bark obtainable in England. He wanted the Captain to get him some genuine store from Portugal or Spain. A family called Thrapp, of whom the Captain might not have heard, wanted news of one Samuel. Was he dead or alive, or sick? No clue was offered as to Samuel's identity, but, astonishingly, Captain Garrick was able to comply.

c

The sequel was rather sad.   Samuel was alive, but in debt, " a small
matter to get clear with his officer ".   His brother, William, sent a
letter for him by David, but not one word of financial help.   From
September to December 1734 Mrs Garrick's health had been wretched.
She kept her bed four months, got " better, but very weak, attended
with Lowness of Spirits, which compells her to drink Wine, which
gives a good deal of uneasiness upon two accounts, as it goes against
her inclination and Pockett ".   In December, David had suggested
that there now seemed about three Christmas boxes owing from
Gibraltar for the family, if not four.   But Mr Walmesley was off for
London again and had no doubt of putting " the finishing touches "
to his business of getting leave expedited.   He seemed to have gone
back to the idea of permission to come over to vote.   Mama said
that if her husband was not restored to her with the Spring she would
take the plunge, and herself go out to the Rock.

> We have had a great many Officers here a Recruiting from Ireland.   I
> was in great hopes I should have Recruited my Self this Spring.   For Mr
> Hervey, who is a Cornett in my Lord Mark Carr's Regiment, had given me
> and Mr Walmesley a promise for his Commission, if his Brother-in-Law Sir
> Thomas Aston had died, who at ye time was struck with a dead Palsie.
> [Mr Hervey being heir to it, through his wife Sir Thomas Aston's sister, or
> rather, she was the heiress].   But Sir Thomas is now perfectly recover'd.

Captain Garrick's complaints that he did not hear enough from home
always provoked replies in copybook vein.   He now demanded
that David should write every fortnight.   He had sent a miniature
of himself, by an artist called Le Grout.   " My poor Mamma sighs
whenever she passes ye Picture."   She said that the presence of the
original would do her more good than all the physicians in Europe.
Meanwhile, the smiling likeness of a military gentleman, not very tall
and " pretty jolly " had turned David's thoughts again to following
in his father's footsteps.

> I can tell my Papa I stand a good chance to get into ye Army.   I have
> the promises of three Lieutenant Colonells to provide for me if they should
> get Regiments.   One is Col: Warburton, Col: Fowkes, and Col: Pyot has
> sworn to make (me) Chaplain to his Regiment if I should be in orders.

The boy was growing up.   He was no longer a stocky, dark-skinned
little lad, stumping across to the Palace to amuse Mr Walmesley—
partly by the *naïveté* of his flood of questions about the great world.
He had become a lithe young man, very engaging in his manners, but
still naïve.   Captain Garrick wrote asking for the dates of birth of all
his children.   This list showed that David was now eighteen.   He
himself said that he was now quite a philosopher, but would gladly be
quit of one accoutrement of that species, viz. a pair of ragged breeches.

He mentioned, not very hopefully, that he had heard velvet was very cheap at Gibraltar.

After April 1735, the supply of David's letters to his father fails. The reason was one for mingled joy and grief. Mrs Garrick's prayers were to be answered, but in a way never foreseen. For her husband was not coming home on King's leave, or any kind of leave. He was coming home as soon as he could travel, to go on half pay again. He had been very unwell.

To the end of his days, David remembered with self-reproach a *gaffe* made by him on the day of his father's arrival. Spirits were running high in the house in Beacon Street, too high. "I dare say, sir, I have now a good many brothers and sisters at Gibraltar." Poor Captain Garrick's looks proclaimed that life, separated from all he held dear, had been killing him. Fresh tears rose in gentle Mrs Garrick's eyes.

Something would have to be done about David. Mr Walmesley thought so too. And this time he had a scheme whereby two of his protégés might benefit.

Samuel Johnson had turned up again. Incredible though it seemed, he had found a wife as extraordinary-looking as himself. At their wedding, Mrs Elizabeth ("Tetty", "Tettsey") Porter had given her age as forty. In fact, she was forty-five, twenty years senior to her bridegroom. But she had a dowry of over six hundred pounds. Mr and Mrs Johnson were taking a large, somewhat decayed country house out at Edial—pronounced Edjal—and Mr Walmesley suggested that Captain Garrick should send David to Mr Johnson's select Academy. Eventually, two young Garricks went, for George, the youngest son, now thirteen, accompanied his brother. One of the young Offleys from Winchnor Park was also collected by Mr Walmesley. Lawrence Offley was a cousin of Mrs Harry Hervey. At first these three were the only boarders, and from the first the success of the experiment seemed doubtful. From David's point of view there were advantages. "When his master expected from him some exercise of composition upon a theme, he showed him several scenes of a new comedy, which had engrossed his time." Mr Johnson was sympathetic, for he too was engaged upon a work for the stage, but a tragedy. He had borrowed from Peter Garrick *The General Historie of the Turkes*, by Richard Knolles, and the scene of his play was set in Constantinople in the fifteenth century. It was called *Irene*, and Irene was a fair Grecian slave, a Christian captive of Mahomet II, Emperor of Turkey. The author brought the first acts to read aloud to Mr Walmesley, who asked how was it possible that the luckless heroine should be brought into yet

more calamity. "Sir," replied Mr Johnson to the Ecclesiastical
Registrar, " I can put her into the Spiritual Court."                    *19*

Edial was only two and a half miles out of Lichfield, to the west.
When a troupe of strolling players presented a farce in the Guildhall,
Mr Johnson took his young gentlemen to see Colley Cibber's *Hob: or
the Country Wake*. The occasion was doubly dramatic, for when the
master left his seat for a few moments, a Scottish officer who disliked
him successfully urged a local innkeeper to occupy it. Mr Johnson
picked up chair and man together and threw them " at one jerk into
the pit ". One of his uncles had been a prize-fighter. The officer
shouted, " Damn him, he has broke his limbs ", but Mr Walmesley
poured oil upon the waters, and Mr Johnson, recovering his place,
" with great composure sat out the play ". David loved recounting *20*
this story of his old master in later London years. Johnson, when
asked if it was a fact, said that David had not spoiled it in the telling.
" It is very *near* true, to be sure."

David thought his master's wife quite atrocious. His two descriptions of her were imparted many years later, when her attractions may have waned, but there could be no doubt that even at
forty-five she was a figure far from romantic in the eyes of a youth.
He spoke of her as " very fat, with a bosom of more than ordinary
protuberance, with swelled cheeks of a florid red, produced by thick
painting, and increased by the liberal use of cordials; flaring and
fantastick in her dress, and affected both in her speech and her
general behaviour ". She was " a little painted poppet; full of
affectation and rural airs of elegance ". But she provided an ideal *21*
subject for mimicry, and so did her bridegroom; for the cream of the
jest was that Mr Johnson always declared, " Sir, it was a love
marriage upon both sides." The young gentlemen of Edial Academy
listened at the door of their master's bedroom, and even peeped in at
the keyhole, and one of David's best performances was a Johnson
bedroom-scene. The master sat composing *Irene*, and reading aloud
good bits, in his sonorous voice, to his exasperated wife. The only
result of her cries that he should leave off and come to bed, was that
he absent-mindedly started to dress again, instead of undressing.
He seized the sheets, and tried to stuff them into his breeches, while
Mrs Johnson, shaking with cold and wrath, tussled to regain them. *22*

In the spring of 1736, Lichfield gossips who had prophesied that
Mr Walmesley would leave at least some of his fortune to Davy
Garrick, found that they were quite wrong. At the age of fifty-six,
Mr Walmesley took a wife, thirty years his junior. The match was
otherwise wholly suitable. Miss Magdalene Aston was one of the
eight sisters of Sir Thomas Aston, baronet, of Aston Hall, Cheshire

(another was the Honourable Mrs Harry Hervey). But Mr Walmesley, as his happiness increased, was not neglectful of two talented young men whose careers seemed in the doldrums. On February 15, 1737, he sat in his Palace, at Lichfield, writing a long letter, in his surprisingly large, round, clear, childish hand.

To the Rev: Mr Colson,
At his house in Rochester, Kent.

By way of London.  A single sheet.

My dear Old Friend,
Having not been in Town since the year thirty-one, you will the less wonder at seeing a letter from me. But I have the pleasure of hearing of you sometimes in the prints, and am glad to see you are daily throwing in your valuable contributions to the Republic of Letters.

But the present occasion of my writing is a favour I have to ask. My neighbour, Captain Garrick, (who is an honest, valuable man,) has a son, who is a very sensible young fellow, and a good scholar, and whom the Captain hopes, in some two or three years, he shall be able to send to the Temple, and breed to the Bar. But, at present, his pocket will not hold out for sending him to the University. I have proposed your taking him, if you think well of it, and your boarding him, and instructing him in mathematics, and philosophy, and humane learning. He is now nineteen, of sober and good dispositions, and is as ingenious and promising a young man as ever I knew in my life. Few instructions on your part will do, and in the intervals of study, he will be an agreeable companion for you. His father will be glad to pay whatever you shall require that is within his reach; and I shall think myself very much obliged to you into the bargain. This young gentleman, you must know, has been much with me, ever since he was a child, almost every day; and I have taken a pleasure often in instructing him, and have a great affection and esteem for him; and I doubt not but you will soon have the like, if it suit with your convenience to take him into your family. You will be so good, as soon as you have considered of this affair, to write to me.

Having changed my condition of life (being tired since the death of my brother of living quite alone) my chances for seeing London are now become more hazardous than ever. But you know I never came thither in my life, without enquiring after you; and therefore I am not without hopes, especially if Davy Garrick comes to be your pupil, but you will contrive to spend a month or six weeks with me at Lichfield in the summer. I shall always have a bed for you, and a stall for your horse; and nothing, I do assure you, will give me a greater pleasure.

Captain Garrick, and the young gentleman, beg your acceptance of their compliments; and I am ever, with the greatest truth, Dear Sir,
Your most affectionate old friend, and
humble servant
Gilbert Walmesley.

Less than a month later, Mr Walmesley was at his desk again.

Dear Sir,
I had the favour of yours, and am extremely obliged to you; but cannot say I have a greater affection for you upon it, being long since so much

endeared to you, as well by an early friendship as by your many excellent
and valuable qualifications; if I had a son of my own, it would be my
ambition, instead of sending him to the University, to dispose of him as this
young gentleman is.   He, and another neighbour of mine, Mr Johnson, set
out this morning for London together: Davy Garrick to be with you early
the next week, and Mr Johnson to try his fate with a tragedy, and to see to
get himself employed in some translation, either from the Latin or the
French.   Johnson is a very good scholar and poet, and I have great hopes
will turn out a fine tragedy writer.   If it should any-ways lie in your way,
I doubt not but you would be ready to recommend and assist your country-
man.

　If I cannot be so happy as to see you here this summer, I shall depend
upon it the next; and your pupil's coming hither then, will, I hope be an
inducement,

I am, ever, Dear Sir,
Your most obliged, and most affectionate
humble servant,
Gilbert Walmesley.      *23*

### 4

Mr Walmesley's second letter supplies the date on which his two
protégés took the road for London.   It was Wednesday, March 2,
1737.   They themselves, in the days of their prosperity, loved to
recall their somewhat ignominious exit from Lichfield.   In a " pretty
large company " which included the Bishop of Killaloe, Johnson,
humorously ascertaining the chronology of something, expressed
himself thus: " That was the year when I came to London with two-
pence half-penny in my pocket."   Garrick, overhearing him,
exclaimed, " Eh?   What do you say?   With two-pence half-penny
in your pocket? "   *Johnson:* " Why, yes; when I came with two-
pence half-penny in *my* pocket, and thou, Davy, with three half-
pence in thine."   Some listeners thought that Garrick embellished a   *24*
little when he declared, " We rode and tied."   This would have
meant that they had a single horse between them, and the drill
would be that one gentleman rode it for a due distance, then tethered
it by the roadside and walked on, until his companion, now the
cavalier, overtook him.

　The first stages of the road from Lichfield to the capital run
through typical flats, against which the figures of travellers can be
seen coming into view for a very long time.   It was the old Fosse
Way.   At Newark they struck the Great North Road, as oddly-
assorted a pair of boon companions as ever ventured upon it.   It
appears that they got on together very happily.   They were going to
conquer London.

## CHAPTER II

## SALAD DAYS

1737–1742

I

GARRICK'S first biographer, Tom Davies, declares that the capital which the young Garrick approached with Samuel Johnson in March 1737 was already familiar to him. " Several of his father's acquaintance, who knew the delights of the stage, often treated him with a journey to London, that he might feast his appetite at the playhouse." All succeeding authors have accepted this. But a journey to London, at this date, was something not at all lightly undertaken, and, as Johnson knew, the boy was " the son of a half-pay officer, bred in a family whose study was to make fourpence do as much as others make fourpence-halfpenny do ". David himself wrote to Gibraltar that he needed new breeches and a waistcoat. And if he was taken frequently to London by rich friends who customarily went for long stays, it is very odd that in his letters to his father, covering three years, although he mentions Lichfield gentry going and coming to Town, and laments his shortage of local news, he never once alludes to such a jaunt being offered to him. There is a possibility that, after his father's return, he went to London with him. This would account for Davies's further statement that some time before the death of his namesake David Garrick II, " his nephew David insinuated to him, that he ought to make some compensation in his will for the disappointment which he had obliged him to incur by a fruitless voyage to Lisbon. The old gentleman was convinced that the remonstrance was just, and bequeathed to David a larger portion of his effects than to any of his brother's children."

Uncle Garrick died on December 16, 1736, at Carshalton, where he was staying with his sister, Mrs La Condé. He had made his will three days before. It was somewhat illiterate but perfectly legal. David Garric (as he wrote himself) left his sister " Laconde " one thousand one hundred pounds, and his sister Fermignac two thousand two hundred. To his nephew and namesake, " son of my Brother ", he left " £1,000, to be put out at interest by the Executors, jointly with my brother, until he is of age, or to be paid before in case there is a good place that offers in given money. If should be disobedient to his father and mother before comes of age the money must be given to the father to doe as he thinks most convenient." He left

" Cousin Cazalet £100, to give her husband what she pleases ", and the same sum to the French Church in Threadneedle Street, for the poor French refugees.  Mr Laconde got his house and all his wine, and Mrs Fermignac his clothes.  Captain Garrick was residuary legatee.      3

Captain Garrick was in London a fortnight later, for he made his will there on New Year's Day, 1737.  He had decided to sell his commission and retire, and before he went home had nearly succeeded in concluding for a sum of eleven hundred pounds.  He left Peter, 4 Magdalene and Jane five hundred pounds apiece, William, who was going into the army, four hundred pounds.  George and Merrial each got three hundred pounds.  " To my son David 1/-"  The sum left to David has given cause for speculation.  Captain Garrick had just learned that David had been provided for by his uncle, nevertheless the wording used by both testators suggests at least suspicions that the young man seemed to be developing a taste for a profession of which they could never approve.  It does not seem likely that David went to London with his father only nine weeks before he set out on his great adventure with Johnson.  Uncle Garrick, though in failing health, may have been to Lichfield.

Whether he arrived as a stranger, or an accustomed visitor, David halted in Town before going on to Rochester and Mr Colson.  He must enter his name amongst " the young beaux " of Lincoln's Inn. On March 9 he was enrolled as a student, and he paid for admission the sum of £3 3s. 4d.  Johnson had got lodgings " with Mr Norris, a staymaker, in Exeter Street, adjoining Catharine Street in the Strand ", who seems to have been a connection of the Baileys of Lichfield, cousins of Mrs Garrick.  Whether David also occupied an 5 upstairs room in this house, or whether other arrangements had been made for him, they were in touch during the next few days, which brought news of disaster at home raining in like those in a Greek tragedy.

Three days after the couple had left Lichfield, Johnson's brother, Nathaniel, a young man of twenty-four, had been buried there, in St Michael's Church.  He had not been a very satisfactory brother, but the news of his sudden death evidently gave Johnson a terrible shock.  He never afterwards was heard to allude to him.  The 6 funeral of the long-ailing Captain Garrick had taken place on March 11.  As he had not completed the contract for the sale of his commission, the next senior lieutenant would get his company free, a situation for which all " eldest lieutenants " lived in hope.

David could not now expect supplies from home soon.  He could not inherit Uncle Garrick's legacy for a year.  He suggested to

Johnson that they should raise a loan, " from a tradesman, whom he had a slight knowledge of, Mr Wilcox, a bookseller in the Strand.  To him they applied, and, representing themselves to him, as they really were, two young men, friends, and travellers from the same place, and just arrived with a view to settle there, he was so moved with their artless tale, that, on their joint note, he advanced them all that their modesty would permit them to ask (five pounds) which was soon after punctually repaid."

<sub>7</sub>

## 2

David Garrick, just turned twenty, betook himself to Rochester and Mr Colson, prepared (when it was forthcoming) to live frugally upon the interest from his uncle's legacy.  Johnson does not seem to have taken up residence there.  Boswell says, " I never heard that he found any protection or encouragement by the means of Mr Colson, to whose academy David Garrick went."  But Garrick did not go to the Free School of which Colson was First Master.  He went as a private pupil to Colson's own house, and Mrs Thrale (a good witness) was sure that Johnson caricatured Colson under the name of Gelidus, in his *Rambler* essay, number 24.  Here the mathematician to whom Mr Walmesley had recommended his young friends appears as a scholar so absent-minded that he hardly raised his head from his books when a flying messenger came in to tell him that a neighbouring town was ablaze.  He had already published *An Account of Negative-Affirmative Arithmetic* and *The Universal Resolution of Cubic and Biquadratic Equations*.  When Garrick arrived he was at work on an introduction to Dr Saunderson's *Elements of Algebra*.  David Garrick and John Colson appear to have had only one thing in common.  Colson had been the son of a vicar-choral of Lichfield Cathedral; Garrick was the grandson of one.  This link did not prove sufficient to produce intimacy between characters so diverse, and David did not linger in a picturesque place but thirty-three miles from London.  He stayed long enough to organize private theatricals, of which " several instances were remembered at Rochester ".  Thirty years later, a fellow lodger reminded him how he used to call in vain to Colson's little niece to desist from making such a noise as she ran about the house.

His elder brother had now retired from a sea-faring life.  David decided to abandon preparation for the Bar.  The Garrick family was already interested in the wine-trade.  The brothers set up jointly as wine-merchants, " Garrick & Co.", Peter in Lichfield, and David in London.

The London office and cellars were in Durham Yard, an area

between the small old streets leading south-east off the Strand towards the Thames.   The district had once been occupied by the town houses of the nobility.   Durham House had been the birthplace of Lady Jane Grey and the residence of Sir Walter Raleigh.   But the nobility had deserted their palaces on the Strand, and moved westward.   The offices of Garrick & Co. overlooked shining reaches of the Thames.   When David Garrick was rich and famous, another actor, Samuel Foote, loved to whisper that " he remembered Garrick in Durham Yard, with three quarts of vinegar in the cellar, calling himself a wine merchant ".

Peter Garrick very much resembled his younger brother in outward appearance, and Johnson, to the last, thought highly of him. " Sir," said he to Boswell, "I don't know but if Peter had cultivated all the arts of gaiety as much as David has done, he might have been as brisk and lively.   Depend upon it, Sir, vivacity is much an art, and depends greatly on habit."   Johnson read aloud to Peter in a single evening at the Fountain Tavern, the whole of *Irene*, which was now ready for production, and Peter, who knew Charles Fleetwood, the aristocratic manager of one of London's two great theatres, offered to recommend it.   Fleetwood refused it, probably, thought Boswell, " because it was not patronized by some man of high rank ". He did not, however, a year later, refuse David's first work for the stage.

It is certain that, in youth, David was in awe of Peter, who did not fail to assert the rights of elder brother and head of the family— moreover a family of French origin.   David would never break the heart of his widowed mother by appearing in anything but private theatricals.   He dutifully took up the profession of vintner, and courted patrons.   On an October day of 1739 he inscribed the order of a Mr Robinson of the Strand for two dozen of red port at eighteen shillings.   He had in him the makings of an excellent man of business.   Red Port, known in its country of origin as *Consumo*, was *vin du pays*, brandied for export, darkened with elder berry.   Canary and Mountain, sweet wines, offered to a morning caller, were always in demand.   French claret—Bordeaux—was very expensive.   Most of the claret supplied to London came from Portugal, and most of the " hock-wine " from the Rhine. . . .   His days were now spent on the wharves, and tasting samples, but he also frequented the coffee-houses of Covent Garden—haunts of authors, artists, actors and critics.   He longed to get the custom of the Bedford.   There were two establishments bearing the name of the nobleman whose town house had once overlooked Covent Garden—the Bedford Arms Tavern and the Bedford Coffee-House.   The coffee-house stood on the north-east corner of the square, opposite the performers' entrance of the Covent Garden Theatre. Covent Garden, called by Richard Steele "the Heart of the Town", and the first of London's great squares, had been laid out a hundred years past at the order of the fourth Earl of Bedford, by Inigo Jones. Its arcades were said to have been intended to resemble those of the Place Royale, in Paris. But the design had not been completed and they bore an Italian name. The Great Piazza occupied the north end of the square, and the Little Piazza, the east. A church, *en suite*, dedicated to St Paul, was on the west side. Covent Garden had been originally the convent garden of St Peter's, Westminster, and had covered seven acres, from the Strand to Long Acre. On the dissolution of the monasteries the land had reverted to the Crown, and presently it had been given to the first Earl of Bedford. Fashionable folk were now living in Mayfair, in Grosvenor, Cavendish and Hanover Squares, but the shops, taverns and particularly coffee-houses of Covent Garden still attracted them, and the district, if much fallen in dignity, was much frequented. Here the artist might meet the patron. After the Play elegant company generally resorted to a Covent Garden coffee-house, " where there is playing at Picket, and the best conversation till midnight. Here you will see blue and green ribbons and Stars sitting familiarly and talking with the same freedom as if they had left their quality and degrees of distance at home." Tom's and Will's coffee-houses were both in Russell Street, the highway from the West-End to theatre-land. At Button's, opposite Tom's, Jemmy Maclaine, the gentleman highwayman, had made daring appearances. Prices for dinner at the " ordinary " in a coffee-house were moderate and portions large. Upstairs rooms catered for more exalted private parties at greater cost.

The market in the centre of Covent Garden still preserved a deceptively innocent country air. It was bright with " sweet-peas and pinks, and scarlet Martagon Lilies, double stocks and flourishing Marjoram ". It was sanded and rolled, and presided over by a famous column, bearing " a curious Sun-Dial, foursquare, having about it a mound, gilt with gold, all neatly wrought in Freestone ". Around the steps of the column were rows of booths, piled with fresh flowers, fruits and vegetables. Quack doctors set up stalls with herbal remedies. Football was also played there, and when the prentices joined in, pedestrians took to their heels, for the game of these cockney athletes was very rough, and their ball was heavy. It often broke windows of the taverns and luxury shops with which the jackals of the entertainment trade had hastened to fill the arcades under the Piazzas after the nobility had ceased to live so near the

City.  It could not be denied that the reputation of the square had
long been dubious.  That of the side-streets surrounding it was
notorious.  They contained no less than twenty-two gambling hells.
In the square itself some fine houses still stood—large doll's houses,
handsomely built in red brick with stone facings.  They possessed
beautiful staircases and delicate panelling and chimney-pieces.  But
painters and players now lodged in them.  No actor of pretensions
lived anywhere but in Covent Garden, close enough to be summoned
to rehearsal by the beat of a drum; and to recognise stage-favourites
off-duty was one of the attractions of the old " Centre of the Town ".  13

David Garrick's principal boon-companion during his first years in
London was one whose appearance and record was enough to make a
loving mother's heart stand still.  " Wicked Charlie " Macklin,
" the wild Irishman ", whose real name was McLaughlin, was a
savage, coarse-looking fellow.  His countenance was perfectly that
of the stage villain.  He had killed a man.  In early youth he had
run away from an Irish saddler, to whom he had been apprenticed,
and had become a servitor in a tavern patronized by strolling players.
He had been a scout at Trinity College, Dublin, played in barns and
booths at Southwark Fair and joined a travelling company at
Bristol.  His first approach to the manager of Covent Garden
Theatre had been ill-received.  " I spoke so familiar, and so little in
the hoity-toity tone of the Tragedy of that day, that the manager
told me I had better go to grass for another year or two."  He
accepted this advice, collected an actress wife and presently was
engaged at Drury Lane.  He appeared first in London under the
name of " Mechlin " as Captain Brazen in *The Recruiting Officer*.  He
was successful, for he was full of energy, though remarkably hideous,
and he was doing well when he had the misfortune, in a green-room
squabble over a wig, to lunge at a fellow actor with a stick which
entered his adversary's left eye and caused his death.  But when all
this has been said, the worst has been said.  Macklin, advised by his
friends to go into hiding, manfully stood his trial and was acquitted
of murder, though convicted of manslaughter.  It does not appear
that he served any sentence.  The reason why David saw so much of
" Dear Mac " was professional.  They had the same, and revolution-
ary, ideas about acting.  Macklin deplored the accepted and
established style, which was what might truly be called " stagey ".
English actors, since the days of Dryden, had copied the French
model.  They came portentously downstage, struck an attitude, and
declaimed.  They wore costume of their own day with strange
additions.  It was quite normal for an actor taking a tragic lead to
wear a lofty headdress of plumes.  The females swept about the

boards in enormous hoops, powdered wigs and much mock jewellery. Tragic characters chanted, lovers moped and whined, comedians clowned. This was what the public expected, and the theatres were crowded. But the theatre in London seemed to both Macklin and Garrick to be in a bad way, and they believed the public was ready for a change—the naturalistic style. There were, when Garrick arrived in town, two principal theatres: Covent Garden, of which Rich was the manager, and Drury Lane, owned by Fleetwood. These rivals were of widely differing types. Old Rich was illiterate and had a disconcerting trick of calling everyone " out of their name " always with the prefix of " Mister ", pronounced " Muster ". He believed himself to be a great teacher, though his voice was poor and his accent was extraordinary. He was capable of knocking down a prompter, and returning from the wings to explain to his audience, " The fellow interrupted me in my Grand Pause." Audiences liked him. He was generally held to be unequalled as Harlequin. Fleetwood, whose euphonious and high-sounding name really was his own, was of an old family, polished, urbane and of a pleasing address. Unfortunately, he was quite unreliable. He had wasted most of his patrimony, before he had bought the patent of Drury Lane (which was going cheap), in a gamester's attempt to recoup himself. Macklin often accompanied him to White's, where both gambled heavily, and when Macklin was in funds and Fleetwood was not, the manager would borrow from the actor " with the manner of sensitive distress which would soften the hardest creditor ". Macklin was openhanded, and an indulgent parent. David Garrick went with him to coffee-houses, and when the occasion offered, amused the company by mounting upon the table and " mimeing ". His imitations of leading actors were " to the life ". He became a familiar figure in green-rooms, " a very sprightly young man, neatly made and of an expressive countenance, and most agreeable and entertaining manners. The stage possessed him wholly. He could talk and think of nothing else."

Although the condition of the theatres was not, in his opinion, good, the supply of actors of ability was large. But, as a class, their reputation was at a low ebb. Covent Garden and Drury Lane enjoyed monopolies. They were the only authorized theatres. In the very year that Garrick arrived in London, performances in premises lacking letters patent from the Crown or not licensed by the Lord Chamberlain had been prohibited by Sir Robert Walpole's Licensing Act. The Little Theatre, Haymarket, in which Henry Fielding had produced anti-government skits, and Goodman's Fields Theatre, Ayliffe Street, had to close. Goodman's Fields, behind the Minories, was in an industrial quarter, where weavers and silk manufacturers predominated. Giffard, who had bought and rebuilt it, at some expense, was a sanguine character, and for many months he believed that the Duke of Grafton, the Lord Chamberlain, would relent. He was of good extraction, and had occupied a post in the South-Sea House until he had run away to become a player. He had a sense of humour. Garrick listened to his tale of woe with sympathy. There was a Mr Webster down at Lichfield who knew a Mr Maddox who had interest with the duke. David thought Peter might approach Mr Webster. When Giffard found that the duke seemed determined to be adamant, he decided to reopen without a licence. The Act was loosely worded. He advertised concerts, for which tickets had to be bought. During the Interval a play was shown, free of charge, to all present. He succeeded in doing this for three years, always in hope of a licence.

One of the coldest winters in man's memory settled down upon England. The Great Frost, which began upon the day after Christmas 1739, endured until the last day of January 1740. A violent storm, with east wind, blew barges and lighters upon the Thames from their moorings, and the tide being heavy, floated ice upon them. At Barnard Castle horse-races were being held upon the frozen Tees. The streets of London were clogged and glassy; two or three horses tugged hackney carriages; coal-carts coming up from the wharves needed a team of eight. His Majesty headed a list of contributors to a Fund for the relief of sufferers from the Great Frost.

David Garrick's first play came to production on April 1, 1740. Fleetwood had accepted a *petite pièce*, which could hardly be said to have a plot, but gave scope for several of his company in rôles written for them. It was called *Lethe, or Esop in the Shades*, and the actors and actresses, in their pale silks and satins, drifted upon a scene which might have been painted by Watteau, or Lancret or Boucher— a grove, with a view of the river whose waters brought forgetfulness. There were two classical characters discovered when the curtain rose: old Esop, the philosopher, and Charon, who had to ferry the visitors. Mercury, who was to conduct them to Elysium, soon joined them, and after a brief, witty interchange of compliments, the three immortals burst into song—

> Ye mortals whom fancies and troubles perplex,
> Whom folly misguides, and infirmities vex,
> Whose lives hardly know what it is to be blest,
> Who rise without joy, and lie down without rest,
>     Obey the glad summons, to LETHE repair
>     Drink deep of the stream and forget all your care.

The first of the walking misfits from middle-earth, who have been heard without calling impatiently "Boat! boat! boat!" is the Poet. He wants to forget the hissing of his first play. But he has written another. (The Poet was cut out in later productions.) The Old Man who follows him wants to forget that he must die, and, to tell the truth, how he got his money. For he has a little money saved, in an iron chest ... Harry Woodward, as "the Beau" or "Fine Gentleman", had a part literally made for him. The Beau said he wanted to forget his modesty and good-nature—for on earth he was helpless when the ladies ran after him, and he was very unwilling to draw his sword to defend himself from other gentlemen. Lord Chalkstone, who came next, well heralded, was a great hit. He was not in the play as originally written, but in later years the gouty old lord was a favourite part of the author.

> None of your waters for me; damn 'em all; I never drink any but at Bath—I came merely for a little conversation with you, and to see your Elysian fields here. (*Looking through his glass.*) Which by the way, Mr Esop, are laid out most detestably—no taste! No fancy in the whole world! Your river there, what d'ye call? Aye, Styx—why, 'tis as straight as Fleet-ditch. You should have given it a serpentine sweep, and slope the banks of it. The place indeed has fine *capabilities*; but you should clear the wood to the left, and the clump of trees to the right: in short, the whole wants variety, extent, contract, inequality. (*Going towards the orchestra, stops suddenly, and looks into the Pit.*) Upon my word, here's a very fine hah-hah! And a most curious collection of evergreens and flowering shrubs.

To see Mr Garrick mincing down to quiz them, set the pit rocking, and the boxes liked the dig at "Capability" Brown, fashionable landscape-gardener. Later, a picture of Garrick as Lord Chalkstone sold well in print-shops.

Mr and Mrs Tatoo, who gave an opportunity for the juniors of Fleetwood's company, were a pathetic couple. They were not yet out of their teens, not three months eloped and quite at loggerheads. They wanted to be divorced—forget it all. The Frenchman, who entered humming a little song, wanted to forget his creditors in England, and that although, over here, he was Monsieur, le Marquis de Pouville, he was in fact Jean Frisson, a hairdresser from Provence. The author played this part, next year, *con amore*. He was followed by Mrs Riot, a foreshadowing of Mrs Malaprop. Kitty Clive, Drury Lane's first comedy actress, was provided with a typical entry.

> A monster! a filthy brute! your watermen are as unpolite upon the Styx as upon the Thames. Stow a lady of fashion with tradesmen and mechanics! Ah! what's this? Serbeerus or Plutus! (*Seeing Esop.*) Am I to be frightened with all the monsters of this internal world?

Esop.   What is the matter, lady?

Mrs Riot.   Everything is the matter, my spirits are uncompos'd, and every circumstance about me in a perfect dilemma.

The world of fashion is Mrs Riot's prey, but she is hindered from entering it by a brute of a husband, who won't leave the City. However, she has got one invitation.

Mrs Riot.   (*Drawing out a card.*)   Lady Rantan's compliments to Mrs Riot.

SONG

The card invites, in crowds we fly
To join the jovial *rout*, full cry;

What joy from cares and plagues all day
To hie to the midnight *hark-away*.

Nor want, nor pain, nor grief, nor care,
Nor dronish husbands enter there;

The brisk, the bold, the young and gay
All hie to the midnight *hark-away* . . .

She makes her exit still singing, and, supported by his tailor, the Drunken Man totters on.   He is Mrs Riot's brutish husband.

Esop.   What in the name of ridicule have we here?   So sir, what are you?

Drunken Man.   Drunk—very drunk, at your service.

Esop.   That's a piece of information I did not want.

Drunken Man.   And yet it's all the information I can give you.

Esop.   Pray, sir, what brought you hither?

Drunken Man.   Curiosity—and a hackney coach.

The Tailor, who wants to forget that he has an unfaithful wife, was cut out of *Lethe* later, but the Drunken Man, played by Macklin on the first night, became one of the great parts of Richard Yates.

The play ends with Charon reporting a hitch.   The gentry waiting for the ferry are having such a quarrel about precedence that they have forgotten their misfortunes.   The immortals decide to discharge those who have already come over, and during a last song, by Mercury, all the characters drift on to the scene again, from the grove. Esop leads them off, to drink to the forgetfulness of vice, and the curtain descends on a moral couplet

'Tis vice alone disturbs the human breast
Care dies with guilt; be virtuous, and be blest.

The Beau and Mrs Riot were so much liked by the public that in due time figures were produced by the Bow Porcelain company, and at Plymouth, of Woodward and Clive as " The Fine Gentleman and Lady ". Garrick, in his prime, had them on a chimney-piece in his country house. The piece was given again, a fortnight later, with a prologue by Johnson. The takings went to Giffard, who had played Esop. It was his benefit night—that is to say, he was allowed by Fleetwood to collect the door-keeper's receipts, less a charge of £60 for the use of the premises.

The spring season was almost at an end. In May theatres closed, and actors with sufficient prestige went across to Ireland to play leads in Dublin, while lesser performers toured the provinces. A Great Drought was following the Great Frost. On July 5 David found time to send a long letter to Peter, who had been up to town.

Dear Peter,
    I received yrs with a double pleasure, yr safe arrival and my mother's better health being mention'd therein. I shall send the sugar as powder, and would have sent the white wine, but I thought the grocer's packing would be better . . .

The despatch of a wig for Peter, and hopes that Giffard was going to get his licence, occupied him for a long paragraph. He asked his brother to pull what strings were possible in Lichfield to help a friend to whom they were both indebted. " I have the custom of the Bedford Coffee-House, one of the best in London, by Giffard's means." He was still very much tied to Lichfield. A Mr Sadal had sent up to town a young nephew, " an understanding youth " with, as yet, " the Staffordshire twang ", who wanted to become a doctor. David was doing his best for him. It was not possible for the lad to enter the hospital he desired until Michaelmas, meanwhile he was to attend lectures. " I will take care of him till then, and preach economy and virtue to him. I have already given him a just detestation of the lewd Night Walkers and vile polluters of Youth. He always smiles when I begin my Lecture and cries ' Flee ye! you talk welly as well as Mr Hinton ' (a favourite clergyman of his at Lichfield)."

David repeated towards the end of this letter his relief that his mother was better. In a second and shorter note, dated a month later, he had to mention that cash was rather low, and one of their creditors wanted his account settled. Would Peter send up supplies as soon as possible? " I am very uneasy till you send me a particular account of my mother, for I hear by several hands she is in great danger. Pray my duty, and I desire nothing may be concealed from me."

Three weeks after he wrote these lines Mrs Garrick died. She

D

was buried beside her husband at Lichfield on September 28, 1740.
For David it was the Order of Release, but he did not immediately
avail himself of it.   The ties that bound him to his family and their
circle at Lichfield were still so strong.


### 3

During his first years in London he met Johnson mostly at the
headquarters of *The Gentleman's Magazine*.   Mrs Johnson had come
to town, but she was not a favourite with her husband's ex-pupil.
The first number of *The Gentleman's Magazine and Historical
Chronicle* had been published in 1731, by Edward Cave, who was its
proprietor, printer and editor.   He had reporters posted in both
Houses of Parliament, to watch the debates, and as the magazine
increased in circulation some members sent him copies of their
speeches.   Johnson reported debates for about three years.   The
miscellany also contained poems, music, correspondence, essays,
biographies, engravings, maps, reviews, news from home and abroad,
and births, deaths, and marriages.   " Printer " Cave was a rough
diamond, over six feet high and very bulky.   He was a strict vege-
tarian and a martyr to gout.   His career had been chequered.   His
headmaster had thought that he was worthy of a University education, but he had been asked to leave Rugby Grammar School for
robbing his headmaster's wife's henroost.   After working as a clerk
in the excise and in the timber trade, he had found his *métier* in the
printing and publishing world.   He had married a widow who had
brought him a little money, and had got, through her influence, employment in the post office, but had been asked to leave that too.   He
was charged with opening letters to obtain news, though this was
never proved.   By the time that he was forty, he had enough capital
to buy a small printing office at St John's Gate, Clerkenwell, and here,
from the beautiful gatehouse of the ancient priory of the Knights of
St John, he began to send forth his magazine.   Its cover was
embellished with an engraving of the premises.   Johnson said that
when first he saw the venerable building so familiar to him from its
likeness, he beheld it with reverence.

He introduced David to Cave, and during the early autumn of
1740 theatricals took place in the large room over the gatehouse of
St John's.   The piece chosen was by Henry Fielding, *The Mock
Doctor*, and David played the Doctor.   It was essentially an amateur
affair.   Some of the printers were called in to read the smaller parts.
The epilogue was written by David, and appeared in the September
number of *The Gentleman's Magazine* signed " G ".   He himself

advanced at the close of the entertainment, stroking his wig, to
speak its three dozen couplets, which opened well—

> How happy chance may alter one's condition,
> Behold poor Gregory a rich physician!
> My axe is chang'd and dwindled to a pen,
> To trees once fatal, fatal now to men . . .

During this second hard winter he had quite a famous man as a
fellow performer in a burlesque of *Julius Caesar* called *Caesar's
Ghost*, got up by two of the playwriting sons of Benjamin Hoadly, the
somewhat worldly Bishop of Winchester. William Hogarth, artist,
was to become a close and dear friend, though he was ten years senior.
As an actor he was not a success, though he was enthusiastic and a
good mimic. Either from stage-fright or absent-mindedness he
could never remember his part. The difficulty was solved by
writing his lines very large on an illuminated paper-lantern which he
bore in his hand. Hogarth was remarkably short, barely five feet
high, and his benevolent brow was adorned by a dramatic scar which
actually recorded no more than an accident in childhood. He wore
a large old-fashioned bushy wig, walked and spoke with a consequential air, carried a rustic-looking stick, and was often attended by
his dog, the pug " Trump ". He was a native of Kendal, and had
had a hard struggle before he had attracted public attention with
what he called " small conversation pieces ". David and he had
noted, and were to record, in their various spheres, much the same
things, and Hogarth, too, was always on the side of the angels.
Although he depicted, in detail, the horrible and the squalid, it was
always to point the moral lesson. *The Harlot's Progress*, his first
effort in this line, had been doubly successful. Lady Thornhill had
caused the series to be conveyed into her husband's dining-room.
On studying them, Sir James had asked the artist's name. On hearing that it was William Hogarth, with whom Miss Thornhill had
eloped, he had drily commented that a man who could do so well
could afford a wife without a portion. But a reconciliation had
followed. *The Rake's Progress* and *Marriage à la Mode* had confirmed Hogarth's talent, and about the time Garrick came to town
he had produced *Four Times of the Day*, and *Strolling Actresses
dressing in a Barn*, which demonstrated that although he was not
blind to their failings, he knew thoroughly, and had sympathy with,
the poor players on whom the Licensing Act of 1737 had just come
down so heavily.

Meanwhile, a theatrical event in which Garrick was deeply
interested was drawing near. Macklin had at last persuaded Fleetwood to let him attempt something which would be doubly a novelty.

He wanted to appear as Shylock, and in Shakespeare's *Merchant of Venice*. The character was familiar to audiences, but in Lord Lansdowne's adaptation, *The Jew of Venice*, first acted in 1701; and the tradition was that the Jew was a low-comedy figure. On St Valentine's Day, 1741, Macklin arrived at Drury Lane looking more than usually awful. The plentiful lines on his nutcracker countenance were heavily scored in black. He was wearing a piqued beard, a red hat and a loose black gabardine. He had been looking up his history and he believed that this was the correct costume for a Venetian Jew of Shakespeare's day. Recounting his emotions afterwards, he confessed that when the last bell rang before the curtain went up his heart " began to beat a little. However I mustered all the courage I could and, recommending my cause to Providence, threw myself boldly on the stage, and was received by one of the loudest thunders of applause I ever before experienced." He played Shylock as a villain, and completely naturally, and an audience accustomed to a comic Jew and the accepted formal style of acting could hardly believe their eyes and ears. But his performance carried conviction. As the first scenes passed he could hear distinctly from the pit, murmurs of " Very well—very well indeed! This man seems to know what he is about." At the close of the third act, for which he said he had " reserved " himself, the manager came forward with outstretched hands, uttering the glad but not grammatical phrase, " Macklin! you was right at last! "

James Quin, who had first appeared at Drury Lane three years before Garrick was born, was playing Antonio. He was an established favourite, and prided himself on being a wit and never opening a book. Shylock had surprised him, too, for at rehearsals Macklin had given no hint of his intention but simply walked through the part. Quin said, guardedly, " If God Almighty writes a legible hand that man must be a villain." The Royal Box at Drury Lane was soon occupied, and it was told that next morning, at a Prime Minister's audience with his sovereign, Sir Robert Walpole had said, " I wish, your Majesty, it was possible to find a recipe for frightening the House of Commons! " " Vat you tink," asked George II, who confessed to a sleepless night, " of sending dem to see dat Irishman play Shylock? " Another figure far more versed in literature, one whose pen would make or kill, was presently observed crouched in a side box to watch a new sort of Jew and acting. The wasp of Twickenham had come out of invalidish retirement. Alexander Pope was reported to have produced a couplet on the occasion.

> This is the Jew
> That Shakespeare drew.

In fact it was not, for Macklin played Shylock as a straight villain without the slightest attempt to gain sympathy, for which the text gives authority.  But he continued to repeat his success for the rest of his life without alteration.  He had been natural, which nobody yet had dared to attempt, and he had made people pack a theatre to see a Shakespeare play.

16  A few weeks after Macklin's triumph, Dick Yates, who was appearing as Harlequin at Giffard's unlicensed theatre, Goodman's Fields, felt too ill to go on.  Nobody in London, far less Lichfield, guessed that on that chilly spring night, the spangled jacket and mask of Harlequin, whose performance lacked nothing of fire and gaiety, had been worn by David Garrick.

Giffard was taking what was called a sharing company down to Ipswich while the London theatres closed for the summer that season.  The theatre in Ipswich had the appearance of a warehouse and was attached to the tavern next door.  In a July issue, a local paper gave the full bill of the company which was to appear on Tuesday, 21st, in a comedy called *The Inconstant, or The Way to Win Him*.  The part of Captain Duretête was to be played by a Mr Lydall.  Mrs Giffard had been a Miss Lydall, so the young actor might well be supposed to be a relation of the manager.  It seems that he had already appeared as Aboan in *Oroonoko*, but as Aboan was a noble savage, with a black face, he might easily have done so without being recognized.  *Oroonoko* had been adapted by Thomas Southerne from a novel by the Restoration authoress, Aphra Behn, and had first been produced in 1699.  The scene was one of hot blue skies and cocoanut groves—Surinam, a colony in the West Indies— and the hero was a dusky prince.  Aboan, one of his counsellors, was not a heavy part, but contained some opportunities.  When he had to work upon Oroonoko's feelings of jealousy for his consort, the blameless Imoinda, Aboan bore a slight likeness to Iago.  But he was not a villain, and he made a good end.  The caste included British officers, ladies who had left " dear England " for their country's good, Indians and negroes.  Aboan did not open his mouth until the first scene of Act III, and after that was off until Scene IV.  In Act IV he had a few lines in Scene II; in Scene IV came his chance— " enter Aboan Bloody ".  This entrance was followed by an embarrassingly protracted suicide.

Ipswich claimed afterwards to have been the first to recognize the genius of England's greatest actor.  Certainly, not only the citizens, but gentry from the surrounding landscape came in to see Mr Giffard's shows.  Mr Lydall was received well as Sir Harry Wildair, Captain Brazen and Osric (to Yates's Hamlet).  He himself said afterwards that he had gone to Ipswich resolved, if he was a failure there, to give up the idea of so dangerous a profession. But he found, as he had hoped, that he could do what he thought. It was quite easy. He had only to proceed. He was a natural actor. Disillusionment awaited him.

On his return to London, Mr Lydall sent in his own name, and expressed his desire for an engagement, to Mr Fleetwood at Drury Lane. Mr Fleetwood, who had been so approachable to a young gentleman in the wine trade who had provided him with a produce-able *petite pièce*, was quite different when confronted with a theatrical aspirant. Mr Fleetwood would not oblige him. Nor, which was less surprising, when he went on to Covent Garden, could old Rich. When Peter Garrick came to London, on one of his periodic visits, he found David unwell and out of spirits, but the state of their business was enough to explain this. In the last week of October 1741, safely home, Peter received two letters, one from his brother, the other from John Swinfen, son of the doctor who had stood god-father to Samuel Johnson. Both told the same story. David had at last betrayed his family. He had taken the plunge.

## 4

David Garrick's correspondence with his brother about his going on the stage was preserved by Peter and eventually came to rest amongst David's papers. In the view of after events the little series is pure comedy, but at the date when they were written they were high tragedy.                                             17

Dear Peter,

        I rec'd my shirt safe and am now to tell you what I suppose you may have heard of before this. But before I let you into the affair, 'tis proper to premise some things, that I may appear less culpable in your opinion than I might otherwise do.

        I have made an exact estimate of my stock of wine, and what money I have out at interest, and find that since I have been a Wine Merchant I have run out near four hundred pounds. And trade not increasing I was very sensible some way must be thought of to redeem it.

        My mind (as you must know) has been always inclined to the Stage, nay, so strongly that all my illness and lowness of spirits was owing to my want of resolution to tell you my thoughts when here. Finding at last both my inclination and interest requir'd some new way of life, I have chosen the most agreeable to myself, and tho' I know you will be much displeas'd at me, yet I hope when you find that I have the genius of an actor without the vices, you will think less severely of me and not be asham'd to own me for a brother.

        I am willing to agree to anything you propose about the wine. I will take a thorough survey of the vaults and, making what you have at Lichfield part of one Stock, will either send you your share I have, or any other way you shall propose.

Last night I play'd Richard the Third to the surprise of Every Body, and as I shall make very near £300 per annum by it, and as it is really what I doat upon, I am resolv'd to pursue it.   I believe I shall have Bower's money, which, when I have it, shall go towards my part of the wine you have at Lichfield.

Pray write me an answer immediately

I am dr. Peter<br>Yours sincerely<br>D. Garrick.

I have a farce [*The Lying Valet*] coming out at Drury Lane.

John Swinfen's letter, of the same date, is in a most beautiful script, but has one distracting feature.   Although, avowedly an old friend of the family, he has not got their surname right.

Dear Sir,

I don't doubt but you will soon hear my good friend David Garwick performed last night at Goodman's Fields theater, and for fear you should hear any false or malicious account that may perhaps be disagreeable to you, I will give you the truth, which much pleased me.   I was there, and was witness to a most generous applause he gain'd in the character of Richard the Third; for I believe there was not one in the house that was not in raptures.   I heard several men of judgement declare it their opinion that nobody ever excell'd him in that part, and that they were surpris'd, with so peculiar a genius, how it was possible for him to keep off the Stage so long.   Many of his country friends, who have been most used to theatrical performances in Town Halls by Strollers will be apt to imagine the highest pitch a man can arrive at on the stage is about that degree of exalted heroism as the Herberts, and the Hallams have formally made us laugh and cry with.   And there are I dont question many others who, because their Fathers were called Gentlemen (and perhaps themselves, the first), will think that it is a disgrace and a Scandal that the child of an old Friend should endeavour to get an honest livelyhood and is not content to live in a scanty manner because his Father was a Gentleman.   I think I know you well enough to be convinced that you have not the same sentiments, and I hope there are some other of his friends who will not alter their Opinion or Regard of him till they find the Stage corrupts his Morals and makes him less deserving, which I do not take by any means to be a necessary consequence nor likely to happen to my honest friend David.

Cousin Peter Fermignac, who also had a neat hand, had been entrusted with the painful task of breaking the news to Aunt and Uncle La Condé at Carshalton.   He chose to send on David's explanation, addressed to him, to Aunt La Condé, who had been born Jane Garrick.

Dear Madam,

The underwritten is a copy of a letter sent me from David Garric who play'd Crook'd Back Richard last night and does it to-night again, at Goodman's Fields.

## THE LETTER

Dear Sir,

I suppose you must have heard by this time of my playing King Richard at Goodman's Fields, and I suppose you are apprehensive I design to continue on the stage. I have troubled you with an account of my intention.

You must know that since I have been in business (the Wine Trade, I mean), I have run out almost half of my fortune, and tho' to this day I don't owe anything, yet the terrible prospect of running it all out made me think of something to redeem it. My mind led me to the stage, which from being very young I found myself inducing to, and have been very unhappy that I could not come upon it before. The only thing that gives me pain is that my friends, I suppose, will look very cool upon me, particularly the chief of them I have at Carshalton. But what can I do? I am wholly bent upon the thing, and can make £300 per annum out of it. As my brother will settle at Litchfield, I design to throw up the Wine business as soon as I can conveniently, and desire youl'l let my Uncle know. If you should want to speak with me, the Stage door will always be open to you, or any other part of the house, for I am Manager with Mr Giffard—and you may always command

Yr most humble servant<br>
D. Garrick.

Peter added a post-script.

This is his letter which I leave you to consider, and am very sorry for the contents, but I thought fit to communicate them to you and am

yr dutyful nephew<br>
Peter Fermignac. Tuesday, October 20th.

Peter Garrick evidently obeyed his brother's request to answer immediately, for although his side of the correspondence is missing, a shower of further explanations from David is available. From internal evidence it is clear that Peter's reception of the news was all that David, in his most pessimistic moments, had feared. For several months he does not even dare to address the head of the family by his Christian name.

October 27

My dear Brother,

The uneasiness I received at your letter is inexpressible. However, 'twas a Shock I expected, and had guarded myself as well as I could against it. And the love I sincerely have for you, together with the prevailing arguments you have made use of, were enough to overthrow my strongest resolution, did not necessity (a very pressing Advocate) on my side convince me that I am not so much to blame as you seem to think that I am.

As to my Uncle's upbraiding you with keeping our circumstances so secret, I am surpris'd at it, for you. Be sure what I have run out has been more owing to my own wilfullness than any great miscarriage in Trade. But run out I have, and let me live never so warily but must run out more; and indeed, the trade we have, if you will reflect very seriously, can never be sufficient to maintain me and a servant, handsomely.

As for the Stage, I know that in general it deserves your censure, but if you will consider how hansomely and how reputably some have lived—such as Booth, Miles, Wilks, Cibber etc—and admitted into and admir'd by the best company; and as my genius that way (by the best judges) is thought wonderful, how can you be so averse to my proceeding, when not only my inclination but my friends, who at first were surpris'd at my intent, by seeing me on the Stage, are now convinc'd 'twas impossible for me to keep off? As to company, the best in Town are desirous of mine, and I have received more civillity and favour from such since my playing than I ever did in all my life before.   Mr Glover (Leonidas, I mean) sent for me and told me as well as everybody he conversed with, that he had not seen such acting for ten years before.   But in short, were I to tell you what they say about me it would be too vain, tho' I am now writing to a brother.   However, Dear Peter, so willing am I to continue in your affection, that were I certain of a less income with more reputation, I would gladly take to it.

I have not yet had my name in any Bills, and have played only the part of Richard the Third, which brings crowded audiences every night.   Dear Peter, write me a letter next post, and I'll give you a full answer, not having time enough at present.   I have not a debt of twenty shillings upon me, so in that be very easy.   I am sorry my sisters are under such uneasiness, and as I really love both them and you, will ever make it my study to appear

Your affectionate brother

David Garrick

By November 16 he has to confess that he has now played more than Richard—but with the same success.

My dear Brother,

I am very sorry you still seem so utterly averse to what I am so greatly inclin'd, and to what the best judges think I have one of the greatest geniuses for.   The great, nay incredible, success and approbation I have met with from the greatest persons in England have almost made me re-solve (though I am sorry to say it against your entreaties) to pursue it, as I shall certainly make a fortune by it if health continues.   Mr Lyttelton, Mr Pitt and several other members of Parliament came to see me play Chamont in " The Orphan ", and Mr Pitt, who is reckon'd the greatest orator in the House of Commons, said I was the best actor the English Stage had produc'd, and he sent a Gentleman to me to let me know he and the other Gentlemen would be glad to see me.   The Prince has heard so great a character of me that we are in daily expectations of his coming to see me.   I am told you are afraid Giffard has had my money.   Upon my honour, he does not owe me a farthing, having paid me long ago what I lent him, which was but thirty pounds.   I receive at present from him (tho' 'tis a secret) six guineas a week, and am to have a clear Benefit.

The jargon of his profession dreadful to Lichfield ears now breaks in.   Pit and boxes are to be put together on his benefit night, and on mere speculation he has had an offer of £120 for the result.   All friends " who still so continue to me " will be present.   He wishes that Peter could be brought up to see him act, and judge for himself. His seat and lodging shall cost him nothing.   He does not dare to say that on this occasion his own name, for the first time, is to appear on the bills.

Letters to Peter seem to have been invariably achieved on Tuesday nights, after returning from the theatre, but the next, dated November 24, shows no signs of flagging spirits.

> My dear Brother,
>     As you finish'd your last letter with saying tho you did not approve of the Stage, yet you would always be my affect Brother, I may now venture to tell you I am very near quite resolved to be a Player, as I have the judgment of the best judges (who to a man are of opinion) that I shall turn out (nay, they say I am) not only the best Trajedian but Comedian in England.

A ray of hope has dawned upon the family horizon. Uncle La Condé is coming round.

> My uncle I am told will be reconciled to me, for even the merchants say 'tis an honour to him, not otherwise.
>     The business is rather better than it was, but my mind is quite turn'd another way. . . . Write, pray, immediately.

Peter evidently also showed signs of weakening, for the next letter, a very long one, announces that, together with the London accounts of Garrick & Co., a copy of *The Lying Valet* is on its way to him by carrier. The date is December 22.

> The Valet takes prodigiously, and is approved of by men of genius, and thought the most diverting Farce that ever was performed. I believe you'll find it read pretty well, and in performance 'tis a general Roar from beginning to end, and I have got as much reputation in the character of Sharp as in any other. . . .

He adds a list of the other parts he has now played—Jack Smatter in *Pamela*, Chamont in *The Orphan*, the Ghost in *Hamlet*, Clody in *The Fop's Fortune* and Lothario in *The Fair Penitent*. He is almost ready to appear as Bayes in *The Rehearsal*, and Othello. It is quite untrue that he has ever played Harlequin at Covent Garden, as some people said. He played a bit of Harlequin's part once, in an emergency, at Goodman's Fields. He is finishing up the London end of the wine business now—shall bottle no more and sell what is left in cask. He regrets there is not such a thing as a Seville Orange in Town, nothing but Lisbon Crabs at threepence apiece, so he will not send any. He has got a heavy cold and is going to spend the weekend with Joe Smith in the country at Stanmore.

On April 19 he announces that he dates his retirement from Garrick and Co. as from March Quarter Day. He has been down to the vaults for the last time—two hogsheads of Port, one and a half of Madeira and one of Claret. Peter shall have them all. He is feeling

better than usual, but will be glad when the season is over.  Something dreadful has happened.  A Lichfield lady, Mrs Brown, had
decided to see young Garrick act, and had found that his name was
not the Open Sesame at Goodman's Fields that she had been led to
expect.  Though Peter had written her desires, Mrs Brown's box had
not been forthcoming.  David has gone into this, and is able to
explain that if Mrs Brown's box had been asked for, there it was.
But the footman of the friend with whom she was guest had asked
for the box in his lady's name—Mrs Dalton.  *Voila!*

The family at Lichfield, who were to be dabbled in the mire by
having a brother a player, numbered six.  Peter, Lennie and Jenny
were aged thirty-two, twenty-seven and twenty-four and all alas!
unmarried.  William, who was twenty-two, was safely in the army,
but George was nearly nineteen and even little Merrial seventeen.

David's last letter to Peter upon the painful subject of his chosen
profession has an awful look, but this is mainly because the same
hand which scored out passages in earlier family letters in this
collection, has been at work with a particularly sooty ink.  Still, it
is clear David's bed is not yet of roses.  Billy, the soldier, has been
in Town, and tales have reached Lichfield that Billy has spoken un-
suitably about Peter's conduct to David.  David lays this ghost
promptly.  Billy has done nothing of the kind.  " It gives me pain
to see you warm upon trifles, and suspicious without foundation."
David has been able to get a place as a clerk in a solicitor's office for
George—Mr Paterson's office, a great favour—and the lad must
come up in October.  An engraving of Garrick as Richard is on its
way to Lichfield, for Mr Vyse, who had asked for it; one for Peter
shall follow.  David is now going to Cheltenham to the Vernons',
friends of the Lichfield Fletchers.  His last letter of this series ends
with a familiar ring—" Best Compliments to Mr Walmesley ".  But
it really mattered no more what Lichfield thought.

5

It is a curious fact that Peter, when inveighing against David's
going on the stage, does not appear to have made use of a serious
argument against his present situation.  Actors performing at the
two licensed theatres were King's Players.  David had come out in
an unlicensed house, and according to the merciless Act of 1737,
persons employed at such establishments were liable to be classed as
" common players of Interludes " with rogues and vagabonds.
Goodman's Fields was not, of course, his choice.  He had accepted
Giffard's offer *faute de mieux*.  He was still good at making the
best of things, and said that if he had been accepted at Drury Lane

or Covent Garden it could only have been for small parts, as a beginner, and probably ones ill-suited to his appearance. He was resolved never to come forth in parts which demanded a " tall fellow ". There seemed to be much in favour of venturing first as *19* crook-back Richard. The play (or Cibber's version of it) had always been popular. Macklin's success as Shylock had shown that there was a revival of interest in Shakespeare, and a public for the naturalistic style of acting. The play-bill for October 19, 1741, was not quite truthful.

At the late Theatre in Goodman's fields, this day, will be performed a Concert of Vocal and Instrumental Music, divided into Two Parts.

Tickets at three, two and one shilling.

Places for Boxes to be taken at The Fleece
Tavern, next the Theatre.

N.B. Between the two parts of the Concert, will be presented an Historical Play, called

The Life and Death of
King Richard the Third

Containing the distress of K. Henry VI.

The artful acquisition of the Crown
by King Richard

The murder of young King Edward V.
and his brother in the Tower

The landing of the Earl of Richmond; and the death
of King Richard in the memorable battle of Bosworth-
field; being the last that was fought between the
houses of York and Lancaster.

With many other true Historical passages.

The part of King Richard by a Gentleman (who
never appeared on any Stage).

The Concert was announced to begin at exactly six o'clock. The house that awaited Garrick's first appearance in a leading part in London was remembered as cold, thin and unexpectant. London was accustomed, since Cibber had retired, to Quin as Richard, and both actors had been notably laborious as the royal murderer. The preliminary music having been endured, the audience prepared to fall into the usual somewhat trance-like condition induced by witnessing tragedians stalking about the stage like classical deities, and uttering in a monotonous sing-song, relieved only " to excite admiration and intrap applause " by a " sudden mechanical depression ", or " the rant ". Macklin, who was amongst the friends of Garrick present on this memorable first night, used to tell that when the new Richard came upon the scene (which he does at once, in this most difficult

# GARRICK as Richard III.

*By William Hogarth* (75" × 98½")

Garrick first appeared as Richard at Goodman's Fields, October 19, 1741. When about to retire, he announced, " I gained my fame by Richard, and mean to end by it," but he eventually ended his career in a comedy part, on June 10, 1776, and appeared as Richard for the last time at a Royal Command performance three days earlier. Sheridan thought his Richard " fine but not terrible enough ", which provoked from Mrs Siddons, who had played Lady Anne, " God bless me! What could be more terrible? "

Engraved by Hogarth and Grignion, 1746.

This portrait was originally bought by Mrs Duncombe of Duncombe Park, from Hogarth, and descended by inheritance to the Earls of Feversham. It was bought in 1956, from Agnews, by the Walker Art Gallery of Liverpool.

*Reproduced by kind permission of the Trustees, the Walker Art Gallery, Liverpool.*

play), he seemed disconcerted, and remained a few seconds without being able to go on. Then he collected himself and in a few more seconds the Rubicon was crossed and his audience realized that this player " seemed to identify himself with the part ".

> The character he assumed was visible in his countenance; the power of his imagination was such that he transformed himself into the very man; the passions rose in rapid succession, and before he uttered a word, were legible on every feature of that various face. . . . The rage and rapidity with which he spoke—
>
> " The North! what do they in the North?
> When they should serve their Sovereign in the West? "
>
> made a most astonishing impression. His soliloquy in the tent-scene dis-covered the inward man. Everything he described was almost reality; the spectator thought he heard the hum of either army from camp to camp, and steed threatening steed. When he started from his dream, he was a spectacle of horror. He called out in a manly tone
>
> " Give me another horse! "

Three other incidents in his performance attracted particular approbation: his love-making to Lady Anne (played by Giffard's wife), his new " business " throwing away the prayer-book after his interview with the Mayor, and the gloating malignancy of his expression and voice when he spoke the too well-known words " Off with his head—so much for Buckingham." But the tent-scene was generally adjudged his best. Five years later his friend Hogarth painted him in this scene, gesticulating horribly. On this first night an audience presented with something so unusual seemed for some moments in doubt whether to hiss or clap, but such doubts did not last long. " Loud shouts of approbation " soon broke out, and " the death of Richard was accompanied with the loudest gratula-tions of applause ". Garrick, according to a printer, Mr Dryden Leach, who was behind the scenes and loved to record the incident, was grateful for the juice of a Seville orange. He had almost shouted himself hoarse by the time Richard was called upon " to throw aside the hypocrite and politician and assume the warrior and the hero ".

Next day the *Daily Post* contained a small significant paragraph:

> Last night, was performed gratis the tragedy of " King Richard the Third " at the late theatre in Goodman's Fields, when the character of Richard was performed by a gentleman who never appeared before, whose reception was the most extraordinary and great that was ever known on such an occasion. We hear he obliges the town this evening with the same performance.

Another criticism from *The Champion* which appeared a little later demonstrates to how low an ebb the theatrical art had fallen. Richard was commended because he neither whined, bellowed nor grumbled, because his mien and gait were neither strutting, mincing, stiff nor slouching, and because " when three or four are on the stage with him he is attentive to whatever is spoke, and never drops his character when he has finished a speech, by either looking contemptuously on an inferior performer, unnecessary spitting, or suffering his eyes to wander through the whole circle of spectators ". 21

He played Richard for three nights in succession, then his old Ipswich part of Aboan for three nights. On October 28 " the gentleman who performed King Richard " was seen in *Love Makes a Man*. On November 2 he was Richard again, and just as he was ready to go on was told that Mr Pope was in the house, brought by Lord Orrery. As on the first night, a moment of hesitation was observed after Richard appeared and before he opened his mouth, but the usual success followed. Garrick said that on entering he was aware of the poet watching him with a serious earnestness. When he dared to look again, during a burst of applause, he perceived Mr Pope's frail hands applauding heartily. Pope pronounced, " That young man never had his equal and never will have a rival," but also apprehensions lest " the young man should become vain, and be ruined by applause ". He came twice more to confirm his first impression, and Garrick supped in his company. By November 26 " house full " was announced at Goodman's Fields soon after five o'clock and several hundred people who had come to see Richard at a theatre so close to the looming Tower of London were obliged to depart westwards unsatisfied. *Lethe* was next put on by Giffard, and then *The Orphan* and *Pamela*, in which " the gentleman who played Richard " was Chamont and Jack Smatter.

December 2 was his benefit night, and at last " Mr Garrick " was announced to appear in *The Fair Penitent*. Tickets were to be had at the Bedford, Tom's and Cary's coffee-houses, at The Fleece adjoining the theatre and Mr Garrick's own lodgings, in Mansfield Street, Goodman's Fields. Footmen keeping seats for their employers were warned to arrive by three o'clock, and that there could be no keeping of seats in the pit. In Christmas week *The Lying Valet* came out, at Goodman's Fields, not Drury Lane, as the author had originally expected. He was an irresistible Sharp. The play was published, and advertised, price 1s., in the December number of *The Gentleman's Magazine*.

He was beginning to get too many letters, but he answered them all very politely. There was a young clergyman, tutor to the family of Lord Carpenter in Grosvenor Square, who was notably profuse in admiration and advice. Mr Thomas Newton, who was Lichfield 22 born, brought his noble employer and " young ladies " to see his fellow townsman act, and finally Mrs Porter, who had returned to Town specially. Mrs Porter, whose name was still spoken with bated breath in green-rooms, had made her first appearance on the stage in 1699, and it was said that she had been seen long before that, as a child actress—the Fairy Queen at Bartholomew Fair. All the stories about Mrs Porter were impressive, including her carriage accident on Highwood Hill, Hendon, when, driving herself home after a performance, she had presented a pistol at an amateur high-wayman, cowed him into submission and presented him with ten shillings. Unfortunately at the close of the scene she had struck her horse too dramatically, with the result that she was bolted with, her chaise overturned and her thigh was dislocated. After that she had always supported herself, on the stage and off, with an effective cane. She had retired in a blaze of glory some ten years past, but made occasional gracious appearances at benefit and command perform-ances. Her comment on the new actor, spoken in the powerful tones for which she was celebrated, was generous. " The youth " was a born actor, better than many who had twenty years' training. " Good God! what will he be in time! " Not all veterans were equally kind. Old Colley Cibber, whose disagreeable son Theophilus was being pushed on by him since his own retirement, persisted that Theophilus was superior to Garrick as Bayes in *The Rehearsal.* Colley sat at Tom's Coffee-House, listening with a wry face when he was told of Mr Garrick being commended by Mr Pope and Mr Pitt, supping with Mr Murray, and dining with Lord Halifax, Lord Sand-wich and Lord Chesterfield. An old General, playing cards with Col-ley, irritated him so much by his recurrences to the subject of the new actor that presently Colley revoked. " Have you no diamond, Mr Cibber? " " Yes, a million, by G—d! " " And why not play them then? " A bystander silkily suggested the crowning insult, " Because *Garrick* would not let him! " Colley affected to believe that when Garrick played Fribble he was so lifelike because he was in fact a Fribble. Most people were surprised that Garrick was so different in his various parts. They were accustomed to going to see Cibber, or Quin, or Foote, who were always recognizable from the moment they appeared, from their pronounced mannerisms, and never much different whatever part they were in. With the new man they had to wait for a thrilling whisper that this was Garrick.

In the green-room at Drury Lane, the elegant Fleetwood asked Cibber when he would have another comedy ready. " But who would take the characters? " asked Cibber dangerously. " Why, sir," he was told, " there's Garrick, Macklin, Clive, Pritchard." " Oh!

yes? I know the list very well—but then, my dear fellow " (taking his snuff very deliberately), " where the devil are your *actors*? "

Mrs Bracegirdle, another retired luminary, and as unrelenting as her name, took Cibber to task. She was in her seventieth year, and had been trained by Betterton, and had certainly been on the stage when she was six. She was wonderfully preserved, and had large, firm, white, even teeth, and a high complexion. She was a leading exponent of the old style. Indeed there was a legend that once, when she had come to the end of a majestic tragic scene, the poor fellow who was supposed to be playing the part of her lover had woken up with a start. " Come, come, Cibber," said Mrs Brace-girdle, " tell me, is there not something like envy in your character of this young gentleman? The actor who pleases everybody must be a man of merit." Old Colley admitted, " Why, faith, Bracey, I believe you are right. The young fellow *is* clever."

Quin, London's favourite tragedian, was naturally sore at his deposition. After his first experience of Garrick, he burst out, " If this young fellow be right, then we have been all wrong." He dubbed Garrick " the Whitfield of the stage ", and said that " Garrick is a new religion; Whitfield was followed for a time; but they will all come to church again." Young George Whitfield, evangelist and leader of Calvinistic Methodists, was also attracting large audiences, some of exalted station, at " a large temporary shed " known as the Tabernacle, in Moorfields, close by. He possessed one of the most afflicting squints ever recorded by artists (the result of measles in childhood), but had a fascinating voice of great compass, audible at great distances, and strong histrionic sense. Garrick, after studying him, said that " he could make men either laugh or cry by pronouncing the word Mesopotamia ". Garrick replied to Quin in verse—

> *Pope Quin*, who damns all churches but his own,
> Complains that Heresy infects the town;
> That *Whitfield-Garrick* has misled the age,
> And taints the sound religion of the Stage;
> " Schism! " he cries, " has turn'd the Nation's brain,
> But eyes will open, and to Church again! "
> Thou Great Infallible, forbear to roar,
> Thy Bulls and Errors are rever'd no more;
> When Doctrines meet with gen'ral approbation,
> It is not *Heresy*, but *Reformation*.

" The young fellow," however, had much to learn yet. Giffard was determined to put on *The Rehearsal*, an elaborate satire on playwrights, critics and actors, by the Duke of Buckingham, who had been prominent at the court of the Merry Monarch. Garrick, cast for the part of the playwright, the ridiculous Bayes, thought that it would be useless to follow the old tradition that Bayes was Dryden, Poet Laureate, who had died in 1700. He had visited the theatres so diligently, and his talent for mimicry (what Johnson disapprovingly called " Davy's buffoonery ") was so acute, that he had no difficulty in presenting to a delighted audience perfectly recognizable caricatures of modern actors—Delane, Hale, Ryan and Bridgewater, all of whom acted in the established style. But he found very soon that he had made a mistake. Hale came to a performance and was cut to the quick. There was a rumour that Delane, whose favourite part was Alexander the Great, drank himself to death after seeing himself as Garrick saw him. But this was generally agreed to be an exaggeration. His " attachment to the bottle " was of long standing, and he survived another eight years. There is a green-room story of this winter based on a single authority, that Garrick had warned Giffard that he must " just glance at him " in his imitations, so as to make some show of impartiality, but that this imitation never was seen again after a rehearsal, and that early next morning a surgeon had to be sent to Mansfield Street to attend a gentleman with a slight wound in the guard arm. *The Rehearsal* had to be postponed for a fortnight, " owing to the indisposition of a principal performer ". Mr Giffard and Mr Garrick, both being gentlemen born, had settled their difference as gentlemen did—with swords, and seconds who kept mum. Whatever the truth, Garrick gave up his imitations of fellow actors and never again so erred.

Certainly, there is a hint of a rapier in an announcement which he sent to *The London Daily Post* this winter. Mr Garrick begged to assure the ladies and gentlemen " who were offended with him without a cause " that he was not at either of the Masquerades this season, which could be proved. If any person had a wish to be further satisfied, Mr Garrick was ready to do so in person, and in the fullest way. In what unbecoming character he was supposed to have appeared at a Masquerade is not disclosed, but inevitably a star so quickly risen was a target for gossip and jealousy, and he was determined to protect his young reputation.

He evidently showed his youth still, though perhaps not inexperience. Dr Young, the author of *Night Thoughts*, who had seen Betterton, found Garrick " only a boy to him ". Lord Cobham, who had also seen Betterton, thought Garrick " not inferior ". Betterton did not sound inspiring. Irreverent fellow-actors said that he laboured under great physical disabilities, for he had been so clumsy he could never take part in even a country dance; his head

E

had been too big for his body, his arms strangely short. He had frequently held forth with his left hand tucked in his breast, while he sawed the air with the other. He had small black-currant eyes in a large pudding countenance, and a low, grumbling voice. The fact remained that when a new actor arose, people instinctively measured him by Betterton, whom old Cibber said had been an actor, as Shakespeare was an author—without comparison. Mr Thomas Gray, whom Johnson did not think a first-rate poet, was avowedly anti-Garrick, " stiff in the opposition ". " Did I tell you about Mr Garrick, that the town are horn-mad after him? There are a dozen dukes of a night at Goodman's Fields, sometimes." But the lively Garrick was not at all likely to appeal to Gray, whom Johnson demolished in a single sentence. " He was dull in a new way, and that made many people think him GREAT." Gray's elegant friend Horace Walpole, with whom he was at present on rather stately terms after an unsuccessful foreign holiday together, admitted Garrick's skill as a mimic, but otherwise found " the young wine-merchant, turned player " nothing wonderful. " It is heresy to say, as the Duke of Argyll says, he is superior to Betterton." Johnson, although he would not allow anyone else to say anything slighting of Garrick in his presence, never let his ex-pupil forget that he was a pupil. Johnson, Garrick and Giffard sat in a coffee-house one evening after a performance. " The players, sir," said Johnson, trailing his coat, " have got a kind of rant, with which they run on, without any regard either to accent or emphasis." Giffard and Garrick leapt to the challenge. " Well now," offered Johnson, " I'll give you something to speak, with which you are a little acquainted, and then we shall see how just my observation is. Let me hear you repeat the ninth commandment, ' Thou shalt not bear false witness against thy neighbour '." Giffard and Garrick both threw their emphasis on the words " false witness ". Johnson pointed out that it should be on the word " not ", and they had to admit he was right.

Goodman's Fields was now " full of the splendour of St James's and Grosvenor Square. The coaches of the nobility filled up the space from Temple Bar to Whitechapel ". The managers of Drury Lane and Covent Garden looked sourly at half-full houses on nights when Garrick was playing in East London, in an unlicensed make-shift theatre surrounded by " a halo of bagnios " with a bunch of grapes hung out over every second door. Fleetwood's company was also being devastated by an affliction to be diagnosed next year as " influenza ". Mrs Woffington, the dashing young actress from Ireland, fainted as she waited to go on as Helena, the woman-doctor, on the first night of *All's Well*. She was a resilient girl, and the play was advertised again in a few days, but by then William Milward, another promising beginner, was stricken. He got up too soon, after his attack, and was noticed shivering miserably when at last the play was produced, with the full cast. He said: " How is it possible for me to be sick when I have such a physician as Mrs Woffington? " But he died, and Mrs Woffington played in March at the benefit for his widow and infants.

Garrick's success, playing the lead in his own farce *The Lying Valet* on the last day of November, was outstanding. The little two-act piece was no more than an up-to-date adaptation of the well-known French comedy *All without Money*, and the character of the helpful but most untruthful body-servant of an impecunious noble-man had appeared in several of Molière's plays. But Garrick's Sharp, an English rogue, was instantly popular. The house was as full for the Valet as for Richard, or " the haughty gallant young Lothario ".

From Grosvenor Square, the Reverend Thomas Newton wrote gravely, admonishing him.

> I was almost angry with you, to see your name last week in the bills for Costar Pearmain. I am not fond of your acting such parts as Fondlewife, or even Clodio; nor should be of the Lying Valet, if it was not of your own writing. You who are equal to the greatest parts, strangely demean your-self in acting anything that is low or little. There are abundance of people who hit off low humour, and succeed in the coxcomb and the buffoon very well; but there is scarce one in an age who is capable of acting the hero in Tragedy and the fine gentleman in Comedy.

28

But David could not resist setting the house in a roar, and he had not yet decided whether he was to choose as his best medium Tragedy or Comedy. To the end he held that Comedy called for the more practised actor. In a good Tragedy, the plot, the language, might carry an indifferent player to surprising heights. But he never resented advice. When he could, he ceased to appear in small, light parts. After long conclaves with Macklin and Giffard he had decided to give London a new Lear, not an Othello, before the season ended. By March 11, he was ready with something over which he had worked hard. It was not Shakespeare's *Lear*, for the version acceptable to London had long been that of another Restoration playwright, Nahum Tate. A happy ending had been thought essential, and therefore Lear had to regain his reason and kingdom, his two wicked daughters were despatched by poison and his good one married Edgar, depicted as her old flame. Even Johnson thought Cordelia's death too shocking. Garrick's first appearance as Lear

was well received, but he himself was not satisfied with it.  He
played it six times, getting worse, he feared, and then not again until
mid-April, when he attempted a *tour de force* on the night of his
second benefit, by displaying himself both as an old mad king and as
a loutish boy of fifteen, " Master Johnny " in Cibber's *The Schoolboy,
or the Comical Rival.*  It was thought that he had made Lear much
more effective, older and feebler.  The audience sobbed.  Years later,
he could sometimes be prevailed upon, in sympathetic company,
to tell how he had worked on his Lear, going to the fountain-head,
however horrible the strain, to study a man driven mad by misfortune.  There was a poor fellow living in Leman Street, near
Goodman's Fields, who had accidentally killed an adored little
daughter by dropping the child out of the dining-room window.  He
had thereupon lost his reason, but as he had some money and was
quite harmless, was allowed to stay on in his house looked after by
two keepers, appointed by his doctor.  David Garrick, wanting to
know how a man who had killed his daughter should be played, went
to Leman Street, and was not disappointed.  The distracted father
passed his days going to the fatal window, playing in fancy with his
little running victim, dropping it, making the house ring with his
maniacal shrieks.  After the storm had passed he would sit down,
looking around him slowly, apologetically, horribly and suddenly old.
His biographer, Arthur Murphy, often saw Garrick arise on request
to give a representation of the unfortunate father of Leman Street.
" There it was that I learned to imitate madness; I copied nature,
and to that owed my success in King Lear."                         29

He was now working too hard.  The season at Goodman's
Fields lasted from Monday, October 19, until Monday, May 23.
During it he made at least a hundred and forty appearances, in
nineteen different characters.  On December 22 he wrote to Peter, 30
" I am not fix'd for next year, but shall certainly be at the Other
End of the Town."  The managers of the two patent theatres,
drawn together by a common interest, were intriguing to get Goodman's Fields closed.  They had called in the aid of Sir John Barnard,
one-time Lord Mayor of London, the original mover of the Licensing
Act.  Giffard bowed to the inevitable.  Mr Fleetwood, always the
gentleman, offered Mr Garrick an engagement at Drury Lane for
next season, at five hundred guineas—a larger sum than had ever
been offered to any actor.  Garrick accepted, but made a stipulation
that both the poor Giffards should also be engaged for Drury Lane.
Fleetwood, on his side, asked that Garrick should appear at Drury
Lane for just three nights before this season ended.  He agreed to
be Bayes on May 26, Lear on the 28th and Richard on the 31st.

Mrs Woffington was to be his Cordelia, and he now knew that he was what is called madly in love with her.

He was still receiving Jeremiads from Peter. In his spare time he had to get down to " those curs'd vaults " and attended by a staring employee with a candle, consider the casks of all that was left of the London end of Garrick and Co., Vintners. He need fear nothing now, so long as he kept his health: but he sometimes felt very ill, and his correspondence was enough to send any man's brain into a whirl. He was getting a good many anonymous letters, but not yet blackmailing ones. They generally awaited him at the Bedford.

By the end of April he knew that he was not going to get a summer holiday. Mr Louis Duval, agent for the manager of the New Theatre in Smock Alley, came over from Dublin with an invitation for him to appear in the Irish capital on most favourable terms. Mrs Woffington was to be his leading lady. He did not hesitate, and the first week of June saw him bowling down to Park Gate near Chester in a post-chaise, to embark for Ireland in exotic company— Signora Barbarini, the ballerina, and Mrs Woffington.

## CHAPTER III

# WOFFINGTON

## 1742–1745

### I

FACTS about the origins of Margaret Woffington (as she signed herself) are extremely hard to find. Legends abound. Even the surname which she made famous has been declared to be one which she adopted for stage purposes in place of the less interesting Murphy. Her date of birth has been given as anything between 1713 and 1720. She never produced any visible relatives except a widowed mother, a devout Catholic, and a very beautiful, much younger sister, Mary, " Polly ". But the name of Woffington was not uncommon in Dublin since 1675, and it seems probable that she was the daughter of one Arthur or John Woffington, a journeyman bricklayer, who died when she was very young, according to one account, by falling off a ladder. If it be true that a Robert Woffington, a Vicar Choral at St Patrick's Cathedral, was her uncle, neither ever acknowledged the relationship. William Rufus Chetwood, actor, prompter and dramatist, owner of a bookshop over Tom's Coffee-House in Covent Garden, and a contemporary, staunchly claims that she was " born of reputable parents who gave her a genteel education ". When Garrick, aged twenty-three, first saw her perform, in 1740, she may have been four years his senior, or three years younger; but her youth had been far from sheltered. It had been spent in dire poverty. Her mother was said to have failed to pay the rent for a huckster's shop on a Dublin quayside and descended to selling watercress in the streets. Charles Lee Lewes, who became an actor when Woffington was in her prime, believed that she had assisted her mother as a street-seller. " I have met with more than one in Dublin who assured me that they remembered to have seen the lovely Peggy, with a little dish upon her hand, and without shoes to cover her delicate feet, crying through College Green, Dame Street and other parts of that end of the town. ' All this fine salad for a ha'penny! All for a ha'penny! All for a ha'penny here! ' " About 1727, a French acrobat, Madame Violante, was performing in a booth-theatre near College Green. Tom King, who acted in Dublin as a beginner when Margaret Woffington was a leading lady, believed that her stage career had begun as a baby, suspended in a basket attached to the feet of Madame Violante in a rope-walking act. As a child- *1* actress she was certainly Polly Peachum in a production by Madame Violante of *The Beggar's Opera* in which all the cast were " lilliputian ". The Lilliputs arrived at the Haymarket Theatre in London in September 1732, with " The celebrated Miss Woffington as Macheath ". She vanishes from records after this for five years, to reappear as Ophelia at the Aungier Street Theatre in Dublin. There is the usual story of a veteran having fallen ill and a beginner pleading to be allowed to take her place. Charles Coffey, playwright, and Thomas Elrington, manager of Smock Alley Theatre, are said to have encouraged her, but Elrington did not engage her. She was playing regularly at Aungier Street in the " dreadful-severe " winter of 1739–40, as Sylvia in *The Recruiting Officer*, and in smaller parts. She made her first outstanding success as Sir Harry Wildair in *The Constant Couple* in April 1740.

She reached London again a month later and attempted to get an appointment with Rich at the Covent Garden Theatre. Rich, who was reported to give an interview to no stranger under the rank of baronet, was eventually surprised by her bursting in upon him, in his private residence in Bloomsbury Square, when he was surrounded, according to his custom, by as many as twenty-seven cats of varying size and colour. He was having his tea and toast. She made a startling impression (" It was fortunate for my wife that I am not of a susceptible temperament "), and was engaged to play Sylvia at a command performance on November 6. Rich afterwards stated that he accepted her because she had " so charming a figure and so handsome a person ", but he had warned her that an Irish reputation would not help her unless she had genuine talent and worked hard. " Perhaps, with some of my help in private, you may do very well." Now Sylvia is a part in which the heroine adopts male costume, a stage device popular since the days of Shakespeare. But the Rosalinds, Violas and Portias of Shakespeare's companies were all in fact boy actors. They were boys, playing girls, disguised as boys. " Miss ", who soon attained the honorary rank of " Mrs " Woffington on playbills, proceeded to give London Sir Harry Wildair, written for a man, and she poached with such success that thereafter the part was her preserve; no man was ever liked in it. " I have played the part so often," she once announced, running off the stage flushed with applause, " that half the house believes me to be a real man." Quin, at his most insulting, replied, " By God, madam, if they do, the other half knows you to be a woman." Rich refused her a rise in salary, and she went to Drury Lane and further triumphs.

She was tall, and had a resonant voice. She was " happily made ", with an alabaster neck, curling dark hair, splendid black eyes and a lovely mouth. Horace Walpole's cousin Conway wrote her down " an impudent Irish-faced girl ". Walpole himself wrote to his namesake Horace Mann, in Rome, in October 1741, " There is much in vogue a Mrs Woffington, a bad actress; but she has life." She had that in abundance, and much more. She was warm-hearted, open-handed and not vain. When the part demanded it, she willingly adorned her face with wrinkles. She was reliable. Benjamin Victor, theatrical manager, gave her a very good character:

> So generous was her conduct, though she seldom performed less than four nights a week, that she never disappointed one audience in the three winters, either by real or affected illness. And yet I have often seen her on the Stage when she ought to have been in bed. [3]

Murphy described her at the date when she set off for Ireland with Garrick:

> He travelled in company with Mrs Woffington, a celebrated actress, in the bloom of youth, possessed of a fine figure, great beauty, and every elegant accomplishment. Her understanding was superior to the generality of her sex. Forgive her one female error, and it may fairly be said of her, that she was adorned with every virtue: honour, truth, benevolence and charity were her distinguishing qualities. Her conversation was in a stile of elegance, always pleasing and often instructive. She abounded in wit.

She always announced that she preferred male company. Women talked " nothing but silks and scandal ".

### 2

On June 8 the *Dublin Mercury* announced

> The famous Mr Garrick and Miss Woffington are hourly expected from England to entertain the nobility and gentry during the summer season, when especially the part of Sir Harry Wildair will be performed by Miss Woffington.

There were two principal theatres in Dublin. That at Smock Alley was the older, though it was now known as the " New Theatre ", since it had been rebuilt in December 1734. It possessed an initial disadvantage in that it was situated in a lane wide enough for one vehicle only and close to the quayside. To see the audience arriving in chairs and carriages for a first-night at Smock Alley was almost as dramatic as the play itself. The scene was a second babel. But both Smock Alley, and the Theatre Royal, Aungier Street, opened in March 1734, claimed superiority over London in one respect. Covent Garden and Drury Lane had merely lobbies outside the boxes. The Dublin houses possessed what were known as " box-rooms ", large, finely decorated saloons outside the boxes in which patrons might meet for conversation while their carriages were called. A great deal of money had been spent in Aungier Street " to build a very sumptuous, but a very bad theatre. In a crowded audience, a great part in both galleries can neither see nor hear." The auditorium at Smock Alley was satisfactory, but unfortunately the stage had been sacrificed to it. It was cramped. No women sat in the pit in either house, and inhabitants of this area were often rowdy.

Four days after the *Dublin Mercury's* preliminary announcement, excitement was kept alive by the news that " Mr Garrick was hourly expected from England ". The redoubtable Madame Violante once endured a passage of a month's duration, by the packet from Park Gate, but on the day of Garrick's first arrival all the omens were propitious. He came in sight of the city known as " the nursery for the English stage " early on the morning of June 13. It was a Sunday. The weather was perfection, and he was about to spend at least two summer months in the company of the woman whom he loved, and in her birthplace. The Irish were renowned for their extravagant way of living and for their extraordinarily hospitable and convivial manners, and already, as the packet came from the bay into the Liffey, a stranger could perceive that this town, divided in two by the river, lined by quays, spanned by ancient bridges and backed by the foothills of blue mountain heights, was picturesque in the style most fashionable. A closer view displayed that distance had lent some enchantment. The silvery Irish light did not as yet pour down upon many Palladian façades; not much Portland stone arose against the cloudless blue sky. Most of what was to be famous as eighteenth-century Dublin was not yet built in 1742. Moreover, already on the quayside, it was obvious that in Dublin the squalor and poverty were even more marked than in London. But a born mime could also observe that these natives were friendly and themselves possessed of strong dramatic sense. He came somewhat under the wing of an Irish actress returning from England as an accepted star. He was kindly welcomed. On June 23 he wrote to Peter from his lodgings in Aungier Street that he was, both on the stage and off, having a success equal to that in London. " Lord Orrery who is a demi-god has sent such affectionate letters to all his acquaintance. Change of air has agreed vastly with me."

Dublin high society revolved around the castle, in which the Lord Lieutenant, always a peer from England, lived in state, holding his court, surrounded by ministers, chaplains, pages, musicians and lustrous friends from England, invited over to see a little of Ireland. The third Duke of Devonshire was Lord Lieutenant at the date of Garrick's first visit. Horace Walpole said " his outside was

unpolished ". He was plain in his manners and in his dress, and
no great patron of the theatre, so his absence in his native land was
not considered a tragedy.

Woffington opened the season on Wednesday, June 16, with Sir
Harry. Garrick followed on the Friday with Richard, and Woffington as his Lady Anne. It was calculated that on this occasion more
people were turned away than admitted to the theatre. He played
the gallant Chamont on the next Monday. On the Tuesday Delane,
whose arrival at Aungier Street had also been much advertised,
boldly attempted Richard, but with humiliating result. Garrick's
first benefit came on Thursday, 24th, when he repeated his old London effort of presenting his audience with high tragedy and low
comedy on the same evening. He was Lear, with Woffington as
Cordelia, and Sharp in *The Lying Valet*. Next evening he appeared
in Ben Jonson's *The Alchymist* as Abel Drugger. " The most critical
as well as the most candid audience in Europe " seemed to prefer him
in Comedy. It is true that it was on this trip that he was first nick-
named Roscius, but Irish gentry, greeting one another, now answered,
" How d'ye do? " with " As gay as Garrick! " His name was given
to something else. The weather, hot when he arrived, was now
oppressive. The epidemic which broke out in a city enthralled by
a new actor was called " Garrick fever ".

He toiled on, playing all the parts in stock plays from his London
season. For his second benefit, on July 8, he gave Richard as the
sole piece. Early in August his appearances for the last times as
Chamont and Sharp were announced. His third and final benefit, in
August, was well planned. He had been billed to make his exit in
*The Fair Penitent*. Suddenly, Hamlet was substituted. He had
never attempted this character before, and Woffington was to be
Ophelia. Dublin appreciated the compliment heartily. When the
great—and very hot—night came, he was carried through on waves
of frantic applause. Upon reflection, although he was said to have
displayed many beauties of diction and action, not all his readings
were approved; but it was prophesied that he would be " the best
and most extraordinary player that ever these kingdoms saw ". He
was considered most moving in his scenes with the Queen, and with
Ophelia. It was remarked that he had scouted tradition in two
instances. The entrance of Hamlet had always been heralded by
slow music. Mr Garrick dispensed with this, and had purged the
play of every word that could shock a modest ear. He had also,
judging by a long letter dated August 14, from " someone entirely
unknown to you ", cut out Hamlet's directions to the players,
and pronounced wind, matron, Israel, villain, appal and Horatio

5 as wynd, metron, Iserel, villin, appel and Horetio. He did not get away without giving Hamlet once more, and he was Captain Plume, with Woffington as Sylvia, on Thursday, August 19. " This is the last time of Mr Garrick, Mrs Woffington and Signora's performing, during their stay in this country."

He set out for England on the following Monday, travelling with Delane, Dr Arne and Mrs Cibber. His companions came from the opposite camp, the Aungier Street Theatre. Dr Arne's sister, Mrs Theophilus Cibber, who had been, with Quin and Delane, the hope of the Theatre Royal's Dublin season, had given a last appearance as Andromache and shaken the dust of Ireland from her feet for ever. It is probable that Garrick must have met her already in London. A future member of his profession whom he certainly met now for the first time was a young Irishman, Thomas Sheridan, a Bachelor of Arts from Trinity College, son of a well-known Dublin doctor. Not all the students who attended the Dublin theatres were welcome. It was said that as many as fifty, who would have been better employed at their books, thronged around the players on the very stage at 6 morning rehearsal. Sheridan afterwards remembered an incident of Garrick's first tour which displayed the atrocity of manners in the theatre of these days. When a performance of *Lear* had reached the last scene of Act IV and the curtain was about to rise to disclose Lear asleep in a tent in the French camp, his head in the lap of Cordelia, a loudly shouting ruffian, inflamed with wine, staggered on to the stage and attempted to force his attentions on the actress. Lear's look was enough to kill, and it may well have been in this moment that Garrick made up his mind that Mrs Garrick should cease to appear on the stage upon her marriage. The bully was removed, but he and two of his friends were heard hallooing behind scenes afterwards, searching for the player who had dared to look at a gentleman 7 so uglily.

This seems to have been the only unpleasant moment in Garrick's first Irish season. A story that he had sought out Dr Barry, the most fashionable physician of the capital, to attend a minor player at Smock Lane, was popular as confirming that one so gay could also be so kind. He had had the good taste to be obviously in love with his Irish leading lady. He had arrived in Dublin almost as a secondary attraction to her. He quitted it without her, and having quite established his own reputation in their profession. But she was following. He was going to Drury Lane, his Mecca, to play leading parts, at an unsurpassed salary. It seemed as if all his dreams were coming true.

### 3

His two months in Dublin in her company had convinced him that he could not live without Woffington. Like Romeo, his bent of love was honourable, his purpose marriage. But he was far from certain that she would accept the rôle of Mrs Garrick. A poem which he may have written to her now, or before, was addressed to her in her character of Sylvia. He kept a copy, and it was found amongst his manuscripts when he died.

> If Truth can fix thy wav'ring heart,
>   Let Damon urge his claim;
> He feels the passion void of art.
>   The pure, the constant flame.
>
> Though sighing swains their torments tell,
>   Their sensual love contemn;
> They only prize the beauteous shell.
>   But slight the inward gem.
>
> Possession cures the wounded heart,
>   Destroys the transient fire;
> But when the mind receives the dart,
>   Enjoyment whets desire.
>
> The senses in your charms enjoy
>   A sweet but short repast,
> But oh! the mind can never cloy
>   The soul's eternal feast!
>
> By age your beauty shall decay,
>   Your mind improve with years;
> As when the blossoms fade away,
>   The ripening fruit appears.
>
> May heaven and Sylvia grant my suit
>   And bless the future hour,
> That Damon who can taste the fruit
>   May gather every flow'r.

He was a young man who had hung about the green-rooms before he had become an actor. The reputation of " Woff " had always been known to him. She was credited with having had as lover every man seen much in her company. There was Elrington, who was said to have helped her in her start in Dublin. Someone must have helped her, but he had been a most respectable family man, and had died ten years past. Charles Coffey had given her her first chance at Aungier Street. He was deformed in person, and seemed to have been a genuine admirer of her talent. His place as her teacher had been taken by old Colley Cibber; and a crony of Cibber's—Owen MacSwinney, haunted her. Old Rich had engaged her at sight. . . . A pamphleteer attacking Cibber had said, " Lo! yonder goes Susannah and the two Elders." But Woffington, although not everyone appreciated this, had a genuine gift for friendship, and her old gentleman attended her to the last. Mac-Swinney left his fortune to her. There was a story about a faithless lover, younger son of an Irish peer, and a broken heart; but that belonged to her extreme youth. The two rivals whom Garrick believed he had reason to fear were Sir Charles Hanbury-Williams and Lord Darnley. Sir Charles was a favourable example of the fashionable young aristocrat of his date. He was unsatisfactorily married to an unoffending heiress, thirty-four, a patron of the arts, highly-strung, though somewhat heavy in appearance, and himself an author. He had addressed several poems to the rising actress which were privately circulated. His " Lovely Peggy ", which was yet to come in 1742, was thereafter indissolubly connected with her name. He could certainly offer an establishment on a handsome scale. He spent the winter in Mayfair and the summer at Coldbrook Park, Monmouthshire. Some of his poems were rather coarse. Garrick found him " hateful ".

Lord Darnley seemed far more dangerous. He was twenty-six, a bachelor, had succeeded to his father's Irish earldom and his mother's English barony. He was immensely rich. It was just possible, though not at all probable, that he could be brought to offer marriage. In that case Garrick's suit was hopeless. He could only retire. But Woffington had said that he had not yet offered and that she would not have him if he did. In his terrible " Epistle to Mrs Woffington " produced three years later, Garrick gave the year of their Irish trip as that in which his hopes had been highest.

> From *forty-two* I take my present date
>   When Darnley's gold seemed void of charms,
> And driven by whim, inconstancy or fate,
>   You flew from him to Garrick's arms.
>
> No mercenary views possessed your mind,
>   'Tis love! cried out the public voice;
> To Sylvia's virtue we have all been blind:
>   By fate a mistress, not by choice.

His plans for the winter season were made. Peter Garrick still got news of his brother from Lichfield friends in London. In the autumn of 1742 they could only have reported that David was to be found at 6, Bow Street, living under the same roof as an actress who never attempted to deny the number of her lovers, and an actor who had been tried for murder. But this sounded much worse than it was. Macklin, Woffington and Garrick were going to set up as a Dramatic Triumvirate, and in their off-time instruct beginners in the new style of acting. They were going to bear domestic expenses jointly: each was to be in charge of the housekeeping for a month at a time. Mrs Macklin kept a sharp eye on her husband, and their daughter was now eight; they may have also been at Bow Street, though nobody mentions this. That so crack-brained an enterprise survived for even six months seems remarkable, and there is no trace that any stage candidates ever presented themselves for instruction by so intimidating a trio.

Garrick's private life at this time lacks documentation, though it is quite easy to discover what parts he was playing on any night. There are no letters to Lichfield. He evidently destroyed any from Woffington, for there are many from other actresses amongst his papers. He never made any allusion to the years in which he had hoped to see Mrs Woffington Mrs Garrick, and never allowed any in his presence. She was not quite so discreet; but she never pretended to be discreet. Cooke's life of Macklin is a rich source, but by the *10* time Macklin confided his most bitter and damaging memories he had had his great quarrel with Garrick. There is a story (told by others also with variations) of an incident when " his lordship ", probably Darnley, found a man's wig on Woffington's dressing-table and upbraided her for unfaithfulness. With her usual *aplomb* she declared it to be a property wig which she was going to wear in one of her male-impersonation parts. She extracted a humble apology. Next day, according to Macklin, Garrick praised Woffington for her presence of mind. " What was still better, Sir," recounted Macklin to Cooke, " he gave us a dinner that same day at Richmond, where we all laughed heartily at his lordship's gullibility." Macklin's *11* tales, designed to show Garrick in the most contemptible light, as one of Woffington's lovers, did not do much harm. What was much more serious was that he started the legend that Garrick was mean, and this ghost was never laid, in spite of ample evidence to the contrary. What nobody ever took the trouble to trace was that at the date when Macklin, and to a much lesser degree Johnson, began to notice Davy being close, his salary was not being paid. He was a leading attraction at Drury Lane, and supposed to be receiving larger recompense than any previous actor. But Fleetwood was not paying regularly or in a manner which begat any confidence for the future. Macklin recalled that when he rode out to Richmond with Garrick, and dined on the way, or even when they came to a turnpike, Garrick would find that he had no money at all on him—had put on riding

breeches that morning—or had only a thirty-six shilling piece which
could not be changed. Macklin made a note of every occasion and
eventually presented a bill, amounting to between thirty and forty
shillings. Garrick was a little put out, and at first took it for a joke,
12 but Macklin got his money.

Amongst the idiotic arrangements for the establishment in Bow
Street was that the trio should have a common purse. They gave
little suppers after the theatre, which of course were very well-
attended and very exhausting. It was noticed that during Woffington's month the company and fare were splendid. She was a born
hostess. Garrick's month tended to be rather quiet and homely.
Johnson said that once when he was drinking tea with his old friend
and Peg Woffington, he remembered Davy grumbling at her for
making the tea too strong. " Why," said Garrick, " it is as red as
blood! " " He had then begun to feel money in his purse, and did
not know when he should have enough of it." What Johnson did
not realize was that Garrick had begun to earn largely and had most
likely saved something considerable, but was living on the edge of
a financial volcano. And the " stock purse " at Bow Street was
sometimes found to be " deficient in some hundreds of pounds ".
Johnson answered Boswell fully on more than one occasion on the
subject of Davy and money. When Boswell asked, " Garrick is a
very good man, a charitable man? " " Sir," replied Johnson, " a
liberal man. He has given away more money than any man in
England. There may be a little vanity mixed; but he has shown
that money is not his first object." *Boswell:* " Yet Foote used to
say of him that he walked out with an intention to do a generous
action; but that turning the corner of a street, he met the ghost
of a half-penny, which frightened him." *Johnson:* " Why, sir,
that is very true too; for I never knew a man of whom it could be
said with less certainty to-day what he will do to-morrow than Garrick; it depends so much on his humour at the time." Mr, afterwards Sir William, Scott, His Majesty's Advocate General, who was
present, dragged Johnson back to the point. " I am glad to hear of
his liberality. He has been represented as very saving." *Johnson:*
13 " With his domestick saving we have nothing to do."

Another of Macklin's tales seems to reflect on Fielding, not
Garrick. The rising actor had now achieved what he had dreamt of
in his vintner days—an attached body-servant. His first recorded
valet was rather a humble character and looked after him primarily
in the theatre, though also in his lodgings, where he waited at table.
The man could only be correctly, though confusingly, described as
his Welsh dresser. He was also, most inconveniently, " Davy ",

though as a surname. After a large dinner-party given by Garrick to Mrs Cibber, Henry Fielding, Macklin and others, Welsh Davy was observed in great glee going over the tips which he had received. " There's half-a-crown from Mrs Cibber, Got pless her! Here is a shilling from Mr Macklin. Here is two from Mr Havard. And here is something more from the poet, Got pless his merry heart! " Fielding's contribution, which was done up in paper, proved to be a penny. Next day Garrick reproved Fielding for playing such a trick on Welsh Davy. Fielding said that he had done the servant a good turn, for if he had given more his master would have pocketed it. A penny, the man had a chance of keeping.

14

As the winter of 1742–1743 wore out, Garrick played fourteen characters, seven of which were new to London and five new to him. He made his first appearance as a regular member of the Drury Lane Company, one of His Majesty's Servants of the Theatre Royal, on October 5. All went well. Chamont was perfectly familiar to him and to many of his audience. He had played him at Ipswich and at Goodman's Fields. Bayes, Richard, Clodio, Plume, Lear and Fondlewife followed. He then gave London his Hamlet, which created an even greater sensation than it had done in Dublin. His simulation of horror on beholding the Ghost was so much admired that it became (with, it is to be feared, elaborate embellishments) a stock Garrick success. A painstaking German critic, who beheld a performance thirty years later, wrote down every gesture employed by the great actor in this scene. But the magic is not communicated. The only result has been to make succeeding generations reflect that if Garrick really acted as described by Professor Georg Christof Lichentenberg, he must have been awful. Samuel Johnson's sense of humour got the better of him when Boswell asked " Would you not, sir, start as Mr Garrick does if you saw a ghost? " " I hope not. If I did, I should frighten the ghost." Fielding's sense of humour did Garrick more service. In *Tom Jones* he sent Partridge, a country type, to see Garrick and the ghost. The result was most gratifying. Partridge was simply terrified. He did not realize that Mr Garrick was acting, or that the ghost was not real. " He the best player! Why, I could act as well as he myself. I am sure if I had seen a ghost I should have looked in the very same manner, and done just as he did. Indeed, though I was never at a play in London, yet I have seen acting before, in the country; and the King for my money: he speaks all his words distinctly, half as loud again as the other. Anybody may see *he* is an actor."

Anonymous letters, of praise and of criticism, continued to rain upon Garrick. They were sent to " the Bedford Coffee-house, under

the Piazza, in Covent Garden ", to " the Piazza, Covent Garden ", to
" The Theatre Royal in Drury Lane " and " the Playhouse, in Drury
Lane ". " Ignoto " was a faithful correspondent. (" Do you think,
Sir, Hamlet would address himself to the Grave-digger so very seriously? ") " P.W.", after a long dissertation as to the correct text,
offered, should his hints (sent to an actor who seemed to him to be a
very good judge of Shakespeare) be thought worth following, to
send further remarks. His sheet was gravely filed " This letter is
answered ". Somebody who did not sign at all, but had been with
three or four friends to see your second night, found Hamlet's
reception of the news of the death of Ophelia inadequate, but Fondlewife, witnessed on the night of Friday, December 3, much over-
acted—" Especially in that sort of feeble trot you seemed to affect so
much. A part over-acted makes the actor look foolish." He ended
hastily " Don't think from any thing I have here said that I am not
your great admirer. I assure you I am; and not only look upon you
as infinitely superior to any thing we have had for many years; but
believe that, with proper care, you may prove as great an actor as
ever England produced."

Archer, in *The Beaux' Stratagem*, a gentleman pretending to be his
valet, was a new part in which Garrick shone. He had not yet acted
with Woffington at the Lane, and the first occasion on which he did so
provided a dreadful memory. Fielding's *Wedding Day* had been
written twelve years before, for Wilkes and Mrs Oldfield, before
Fielding gave up the stage for domestic felicity. At Fleetwood's
earnest request he had furbished it up for performance on Valentine's
Day, 1743. Before the fatal night there were signs of a storm.
Fielding was in a bad way—" Laid up with the gout, with a favourite
child dying in one bed, and my wife in a condition very little better in
another, attended with other circumstances which served as very
proper decorations to such a scene." The bailiffs were in, and Fielding was working against time. He was to lose his wife, but not for a
year, and his grief was to be so great that his friends must fear for
his reason; but he was to marry again—his children's nurse—and
write *Tom Jones*.

The Lord Chamberlain's office had insisted on alterations in *The
Wedding Day*. Mrs Clive had flounced out of the part of Mrs Useful,
whose name proclaimed her profession. Woffington was not the
heroine. She was the *ingénue*, but had one good scene, masked, with
Garrick, who took her for a lady of the town.

> Millamour. Lookye, madam, it is in vain to resist. So, my dear
> artificial Blackamoor, I desire thee to uncover.
> Charlotte. No, sir. First hear my history.

F

Millamour.   I will first see the frontispiece of it.
Charlotte.   Know, I am a woman of strict honour.
Millamour.   Your history hath a very lamentable beginning.

Mrs Pritchard was Clarinda, the heroine, but a somewhat battered heroine, already betrayed by Millamour, and having on the morning on which the curtain rises, consented to a *mariage de convenance*, gone through a legal ceremony with a man old enough to be her father, who does, in fact, turn out to be her father.   She is his nameless child by the deserted Mrs Plotwell, once the victim but now a rival in the profession of Mrs Useful.   Fortunately, Mrs Pritchard, an actress of sterling character and much reliability, never read any part in a play except her own.   That was her rule.   So, if she did not have to make another appearance after Scene I of Act V, as happily arranged in *Macbeth*, she went home, in comfortable security, to have her supper, regardless of her neurotic husband's due end.

Garrick had begged Fielding to make Millamour less unsympathetic.   Some of the lines he had to speak gave him the shudders.   He knew how flat they would fall—if indeed that was the worst he had to fear.   Millamour, to be sure, had loved his Clarinda before the play began and agreed, in scuttling haste, to marry her before it ended, but he was a cold fish even in his wit, not even a gay Lothario.   Fielding refused to make the cut Garrick asked.   " No, d—n them! If the scene is not a good one, let them find that out."   Many theories exist as to exactly what had happened before the curtain rose on that dreadful first night to display the unexpected figure of Macklin beaming at a full house.

GENTLEMEN AND LADIES
We must beg your indulgence, and humbly hope you'll not be offended
At an accident that has happned to-night, which was not in the least intended,
I assure you; if you please, your money shall be returned.   But Mr Garrick, to-day
Who performs a principal character in the play,
Unfortunately has sent word, 'twill be impossible, having so long a part,
To speak the Prologue: he hasn't had time to get it by heart.

This did not sound like Garrick, nor, as Act I, set in Millamour's lodgings, unfolded, did the audience at all relish their favourite. Fielding, according to Arthur Murphy, was seated in the green-room, stretching his six foot of misery, defiantly sipping champagne and smoking tobacco, when poor Millamour entered to him, absolutely shattered.

" What's the matter, Garrick?   What are they hissing now? "

" Why, the scene that I begged you to retrench, I knew it would not do; and they have so frightened me that I shall not be able to collect myself the whole night."

" Oh! damn them. They *have* found it out, have they? "

The young actor, who had never been hissed before, pulled himself together and did play the leading part out, but the piece was withdrawn after half a dozen performances, and on the last night it 15 was recorded that there were only five ladies in the house.

A fortnight later he heard the applause to which he was accustomed when he essayed Lord Hastings in *Jane Shore* for his own benefit; and for *The Lying Valet*, in which he was to take the title rôle, seven rows of the pit were turned into boxes, and extra boxes were provided, actually on the stage. His popularity seemed reestablished. But another failure was coming. He was to be seen with Woffington on March 17 in *The Constant Couple*. The occasion was her benefit. For some reason, mysterious to the public, she was not going to play Sir Harry Wildair, her most famous part. She was going to be Lady Lurewell. She had relinquished Sir Harry to Mr Garrick. After two nights, Mrs Clive was Lady Lurewell and Woffington disappeared from the caste. Still, Garrick as Sir Harry would not do. The part was written for an attractive young man, and he was that, and Woffington was only a young woman playing a young man, but by general consent she was the ideal Sir Harry. It was noticed that Garrick had seemed from the first uneasy in the part—as well he might, for his lovely Peggy had prompted him rather audibly. With his usual glorious common-sense he accepted the judgement of his public and dropped Sir Harry for ever. He had something else ready, something which no actress would ever covet or attempt—Abel Drugger, tobacconist's assistant. He would show he had versatility.

He appeared as Abel Drugger for the first time in England on March 21, and made the part his own for life. Ben Jonson's *Alchymist* was not a cheerful play, but it was one of those which can never quite die. London, nerve-wracked and half-deserted, during the days of the Great Plague before the Great Fire, was the lurid background for the figure of little Abel, simple, sly, horribly natural. " You are in your element," said Hogarth, after witnessing Abel, followed by Richard, " when you are begrimed with dirt, or up to your elbows in blood." Another artist, who was to become an even greater friend, was to immortalize Garrick as Abel, in a picture of Scene VI, Act 2, " attended by Burton as Subtle and Palmer as Face ", actors whose names and faces have therefore descended to posterity. William Cooke, biographer of Macklin, got from Johnson, a favourite Garrick story, connected with Abel. A Lichfield grocer

came up to town, and Peter Garrick gave him a letter of introduction
to David.   On his return Peter inquired how his friend had found his
player brother.   After some hesitation the worthy tradesman said
that on the night of his arrival he had seen Mr Garrick's name in
the bills at Drury Lane to perform as Abel Drugger, and had paid for
a seat in the two-shilling gallery to see him.   But after that experience he had not chosen to deliver his letter.   " Well—by God!   Mr
Garrick, though he be your brother, he is one of the shabbiest,
meanest, most pitiful hounds I ever saw in the whole course of my
life."                                                                                                                      16

Abel was Garrick's last new part in the season of 1742–1743.
Upon the surface, it appeared that he had done very well, and had
no reason to fear the future.   Not many people outside the theatre
knew that ruin was threatening Drury Lane, and that his love affair
was going very ill.

4

Fleetwood seemed to his alarmed company to be getting rather
depraved.   Racked with gout and drinking heavily, " he was seized
with an unaccountable passion for low diversions and took a strange
delight in the company of the meanest of the human species ".   He
was seeking the society of boxers and horse-copers.   He was to be
seen much with Broughton, the famous pugilist.   He frequented the
prize-ring at Hockley in the Hole, and the bear gardens.   In the
theatrical world, rope-dancers, fire-eaters and dancing-monkey proprietors were his chosen companions.   He was known to be in debt,
and must have mortgaged not only his patent but also the clothes
and scenery at the theatre, for during the late season bailiffs had
appeared in the house more than once.   Garrick's faithful Welsh
dresser had found them about to lay hands upon the rich cap worn
by his master as King Richard—the head-dress bearing the crown
which was to be lost at the battle of Bosworth.   Its jewels were
paste, but large and brilliant.   "You must not take that," said Welsh
Davy in his quick pattering speech, " look you!   It belongs to the
King."   The officers of the law, thinking it was the property of
George II, resigned their prey, awestruck.                                                         17

A creature called Pierson was Treasurer for Fleetwood.   He was
insulting to the lesser actors when they demanded their long-overdue
salaries.   Macklin, who was called " the Prime Minister ", chose the
plays and players, and was still very close friends with Fleetwood.
Garrick was no longer living under the same roof as Macklin.   After
" some starts of suspicion " he tackled Macklin on the subject of their
finances, but got so little satisfaction that he came to believe the

story that Fleetwood was paying Macklin a subsidy to keep the disaffected company together on reduced salaries. Garrick's salary as the season drew to a close was over six hundred pounds in arrears. After much consideration he decided to sue Fleetwood. There was nothing else for it. He invited himself to breakfast with the manager on a promising date, a Sunday morning, and set out determined to tell him of his intention. But he found Fleetwood, not only cold sober, but so entirely charming and reassuring that he departed, having spent a very enjoyable morning without having mentioned money.

At the beginning of May 1743 he summoned more resolution. He refused to appear at the theatre, and kept his word for three weeks. He next invited his fellow players to his lodgings to discuss action against Fleetwood. His lodgings were in James Street, Covent Garden, over the premises of a periwig-maker. Garrick, aged seven and twenty, was businesslike. He explained what he believed to be their situation to such members of the company as had mustered, and urged them to sign a document, agreeing to secede from Fleetwood and stand together. His suggestion was that they should all apply to the Duke of Grafton, Lord Chamberlain, for a licence to open a new theatre. The Opera House seemed a possibility. He had good reason to believe that when the duke understood their situation and grievance he would grant their request. There was, even, a precedent, for the Earl of Dorset, when Chamberlain, had so obliged actors oppressed by old Christopher Rich. The meeting was attended by Macklin, the two Mills's, Leigh, Havard, the Pritchards, Berry and Woodburn, all valuable members of the company. But it does not appear that three of his greatest friends, Yates, Giffard and Woffington, were there. Woffington had known what it was to have the wolf at the door. She had arrived in London with her Sir Harry suit and one gown. Garrick's scheme was received with much relief. Only Macklin put a spoke in his wheel by demanding that before they sought out the duke they ought to warn Fleetwood what they were about. Garrick was entirely against this. He said that if they showed Fleetwood their hand he would undoubtedly get round them in some way, probably see the duke first. He knew the manager as a master of dissimulation. Macklin found himself in a minority and the paper was signed by all. The great day of the players' reception by the Lord Chamberlain duly arrived and Mr Garrick, at his best, headed the deputation. Charles Fitzroy, second Duke of Grafton, had a lofty person, with great dignity. He was harsh-featured, and black-a-viz'd, as befitted a grandson of Charles II. But he was not at all merry. Garrick's humiliation was great. " Put not your trust in princes." All that he had been told of the

Chamberlain's benevolence appeared quite mistaken. Nothing could have been more frigid than his grace as he enquired what income Mr Garrick was making by his acting. Garrick ventured to mention five hundred pounds a year. "And do you think that too little! " exclaimed the nobleman. " When I have a son who has to venture his life for his country for half that sum." The deputation was dismissed, their application refused. 18

The situation at the Lane increased in tension. Fleetwood got together " fresh troops "—recruits from all the strolling companies in the country, and announced his autumn opening. Curiously enough, his chief anger was directed, not against Garrick, who was the mainspring of the revolt, but Macklin. He had supported Macklin " all through his difficulties ", to wit when the actor had been tried for murder. Garrick considered joining with Quin (reputedly difficult) and taking the old Lincoln's Inn Theatre. Macklin approached Covent Garden, but without satisfactory result. He appeared disturbed by Fleetwood's animosity and told Garrick that if they could not get employment in London they had better set off for Ireland to get money there. This, however, he mentioned as " le dernier ressort ". He knew well that Fleetwood was making Garrick large offers to return.

The quarrel between Garrick and Macklin, which was inevitably on a much larger scale than that between Fleetwood and Macklin, now began to threaten. It was bound to be terrible, for in his " Dear Mac " Garrick knew he had a very powerful adversary. The condition of the inferior players, as the strike organized by Garrick failed, was pitiable, and they told him so repeatedly. Fleetwood had offered to take all except one of them back, some at their old salaries, others on half-pay. Garrick went to see Fleetwood again. He was offered a hundred guineas a year more than before. He retaliated by offering to play for a hundred guineas less, provided Macklin was taken back. Fleetwood said that the man Macklin should never again enter his theatre. Macklin said he was not going to be made a scapegoat: the players must honour their bond. He was Shylock to the life. Garrick went on to Covent Garden and got Rich to offer Mrs Macklin an engagement at three guineas a week, to which he promised to add six from his own salary until Fleetwood agreed to re-engage Macklin. He offered to add more. But Macklin was now out for blood. If Garrick deserted from their pact he was going to ruin him! A whisper that Macklin was taking Garrick to Dublin, and they were to be left stranded, reached the unfortunate strikers of the late Drury Lane company, and they sent Garrick a joint plea, telling him that he was as much bound to them as to Macklin.

Should they not all go back? "This punctilio of honour" would mean starvation for them. They also wrote to Macklin pressing him to release them.

Fleetwood's season opened in September. Two months passed without a mention of Garrick in his bills, then Mr Garrick as Bayes was announced for December 5, and simultaneously, a letter from the young actor was published in the leading London journals. Mr Garrick believed it was his duty to acquaint a public which had always shown him such indulgence that it was not obstinacy or exorbitance which had withheld him from their service, but a necessity to bring about a reconciliation between his manager and the company. This was now almost accomplished. He did not apparently see Macklin to explain his action.

December 5 made stage history. In the morning appeared *The Case of Charles Macklin, Comedian*, probably written mostly by himself, and violently denouncing Garrick for treachery. Handbills, signed by Garrick, begging the public to suspend judgment until he could produce his answer, were hastily circulated around and in the theatre. Before the curtain rose it was clear that Macklin had managed to pack the pit with supporters who meant to make trouble. A party from the Horn Tavern, Fleet Street, led by the notoriously dissipated Dr Barrowby, led the tumult. When Garrick appeared, hisses, boos and cries of "Off! Off! Off!" were the only words heard. Again and again he bowed, and was understood to be asking to be allowed to speak. The play proceeded in dumb-show. Rotten eggs, apples and peas (to make the actors slip) began to descend upon the stage. Garrick, seemingly calm, moved high up-stage to avoid them. After a few minutes, during which the situation promised to become very ugly, the curtain was let down. Garrick's *Reply* to Macklin was ready two days later. He had called in the assistance of a professional, a member of *The Gentleman's Magazine* staff. William Guthrie, of an impoverished Jacobite family, has been dismissed as "a hack-writer", but Johnson had a good word for him. "He is a man of parts. He has no great regular fund of knowledge; but by reading so long and writing so long, he no doubt has picked up a good deal."

Mr Garrick as Bayes in *The Rehearsal* was announced again for the night of December 9. "The sea in a storm was not more terrible and boisterous than the loud and various noises which issued from the pit, galleries and boxes." But before the overture had ceased an enormous figure, supported by many more of the same build arose in the middle of the pit, and spoke in a loud voice. "Gentlemen, I am told that some persons here are come with an intention not to hear the play. I come to hear it. I paid my money for it. And I desire that they who come to interrupt may withdraw and not hinder my diversion." The words were reasonable, and the speaker looked impressive, but there were plenty of Macklin's party present. The thirty bruisers organized by Broughton, who had been imported into the house by Fleetwood in conjunction with William Windham, a patron of " The Fancy " and friend of Garrick, knew where to land their blows. They fell upon Macklin's party and drove them out of the pit. The fray was soon over, and when Garrick appeared he was allowed to play without interruption.

Macklin did not yet think his case desperate. On December 12 he issued a *Reply* to Garrick's Vindication. It " fell dead-born from the press ", and he found that he was left with the last word, but that was all. It was not nearly the end of Macklin. He went off and set up his Dramatic Academy: he became proprietor of a tavern in the Piazza: he went bankrupt. His record of quarrels became formidable. He was still playing, aged eighty-nine: he survived to the age of, possibly, a hundred. When Garrick became Manager of Drury Lane in 1747, he invited his old friend to join his company, and some sort of a reconciliation was patched up. " Garrick, like a true politician, neither loved nor hated in the way of business." But too many terrible things had been said by them to one another in those dark days of 1743–1744. Macklin's senile mutterings against Garrick, eagerly noted down by his biographer William Cooke, became the fountain-head of anti-Garrick stories.                                  1

Meanwhile, the season of 1743–1744 remained to be faced, with Mr Charles Fleetwood in a triumphant mood. Garrick was going back to the Lane, to play five new parts. Two of them, Regulus, in a tragedy of that name, and Zaphna in *Mahomet*, were declamatory classical stuff. Fleetwood ought never to have accepted them. But good William Havard, one of the late rebels of the company, had written *Regulus*, and *Mahomet*, translated by the Rev. James Millar, had been a success at the Théâtre Français the year before last. When Quin at Covent Garden heard that Garrick was going to play Macbeth " as written by Shakespeare ", he was surprised. " Don't I play Macbeth as written by Shakespeare? " He did not. The version to which London was accustomed had been produced by the great Davenant, poet laureate to Charles I. The three witches were comic characters, two grand-dams and a Vampire, attended by Furies, all straight out of the property box. They danced and sang. Much else had been " improved ". Garrick made some alterations, but not enough to shock London. To protect himself he published, anonymously, a pamphlet criticizing his boldness in doing as much as

he had.  London made no objections.  Mrs Pritchard had gone off
to Covent Garden, so he had the mild and long-suffering Mrs Giffard
as his Lady Macbeth.  He was considered to play a highly neurotic
character very movingly, as well he might.  His " Biron " in
Southerne's *Fatal Marriage* was also very moving.  But it was as
Lord Townly in *The Provok'd Husband* that he pleased most this
season.  Woffington was Lady Townly.

> Lady Townly.  My lord, my lord—you would make a woman mad!
> Lord Townly.  Madam, madam, you would make a man a fool!
> Lady Townly.  If Heaven has made you otherwise, that won't be in
> my power.
> Lord Townly.  Whatever may be in your inclination, madam, I'll pre-
> vent your making me a beggar at least.
> Lady Townly.  A beggar!  Croesus!  I am out of patience!—I won't
> come home till four tomorrow morning.
> Lord Townly.  That may be, madam; but I'll order the doors to be
> locked at twelve.
> Lady Townly.  Then I won't come home till tomorrow night.
> Lord Townly.  Then, madam, you shall never come home again.
> (*Exit.*)

Garrick and Woffington, playing man and wife, were perfection.
But he knew by now that they were never to be man and wife.

## 5

Sir Charles Hanbury-Williams was a gentleman of regular habits.
He came to London every year in December and stayed till May.
In the winter of 1742 he completed his legal separation from his wife.
He could not re-marry, but he displayed no signs of wishing to do so.
He did not even, as yet, settle to a mistress.  In the winter of 1743 he
decided upon Woffington to fill his vacancy.  He had admired her
for three years, but believed Lord Darnley was in possession.  This,
she gave him to understand, was now a thing of the past.  Like
Garrick, he had been attracted by her mental capacity.

> 'Tis not her form alone I prize
> Which ev'ry fool, that has his eyes
>     As well as I can see;
> To say she's fair is but to say,
> When the sun shines at noon, 'tis day,
>     Which none need learn of me.
>
> But I'm in love with Peggy's mind,
> Where ev'ry virtue is combined
>     That can adorn the fair,
> Excepting one you scarce can miss
> So trifling that you would not wish
>     That Virtue had been there.

She who professes all the rest,
Must sure excel the prude whose breast
    That Virtue shares alone;
To seek perfection is a jest,
They who have fewest faults the best,
    And Peggy has but one.                        *20*

He had her portrait painted for his country house.   The affair
seemed likely to become permanent.   Late in May it was so much
the talk of the town that Lord Lincoln, leaving a note at Sir Charles's
house in Conduit Street, to tell him that His Majesty had been
pleased to name him a Knight of the Bath, added waggishly, " The
king insists upon Mrs Woffington being knighted this very evening! "
But the talk of the town was behind events.   It was true that
Darnley seemed to have receded, but still Sir Charles found he had a
rival—one of her fellow players at the Lane, rather a well-known one,
it must be admitted, but to Sir Charles he was " young Foppington ".
Lord Foppington in *The Careless Husband* was one of the early parts
played by Garrick in his East End days, at Goodman's Fields.
Moreover, the ridiculous Foppington had been an unsuccessful
suitor of Lady Betty Modish—a character in which Woffington was
brilliant.

There is a story that having denied to Sir Charles that she had
seen Garrick for ages, her lover taxed her with having parted from
him that morning.   She languidly asked, " And is not that an age
ago? "   But her little player lover was serious—gloweringly so.   He *21*
wanted to marry her.   The situation was ludicrous.   Sir Charles
bowed himself out.   In any case he was leaving town at the end of
May.   But he was disappointed to be leaving alone.   On June 26
Horace Walpole wrote to him, " I have never seen Mrs Woffington,
but enquired and hear she lives at Teddington.   Rigby will have
told you that Lord Darnley is on the tapis again."   In August, from
his country seat, Williams sent another old friend, Stephen Fox,
rather a pathetic letter.   He had always suffered from headaches.
Some of his acquaintance told him he alternated unwisely between
violent exercise, and eating and drinking too much.   He was putting
on weight.   He was very sorry for himself.

I recover strength slowly, and look pale and mighty fair.   I believe if
Mrs Woffington saw me she would venture from Darnley for half an hour's
conversation.   I am glad the man has got his mare again.   She is so handsome that anybody must like her, and he is so rich that any woman must
like him.   I am forced to be content with her picture, which I have hung up
in my room in the wood, which is very like her and very handsome.   I sit
and look at that and my paper in turns, and I believe pleasant subjects to
look at inspire very well.

Fox replied:

> I did not know Lord Darnley had got Mrs Woffington again. It surprises me; for 'tis hard to think he gives her more money, and much harder to imagine any other reason for her leaving you. But I can't bear you should care about it, as I see you do.

Fox was right in being surprised, but Williams did not enlighten him. He may even have hoped that his successor was the very rich young peer. He tried to pass off his mistake lightly. When he came up to town again for the 1744–1745 season his attitude was perfectly that of the man of fashion. " My winter's diversions will consist in hunting after and getting a new mistress—unless my old one is disengaged." But his last poem shows that she had not been disengaged.

> To heights like these your Muse should fly,
> To others leave the middle sky,
> Whose wings are weak and flabby:
> Leave these to some young Foppington,
> Who takes your leavings, Woffington,
> And tunes his odes to Peggy.

<sup>22</sup>

Garrick's part in this story is much less well-documented than that of Hanbury-Williams. No letters from him on the subject have come to light. The sole sources are a couple of poems from his pen, some comments from Lord Rochford and stories retailed by Murphy and Macklin's biographer Cooke, probably emanating from Woffington, though not very kind to her. According to Murphy, Garrick went so far as to buy the wedding ring, and tried it on her finger. She had agreed to marry him. She said that she had dismissed Darnley and Williams. But when he came to London for the winter season of 1743–1744 it was soon obvious that she had not dismissed Williams, and though the most fascinating of women, she was certainly a difficult one. Her celebrated voice was very resonant. When, as Portia, she had to speak the lines " He knows me, as the blind man knows the cuckoo, by the bad voice," the audience laughed and she laughed with them. Some people professed to admire even her " croak ", but she was known as " the screech-owl of Tragedy ". A voice, like a wife, is a life-sentence.

It was quite true, as Williams had heard, that in June 1744 she had taken a house in Teddington. The moment had arrived when she needed a background of at least outward conventionality. Mary Woffington was coming home from the convent-school in which her actress sister had maintained her, with pin-money equal to that supplied to the daughters of the nobility. Mary was sixteen, her features were more regular than those of Margaret. She had

acquired French polish, and wanted to act.  The great Woffington's
ambitions for her little sister were quite simple and entirely creditable.
She wanted Polly to have all that life had denied to her—an early
marriage to a young gentleman of good reputation, who could give
her a happy home and children.  If possible she should also have a
title and fortune.  As Mrs Garrick she would have been able to help
Polly in her theatrical aspirations, but Garrick was behaving exas-
peratingly.  He had led an unsuccessful actors' revolt against his
manager; his career seemed in jeopardy.  He had played her
aristocratic lovers off the stage.  She believed she could whistle
them back, or others, but that would mean losing Garrick for ever.
She invited Garrick to take part in a play which she was going to
have acted in a barn adjacent to her Thames-side house during the
dead months of the theatrical season.  Garrick obeyed, and played
Orestes in Ambrose Philip's *Distress'd Mother*, a translation of
Racine's *Andromache*.  Polly was Hermione, and another very
pretty young girl, daughter of a Mrs Bellamy, was Andromache.  All
the neighbours were invited.

He set off for a round of country-house visits in less than his usual
spirits.  He had three ports of call in East Anglia—William Windham at Wenham, near Capel St Mary, and Richard Rigby at Mistley,
on the Stour, were bachelors; but at Easton Hall, near Ipswich,
there was a châtelaine, aged one and twenty, who embodied his ideals
of a stately peeress.  Lady Rochford, described by Horace Walpole
as " one of our court-beauties—large, but very handsome, with
great delicacy and address ", was said to have refused " all the
royals ", especially the Duke of Cumberland.  Lady Rochford, who
was delighted to hear that he was coming to them for her lord's
birthday, on September 13, wrote sympathetically.  " I wish it was
as much in my power to hinder your attendance on Mr Fleetwood and
settle you in a pretty farm, agreeable to your wishes, in Suffolk at
£200 a year."

He made his first appearance in the 1744–1745 season in October.
When Quin heard that Garrick was going to play Sir John Brute, he
made another of his strictures.  " He may possibly act Master
Jacky Brute, but he cannot possibly be Sir John Brute."  Quin was
again mistaken.  Garrick's representation of a drunken country
gentleman was a most horrible piece of nature.  This part, at which
he tinkered for years, adding and cutting scenes, became one of his
stock successes.  And it was one in which he improved with age.

But however popular he might be, Drury Lane Theatre was going
through dark days.  In one of his last efforts to avoid bankruptcy,
Fleetwood decided to raise the prices of admission.  The first riot

took place when Woffington was playing Phillis in Steele's *Conscious Lovers*. She bravely and soothingly received a deputation from the pit which was calling angrily for the manager, and the play proceeded. Two nights later, when Garrick was playing Sir John Brute, trouble became more serious. The play had to stop and could not be resumed. Seats were torn up, sconces were pulled down and cast on the stage, and the rioters threatened to come behind and burn the scenery. Fleetwood promised concessions, but it was clear that his race was almost run.

In March, Woffington gave up her benefit night in order that her sister might make her début. She chose *The Beaux' Stratagem*, and for Polly the part of Cherry. Garrick appeared as one of his low-life characters—Scrub, man-of-all-work to Lady Bountiful. He was superb, but the critics were far from enthusiastic about the younger Woffington. Polly had sense. She never acted again. She decided upon matrimony, and in November of the following year the Earl Cholmondeley was to be seen hastening south to break a match stolen between his second son, Robert, who was still a minor, and " a player's sister ". The earl, who was himself not yet four and forty, but alarmingly in debt, was ushered in to Mrs Margaret Woffington, and found himself received by Portia. When he discovered further that his new daughter-in-law would bring an adequate dowry, he was even more pleasantly surprised. Woffington had the last word, " My lord, I have much more reason to be offended than you. For whereas I had before but one beggar to support, now I have two." The Woffingtons appear to have captured a weakling, at least a man of peace. Boswell says that as an ensign in the Guards at the Battle of Fontenay he " fairly hid himself, for which he was disgracefully broke at the head of the Army ". He sold his commission in 1755, took holy orders and became a non-resident Hertfordshire Rector. The marriage appears to have been happy, and nine children were born, of whom four survived. Polly Woffington, " a very airy lady " according to Boswell, moved elegantly in literary and artistic circles. " The only person I flatter is Garrick; and he likes it so much that it pays one by the spirits it gives him." The Honourable and Reverend Robert Cholmondeley more than once applied successfully to Garrick for funds.

6

During the 1744–1745 season Garrick appeared as a pamphleteer. His little effort cost sixpence, and was entitled *An Essay on Acting, in which will be considered the Mimical Behaviour of a certain fashionable actor etc: to which will be added a short criticism on his acting Macbeth.* It was anonymous. In the preface he represented himself as a critic who had made the stage his study and entertainment for twenty years or more. But he was only twenty-seven, and his spirits ran away with him. In the section headed *What Acting ought to be and what our present Favourite is not,* he found Garrick quite unsuited physically to Macbeth and mentally ready for Fleance, or one of the Infant Shadows in the Cauldron Scene. Garrick actually played Macbeth the very opposite of what Shakespeare intended. Why did he wear a tie-wig and a plain hat, whereas Banquo wore gold lace? In the dagger scene he wore a frippery flowered dressing-gown, more suited to a Foppington. He should have worn crimson damask. The banquet, too, was poorly mounted. Ought not there to be several bishops and inferior clergy, and on the table, not merely a few trashy apples and oranges? Macbeth was a king, and should have been served with hot costly viands, and large pyramids of meat, sweetmeats and savoury biscuits. " Garrick must be allowed all the merit that Mimicry can give him—which to be sure is very pleasant, over a bottle, tho' despicable on the stage. Why being a good mimic should entitle him to be a great actor cannot easily be comprehended."

It was a very slight performance, and except in a few sentences about a player's training, all chaff. He did admit that a player should " go about much, observe humours of every kind, digest and transplant them ". He never could resist publishing an attack on himself, in a style that threw the ridicule on attackers.

A letter, full of pomposity, had come last spring from Thomas Sheridan, to whom Garrick had written kindly in congratulation on his appearance on the Dublin stage. Mr Sheridan had thanked Mr Garrick for his kind invitation to spend the " dead " summer season with him at a rural retreat at Walton-upon-Thames and join Drury Lane's players, but he had hardly time to write. In the last fortnight he had to study three new characters as well as perform nightly. His cool suggestion had been that as Richard, Hamlet and Lear seemed to be Garrick's favourite parts also, they should not appear in them in the same town, in the same season. " In plain English, what think you of dividing the kingdoms between us; to play one winter in London and another in Dublin? " His scheme, which he had the grace to admit might seem a little strange at first view, would, he believed, turn " to both our advantages ". He had come to London, and, as Garrick had originally suggested, got an engagement at Drury Lane. Here he had played all his (and Garrick's) favourite parts, and as another " gentleman-player " and a novelty, gained considerable applause. His features were stiff and his voice was inharmonious. Johnson summed him up with deadly accuracy. " Why, sir, Sherry is dull, naturally dull; but it must have taken him a great deal of pains to become what we now see him. Such an excess of stupidity is not in nature." At the end of the 1744–1745 season he returned to Dublin to institute reforms in the theatre there.

Garrick toiled on, appearing in ambitious new parts, none of which were much liked. If knowledge of jealousy helped a man to play Othello well he should have succeeded there. He was good, audiences had to admit, but he was not London's idea of Othello. He was too violent in gesture. There was an unfortunate incident at the first night which was said to have poisoned the part for him. Hogarth's set of conversation pictures, *The Harlot's Progress*, had recently been engraved and were at the height of their fame. In one of them, where the lady is upsetting the tea-table to distract the attention of one lover from the exit of another, a small negro page, a " Pompey ", is prominent in the foreground, advancing with the equipage. When Garrick entered as Othello, dressed in the scarlet coat of a Venetian general, his face blacked and his head surmounted by an impressive turban, Quin turned to Dr Hoadly and said audibly, " Here's Pompey! But where's the tea-kettle and lamp." Years later, Garrick, turning over his " own choice folio of Hogarth's prints " in retirement, burst out laughing when he came to the one including little Pompey, " Faith! it is devilish like."

Garrick's wicked King John was not considered anything like as good as his wicked King Richard, although he had the support of an ideal Constance. This was Mrs Theophilus Cibber, returned to the Lane after nine years. She owed her engagement to Quin, for when Garrick had been expressing doubt as to her capability Quin had fired up in her defence. " Don't tell me, Mr Garrick! That woman had a heart, and can do anything where passion is concerned."

Poor, poor Susannah Arne was not one of those players whom Garrick could have quoted to Brother Peter as an example of a blameless private life. But it was generally accepted that she had been far more sinned against than sinning. She was the sister of Dr Thomas Arne, musician, and had made her name in opera. Handel had written the contralto arias in his *Messiah* and the part of Micah in *Samson* for her. Her voice, although naturally small, was well-trained and possessed a haunting sweetness. But at the age of nineteen she had most mistakenly married the actor son of the great Cibber, Theophilus, mean in stature as in mind, a widower with extravagant tastes. Four years after their marriage he had come

back from a trip to France (undertaken to escape his creditors) and
had startled the theatrical world by bringing an action against a
young Berkshire landowner called Sloper, for seducing Mrs Cibber.
He claimed five thousand pounds damages, but the jury assessed
them at ten pounds. During the course of the evidence it had become glaringly apparent that Theophilus had deliberately connived
at Sloper's intimacy with his wife. He had introduced the young
man to her as " a good-humoured boy ", borrowed largely from him,
taken lodgings for them all, and left Susannah with their lodger, who
was, in fact, paying all their expenses. Tom Arne supported his
sister throughout two legal actions—for Theophilus brought a second
for detention of his wife, claiming ten thousand pounds damages and
got five hundred pounds. Her wedlock had become a deadlock.
She settled to live with Sloper, when she was not acting, and by the
time Garrick first played with her the connection was almost
hallowed by antiquity. It had endured eight years. She was the
reverse of Woffington in every imaginable way. Her voice, sweet
and low, enchanted the ear. She was small, dark, slight and slender,
easily alarmed, painfully apologetic. People said that from their
appearance Garrick and she might have been brother and sister—
and brother and sister it seemed they were to stay, although it soon
appeared that Mrs Cibber liked her new stage partner extremely.
Little notes began to shower upon him—

Sunday morning, May 1st, 1745

Sir,
      I am very glad to hear you are better and, if you dare venture out,
shall be glad of your company at dinner. As you are an invalid, pray send
me word what you can eat, and at what hour you will dine. I shall send
Tom to meet you . . .

Friends outside the theatre commented on Garrick having found
a new leading lady who was a great tragic actress. " But how agree-
ably you surprise me ", wrote Lord Rochford, " in telling me we
shall see you and Mrs Cibber together. But how will Woff relish
that? Or, to speak more properly, how will you relish it? For to
tell you my mind, I believe the other party can wean themselves
much easier than you can, or I have no skill in woman's flesh."
Garrick had not weaned himself easily. It seems from internal
evidence that the famous quarrel-scene with Woffington detailed by
Cooke must be assigned to this summer. Woffington, according to
Cooke, was now " soliciting to be made an honest woman of ". A
morning came when Garrick was in no humour to think of wedding
bells. He told her, hesitantly, that he had been thinking it over all
night, and he thought this marriage might be a very foolish thing for

two people who might do better in their separate lines. And that for his part, although he loved and respected her, and ever should do so—as an admirer—yet he could not answer for himself in the part of Benedick. Woffington, with her usual courage, took the bull by the horns. "And pray, was it this which has given you a restless night?" "Why, to tell you the truth, my dear Peggy, as you love frankness, it was; and in consequence I have worn the shirt of Dejanira for these eight hours past." "Then, Sir," said she, raising her voice, "get up, and throw it off! For from this hour I separate myself from you, except in the course of professional business, or in the presence of a third person."

Cooke succeeds in giving the scene a slightly comic turn, but the shirt of Dejanira was no joke. It was a horrible simile. It rings true, and draws the curtain on much suffering. So does the long "copy of verses, Epistle to Mrs Woffington, sent to her in June 1745" left amongst Garrick's MSS. the only record from his pen of an affair which had lasted for three years.

He opens very fiercely—in a metre very different from that of earlier and happier love-poems.

> Sylvia, to you I dedicate my lays,
>    —No flattering bard or love-sick youth;
> Regardless of your censure or your praise,
>    I come to expose the naked truth.

The naked truth is a catalogue of her conduct since he had become her lover in their sunlit Dublin season.

> I know your sophistry, I know your art,
>    Which all your dupes and fools control;
> Yourself you give, without your heart—
>    All may share THAT, but not your soul.
>
> But now her thirst of gold must be allayed,
>    The want of show her pride alarms,
> It must, it shall, be gratified, she said,
>    Then plunged in hateful Williams' arms.
>
> Oh peer! (whose acts shall down time's torrents roll,)
>    If thus you doat, thus love the dame,
> In nuptial bonds unite her to your soul,
>    And thus at once complete your fame.

Darnley is obviously the peer, but a new candidate has been introduced by her, whose name now appears for the first time in the story.

> But now, advice apart, the theme pursue,
>    Follow the damsel in her wild career,
> Say what gallants, what keepers are in view—
>    Behold the Colonel in the rear!

Some say you're proud, coquettish, cruel, vain,
Unjust! she never wounds but cures.
So pitiful to every lying swain—
Flatter or pay, the nymph is yours.

Cooke adds another anecdote designed to show Garrick as mean. Woffington returned all his gifts. He returned all hers except a pair of diamond shoe-buckles. After a month she sent him a reminder. He answered that as they were all he had left to recall many hours of happiness he hoped she would let him keep them. He wore them to the end of his career.

The break had not come suddenly, but it was final. They had to meet again, and they played together again, but Cooke says that Garrick was thereafter perfectly cold, treating her as if she was a mere acquaintance, and that Woffington felt it. She was accustomed to keep her lovers as friends. She was always alluded to by Sir Charles Hanbury-Williams in most unctuous tones as " My dear Mrs Woffington ".

Since she gradually faded from Garrick's life, the end of her story may be told briefly. The Colonel, object of Garrick's last jealousy, became a permanency. He was a Colonel Caesar of the Guards. Horace Walpole says he was directly descended from the Sir Julius Caesar, Master of the Rolls to James I. He came of an aristocratic Italian family. He was not a peer, or even a baronet, and no marriage took place, but he was her shadow for the remaining fifteen years of her life, and was left rather shabbily in the end, for Polly descended on her sister's death-bed and bore off all property possible, despite some sort of a lovers' pact, void in law, that whichever died last should inherit all. As Garrick had prophesied, Woffington continued a highly successful career without him. She staggered off the stage, screaming with agony, in her thirty-seventh year, when speaking the epilogue as Rosalind in *As You Like It*. She never acted again. She lingered three years, her intellect unclouded, but her physical powers gradually decreasing. Arthur Pond, who had painted her before, in her youth, performed a last portrait of her, lying in bed, still elegant, still beautiful.

Her other two principal lovers also came to untimely ends. Darnley died, a bachelor, in 1746. Hanbury-Williams took up a diplomatic career, was a success in Germany, but suffered a mental breakdown while Ambassador to the Court of Catherine the Great. He returned to England, and made a partial recovery, but Miss Bellamy, in a most distressing book of memoirs, recounts that after appearing quite normal when attending her performance in the name part as Cleone at Covent Garden, he went for her with a breakfast knife. He died insane, aged fifty.

## 7

In one of Mrs Cibber's arch and persistent letters of this period, the name of a man with whom Garrick was to be associated professionally for the next twenty-three years makes a characteristically inconspicuous entrance.

> I hear we are both to be turned out of Drury Lane Playhouse to breathe our faithful souls out where we please. But as Mr Lacy suspects you are so great a favourite with the ladies that they will resent it, he has enlisted two swinging Irishmen of six feet high to silence that battery.

Her letters and invitations to come for a prolonged visit to Mr Sloper's country seat, Woodhay, near Newbury, " a most sweet place ", to improve his health and " talk over stage affairs at leisure " pursued Garrick to spas far distant from one another. The failure in health which he had always dreaded, as the one thing that might wreck his career, seemed to have overtaken him. As far as the world knew he was still entirely successful, and of growing reputation; only he knew that he was burning himself out. He was unsettled, apprehensive, miserable. He was to suffer from recurrent bouts of illness, apparently due to nervous exhaustion, until he had a home of his own; but the woman who was to make that possible had not yet arrived in England.

Benjamin Victor, who had begun life as a barber, " within the liberties of Drury Lane ", always hankered for the stage, and was soon to give up the linen trade to become manager for Thomas Sheridan in Dublin, tells, at length but without clarity, the admittedly confused tale of the sale of the Drury Lane patent.

Fleetwood now only expressed a wish to retire, with all possible dignity " to the South of France as a Retreat from all his complicated Misfortunes ". He had mortgaged his patent to a Sir Thomas de Lorme and a Mr Masters, and unknown to them further induced a Mr Hutcheson Meure to advance him money for its redemption. Mr Meure was presently startled by seeing in the newspapers that the Drury Lane patent was up for sale by an order in Chancery. In fact he owned the theatre, its scenery and other properties, but without a licence or patent. A couple of city bankers, Messrs Green and Amber, interested in theatrical speculation and known to be men of substance, came into the market and invited James Lacy, at present stage manager for Rich at Covent Garden, to join them and undertake the management at the Lane. They would find two-thirds of the patent money, and he should pay his third gradually out of his share in the profits. After considerable but unavoidable delays Lacy agreed, and was detailed to get Fleetwood to accept an annuity and Mr Meure not to press for his mortgage.

Mrs Cibber's latest *billet-doux*, which had reached Garrick at " Buxton Hall, near Chapel-le-Frith, Derbyshire ", had painfully suggested that in their present melancholy situation they had better set up a company of strolling players and show Lacy that they could get their bread without him.

Mid-October found him at Bath, with his elegant friend, William Windham. Windham, who was almost exactly his own age, might have come out of a contemporary play. He was a very handsome young gentleman, of a family which had been settled in Norfolk since the fifteenth century, and he had a beautiful ancestral home, Felbrigg, near Cromer. But he also had a stern sire, with whom he had quarrelled so much that he lived mostly in London, in a picturesque habitation in Suffolk, well known to Garrick, or on the Continent. Four years ago he had written an account of his adventures amongst the glaciers and ice-Alps of Savoy. At breakfast, one morning, after looking through the post which had followed them from London, Garrick put a letter into his gay companion's hand saying, " This is the oddest epistle I ever saw in my life." Windham read it, and pronounced, " It may be an odd one, but it is surely an honest one. I should certainly depend upon a man that treated me with that openness and simplicity of heart." Thomas Sheridan, with whom he had parted on not very good terms, had written with all his accustomed heaviness to say that he was now sole manager of the Irish stage and should be very happy to see Garrick in Dublin. He had heard that Garrick was thinking of another Irish season. He would be ready to give him all advantages and encouragement which he could in reason expect. His offer was to divide all profits with him, after deducting expenses. He added that Garrick must expect nothing from his friendship, for he owed him nothing. But all that the best actor had a right to command, he might be very certain should be granted.

Garrick had indeed been thinking of Ireland, but rather as Macklin, in his most desperate moments had styled it, as *le dernier ressort*. To go on Sheridan's invitation would suit him very well, much better than Mrs Cibber's next proposition, which was that he and she and Quin " playing without salaries " should collect a company, in hopes of getting a licence, " for fifty, sixty, or any number of nights you agree upon ". He shrank from such a notion, and he decided, if he left England, not to see her before he set out, for she was full of dark hints as to a further proposition, too secret to be put on paper. He had not a doubt, and time proved him right, that she was going to suggest that he should offer for the Drury Lane patent. She was in constant touch with his friend, Somerset Draper, partner in the publishing business of Jacob Tonson, whose father had died worth a hundred thousand.

From Bath he had gone to Lichfield. He had gone home, after eight years, to " castle on the bridge " to stay with Lennie and Jenny and Merry and Peter, to hang on the bridge, and watch the world go by, to meet the neighbours at cathedral-close tea-parties, and entertain them with his imitations, to slip across to the Palace for an hour with Mr Walmesley, who was very old now, and much vexed by his gout, and proud of his protégé, but full of sage warnings against over-work. " Davy " Garrick had now been hissed off the stage, and egged off the stage. He had been in love, and was now out of love. But he was a success, and could afford to show himself at home now that he had made up his mind, and could announce that he was resting after a London season and before one in Dublin. But before he could leave England he must get a reply to a letter about another matter which might change not only his plans but those of the whole country.

Amongst Mrs Cibber's inaccurate prophecies was a casual mention, " The Rebellion is so far from being a disadvantage to the playhouses that I can assure you it brings them very good houses." She wrote on October 24. Prince Charles Edward Stuart had landed on the wild west highland coast on July 23. Within a month he had been holding his court in the palace of Holyrood House, but such was the state of communications that Sir Charles Hanbury-Williams, shaken out of his usual routine, was languidly greeted by friends in London in the first week of October as bringing tidings of " Scotch affairs " from the north. The news of the Prince's success at Prestonpans had brought a run on the Bank of England, but in Thamesmouth troops recalled from Flanders, under the command of George II's soldier son, the Duke of Cumberland, were disembarking. At Drury Lane, Benjamin Victor had presented Mrs Woffington with a superb costume in which to speak a patriotic epilogue as Britannia. Lacy was being very active. A press announcement at the end of September had reported that he had applied for leave for Drury Lane to raise two hundred men for the defence of his Majesty's person and government. David Garrick might no longer be a member of his Majesty's company, but he was by descent a Huguenot, and the Huguenot merchants were coming forward solidly with offers of support against a Catholic prince, come from France, who would bring back to England, they believed, the religious persecution from which their grandsires had fled.   David's father had served the *3* House of Hanover in the army; his younger brother, William, had followed his example.   David had no doubt that he must at least offer to play the part of Captain Plume in earnest.   But he did not intend to enlist under Lacy's banner.   If he was to serve, it must be under one of his friends totally unconnected with the stage.   On a scheme proposed by the Duke of Bedford, noblemen were raising on their own estates regiments for short service.   On October 4 the Marquis of Granby was gazetted colonel of " The Leicester Blues " raised by his father the Duke of Rutland.   The regiment was coming to Lichfield camp.   David had settled upon Lord Rochford.   On *3* October 31 Lord Rochford replied at length.   His first paragraph was given up to apologies, but offered no reason for his long delay. It was painfully clear that his dear Davy's patriotic gesture had caused a young Whig peer, a lord of the bedchamber, embarrassment.

> I must commend your laudable zeal in offering your services for the suppression of the Rebels, and thank you more particularly for shewing your inclination to fight under my command.   Had I a design to raise a regiment, or to raise a troop, on this occasion, I know nobody I should be so proud of commanding as yourself.   But, thank God! we have now old regiments 'enow at home to quell the sad remains of those rash traitors, without raising any new ones; for, I flatter myself, before you receive this (or very shortly) Wade will have given us a good account of them.   If he should not succeed, I much doubt whether anything that could be raised here would prevent a mischief, which I hope Heaven will avert.   I heard an account to-day that the Young Squire was travelled off to Dunkirk, which I am very sorry for, as I was in great hopes he would have been the turnkey of Newgate's guest.
> But damn! all politics, I have worse news for you . . .

His worse news was that Fleetwood's absurd shows were dragging Drury Lane into the mire.   " For God's sake, come to town.   Slay him, and take the command of his army yourself."                                                             *3*

On the day after Lord Rochford wrote his letter, the Young Squire began his march south.   On Sunday, November 17, he left Carlisle and continued his unopposed entry into England, on foot, through the snows, at the head of his infantry.   He was a hopelessly dramatic and romantic figure.   In England drawing-rooms were being shocked, families rent, by sudden disclosures, or, what was worse, dark suspicions, of long desire for a glamorous Royal Stuart. In Garrick's own circle a most unexpected figure, Samuel Johnson, was believed to cherish such an attachment.   London, on Black Friday, December 6, was not an edifying spectacle.   News had arrived that the Prince had reached Derby.   He was within a

hundred and fifty miles of the capital.   There was a second run on
the Bank of England; the Duke of Newcastle, shut up in his apart-
ments, was refusing to see anybody, and there was a rumour that
George II had packed his portmanteau for return to Hanover.   But
England had shown no signs of a general rising, and the French had
not yet landed.   Marshal Wade was at Wetherby, the Duke of
Cumberland had reached Lichfield, and a third army waited on
Finchley Common, ready to protect London.   William Hogarth was
painting one of his best crowd pictures, *The March of the Guards to
Finchley*.   Garrick had gone direct for Ireland from home, and
arrived in Dublin on Sunday, November 24.

## CHAPTER IV

# ROSCIUS

## 1745–1749

### I

ABOUT the end of February 1746 a party of young Scotsmen took the packet for Harwich from Helvoetsluis. One of them afterwards wrote his autobiography. He was called Alexander Carlyle, was twenty-three years old, and destined for the ministry. He had spent two winters studying at Glasgow University and was due for a third, at Leyden, when Prince Charles Edward had arrived in Scotland, whereupon he had become a volunteer for the defence of Edinburgh. Edinburgh had let the Prince come in quietly, so, despite the very unsettled state of the country, Alexander had left Scotland, as always arranged, in November '45.

The rascal of a landlord at the Helvoetsluis inn had told Dr Monckley, treasurer and director of the young travellers, who was very fat, that he had often known packets becalmed at sea for a week, so Monckley had provided them with a cold ham, a couple of fowls, a sirloin, nine bottles of wine and three of brandy. They never touched anything, except a little of the brandy, as they were soon so sea-sick that they could hardly lift up their heads.

> We had one cabin-passenger, who was afterwards much celebrated. When we were on the quarter-deck in the morning, we observed three foreignors of different ages who had under their care a young person of about sixteen, very handsome indeed, whom we took for a Hanoverian baron coming to pay his court at St James's. The gale freshened so soon that we had not an opportunity of conversing with these foreignors, when we were obliged to take to our beds in the cabin. The young person was the only one of the strangers who had a berth there, because, as we supposed, it occasioned an additional freight. My bed was directly opposite to that of the stranger but we were so sick that there was no conversation among us till the young foreignor became very frightened, in spite of the sickness, and called out to me in French, if we were not in danger. The voice betrayed her sex at once, no less than her fears. I consoled her as well as I could.

Next morning, at Harwich, the eldest of the three attendants on this lady in disguise introduced himself as her father, explained that she was Violetti, the dancer, engaged to appear at the Opera at the Haymarket, and expressed a hope that the young Scottish gentlemen would witness her first night and benefit. The whole party spent the night at Colchester where the foreignors were likely to be roughly treated, as the servants at the inn took offence at the young woman in men's clothes, as one room was only bespoke for all four. We interposed, however, when Monckley's authority, backed by us, prevented their being insulted. They travelled in a separate coach from us, but we made the young lady dine with us the next day, which secured her good treatment. We were so late in getting to London that we remained all night together at an inn in Friday Street, and separated next day, with a promise of seeing one another often.

Carlyle, who loved the stage, duly attended twice at the Haymarket and found that Violetti, who was the first dancer, performed exquisitely. Otherwise, he was disappointed in what London had to offer. " The theatres were not very attractive this season, as Garrick had gone over to Dublin."

He never saw Violetti again until 1758, by which time she had been Mrs Garrick for twelve years. He did not remind her of their first meeting and she evidently did not recognize him, which he thought small wonder, " having thrown away my bag-wig and sword,
1 and appearing in my own grisly hairs ".

2

Garrick had gone over to Dublin. His partnership with Sheridan opened somewhat inauspiciously, for at their first meeting he asked for a stipulated sum for his performances during the season. Sheridan objected, and repeated his original offer of dividing profits after deduction of expenses. The dispute was settled by Sheridan taking out his watch and giving his visitor " a few minutes " in which to
2 make up his mind. Garrick gave way.

The season did not open for another fortnight, so he had leisure in which to call upon old acquaintances and meet many more people eager to entertain London's first actor. His circle soon included characters whose names sounded as if they came out of a contemporary comedy, but were in fact to be enduring friends—Lord Bellamont, Lord Milltown, Lord Forbes and Lady Doneraile. Colonel Thomas Butler, brother of Lord Lanesborough, had a vivacious lady, a town house on St Stephen's Green, and a country one on the coast, at Clontarf. Garrick bought an Irish horse for expeditions to Irish country houses and wrote to Mrs Cibber that Lord Blessington and Doctor Barry had drunk her health and wished, as he did, that she had come to Ireland. He said that he sadly wanted to make love to her again. He had not told her of his departure as she was one of those of whom he did not care to take leave. She replied quickly that what she had needed to see him about was a suggestion made to her a fortnight past that he should buy the remainder of the Drury

Lane patent. " I desire you always to be my lover upon the stage and my friend off it." 3

He made his first appearance on December 9, and Sheridan and he entered together upon a partnership of remarkable prosperity. Both appeared alternately as Hamlet and Richard. In *Othello* they took it in turns to play the Moor and Iago. Garrick's first benefit took place on Christmas Eve, when he acted Bayes. It was believed that one of the circumstances which had attracted him to Dublin was that the Lord Lieutenant was now Lord Chesterfield, famous as a patron of the arts, but upon whom Johnson was to deliver one of his most annihilating pronouncements. If Garrick had hoped for encouragement from this quarter, he too was disappointed. Sheridan and he, in accordance with custom, on this brilliant occasion, escorted the Lord Lieutenant to his box with wax candles. Lord Chesterfield spoke easily to Sheridan but took not the slightest notice of Garrick, although he had met him at dinner in London. He did not even return the bow of poor Bayes. It was suggested that the new Lord Lieutenant was at work to patronize exclusively everything Irish, and Sheridan was truly a son of Dublin. This was a credible explanation; for though during Lord Chesterfield's Vice-royalty, Sheridan was frequently invited to Dublin Castle, when they met in London a few years later he was received coldly. 4

Christmas week 1745 brought letters with black seals from Lichfield. Poor Jenny had been buried in the cathedral beside her parents on December 15. She had been but twenty-seven.

A new actor also appeared as Othello during Sheridan and Garrick's management. " Spranger " Barry was the son of a Dublin silversmith. He had lost his fortune, which had been considerable, and made a first tentative appearance on the boards last year. He was very tall, very handsome, with a melting voice and refined melancholy air. He looked as if his disposition should be charming, and when, next year, he came to London and was passed off by Macklin, for a jest, as " the Earl of Munster ", nobody doubted it. He was three years younger than Garrick and, as yet, deferential. One of the first letters received by Garrick on his return to London was from poor Barry, explaining that as he had not had his salary paid from the moment his " guardian angel " had left, he could not yet repay the loan Garrick had so kindly advanced. Garrick had acted with the generosity traditional in their profession and written home that the new actor was the best lover he had ever seen on the stage. Barry awaited Garrick's advice as to whether to accept an offer made by a myrmidon of Lacy to appear at Drury Lane.

Lacy, who had been much chagrined by Garrick's disappearance from London, and had written to Sheridan to complain of it, was in Dublin to witness his first appearances there.   He had come over, it seemed, although the London season should have been in full swing, to collect new material for what Mrs Cibber acidly called his " ragged regiment ".   On the very Black Friday that London had heard of Prince Charles Edward's arrival at Derby, and had taken panic, the Prince had turned back for Scotland.   He was understood to be wintering near Glasgow, waiting for the spring to open a new campaign, it might be.   Meanwhile London's theatrical season drooped and pined.

Amongst the players with whom Lacy had travelled to Ireland was the little Bellamy, with whom Garrick had performed in amateur theatricals in Woffington's barn.   She had not hesitated after that success to press her services at Covent Garden, and it may well have been that her head had been turned when, after her début as Monimia in *The Orphan*, old Rich had tossed her up in his arms, crying, " Thou art a divine creature and the true spirit is in thee."   Her mother, who had eloped from boarding-school, had been on the stage; her father, who acknowledged her, and had paid for her education in a French convent, was Lord Tyrawley.   She was probably by now eighteen, though in an autobiography pathetically entitled *An Apology for the Life of George Anne Bellamy*, produced by her in her days of destitution, she subtracted several years from her age.   She was a *petite* sugar-blonde and continually a victim of untoward circumstances.   She had already been run away with once, and was to be again.   Even her extraordinary Christian names had been bestowed by accident.   She had been born on St George's Day and it had been intended to christen her Georgiane, then pronounced Georjianne; but apparently an unintelligent clergyman had bewilderedly named this child George Anne.   George Anne (as soon as she learned of the mistake) she remained.   Her book provides many anecdotes of Garrick's second Dublin season, at least founded upon fact.   Her first brush with him came over the production of *King John*.   It was her ambition to reduce Dublin to hysteria by her performance as the widowed Constance Plantagenet, mother of Prince Arthur—high tragedy.   Garrick and Sheridan thought that with her popping curls, saucer-eyes and page-boy figure she would be better cast as little Arthur.   Besides, there was the consideration that if she took Constance, Mrs Furnivall, an experienced actress whose countenance and proportions were very ill-suited, would have to be little Arthur.

Bellamy, who had been introduced into the best Dublin society by her father's sister, Mrs O'Hara, flew to that leader of playgoing ladies of fashion, Mrs Thomas Butler, with her tale of woe and wrong, and Mrs Butler canvassed the drawing-rooms, with the result that the first night of *King John* was a flat failure. Nobody went. Delighted that she had given " the immortal Roscius his first humiliation ", George Anne graciously consented to appear once more in *King John*—as Constance. Mrs Butler put her operation into reverse and for this performance crowds had to be turned away from the theatre.

Bellamy had a further triumph when Garrick invited her to undertake the name part in *Jane Shore*. She replied that she feared she was too juvenile. She was gaining some popularity with Dublin audiences, for in spite of her inexperience, her appearance was very effective in such unintellectual parts as the Orphan and Ophelia. Garrick sent her a playful note, saying that if she would oblige him by being Jane he would write for her " a goody goody epilogue, which with the help of your eyes, should do more mischief than ever the flesh or the devil have done, since the world began ". He addressed it " To my Soul's Idol, the beautiful Ophelia ", and gave it to his servant, Welsh Davy, who unfortunately delivered it to a messenger from the Press. Next day Mr Garrick's letter to Miss Bellamy blossomed in the Dublin newspapers and Garrick, according to Bellamy, was " not a little mortified at its publication ". She played Jane, but was not called upon to speak any epilogue. Garrick himself took the opportunity, since this was his last benefit, to record his thanks to his Irish audiences. A poem, dated from Dublin on St Valentine's Day 1746 and reprinted in *The Gentleman's Magazine*, reflected what Dublin thought of him.

> In the force, the fire, the feature
> Usher'd from a feeling heart,
> Garrick is the child of Nature,
> Mankind—only acts a part.

Mrs Cibber was still writing.

> I know you reckon yourself a very politic prince, with your journey to Ireland; and I think the great Garrick never acted so simply since I had the honour of knowing him. You were out of the way at the very time that the fate of the stage is depending.

He had countered by suggesting that she should come to Dublin; but she dreaded the sea passage.

April 15 was a gala night in honour of the birthday of His Royal Highness, William, Duke of Cumberland. Lord Chesterfield, whose health had been indifferent, was going home on a leave, from which he was never to return. He attended the performance of *Orestes* in state, with his court, and Garrick spoke an epilogue which included praise of the martial prince and Hibernia's grief at losing her Viceroy. On the next day, " a dark, misty, rainy day ", the Jacobites were finally defeated on Culloden Moor. The situation had been causing anxiety in England, for on January 17 Prince Charles Edward had won a victory at Falkirk. The news of his soldier son's success at Culloden was brought to George II at Drury Lane theatre, and the audience were startled by the sudden apparition of their sovereign, waving a paper at them from the Royal box, but unable, from excitement, to get out a word of the King's English except " Hey! hey! hey!" An equerry tactfully recovered the despatch and read it aloud. The news spread quickly and that night the streets of London presented an ugly scene. Young Alexander Carlyle, who happened to be out with another Scot, Tobias Smollett, in a coffee-house, had difficulty in getting home to New Bond Street, where he was staying with his cousins, the Lyons from Perthshire. " The mob were so riotous and the squibs were so numerous and incessant that we were glad to go into a narrow entry to put our wigs into our pockets, and to take our swords from our belts and walk with them in our hands." Smollett cautioned Carlyle against opening his mouth, lest his speech betray him. " For John Bull is as haughty and valiant tonight as he was abject and cowardly on the Black Wednesday when the Highlanders were at Derby." When Carlyle reached his goal he did not find his host, although an officer in the Guards and perfectly loyal, as delighted at the victory as he had expected. " What's the matter? " asked Carlyle. " Has your Strathmore blood got up that you are not so pleased with the quelling of the Rebellion? " Captain Lyon said heavily that he heartily rejoiced it was quelled, but he was sorry that it had been accomplished by the Duke of Cumberland.

Garrick, who had spent a few days in Dublin making his farewells after the theatre closed, travelled home with Benjamin Victor, who was going over to England to disengage himself from business in the Irish linen trade, fetch his family and settle in Dublin as Treasurer and Deputy Manager to Sheridan. Garrick's parting with Sheridan was only moderately cordial, although from the financial point of view their partnership had been a complete success. Rumour credited them with having reaped a golden harvest while the London companies were nigh starving. Garrick's share of the profits for six months were, in fact, six hundred pounds. The travellers set out on May 3 and reached London on the 10th. The spring weather was extremely cold and wet, and the theatrical world to which they had returned was also miserably unsettled. Amongst the victims of the

run on the banks owing to the Rebellion scare had been Messrs
Green and Amber. They had failed. Mr Meure had appeared in
January to tell the Drury Lane company that they must expect no
more salaries. Lacy was struggling to bring order out of disorder,
and the poor players' demands for payment were being met for the
present; but Garrick did not return to the Lane. The news soon
spread that he had gone over to the other house. He engaged himself to play for old Rich at Covent Garden next winter. As he had
done before, when joining the Drury Lane company, he agreed to give
half a dozen performances at once. Rich reopened his theatre, and
Garrick appeared between June 11 and 27, in rapid succession as
Lear, Hamlet, Richard, Othello, Archer and Macbeth. Victor heard
that, sharing the profits with Rich, he got no less than three hundred
pounds for these efforts. Three of the performances—*Richard III*,
*Othello* and *The Beaux' Stratagem*—were by command of His Royal
Highness, Frederick, Prince of Wales.

A heavy but handsome martial hero was being shown the sights
of London. The Prince of Hesse had been on the staff of his brother-
in-law Cumberland in Scotland. Cumberland was still in the north,
doing what he called " a little blood-letting " of " a more stubborn
and villainous set of wretches than I imagined could exist ". Society
had to express their relief and admiration to the Prince of Hesse.
He arrived on June 2 and was ceremoniously presented by His
Majesty at Kensington Palace with a sword of curious workmanship
set with diamonds of very great value. At the Opera, he was
observed to change his box for that of the Prince of Wales in order
to get a better view of " the last dance " performed by Mademoiselle
Violette. He appeared at Ranelagh, to sup, and went up to Mr
Garrick and spoke to him.

Mrs Cibber wrote on June 8 to say that Garrick had been so silent
that she had feared him sick, dead or returned to Ireland. She
repeated her invitation to Woodhay.

> If you design riding when you are here, why would you not send back
> your horses? As for your man, you may put him in your pocket, if he is the
> same I remember; a little crumpling won't spoil him. The chaise shall meet
> you at Reading or Newbury. Don't forget what the Prince of Hesse said
> to you at Ranelagh, for I shall expect every word from you. Bring fine
> weather, health and spirits with you and stay a good while. 7

He went to Old Alresford first, and stayed with Hoadly *père*,
Bishop of Winchester. Announcing his intended visit in a letter
dated " this ? day of July, from the barber's shop, up two pairs of
stairs ", he said that he was coming with Hogarth, and they would
have another travelling companion.

Your French cook is safe and sound, and shall come with me, but pray let us have no kickshaws. Nothing but laugh and plumb pudding for your sincere friend and Merry humble servant.

He went on to Cheltenham, where he made very merry amongst a party of old friends with Lichfield connections. One matron, " for her own comfort and the misfortune of her acquaintance ", got into " rantipole spirits " from drinking no more than the waters. In a letter to George, announcing himself returned to London for a week, he opened, " Yesterday I left Elysium and arrived at Hell, about six o'clock in the evening, blasted with the wind and drench'd with the rain."

At Alresford, where he had enjoyed himself much, Benjamin Hoadly, junior, had presented him with a play *The Suspicious Husband*, with a part, " Ranger ", written for him. He had been guarded about this, and had written from Cheltenham, " whether Ranger will appear next winter or sleep for ever in the 'scritoire " he could not yet say. He had been looking at *Philaster, or Love lies Bleeding* by Beaumont and Fletcher, but found it " very indecent ". It would 8 require great alteration.

A very fine late summer had followed the inhospitable spring, and another foreigner, who did not attract nearly as much attention as the Prince of Hesse, was recording his impressions of the London that Garrick knew, in floods of sunshine. Giovanni Antonio Canale, to be better known as Canaletto, had arrived towards the end of May, furnished with a letter from Mr Joseph Smith, British Consul in Venice, to Woffington's old *beau*, Owen MacSwinney, asking that the artist be introduced to the Duke of Richmond. He immediately received a ducal order to paint two views, one of the Thames and the other of Whitehall, as seen from the windows of his Grace's London house. He set up his easel in the dining-room overlooking the gardens, which ran down to the river, and in the foreground of his picture were ladies fluttering like butterflies in fly-away muslin caps and aprons, and spreading silk hoops of coral and turquoise. Gentlemen, wearing wigs and tricornes and long amber and wine-coloured coats, attended them. London as Canaletto saw it in the summer of 1746 was a place of infinite charm, but to more than Garrick, at present, it was Hell. Prince Charles Edward, after romantic wanderings, escaped, just as Lord Rochford had always prophesied, to France in September, but all summer the mouth of the Thames was blocked by transports in which wounded clansmen lay in darkness and semi-starvation awaiting death or transportation. In Westminster Hall scaffolding was being set up for the trials of Lords Kilmarnock, Cromartie and Balmerino. Fear begets cruelty, and

London had been very badly frightened.  To go to look at the Scotch in the Tower or New Gaol, Southwark, became quite one of the diversions of people of fashion.  On Tuesday, July 29, a peer and a ballet-dancer arrived on this errand—the Earl of Burlington, celebrated for his architectural tastes and patronage of men of letters, and Mademoiselle Violette from the Opera, who was living at Burlington House.  As they entered, her companion instructed the young foreign lady, " Everyone that we shall see now is to be executed to-morrow."  The prisoners were then brought in, and amongst them was " Jemmy Dawson ", considered a most interesting case.  He had run away from the University, where he had got into a scrape, and got himself into a worse one by joining the Prince at Manchester.  His father, who was a respectable Lancashire man, was going to be allowed to see him to-night before he was dragged on a hurdle to execution on Kennington Common to-morrow at 11 a.m.  There was an even younger rebel; he looked a mere boy; his name was James Wilding.  He was a Roman Catholic.  With the grace natural to her profession, Violette flung herself at the feet of her attendant milord and begged him to use his power to save young Wilding.  Lord Burlington was not proof against her vehemence.  Some seventy years later, an ancient spinster in Liverpool, almost the last of the Wilding family, asked an acquaintance going to London to search out and offer thanks, though late, to Mrs Garrick.

At some date this winter, if not before, Garrick and she first saw one another; most probably each watched the other performing.  She was holding her place as principal dancer at Drury Lane; he was drawing packed houses to Covent Garden.  According to tradition her first experience of seeing Mr Garrick perform was fatal to the peace of mind of " La Violette ".

3

The season in 1746–1747 promised to be brilliant.  Both theatres offered new attractions.  At Drury Lane, Lacy announced Spranger Barry, the young Irish star, who had never before appeared on the English stage.  He was being coached by Macklin, and presently was to accept the advice of the Prince of Wales to take lessons in deportment from his dancing-master, Mr Denoyer.  Lacy also had London's two leading comedy-actresses, Clive and Woffington.  Unfortunately, according to Davies, " No two women of high rank ever hated one another more unreservedly than these great dames of the theatre. . . . Woffington was well-bred, seemingly very calm, and at all times mistress of herself.  Clive was frank, open and impetuous."  When Clive, after one of their " clashes " in which she had been very

frank, pondered upon the airy and apparently civil replies of Woffington, she realized, with sudden pangs, deadly sarcasm.

Rich had secured for Covent Garden the most popular leading
exponents of the old style of acting, and of the new, Quin and
Garrick; he also had Woodward, a great comedian, and both the
famous tragedy queens, Mrs Pritchard and Mrs Cibber. Quin was
now fifty-four, but looked much more. He had been a favourite for
thirty seasons and on the stage some years before that. He had lost
his figure, and he had never had any looks, but he could still be
tremendous—especially when he spied an unfortunate stage-hand
within two yards of the wings. (" Get away, boy! " was then
accompanied by a terrible slash with his cane.) But when he opened
the season as Richard, the result was disappointing. Quin's name
" could scarce draw together a decent appearance of company in the
boxes ". Garrick was billed for Richard a week later and the house
was packed. Another novelty had to be tried—Garrick and Quin
in the same play. *The Fair Penitent* was chosen for November 14—
Quin as Horatio and Garrick as Lothario. Covent Garden was again
packed, but the rival actors found themselves playing to a very
difficult house. When in Act II they first met on the boards, for the
first time in their lives, repeated shouts from supporters of each
egged them on to gladiatorial combat. Quin was observed to change
colour, although he laughed it off: Garrick afterwards admitted that
he had been disconcerted. There was a ridiculous incident when
Quin made one of his famous dramatic pauses before accepting
Lothario's challenge. He waited so long, pondering the words " I'll
meet thee then! " that a ribald voice from the gallery was able to
interpose, " Why don't you tell the gentleman whether you will meet
him or not? "

A scholar from Westminster School, a clever dark boy with a big
nose and a long sad countenance, who had been writing about
Shakespeare before he was twelve, witnessed that first night, and
afterwards, when he was a reverend gentleman and a prolific author
of plays for Garrick, recorded his memories. Quin, in his usual
green velvet coat, enormous periwig and high-heeled square-toed
shoes, " paved " out his periods in full heavy monotony, accompanying them with a weary sawing motion. Mrs Cibber " recitatived " in
a high-pitched sweet key, which made every speech sound like an old
ballad. " But when, after long and eager expectation, I first beheld
little Garrick, young and light and alive in every muscle and every
feature, come bounding on the stage, and pointing at the wittol
Altamont and heavy-paced Horatio—Heavens, what a transition!
it seemed as if a whole century had been step't over in the transition

H

of a single scene." Richard Cumberland, aged fourteen, thought
Garrick a " heaven-born " actor. Another member of the audience, 12
old Lord Conyngham, over from Ireland, described the contest between Quin and Garrick as resembling one between an old unwieldy
man-of-war, a three-decker, slow in manœuvring to bring her broad-
side to bear, and a little frigate, easy to handle and able to land her
shots where and when she chose. Mr Walmesley was at Bath, where
he found himself " a very insignificant person " since his whist was
only good enough for a ladies' table. " But I must not forget to tell
you what Lord Chesterfield said of you. He says you are not only
the best tragedian now in the world, but the best, he believes, that
ever was in the world." Characteristically, Lord Chesterfield had
added that he did not like Garrick in comedy, and spoken much in
praise of the young Irish wonder, " Silver-tongued " Barry.
Walmesley had not neglected to say that he hoped Lord Chesterfield
would give his Dear Davy his protection, to which Chesterfield had
replied that Garrick needed no protection. He thought Barry
merited encouragement but made quite a joke of his rivalling or
hurting Garrick. Some widow would soon take so very handsome a
young fellow from the stage. Mr Walmesley, whose gout was so bad
that he had been unable to use his pen for two or three months, and
would be miserable at Bath, but for the coffee-house and a good bookseller's shop, urged his dear Davy not to hurt his health by playing
more than he could bear, and sent a sad message to his other Lichfield protégé Mr Johnson, who did not seem to be succeeding. " Tell
him I esteem him as a great genius—quite lost to himself and the
world." 1

Quin's hour of triumph came with *Henry IV, Part I*, for " Quin,
with a bottle of claret and a full house, the instant he was on the
stage was Sir John Falstaff himself ". It was noted that he had not
stopped at padding his figure; his voice also was padded. Davies
claims that " Mr Garrick and Mr Quin had too much sense and temper
to squabble about trifles ", and Murphy agrees that they " carried on
their business in perfect good humour with each other and had no
kind of difference throughout the season ". Garrick tactfully said
that he considered Quin's Falstaff the perfection of acting. He
played Hotspur himself, and made no particular hit, it may have
been because he was not feeling well. Havard undertook the part
after the first five performances, and Garrick never appeared in it
again. But Covent Garden cherished a story that when Quin, as
Falstaff, bore the gory corpse of Garrick, as Hotspur, from the scene,
dreadfully grunting " Come thou along with me! ", he added,
audibly to all in the wings, " Where shall we sup to-night? " 1

*Miss in Her Teens* brought Quin and Garrick as near to disagree-
ment as they ever came.   Encouraged by the success of *Lethe* and
*The Lying Valet*, Garrick had put together another *petite pièce*.
Neither the plot nor the characters were new, but they had been
popular before and, he thought, might be again.   The cast was small.
There were six men—old Sir Simon Loveit, a widower, who wanted to
marry Miss, his son, Captain Bob, who by a most unconvincing
chance had won her heart, under the alias of Rhodophil before he
went to the wars in Flanders, two wicked old soldier servants, Jasper
and Puff, and two more suitors for Miss, whose names explained
them, Captain Flash and Mr Fribble.   Puff's deserted wife, whom
Jasper had been courting, was maid to Miss's old aunt, a benevolent
dowager, and Miss herself was a hoyden, who slapped her suitors on
the back and brought out the most *risqué* remarks with round-eyed
innocence.   Bellamy would have been an ideal Miss, but she was
now a leading lady of Sheridan's company in Dublin.   Miss Biddy
Bellair was created by Miss Jane Hippisley, who, to tell the truth,
was no longer in her teens.   She had been on the stage twelve
years, and had played Ophelia to Garrick's Hamlet in his Goodman's
Fields days.   But she was an old friend, and the part almost played
itself.   Her father was cast for Sir Simon, and Woodward had, in
Flash, a part written for him.   But the success of the piece was
Garrick as Fribble.   Roars of laughter greeted him on his first
mincing entrance, attired in a costume which was a caricature of the
height of fashion.   For Fribble was the most ladylike of gentlemen,
terribly nervous for his health, belonged to a sewing-club, and brought
to Miss, on bended knee, as a courting gift, a pot of his own lip-salve.
"The ingredients are innocent, I assure you!"   *The Gentleman's
Magazine* reviewed Mr Garrick's farce, quoting passages, and print-
shops soon produced pictures of the duel scene.

Only Quin, according to Davies, resolutely refused to attach
himself to such nonsense.   The little piece was too short to be presented as a full evening's entertainment.   It would have to be
played before something longer in which Quin would appear.

> He complied at first, but soon after repented; he surlily swore that he
> would not hold up the tail of any farce.   "Nor shall he," said Mr Garrick,
> when he was told what Quin had said; "I will give him a month's holidays."
> He picked out of the prompter's list of plays all such as could be acted
> without Quin, and "Miss in her Teens" was tacked onto them every night
> for about five weeks.

Quin sometimes called at the theatre during that time, and on being
told that the house was full would retire with a growl.   Garrick, in
fact, had not at that time the power to choose what plays should be

performed. The correct explanation of his witticism is that he foresaw that *Miss in Her Teens* was going to run. If Quin would not appear on any night when it was offered, then he would get a rest.

As Hastings in *Jane Shore* Garrick was considered to have quite cut out Quin, who was Gloucester. In a new part in a new play he was to create a character which was to remain in his répertoire for life. He had decided to produce Benjamin Hoadly's *Suspicious Husband*, pressed upon him at Old Alresford last July. He had given it a prologue and epilogue. Quin refused the title rôle. The play was a resounding success. His Majesty had laughed so much that he sent a hundred pounds to Dr Hoadly in gratitude and allowed the comedy to be dedicated to him. *The Gentleman's Magazine* loyally devoted seven pages of its March issue to a review and excerpts, but thought Mr Garrick, as Ranger, made a vicious character too attractive. Ranger was, as his name suggests, a gay young man-about-town, taking his pleasures where he found them, but not yet quite lost to a sense of sin. The great moment of the play did not come until Act III when the *ingénue* Jacintha, who has decided to elope dressed as a boy, is disturbed after she has left a rope-ladder dangling from the bedroom window of her blameless and lovely chaperone Mrs Strickland, wife of the Suspicious Husband. Ranger, sauntering home from the Piazza by full moonlight, comes upon it.

> Now I am in an admirable mood for a frolic; have wine in my head, and money in my pocket, and so am furnished out for the cannonading of any countess in Christendom. Ha! what have we here? a ladder!—this cannot be placed here for nothing—and a window open! Is it love or mischief, now, that is going on within? I care not which—I am in a right cue for either. Up I go, neck or nothing. . . .

After looking in and perceiving " a light and a woman! by all that's lucky, neither old nor crooked ", he steps softly in at the window, and " for fear of the squalls of virtue and the pursuit of the family ", takes the precaution of pulling up after him the ladder. " Now fortune be my guide! "

Ranger added greatly to Garrick's reputation, and eventually his own farce was produced on a night when Quin was appearing in a serious piece. On the night of Quin's benefit, a letter from Garrick, printed at the head of the playbill, announced that he had not the strength to go through the part of the revengeful Jaffier in *Venice Preserv'd*. But sooner than disappoint his friend by failing to appear at all on such an occasion, he would act in his own farce as Fribble. This statement caused a flutter in Mayfair. Fribble was ill! Ranger was ill! " Flocks of footmen " sent to inquire for Mr Garrick, arrived at the doors of his lodgings over the periwig-makers in Little James

# GARRICK as Ranger in "The Suspicious Husband".

*By Francis Hayman* ($27\frac{3}{4}'' \times 35\frac{1}{2}''$)

Hayman was the principal scene-painter at Drury Lane, in the early days of Garrick's career there. Garrick created the part of Ranger, in Benjamin Hoadly's comedy, on December 4, 1747, and appeared in it last on May 23, 1773. Another version of this conversation piece, of which this reproduction is a detail, is the property of the Garrick Club.

*Reproduced by kind permission of the Trustees, The London Museum.*

Street. It was recollected that he had already, several times this
season, been obliged to retire from parts. Nevertheless, he had
played on ninety occasions. It was understood that a neglected cold
had " settled on his lungs ". He was indeed out of health, but as
usual his illness had been increased by what he called " lowness of
spirits ". The time had again come for him to take a plunge. In a
few weeks his engagement with Rich would end. Covent Garden had
enjoyed the most successful season in its history, and largely owing to
his performances. But the older theatre was his first love and Lacy
still wanted him for Drury Lane, and as more than an actor. Moreover Lacy's situation had altered it seemed for the better. Garrick,
who had been feeling so ill that he almost wished himself in another
world, decided that this world was too interesting. On April 9 he
arose from his sick-bed and went along to keep a business appointment with Lacy.

The eyes of London that day were not turned towards theatre-
land. Tower Hill was offering a rival attraction. Simon, Lord
Lovat, aged eighty, last of the rebel Scotch lords, was being executed
that morning. Hogarth had posted out to the White Hart Inn, St
Albans, when he heard that Lord Lovat had arrived there under
guard on his road from Scotland, and had obtained a remarkable
likeness of the foxy old peer, counting the clans on his fingers. To
witness his trial, in Westminster Hall, Lady Burlington had taken
17 her charming protégée, Violette, the dancer.

Garrick may later have acted better than he did in his Covent
Garden season, for with years he gained ease and experience; but
judging by contemporary reports he never acted more poignantly
than he did when he was half distracted by the problem whether to
engage with Rich again, or try Ireland again, both of which would
be literally playing for safety, or whether he should go into partnership with Lacy, become manager of Drury Lane, perhaps lose all he
had or perhaps succeed, become rich, and marry. For he now knew
that he was in love again.

4

Various stories were told as to how James Lacy had come into
favour with the Duke of Grafton, Lord Chamberlain. He was a
large, well-favoured person, with smooth features and a clear blue
eye. Benjamin Victor, who had known him before he had displayed
" a theatrical bias ", believed that the duke, descendant of Charles II,
paid a particular regard to all those whose families had suffered in
the cause of King Charles the Martyr, " and it was not unknown to
his Grace that the Lacys of Ireland, from whom the gentleman we

are speaking of was descended, were absolutely ruined by their
Attachment to that Monarch, having lost a vast Estate and been
obliged to follow Fortune in almost all the different Services of
Europe ". Tom Davies believed that Lacy, who rode well, had
ingratiated himself with the duke in the hunting-field, and there were
further legends that he had offered the duke a horse which his grace
had admired, and that he had resourcefully produced " savoury
refreshments " when the Croydon hunt had killed far from home.
The facts were that the old Drury Lane patent, granted in 1732, had
now only six years to run, and the lease of the theatre five: but a
lease without a patent was useless. However, it now appeared
reasonably certain that the duke would renew it if Lacy could find
a solid partner. Lacy's career, so far, had not been reassuring. He
had failed in business in Norwich, and he had been most unfortunate
over the Rotunda, at Ranelagh. That building " a standing monument of his taste and ingenuity ", still stood, and was vastly popular.
It coined money. But he had been " yoked with a wicked partner ",
and had been lucky to escape from his Ranelagh scheme with four
thousand pounds profit. He had acted in Fielding's satire at the
Haymarket which had been largely responsible for the fatal Licensing
Act, and he had not even been a success. There were no two opinions
that he had " entirely mistaken his talent by exposing himself on the
stage ". But he clearly had a flair for the entertainment trade.
Davies thought he had a good understanding, uncultivated by
education, that his observations on men and manners were judicious,
and that if his own manners were sometimes boisterous " he was one
of those whom no repulses of fortune, or checks of disappointment
could intimidate or divert from his purpose ". He had also other
powerful patrons—" the Lady Burlington who was a Friend to no
Body by Halves ", Lord Hartington, heir to the Duke of Devonshire,
Mr Roberts, Secretary to Mr Pelham, at the Treasury. Of course,
he had for the last eighteen months been trying to attract " the great
theatrical loadstone " whom everyone assured him would be his
ideal co-patentee. " Mr Garrick had Money, Reputation and
Ability; all were Requisites." But Garrick had thought the time
unripe, and indeed the risk was great.

The Agreement concluded on April 9, 1747, described the signa-
tories as James Lacy, of Great Queen Street, near Lincoln's Inn
Fields, in the county of Middlesex, gentleman, and David Garrick, of
James Street, Covent Garden, gentleman. It banished from the
scene for ever the mortgagees, Mr Hutcheson Meure and Messrs
Green and Amber, late of the Strand. The liabilities of the theatre,
including the arrears due to tradesmen and actors, were reckoned at

about twelve thousand pounds. Nobody who had known the wiles of Charles Fleetwood Esquire would be surprised to note that he too was bowed out very handsomely. He got an annuity of five hundred pounds with which to pursue a career of dignified retirement in the sunny south of France. Garrick had been repeatedly to see three friends of substance, two of them in the City. Mr James Clutterbuck was a mercer, Mr Somerset Draper, a publisher. Mr Samuel Sharpe, surgeon to Guy's Hospital, was in the habit of delivering lectures in Covent Garden, and had literary aspirations. Garrick, in his thirtieth year, had found eight thousand pounds. Lacy, provided that he got the new patent before the end of May, was to find four thousand, and, if the liabilities appeared at more than the twelve thousand reckoned likely, was to settle the excess out of his profits. Each patentee was to receive five hundred pounds a year, and Garrick a further five hundred pounds as his salary for acting. It was also agreed, although the document did not state this, that Garrick was to undertake, principally, stage management and the choice of players and plays, and that Lacy, assisted by young Brother George Garrick, now aged twenty-three, would deal with business management. Soon after Garrick was to regret that the same delicacy which had made him unable to broach the subject of his unpaid salary to Fleetwood, had detained him from pressing Lacy to be more precise as to their respective duties. A Mr John Paterson, in whose office George had received his legal training, had to be called in to arbitrate, and produced a document providing for questions in continual dispute. It was arranged that " cuts " made by Garrick at rehearsal should be sent immediately to Lacy, by the prompter, for approval. Garrick sadly filed " Some letters that passed between Mr Lacy and me upon a difference between us ". Lacy's contributions, written in a surprisingly niggling hand abounded in such lordly and stormy passages as " When you were received by me as a Partner ", and, " I say NOW what I said when I admitted you FIRST, that no partner shall have
18 a greater share of POWER " etc.

The Covent Garden season closed on May 27 and three days later Brother William, now a Lieutenant in the Young Buffs, engaged on coast defence at Newhaven, wrote to Brother George " at Mrs Farington's, nearest House to the Church in Mark Lane, London ".

> Yesterday I received yours, with the Sword, wich I expected last week, but as I did not receive it, I thought you had taken up your bed and walkt; but am very sorry I am deceived, and to hear of your being in so much pain.
>   I am very sorry my dear Brother has engaged himself with Mr Lacy, who
19   I am afraid will give him a great deal of trouble and uneasiness.

5

An empty theatre is inevitably somewhat ghostly, and the house
to which Garrick and Lacy repaired together at all hours in the
summer of 1747 was in addition the oldest in London.  It was
seventy-three years old, plain-faced and decidedly shabby.  The
June sunshine, slanting in, and the light of a few tallow candles,
displayed much that new brooms should sweep clean.  The first
theatre on the site had been burnt down in 1663, nine years after its
opening; the present building had been designed by Sir Christopher
Wren.  Legend said that he had incorporated into his house some of
the original fabric.  Down in the basement were walls that Nell
Gwyn had known.  He had built strongly and the arches on which
his theatre rested were to survive two more re-buildings and another
fire.                                                                    20

It was two years since Garrick had been into Drury Lane, except
as a visitor, and as the house was now closed for the summer, few of
the staff on Lacy's payroll were in attendance.  This list looked
alarming—men-dressers, women-dressers, office-keepers, numberers,
boxkeepers, doorkeepers, scene-men, sweepers, porters, a messenger.
There were even troops.  Soldiers on guard outside the theatre
during performances had been a rule since the Lincoln's Inn riots of
1721.  The house also had a couple, male and female, in charge of
properties, a barber, a laundress, candlewomen. . . . It would not
be possible to cut down on any of these and some were old friends,
with a broad smile for young Mr Garrick.  With two important
employees he was on very good terms—Mr Hayman, who painted
scenery (and had painted him and Windham, in a landscape, in off-
duty hours), and Mr Cross, the prompter.

The Theatre Royal, Drury Lane, was, compared with Covent
Garden, historic, but it could not be denied that the junior house,
which was only fifteen years old, had modern advantages.  " Lun "
Rich's new theatre had been much advertised at the date of its opening, and Hogarth had produced a caricature, ' Glory, or the triumphant entry into Covent Garden ', in which " Lun ", attired as a
Roman conqueror, rode in a chariot towards a palatial pile, flying a
flag inscribed " Rich for ever— ".  The uniformity of the houses surrounding the large open space in which it arose gave it a curiously
continental air.  Its interior, decorated by an Italian artist, was
" shining all with gold ".  It was much larger than the Lane, upon
which visitors came suddenly, through small streets.  Lacy thought
he could do something about the approach to their theatre.  Anything that would ease traffic congestion and consequent late arrivals

would be a boon. It was flattering, and it was thrilling, on a night when Garrick played, to see chairs and chaises waiting all round the Piazza and Southampton Street, and half way up Maiden Lane, but on nights when the rain was coming down steadily upon the silent vehicles packed tight in the glistening streets, the confusion and misery as soon as the curtain fell were at once tedious and alarming. Garrick would like to alter the façade of the theatre too, but not yet. (Brother Billy had written airily to Brother George that he heard David and Lacy were going to pull down the old house and while it was re-building, play at Lincoln's Inn Fields.)

With much of the scenery which was kept in an adjacent building in Old Vinegar Yard the new patentee was all too familiar. It consisted mainly of flats and shutters, which could be pushed across the stage and removed to display a further scene behind. There were some " relieves ", moulded scenes, and " cuts " which showed perspective. They were all used again and again, and he had played in the same parlour as Archer, and Foppington, and Plume, and beneath a balcony which belonged to Mr Strickland, and Shylock, and Juliet, and on a blasted heath which was also, when occasion demanded, Bosworth Field and the cliffs near Dover. The theatre machinery littered the house in the dead season—winding-drums, ropes and pulleys, levers, counterweights and blocks. Drury Lane was rich in traps, wires and transparencies, for supernatural appearances. These were a legacy from the days when it was having to compete with " Lun " Rich's pantomimes, and lovers of the classic drama had held up hands of horror at the antique house so degrading itself. But Garrick, who had himself bounded on to the stage first in the spangles and mask of harlequin, had no particular dislike of a pantomime. The immortal Shakespeare had himself introduced something of the kind in several of his plays—for example, *Midsummer Night's Dream*, and *The Tempest*, both of which ought to be intelligently revived.

Drury Lane had one feature which was unique. Wren's stage projected in an oval up to the front row of the pit. There had originally been seventeen feet of it beyond the proscenium arch, and fifteen behind. The actor who had been " discovered " against his appropriate background when the curtain rose, would desert it happily, sally down on to the " apron ", and there, striking his attitude, begin to hold forth, in the style of his day. The " apron " had its advantages, for actors on it could be seen and heard from every part of the house, but the destruction of illusion was great, and it was clearly not designed for the new style of acting—Mr Garrick's new, easy style, which he intended to instill into all his performers. (" Mr Wignall, why can't you say, ' Mr Strickland, your coach is ready ', as an ordinary man would say it, and not with the declamatory pomp of Mr Quin playing tyrants? "  " Sir, I thought in that passage I HAD kept down the sentiment.") Moreover, the heavily raked stage, on 21 which Garrick and Lacy walked in eager conclave, amongst dusty coils of rope, in echoing blue gloom, had been shortened by four feet about fifty years ago, in order to enlarge the pit.  This had been one of the cheese-paring " improvements " of " Lun " Rich's father, Christopher, of whom old Cibber said terrible things.  Christopher, who had been bred an attorney, had fought the Lord Chamberlain and his poor players, with considerable success, but in the end reduced the Lane to silence.  *The Tatler* had published in 1709 an imaginary catalogue of the " contents of the palace in Drury Lane, of Christopher Rich, Esquire, who is breaking up housekeeping ". This had included such things as " a rainbow, a little faded ", Roxana's nightgown, Othello's handkerchief, " the imperial robe of Xerxes, never worn but once " and " a basket hilted sword, very convenient to carry milk in ". . . . Chris Rich's name was not a lucky one for a new patentee to ponder, as he dubiously surveyed a stage which had been tinkered with so that more violent gesture and louder voices than he approved would have to be the order of the day, for the present, at any rate.  Two of the four proscenium doors by which the actors had been accustomed to make their entrances and exits on to the apron had been turned into stage boxes under old Rich's orders.  By this alteration the house had been made to hold ten pounds more than before.  Lacy now thought that by re-arranging the seating he might contrive to increase their accommodation by forty pounds a night.  The auditorium was three-tiered.  The pit with its backless fixed benches, covered with green cloth, had three tiers of boxes enclosing it.  In the music-box sat the orchestra.  Old Rich had sent that aloft.  There were two galleries, middle and upper. . . . The whole interior must be re-decorated.  Fortunately the season was warm, and they had three and a half months in hand before their opening.

They discussed other things before they left the empty house to the bricklayers, the carpenters and the painters.  They were agreed to abolish the pernicious custom of " tasting " a play—return of entrance money if the spectator left at the end of the first act, and half price for the third act only.  With their second reform they felt they were not on such sure ground, but it must be tried for a month, and announced on play-bills—no admittance behind the scenes. After reform of the audience came reform of the company.  Garrick was determined to call together something outstanding—all the best players in the country, all his old friends, and no old feuds. He was going to give the public Macklin as the Jew, Woffington as Sir Harry, and Barry as Othello. But his players were going to find his rule stricter than any to which they had been accustomed. "Order, decency and decorum" were to be the watchwords under his management. Punctuality at rehearsals was going to be observed, and at rehearsals the cast were to behave as if they were playing to an audience. This rule should solve many difficulties and save much time. He was not going to allow persons who had failed to learn their parts to "supply the defect by a bold front and forging matter of their own". (Yates was a notorious offender in this line, and he must have Yates.) Finally, for this was enough for the moment, he was going to revive much more of the work of Shakespeare purged of the additions of Davenant, Dryden, old Cibber and the rest. The name of Garrick should be remembered together with that of Shakespeare.

When he had given over the theatre to the workmen, he set off for Lichfield. This was bound to be a trying visit, for Cassandra-like prophecies of disaster in his new venture must be expected from Peter. He reached home, in the end, in poor shape, had to take to his bed at once and send for the apothecary to bleed him. However, his fever abated, and he thought he could trace the source of this unmerited attack. Upon reflection he distinctly remembered damp sheets at Dunstable. His very sore throat, dreaded malady for an actor, had developed at Coventry.

He could not stay away from the theatre long. He was back in London on Friday night, July 11, and found awaiting him the sort of letters to which a manager must become inured. One was in a familiar hand, the second was signed, "A.B. till I see how you can keep a secret." Mr Pritchard, who was down at Bristol, was on the war-path. Somebody had told his wife (quite inaccurately) that although she had been engaged for the new company at the Lane, it would be to play second fiddle to Mrs Cibber. "A.B." supplied the inner story. Rich was making an effort to detach Mrs Pritchard. Her husband, who loved her, was to be "blown up" by being told that Mr Garrick made such a difference between her and Mrs Cibber, with whom he always preferred to play. "Mrs Cibber's name never appears in the bills but in principal parts, and her name always in the largest letters."

Next morning, on his return from the theatre, where the premises were in a state of confusion which looked hopeless, Garrick sat down to write a very good letter to Pritchard. To the end of his days, he could not resist writing long, tactful, very kind, firm letters to troublesome correspondents, of which he kept copies. He was very fond of Mrs Cibber, and by no means unappreciative of her talents for tragedy, but in private life her drooping pose, her melancholy gaze, told him that all flesh was grass, and he was only just out of his twenties and liked women to be cheerful. If affairs in his private life went as he longed for them to do, his " little wife " (on the stage only) would certainly be wounded. She must, by now, have heard of his new partnership in business. He had not faced telling her of it himself, for she would not like his engaging with Lacy of whom she had always nourished the darkest suspicions. She would also, no doubt, quarrel with Clive and Woffington. But his unfailing good-humour and energy would bind his widely-diverse leading ladies together.

He wrote to Pritchard nobly.

> I have not engaged Mrs Cibber as yet, and if I should, you may depend upon it that no stupid article such as playing with her (solely) should be part of the agreement. If you will consider the falsehood, you may know that such clauses are incompatible with my interest and inclination, and I am sorry they should be thrown out to spoil the harmony I intend shall subsist in our company.

In his second sheet he became majestic.

> I have a great stake, Mr Pritchard, and must endeavour to secure my property and my friends to the best of my judgment. I shall engage the best company in England, if I can, and think it to the interest of the best actors to be together. I shall to the best of my ability do justice to all, and I hope Mr Pritchard and his friends will be the last to impeach my conduct.

He was a little hard on Pritchard when he suggested that he would find he ran as little " risque " of ill-treatment from his present managers as from his former. He begged him, if he and Mrs Pritchard were at all uneasy, that they would to let him know by the next post, in which case he would use his endeavours with Mr Lacy to discharge them from their agreement. He admitted that he was himself " a little vexed ", and in his postscript asked if Havard had received a letter from him. For although Havard was no novelty, and had a dreadful vein of dullness, he was an old friend, and a good, steady man, unlike Delane, whom he had also engaged.

Having settled the Pritchards, for the moment, and satisfied himself that he could do nothing more amidst his " alterations and mortar " he betook himself to a watering-place where the arrival of England's youngest actor-manager could not be amiss. For he did not find that the changed régime at Drury Lane was, as yet, attracting all the comment he had expected. Tunbridge Wells had been made fashionable by Charles II. " At a little distance, it bears the appearance of a town in the midst of woods, and conveys to the imagination the soothing idea of a rural romantic retirement, while it actually affords all the conveniences of City life." It was only thirty-four miles from Town and got the London papers on the day of publication. It had rows of little shops along its principal promenade, offering London luxuries at Spa prices, and journalists came there to pick up news, and sketch. When Bellamy made her first appearance there it was in the style the absurd creature deemed suitable for a leading lady—in a coach and six, with her maid and two mounted footmen, four of her steeds being " bright bays ". Next year Mr Garrick was to be depicted by a caricaturist at Tunbridge, lounging on the " pantiles " in an assemblage which included Lord Harcourt, the Bishop of Salisbury, the Duchess of Norfolk, Signora Frisi from the Opera, old Cibber, Lord Burlington and Mr Samuel Johnson.

He wrote to George from Tunbridge, on July 26, from a very noisy coffee-house.

> I have drunk the waters, and they agree with me. I am taking an ounce of Bark with them, and hope they will strengthen and recruit me. There is very good company here, and I have been with them all round. . . . If there is any news, or Mr Lacy has anything to say, let me know. I go to bed at eleven, rise at seven, drink no malt liquor, and think of nothing. Old Cibber is here, and very merry we are. Mr Lyttelton and I are Cup and Can . . . I have played at E.O. and won. I don't dance but I sleep without my cold sweats and eat like a ploughman.

Drury Lane, under new management, opened on September 15 and the list of favourites engaged was enough to take the heart out of Covent Garden. The stars included Macklin, Woffington, Barry, Clive, Delane, Mrs Cibber and Mrs Pritchard. Amongst lesser luminaries, but some much loved, were Ned Shuter, invaluable as a low comedian, Havard, Yates, the Millses, the Sparkeses and Miss Hippisley, now Mrs Green. Woodward was coming as soon as he could leave Ireland. " Lun " Rich was left with Theophilus Cibber, Foote, Ryan and Giffard. Foote intended to give what he called his " tea-parties," a form of entertainment begun by him at the Haymarket, when he had invited audiences to drink tea with him and witness his imitations of theatrical rivals. Strange to say, Rich did not seem at all interested in his predicament. He had parted with his best performers without a pang. Not all members of his company had applauded when he had knelt down upon his stage to give a ridiculous imitation of Garrick as Lear. He had seemed rather to resent the full houses which Garrick and Quin had brought him. Although not very old as yet, but sixty-five, he was getting more and more eccentric.   Tom Davies heard that he used to peep through the curtain at the packed house awaiting his great performers, and retreat muttering, " Ah, you're there, are ye?   Much good may it do ye."   As the season advanced Quin, who had not been re-engaged, wrote to him from Bath, " Dear Sir, I am at Bath.   Yours James Quin ". to which he replied, " Dear Sir, Stay there and be damned; Yours John Rich."   2

The first play produced by Garrick and Lacy was *The Merchant of Venice*, with Macklin as Shylock.   The prologue, spoken by Garrick, had been written by Johnson, and was to become historic. Years afterwards, Johnson said that its entire sixty-two lines were clear in his head before he wrote down a single couplet.   He did not afterwards change more than a word, and that was done at the remonstrance of Garrick.   " I did not think his criticism just; but it was necessary that he should be satisfied with what he was to utter." The prologue, however, bears strong internal evidence of having been composed after much confabulation with Garrick, for it clearly expounds all his leading principles.   Its opening verse extolled the immortal Shakespeare; it proceeded to deplore the low morality of the playwrights following Ben Jonson, and the declamatory style of acting, and it rousingly appealed to the audience to demand better fare.

> Ah! let not censure term our fate our choice,
> The stage but echoes back the public voice.
> The drama's laws the drama's patrons give,
> For we, who live to please, must please to live.
>
> Then prompt no more the follies you decry.
> As tyrants doom their tools of guilt to die.
> 'Tis yours this night to bid the reign commence
> Of rescued nature and reviving sense.

After the first few performances Garrick was announced unwell, and the prologue was omitted, but it was published, on October 8, without the author's name, and together with the epilogue, spoken by Woffington.

Three years ago, Samuel Johnson had got himself into hot water with his hagiography of Savage, for which he had failed to verify his facts, and Mr Harte, tutor to Lord Chesterfield's son, said that when he went to visit Cave at St John's Gate, a dish from their dinner was sent behind a screen for an employee of *The Gentleman's Magazine* who deemed himself too shabby to appear.   Johnson had now got what sounded like employment for some years.   He had signed a contract with a solid group of booksellers to produce a dictionary of the English language.   He had taken a house, in Gough Square, had engaged assistants, and was receiving some advances to meet his expenses. Directly he had gone into partnership with Lacy, Garrick had shown signs of being a good friend. In April he had read aloud passages from Mr Johnson's tragedy to literary friends. He now thought he would have to defer production until next season. Mr Johnson's luckless *Irene*, bane of his pupil's Edial school-days, had now been awaiting her début for ten years. But Garrick meant to give her a trial, and with every advantage, for whatever he thought of her, and despite all evidence to the contrary, he could not rid himself of the conviction that there was something great slumbering in Johnson. Another failed schoolmaster had sent him a play which he was going to launch without delay. But Edward Moore's *Foundling* was a comedy, and young Belmont, a variant of Ranger; also Mr Moore had as patrons Mr Lyttelton and Mr Pelham. Mr Walpole was to declare the piece " far from good, but it took ".

After Macklin as the Jew, Garrick gave London *The Beggar's Opera*, always popular, then Barry as Hamlet. The house was disappointed that the new patentee did not appear to speak the prologue to *Hamlet*. On October 8 he published it, together with the epilogue " Mr Garrick being disabled by illness ". He had appeared five days earlier introducing the first (and last) performance at the Lane of *Albumazar*. Albumazar had, in fact, been an Arabian astronomer who had flourished in Baghdad in the ninth century. He was represented in this comedy, which had been first performed before James I, as a rascally wizard. Dryden, whose prologue Garrick spoke, charged Ben Jonson with having appropriated the character for his *Alchymist*, but wrongly, for Jonson's play had been in the field first, by four years.

Garrick reappeared on October 15, in a part which put no great strain upon him, and in which he was always liked, Archer, in *The Beaux' Stratagem*. Woffington played Mrs Sullen. As the season advanced, and plays were given five times a week, instead of three, he repeated all his established successes—Abel, Hamlet, Lear, Macbeth, Richard, Hastings, Sir John Brute.

It may have been on one of these occasions when he was wringing hearts as Lear that Mrs Clive, who had just emerged from one of her standing fights with her manager, was heard to announce to the wings, " Damn him! he could act a gridiron! " He cautiously left Othello to Barry, and Sir Harry Wildair to Woffington. The only new parts which he attempted in his first year as manager were Jaffier in *Venice Preserv'd*, which he thought exacting, and Moore's Young Belmont. But he produced other plays new to the house— *King Henry V* in which he appeared as prologue and chorus, and *The Tempest*, still in Dryden's version.

On December 12, William Windham, who had been staying in Lichfield, reported to Brother Peter:

Now I must give you an account of David. He is very well, in very high spirits, constant full houses and as admired and followed as ever, or rather more so, for no one has the assurance to pretend to any competition with him. The affairs of the Theatre appear to go on extreamly easy. Everything is done with the greatest order and regularity, and there is a most exact discipline observed by all belonging to the house. Lacy and he agree very well, and every thing is done just as David pleases, so that he seems to have little disagreeable work. He has made a regulation for the boxes which is of great advantage to the managers, as it prevents bilking, and to the audience, as it prevents the continual disturbance there was in the boxes, opening and shutting doors and frisking in and out. For he makes people pay at coming in to the box. No manager but himself would have dared to have attempted such a thing, but he had all the people of fashion strenuously for him, as indeed they are in everything, and no people seem displeased with him and his management but that pack of scoundrels the . . .

At this point the name of the pack of scoundrels has been expunged from Windham's letter to Peter in the same sooty ink which made obliterations in David's early letters to his father. The pack appear to have introduced Windham to the Garricks which makes the affair the more deplorable, and Windham only waits to knock somebody down. His letter reverts to a picture all *couleur de rose*. Rich is in a very bad way. Foote " gives tea " at Covent Garden, and was to come out this week " with an abusive satyr on David ", but Lacy has been to see Chetwynd, the licencer.

There is a satisfaction and joy in all the folks at Drury Lane Theatre, that show they are under a good government, and in a thriving way; I think every year must make it better. David had a charming lodging in King Street, furnish't very neatly in a mighty elegant taste, and seems to me more pleased and contented than ever I saw him.

Six weeks after this cheerful letter was written, the young patentee was to be seen, on the morning of January 24, 1748, ruefully surveying one of those scenes of disaster which proved that however contented his company, he had also to contend with a rough public. There had been what the press mildly described as " a disturbance " at the playhouse last night. Two of the principal dancers had not appeared to perform at the end of the entertainment, " whereupon several gentlemen in the boxes and pit pulled up the seats and flooring of the same, tore down the hangings, broke partitions, and all the glasses and sconces ". (Almost exactly the same thing, but worse, had happened in 1736, but on that occasion, when even the Royal arms had been torn from the Royal box, a penitent marquis, who had led the assault, had sent round to the theatre next morning, a hundred guineas.) The situation was serious, for Moore's *Found-ling* was to be produced in less than a fortnight. The young actor-manager boldly pitted his strength against the young bloods of Mayfair, and won. Horace Walpole was present on a first night when disaster threatened.

> Lord Hobart and some young men made a party to damn it, merely for the love of damnation. The Templars espoused the play and went armed with syringes charged with stinking oil, and sticking plasters; but it did not come to action. Garrick was impertinent, and the pretty men gave over their plot the moment they grew to be in the right.

The Royal box had been occupied no less than seven times during this first season of Garrick and Lacy's management. The Prince and Princess of Wales had been to see Barry in *Hamlet*, and next week there arrived what Lacy's accounts described as " The King and Princess Emilia too ". The same party, with the addition of the Duke of Cumberland, had witnessed *The Suspicious Husband*, which His Majesty had seen last year. On January 8, after a per-formance of *Jane Shore*, accounts showed " Christmas boxes to the Duke's footmen, and Prince and Princess of Wales's chairmen ". Finally King, Prince and Princess of Wales on separate occasions had witnessed Garrick as Sir John Brute and Abel Drugger. The charge for wax candles, with which the managers met and escorted their Royal guests into a house glowing with the same expensive light, was also carefully noted.

As the season drew towards its close, the massive figure of Mrs Pritchard increased in significance. Johnson scorned her as a very stupid woman, but she was teachable, and had found a manager willing to take pains with her. Unfortunately, the rise in popularity of Mrs Pritchard was not reflected in the green-room. When the theatre closed for the summer, in May, Garrick knew that he was going to have losses from his company. The first to announce her departure was Woffington. This was not surprising, but the "induce-ments of mixed character " suggested by contemporaries can hardly have included the approaching marriage of Mr Garrick. His mar-riage that season seemed to be rather receding than approaching. He had not persuaded Violette to appear under his management. Other ladies of foreign name filled her place—Mesdemoiselles Auretti and Foulcade, Mesdames Mariet and de la Conti. Violette lived at Burlington House, apparently retired on her laurels, and Lady Burlington, who disapproved of him, kept so close a watch that he could hardly gain a word with her. Violette, in later years, was wont to relate that at a desperate moment of his courtship Mr Garrick had disguised himself in women's clothes, in order to convey

I

a letter into her chair, outside the theatre after a performance. If
this romantic incident took place during the run of *The Provok'd* 28
*Wife* in November 1747, he need not have troubled to change his
dress, for in his latest additions to that piece Sir John Brute had to
appear in a lady's gown and riding-hood. In October, Horace
Walpole, reporting that the King was said to have got a new mistress
in Hanover, and that Henry Fox had certainly got a bride with a
fortune of ten thousand, added to his catalogue " and the Violette,
as it is said, Coventry for a husband ". The Earl of Coventry was a
widower and past sixty, and at a recent masquerade given by the
Duchess of Queensberry he had been observed following the little
*danseuse* with extraordinary persistence. Lady Burlington, walking
with her charge tucked under arm, had drawn off her own left-hand
glove, and ostentatiously moved her wedding-ring up and down her
fourth finger.                                                        29

The early spring brought one ray of hope to the anxious Garrick.
On March 28, William Cavendish, Marquis of Hartington, married
Lady Charlotte Boyle, only surviving child of the Burlingtons. The
alliance, which was also a love-match, had been mooted three years
past, but the bride had been considered too young then. She was
now rising seventeen. Lord Hartington was tactful, and a friend.
To the end of his days, Garrick never forgot the obligations he was
under to the family of Cavendish. He visited Chatsworth for the
first time this summer. The impression made upon him by this
house was also ineradicable. It had been conceived grandly by a
Whig earl who had found that the air of Derbyshire suited him best
while a Catholic monarch sat on the throne. It was built in the local
stone, and within there had been lavish introduction of the local
alabaster. It was indeed a palace, with a state suite, much fine
carving of trophies and garlands, and a painted hall with a wrought-
iron grand staircase. Mortlake tapestries hung on the walls, and
much of the furniture was old, though the first Duke of Devonshire
had banished a houseful to another of his northern fastnesses—
Hardwick. But what Garrick marked most were the garden vistas of
staircases, terraces and fountains, sparkling in the crystalline air.
An abundant high-level supply had made Chatsworth an ideal site for
water-effects. The principal cascade was dramatic—six hundred
feet long, with a drop of sixty feet. He was to see four generations of
Cavendishes in this house.

## 6

Rich, who had been biding his time, opened at Covent Garden on
October 17, 1748, with the first part of *Henry IV*. He had got Quin

back to play Falstaff, and Woffington was to appear as Lady Percy. Two other names prominent on his playbill had explanatory notes under them. Mr Sparks (Henry IV) was appearing for the first time on this stage. Mr Delane (Hotspur) was returning to this stage after seven years. Both were seceders from Garrick and Lacy's company, and drinking too much. Covent Garden's playbill showed that one more thing had come to them from the rival house, but this was a detail of administration. " No Persons to be admitted behind the Scenes, or any Money to be returned after the Curtain is drawn up."

Drury Lane also opened with Shakespeare, but offered two plays long neglected. Garrick and Mrs Pritchard were unanimously voted brilliant as Benedick and Beatrice in *Much Ado about Nothing*; Barry and Mrs Cibber were heartrending as Romeo and Juliet. With this play Garrick had taken great liberties, explained by him when he published his version two years later. He had cut out the whole incident of Romeo moping with love for Rosaline just before meeting Juliet. It was dreadfully true to life, but he did not consider it highly romantic. " Many have held it a blemish." He had added a scene at the end which he thought Shakespeare would have included had he known that it had been in Bandello's original Italian story. He explained that Otway, who had heard of it, had made use of it in his *Caius Marius*, a tragedy taken from *Romeo and Juliet*. Parts of the scene, which he considered most affecting, had been taken from Otway, and parts from Congreve's *Mourning Bride*. Juliet was now made to awake in the tomb to witness the death of Romeo before following him to eternity. This gave the opportunity for a lovers' farewell, and long-drawn-out death agonies in which Mrs Cibber and Barry excelled themselves. Apparently nobody who witnessed *Romeo and Juliet*, which had not been seen for eighty years, questioned the improvements made by Garrick.

Johnson's *Mahomet and Irene* was next put into rehearsal, and meanwhile Massinger's *New Way to Pay Old Debts* was revived. Neither Sparks nor Delane had been a great loss to Drury Lane and Garrick had been looking out, successfully, for new blood. Mr Thomas King as Allworth was disingenuously announced as " appearing for the first time in any character ". He was not doing that, for he had been playing in a barn at Windsor with Yates during the " dead " summer months; but he was very young, just eighteen. He was the son of a London tradesman of good north-country stock, had been educated at Westminster and had run away from a solicitor's office. He had beautiful chestnut eyes and a good shape. Yates had recommended him. He was to become a mainstay of Garrick's company.

As must be expected, Samuel Johnson was proving one of the most difficult authors ever to come behind the scenes. As rehearsals proceeded he began to take a less unfavourable view of actors and particularly of actresses, but his disputes with his ex-pupil David over alterations in his sacred text became so unbearable that a good friend of both, the Rev. Dr John Taylor of Ashbourne, school-mate and college-mate of Johnson, had to be called in to pour oil on the waters. In the first place, Johnson wanted Garrick to play Demetrius, merely because, in the first rush of inspiration, he had happened to put some of the most striking passages in his tragedy into the mouth of this lesser character. This could not be helped or altered. Nobody but Garrick could do justice to them. Garrick had naturally expected to be asked to undertake the title-rôle. But Mahomet, he thought, lacked colour. " Sir," objected Johnson, " the fellow wants me to make Mahomet run mad, that he may have an opportunity of tossing his hands and kicking his heels." Eventually Barry played Mahomet and Garrick Demetrius.

Accounts of the great first night on February 5 differ considerably. According to Dr Adams, Master of Pembroke College, there were catcalls and whistlings from the pit and gallery before the curtain rose, which alarmed friends of the author. The Prologue, " written in a manly strain ", and spoken by Garrick at his best, either soothed or awed the audience. The play went off tolerably until the last scene, when Mrs Pritchard, as the luckless Irene, was to be strangled with a bow-string upon the stage. The audience called out, " Murder ! Murder ", and, after several attempts to speak her dying lines, Mrs Pritchard had to go off alive. On succeeding nights she was carried off to be put to death out of sight. An attractive young organ-student, Charles Burney, a pupil of Dr Arne, who was also present, was enthralled by play, actors and production. Garrick had not spared expense on scenery and costumes, and there was applause when the curtain rose to display " Gardens belonging to the palace in Constantinople, where Mahomet held his court, immediately after his conquest of that capital, since fortified, and called the Seraglio ".

*The Gentleman's Magazine* loyally printed " a plan and specimens from Mr Samuel Johnson's tragedy, acted from Monday, February 6th to Monday February 20th inclusive ", and young Burney, who went to most of the nine performances, said he could not understand what Sir John Hawkins meant by saying it had been coldly received. Johnson himself was observed, both behind the scenes and in a side box, almost unrecognizable. He had conceived the idea that the author of a classic tragedy, perhaps destined to bring him fame equal

to that of Addison, must be suitably attired.  He appeared in a
scarlet waistcoat with rich gold lace and a gold-laced hat.  But he
was soon under no illusions as to his future as a writer for the stage.
When asked how he felt upon the ill-success of his tragedy, he replied,
" Like the Monument ", and when told that Mr Percivall Pott,
surgeon and author, had said *Irene* was the finest of modern tragedies,
30 he commented, " If Pott says so, Pott lies ".

After *Irene*, Garrick played Iago to Barry's Othello, and three
parts in a refurbished edition of his own old farce *Lethe*.  An outside
event was calling for recognition, and Drury Lane next announced
*The Triumph of Peace, a musical entertainment, by Mr Dodsley*.  The
Peace of Aix-la-Chapelle had been proclaimed on February 2 in the
cities of London and Westminster, by the heralds, at St James's
Gate, Charing Cross, Temple Bar, Chancery Lane, Wood Lane,
Cheapside, and finally the Royal Exchange.  Great Britain had been
at war on the Continent for nearly ten years, and the struggle over
the Spanish succession had come to be regarded almost philosophic-
ally.  In Lord Rochford's drawing-room, her ladyship's Mama did
nothing but call the King of Prussia names, and in many drawing-
rooms there was a mistaken belief that the young Queen-Empress
Maria Theresa was a meek, gentle, persecuted figure.  But whatever
views were held on the pragmatic sanction, the peace was greeted
with universal jubilation.  It was likely to provide an excuse for a
very gay summer.

The moment seemed rather an inappropriate one for the soldier
of the Garrick family to ask for a loan—a substantial one, six hundred
and fifty-six pounds.  However, David obliged William on April 4.
The bond witnessed by George provided for the repayment of half
twelve months hence.

On April 15, when Mr Aaron Hill's *Merope* was produced at
Drury Lane, there was a rival attraction in the shape of the arrival
of the fireworks in St James's Park.  A rehearsal at Vauxhall Gardens of the music for the fireworks was so well patronized that London Bridge was blocked by carriages for three hours.  The structure
in St James's Park, begun on November 7 on the news that the treaty
had been concluded, was not ready until April 26.  It was a lath-and-
plaster temple, a hundred and fourteen feet high, adorned with
figures of the Kings of Great Britain, France, Germany and Spain
embracing, attended by Neptune, Prudence, Plenty and Thames
(denoting the return of Trade), and many other helpful allegorical
persons.  The fireworks included Caduceus Rockets, Honorary
Rockets, Air-Balloons, Girandoles, Tourbillons (copied from the
Chinese), Pots d'Aigrettes and Marrons (of French extraction).  The

Duke of Richmond, watching with the royal family from the window of the library in St James's Palace, determined to give a fireworks party himself as soon as the weather was more suitable for al-fresco entertainments.   Late frosts were said to have killed all the walnut trees in Hyde Park.

*Merope* at Drury Lane, another classical tragedy, taken from the French of " the inglorious Voltaire, who has represented the English as incapable of writing Tragedy ", caused Garrick almost as much trouble in rehearsal as *Irene*.   Mr Hill was not difficult in at all the same way as Johnson; he was a charming garrulous old gentleman, most grateful for the prospect of financial relief, but he had ideas as to casting.   Mrs Cibber refused the title-rôle.   She was not going to appear as the widow of Sisyphus and Mr Garrick's mother.   Although now in her thirty-sixth year she was justly proud of " her maidenly slim figure ".   Mrs Pritchard, who suffered from no such disability, gallantly accepted Merope and was rewarded by a remarkable personal success.   Mr Hill pressed the part of the amorous Polyphontes, General of Mycenae, upon Barry, and when that spoilt fellow disliked it, imprudently offered him " Narbas, a faithful courtier ".   Havard accepted Polyphontes, and Barry silkily declared himself well pleased with a part so small that the boxes would be disappointed.   Garrick as Eumenes, a dispossessed princeling, " played like an angel ", and the boxes certainly were not disappointed in his performance in a dull play.   He had been unlucky in his classical tragedies this season, for they were still a popular form.   When the royal children had acted at Leicester House in January, *Cato* had been chosen, and Quin, master of the old style, had been summoned to teach the unfortunate infants how to stride and declaim.   Prince George, eldest son of the family, was a nice-looking little boy with bright pale blue eyes, flat flaxen hair, pink pincushion cheeks and a diffident manner.   In the Prologue he announced his pride in being " a boy, in England born, in England bred ".   For his eleventh birthday, on May 25, a grand gala was planned.   At seven p.m. a silver cup, value twenty-five guineas, presented by His Royal Highness, was rowed for by seven pairs of oars, from Whitehall to Putney.   His parents, with many of the nobility, preceded the wager-men in a separate barge.   Prince George's magnificent new-built craft, of Venetian design, was manned by attendants in Chinese habits.   Chinese taste was coming into fashion.   On May 15 the Duke of Richmond's fireworks party took place on exactly the scene painted by Canaletto from his Grace's library.   It was indeed " a grand entertainment ".   It was given in honour of the visiting Duke of Modena, who was a somewhat disconcerting figure, as he had painted his face bright red and white.

Above four hundred persons of distinction had been invited, and after a concert of water-music, the fireworks, let off in the Privy Garden and on the Thames, included two hundred water-mines, air-balloons and fire-trees, five thousand sky-rockets, twenty suns and a hundred stars. A choice supper was served; the skies had a velvet warmth, and the revelry endured until 2 a.m. The King and Princess Emilia attended in their barge; the Duke of Cumberland mingled with the duke's guests on his terrace. The banks of the river were black with spectators. Horace Walpole was there, taking notes.

> There was an admirable scene: Lady Burlington brought *the Violette*, and the Richmonds had asked Garrick, who stood *ogling* and *sighing* the whole time, while my Lady kept a most *fierce look-out*. Sabbatini, one of the Duke of Modena's court, was asking me who all the people were, " And who is that? " " C'est miladi Hartington, la belle-fille du Duc de Devonshire." " Et qui est cette autre dame avec? " It was a distressing question; after a little hesitation, I replied, " Mais, c'est Mademoiselle Violette! " " *Et comment Mademoiselle Violette! J'ai connu une Mademoiselle Violette par example.*" I begged him to look at Miss Bishop.

Suddenly, in the same number of *The Gentleman's Magazine* which published accounts of the prince's and the duke's water-parties, there appeared under the heading of Marriages—" Mr Garrick, the comedian, to Mademoiselle Violetti, the famous dancer ". The date given was May 25. It was not true. But it was very nearly true, and David was preparing Brother Peter to accept as " your sister " a Viennese opera-dancer, a strict Roman Catholic, who spoke very little English as yet. For, in the next issue of the magazine, under the date of June 22, came a correct entry " David Garrick Esq: (not before) to Mademoiselle Eva Maria Violette, £10,000 ". *The General Advertiser* on June 23 gave more details— " Yesterday was married by the Rev: Mr Francklin at his chapel,
31 Russel St, Bloomsbury, David Garrick Esq to Eva Maria Violetti."

Engraved portraits of the bride and bridegroom appeared in *The London Magazine*. Even allowing for the difficulty of hasty production it must be hoped that they were what Spranger Barry called " damned unlike prints ". For Mr Garrick, the editors had been obliged to fall back upon the early head and shoulders by Arthur Pond. The player's background included a mask, crown, trumpet and sword. Mademoiselle Violetti's attributes were a fan, a tambourine and a floral wreath, and she was depicted sitting very upright, wearing a lace cap and a sacque gown. Her rosebud mouth was
32 pursed, her expression was resolute.

## CHAPTER V

## 27, SOUTHAMPTON STREET

### 1749–1751

I

WEDDINGS, in the mid-eighteenth century, did not take place with quite the same speed as in the days of the immortal Shakespeare, when Capulet, late on Monday night, decided that Wednesday would be too soon for Juliet's marriage and therefore settled upon Thursday. Garrick, according to the witness of Horace Walpole, was not yet the accepted suitor of La Violette at the Duke of Richmond's water-party on May 15, 1749, but there was not time for banns to be called before his wedding. A licence was issued on June 17 " for the chapel in Russell Street, Bloomsbury, or the chapel of Burlington House ". (In any case, Lady Burlington is likely to have insisted *1* on her protégée's marriage taking place, as was usual in high life, by special licence.) On June 20, attended by his lawyer, Mr Paterson, Garrick signed the marriage articles imposed by the Burlingtons. These provided for the bride very securely. She received the annual interest of £5,000 charged on Lady Burlington's Lincolnshire estates. Garrick agreed to settle upon her £10,000 and £70 per annum pin-money. Horace Walpole wrote, three days after the wedding, *2* " Garrick is married to the famous Violette, first at a Protestant, and then at a Roman Catholic chapel. The chapter of this history is a little obscure and uncertain as to the consent of the protecting Countess, and whether she gives her a fortune or not." He had got his facts better than most of his contemporaries, in that he believed that some provision had been made by Lady Burlington. For gossip at the date of the marriage, which persisted with extraordinary vitality, declared that Lord Burlington had given to Garrick, with a large dowry, a natural daughter. One of the chief difficulties in discovering *3* the truth was the longevity of La Violette. She survived, in excellent command of her faculties, until 1822. Biographers of her husband were therefore faced with the choice of asking her for evidence, producing what guess-work they could, or ignoring her origins. Tom Davies, in his two-volume *Memoirs of the Life of David Garrick Esq*, published in 1780, took the least satisfactory line. He neglected to mention that his hero ever married, although Mrs Garrick inevitably appears as his narrative proceeds. Arthur Murphy, publishing in 1801, opened the fifteenth chapter of his first volume cautiously, though not correctly.

In the month of July Garrick entered in a new scene of life. He married the fair Violetti, a native of Vienna, who chose to grace herself with an Italian name. She was an elegant figure, and, as a dancer, greatly admired for the uncommon charm, which she displayed in all her movements. Previous to this match, it is certain that Garrick was on the point of marrying Mrs Woffington. This writer has heard her declare at different times, that he went so far as to try the wedding-ring on her finger. But Violetti was patronized by Lord and Lady Burlington, who, it is generally understood, gave her a fortune of six thousand pounds, the sum bequeathed to her by Garrick's will, in addition to other considerable legacies.

Four years later, in the second volume of his Memoirs, Charles Lee Lewes produced under the heading of " Mr Garrick's Marriage etc." an amazing mixture of fact and fiction. After expressing his surprise at the taciturnity of " Mr Davis " (sic) and Mr Murphy on the subject of the wedding of Roscius, he announces his good fortune in having it in his power to give " a circumstantial and authentic account of his courtship and marriage, as I received it from an aged domestic, who lived at the time it happened, at Burlington House, Piccadilly ". The aged domestic's tale, related by Lewes, was colourful. Lord Burlington had, during " his tour through Italy ", had an amour with a young lady of family in Florence. After his return to England and marriage to Lady Dorothy Savile, he had provided for his Italian child, " a lovely girl ". But " a person at Florence " whom he had entrusted with the funds, had, after the untimely death of the mother of the lovely girl, embezzled most of them. This monster had got the innocent young female an engagement to appear as a dancer in the opera-house. Lord Burlington, hearing of his daughter's plight, had sent for her to come to Drury Lane, where she was engaged by Mr Garrick, manager. His lordship had a legitimate daughter, Lady Charlotte Boyle, afterwards married to Lord Hartington, who was a few years younger than his Italian offspring. After a visit to the theatre in company with Lady Burlington and Lady Charlotte to see the Signora Violetti, he had suggested her appointment in their house as a tutoress in the Italian tongue. Lady Charlotte almost anticipated his wishes, and the Signora was taken home by them that very night to Burlington House. Here her charms enraptured all, but she began to fade and pine in an alarming manner. Dr Mead was summoned in vain. Lady Burlington eventually drew from the invalid the true cause of her malady. " Mr Garrick was the object of her esteem ", but entirely ignorant of it. Lady Burlington unpromisingly commented " that Mr Garrick was a young fellow universally caressed by families of the first distinction, and one who had already been suspected of aspiring to rank and fortune in a matrimonial alliance ". Lord Burlington, however,

solved the problem.  He sent for " Doctor " Garrick instantly,
assured him that Signora Violetti was a lady of family and virtue,
and offered with her hand a portion of ten thousand pounds.  " The
enraptured Garrick gave his lordship ten thousand thanks " and
declared that he had long felt " a more than a common interest " in
the young lady, whereupon Lord Burlington admitted his paternity.

The next author to approach the subject was James Boaden in
the biographical memoir prefaced to his edition of John Forster's
collection of Garrick's private correspondence published in 1831.
Mrs Garrick had now been dead nine years and an authoritative
obituary article, produced by her executors, had appeared in *The
Gentleman's Magazine* for November 1822.  Boaden quoted from it
(without giving his source) almost wholesale, and followed them in a
mistake about the extent of Garrick's contribution in the marriage
settlement.  He stated that " Violette " had been born in Vienna
and educated as a dancer.

> Her name was Violette, not, as it has been usually written, Violetti,
> and she assumed it by command of the Empress Queen Maria Theresa—
> the name of her family being Veigel, which, in Vienna *pâtois*, signifies
> Violet.  She was introduced at the court of Vienna in all probability by
> the *Maître de Ballet*, M. Hilferding, with other young ladies, to dance with
> the children of Maria Theresa, for it does not appear that she ever danced
> on the public stage at Vienna.  Mademoiselle Violette came to this country
> accompanied by a family named Rossiter, who visited England to look
> after some property.  A lady of fashion, to whom Mrs Garrick bequeathed
> a token of remembrance, told the reverend gentleman, her executor [Rev:
> Thomas Rackett], that she had the following account of her journey to
> England, both from her own mother and others.  " The Empress Queen,
> perceiving that her husband, the Emperor Frederick I, regarded Made-
> moiselle Violette with marked attention, to prevent any unpleasant circum-
> stances proposed this journey to England, and forwarded powerful recom-
> mendations in her favour."  It was no doubt owing to such introduction
> that His Majesty George the Second commanded the play on her first appear-
> ance, and honoured her benefit also in 1748, with his presence. . . . She
> probably resided at this time at Burlington-house, and indeed so precious
> had she become there that the Countess herself attended her to the theatre,
> and with maternal care used to throw her pelisse over her when she came
> off the stage. . . . The very extraordinary favour shown this lovely creature
> by the Burlington family gave rise to a story that she was really a daughter
> of the Earl, by a lady of the greatest merit at Florence; and when after-
> wards a portion of six thousand pounds was given with her hand to Garrick
> in marriage, the story seemed confirmed past reasonable doubt; nay, it was
> said his Lordship had acknowledged her to Mr Garrick as his child.

But Messrs Rackett and Beltz in their obituary notice had already
given the death-blow to the legend that she was a daughter of Lord
Burlington.  The earl had been married two years before she was

born, and had since been uninterruptedly in England, where his presence was attested by Journals of the House of Lords.

She was born at Vienna, on the 29th February, 1724–5, as appears by the registry of her baptism in the Cathedral Church of St Stephen. She was one of the three children of Mr Johann Veigel, a respectable inhabitant of that city, and named after her mother, Eva-Maria. Her brother, Ferdinand Charles, showing himself talents for dancing, became attached to the Corps de ballet.

4

In 1845 John Thomas Smith published his *Book for a Rainy Day*. In October 1829 he had made a pilgrimage to Garrick's country house, and asked questions of the then owner, Mr Thomas Carr, solicitor to Mrs Garrick. Mrs Carr had been " inseparable from Mrs Garrick for the last thirty years of her life ". Smith asked the couple whether Lee Lewes's story was true. Carr, who seems to have missed Rackett and Beltz's obituary notice, replied that " there was certainly a mystery as to who her father was ". Mrs Carr said that when Mrs Garrick had read Lee Lewes's book she had " exclaimed, with her usual vivacity, ' He is a great liar; Lord Burlington was not my father, but I am of noble birth '." " Is it true," asked Smith, " that Lord Burlington gave Mr Garrick ten thousand pounds to marry her? " " No," he was told. " Nor did Mrs Garrick ever receive a sum of money from Lord Burlington; she had only the interest of six thousand pounds, and that she was paid by the late Duke of Devonshire." The late Duke had been the Burlington's son-in-law.

5

Percy Fitzgerald, whose biography of Garrick was published seven years later, had seen Boaden's researches and knew that the story of Violette having been a daughter of the house of Burlington was quite false. He had seen Thomas Rackett. By 1899, when he produced his revised edition, he had one more scrap of evidence to offer about Garrick's courtship. A play about Garrick had been produced in Germany, which had been so successful that it had been adapted for the English stage. In the German piece Violette's father was a baronet, in the English she was " Ada Ingot ", the child of a wealthy City man. In both she was made to have fallen in love with Garrick across the footlights. The German narrative introduced the name of a Mr Bingham, of Lincoln's Inn, with whom Garrick had studied law; such a person had existed, moreover an octogenarian gentleman had been " told by Mrs Garrick herself that the story of which the German dramatist availed himself was a fact, not a fiction ". She had indeed pined away, in despair, until nothing but " Doctor Garrick " could reclaim her, and it was his entirely manly and disinterested attitude, when summoned by

6

the Burlingtons, that had at last brought them round. She did not expand as to whether he had, as in the plays, tried in vain to disillusion her, by acting drunk, but only succeeded in proving that even in his cups he was a gentleman.

The Heralds' College, in the Pullman MS., offers confirmation of [7] Eva-Maria Veigel's origin. Her father was one " Feigel, *anglicé* Violet, an officer in the Dutch service ", and the coat of arms of Feigel or Feiger was impaled and quartered with that of Garrick by her husband. She had a sister, Mrs Theresa Fürst, and a niece Elizabeth Fürst, who married one Peter de Saar, *Conseiller des Comptes* in the Department of the Post Office, Vienna. A great nephew of Mrs Garrick, Louis de Saar, was a lieutenant in Prince Hohenlöhe's dragoons, in the Austrian service, and a great-niece, Louisa, married Arthur de Pocorny, also of a government department in Vienna. All left issue. [8]

2

After Eva-Maria Veigel, disguised as a boy and escorted by the Rossiters, parted from the Reverend Alexander Carlyle at an inn in Friday Street, in February 1746, her career until 1749 must be traced from play-bills and chance contemporary mentions. She had come with good introductions, was a good performer, and had marked personal charm. She had an immediate and great success. At her first appearance, according to a letter from Lord Strafford written on March 27, she surprised the audience.

> For at her beginning to caper, she shewed a neat pair of black velvet breeches, with roll'd stockings, but finding they were unusual in England she changed them next time for a pair of white drawers.

Horace Walpole wrote of her three months later:

> The fame of the Violette encreases daily. The sister-Countesses of Burlington and Thanet exert all their stores of sullen partiality in competition for her. The former visits her, and is having her picture, and carries her to Chiswick; and she dines at Bedford House and she sups at Lady Cardigan's, and lies—indeed I have not heard where, but I know not at Carlton House where she is in great disgrace for not going once or twice a week to take lessons of Denoyer, as HE bid her. You know that is politics, in a court, where dancing masters are ministers. [9]

' He ' was Frederick, Prince of Wales, whose reputation with women was bad, so Eva-Maria's refusal to accept tuition from his favourite dancing-master was no doubt prudent; she had already in her own land experienced the inadvisibility of attracting the attention of a royal prince. The Prince of Wales showed his chagrin by suggestions that she did not dance so very well. His crony Lord Middlesex held sway at the Opera House, and there was further trouble when the fame of La Violette threatened to eclipse that of his mistress, La Nardi. Next season Violette left the Haymarket for Drury Lane, *faute de mieux*. Lord Middlesex had dismissed the chief musician without his salary (" on pretence of his siding with the Violette "), and seen to it that the principal male dancer was arrested for debt. Even the Violette, " the finest and most admired dancer in the world ", had not, according to her champion Horace Walpole, who had always approved of her in every way, been paid.

At Drury Lane she soon learnt what it was to disappoint in a wider sphere. At the foot of the play-bill for January 17, 1747, was printed a note supposed to emanate from her.

> Mademoiselle Violette humbly begs leave to acquaint the public that she is very much concerned to hear that she is charged with having been the occasion of the noise at the play-house in Drury Lane on Wednesday night. As she was entirely ignorant that three dances had been advertised until it was too late to prepare herself, and as she cannot possibly be guilty of an intention to disoblige or give offence to an English audience (from whom she has received so much applause) she presumes to hope they will not impute to her a fault which she is not capable of committing, and especially where she has met with so much indulgence, for which she retains all possible gratitude.

Lord Bury and some men of fashion had begun the disturbance, insisting that she should be sent for from Burlington House. Lord Hartington used all his influence to secure a good reception for her at her next appearance and she was not hissed by Lord Bury.

The Drury Lane Account Books for 1746–1747 show that she made five appearances under Lacy's management that winter, between November 24 and February 9. Her salary was £400. " Signior Violetta " (sic), perhaps her brother Ferdinand-Charles, also a dancer, received thirty pounds for his performances on Christmas Eve. The King attended her benefit, on February 11, for which Lord Burlington had the tickets designed by William Kent and engraved by George Vertue. Nobody in London seemed particularly surprised that Lady Burlington, who was, to put it mildly, extremely eccentric and a law unto herself, showed so much solicitude for a Viennese *danseuse* who had come with Imperial recommendations and was moreover a character of great charm. But far from regarding Garrick as likely to hope for a better match, Lady Burlington scorned him. " Marriage and a coach," preferably with a coronet, was her intention for her charge. But by this time Garrick was no longer a mere player circulating between the rival London houses and

Dublin.  He was a manager of Drury Lane, a secure favourite and much commended as the witty author of a number of prologues and epilogues and two popular farces.  He had long been received as a friend in many great houses in London, but it does not appear that until Lord Hartington took his part he was ever welcomed at Burlington House.  At that renowned edifice in Piccadilly, designed by its owner, the atmosphere was notoriously chilly.  It had been well described by a critic of the architect Earl as:

> Possessed of one great hall of state,
> Without a room to sleep or eat.

It seems that the winter of 1748–1749 must be the date when La Violette as described by Lee Lewes's " aged domestic at Burlington House " took to her couch heartbroken that she must not declare her love for Garrick.  Her patroness was kind, but accustomed to ruling all about her with a rod of iron.  According to her uncle, Lord Winchester, Lady Burlington had been, in her youth, " the wickedest mischievous jade upon earth ".  She delighted in intrigue, and in wielding the power given to her by her birth and her position.  Her uncle wished her husband would " send her down into the country " —the worst fate reserved for a woman of fashion.  But in Garrick she met her match.  He had evidently opened negotiations with the Burlingtons by May 1749, for the same number of *The Gentleman's Magazine* which printed a premonitory notice of his wedding, included a poem, " To Mr G-----K, on the Talk of the Town."  This opened dramatically:

> No, no;  the left hand Box in blue;
> There!  don't you see her?  *See her!  Who!*
> Nay, hang me if I tell.
> 　　There's G - - - - - k in the Music-box!
> Watch but his Eyes—see them!  Oh!  Pox!
> 　　" Your Servant, Ma'moiselle."

The poem was attributed to Edward Moore, who had written a play produced at the Lane, but there was a belief that Garrick himself, to forward his courtship and anticipate criticism, had had a hand in it.  Ladies of fashion, wild as the witches in *Macbeth* at the prospect of their favourite actor married, were described as venting their spite.  Was he not nearly done for in any case; growing out of fashion?  Last night as Archer he had hardly spoken a line right. It was whispered that old Cibber hoped he was going to drop the part of Richard, as he had dropped Bayes.  He had been well enough as Ranger, for the part suited him, and in *Merope* he had certainly looked young; but to see " such a shrimp " attempt to ravish the massive Mrs Pritchard in *Jane Shore* had been laughable.  If he married, he might in future be allowed two of his parts only—Sir John Brute all day, and Fribble all night.

> The clergy too have join'd their chat,
> " A papist!  Has he thought of that?
> . Or means he to convert her?
> Truth boy, unless your zeal be stout
> The nymph may turn your faith about
> By arguments experter."

The last stanza bade him not to heed the talk of the town, and wished Benedick well with his Ma'amselle.

> The fops that join to cry her down
> Would give their ears to get her.

From the moment that he was accepted, it is clear that the Burlingtons took charge of his wedding, and that they drove a hard bargain on behalf of their favourite.  If she was determined to ally herself with a member of a profession which they considered most precarious, she must be protected.  A separate document, when her marriage settlement was drawn up, assigned her jewellery and personal belongings to her absolutely.  Garrick began to experience what he was to realize increasingly during the next few years: that to be accepted by the Burlingtons was almost more oppressive than being scorned.  Eva-Maria was a devout Catholic, therefore there would have to be two wedding ceremonies.  Garrick called in an old friend, Thomas Francklin, the future author of many indifferent plays, to perform the Church of England ceremony.  Francklin's father kept a well-known bookshop, haunt of literary men, near the Piazza.  Francklin, who had been educated at Westminster, was now a Fellow of Trinity College, Cambridge, and engaged on translations from the Greek.

Eva-Maria Garrick loved to recall her wedding day.  In extreme old age she gratified the curiosity of John Thomas Smith.

> I suppose now, Sir, you wish to know my age.  I was born at Vienna, the 29th of February, 1724, though my coachman insists upon it that I am above a hundred.  I was married at the parish of St Giles's at eight o'clock in the morning, and immediately afterwards in the chapel of the Portuguese ambassador, in South Audley Street.

She always preserved a piece of her wedding dress—" a cream coloured silk apron edged with guipure ".  Four months after her husband had been buried with unprecedented pageantry she noted in her diary, " I went for the first time to Westminster Abbey, to my dear Husband, being our wedding day."

She was twenty-five on that early June morning, and Garrick was rising two and thirty.   His courtship of Woffington, which had lasted for three years, had ended in failure.   His courtship of La Violette had lasted about the same time.   Lady Burlington majestically but not very generously gave the bridegroom a prayer book.   He took it in the best possible manner and wrote inside one of the verses liked by his audiences:

> This sacred book has Dorothea given
> To show a straying sheep the way to Heaven;
> With forms of righteousness she well may part
> Who bears the spirit in her upright heart.

Amongst his papers, on his death, was found some other poetry belonging to this date.

### " VERSES SENT TO ME ON MY MARRIAGE."

> What!  has that heart, so wild, so roving,
> So prone to changing, sighing, loving,
> Whom widows, maids, attacked in vain,
> At last submitted to the chain?
> Who is the paragon, the marvellous she,
> Has fix'd a weathercock like thee?

His reply was attached.

> 'Tis not, my friend, her speaking face,
> Her shape, her youth, her winning grace,
> Have reach'd my heart;—the fair one's mind,
> Quick as her eyes, yet soft and kind,
> A gaiety with innocence,
> A soft address, with manly sense,
> Ravishing manners, void of art,
> A cheerful, firm, yet feeling heart,
> Beauty, that charms all public gaze,
> And humble, amid pomp and praise. . . .
> These are the charms my heart have bound,
> Charms often sought, so rarely found!
> Nor think the lover's partial voice
> In flattr'ing colours paints his choice.
> When you MARIA hear and see
> You will not wonder such a she
> Has fix'd a weathercock like me.

### 3

The newly-wed couple were to honeymoon at Chiswick, Lord Burlington's famous country retreat outside London, and they would be tactfully, but also inevitably, left to themselves, for the noble owners had gone north at this season.   Chiswick House, designed by Lord Burlington, was beyond doubt an ideal scene for a honeymoon. Lord Hervey had said with his usual satire that it was too small to live in and too large to hang from your watch-chain. It was a miniature Italian palace, near the Thames, based on the Capra villa, built for Paolo Almerigo, near Vicenza, at a date when Elizabeth Tudor reigned in England. The visitors bowled in through a great gate guarded by sphinxes over much smooth yellow gravel towards a south entrance in the centre of an impressive classical elevation. On either side of a flight of steps stood statues of the owner's architectural masters, Inigo Jones and Andrea Palladio. When Lord Burlington had enlarged and altered a Jacobean mansion which had been the home of the ill-fated Duke of Monmouth, accommodation for a family had been of no interest to him. Consequently, he had left the original deep mullioned windows on the first floor, where the only available bedrooms were few and dim.

Critics found Chiswick an exotic, ill-suited to the English climate and habits. It had a dome. But the earl had not forgotten that in Middlesex the sun was not so fierce as in Tuscany. The eight principal reception-rooms, all of which opened out of one another, received ample direct light. The long gallery, entered from the central, domed hall, led on the east to an octagon room, and on the west to another novelty, a room which was completely circular. Carrara marble consoles and chimney-pieces with staring female faces, ribboned wreaths of foliage, fruit and flowers, pedimented doorways and exuberantly painted and gilded ceilings, reflected subdued light from a green world outside. Lord Burlington had called in William Kent, painter, sculptor and landscape gardener, whom Hogarth held in contempt. The earl in Rome, on his Grand Tour, aged one and twenty, had met and liked a sturdy Yorkshireman who had started his professional career as apprentice to a coach-painter. He had begun by engaging him to provide a suitable background for the collection of Italian paintings which he was forming. This had now expanded to become one of the best in England, in Europe, Garrick believed. It was disposed upon the brocaded panels of the quiet, glittering, intercommunicating ground-floor salons, and the young actor had viewed it with so much reverence and appreciation that the open-handed earl had presented him with a picture suitable to his avocation—a Guido Reni of a scene from *Orlando Furioso*. Kent had been to Rome twice more, on behalf of his patron, and taken charge of the decoration, furniture and gardens of Chiswick. Within, there were porphyry vases, and tables, for each of which, it was said, Lord Burlington had given a thousand crowns in the Eternal city. Without, there was abundance of classical statuary, old and new, some bought at the same time, on the same scale.

K

There were bird-haunted, shadowy groves, verdant alcoves, avenues of sweet-smelling cedar, long gravel walks between yew hedges, and a shining placid great canal. " Chiz river " was spanned by a classical bridge, and overlooked by a circular temple. The Garricks, when they chose to step out of the central Venetian windows of the gallery and down a double staircase of the north front, found themselves in a paradise planned for large *fêtes champêtres*.

The month was June, they had been very unhappy, and now they were happy and alone in a little palace that seemed to come out of a fairy-tale. But it was only a fairy-tale, for the house was not theirs, and they would have to return to the world again. Fortunately, this was the world of the theatre, and they were players.

When the curtain rises on them again they are in a cottage at breakfast. Garrick did not intend to remain dependent on the Burlingtons for the rest of the summer. He had hired a lodging in Merton, Surrey, and it was from this address that he set himself down on August 3 to write a five-side letter of due gratitude to the benefactress. Lady Burlington's letters had been missing them—two letters, sent to the care of the porter at Burlington House. He tactfully acquitted the porter, and hastened to ingratiate himself. " Your desire, Madam, of receiving news from us and about us cannot possibly equal our joy and pride in sending it." A " most worthy friend " had ventured to ask " whether Lady Burlington was for or against me ", and on hearing of her " great and generous behaviour ", had not been surprised as he had always suspected she was one of those who had great souls. The Garricks were always talking of her ladyship, when alone—" which we think our happiest moments " and to find himself accepted as " *gendre* " and " *beau fils* " made him vain. He had already sent Lady Burlington a copy of the *Verses to Mr Garrick on the talk of the Town*, and he would write also to Eva-Maria's home:

> Our mother at Vienna (for whom I have the greatest tenderness) shall be made happy with regard to her daughter. Did she know my thoughts, she would be very easy, but as it is very natural for her to have apprehension, so I shall look upon it as my duty to quiet 'em as soon as possible. I love and regard everybody that belongs to her, and I flatter myself that they will have nothing to be sorry for but the loss of her, which (I can feel) must be no small matter of concern to 'em.

The gardener had sent delicacies from Chiswick down to Merton, a pineapple and a melon, and they had had Mr Blyth, who had performed the Roman Catholic service at their wedding, to dine. (Mr Blyth had hinted that he would welcome some franks for letters from his lordship when the occasion offered.) The married man's first

letter to a peremptory aristocrat who had indeed, according to her
lights, been very kind to his bride, ended as it had begun, in fulsome
vein. He described the arrival of her ladyship's letters at their
breakfast table:

> I could heartily wish you had seen the sudden change of our faces, and
> of the whole economy of the tea-table—each has to read the other's letter.
> Breakfast was at a Stand. Mr Maud's best green cool'd in the cup, the two
> slices of bread and butter (round the loaf and proportionately thick) which
> are cut and eaten by Madam Garrick every morning, lay neglected and
> forgot. Mr George, who had been out shooting, and ready to eat his
> fingers, sat with his mouth open.

He was glad that Lady Burlington approved of their having refused
to go to Lord and Lady Cobham. The truth was that they hated to
dine from home. Lord Radnor had been their only exception, and
friends seemed to understand that nothing but Chiswick would do.
They had been, in imagination, to Londesborough, the other night,
" and a sweet journey we had ". But that pleasure in fact would
have to wait till next year. From Merton, next month, they were
going home.

A letter to Peter had been written a week earlier.

> Your Sister and I return you thanks for your wishes of Joy and
> Happiness. She would have written to our Sister Magdalen, had she the
> skill enough to undertake it. She speaks and reads English well but our
> Characters are so different from the German (which is her native Language)
> that what with them and the Spelling, she is a little puzzled. But in time
> she will do that, as she can make herself mistress of anything she pleases.

15 He described himself as never in such health and spirits.


## 4

27, Southampton Street, which was to be the Garricks' town
house for twenty-three years, and for four and a half years their only
house, was also essentially a home and, for a young couple, a handsome one. Garrick, searching against time to produce something
worthy of a bride coming from Burlington House, had not stinted.
Mr Joseph Cradock, a young Leicestershire man of fortune, who came
to lodge opposite a decade later, believed the bridegroom to have
16 been " rather over-reached in his bargain with Mr Sheldon ". His
bargain, however, had advantages. Its situation was excellent from
the point of view of a manager of Drury Lane. It was not more than
ten minutes' walk from the theatre, by either of two routes. It
stood at the top, and therefore quieter, end of one of the streets

leading north off the Strand.    (George Anne Bellamy was first carried
off by a nobleman's carriage waiting at the bottom of this street.)
In the small hours, when traffic had ceased to flow around the pearl-
grey walls of St Mary-le-Strand, and the delicate steeple of that
church was printed against empty skies above almost empty streets,
this stretch of the Strand was as calm and pretty as a backcloth in
stage scenery.    But Southampton Street was very close to the river,
and in fact the continuation of an ancient lane across the Strand,
leading up from the banks of the Thames.    Number 27, a thin house
of warm red brick, stood on a distinct incline.    It had four storeys,
and fifteen small-paned front windows, facing east. · There were
three dignified, tall windows on street level, four similar on each of
the next storeys, and four smaller and squat, denoting attic bedrooms.    It had good cellars with a well, from which Thames water
was drawn from a tank embossed with the date 1710.    The front
door was solid, and bore a knocker in the shape of a classical female.
It was not a large house; there were no rooms to the right of the
front door, but it was not small, and the rooms were so lofty and well
proportioned that they gave the impression of spaciousness.    It was
well designed for the entertainment of a large number of guests.
The principal rooms were panelled, and the chimney-pieces and doors
were elegant.    Out of the entrance-hall arose a staircase with delicate balustrading and shallow, broad treads, wide enough to admit a
lady in the largest of hoops.    There were window-seats on every
landing, and in every reception room, so that Eva-Maria, sitting in
the window of her drawing-room, could watch for the figure of her
actor-manager, hurrying up Tavistock Street opposite, or round the
corner from the Piazza, on his way home from his theatre.    On the
ground floor there was one very fine front room, destined to appear
in innumerable anecdotes of theatrical and literary life—the study
of Roscius.    Behind came the breakfast and dining-room, looking
towards Maiden Lane, and conveniently close to the kitchens.    The
second-floor contained one large bedroom and two lesser.                    17

Roscius, hastening home, sure of a sympathetic audience, had a
peck of troubles to pour out in the late summer of 1749, and on one
occasion, it seems, his bride had a tale of horror to unfold.    According to Lee Lewes (who reproduces a document which he is unlikely to
have seen), within a few weeks of their wedding she had received an
anonymous letter.    Her unknown correspondent told her that he
could no longer conceal the passion which her beauty inspired, and
that although reason whispered that she now belonged to another, the
same reason whispered that she had chosen unwisely—" a wretch, as
incapable of love as generosity—a pitiful little animal, who has no

other passion but avarice and no other mistress but a guinea. Your Answer will reach me in safety if addressed as follows."

What steps Garrick took to discover the writer are not detailed by Lee Lewes, but in his opinion Garrick, without ever being able to prove it, always believed the advance to have come from Spranger Barry, and " ever afterwards conceived against him the most inveterate hatred ". Barry may have admired La Violette and have been mad enough to tell her so, but the overweening personal vanity of the young man was in any case quite sufficient to explain Garrick's dislike of him dating from this time. During this year he became a nuisance in the company. He suffered from a conviction that Garrick was jealous of him, especially of his Romeo. In vain, Garrick gave up to him Othello and many of his other favourite parts. Barry complained that he was called upon to act " at improper seasons, and on unlucky days; such as when a great lady had summoned a prodigious company to a concert of music, or some public assembly was announced ". Garrick let him choose his own days, and Barry subsided temporarily. (" Very well, that is all that I can ask.") But Garrick's Hamlet still drew the larger houses. Barry began to develop sudden indispositions, and was indignant when their genuineness was questioned. He insisted on inserting a paragraph at the head of play-bills stating that he " scorned all trick and evasion ", and the London press hastened to copy this. Susannah Cibber was also behaving like a spoilt child. She did not think she would play at all next season. Woodward seemed likely to be going to play almost too well.

Eva-Maria Violette slipped into the rôle of Mrs Garrick with astounding ease. There is not the slightest evidence that she ever regretted her retirement, or Burlington House. The part of Mrs Garrick occupied all her energies. She attended the theatre regularly, and it soon became known that the manager's wife was a character with whom it was wise, as well as agreeable, to be on good terms. She read the plays sent to her husband, and commented on them; she saw all the costumes, she entertained and scrutinized the extraordinary variety of human beings, often in a strange state of mind, who presented themselves under her roof. There was no question of Garrick, on his marriage, falling out of the fashionable and intellectual society in which he had been a popular figure. The Garricks were asked everywhere together, and of the pair she was considered by many the easier guest. At first her English was inadequate and her foreign accent was pronounced. Garrick was well amused when, at an auction, deeming it prudent to give the name of her Welsh maid, Betty Price, she announced, in her excitement

at getting her bargain, that she was "Potty Brice". But incorrect accentuation and a limited vocabulary, however excusable
in a young and pretty woman, are apt to become less interesting with
years. Eva-Maria, who had great good sense, set herself to master
the English tongue, and succeeded so far that even in her Journal, to
which she briefly confided daily events, she wrote in English, and
far better English than most English ladies of her day. It seemed
that she had even come to think in the language of her adopted
country.

As an ex-member of London companies she knew what to expect
as the annual routine at Drury Lane. The season would open in
mid-September, and this was the time for introducing new performers, or welcoming back an old favourite. The audience would
consist mostly of critics, merchants, barristers, other players, and
particularly countrymen in town, unmistakable by their dress and
manners—a light grey or dun suit, slouch hat, lank hair; people
slow to applaud but not lacking mother-wit. Although the curtain
did not rise until six o'clock the theatre was a scene of activity on a
popular night from three onwards, as anyone desiring a good seat
might arrive as soon as the doors opened. At the height of the season people of quality sent their footmen to hold seats; humbler folk
sent even humbler folk. During the early autumn weeks performances took place generally only on Tuesdays, Thursdays and Saturdays, alternating with those at Covent Garden. By mid-October
six performances a week were given, and November or early December were often enlivened by the production of a new play or one of
those old, and once-popular, plays which Garrick thought might
succeed again. January and February were the most important
months. Town was full and the first nights were of pieces designed
to attract the fashionable and influential. Benefits began in the
middle of March, " and then " as David told Brother Peter, " Farewell to all the *Pleasures* of the theatre." They were designed primarily to bring in a good profit for the actors or actresses concerned,
and naturally much heart-burning took place on such competitive
occasions. The season generally ended, late in May or early in June, 19
with Garrick in a series of his best-known parts.

His last appearance before his marriage had been on May 18 as
Benedick, and it was as Benedick that he first appeared twelve days
after the opening of his autumn season of 1749. A critical house
awaited him, but by the time he spoke the words, " When I said I
would die a bachelor I did not think I should live till I were married ",
it was clear that he had nothing to fear. As " the married man " he
was just as much liked as he had ever been. His " several strokes

of humour " in the passages applicable to his own situation " aroused
infinite mirth ", his performance was " a complete triumph ".  Vic-
torian, and later, critics uttered severe strictures on his " characteristic bad taste " in choosing such a part at such a moment, but no
contemporary shared this delicacy and an actor manager who needed
full houses got them.

*Edward, The Black Prince, or The Battle of Poitiers,* his first new
piece in the New Year, in which he played the title rôle, seemed a
reasonable venture.  He had had a success with Henry V, another
national hero, although he had left the part to Barry.  There was a
beautiful dance of medieval children, led by Master Maltere; and
Cross, the prompter, noted in his diary that the boy danced well.
But William Shirley was not William Shakespeare, as critics were
quick to discover.  The play was condemned as defective in unity of
action, though its language and sentiment were approved.  The
idealized Edward was " too uniform, too cold and tame, for such an
actor as Mr Garrick ".  He laid Edward aside and never tried it
again.

The New Year had opened somewhat unpropitiously, and two
more vexations, one wholly unmerited, awaited him.  Otway's
*Friendship in Fashion* had been considered " very diverting " and
had won general applause when it had first been seen.  But the date
had been 1678.  His immediate cause for anxiety as January 26 drew
near, however, was not whether public taste had changed, but
whether Foote was going to organize a riot.  Foote, the last person
who should have objected to being caricatured, had heard that
Woodward (returned from Ireland) was going to " dress at him ".
Foote's letter to the manager of Drury Lane showed every sign of
having been composed under stress of strong emotion on the spur of
the moment, and probably after dinner.

To Mr Garrick.

Sir,
     It is impossible for me to conceal a piece of intelligence that I have
received this minute from either a friend or an enemy.  I am told that on
the revival of a comedy called " Friendship in Fashion " a very contemptible friend of yours is to appear in the character of Malagene, habited
like your humble servant.  Now I think it is pretty evident that I have as
few apprehensions from the passive wit of Mr Garrick, as the active humour
and imitation of Mr Woodward; but as we are to be in a state of nature,
I do conceive that I have a plan for a short farce that will be wormwood to
some, entertaining to many, and very beneficial to, Sir

Yours<br>Samuel Foote.

If your boxkeeper for the future returns my name, he will cheat you of a
sum not very contemptible to you—viz five shillings.

Foote could be what is called " an ugly customer ".   Last year
Lacy had threatened to break his head, and many years later Johnson, when asked by Boswell if Foote had ever imitated him, awfully
replied, " Sir, fear restrained him: he knew I would have broken his
bones."   Garrick, as usual, when trouble threatened, wrote one of
his long, polite, painstaking letters.   He stood up for Woodward's
reputation, refused to interfere in " a mimical war " and answered at
length the jeer about the five shillings.   Foote's threat was not 21
brought into execution, for it was not needed.   Taste had changed
since the days of James II, and the actress playing Lady Squeamish
was hissed into silence.   But she was Kitty Clive, who knew London
audiences through and through and had the spirit of a lioness.   In
the last act the audience broke into something like a riot, to the
amusement of the French ambassador, who had come to see a play
said to be *risqué*.

The earthquake took place on February 8, the day before the
first Royal Command performance of the year at Drury Lane.
Westminster Hall was expected to collapse, and from the new
houses around Grosvenor Square people ran out screeching to seek
safety in the fields.   Chairs were set dancing and pewter rattling,
and Mr Walpole felt his bolster rise behind his head.   It was soon
remarked that the dreadful tremors had been confined to the fashionable quarter of London, and Mayfair and St James's were warned,
by sensational preachers, that they were about to share the fate of
Sodom and Gomorrah.   Mr Aaron Hill, unlucky to the last, died
peacefully a few hours before his *Merope* was produced at Drury Lane
for his benefit.   He expired " in the very minute of the earthquake,
the shock of which, though speechless, he appeared to feel ".   He
had been a beautiful character, in some respects, and certainly a
very unusual one.   When lamenting, with reason, his financial
situation, he had presented Garrick and Lacy with scenery for
*Henry V*, for which, Benjamin Victor was ready to swear, he had
paid two hundred pounds.   His schemes for establishing plantations
in South Carolina, and of extracting timber for the Navy from the
forests on the Duchess of Gordon's estates, had not won him the
least addition of fortune.   He believed he had brought to perfection
the making of potash equal to that imported at a large annual cost
from Russia, and of oil from beechmast.   He had long urged upon
the Prince of Wales, who was to be patron, a project for a Tragic
Academy.   The Prince had done what he could in ordering a Royal
Command performance of *Merope*.   For Garrick the removal from
the world of the theatre of Mr Hill brought immediate relief.   The
old elegant man had never ceased to plead, by pen and in person, at

inordinate length, that Britain's first actor would appear as " his great idol, Caesar ". (Mr Hill, practising what he preached, had christened his own surviving children Julius Caesar, Caliope, Urania and Minerva.) There was, he told Garrick, " but one walk in acting which you have left untrodden; the walk I mean is the sublimely solemn. . . ."

The weather was extraordinarily mild. On February 28 spring seemed to have come. The press announced wall-fruit in blossom, a swarm of bees taken and hived at Bisham, and " the Lady-bird insects " in plenty about London, where the roads were very dusty. Four days later came a first night which suggested that the persuasiveness of Mr Hill had left its mark.

Garrick had evaded Julius Caesar or Cato, but succumbed to *The Roman Father* of William Whitehead. This tragedy was founded " on the story in Livy ", and Corneille had already used it. Mr Whitehead had been educated at Winchester and was a fellow of Clare College, Cambridge. He was a friend of many young men of fashion, including Charles Townshend, and had been tutor to Lord Jersey's heir. He had addressed a tactful, graceful poem to the new manager of Drury Lane. Garrick as Horatius, father of the Horatii, proved that Hill had been right. Although the play was not good, it took very well. Garrick kept it in his repertory for sixteen years, and long before that Whitehead, who had proceeded to write better classical tragedies, was Poet Laureate.

The earthquake continued to be a nuisance. There was a rumour that it was going to be repeated, on a much grander scale, exactly a month after it first threatened sinning London, and again a month later. Ladies ordered warm " earthquake " gowns, and drove ten miles out of the capital before dark, to sit up all night at country inns playing cards. People with less money took refuge in boats upon the river. There was a considerable evacuation. But Holy Week, in which the theatres would be closed in any case, began on April 9.

On April 5 Garrick produced *Comus* for the benefit of a granddaughter of Milton, and himself spoke a prologue written by Johnson. The Masque was followed by *Lethe*, always liked, and Mrs Foster, only surviving descendant of Milton, received one hundred and thirty pounds, which greatly surprised her, as she had never heard of a benefit.

The annihilation of London faded from the public mind just in time for the remaining members of the company. To oblige Mrs Clive, Garrick himself had appeared as Hamlet. The flood of benefits drew to a close with something new to London. *The Provok'd*

*Wife* was produced on May 7, " being the first Application of this Kind " " On behalf of the Prisoners confined in the Marshalsea-Prison, Southwark ".

## 5

The circle of friends whom Garrick had been accustomed to visit as a bachelor during the three months while the theatre was closed for the summer had suffered some changes since his marriage. The Rochfords were now unavailable. They were in Italy. Lord Rochford had been appointed to a diplomatic post—British Envoy to Turin. William Windham's father had died and he had succeeded to Felbrigg, and married, to the annoyance of his family, a beautiful widow, Mrs Lukin of Braintree. The wedding took place in February, 1750, and William Windham, junior, appeared three months later.

Garrick had no time for a trip to Lichfield this summer. He liked to have his arrangements for the forthcoming season planned and fixed well in advance before he left London in July, and this year he was faced by difficulties. That Barry and Macklin should leave him and engage with Rich at Covent Garden was not a surprise, but that Mrs Cibber, who had not appeared for a year, should also go over to Rich was serious. The combination of Barry and Mrs Cibber had been a leading attraction at Drury Lane. He considered the material available, and told Lacy, who had a house at Isleworth, to go over to Richmond and see George Anne Bellamy, who was living there in some style, but with no very visible means of support. On her daughter's arrival in England in 1748 after her successes in Dublin, Mrs Bellamy had notified Garrick, and he had invited the pair to dine at his lodgings in King Street. George Anne had come, the pink of propriety, accompanied by her mother. " He received us with that cheerfulness and civility which constituted a part of his character." But he had regretted that at present Mrs Cibber, Mrs Clive and Mrs Pritchard engrossed all the leading parts in his productions. Later, Bellamy heard with rage that Garrick had sworn that never would he engage her upon any terms. She believed him to nourish eternal resentment that she had refused an offer made by Delane on his behalf while she was in Ireland. She had gone on to Rich, and presently disobliged her manager, and particularly her old friend Quin, by eloping to Yorkshire between the fourth and fifth acts of a performance of *The Provok'd Wife* with a rackety young Mr Montgomery, who later took the name of Metham and eventually inherited a baronetcy. Quin had to go before the curtain and make apologies and what explanations he could of the little leading lady's

sudden disappearance.   Probabilities of marriage with Mr Metham
had receded disappointingly after the birth of a son " my ever-
regretted George " of whom Mrs Bellamy took charge in Yorkshire
while her daughter came south to play at Covent Garden again.   Mr
Metham, who also loved cards and horses, pleaded a bad run at
Scarborough and at York races as his reasons for being unable to
undertake any further financial commitments.   He wrote that at
Lord Burlington's he had met Mr Garrick, who wished he could
number Miss Bellamy amongst his players.   Metham also introduced
her to " an amiable French nobleman, the Marquis de Verneuil ", and
" Madam Brilliant ", one of the actresses who had come over with a
French company to the little theatre in the Haymarket.   The French
visitors had not been received favourably and Madam Brilliant was
in the greatest distress.   On the suggestion of the Marquis, Bellamy
and " the Brilliant " hired the Assembly Rooms at Richmond and
gave several performances in French, and Bellamy next took a
furnished house in Frith Street, Soho, at which gentlemen could play
high at Faro and enjoy suppers created by a French chef.   The
Marquis, helpful as ever, presented her with some porcelain figures
from the new factory at Chelsea to lend an air to her drawing-room
chimney-piece.   But the thought of having to sell her diamonds, in
order to raise her share of the capital to be invested in this venture,
was vexing her as she travelled down to her Richmond house on a
midsummer morning.

> I had scarcely got out of the chaise before Mr Lacy, joint manager
> with Mr Garrick of Drury Lane Theatre was announced. . . . To my very
> great surprise he informed me that Mrs Cibber was engaged at Covent
> Garden, together with Mr Barry;  and that Mr Quin, from some disgust,
> had quitted the stage.

Enraged at one more proof of " Mr Rich's repeated duplicity ",
Bellamy signed on the spot an agreement for three years at Drury
Lane which Lacy had brought with him.   She had no sooner done
the irrevocable deed when Lacy, with a malignant grin resembling
that of the Demon in *Faust*, admitted that he could not say that the
report of Mrs Cibber's engagement was confirmed.   " However, at
all events you must be a gainer by playing with my partner, whose
consequence stamps merit where there is none and increases it where
there is."   According to Bellamy, Rich arrived a few hours later to
invite her to act with Barry, and only descended to Mrs Cibber in disgust.   Whatever the truth, it was soon a fact that Barry and Cibber
were going to be brought on by Rich as Romeo and Juliet.   Garrick
spent many hours of the remaining weeks before September in

coaching Bellamy to act Juliet to his Romeo, a part he had never before attempted.

Drury Lane opened on September 8 with *The Merchant of Venice*, to which Garrick had added a new occasional prologue, spoken by himself and glancing cheerfully at the defection of his performers of last season.

> Strength'd by new allies, our foes prepare,
> Cry Havoc, and let slip the dogs of War.
> To shake our souls, the papers of the day
> Draw forth the adverse bands in dread array,
> A pow'r might shake the boldest with dismay. . . .
> To keep the field, all measures we'll pursue,
> The conflict glorious! since we fight for you.

Barry replied at Covent Garden rather unhandsomely.

> When kings allow no merit but their own,
> Can it be strange that men by flight prepare
> And seek to raise a colony elsewhere?

The fight began in earnest on September 28, when *Romeo and Juliet* was announced at both houses, and it continued for twelve nights. Rich gave way first, offering Mrs Cibber's exhaustion as his excuse, and Garrick did keep the field by one performance. Naturally, both houses were crowded, and London was flooded by epigrams.

> " Well, what's to-night? " says Angry Ned,
>      As up from bed he rouses;
> " Romeo again," and shakes his head,
>      " Ah! pox on both your houses."

An inconvenient result from the point of view of the box-keepers was that people went to see half of the play at one house and half at the other.

Opinions as to the merits of the two companies varied. Barry was so tall, so musical; he seemed the maiden's dream; but Garrick seemed to have thought more. Garrick made his audience feel with him; Barry reduced it to sobs. A female critic whose *bon mot* was much repeated said that if she had been Juliet she would have wished Mr Garrick to climb up into her balcony, but she would have jumped down to Mr Barry. With regard to the ladies, the positions were reversed. Mrs Cibber was all pathos and an experienced actress, Bellamy was younger and very pretty. (She was now a passionate Italian brunette.) As Mercutio, Macklin was much less liked than Woodward, although, according to Bellamy, Woodward was appearing at a disadvantage in a company which included her. She had, on her début, many years before, refused the offer of his hand in marriage.

The ladies who had left his company (and also the ungrateful Bellamy) called Garrick a little tyrant. He was indeed deciding to make another departure from tradition at his theatre. On Lord Mayor's Day it had been customary to present a popular, but very coarse, piece, *London Cuckolds*. After 1750, without any explanation, it was never again played at Drury Lane. Nobody complained. On December 3 Garrick appeared for the first time this season in a new part, Osmyn in Congreve's sole tragedy *The Mourning Bride*. " Osmyn " was the very improbable name adopted as a disguise by Alphonso, Prince of Valencia, who had been unlucky enough to be taken prisoner by the King of Granada. Mrs Pritchard was Zara, a Moorish queen, in love with Osmyn, but repulsed by him, and Bellamy, Almeria, daughter of the King of Granada and secretly married to Osmyn. The discovery of his daughter's marriage so infuriated the King of Granada that he ordered Osmyn's execution, and to punish his daughter further, took the victim's place in his cell, so that Almeria might be disappointed and mocked by him when she came by stealth to release her husband. But by mistake the King himself was decapitated, and Zara, finding a headless body attired in Osmyn's garb, took poison in despair. A tragedy offering such rich fare was an instant success. It was given for nine successive nights in December and four more times that season, and was added to Garrick's repertory until his retirement. It contained some memorable lines—" Musick hath charms to soothe a savage breast ", and " Heav'n has no rage like love to hatred turned, Nor Hell a fury like a woman scorn'd ".

Arthur Murphy said that Garrick always declared with emphasis that " a Good Play was the *roast beef of Old England*, and that song and gawdy decorations were the *horseradish* round the dish ". But with this Christmas he provided something exotic at Drury Lane. Rich at Covent Garden had always prided himself on his pantomimes. On Boxing Day Garrick gave *Queen Mab, A New Entertainment in Italian Grotesque characters*. Woodward, the author, played Harlequin, loyally attended by Ned Shuter, a species of Scaramouche. A production which had entailed much labour and expense in a house hitherto unused to such things, was played for forty-five nights, and a cartoon appeared commenting on the state of war between the rival houses. It was named *The Theatrical Steelyards of 1750*, and showed Garrick in the scales, waving his cap in triumph, with the balance already so much in his favour that he does not need to hoist in Queen Mab, offered by Woodward. Woffington, Barry, Mrs Cibber and

Quin weigh so little in comparison, that Rich, in his Harlequin's costume, lies in the dust, weeping.

In February, as usual, Garrick brought out a new play by a rising author of influence. *Gil Blas*, by Edward Young, in which the manager played the name part, ran for less than the necessary nine nights and must be regarded as his first failure of this season. The masque of *Alfred* by James Thomson, a protégé of Pope and Lyttelton, and David Mallet, writer of popular ballads, had been first performed in his gardens at Cliffden House, at the request of the Prince of Wales. Garrick mounted it splendidly, and as the vocal and instrumental music was pronounced by experts to be charming, a brilliant success was prophesied. One song from *Alfred* descended to history, and for that, Mallet said, Thomson must be thanked. It was called *Rule Britannia*.

On March 7 Drury Lane was lent for a performance entirely by amateurs. Such interest and curiosity were excited by this prospect that the House of Commons rose at three o'clock so that members could attend. Sir Francis Delavel of Seaton Delavel and Ford Castle, Northumberland, of Doddington, Lincolnshire, and Cannon Park, Hants, had been so much admired as Othello, supported by a company of talented friends (including two gentlemen of his own family, as Iago and Cassio), that after delighting guests at his brother-in-law Lord Mexborough's house he had attempted to hire the Little Theatre in the Haymarket. That proposition had failed, but Garrick had stepped into the breach. He was to be paid one hundred pounds for the loan of his house for the one night. Costumes, scenery and lighting the house by wax eventually amounted to a bill for one thousand pounds. What was most remarked on the night of March 7 was nothing to do with acting. The audience gathered together was the most dazzling that had ever been seen. Even in the footmen's gallery, persons wearing the stars of noble orders were observed. Outside, the scene was one of indescribable confusion, and a large mob was gratified by watching the quality in their finery leaving their chairs and coaches in despair and picking their way on foot through the mire of a wild, wet night. Horace Walpole, of course, was present and knocked off the amateurs' performance in a sentence: " They really did so well that it is astonishing they should not have had sense enough not to act at all."

On March 21, when actors and actresses were beginning to think of their benefits, came a thunderbolt. " The Lord Chamberlain sent Orders to the Playhouses to forbear acting till further Orders." The Prince of Wales had died suddenly, of pleurisy. He had not been a popular prince and a contemporary ballad was sweepingly disloyal.

Here lies Fred
Who was alive and is dead.
Had it been his father,
I had much rather.
Had it been his brother,
Still better than another.
Had it been his sister,
No one would have missed her,
Had it been the whole generation
Still better for the nation.
But since 'tis only Fred
Who was alive and is dead,
There's no more to be said.

At Leicester House, Prince George, who was soon to be created
Prince of Wales in his father's place, showed signs of sensibility
which were eagerly repeated. " I feel," said the boy, laying his
hand on his breast, " something here—just as I did when I saw the
two workmen fall from the scaffold at Kew." All playhouses were
equally hit by the prohibition, and there were stories that Covent
Garden would never rally again.

As Garrick had expected, Rich's vaunted acquisitions from Drury
Lane were costing him dear. The scenes of delicately veiled dislike
in the green-room between Mrs Woffington and Mrs Cibber were said
to be better than anything these ladies played before the footlights.
Mrs Cibber was genuinely ill. Barry also was ill. He had his delicate throat to consider, especially when playing with Quin. Relations between him and Quin became so strained that they could not
be brought to rehearsal together. One or the other, sometimes both,
failed to appear, which made rehearsals sad affairs. Garrick decided
to go for a little jaunt, with his wife, to Bath.

### 6

He had been to Bath before, of course, but never in a chariot, with
a pretty woman by his side. He almost felt as if he had eloped with
Eva-Maria. But he had also never before left behind a house of his
own, and a staff. He wrote to George, from Marlborough, urging
him to keep a watch upon Southampton Street, and particularly
Molly, our housemaid. She sat heavy upon his soul. She was " the
greatest peeper in papers " that ever he had known, and had " all
kinds of people following her ". George must drop in, and if he found
that Molly, left to her own devices, was behaving as David feared
likely, George had authority to give her notice. He told George to
write to him at Bath c/o Mrs White at North Parade, and tell him if
it was true that Covent Garden was for sale. Otherwise, he had no

anxieties. He had " lost all my Devils. Nothing hurts me but London worries ".

He wrote to George again on March 31. They had got into Bath safely on Friday evening, by seven o'clock.

> Your sister was much jolted for the last ten miles, and bad roads they are, tho' not dangerous. The moment you have the least intelligence when we open at the Playhouse let me know, for if we don't begin Easter Monday, I will drink the waters. . . . Pray call now and then in Southampton Street and look into the stables, and see if Robin is neat and tight and take care of things. I believe he is honest, but he has a great trust, and a wary eye will not be amiss. A word to the wise!—Now for your affair. . . .

George's letters, which he had found awaiting him at North Parade, had contained a bombshell. George wanted to get married. On the face of it this seemed a reasonable thing, for he was now twenty-eight. Unkind people at the theatre said that George's salary was " Hush-money ", for what he did, except go round saying " Hush " when the manager was about to perform, nobody could discover. George wanted to propose to Miss Elizabeth Carrington. She was the daughter of a gentleman in a good position. Mr Carrington was a King's Messenger and resided in Somerset House. George did not seem to think it at all unusual that he had not yet been introduced to the lady. His good friend Mr Squire, who knew the family, was going to do that, and he wanted David to draft him a proper proposal. This romantic situation shook David.

> I must beseech you to look narrowly into things, and be sure of matters, before you engage. Your whole [life] depends upon it, and should you be deceiv'd (I only say should you), you will certainly be worse than you are and miserable. Therefore, I say, Take Heed. But when you are well assur'd of your Point, and you like the Party, it will prove a very lucky incident of your life. However, if you consult with your good friend Mr Squire you cannot err in one part, and if you consult your own Heart and find it willing, in the other, you may be a very happy man. I have drawn you out a letter which you may alter, or omit parts of it as will best suit most the circumstances of the affair.

His draft letter opened well:

> Madam, Tho' I have not the pleasure of knowing you but by sight, yet from that little knowledge of you, I have often wished for more. . . .

But the postscript contained the gist of the matter:

> If my proposal were not thought too importunate, I could wish to have your leave to desire your Mama's permission that I may wait upon you some day this week.

He ended his own letter by begging George to consult again with Mr Squire:

Now dear, George, let me desire you for your own sake to enquire into her character, and that of your Friend. You cannot be too circumspect in this grand affair of your life.

Strange to say, George's suit prospered. Miss Carrington liked him well. But her father was to prove a tougher proposition. He was to haunt the Garrick family for the rest of their lives, and when George's wife died, leaving five infants, George was to continue to live in Somerset House.

Drury Lane reopened, with *Queen Mab*, on April 8. *The Recruiting Officer*, *Much Ado*, *The Suspicious Husband* and *Lethe* followed—all popular stuff. The benefits concluded on May 22, when the object of charity sounded pathetic: " Benefit of the Widow Reinhold and her four small children." Garrick had been generous in his list this season and he, who had begun his career in a play by Farquhar, advertised before a performance of *Lethe*: " Tickets delivered out by a Daughter of Mr Farquhar's in great distress, will be taken this night."

The weather that early summer was very warm—like the East Indies. London heard that at Versailles the royal guards were dying at their posts from heat-stroke. But when Drury Lane closed the manager was already gone on holiday. He had gone to France.

L

## CHAPTER VI

# HAPPY DAYS

## 1751–1755

### I

THE Garricks set out from London on May 19, 1751. They had an experienced travelling companion. Mr Charles Denis had spent eight years in Paris before the War. He was by profession a surgeon, and one of the talented sons of a French Protestant minister who had been obliged to fly his native land on the revocation of the Edict of Nantes. Eva-Maria's sole experience of a sea-passage had been so terrible that it had given her a horror, for life, of quitting terra-firma; however, cheerful people said that, given a fine day, Dover cliffs might sink below the horizon no more than four minutes before the voyager perceived the Haute Ville of Boulogne rising to greet him. A crossing might take anything from three to ten hours, even in good weather, for there were always the possibilities of a difficult landing if the tide was low, or if there was a land breeze. The Garricks were lucky in that their passage took three and a half hours, but in Boulogne they were bullied. The custom-house officers were most uncivil, in spite of the presence of a lady. After the customs, there was trouble about post-horses. David had brought a small book, a quarto volume, which he was later to have bound in red morocco with gilt tooled edges. Although he was going to report *1* from France, where New Style was used, he was going to stick to Old Style, which made dates twelve days earlier. His French was fluent, but oddly spelt, and where he could get a French name wrong, he did. But he was equally guilty of that in English. He wrote his diary on the left-hand page and used the clean sheet opposite for second thoughts, memoranda and engagements. Boulogne was noted by him for dirt, beggary, imposition and impertinence. " Everything as disagreeable as it could possibly be."

The shortest route to Paris was by Amiens and Chantilly, so the Garricks took that. The roads were for the most part good, but the inns very bad; Abbeville had the best. But people were civil, the wine was very good and the bills were reasonable. There were very few buildings on the road to Paris, but many churches, convents and calvarys, and it amused David to see that as they drew nearer to the capital, the post-boys, who in Picardy had bared their heads at every crucifix, began to cock their hats, and dash on, whipping up their horses, at the sight of one. In England there would have been noblemen's seats to admire from the high-road, but they did not see any in France until they got to Chantilly, where the Prince de Condé was in residence, so they saw the gardens only. They dined at St Denis, and made the due pilgrimage to the abbey which was the burial-place of so many French monarchs. They clattered into Paris between six and seven on Thursday evening, May 23, " and did nothing that night but clean ourselves and stare out of the window of our Hotel d'Estrangers, which looks on the Palais Luxembourg ". Paris, even as seen from the window, was very unlike London. Everyone seemed to be on the run. The houses in the better streets were built of hewn stone, and six or seven storeys high, with windows opening like folding doors. There were no flagstone pavements and there seemed to be nothing much between very narrow streets, in which traffic-blocks and swearing of waggoners and coachmen were continual, and very fine wide ones—boulevards, adorned with rows of stately trees, with a broad road in the centre for coaches, and at the sides, walks used by pedestrians. On the margins of the boulevards were coffee-houses and shops. The shops of Paris were famous, especially for their gold and silver lace, silks, velvets, ribbons, tapestry and glass. Eva-Maria intended expeditions in search of Paris novelties for friends at home. The noise of Paris, like the speed, was perpetual. Water-carriers, oyster-mongers, street-porters and vendors of ginger-bread or oranges (" Portugal! Portugal! ") never stopped shouting. When the cries of the lantern-bearers ceased, the milkmaids began to come into town. Church and convent bells, of course, tolled remorselessly night and day.

But the visitors from England were young, and on holiday, and in Paris for the first time, in May. They entered at once upon a programme which displayed that they were both ardent sight-seers and possessed of remarkable constitutions. They made the sort of mistake that tourists do in a strange place by hastening to the Comédie Française on their very first evening, and saw Molière's *École des Maris*, very ill-acted. It appeared that all the best actors were resting after a performance, last night, of a tragedy called *Zarès*. David noticed, with a manager's eye, that the lighting of the stage with candles instead of lamps had a mean effect, that only one piece of music was performed before the curtain rose, and that by an orchestra numbering only ten.

A call at the British Embassy, to leave their names, was their next duty, after which they called upon the Burlingtons' kinsman, Mr Boyle, and proceeded to the Comédie Italienne. Here the acting was better, but the dancing would, in the opinion of the English

experts, have been hissed off any stage in London. They spent
their first Sunday afternoon in Paris doing something very suitable
for the day of rest. Lady Sandwich, to whom they had brought
an introduction, was connected by marriage with the Burlingtons,
and a very old lady. She was indeed the daughter of the great, but
licentious, Earl of Rochester, favourite of Charles II and patron of
Dryden. Since her widowhood she had chosen to live in Paris, and
it was clear that she appreciated the French and their foibles perfectly, while retaining all the sentiments of an Englishwoman. She
was very polite in instructing the young visitors. Sunday, according
to the ungodly custom of the French, was also the day for fun, so they
went on to the Opéra in the Palais Royal, but saw what David called
a very *raw* entertainment. On Monday morning, Paris began to
grow upon him. Notre Dame was the most splendid church he had
ever seen, and a Pietà by Nicolas Coustou, behind the high altar, the
finest piece of sculpture he had ever seen. (Upon second thoughts,
he crossed out the second " finest " and substituted that it was just a
most fine Pietà.) At the adjacent orphanage, the Enfants Trouvés
were surprisingly handsome and neat. There were six thousand
nameless children deposited every year, he was told, in the establishment adjoining the cathedral. That the children should be so
good-looking was additionally surprising, as so far he had been
struck by the remarkable ugliness of all the people he met in the
streets, gardens and other public places. The women, to be sure,
were all heavily painted, which he found most disagreeable. He
had to admit that their manners were attractive, gay and easy, and
they were well shaped, " They tread much better than our ladies."
Four days later, when he went for a morning's ramble on foot with
Denis, leaving Madam Garrick at home to rest, he came to the con-
clusion that the elegant gait of the Parisiennes might be attributed to
the fact that they mostly seemed to have better legs than were usual
in London. This must help. He succeeded in witnessing *Zarès*
that night, presented in the traditional manner of French classical
drama. It was really *Zaïre*, and by Voltaire, and that old Moorish
queen again. Congreve had put her on the stage when Voltaire was
three years old, and Aaron Hill, fifteen. As a play, it certainly gave
scope for players. With regard to French acting, the manager of
Drury Lane was withering, in his diary. He really was no judge of a
manner of speaking and acting so different from that to which he was
accustomed, and which he thought could not be agreeable to the
performers or to the natives. At the Opéra next night he gave
Rameau's *Indes Galantes* praise for exceedingly expensive mounting
but found the singing execrable. At St Germain des Près, the oldest

church in Paris, Eva-Maria had to be left behind in the nave to survey Romanesque architecture while her husband was shown over the library by monks whom he found very conversable. The rule of the Benedictines admitted no females to their penetralia. But she may well have been glad of the pause, for they had already seen the Invalides and the Collège Mazarin, of which David had admired the first but not the second, and they were going on to St Sulpice (which was the newest church in Paris, and would be handsome when finished), and after that to see the justly praised Rubens pictures at the Palais Luxembourg. That night, at last, David saw a French actor whose performance appeared to him to have feeling and spirit. Le Kain was short, stout and ill-made, especially about the jaw, so that he seemed to be swallowing his words; but although his voice was not pleasant its range was tremendous.

Wednesday May 30 was the Feast of Corpus Christi, and they had been told that they must on no account fail to visit the Gobelins factory, as this was the week in which the merchants hung out all their best tapestries. Unfortunately, several hundred other people had decided to make the same expedition. After a glance at the streets, David decided that nothing would persuade him to take his wife out that day. They watched the Corpus Christi procession from their hotel windows, and he thought it not so good as that which he had witnessed in Lisbon when he had been eleven years old. He filled in the afternoon by visiting five more churches, including that of the English Benedictines, in which the exiled James II of England was buried, and afterwards went for a drive up to a pleasant view-point on a hill outside Paris. This was called L'Étoile, because of its twelve radiating avenues, and from it Paris looked lovely. The air was crystalline. No pall of smoke hung over this city because, unlike London, it burned wood, not coal. He appreciated this effect of light and gaiety again next morning when he went up to the top of Notre Dame with Denis, after a horrible expedition to the Hôtel Dieu, the most ancient hospital of the city. Nearly everything that they did that morning would have been unsuitable for Eva-Maria, for after the hospital and the ascent of Notre Dame, they went on to the Place de Grève, the Tyburn and Tower Hill of Paris, surrounded by a labyrinth of narrow and squalid streets, the Hôtel de Ville, three more churches, and finally the Bastille, which " had a horrid appearance and looks the thing it is ". David was disappointed that they could not get in at the Hôtel de Soubize, as the Rohan family had not yet departed for Versailles. Their mansion seemed to him to have more the look of Burlington House than anything he had yet seen. He was cheered by having observed that morning two very pretty clean faces unpainted, " which was a greater curiosity than any I had yet seen in Paris ". But even he admitted himself " tired to death with our walk ". He took Eva-Maria for a mild outing after dinner, to the Luxembourg again, so conveniently close to their hotel, and afterwards to the Comédie Française again.

Next morning they achieved a trip to the Gobelins, which were well worth seeing, and went over the Sorbonne and the General Hospital, where the stinks were not so bad as at the Hôtel Dieu. After a tour of the King's pictures at the Louvre they agreed not to attempt any theatre that night. They went for a drive after dinner up and down the Cours la Reine, which was five hundred feet long, with the main road to Versailles running through the middle, the Seine on one side and well-grown plantations on the other. It had been laid out by Marie de Medicis, and the present monarch's favourite, the Marquise de Pompadour, was going to have the plantations cut down, and the district, which was often flooded by the river, entirely re-planned, regardless of cost. There were strong evidences of poverty in the streets of Paris, and David had been shocked when he was told what had been spent to provide Louis XV with young peas, when he had been at his hunting palace at Cressy last month, for a single night. His Most Christian Majesty was now fifty-two, but judging by his portraits, looked much more—a tall, heavy, handsome man, with a great air, melancholy black eyes and a livid complexion, almost olive.

The English visitors had learned that on Sunday mornings they ought to attend at the British Embassy chapel. The Ambassador, who had been appointed on the signing of the peace two years past, appeared to fill his part admirably. Lord Chesterfield said that Lord Albemarle had become a colonel of the Guards, a Groom of the Stole, Governor of Virginia, and finally Ambassador to Paris, solely on account of his address and graces; but this seemed spiteful, for he was held to have acquitted himself with distinction at the battle of Fontenay. Reward for the Garricks came two days later in an invitation to dine at the Embassy on the night of June 5. It was not very convenient, as the weather had now grown very hot, and that was the day on which they were to leave for Versailles, twelve miles outside the city. However, they could drive out in the cool of the evening after dinner. They had met several of the Embassy staff by now. Mr Mildmay took Mr Garrick to the Comédie Italienne to see *Arlequin Scanderbeque*, and was so horrified at having carried London's finest actor to so poor a show, that he soon suggested they did not sit it out. Mr Charles Yorke was visiting his brother, Joseph, who was said to provide the brains at the Embassy. In the same circle revolved lively young Lord Huntington, and Lord Stormont (rather silent, but possibly more able), Mr Philip Stanhope, Lord Chesterfield's son, and Mr Hans Stanley. Garrick had arrived determined not to make the mistake of seeing too many of his countrymen in Paris, but when he came to look at the list of English acquaintances to whom he must make calls *pour prendre congé*, he found that already it numbered no less than twenty.

The Garricks had taken rooms at the hotel at Versailles for three nights, which they would never have done had anyone warned them. Disgraceful though it might seem, it was a fact that the best hotel in a town which had grown up around the most magnificent of French palaces, was very bad indeed. David was in no mood to admire when he found himself confronted at dusk by the vastest royal residence in his experience.

> I was struck by the view from the terrace down to the lake. The Building is large and extended, but in my opinion inelegant. We saw the Dauphine and Mesdames return from their walk, and then we returned to our dirty lodgings and supper.

They saw one more royalty on their way home, Louis XV, also not at his best. " The King came from Cressy this night, and we saw him enter the palace, with great haste and a very dirty, dusty retinue." Next morning they were at the palace again betimes. Inside, there were indeed many fine pictures, and the Great Gallery was magnificent. The newly-appointed Venetian Ambassador was arriving that day, to present his credentials. They had already seen him " make his entry " to Lord Albemarle, and had not been much impressed by his state and circumstance, but he recognized them at once this morning, paid David many compliments and was altogether particularly civil. In the evening they went to see the King, Queen, Dauphine and Mesdames at chapel. All these royal ladies, unfortunately, were entirely insignificant. The Queen had no influence; the five princesses, aged from fourteen to twenty-four, varied in their degree of good looks, but their father was not finding them husbands, and never would. The Dauphine was believed to have some parts, but until she presented her sickly husband with an heir would not gain in prestige. She had miscarried last year, but was expecting again in September. The famous fountains were playing in the gardens, but David beheld them, more fatigued than satisfied. " No cascade was as large as that at Chatsworth, nor any jet d'eau the equal of those I have seen there." Next day he saw at last the uncrowned queen of France. The heat was so great that they chose to see the Trianon palace and the Ménagerie before breakfast. The Venetian

Ambassadress paid her ceremonial call upon the royal family that morning, and they saw her making her curtseys to the Dauphine. The poor dowdy little Saxon princess was surrounded by the first ladies of the French court. " I beheld La Marquise Pompadour." The etiquette of the reception of the Ambassadress was incredibly stiff. " Scarce ten words passed on either side." Not a single word as to what he thought of La Pompadour was confided to the diary, but it proceeded in no approving vein. " Then I saw the Dauphine dine, which as I was very hungry myself, was not very agreeable. So after *she* had picked a bit, I gave my wife a wink and we retired to the same ceremony." The rest of that day was spent in an expedition to the royal châteaux of St Germain-en-Laye, which looked like a palace, and Marly-le-Roi, where the gardens were neat. On Saturday, June 8, the Garricks surpassed themselves. They saw Meudon, which belonged to the Dauphin, Bellevue, just built by the Pompadour, St Cloud (where they dined) and Madrid, both of which belonged to the King. Of the four David liked the last best, but then it had a very pretty theatre. He was told that when actors were summoned there, they got from the King a bottle of wine, a pair of silk stockings and their coach hire. The prospect from this place was absolutely beautiful, and the furniture was elegant, but not showy. The château was nearly two hundred and fifty years old, and Francis I was said to have named it in memory of his captivity in Spain.

It was quite a relief to be safely back in the Rue Racine watching Paris on the go, from a French window, and going to the Embassy chapel again and to see the interior of some noble town houses. The Duc de Penthièvre's Hôtel de Toulouse was worth seeing, and at the Hôtel de Tallart a very polite owner, who was a Marshal of France and lame, came himself in a wheel chair, spinning over the parquet, to greet them and show them round. One of the attractions of these Paris great houses was that nearly all had gardens, a thing seldom seen in London, except at Burlington House.

David's thoughts returned to the Burlingtons again when he saw the vaunted picture gallery at the Hôtel de Matignon. " No Hôtel has so good a collection of pictures as there is at Chiswick—in general Rubbish to 'em." He was sitting for his portrait nearly every morning this week in the studio of an artist known as " le peintre Turcq ", owing to his habit of wearing a turban, a relic of long residence in Constantinople. M. Liotard, who proved on closer acquaintance a sensible, unaffected man, was said to be very apt at catching a likeness. Monsieur de la Noue was another French friend whose name now made constant appearances in the diary. He was

an actor, a comedian, not of the first order, wrote David ruthlessly.
Seated alone with an English manager in the security of the Hôtel
des Estrangers, poor de la Noue poured out terrible things of the
tyranny that French actors had to endure, and how disagreeably they
were dependent upon the Lords of the Bedchamber.   He himself had
been sent to prison for a month.   He invited the most celebrated
actor in England and Director of the London play-house, to a little
supper, to meet other members of his profession, and absolutely laid
himself out for the honour of France.   David was splendidly entertained.   He also dined to meet M. Alexandre Piron, the dramatic
poet who hoped to surpass Voltaire in tragedy, and was a man of
sixty-two, of great wit and spirit, though incapable of appreciating
Shakespeare.   No actresses were present at these parties, but only
two had found mention in the diary—Mlle Dumesnil, France's leading tragedy queen, whom he found " violent ", and Mlle Clairon, a
comparative beginner, " who pleased me more than any actress I
have yet seen ".

By June 21 David had made his last entry in his Paris diary.
His catalogue of things seen was impressive.   He had visited fifteen
palaces, châteaux and hôtels, and seventeen churches, and had been
to the theatre thirteen times.   The diary ends abruptly, but he was
still in Paris a week later, for M. Charles Collé who composed
comedies for the private theatre of the Duc d'Orléans, and also kept
a diary, dined to meet him, and after the meal the company was
indulged with the dagger scene from *Macbeth*, which all present
thought quite masterly.   David, pressed to give his opinion of
French actors, said he considered them all, from the highest to the
lowest, bad, and a party of gentlemen of the politest nation in the
world fully agreed with him.   It is possible that he deserted the
diary for no other reason than the hurry preceding departure.   But
there was certainly another and more sinister reason for his ceasing
to write down things.

2

On Tuesday, June 4, he had mentioned in his diary " Saw
Dévisse ".   It had been a hot day, so hot that he had not stirred out
all morning.   About a fortnight later M. Louis Basile de Bernage,
Provost of the merchants of Paris, was writing confidentially to M.
Berryer, Commissioner of Police:

> On what you were good enough to acquaint me with, Monsieur, as to
> the design which brought to this place Messieurs Garrick and Levié, I have
> had them sought for but have not succeeded in discovering them.   You
> had given me hopes of sending me information should anything come to

your knowledge on this subject, so I am led to believe that you have heard no more of the matter. But *I know without any doubt that one of our dancers, named Dévisse, who left furtively in the month of August last year, and passed into England*, is at present in Paris. One of our actors assures me that he saw him and spoke to him in this town only a few days ago, and I have reason to believe that the object of his voyage, about which he addressed certain entreaties to me, alleging business affairs, is to help forward by his special knowledge, the steps that Messieurs Garrick and Levié may take to entice some of our actors and actresses and to carry them off with them; perhaps he has already taken measures to succeed in that.

I hope, Monsieur, that independently of these reasons, his infringement of the Regulations and orders of the King will decide you *to give orders to have him arrested and carried to Fort l'Evêque*. Monsieur le Duc de Gesvres, to whom I have reported this, is of my opinion; and Monsieur d'Argenson will approve your action. The example is absolutely necessary, first to keep our actors and actresses within bounds and to assure that the public service be properly carried out, and secondly to forestall M. Dévisse's evil intentions, and the manoeuvres of these foreigners.

A warrant was issued against Dévisse, but he was not arrested until September. He had been employed by Garrick since November 1750. Leviéz had been in England for years, first with Rich's company and then at the Lane, where Garrick had found him established as ballet-master. His name never appears in the Paris diary, but then that of Mr Charles Selwyn, Garrick's Paris banker, makes a single appearance, on the last page, and M. Jean Monnet, impresario, whom Garrick had befriended in London, and who was certainly amongst his Paris friends, is also never mentioned. Monnet had brought over to London, on the suggestion of Rich, the unfortunate troupe of French comedians which had included Bellamy's Madame Brilliant. On arrival in London he had been unable to come to an agreement with Rich, so had gone on to Garrick, and on his and other advice, hired the little theatre in the Haymarket. The anti-Gallic riots there had been so formidable that the Lord Chamberlain had finally been obliged to close the theatre; but the Duke of Grafton, always magnificent, had seen to it that Monnet did not go to gaol for debt, and Garrick had given him a benefit night which had produced another hundred guineas. Had Monnet been sent to Newgate, it would not have been his first experience of immurement. He had already been in the Bastille. Far from seeming anxious to engage French dancers for Drury Lane, Garrick, in the diary, only once mentions a performance by them, and then with contempt. But it is a curious coincidence that the diary ends abruptly, and that when the Paris police came to look for him, to charge him with the political crime of enticing members of the French Royal Opéra, he was nowhere to be found.

He was, in fact, quietly back at Chiswick House, and writing home.

Dear Peter,
        Your sister and I are much obliged to you for your wellcome home letter and kind invitation to Lichfield. I assure you we had sincerely intended to steal down to you and sisters this month, and to have crossed the Country, and met Lord and Lady Burlington upon the Yorkshire road. But when we came to hint it to the Family here we had grave faces and cool answers, so that we thought it wisest and best, knowing we can make freer with you than greater folks, to defer our expedition to Staffordshire, which upon my word shall be the first opportunity. For our hearts and wishes tend that way. We have the greatest obligations to our friends here, and as we eloped from 'em at the beginning of the summer they expect (and with reason) that we should stay with 'em the remaining part, and so we shall. We are at Chiswick at present; I expect every moment an order for Yorkshire, which tho' a little too late in the year for my affairs, must be complied with. I have lent George a little horse and he intends seeing you soon. . . . George will be bringing you and my sisters some Trifles from France, which we hoped to have delivered ourselves, but I have told you what has prevented that, so I shall say no more. We shall not be at Chatsworth this summer, but go directly to Londesborough, Lord Burlington's seat. Lord and Lady Hartington who are here with us set out for Chatsworth by Sunday. If you make a visit to Mr Boothby in a fortnight's time, I would have you by all means go there on a public day. They will receive you well, I am sure. I have had the greatest kindness shown me by that whole family. Is not the Mr Boothby you mention the one who married Miss Hollins? If it is, I am sure he must be happy, for when I knew her at school she was a pretty sweet-tempered and most agreeable creature. I met Mrs B— and Miss P— S— in Ranelagh Gardens and came up and talked with them, and they seemed pleased, for I left Lady Hartington and my wife and their company to entertain them.
        You ask me how I like France. It is the best place in the world to make a visit to, and I was indeed much satisfy'd with my journey; the particulars of my liking and dislike you shall know when you see me. I had much honour done me both by French and English, and everybody and everything contributed to make me happy. The great fault of our countrymen is, that when they go to Paris, they keep too much among themselves; but if they would mix with the French, as I did, it is a most agreeable jaunt.

In his postscript, he asked Peter to supply his date of birth, and sent his respects to Mr Walmesley. It was the last time that he had to remember such a message, for his first patron died in the following month. To John Hoadly, to whom he also wrote before setting off north, he reported himself " returned with my better half, safe and sound from Paris, and as true an Englishman as ever ". He repeated that he had been very pleased with his jaunt, and added that he meant to take another for a month longer, when business allowed.

        Business at Drury Lane went well that season. He had lost Barry, but he had three new actors from the Dublin nursery. He intended that they should fill his house for him, even when he was not himself appearing. Of the three, Dexter seemed to him likely to go furthest. He was brought on as Oroonoko. He was too tall, and thin, and his voice seemed somewhat thin, too, but he had remarkable *sang-froid*. On his first night he was " so far master of himself " that he was still chatting to friends in the pit while the second overture was being played. Just in time, he tore himself away to go behind and get made-up and go on. He gave an incredibly polished performance, and the piece was played for the next five nights, and after that, five times more before the season closed. But his admired languor increased. It was natural, and physical, no affectation. The whisper spread that Dexter lacked staying power. Two London seasons wore him out, and he retired to Dublin and a less exacting programme. This was disappointing, for he had regular habits and, given a better physique, might have soared.

David Ross was introduced as young Bevil in Steele's *Conscious Lovers*, and was very well cast. He was the son of a Writer to the Signet in Edinburgh, and rather fond of explaining that he came of one of the best families in Scotland. He had been educated at Westminster School. He was good-looking, in a slightly heavy way, and played in the easy, natural style approved by his manager. He made an instant hit, and went on to secure good opinions in several parts hitherto the perquisite of Garrick at the theatre—Lord Townly, Altamont, Plume. A " polite and distinguishing audience " congratulated themselves that Ross brought back to the stage a character they had feared lost, " the real fine gentleman ". He went much into influential society; but he was also liked by the pit and gallery, for he seemed equally at home in genteel comedy and tragedy. His solemn cast of countenance was a help. To a manager's eye, which must notice everything, he displayed also a tendency towards extravagance and laziness. But he was an excellent *raconteur*, and looked as if he was going to stay.

Poor Harry Mossop was handicapped. He had a ridiculous name, gauche manners and an awkward figure. Neither Garrick nor Rich would engage him when he first presented himself, having emerged a loser from a spiritual conflict, and decided against holy orders. He had gone back to Dublin (where he had received his education at Trinity College), and he had learned much there. Garrick cast him first for Richard III, in which his ungainly movements would not be a disadvantage. He had a harmonious voice, not so lovely as that of Barry, but of great range. " He excelled most in parts of turbulence and rage, of regal tyranny and sententious gravity." His favourite attitude was to stand with one hand on his hip and his other arm

extended; so audiences quick to detect mannerisms called him
" the teapot actor ". He needed very careful handling, for, unlike
Ross and Dexter, he was highly neurotic, and had no sense of humour.
He never pretended to be anything but a great tragic actor. Tas-
well, another member of the company, produced some lines on Drury
Lane's young gentlemen.

> The Templars they cry up Mossop.
> The ladies they cry Ross up,
> But which is the best, is a toss-up.

Of course it was rumoured that the manager was nettled at the outstanding success of his beginners. He may, as an actor, have felt a
pang, but as a manager he could only congratulate himself. Praise
of Mossop's Richard was effusive, but nobody seriously considered
that he outshone Garrick. He was to be placed, for life, as a good
third to Garrick and Barry.

The managers were always in need of characters to " walk on ",
men, women and children, " cupids ". They had inherited, together
with their theatre, a " very whimsical fellow " by name Stone, who
never himself aspired to tread the boards, but was always ready to
offer his assistance in finding " a considerable recruit of low actors ".
Stone, of course, expected remuneration per head for the characters
found, and equally, of course, took a trifle from them for getting them
their engagement at Drury Lane. Grubby notes signed W. Stone
pursued Garrick.

Thursday morn.
Sir,
      Mr Lacy turned me out of the lobby yesterday, and behaved very ill
to me. I only ax'd for my two guineas, for the last Bishop, and he swore I
should not have a farthing. I can't live upon air. I have a few Cupids
you may have cheap, as they belong to a poor journeyman shoemaker, who
I drink with now and then.
                              I am your humble servant.

Garrick's answer was prompt.

Stone,
      You are the best fellow in the world. Bring the Cupids to the theatre
tomorrow. If they are under six, and well made, you shall have a guinea a-
piece for them. Mr Lacy himself will pay you for the Bishop. He is very
penitent for what he has done.
      If you can get me two good Murderers I will pay you handsomely—
particularly the spouting fellow who keeps the apple-stand on Tower Hill;
the cut in his face is just the thing. Pick me up an Alderman or two, for
Richard, if you can, and I have no objection to treat with you for a comely
Mayor.
      The bearer will not do for Brutus, although I think he will succeed in
Mat.
                                        D. G.

Stone seemed to have discovered an actor, in a man enrolled when *Henry VIII* was in rehearsal. The play was to be produced as a pageant—a fine crowd scene was planned for the coronation of Anne Boleyn. One of the men engaged to take the part of a cleric looked the part so well that he was rehearsed as Gardiner, Bishop of Winchester, and promoted to this speaking part. But on the night of April 10, 1752, a dreadful line reached Garrick.

> Sir,
>         The Bishop of Winchester is getting drunk at the "Bear" and swears d—n his eyes if he'll play tonight.
>                                 I am yours W. Stone.

Garrick's reply was succinct.

> Stone,
>         The Bishop may go to the devil, I do not know a greater rascal, except yourself.
>                                                         D. G.      7

Taswell, who knew his Shakespeare through and through, appeared as the Bishop of Winchester, at short notice, though "a gentleman who had never appeared on any stage" had actually been advertised.

Garrick added one new part to his own répertoire before Christmas —Kitely in Ben Jonson's *Every Man in his Humour*. He had cut the old play about, to make it acceptable to a modern audience, and added a scene to the fourth act. He always did well as a jealous man, and was very moving as Kitely, brilliantly supported by Woodward and Yates and, of the new-comers, only Ross, as "Young Knowell". He had found, in Mossop, a strong reinforcement. He could now reappear as Jaffier in *Venice Preserv'd*, having got a Pierre to replace Barry, and as Lothario in *The Fair Penitent*, with an adequate Horatio. In the Christmas holidays he gave Woodward his chance with another pantomime. *Harlequin Ranger* opened on Boxing Day, continued for three weeks and became an annual dish. It was twice interrupted by performances of a new comedy, *Taste*, by Samuel Foote. Garrick had met Foote in Paris, and agreed to produce a little satire on modern affectations. He wrote a prologue, and delivered it in person, in the character of an auctioneer. *Taste* was witty, but it was "relished by the boxes only", and not all gentlemen who had come back from a Grand Tour with maimed classical statues and dusky Old Masters, nor all less well-to-do gentlemen who had assisted them to buy them, were much amused by seeing themselves as Lord Dupe and Mr Puff.

An artist was a constant visitor at Southampton Street this winter, and John Hoadly reported to Joseph Warton comfortably:

# DAVID GARRICK and his wife.

*By William Hogarth*

This picture, begun in 1752, was sold on the death of Mrs Garrick seventy-one years later, for £75 11s. 0d. to Mr Locker of Greenwich Hospital. It has changed hands only twice, as on Locker's death it was bought by George IV and added to the Royal collection at Windsor. Hogarth evidently kept it unfinished in his studio until 1757, when Dr John Hoadly wrote to Dr Thomas Warton, on April 21, " Hogarth has got into portraits, and has his hands full of business, and at a high price. He has just finished a most noble one of our sprightly friend David Garrick and his wife; they are a fine contrast. David is sitting at a table, smiling thoughtfully; Madam is, archly enough, stealing away his pen." The picture appeared in Christie's catalogue, June 23, 1823 as " Portrait of Mr Garrick, seated at his writing table, composing the prologue to ' Taste '; and of Mrs Garrick behind, interrupting his reverie; painted with great truth and spirit ". " Taste ", by Samuel Foote, was produced on January 11, 1752, and was performed only seven times.

*Reproduced by gracious permission of Her Majesty The Queen.*

Hogarth had got into Portraits, and has his hands full of business, and at a high price. He has almost finished one of our sprightly friend David Garrick and his wife. They are a fine contrast. David is sitting at a table, smiling thoughtfully, Madam is archly enough stealing away his pen, unseen behind.

The likeness of Eva-Maria was wholly charming, but according to George Steevens, her husband so much disliked the expression of his countenance that Hogarth blacked out the face and walked off with the picture, in dudgeon. After Hogarth's death his wife sent it to Garrick as a gift. The manuscript under his hand at his " 'scritoire " was the prologue to *Taste*.

Southampton Street received valued guests on a visit of ceremony early in the New Year. The Lichfield Garricks came up to stay. There were now only two available. William was overseas with his regiment. George, who in any case lived in London, had now married, and dwelt with his father-in-law in Somerset House. Peter, Lenny and Merry remained, and of these Merry, now eight and twenty, was Mrs Thomas Docksey, wife of a merchant of her native city.

*Eugenia*, David's last new play this season, was presented on February 17 to an unappreciative house. He was Mercour, and Dexter, Clerval. It was a solemn piece by one of the stage-struck clergy whose dramatic works steadily rained upon him. Mr Philip Francis was a son of the Dean of Lismore, and himself supposed to be in charge of a cure of souls in Norfolk, and a school at Esher. Actually, he spent much time at the Bedford Tavern and other haunts of theatrical and literary society. *Eugenia* was " from the French ", but Madam Graffigny's *Cénie* had been a comedy. After six nights, the unhappy exile was laid to rest, never to be resurrected.

By March 21 the theatre had closed for Holy Week and David wrote to Peter:

> I am glad you and Co: got safe to your dear beloved Lichfield, and am glad that you found all well at the castle on the bridge.

But all was not perfectly well, and David would have to write more letters on this subject. It had been brought to his notice during the family reunion that he ought to do something for Peter. There must be people whom he could approach with a view to a salaried appointment. For the rest of his life, he was to continue this brotherly task. For when he had temporarily abandoned the search for something for Peter, there was George in the offing, and although at the date of their marriage Thomas Docksey had been represented as in a thriving way of business, Merry presently needed assistance. He dealt with these applications so delicately that it is not always easy to discover for which relative he was at work.

London was interested this New Year in two novelties. The Gunnings had burst upon society in the previous September. They were Irish girls of surpassing beauty and charm, without fortune. Bellamy told fearsome stories of their extreme poverty when she had come across them, in Dublin, and treasured a letter written to her by Elizabeth Gunning which was familiar and quite illiterate. It was said that when they had been presented at the Lord Lieutenant's drawing-room, their finery for the evening had come out of the property box. Mrs Woffington had lent them gowns. On Valentine's Day of this year, the Duke of Hamilton had married the younger Gunning, according to Horace Walpole " with a ring of the bed-curtain, at half an hour after twelve at night ", and what he thought even sillier, was that now, he heard, young Lord Coventry was going to marry the elder. His fears were justified within three weeks.

London's other leading topic for discussion was the New Style. This, according to Act of Parliament, had come into operation on January 1, and this year the day after September 2 would have to be reckoned as September 14. Previously, the English legal year had opened on March 25. David, who had always believed that he had been born on February 19, 1716, wanted to know how old he must now call himself. By the new reckoning he had been born in 1717. He had begun to consider this in France, where New Style had long been accepted. Eva-Maria had been born on February 29, continental style. The Garricks fell into line and kept dual anniversaries henceforward, New Style; but Johnson waited twelve months before he entered in his diary " January 1st 1753, N.S. which I shall use for the future ".

Johnson had lost his wife this March, and to the amazement of his friends appeared to regret a companion whom they had thought quite intolerable. But he did not as yet come much to Southampton Street, for David had taken a wife of a very different stamp, and Johnson's ideas of the courtesy which must be shown to an elegant female were exacting. David had heard that the widower had been knocked up by two young bloods of their circle, Topham Beauclerk and Bennet Langton, at three o'clock the other morning, (" What is it you, you dogs! I'll have a frisk with you."). After a bowl in a tavern in Covent Garden, where the greengrocers and fruiterers were just beginning to set out their hampers, the party had taken a boat to Billingsgate. " I heard of your frolic t'other night," said Garrick to Johnson. " You'll be in the *Chronicle*." Johnson, after David had gone, said slyly, " HE durst not do such a thing. His WIFE would not LET him! " His wife made no objection, however, to David's dining fairly often from home, especially in the business world. He kept in touch with his City friends at Tom's coffee-house in Cornhill, " the usual rendezvous of young merchants at ' change time ' ". He was often seen at the Queen's Arms in St Paul's church-yard, where he met Mr Samuel Sharpe, the surgeon, and his old friends Paterson, Draper and Clutterbuck. " They were none of them drinkers, and in order to make a reckoning, called only for French wine." At Batson's coffee-house he met another medical friend, Dr Wilson, a physician with a comfortable fortune and no practice, who always had his own seat in the pit at Drury Lane.

On May 12 David sent Peter a long letter, opening " My wife has spoken to Lord Hartington ". He had not forgotten his promise, and Eva-Maria was playing her part. He reminded Peter again, " Send me my age." He knew where it was written down, at home, in the old Family Bible. He did not think that Lenny would object to the search, for, if he was now only thirty-five, not thirty-six, she too was a year younger. For London news, he could only report that they had closed for the summer at the theatre that day, and that he feared his dear friend Draper (one of his backers when he took over the joint-managership) was very ill. George's wife, who was expecting, was very well, but George had a bad cold. Horace Walpole, writing to Rome on the same day, drew the picture of London out of season in a sentence: " Town is empty—nothing in it but flabby mackerel, and wooden gooseberry tarts, and a hazy east wind."

The life of David Garrick seemed to be settling into a regular pattern. It was of success and prosperity, but attended by much toil and uncertainty. In the new year the public always expected new plays at Drury Lane, so he had to provide them with what was supposed to be liked. This meant that he must produce at least a couple of the classical tragedies which still held the stage of France. But the public were ungrateful, and if the new plays were not re-markably good, they went to see them once only, which meant that he lost on these. Collections of his belongings which have survived, abound in little water-colour sketches of an unmistakable, dark-eyed, gesticulating figure attired as a Roman general, as a dusky potentate, an Early English hero, all leading parts in new plays which went back " into 'scritoire " after a few performances, and were never added to his répertoire. New plays came principally from three sources: very dear old friends, such as Sam Johnson, and their hangers-on; gentlemen, young and old, in holy orders, some of whom had mistaken their vocation, and haunted London literary circles in the taverns of theatre-land; literary ladies, who were at work to keep the wolf from the door. There must surely, somewhere, be Shakespeares scribbling in garrets, but if so the results of their

M

labours did not penetrate to him. He wanted to produce much more Shakespeare, altered to suit modern taste, but had not been able to do this for some seasons. He had now, dubiously marked for production, a typical collection. Edward Moore had achieved a third tragedy. It was promisingly entitled *The Gamester*, and would need a Garrick prologue and a good deal of alteration. Beverley, the hero, was a poor weakling lured to destruction by a villain, Stukeley —a part the manager intended to bestow upon Tom Davies, who was a new-comer to Drury Lane but not to the stage, and had a very pretty wife, also a player. Beverley had to end his miserable existence by swallowing a dose of poison, which would give an opportunity for "great agonizing feelings". The fate of *The Gamester* was curious. It was brought on early in February 1753, prefaced by rumours that it was "an honest attack upon one of the most alluring and most pernicious vices to which mankind in general, and this nation in particular, is unhappily subject". Arthur Murphy, sitting in a front box near a gentleman notoriously addicted to gambling, heard this expert pronounce loudly at an early stage in the performance that Beverley was such a poor thing nobody would play a single rubber with him. It was generally agreed that throughout the play Garrick "almost rose above himself", but the chief praise went to Mrs Pritchard, as the gambler's wife. "She did not appear to be conscious of an audience before her. She seemed to be a gentlewoman in domestic life, walking about in her own parlour, in the deepest distress, and overwhelmed with misery." *The Gamester* lasted for twelve nights only, which was disappointing. Some people thought it had been too harrowing, others that spectators both from the West End and the City did not care to see their ruling passion attacked by moral Mr Moore. But it could not be classed a failure. It was marked for further production.

*The Brothers*, by the Reverend Edward Young, was from the first a source of trouble. Bellamy got hold of the manuscript from the guileless author, alleging that she was indisposed, and feared the part of the heroine, Erixene, was very long: perhaps it would be too much for her in her present weak state. Garrick, who had cast Mrs Pritchard for Erixene, was justifiably angry when he heard of the trick played upon him, and according to Bellamy sent her an unsparing rebuke. "The liberty you have taken in asking to peruse Dr Young's piece is unwarrantable, and I will convince you that I alone am the person to be addressed in whatever concerns the theatre." The company arrived for rehearsal in an apprehensive frame of mind, and the manager's first words to Bellamy since what she called their "declaration of war" were not reassuring. "Ah! ah! ah!

madam. . . . You are come at last. It was unfortunate for us that the doctor insisted upon your being his heroine." Bellamy, at her most sugary, agreed with every word he said. She really thought Mrs Pritchard would have been much more suited. " I have such a natural dislike to hautiness that it is with difficulty I can assume it." She would like to relinquish the part to " his favourite ". Upon this, Dr Young cried out " No! no! " and the manager's brow darkened. Dr Young's brow also darkened when Erixene began to suggest alterations in his text, particularly the omission of one line which he thought the most forcible and best he had ever written. The little actress, struck to the heart, went up to him and, taking his hand, asked with swimming eyes for the forgiveness of the writer of that divine work *Night Thoughts*, which had convinced the world of the mistake of giving way to immoderate anger. Dr Young, after striding about the room two or three times, took his pen, and to the astonishment of Mr Garrick struck out the offending line. At the close of the morning's labour the old gentleman asked himself home to dine with Bellamy.

*The Brothers* had been written more than thirty years past, and had been put into rehearsal in 1726, but withdrawn at the request of the author, as he had meanwhile been ordained. He was now seventy, and a most melancholy widower. He said he was in no particular need of the profits and wished that it should be announced that they would be devoted to the Society for the Propagation of the Gospel. He reckoned that his share would be not less than one thousand pounds, and when it proved four hundred pounds, he made up the deficit out of his own purse. For *The Brothers*, in spite of great expectations, and much fire and energy displayed by Demetrius and Perseus (Garrick and Mossop) and floods of tears from their father, Philip (Barry), ran only eight nights. After the first night Dr Young was again immoderately angry, and this time with the manager. Kitty Clive, at her sauciest, had spoke a somewhat ribald epilogue. After the failure of *The Brothers*, everyone agreed with Bellamy that she had been mis-cast.

She was a dreadfully untruthful girl, and a nuisance in a company, and Garrick would, upon the whole, be glad to be rid of her, particularly as, during this summer, he had hopes of the return of Susannah Cibber. The poor Cibber was in a lamentable state of health, but he had two new plays in which he could urge her on, in unexacting but important parts.

Richard Glover, the author of much admired blank verse, had lost his chief patron on the death of the Prince of Wales. He took himself very seriously as an author, and had refused to collaborate

in a life of the great Duke of Marlborough.   The duchess had left
him a sum of five hundred pounds in her will if he undertook the work,
but although he admitted he was not in funds, he would not comply.
He had now written a tragedy, *Boadicea*.   It might be that any play
about the luckless Queen of the Iceni would draw audiences, but
even the name of the character allotted to Garrick sounded depressing—Dumnorix.   Garrick decided to risk it, and Glover was invited
to attend a reading of *Boadicea*.   Tom Davies, who tells the tale of a
social disaster, does not say whether the scene was the famous back-
parlour at Southampton Street or the green-room, but Southampton
Street was usual for small first gatherings of principals only, and the
theatre during the dead season of 1753 was unavailable.   Garrick
and Lacy were at last doing something which they had intended since
they went into management together, and when Drury Lane re-
opened, in September, the *Public Advertiser* was to make an announcement that the premises had been new-painted, gilded and provided
with fresh scenery.   The company assembled to hear *Boadicea*, and
Mr Glover began to read.   It was at once evident that whatever the
merits of his play, this author had such a harsh and disagreeable voice
that nobody could listen without pain.   Garrick politely interrupted,
as soon as possible, with an offer to relieve him by reading an act or
two, but Mr Glover was adamant, and the players, in stunned silence,
heard every word of what appeared to be a remarkable effort.
Glover had managed to make *Boadicea* dull.   There was a quarrel
between Dumnorix and Boadicea in the first act which might be
effective, and it might be that Mrs Pritchard could work wonders
with language that was certainly pure and classic, and sentiments
that were elevated.   But Mr Glover, who had leanings towards historical accuracy, had made his heroine an unsympathetic character.
Boadicea was quite detestably cruel, and Venusia (Mrs Cibber)
sentimental to the verge of idiocy.   Nobody could be anything but
relieved when Venusia, introduced by her husband, Dumnorix, to a
dish of poison, drank if off obediently, whereupon the widower fell
upon his sword in the high Roman fashion.   The session ended, *11*
however, with *Boadicea* chosen for production before the year was
out, and Garrick, his plans laid, wrote one of his holiday letters to
Lichfield before packing for the north.

Chiswick, July 4th, (1753)
    I have just heard that there is an estate belonging to one Mr Boothby
(I don't know if it is your friend or not) near Ashbourn, of about £300 per
annum, to be sold, and has been upon sale near two years.   Dr Taylor, the
physician, tells me it is one of the prettiest freehold estates in the County of
Derbyshire.   I wish you would make some enquiries about it, and let me

know the particulars as soon as you can.  Pray inform me if there is the
River Dove near the house, and what kind of a house, what wood, what
prospect etc etc.  I should be glad to purchase a good thing in Derbyshire
that I might serve the Devonshire family upon occasions.  I should be glad
if you could get the best information you can, but not mention my name
yet, for fear they should rise upon it.  [Dr Taylor, once of Ashbourn, now
of Westminster, brother to Dr Taylor, physician, had told him of the
possibility.]  They say it is the prettiest thing next to Mr Oakover's in the
County.  I own I love a good situation prodigiously, and think the four
great requisites to make it—wood, water, extent and inequality of ground.
I should be glad to know if this place has any, or all.  Should you hear of
any good thing besides this, may be had reasonably, and has taste in it (for
do you mind me, there must be a little taste for us) I beg you will let me
know.  But first enquire about this estate of Mr Boothby's.  I think the
River Dove washes his land, which would be a great inducement to me, for
I must have a river. . . . I am writing now in the greatest haste and with
the damdest pen you ever saw.

He added that they would be leaving for Yorkshire, Monday, and, as
postscript, " How does Lenney do? "  The fancy for getting something of his own, in the country, was growing upon him, and the time
for a decision was drawing near, but events beyond his control were
to direct him to a very happy choice, much nearer London than
Derbyshire, with which for a time his links were to be suddenly
severed.

Boadicea, with new music between the acts, was produced on
Saturday, December 1, and on Monday, Lord Burlington died at
Chiswick.  Garrick played Dumnorix on the night of his patron's
death, and for eight further performances.  A play that was undra-
matic was then withdrawn, and early in the new year of 1794, the
actor-manager's coach, well-loaded, was to be seen taking the road
west.  But after Hammersmith it did not halt at Chiswick.  It
swept on, through Brentford, past Twickenham, home of the late
Mr Pope, past Strawberry Hill, Mr Walpole's fantastic residence, to
Hampton on Thames.  He had taken a lease of Hampton House.
The owner was a Mr Lacey Primatt, whose last tenant had been Lady
Furnace.  The situation was very good; the house and gardens held
possibilities.  It was thirteen miles from Hyde Park Corner, a com-
fortable-looking family country house, near a village which was still
a village.  It faced south, and overlooked, from the Middlesex bank,
a particularly picturesque, glittering stretch of the Thames.  Eva-
Maria, sixty years later, told young Mr Rackett (who scribbled his
notes on the back of a play-bill) that she remembered her husband
hired the house, ready-furnished, gardens, drying-ground and stable-
yard all included, for sixty pounds per annum.  " Next year he
purchased the whole; for how much I do not know."

In July 1754 the name of the new owner of Mr Primatt's villa was still so unfamiliar to the authorities of Hampton that he appeared in the local rate book as " David Garraik ". This was just what he wanted.                                                                    13

### 3

One result of his buying a country house was most valuable to his biographers. He began to keep letters. He now had storage room,  14 and into the chariot bound for Hampton on Saturdays, together with Mrs Garrick's lap-dog, and his country clothes, and his new fishing gear, and London delicacies for the table, and gifts for the garden, and plays to be read, went a formidable package of written matter. The letters received by him were of varying size and quality, and some, which had been stuffed in a pocket for several days, were the worse for wear. He also kept copies of some of his replies. The Garrick collection of private correspondence gave at first sight a fallacious impression of orderliness. He often endorsed, with a pithy note, the cover of something perfectly ridiculous. But study of his replies revealed a dreadful chaos. He was always in a hurry, just stepping into his carriage, just back from the theatre. He knew he had the letter to which he referred safe, somewhere. . . . The Hampton villa came in good time for him. His circle of acquaintances, like his correspondence, was getting very large, and beyond his control, and must, given good luck, increase. Some old friends failed to realize this. Artists were notoriously touchy. Benjamin Wilson, to whom he had given sittings in a studio in Great Queen Street, for a fearsome picture of the tomb scene from Romeo and Juliet, said something which sent him to his desk in one of his hurries.

My dear Hogarth,
      Our friend Wilson hinted to me the last time I saw him, that I had been remiss in my visits to you—it may be so, though upon my word I am not conscious of it; for such ceremonies I look upon as mere counters, where there is no remission of regard and good wishes. As Wilson is not an accurate observer of things, not even of those which concern him most, I must imagine that the hint came from you, and therefore, I shall say a word or two to you upon it.
      Montaigne, who was a good judge of human nature, takes notice that when friends grow exact and ceremonious, it is a certain sign of coolness, for that the spirit of friendship keeps no account of trifles. We are, I hope, a strong exception to this rule. Poor Draper, whom I loved better than any man breathing, once asked me smiling—" How long is it, think you, since you were at my house? " " How long? Why, a month or six weeks." " A year and five days," replied he; " but don't imagine that I have kept an account; my wife told me so this morning, and bid me *scold you for it*." If Mrs Hogarth has observed my neglect, I am flattered by it;

but if it is your observation, woe betide you! Could I follow my own wishes, I would see you every day in the week, and not care whether it was in Leicester Fields or Southampton Street; but what with an indifferent state of health, and the care of a large family, in which there are many froward children, I have scarce half an hour to myself. However, since you are grown a polite devil, and have a mind to play at lords and ladies, have at you.

I will certainly call upon you soon, and if you should not be at home, I will leave my card.

Dear Hogarth
Your's most sincerely
D. Garrick

15

His family at Drury Lane was indeed being rather froward just at a moment when he needed peace. Bellamy was the chief offender. He had sent Clutterbuck down to see her at a country retreat at Twickenham, "a little box" called Ragman's Castle where she was now living with a wealthy politician, Calcraft, whom she did not like much. The offer which Clutterbuck had been empowered to make for the season of 1754–1755 had been handsome—an increased salary, and the parts of Juliet, Desdemona and Calista. But Bellamy had conceived herself much too valuable to accept the leavings of Mrs Cibber, and said that she deemed her present engagement void by the manager's introducing a new leading lady. She had considerable skill and experience now, and amongst the considerations which Garrick could not mention was that she was *petite*. Against the advice of all her friends, she refused to continue at the Lane. In one of the few lucid intervals in her memoirs, she admits that in leaving Garrick's company she made the mistake of her life. Continuing to play with him would have improved her, and she had failed to realize that Mrs Cibber's frequent illnesses were not feigned. She went over to Rich, to play with Barry, and was elated when she heard the manager proclaim, "I have the Juliet now as well as the Romeo." But she was snubbed by the old man when she congratulated him on their full houses. Rich attributed these to the new procession which he had introduced into the production. Bellamy appeared on the stage with Garrick only twice more, in a career which ended sadly. Until he got Mrs Abington, whom he liked even less, he never quite replaced her.

He kept up receipts at the Lane, on the year of his buying Hampton, by playing often in his most popular parts. He was Richard, Macbeth, Benedick, Romeo, Lear and Fribble. He played ninety-three times. His new parts were only two, and both classical— Virginius in *Virginia*, and Aletes in *Crëusa, Queen of Athens*. *Virginia* was a forced card. A lady who had begged to see him for one moment of business was announced to him one morning at Southampton Street: the Countess of Coventry. She had been one of the beautiful Gunning sisters—the silly one. She was sitting in her chariot, outside his doors, and when the manager appeared she pressed into his hands, with a famous smile, "A play which the best judges tell me will do honour to you and the author." It was *17* *Virginia* by the Reverend Samuel Crisp, and he had seen it years ago. It had indeed been praised by Mr Pitt, but it was not, in Garrick's opinion, likely to be a success on the stage. However, a lady who must be obeyed " as if she had been a tenth muse ", had bestowed it upon him, with the words, " There, Mr Garrick! " He steeled himself to play a Roman sire, who plunged a dagger in the breast of his daughter (Mrs Cibber) sooner than see her delivered to slavery and worse by the tyrant Decemvir Appius (Mossop). He was able to bring on, in the smaller part of Marcia, a new actress, Mary Ann Graham, whom he feared was a majestic but wooden creature. Two years later she married his old friend, Richard Yates, comedian, who was old enough to be her father, and instructed by him quite surpassed her mentor, and became a valuable, reliable and really remarkable actress, a pillar of Drury Lane. At her best she could make Garrick shed a tear. But charm was beneath her.

*Virginia* added one anecdote of Garrick to theatrical history. While the hireling Claudius (Tom Davies) was claiming Virginia before the tribunal, as a slave born in his house, Garrick stood on the opposite side of the stage, with his arms folded across his breast, his eyes riveted to the ground, mute and lifeless as a statue. On being told to defend his daughter's cause, he continued in the same attitude, but raised his head to glare in speechless agony at the audience. When he slowly turned his dreadful gaze on the iniquitous Claudius, and spoke the simple words " Thou Traitor! " the effect was awful. " He uttered in a low tone of voice that spoke the fulness of a broken heart." After a pause, during which they seemed to have been struck by lightning, the audience broke into " a thunder of applause such as had never been equalled in the theatre ". *18*

*Crëusa* was another tragedy by William Whitehead, and surpassed *Boadicea* in poisoned goblets and mortal wounds; but it was well written and gave a great chance for Mrs Pritchard, and for Garrick, in a new line. His paternal scenes with his infant son (Miss Macklin) touched all hearts. Horace Walpole thought *Crëusa* worthy of the highest praise, while *Boadicea* and *Virginia* had merely been carried by the good acting, especially of Garrick, the dresses and the music. *Crëusa* was put on the list for further performances.

A great statesman had died and Garrick published an *Ode on the*

*Death of Mr Pelham.* He had very happy memories of a Chancellor of the Exchequer who had once obliged him very much in an application for a miscellaneous writer who, as well as producing unproduceable plays, had used his pen against the government. " As Mr Ralph is your friend, Mr Garrick, I shall with pleasure, and to oblige you, grant him a pension." The sequel was depressing. Four years later, Ralph, who was still having his plays refused, attacked his benefactor savagely in a pamphlet *Case of Authors by Profession.* Garrick thereafter shunned him, and when asked by Lord Camden to dine on an occasion when Ralph was expected, begged to be excused from sitting in company with " the most ungrateful man in the kingdom ".

The season closed on the last day of May, and this year Garrick was not bound for Londesborough, which had become an annual penance, or for Chatsworth, which had always softened the blow. Lady Hartington had succeeded on the death of her father to the Barony of Clifford, with Bolton Abbey and Londesborough, and to Lismore Castle and large estates in Ireland. Lord Hartington had been appointed Lord High Treasurer of Ireland, and Governor of County Cork.

### 4

Garrick had two principal occupations during his summer holiday of 1754: the alteration of Hampton House and the alteration of Shakespeare. Upon Shakespeare he had already made a start. *Catherine and Petruchio* had been produced in March, " altered from William Shakespeare's *The Taming of the Shrew* by David Garrick ". He had removed all scenes except those directly concerned with Catherine and Petruchio. Bianca was already married when the curtain rose, and played a very small and unamiable part. He had an ideal Shrew in Kitty Clive, and Harry Woodward, supported by Ned Shuter as Grumio, was a dashing Petruchio. Members of the audience familiar with green-room gossip found the casting delightfully piquant: Clive and Woodward were known to lead a cat-and-dog life as members of the Drury Lane Company. When Petruchio whacked this Catherine he did it with a good will. The action went at a smart pace, and the success of this experiment had encouraged Garrick to plan others. His immediate prey was *A Midsummer Night's Dream. The Winter's Tale* and *The Tempest* were to follow. All were to be light operas. He categorically denied that he had himself performed the business of turning *A Midsummer Night's Dream* into *The Fairies.* The music was composed by a Mr Smith, pupil of Handel. Whoever produced the " book " deserved small praise. Shakespeare's clownish artisans were completely removed from view.  With them went all the salt of the play; and as, of course, it was necessary for Titania to fall in love with something ridiculous, their existence had to be mentioned in four huddled lines:

> My mistress with a patch'd fool is in love.
> Near to her close and consecrated bower,
> This clown, with others, had rehears'd a play
> Intended for great Theseus' nuptial day.

But if the innovator had annihilated Bottom, and the best scene in the comedy, he had been generous with songs.  The play had three. He needed twenty-eight.  He plundered the works of Sir Edmund Waller and John Dryden.  He haled in " Where the bee sucks " from *The Tempest*, " Orpheus with his lute " from *Henry VIII*, " Sigh no more ladies " from *Much Ado*, and a very pretty piece from *L'Allegro* by John Milton.  Lysander and Hermia were performed by two Italian singers, Signor Guadagni and Signora Passerini, and all the supernaturals by juveniles.  Garrick in his prologue was arch:

> I dare not say WHO wrote it—I could tell ye,
> To soften matters—Signor Shakespearelli.

*The Fairies* drew full houses and, as yet, very little unfavourable comment;  but nine years later, while Garrick was on the continent, *A Midsummer Night's Dream* renamed *A Fairy Tale*, adapted by George Colman, was produced at Drury Lane.  All the clowns had come back.

With *The Winter's Tale*, which he intended to produce early in 1756, he knew he had been ruthless.  *Florizel and Perdita* dealt with the young lovers only.  It began at Act IV of the original play.  He tried to forestall criticism in his prologue.

> The five long acts from which our three are taken,
> Stretch'd out to sixteen years, lay by, forsaken,
> Lest, then, this precious liquor run to waste,
> 'Tis now confin'd and bottled for your taste,
> 'Tis my chief wish, my joy, my only plan,
> To lose no drop of that immortal man.

He was himself playing Leontes, a part which would have given him great scope in the jealousy scenes.  But these were exactly the scenes which he had cut out.  He never seems to have regretted his dreadful deed.  *Florizel and Perdita* was a success.

*The Tempest*, which came next on his list, was known to London audiences in two versions, those of Dryden and Davenant.  He had already produced it at Drury Lane in his first years as manager.  He denied having lent his pen to turn it into " a new English opera " and two years later offered it at last " as written by Shakespeare ".  He never appeared in any version of it himself. Prospero was never amongst his parts.

He had to alter another old favourite before the 1754–1755 season opened. George II had expressed a desire to see *The Chances*, a Beaumont and Fletcher comedy, rearranged to suit Restoration taste by the Duke of Buckingham. Garrick's task consisted mainly in rearranging the duke's version to suit a royal command performance at a theatre where the manager was famed for his propriety. He had difficulty over his casting. The piece contained two ladies both called Constantia who had to be mistaken for one another. Miss Macklin could be the first (and less important), but she was only half the size of Mrs Pritchard. To his dismay, Mrs Cibber, who, as far as size went, could pass as the double of Miss Macklin, claimed the part. She appeared to have become obsessed with an unfortunate desire to shine in light comedy. After a few performances she wisely retired in favour of a younger actress. Garrick, as a gay and carefree Don John, carried the production to success on his own shoulders. But he had needed Bellamy.

He had every reason to congratulate himself, both as actor and manager in the year that followed his purchase of a country villa. As an actor he seemed to have found the recipe, and had only to exercise his growing skill on suitable new parts. He had been Don Carlos (in Vanbrugh's *Mistake*) and Achmet in *Barbarossa*, this season. (*Barbarossa* was another classical tragedy, written by a somewhat unbalanced young clergyman, called Brown, and, surprisingly, had been so well received as to be put on the permanent list.) As a manager, whose business was flourishing, he had only one outstanding anxiety in the spring of 1755. It looked as if Britain was going to war with France again. He met the situation with *Britannia*, a masque by David Mallet, and wrote a prologue, in which he himself appeared as a British tar, " fuddled, and talking to himself ". Garrick, as a drunken (but of course very patriotic) sailor, was so much liked that the prologue was often called for even when the masque was not being played. He took the precaution of being dressed for the part, so that if the roar from the front became intolerable, he could lurch, as if absentmindedly, on to the apron stage. Britain's first actor thought himself so secure in public favour that he ventured to give advice to his audience. When rambling off the stage, he stopped, as if he had forgotten something.

> I wish you landmen, ho! would leave your tricks,
> Your factions, parties, and dam'd politics,
> And like us honest tars, drink, fight, and sing,
> True to yourselves, your country, and your king.

He was so popular.   It seemed that he could not guess wrong.
It seemed that he could divine what London was thinking.

His great friend George Lyttelton, who had refused to join Pitt in
opposing the Duke of Newcastle's administration, wrote to ask if he
did not intend going into Parliament.   He replied in verse that if he
ever quitted Drury Lane, it would not be to play the fool on any
other stage.

## CHAPTER VII

# DANGER

## 1755-1756

### I

At a difficult moment in the winter of 1754, when a theatrical manager must be at his busiest, Mr John Cleland, novelist, asked Mr Garrick to be kind to a young French visitor to London, author of a comedy, an Anglo-maniac, and an adorer of Shakespeare. M. Claude Pierre Patu, a little French banker with a weak chest, had most unwisely chosen November for his first trip to a country he so much admired. His admiration extended to having learned enough English to write a letter in that tongue, though when he discovered that Mr Garrick understood him in French he gladly relapsed; for his letters were very long. Cleland, who had social sense, enclosed to Garrick an English letter from M. Patu which showed he was appreciative.

> I long to wait on Mr. Garrick, and return him *viva voce* my sincere thanks for his *truly French* politeness. My being civil or uncivil towards him is entirely in your power, since you may, at your pleasure hasten or delay the time of your leading me to his house. If you get any occasion of seeing him before, I shall be obliged to you to assure him that I am not a stranger to his talents. . . .

Cleland had not exaggerated. Patu was a charming character. It was only a little disappointing that he proved not to know M. Jean-Georges Noverre. Garrick had been in correspondence with that person since September and wanted an independent opinion upon him. He was Jean Monnet's *maître de ballet* at the Opéra Comique, and Garrick was thinking of inviting him to London. Monnet, to be sure, Garrick knew well, but Monnet could hardly be asked to recommend for London employment a member of his company who had just scored a resounding success. If he came to business, Garrick meant to employ as intermediary his own Paris banker, Charles Selwyn. Monnet had a flair for discovering talent, and Noverre's ballet *Les Fêtes Chinoises* produced in Paris on July 1, 1754, had received wonderful notices in the press of that capital. Drowsing in the country peace of Hampton, while the Thames flowed peacefully by, in the dead season, Garrick considered something which might make Covent Garden green with envy. *Le*

*Nouveau Calendrier des spectacles de Paris, 1755,* gave a very full description.

> The scene represents at first an avenue ending in terraces, and in a flight of steps, leading to a palace situated on a height. This first set changes, and shows a public square, decorated for a festival. At the back is an amphitheatre on which sixteen Chinamen are seated. By a quick change of scene, thirty-two Chinamen appear instead of sixteen, and go through a pantomimic performance on the steps. As they descend, sixteen other Chinamen, mandarins and slaves, come out of their houses and take their places on the steps. All these persons form eight ranks of dancers, who, by bending up and down in succession, give a fair imitation of the waves of a stormy sea. When all the Chinese have come down, they begin a characteristic march. In this is to be seen a mandarin, carried in a rich palanquin by six white slaves, while two negroes drag a car in which a young Chinese woman is seated. They are both preceded and followed by a crowd of Chinamen who play divers instruments of music in use in their country. . . .

After this procession came a ballet, ending in a round dance, at the end of which the scene reverted to that before the procession. The amphitheatre, however, had become a Chinese porcelain factory. Thirty-two Chinese vases arose upon the stage and eclipsed the original thirty-two Chinamen.

> M. Monnet has spared nothing that could possibly assist M. Noverre's rich imagination. The dresses were made from M. Boquet's designs.

In July, in his garden at Hampton House, in September back in Southampton Street, Garrick had *The Chinese Festival* continually in his mind's eye. The taste for *chinoiserie* in decoration was growing. A ballet in which the artistes tried to represent something, instead of merely capering in becoming costumes against an appropriate background, was also new. He could hear the tinkling Oriental music, the running of the light bamboo cars across the stage. He saw the rich gleam of Chinese colours on vase and screen—sealing-wax scarlet, jade-green, turquoise, clear amber, ivory, royal-blue, rose, and of course much gold. He must have Noverre.

Patu returned to Paris, armed with an introduction, and reported cautiously. He was very much inclined to like Noverre; as yet he had not been able to judge of his talent. Madame Noverre was amiable, gentle, affable. . . . This was encouraging, for Noverre himself, as his negotiations with Garrick proceeded, seemed, for a person so artistic, rather exacting. He waved away an offer of two hundred pounds for the season, with a benefit. He wanted three hundred and fifty, and the benefit to take place immediately after those of the two chief members of Garrick's company. He wanted Garrick himself to appear on the occasion, and in a capital part. Charles Selwyn (whom Noverre always called " M. Silvain ") thought that Garrick had better close with this.

> Nobody could be so fit to manage it as he is, if you could confide in his discretion, which I should, to judge from his countenance and manner of expressing himself. It seems he is of Lausanne, and a Protestant, and not much attached to this country; so that it would be possible to fix him with you, if you liked him, and could make it worth his while.

The contract signed on the last day of January 1755 gave Noverre the terms he asked and Garrick the option of continuing his engagement for two or three years. Noverre had in his first letter mentioned *en passant* that he had a sister, a pretty dancer, for whom he would desire a hundred guineas for a season, and she was engaged for solo performances and *pas de deux*. He promised to be in London, with his dancers, by October 15; but Garrick wanted to see him as soon as possible, and empowered Selwyn to offer him twenty louis for travelling expenses. Noverre said that the pleasure of making the acquaintance of M. Garrick caused him to shut his eyes to the sacrifice he would be making by failing to earn in the provinces during the weeks between the two great fairs in Paris. He could leave on April 1, but feared he could not achieve his journey on twenty louis. When Garrick agreed to engage also de Laître, a pantomime *danseur* who had always given much pleasure in Paris, Noverre announced that despite heavy pressure of work he would leave Paris on Sunday morning, March 23. Garrick had wanted him to come during Holy Week, when Drury Lane would be closed. They could then prance about the theatre together, undisturbed by the prospect of an evening performance. They could repair to Hampton for discussions. When the theatre had been closed for three days M. Noverre arrived.

He was a muscular little French-speaking Swiss, with pink cheeks, black eyes and a nose with a hook in it, which would with years become pronounced. He was twenty-eight, and his father, who had been an adjutant in the army of the King of Sweden, had intended him for the military profession, and had given him a liberal education. But his love of art had proved invincible. Lacy had disliked him before he saw him, but he seemed thoroughly to know his business, and when he talked of his garlands and cradles of artificial flowers, the Chinese musical instruments and the costumes of taffetas, gauze and chenille—for which he had brought designs by M. Boucher—his enthusiasm was inspiring. He had plenty of assurance, and before he left (in a hurry as he had come) he had witnessed Garrick as Sir John Brute, and Archer. (" *Garrick, comme acteur, est étonnant.*") From the first it seemed clear that as artists the couple must admire one another, but that they were unlikely to become friends. For, back in Paris, Noverre became very business-like. M. Boquet, decorator and designer of costumes, who was at the head of all fêtes at the court of France, sent an alternative proposition for his services, which was enclosed. Noverre had already engaged three good dancers who would not dishonour their nation, and was looking for three more, but not at the salaries suggested. A child dancer would be needed for the part of l'Amour. He had found one. Should he engage it? Twelve more children would really be needed. M. Monnet, by negligence, had lost his *première ballerina*. There would be no question of taking her from the Opéra. She had already left. There had been an irreparable row. He would need a *corps de ballet* of a hundred. Finally, he must bring his wife, " without whom I cannot live at London ". " I have had much vexation since my return. I have lost two rings, worth sixty louis, which my wife put on my watch-chain without fastening the clasp; and I lost them when I went to see M. Silvain. . . ."

Garrick sent an advance, and resigned himself to the fact that a large family party were clambering on the waggon for Drury Lane— a brother, Augustin, was presently added—and Noverre's next letter was rapturous. He was extremely sensible of the marks of esteem sent in the manager's charming reply. " In fine you are a divine man, and all the artists and *savants* of this country would be glad to have the happiness of knowing you."

But by now there were clouds creeping up in the heaven of the divine man. " This country," with which Noverre evidently identified himself, was France, and war with France was threatening. Lacy, who had always thought that *The Chinese Festival* would be very expensive, looked gloomy. Garrick took the precaution of publishing a press announcement that M. Noverre was a Swiss Protestant and his wife a German, and that the company he was bringing would contain Italians, Swiss, Germans and very few French. It was quite untrue that the grand entertainment proposed, on which no expense had been spared, was to be produced by means of the importation of French dancers, costumiers and even carpenters. All the scenery and dresses, which were very rich, were being made in London.

Meanwhile letters from Patu, who had been making inquiries amongst his stage acquaintances, were disconcerting. He added a postscript in English to one. " I hope, my dear friend, that your friendship and good sense kept you from showing my last letter to M. Noverre, as I am not to forget this gentleman's politeness. The severe, though unfeigned description of his temper is a thing I would by no means have him acquainted with." Noverre, who was temperamental, was lavish in his praise when things went well, but much feared by his employees. There was an anecdote that once, on a first night, he had espied another person whom he concluded to be a carpenter, also watching from the wings, but visible to the audience. He had rushed on the intruder and given him such a kick that he had landed flat on the centre of the stage. Unfortunately, the person had been the Manager of the Opéra.

The caravan from Paris arrived in London on a night when Garrick was playing Richard. *The Chinese Festival* was announced for a fortnight later—Saturday, November 8—and it would be a command performance. The king was coming. Three members of the profession left records of that first night and the five performances which followed—Arthur Murphy, who was in the green-room on the 8th, young Tate Wilkinson, who was in the audience on the 18th, and a French sufferer who gave his very full account to his native press and was evidently one of *corps de ballet*, perhaps Noverre himself.

The programme looked reassuring. " By His Majesty's Command, Theatre Royal, in Drury Lane." An established light comedy, *The Fair Quaker of Deal*, was the first piece on the bill. " To which will be added a New Grand Entertainment of Dancing, composed by Mr. Noverre." In a cast of sixty principals only fifteen were undeniably foreign, and all the Noverre family had been anglicized and appeared as " Mr.", " Mr. junior," " Mrs." and " Miss ". The house was packed, and His Majesty was greeted " with much joy but little respect ", thought the French reporter. No sooner had the curtain fallen on the comedy than signs of unrest in the audience became noticeable. When the charming music heralding the ballet began to be played, nobody could hear it. " The dancers began to go through their motions, but all was noise, tumult and commotion." The king appeared surprised by the uproar but smiled cheerfully. Murphy believed that His Majesty had been told that the audience was noisy because it hated the French. The French commentator believed that the king had retired delighted with the ballet, but dissatisfied with his subjects' want of respect for his royal person. There was instant applause from the boxes and more expensive parts of the house when the first scene was displayed, and such encouragement continued doggedly, but with it were mingled rude whistling, and shouts from the third balcony " No French dancers ", rivalled by suggestions that the interruptors should be thrown into the pit. On Wednesday, November 12, the people determined not to let the show proceed seemed rather more numerous. The French journalist was told that these were failed

N

actors and authors, the scum of the profession, and people hired by the managers of other theatres. The hissing was worse. A man was thrown from the gallery into the pit, and several gentlemen drew their swords upon the malcontents. A number of innocent spectators fell victims to " the nobles " who had lost patience, and struck out at all without distinction. The auditorium presented an alarming scene of broken arms and heads, some very bloody. On the stage, the dancers cowered to a halt. The music ceased. Presently the warlike gentlemen returned, having driven the rioters out of the premises, would-be spectators raised their hats and cried " Huzzah ", and the ballet began again to a sound of loud clapping.

On the following evening it really began to look as if Garrick had won. He had ordered *The Provok'd Wife* to be given as the comedy, and himself appeared as Sir John Brute. At an early stage in the ballet, a man who began to be disagreeable was flung down three flights of stairs and had to be removed, insensible. Nobody else made any disturbance that night. The manager did not appear on the Friday, and the audience was very inferior in quality. All the " milords " were absent attending the opening of Parliament. The ballet was hooted from start to finish and not a note of the music could be heard. Saturday night was startling. Garrick had advertised *Much Ado*, with himself as Benedick. The French observer had heard that the rough people who were behaving so badly were known as " blackguards ". On Saturday, " *les blagards* " were victorious. They tore up seats in the pit, broke the mirrors and chandeliers of the auditorium and tried to get on to the stage " to kill all the troupe ". But Messrs. Garrick and Lacy were not taken unprepared. Within three minutes, so admirable was their organization, all scenery had disappeared, all the traps were open and in the wings waited an army of bravos armed with cudgels, swords and pikes. A great tank, behind the stage, was ready to be set running to fill the cellars into which intruders might fall through the traps. But the rioting went on until midnight, and was only quietened by an appearance of Lacy to promise that the French ballet should not again be shown. He had wanted to make this announcement after the first performance.

" *Les blagards* " spent Sunday in peace, but they were all there again when the curtain rose on Monday night, and so were the " milords ". Above elegant provocative cries for " *Les Fêtes Chinoises* ", and deep growls of " No French dance ", calls for the manager gained prominence. Garrick came in front and made rather a poor impression. The ballet had not been advertised for tonight, but he was loath to disappoint his patrons. The fatal tinkling music began, and with it came a frightening incident. One of the milords seized a ring-leader of the rioters, held him up in the air and seemed to be about to strangle him. Garrick intervened, and the man was released. The aristocrats demanded that the matter be put to the vote, and as they threatened to fall upon all who were not of their opinion, they carried the day. Garrick promised that the French dancers should perform again tomorrow.

Tuesday, November 18, 1755, made history in Drury Lane Theatre. By three in the afternoon it was impossible to get into the house. To pass three hours of waiting, the audience whistled, sang songs and called for the orchestra to play national airs, particularly " The Roast Beef of Old England ". At six o'clock, with the rise of the curtain, a milord leapt from a box upon the stage and began to make a speech evidently intended to be important, which was quite ruined by a rotten apple, deftly thrown, exploding upon his countenance. This was the signal for pandemonium. Broken arms, legs and heads surpassed those of last Wednesday. People who did not want to sustain such injuries got badly crushed under their seats. On the stage, the poor artistes, in their Chinese habits, tried to hide behind the scenes. A torrent of dried peas and tin-tacks rained upon the boards. In the boxes, ladies of spirit helped their cavaliers by pointing out trouble-makers in the pit. A contingent of " blagards " from the gallery won the pit back. They were driven out, but the story quickly spread that they had gone off to Mr Garrick's home to break his windows. A large number of rascals from Whitechapel who had been hanging about outside had joined them. They were going to burn down Garrick's house and murder him. All the leading French dancers were enemy officers in disguise. [2]

2

Surveying the bright and the dark side of the picture after the last performance of *The Chinese Festival*, Garrick was realistic. The mob had not burnt down his house, or his theatre. He was sitting next morning in a house without a single pane of glass in its windows, and he had been obliged to ask for troops to save it; but Drury Lane company would play again tonight. Carpenters had been at work throughout the small hours. He had lost most of the scenery and properties of his beautiful ballet. He reckoned he had lost, in hard cash, about four thousand pounds. He had lost far more in prestige; but nobody yet had dared to point out that he was himself of French origin, or that Madam Garrick was a foreigner and a Catholic. He had got to find fresh lodgings for about a hundred nervous foreigners. Augustin Noverre, in the *mêlée*, had run through a man who had been carried off, said to be dead. But the " *blagard* " had not been killed, and seemed likely to survive.

*Merope* was followed by *Oroonoko*, another piece in which the manager never played nowadays. He ordered *The Beaux' Stratagem* for the following night, and the bills to announce " Mr Garrick as Archer ". On Tuesday, November 21, he passed majestically from a house which had all new glass in its windows, towards Drury Lane, perhaps for the last time. A very large audience awaited him. Archer had to speak the first words of the gay comedy in which Garrick had so often delighted London. He was discovered, when the curtain rose. But the expected words were not heard. He was not about his usual brisk business. He was utterly and awfully silent and motionless. A murmur came from the house. It sounded like " Pardon! " " Pardon! " But he was not going to ask pardon from anyone. He came on to the apron, and regarding his patrons with a countenance representing immeasurable grief, began to speak. He had been injured, by the wanton and malignant conduct of some wicked men, injured in his property, in his fame—in his character. He wished to acknowledge that he had long received many favours. He had also a decision to announce. He was above want, and superior to insult. Unless he was, this night, allowed to perform his duty as an actor to the best of his ability, this would be his last performance. He would never, he repeated never, appear on the stage again.

While he was speaking, there was a calm as if after a storm. When he had finished, his rebuked audience " burst into such an universal according applause as for several minutes shook the fabric of Old Drury ". He bowed gravely, retreated and began to play Archer very cheerfully. He had won. He played Ranger three nights later, and Osmyn the next night. Hamlet, Richard and Lear followed. Barry was back from Ireland, and appearing at Covent Garden.

> The town has found out different ways
> To praise the different Lears.
> To Barry they give loud huzzas,
> To Garrick—only tears.
> A King, nay, every inch a king,
> Such Barry doth appear,
> But Garrick's quite a different thing,
> He's every inch King Lear.

It was hard work, especially when a man was feeling very ill; but it was necessary. For he had seen the red light of danger, and he would never, never forget that.

Early in the New Year of 1756 it seemed that he had got Drury Lane back on to an even keel.

3

The tidying up after his expensive failure was tedious and sad. Patu, having seen accounts in the French press, and friends from London, wrote in agony. He was a singularly naïve person. This was part of his attraction. ("Please send me your sentiments on the Dictionary of Mr Johnson and the poem of *Night Thoughts* by Mr Young." "Give me some news of your stage, your warm interesting stage, the remembrance of which still strikes to my very heart.") His last letter to Garrick ended with the words of the Ghost in Hamlet, "Adieu! *Remember me!*" He had gone to Italy, for his cough. He feared that in view of London's fogs and England's war with his country, he would never again see his very-dear Garrick. He was right, and Garrick in 1757 tied up and endorsed a sad little bundle, "Letters of that poor Patu."

Parting with the Noverre family was not nearly so easy; indeed Garrick never really lost "Mr Noverre, junior"—Augustin. Incredible though it might seem, his experience of England during the black fortnight of *The Chinese Festival* had convinced this young man that here was a most desirable country in which to settle. He did so, was long attached to the ballet at Drury Lane, and ended his days as a valued member of cathedral city society—Mr Noverre, the first dancing-master in Norwich. Madame Noverre's amiability wore thin, after her return to France, and she sent Garrick a very angry incoherent letter complaining of his treatment of her husband. Garrick kept an English draft of a reply, which began by pointing out that her letter was undated and bore no address, and ended by explaining that although in England the ladies were as much honoured as in France, business matters, such as she attempted, were always transacted with the husband. "The act and deed of the wife, in such cases, pass for nothing." He had, in fact, behaved towards the Noverres with great liberality. He gave Noverre leave to retire to Paris "to wind up his affairs", and fifty guineas in lieu of his benefit. Presently, Noverre volunteered to return to London for the next season, which opened on September 15. Garrick, supported by Brother George and Lacy, strongly advised him not to do so. He did not appear until December 1, whereupon Lacy ruled that he had forfeited part of his agreed salary. He then departed for ever in wrath. Garrick gave him a benefit, though he was not in the country. Unfortunately the weather was very cold and Mrs Cibber failed through illness. The result was meagre. Jean-Georges Noverre passed from the life of David Garrick to become " caressed at the first courts of Europe " (at Milan he was created Chevalier), and to descend to history as the first name in modern choreographic art. In his latter years he spoke disparagingly of *Les Fêtes Chinoises*, earliest exercise of his budding talent. But to the last he stuck to it that the performances of " Mr Garrick the celebrated English actor " had convinced him of the possibility of dancers, by means of gesture and movement, telling a story. After watching the facial expression of Garrick he had abolished masks for his troupe. Garrick, for his part, had styled the inventor of a new ballet form " The Shakespeare of the Dance ".

An inevitable result of Garrick's late failure was a dribble of worthless pamphlets. (*The Dancers Damned, or the Devil got Loose at Drury Lane.*) Such things he could disregard, but it was vexing when enemies thought the moment suitable to attack him for his treatment of Shakespeare. Theophilus Cibber, whose own father had been an arch-offender, delivered a lecture at the Haymarket ridiculing Garrick's alterations. " Were Shakespeare's ghost to rise, would he not frown indignation on this pilfering pedlar in poetry, who thus shamefully mangles, mutilates and emasculates his plays? *A Midsummer Night's Dream* has been minc'd and fricasseed into a thing called *The Fairies*, *The Winter's Tale* mamoc'd into a droll, and *The Tempest* castrated into an opera." However, people were going to see these productions, and Dr William Warburton, a voluminous correspondent, and an editor of Shakespeare who was violent against other editors of Shakespeare, did not at all disapprove of Garrick's efforts. " Besides your giving an elegant form to a monstrous composition, you have, in your own additions, written up to the best scenes in the play, so that you will imagine I read the reformed *Winter's Tale* with great pleasure."

A steady flow of gentle letters came from Lord Hartington, who had now become Lord Lieutenant of Ireland; but the poor man was broken-hearted. Lady Hartington had died suddenly, " of a small-pox ". She had been but twenty-three, and they had been ideally matched. He wrote that his loss was never to be repaired or forgotten, and he was to keep his word. He said that when Garrick had first known him, he had been a happier man than he should ever be again. He hoped that Mrs Garrick's " Biddy " had liked her husband, " Sweet-lips ", also a Burlington House dog. Biddy, promoted " Mrs Biddy ", was very small, a fashionable miniature black-and-white King Charles spaniel. Her first labour was long, and provoked David to a poem. As he watched the poor little animal suffer, he realized what a part of the family she had become. If her

master were ever sullen, and her mistress snappish (a rare thing),
Biddy had always been the peace-maker.

> Goddess Hygeia, hear our prayer,
> Descend, our little Bid to save!
> Comfort her with a loving pair.
> Biddy's the only child we have.

Biddy was repeatedly successful as a mother, and one of her sons,
Phill, became Garrick's personal attendant.

The Duke of Devonshire died, and Lord Hartington succeeded to
the title. His cares were already many. The problem of his mother-
in-law, Lady Burlington, was a continual worry to him. She had
always been overbearing. Without husband or daughter to control
her, she had become impossible. She seemed to have fallen under
the influence of a designing member of her staff, of a most undesirable
character, who was making hay while the sun shone. Mrs Garrick
did not care, any longer, to visit Burlington House or Chiswick, and
Garrick had trodden out of one of these lordly pleasure houses, wiping
its dust from his feet for ever. The duke, who regretted what he
mildly called " the coolness ", tried to play peace-maker. " I had a
letter from Lady Burlington, with an account of the affair you mention, and that she was afraid you were gone away for the last time."
He had pleaded that Garrick was warm-tempered, but had her in-
terests more at heart than anyone. " That you were indeed an
impetuous man, but a very honest one, and that I hoped it was made
up and that you were friends again. Indeed I do, most sincerely, for
if you and Mrs Garrick have not some influence, and she is left
entirely in the hands of that woman, to be guided by her, I am sure
some mischief will ensue."

Lady Burlington died in 1758, and the two houses which Garrick
had known so well in the days of his courtship, stood silent. Chiswick now belonged to a child aged ten, and Garrick was to enter it no
more until that young man married, after which he came to know it
very well again. The duke, when on leave from Ireland, always
reported himself at Southampton Street or Hampton, and they were
3 going to visit him at Chatsworth when he retired.

The spring of 1756 was cold and late, after a hard winter.
" Tempests, storms, hurricanes, thunder, lightning, and other terri-
fying phenomena have never been so frequent throughout the
kingdom." Garrick was over-worked, but acting, and writing. He
wrote a topical trifle, *The Modern Fine Gentleman*, for Woodward.
He had introduced a new character for himself into *Lethe*, Lord
Chalkstone, a shocking old man. The part was small; he played it

often.   One night, this spring, he did something which was unusual
for him.   He accepted an invitation to dine at a great house, before
playing.   He was persuaded to stay too long at table; but he got to
the theatre, just in time.   "When he came upon the stage, he
appeared all spirits, laughed as he attempted to act, but could not
articulate.   Many in the house did not perceive what was the matter;
for his friends endeavoured to stifle or cover this trespass with loud
applause."   Next morning, while dawn broke over theatre-land, he
recognized, for the second time in that season, the red light of danger.
" I am fully aware of all that happened.   I was absolutely tipsy."
He formed, then and there, a resolution.   He was never going to
dine again before he played.   He kept to this rule strictly to the end
of his career, and was able to tell a young friend, as an amusing
anecdote, many years later, that he had only once played " in
liquor ".                                                                             4

Brother George's family were constant guests at Hampton and
Southampton Street.   Mrs George had Carrington, named for her
stern sire, in the year after their wedding.   Arabella, named for
George's mother, came next.   The second boy, now rising two, was
David.   Nathaniel and Catherine were yet to come.   Merriel, Mrs
Docksey, had one child, also Merriel.   The David Garricks had now
been married seven years, with nothing to show for it, and they were
pronounced child-fanciers.   In the spring of 1756 both the Duke of
Devonshire and Dr Warburton sent condolences on Mrs Garrick's
illness.   Warburton, who was sixty, had just become father of a son   5
and heir, after eleven years of matrimony.   It may have been that
he felt his own success tactless in view of Mrs Garrick's disappointment, and was therefore curt in his acceptance of Garrick's congratulations.   But no other available source confirms this.   In any
case, the Garricks were both still in their thirties, quite young enough
for hope.

Garrick was planning something for children for next Christmas—
" Lilliput, with the entry of Captain Gulliver into Millendo.   New
music, habits, scenes and other decorations, By command of the
Prince of Wales ".   It was a one-act pantomime, extracted from
Swift's famous work, and to be performed entirely by children,
trained by the manager himself.   There were to be a hundred young
masters and misses chirruping at Drury Lane.   This venture brought
him one promising child.   Pope, the wigmaker to the theatre, supplied
a couple of his brood, Jane, aged fourteen, and a boy, even younger.
Three years later, Jane made her début as an adult.   She became a
principal soubrette, always stout and good-natured.

Meanwhile, Garrick was Athelstan, in a very patriotic, dull new

classical play of that name.  The failure of *Athelstan* could be written
off against a couple of unexpected successes.  Arthur Murphy was
not an attractive-looking young man.  He was fairly well-built,
but narrow-shouldered, with full light eyes, and a sensitive oval face,
marred by the small-pox.  He had already deserted banking and
journalism for the theatre.  Unfortunately, he wanted, as well as
being a member of Garrick's company, to have his literary efforts
produced at Drury Lane.  He excelled in the quarrel by correspondence, and lofty screeds from him poured in upon his manager, to be
patiently endorsed, together with a reasonable reply, " an answer of
6 mine to a wrangling letter ".  In the end, Murphy won.  *The
Apprentice*, a satire upon the ambitions of the uneducated to act,
was very good fun.  Woodward, as Dick, created a part which held
the stage for ten years.  *The Upholsterer*, a two-act farce, in which
Garrick played Pamphlet, was equally liked.  Murphy retired from
the stage, returned to journalism, began to read law and pressed
Garrick to produce his tragedy *The Orphan of China*.  He had very
little originality, and this was a barefaced adaptation of Voltaire's
play of the same name which had captured the fancy of Paris last
year.  It might have been thought that anything reminding him of
China would have been anathema to Garrick, but Murphy had no
tact.  (" P.S.  To save you the trouble of answering this, I will wait
upon you, behind the scenes, the first night you act.")  At one
moment, it almost seemed Garrick had got rid of him.  He had
offered his tragedy elsewhere.  But it was not accepted elsewhere,
though Mr Fox, Mr Walpole and the Poet Laureate thought highly of
it.  Murphy had brought pressure to bear from high circles—Holland
House.  He was proud of his paper-war.  He continued to nag, and
Garrick at the end of three years gave way about Murphy's tragedy
too, wrote a prologue for it, and appeared as Zamti, which had to be
added to his repertory.  For *The Orphan of China*, though it achieved
only the necessary nine nights, was not damned.  This was chiefly
attributed to the unexpected competence of Mrs Yates, who had
come in at short notice to replace Mrs Cibber.  Henceforward,
she was an established favourite.  On May 12, 1756, Garrick played
his last new part of the season for Woodward's benefit, Leon in *Rule
a Wife and Have a Wife*—" altered from John Fletcher ".  Five
days later His Majesty announced to both Houses of Parliament,
heavy but not unexpected news.  " The unwarrantable proceedings
of the French in the West Indies and North America " left Britain no
choice but to declare war on France.  This war, which was to last
seven years, was to be fought out on the Continent, and far beyond—
in the mouth of the Hooghli, on the heights of Abraham. . . .

Messrs Garrick and Rice of Lichfield and London had long been in a far from flourishing condition. Trade with France would now be at an end, and although light Lisbon wine, port and madeira would still be obtainable, French privateers would make wine shipping very difficult. On October 7 David wrote to Peter:

> Though I have been much fatigued all day, and have a new character to play to-night, yet I cannot forbear writing a little good news to you.
>
> His Grace of Devonshire was at our house in Southampton Street yesterday. I happened to be from home, but I went to him this morning by nine o'clock, and breakfasted *tête-a-tête* with him. He is made First Lord of the Treasury, much against his will, but intreated to it by His Majesty. He told me, among other things, of his intentions to serve you, and you may depend upon it that he will keep his word. I would, therefore, advise you to look into the state of your affairs, and cast about to dispose of them to the best advantage. I mean not hastily, but surely and considerately. . . . Estimate your property, and if an opportunity, a good one, offers to you, for the disposal of it, lay hold upon it. Should you want my advice, write as often as you please. Nothing will give me more pleasure than to contribute to your ease and independence, and to drag you out of that melancholy, disagreeable situation you are at present in. Indeed, it is unworthy of you, and I hope my noble friend will give you his finger to take you out of those cursed vaults.
>
> Excuse hurry; say nothing of this to the sisters, and let me hear soon from you.                                                                                          7

Nothing came of this well-meant suggestion. In imagination, David had so far sold up Peter's business, and moved him to London, that he had thought of a tenant for the family house at Lichfield, (" Mrs Richardson and the girls "). Peter stayed at Lichfield, and the duke did not long retain his new appointment, which carried with it the duties of Prime Minister. The majority of His Majesty's servants were demanding Pitt to lead Britain at war, and Pitt absolutely declined to serve under the Duke of Newcastle. In this dilemma, the Duke of Devonshire had been summoned from Ireland. He was young, of very high rank, immensely wealthy and of unexceptionable private character. To be sure, he had never displayed any outstanding political ability. At the end of six months, Pitt recognized the necessity of making up his differences with the Duke of Newcastle. The Duke of Devonshire was bowed out handsomely. He was made Lord Lieutenant of Derbyshire, a Knight of the Garter and Lord Chamberlain of the Household—which would mean reading many plays. He was thirty-two, and generally held to be rather a stick; a stiff, solitary man. As he had no lady of his family to assist him, he wrote to the Garricks when he wanted to order a court suit, which he only desired should be rather plain. " I do not much relish either trimming or embroidery."

James Clutterbuck thought that the opening of the Seven Years War was a propitious moment for an Englishman to invest in land. Garrick wrote to Warburton, who lived near Bath, to inquire about a property there, at Weston, on the Avon. There was an old, large manor-house, but in decay, and although on an eminence, with a disappointing prospect. There were excellent rides on the hill, hanging above—Lansdowne. But Clutterbuck had something better to suggest. William Herbert, fourth and last Marquis of Powis, had died in 1748, and after eight years his trustees had empowered Mr Langford, auctioneer, of the Piazza, Covent Garden, to dispose of his estates. Garrick, although suffering from a loss over *The Chinese Festival*, took Clutterbuck's advice, and followed his example. He apparently never regretted it, for nine years later, he reminded his " dear Clut " that he wanted a farm, to add to his Hendon property. He then bought from Clutterbuck further land which carried with it the lordship of the manor of Hendon, and the vicarial patronage of the village church of St Mary. When George Garrick's eldest son took holy orders, his uncle presented him to the living.

## CHAPTER VIII

# GARRICK'S VILLA

## 1757–1760

### I

ON a fine spring morning of 1758 a portentous-looking party set out from London to spend the day with Mr Garrick at his Thames-side villa. There were seven of them, packed in a single landau, so their golf-clubs, which they had been told to bring, protruded very visibly. As they passed through Kensington, the Coldstream regiment were changing guard, and on perceiving the clubs, the troops gave the travellers three cheers, " in honour of a diversion peculiar to Scotland ". The gentlemen, all of whom were Scottish, opened their purses and gave their countrymen " wherewithal to drink the Land o' Cakes ". This diversion made them a little late, and they encountered Mr Garrick " by the way " looking out for them eagerly. They were at once ferried across the river to Molesey Hurst course, on the Surrey side, where they found the golfing ground surprisingly good. Only three of the party, which had now swelled to nine, could play golf. Mr John Home, who was in charge of this contingent from London, had interpreted rather liberally Mr Garrick's invitation to bring his friends to a dinner. Everyone had jumped at a chance of seeing the great actor in his country retreat to which, they were told, an invitation to dine was something which was issued but seldom. Mr Home, who was fifty-seven, was a famous playwright, but not thanks to Garrick. He had offered his *Agis* eleven years ago, and it had been summarily rejected. He had offered his *Douglas* three years ago, with the same result. But *Douglas*, after a good reception in Edinburgh, had been the success of the season at Covent Garden. Arthur Murphy said that Garrick had not seen a part for himself in the play. The hero did not sound much like him.

> My name is Norval; on the Grampian hills
> My father feeds his flocks; a frugal swain,
> Whose constant cares were to increase his store.

Barry had been very touching as young Norval, and Mr Home had found himself appointed private secretary to Lord Bute, who had always been his patron, and tutor to the Prince of Wales. Garrick had then accepted *Agis* and produced it, with no expense spared, and the full strength of his company, in February of this year. He had

himself played the principal part, Lysander.  The plot was drawn
from the works of Plutarch, and it was, by general consent, not so
thrilling as *Douglas*.  But Lord Bute had taken the prince to see it
twice, and it could not be said to have failed.  " The boxes were
brilliant."  Also, Mr Home now had another tragedy on the stocks.
Of the friends whom he had brought with him only one was a contemporary.  Dr William Robertson, who had come south to see the
publishers about his *History of Scotland*, had been at school with him.
He had a remarkably large chin and was a great talker.  The brothers
Adam, " Bob " and James, were already well known to Garrick.
They were architects, like their father and two brothers.  Robert
had noticed that, in the prevailing vogue for copying classical
architecture, only public ancient buildings had been studied.  He
had recently returned from Spalato in Venetian Dalmatia, where he
had taken careful notes of something domestic—the ruins of the
Emperor Diocletian's palace.  He had been employed by Garrick to
1  provide Hampton House with a new front and an orangery.  The
Adams were very polite, neat-looking young men, not yet in their
thirties.  They did not say much.  The brothers Wedderburn were
even younger.  Alexander, the elder, had been called to the English
Bar last November, and was going to take lessons in elocution from
Sheridan and Quin, so that a Scottish accent should not be too noticeable in a future Lord Chancellor.  His brother David was in the
army, and a very much more gay, sociable person.  The Rector of
Hampton, the Rev. John Black, from Aberdeen, who had been an
army chaplain, had been called in by Garrick.  He could play golf,
as could Home, and the last member of the party, who wrote down
2  the whole story in his autobiography.  The Reverend Alexander
Carlyle had met Garrick before in town, and had been to see him act
in all his principal parts, both tragedy and comedy.  He was extremely curious to see what twelve years in England had done for
Mrs Garrick, whom he remembered perfectly, as a very seasick
Viennese *danseuse*, disguised as a Hanoverian baron.  She was the
only lady at the dinner which followed, and he saw at once that she
had not the faintest recollection of him.  Her figure, to be sure, was
not so ethereal as it had been in the days of her pirouetting, but she
was still very lively, and being a woman of uncommon good sense,
and now mistress of English, a most agreeable hostess.  The dinner
provided was " sumptuous ", and after it they adjourned to drink
wine in Shakespeare's Temple, out of compliment to Home, the
playwright.  The Temple was an octagonal building, with a Greek
Ionic portico, and within it were a statue of Shakespeare by
Roubillac, for which Mr Garrick had given three hundred and fifteen

pounds, and a lead tank, bearing the initials of David and Maria Garrick. There were also Shakespeare relics, which were, with years, to increase in number; for he never could resist anything said to have belonged to his idol—a leather glove of faded doe-colour, with pointed fingers and blackened metal embroidery about the cuff, a quite coarse salt cellar of Delft manufacture, painted in garish royal blue and yoke-of-egg yellow, a signet ring engraved with the magic initials W.S. . . . Experts agreed that they were of Elizabethan or Jacobean date. 3

Garrick's Hampton property possessed one disadvantage. It had a riverside frontage with a landing-stage, and a lawn of more than an acre, on which stood the Temple; but between this and the house ran the main road from Staines to Kingston, with a turnpike in the middle. The owner had suggested to " Capability " Brown, who was engaged on work at Hampton Court, that he should fling over the road an ornamental bridge similar to the one that he had constructed at Paine's Hill in Surrey. Brown had been all for a tunnel, of which at first Garrick had not liked the sound. Samuel Johnson had clinched the matter. " David! David! what can't be overdone may be underdone," and a tunnel had been dug. But it was no 4 ordinary tunnel; it was a Grotto Arch, having at the west end a bath-house, with three rooms, supplied by a spring of excellent water. The dazzling silver flood of the Thames, seen on a day of blue skies through the dripping black grotto arch, in which voices echoed weirdly, was highly dramatic, and emerging from it on to the Temple Lawn was like stepping into fairyland.

Gazing at the grotto arch as they waited for the servants to prepare their collation in the Temple, Carlyle offered to surprise his host by " a stroke at the golf ". He promised that from a mount opposite the arch, he would drive a ball through it and into the Thames. He had measured the distance with his eye, and accordingly made the ball alight in the mouth of the tunnel and run obediently down the sloping green lawn to fall plop in the water. It was just the incident needed to set the seal of success on a thoroughly enjoyable entertainment, and Garrick begged, as a memento, the club with which the feat had been performed.

He had told Carlyle that he was more at home in comedy than in tragedy, and Carlyle had agreed diffidently that, " I could conceive something more perfect in tragedy, but in comedy he completely filled up my ideas of perfection." Johnson once said that he considered Garrick's best part was the host. " Madam, I thought him less to be envied on the stage than at the head of a table." When 5 they drove away into the sunset, after a very happy day, Carlyle could not decide who had been the happiest, the landlord and hostess, or the guests.

Home was quite correct in believing that such occasions were a rarity. Rather a lot of people came to Garrick's Villa, but mostly country neighbours. Great folk from London had to be asked for the day, which was perfectly exhausting for all, and almost worse than the continual droppers-in at Southampton Street. Old friends, artists, came and stayed. Quin was a regular guest, and was given the keys of the cellar, which ran the whole length of the house. Johnson came, frequently unheralded, and after dark, roaring for his supper. His Dictionary had been published in March 1755 and recognized as a standard authority. He was shown over the Villa and expressed himself with characteristic gloom. " Ah, David! It is the leaving of such a place that makes a death-bed terrible."

A little beginner called Zoffany came furtively. It was said that Garrick had first detected his work in the studio of Benjamin Wilson in Great Queen Street, which had once been the studio of Sir Godfrey Kneller. Wilson, who had painted Garrick as Hamlet, and Romeo, gesticulating much, employed the young Bohemian as a drapery-painter. Enemies said that Zoffany painted much more than the draperies. Garrick received a letter, hardly to be called anonymous as it was signed " Timothy Lovetruth ", complaining of his luring away Wilson's employee.

> On coming to town this morning, I could not resist the temptation to inquire after my very worthy brother artist Zoffani. But alas! how unlucky! he had left his work, and was gone to breakfast loaded with pencils etc, in an invisible conveyance. As you will chance to see him before I shall, you will oblige me by desiring him to fulfill his engagements, and act, if he can, like an honest man.

Of course, it came from Wilson, who, like Hogarth, suffered from the green eye of jealousy. Garrick replied that " if your friend, Mr Wilson ", sent any more spies to report on Zoffany's visits to Hampton, he would have them thrown into the Thames.

Zoffany painted Garrick " in character ", which won him the approbation of Lord Bute, and an introduction to the royal family, and twice *con amore* in a conversation group, at Hampton, complete with guests, staff and dogs. Later, he portrayed him in many dramatic conversation pieces, as Abel Drugger, as Jaffier, as the Farmer, in *The Farmer's Return*, as Sir John Brute, as the Poet and Lord Chalkstone from *Lethe*, and best-known and least flatteringly, as Macbeth in the dagger-scene, with an enormous Mrs Pritchard as Lady Macbeth urging him on to the slaughter with the expression of an angry cook in full evening dress. Zoffany, whose real name appeared to have been Zauffely, was highly temperamental. He had been painting clock-faces in Seven Dials before Wilson engaged him at forty pounds per annum. He was a melancholy-looking young man, with large luminous eyes; but very little trouble about a house. He took to green-room society like a duck to water.

Horace Walpole, mincing down from Strawberry Hill, had been one of Garrick's first callers at Hampton. He reported first in August 1755. " I have contracted a sort of intimacy with Garrick, who is my neighbour. He affects to study my taste. . . . He is building a grateful temple to Shakespeare." He was soon asked to dine, and this was evidently one of the occasions for which Mrs Garrick was told to kill the fatted calf.

> I din'd to-day at Garrick's. There were the Duke of Grafton, Lord and Lady Rochford, Lady Holdernesse, the crooked Mostyn, and Dahreu, the Spanish minister. Two regents, of which one is Lord Chamberlain, and the other Groom of the Stole; and the wife of a Secretary of State!

Walpole pronounced the company " *assez bon ton* for a player ". The Rochfords were, in fact, very old friends, and had Walpole come next year he might have met the next Lord Chamberlain, the Duke of Devonshire, an even greater friend. But Walpole, whom Warburton (now Bishop of Gloucester), described with his usual violence as a " half-man " and " sicklied over with affectation " was not created to like Garrick.

> Don't you want to ask me how I like him? Do ask, and I will tell you. I like her exceedingly; her behaviour is all sense, and all sweetness too. I don't know, he does not improve so fast upon me; there is a great deal of parts and vivacity and variety, but there is a great deal too of mimicry and burlesque. I am very ungrateful, for he flatters me abundantly; but unluckily I know it.            7

Garrick's villa was built in yellow brick, of a pleasant colour, between lemon and sand. Robert Adam's " uniform front " was dazzlingly white " with an Arcade and a Portico, and Pediment over, and Stone Pilasters and Cornice corresponding ". The entrance court was on the west side, and the new owner had bought some adjacent livery stables, once belonging to Hampton Court, so as to be able to accommodate the horses and carriages of his guests. The front door, under the arcade, led directly into the hall, with a fine staircase ascending from it. On the left was the dining-room, twenty-five feet by seventeen, and on the right a smaller ante-room leading to the Bow room, in which Samuel Johnson had his favourite chintz-covered sofa. On the walls here on each side of the fireplace hung four oil-paintings by Hogarth, which gave an idea of the rough-and-tumble, bribery-and-corruption attendant upon a modern Election. Hogarth had taken much trouble over this series, which had occupied him for three years, and it had been a blow to him when nobody seemed willing to give the price he asked for the set—two hundred guineas. He had sadly decided to put them up for raffle, and Garrick had put his name down for tickets. But upon reflection Garrick had found he could not bear that his old friend should have to undergo such humiliation. He had returned to the studio and bought the lot. They were not to be called pretty, not the thing for a lady's drawing-room, but they were splendid for the Bow room, which was the most companionable room in the house. It was of a good size—twenty-six feet by twenty—and the big window from which it took its name faced east, over the garden lawn, so, being rather low in the ceiling, it was always full of reflected greenery. Behind the Bow room came his study, into which he was putting book-cases to house his growing collection, particularly of old plays. He had ordered his own book-plate from Isaac Wood. A bust of Shakespeare presided above a quotation from *Menagiano* (vol. IV), a floral cartouche and a disarray of masks and musical instruments. He was proud of his fine bindings and one day, after dinner, when he had retired to his library with Foote, Holland, Woodward, Johnson and some others, he was nettled by the behaviour of his oldest friend. Johnson's eye was attracted " as the needle to the pole " by the books, and presently, rising on a tour of inspection, he pulled out, one after another, about twenty of the best bound. Muttering low, after running a finger down the middle of each title-page, he dashed the volumes open on the floor. " Damn it, Johnson! You will destroy all my books! " " Lookee, David, you do understand plays, but you know nothing about books."

The study also faced the lawn, which was not to be confused with the Temple Lawn, across the road. It had been skilfully re-constructed by " Capability " Brown and gave the impression of being much larger than it was—a little more than two acres. It was decorated with ornamental and forest trees, and choice plants. Eva-Maria had planted a cypress and a cedar of Lebanon with her own hands; a Shakespeare mulberry and a tulip-tree were to follow. Serpentine walks traversed the garden lawn on either side, and at the top was the Orangery. Garrick liked to give the impression that in the country he lived on simple fare, but in addition to the existing kitchen garden, which was walled and in a productive state, he had bought another, adjoining. He had a grapery, a greenhouse, mushroom sheds, and cucumber and melon beds. The very names of the fields above the house sounded romantic, though they were in fact no more than the names of former owners—Morshead's Paddock,

o

Pomfret's Paddock. . . . There were three cottages and some cow-
sheds leaning against the wall of the lane that led across the High
Street at the top of Morshead's, to the Sunbury road.

He had decided upon some country servants, for a country house,
and had written to Peter last autumn about a Lichfield man.

> I should be glad to see him settled before I repair to London to begin
> the acting season.  I hope he has a good character in the neighbourhood,
> for he will be left in trust of everything—house, garden, workmen etc.  We
> shall have no occasion for a Laundry maid, so I shall spare you the trouble,
> for my wife has attended to that scheme, at least for a time.  But if you
> should know of two maids, between then and next spring, one for Laundry
> and the other for our Dairy, and the chickens, (which are prime in their
> way) we should be greatly obliged if you would give us notice of them, and
> secure them for us.

The kitchen, scullery and larders, with servants' rooms above,
were detached, facing on to a court of their own.  There was an
excellent drying ground.  There were five spare bedrooms on the
second storey of the villa itself (one of them slightly overshadowed by
Adam's pediment) and attics in the roof.  He had plenty of room.

The Adam brothers would design anything to match their houses,
from a sedan-chair to a knife-box, but he had decided against
furniture in the classical style.  He had bought the villa ready
furnished, and would gradually replace.  He was going to have some
*chinoiserie*—a four-poster, wardrobe, chairs and cupboards *en suite*,
in straw-coloured lacquer, painted with green landscape scenes and
birds.  He was going to have a Chinese wall-paper.  Oriental chintzes
would suit well for the hangings, and there were some on the way to
him—from India, a gift.  Part of the chintzes failed to arrive, and
provoked a typical Garrick letter to the Secretary of the Customs.

> Dear Sir,
>           Not Rachel weeping for her children could show more sorrow than
> Mrs Garrick:—not weeping for *her* children: (she has none) nor indeed for
> her husband:—thanks to the humour of the times she can be as philo-
> sophical, on that subject, as her betters:—What does she weep for, then?
>      Shall I tell you?
>      It is—it is for the loss of a chintz bed and curtains!
>      The tale is short, and as follows.
>      I had taken some pains to oblige the gentlemen of Calcutta by sending
> them some plays, scenes, etc., and by doing them other services in my
> power.  In return, they have sent *me* Madeira, and *poor Rachel* the un-
> fortunate chintz.  She has had it for four years, and, upon making some
> alterations in our little place *at Hampton*, intended to *shew away* with her
> prohibited present.  She had prepared paper, chairs, etc. for this favourite
> token of Indian gratitude; but alas! all human felicity is frail.  No care
> having been taken on my wife's part, and some treachery being exerted
> against her, it was seized, *the very bed*, by the coarse hands of filthy dungeon

ruffians, and thrown amongst the common lumber. If you have the least pity for a distressed female; any regard for her husband—for he has a sad time of it—or any wishes that the environs of Bushey Park may be made tolerably neat and clean, you may put your finger and thumb to the business, and take the thorn out of Rachel's side.

Thomas Chippendale's bills began to come in—for a book-case, japanned blue and gold, for a mahogany breakfast tray with brass hoops, for a coach-hire and lodgings for men and women coming to Hampton to cover two sofas and ten chairs with tapestry, and put up window curtains.

The first-floor rooms owed most to Robert Adam. The drawing-room occupied the same space as the combined bow-room and ante-room below. It had a south window as well as a bow, which had a prospect as far as Bushey Park. There was an adjoining Picture Room over the study, and what the architect's plans somewhat ostentatiously called the State Bedroom. Eva-Maria had curtained off the bed in its recess, in continental fashion. The rooms over-looking the river were flooded with light. Between the Blue Room and the principal Drawing Room came " a spacious gallery, com-municating with the Balcony ". The Balcony stared forth between four Corinthian pillars over the road and the Temple Lawn, to one of the loveliest pieces of back-water in the river. Hampton Deeps was considered a first-class fishing-station, and there were nine hundred and sixty yards of it from the Temple to Tumbling Bay. A little island, Ashen Eyott, lay picturesquely below the house, almost level with the Temple. It contained a miniature meadow, osier beds haunted by otters, and sentimental-looking weeping willows. Up and down the river, all day, passed pleasure-craft, sturdy rowing-boats, lighter boats with white sails like butterflies, dark-hooded wherries. In the wide, ever-changing skies above, birds swooped and cried. There were wild duck on the banks and bobbing in the stream, and swans sailing serenely. It was an inspiring scene to which to return after a hot night at Drury Lane, dog tired. It seemed that there was no sound in the world, except of horses' hooves taking a chariot round to the stables. There was very little traffic on the highroad after midnight, and villagers in Hampton, turning in their beds, hearing a carriage coming in late could tell themselves with some certainty " Mr and Mrs Garrick home from Town ".

### 2

Brother Peter had not sold the wine business. He was struggling on bravely, how bravely David had not quite realized until he sug-gested that, when the acting season of '56–57 was over, Eva-Maria and he should take a trip down to Lichfield.   It would have been convenient to be away from Hampton for some weeks for they were "over head and ears in dirt and mortar" while the villa was being improved.   He hastened to reassure Peter.

> If we should come to you, our stay will be but short, and in about a month or three weeks time.   Whatever little tightening to your house may be wanted for our reception, and can be done in the time, I beg it may be done at my expense.   Our wants, you know, are very small.   Our pleasure will be to see you and your family.   A clean room and a joint of meat will be the utmost of our wishes.   I am you Dear Peter, yours most affectly.
>
> P.S. Our love to Sisters.

He had played only one new character this season, and in an old play, Mrs Centlivre's *The Wonder*.   But his Don Felix had been, by general consent, one of his best comedy parts.

The war had opened very badly for Great Britain.   There had been an outcry from the Press, and grave faces in the Ministry, when Admiral Byng had failed in his attack on the French Fleet off Minorca. The Admiral had been brought home, under close arrest, and had been confined in Greenwich Hospital for seven months.   But the Navy was loved by a sea-faring nation, and opponents of the Ministry now declared that a brave man was going to be used as a scapegoat. Byng's courtmartial was still proceeding when Garrick produced *The Reprisal, or the Tars of Old England*.   This had meant settling scores with Dr Tobias Smollett, who had been offering him for many years plays totally unfit for the stage, and had taken his revenge in two highly successful but characteristically undisciplined novels. In *Roderick Random*, and *Peregrine Pickle*, Smollett had caricatured the manager of Drury Lane theatre under the name of "Mr Marmozet"—the type of man who, after praising a play to the writer's face, asking for alterations, and promising to consider it for next season, suddenly blew cold, and threw it back.

> It is not for the qualities of his heart that this little parasite is invited to the tables of dukes and lords, who hire extraordinary cooks for his entertainment; his avarice they see not, his ingratitude they feel not, his hypocrisy accommodates itself to their humours, and is of consequence pleasing; but he is chiefly courted for his buffoonery, and will be admitted unto the choicest parties for his talent of mimicking Punch and his wife Joan.

There was just enough truth in this to wound, for Garrick, who liked to please, did often find it difficult to refuse a play outright, and would prevaricate before the final decision.   He did, in congenial company "on the least hint" oblige with imitations.   With a light in his eye, he would "suddenly leap up, and placing himself behind a chair, and leaning on the back of it, start his rounds".

In his youth, after having been amongst strangers for a very short while, he could show them all themselves, so like that they hardly knew whether to laugh or cry. Nowadays he usually obliged with a dagger scene, or recognition of his father's ghost. When Garrick had accepted *The Reprisal*, Smollett had found himself in a quandary. He was very much afraid that gossips would have told the manager that he had gone about saying that a play had been obsequiously solicited from him. He was about to publish the first volumes of a History of England. He hastened to insert praise of the exquisite entertainments provided by a modern genius " who surpassed all his predecessors of this, and perhaps every nation, both as actor and manager ". Garrick, " who neither loved nor hated in the way of business ", behaved very civilly to an author who had brought him a naval piece at the moment he needed one, and had got his stuff correct. (Dr Smollett had been to sea as a ship's surgeon.) He went out of his way to give the playwright the fourth night of the benefit season, instead of the ninth, to which he was entitled, and he acted on the occasion himself. When he found that Smollett had been the first to suffer in a new arrangement about author's percentages, of which he might not have been aware, he hastened to send a personal letter of apology together with " a draught on Clutterbuck " for the sum deducted. During the run of *The Reprisal* Admiral Byng was condemned " for error of judgement " with a strong recommendation to mercy, but the King was obdurate, and the unfortunate officer was shot on the quarter-deck of a man-of-war in Portsmouth Harbour. *The Reprisal*, which was not a very good play, remained popular for years.

A farce by Foote was produced a fortnight after that by Smollett, and on a spring morning a few weeks later, a gentleman asking for satisfaction as a gentleman walked into the manager's office. A challenge was not a novelty to Garrick. According to Alexander Carlyle, he had twice asked Home to be his second when he had been called out by Mr John Calcraft, Bellamy's protector. (No duel had taken place, but Home had been flattered by the invitation.) Mr A'Preece, or Ap Rhys, who was now announced, was an extraordinary figure. That rascal Foote had been at his tricks again. In *The Author* he had himself played the part of a Welsh gentleman " Cadwallader ", which was so like Mr A'Preece that this worthy was now unable to walk in the park or enter a coffee-house without being pointed at, and hearing rude titters. What cut him to the heart was that, until he had realized the perfidy of Foote (whom he has once regarded as a friend), he had himself been to Drury Lane and laughed heartily at Cadwallader. This seemed incredible, but

Garrick accepted the fact. The challenge he hesitated to accept. Regarding very gravely the mountain of flesh before him, he begged Mr A'Preece, who was, he agreed, a person of fortune, allied to many families of distinction, to reconsider his cruel decision. Mr A'Preece was somewhat more advanced in years than himself, and even if David Garrick was vanquished in single combat, the matter would not be at an end. He was only a sharer in the production. Mr A'Preece would have to proceed to call out Mr Lacy, joint-manager, and Mr Foote. But, as he really felt very much for him, he would like to offer a suggestion. He advised his injured visitor to apply to the Lord Chamberlain, " a nobleman who, he was sure, had too much humanity to suffer any gentleman to be hurt by personal representation ". A word was spoken to the Duke of Devonshire. Yates took over the part of Cadwallader for the last five performances, after which, the season being ended, the play was withdrawn. Next season, with Foote back again, it was revived, altered.                        11

*The Male Coquette*, who had the delightful name of Daffodil, came from Garrick's own pen. It was often revived as *The Modern Fine Gentleman*, and as the hero was of a very common type, and far from addicted to bloodshed, no challenges followed this production.

The season ended, the workmen came in at the Hampton villa, and the Garricks set off on holiday. In mid-August they went to Lady Cobham, at the Manor House, Stoke Poges. This was one of the acquaintances discouraged by Lady Burlington. But that imperious lady was now no more. Neither was Lord Cobham, who had loved to entertain in great style at Stowe. Lady Cobham who had been born the daughter of a valuable brewer of Southwark, had asked to meet the Garricks a solemn and very touchy poet who was on a visit to his widowed mother and sisters in the neighbourhood. Mr Thomas Gray had written a beautiful elegy about the churchyard. Sixteen years ago, he had not thought much of Garrick as Richard. Now, the gay player startled the sad singer into laughter, and Gray wrote to Walpole, " If you see him, do not fail to make him tell you the story of BULL & POKER." The pleasure of the acquaintance was mutual, and Garrick composed a congratulatory set of verses on the production of Gray's collected odes.                        12

The Rochfords were back in England, and settled at St Osyth. They had brought back from Turin, tied to their carriage, a Lombardy poplar, which they proposed to introduce to their native land and bestow upon General Conway at Park Place, Henley on Thames. After Lichfield, the Garricks went for an East Anglian tour, reminiscent of David's bachelor days. William Windham was now

Lieutenant-Colonel of a regiment of Norfolk militiamen raised to repel invasion, and the model of a country gentleman. David wrote to Peter somewhat uneasily after he returned from Felbrigg. " We were indeed most happy at Windham's. All was Mirth, Joy, Love, Elegance and What Not. He desired his best wishes to you most affectionately. He seems thoughtful; at times greatly so, and I 13 don't absolutely like his looks or cough."

Four years later Windham died " of a consumption ", and the manager of Drury Lane found himself appointed one of the guardians of young William, aged eleven, and as quick with his fists as his father had ever been. The boy was sent to Eton.

### 3

The manager came back from his holiday of 1757 with his plans for the season made, as he liked. He was going to appear in Christmas week as Wilding, in a new version of Shirley's *Gamesters* which he had re-written. The Duke of Cumberland's troops had been driven out of Hanover, and he had come home to be received by his royal sire with the words, " Here is my son, who has disgraced me and ruined himself." Garrick prepared a patriotic military piece for the pantomime season, *The Prussian Camp*. He was due to perform in Home's *Agis* and Murphy's *Upholsterer*, and fairly late in the spring of 1758 he would appear in a new Shakespeare part, the King in *Henry IV, Part II*. Woodward would play Falstaff. He had not foreseen, as he arranged his programme, that he was going to lose Woodward. This was a blow. Harry Woodward had been a mainstay of Drury Lane company since Garrick and Lacy had gone into management. But Barry, whom old Rich said could wheedle a bird out of a tree, to crush it to death in his fist, had suggested to Woodward that they should go to Ireland together, and open a new theatre. Woodward had hesitated. He had saved four thousand pounds. Mrs Woodward did not want him to risk it. He came to Garrick and told him of Barry's offer. He would not accept it if Garrick would agree in future to give him a salary higher than that ever given, or to be given, to any actor or actress. Garrick and Lacy thought this proposition unreasonable. They refused, and Woodward went off to Dublin. It was part of Garrick's creed that no actor in a company should be irreplacable. He had always thought Ned Shuter the best living comedian. But Shuter excelled in low comedy, and Woodward had been the ideal Mercutio, Petruchio, etc. Socially, he had never been an asset. Off the stage he was curiously dry and silent. On the first night of one of his pantomimes, however, he was a tyrant. He terrified the carpenters and scene-

shifters by his shouting.  He returned from his disastrous venture
four years later, but not to Drury Lane.  He never again appeared
there, except on a single occasion, at a benefit.  Younger men had
stepped in.

His defection caused a stir in the world of the theatre.  " The
loss of that gentleman was such as to put so dangerous a hatchet to
the tree as made the old bark tremble.  Had they not at that
juncture been remarkably feeble at Covent Garden, by the loss of
Barry and others, the tears of Old Madam Drury would have had
additional cause to flow."  With Barry and Woodward had gone
four experienced performers, and others reckoned useful, " a severe
cut in a regular catalogue of stock-acting plays. . . . But Garrick's
name was a tower of strength ".  He was not short of young actors, 14
but he was still dismally lacking in young actresses.

Susanna Cibber lost her ill-disposed husband this autumn, no
cause for regret, but the manner of his departing was horrible.
Theophilus Cibber sailed from Parkgate on a night of storm in October
1758 with a party of auxiliaries for the Irish stage.  After a painful
interval, the body of a woman, the wife of a well-known Dublin
tradesman, was washed up on the Scottish coast, together with a
chest of men's clothes and some books.  The Earl of Munster had
taken a passage with a young son, and the noble family equipped a
search vessel.  Some gentlemen who had quitted the missing ship in
the Dee, when she was under sail, much overcrowded, affirmed that
they had seen Cibber on board and " Harlequin Maddox " and other
members of the profession.  Benjamin Victor shed tears when he was
asked to identify some papers, of no worth, Cibber's clothes, and a
part in a play, with his name written on it.  The loss of Maddox was
almost irretrievable, for with the poor Harlequin went the music,
business and plot of the pantomime, and his assistant " the man who
played on the twelve Bells, fastened to his Head, Hands and Feet ".
For the Irish manager there was only one alleviating circumstance.
The carpenter who was to have fitted the English scenery to the
Dublin stage had missed the fatal vessel by three hours.  The winds
of that autumn blew so wildly that " all the scenery, machinery etc."
shipped from the mouth of the Thames arrived in Dublin in four
days " a passage seldom made in less than a month ".          15

Garrick had two new young men in his company.  William
O'Brien, who appeared first as Brazen, in *The Recruiting Officer*,
seemed a gift from the gods.  He was as handsome as Barry and a
much more amiable character.  When he whipped his blade from the
scabbard, he did it with such skill and grace that it was easy to believe that he was descended from the Earls of Clare, a family who

had lost their fortune in the Stuart cause. His father had been a fencing master.

Tate Wilkinson was an *enfant terrible*. He first appeared a fortnight after O'Brien, in October 1758, in Foote's *Diversions of a Morning*. He had called upon Garrick on May 25, 1757 (he never forgot the date) and had passed 27, Southampton Street three or four times before he had the pluck to rap at the great man's door and ask if Mr Garrick was at home. Mr Garrick was, and while his letters of introduction were carried in, the caller was asked to wait. He was a plain, ill-dressed youth, nearly eighteen, and as his letters from the Honourable Miss Foley and Lord Mansfield explained, the son of an unfortunate clergyman. The Reverend William Wilkinson's name was unpleasantly familiar to Garrick. This person had continued to solemnize marriages at the Savoy Chapel in defiance of the Marriage Act. His affairs had been for some time greatly embarrassed, but he had become rich once he had decided to flout the law. The sequel was inevitable, and when he had heard that the King's Messengers were after him, he had fled to Kent, and engaged a curate—Mr Grierson—to continue performing ceremonies for which he had granted the licences. While Grierson had been officiating, he had married two somewhat unsatisfactory members of Drury Lane Company, a Mr Vernon ("a rambling rover") and Miss Poitier from Paris (who "liked a variety of husbands"). George Garrick, who lived in the house of his father-in-law, Mr Carrington, King's Messenger, summoned Vernon to explain himself. "King David", who looked upon his company as his family, had been present at a very unpleasant interview, in which he had insisted on seeing the marriage certificate. George Garrick had then taken it to Mr Carrington. Both Grierson and Wilkinson had been arrested and sentenced to transportation. Wilkinson had perished, perhaps by his own hand, on board a ship bound for America.

The youth who had called upon the manager of Drury Lane a couple of months after these dreadful happenings, had displayed some talent upon the stage while at Harrow, and had offered his services at Covent Garden, but Rich had been blighting. ("You are unfit for the stage, Muster Whittington, and I won't larn you.") Rich had not been quite right, for Tate was to persevere; but this seemed unlikely. In four volumes of memoirs published more than thirty years later he recounted anecdotes which were to connect his name for ever with that of Garrick.

Garrick, at their first interview, after glancing from the letters in his hand to the aspirant, opened calmly. "Well, Sir! Hey! What, now you are a stage candidate? Well, Sir, let me have a taste of your quality." Tate, " distilled almost to jelly ", attempted some speeches from *Richard III* and *The Earl of Essex*. Garrick commented kindly that his visitor was so much alarmed that it was difficult to form an opinion of his abilities. But nervousness was not a bad omen, by no means a sign of want of merit. Tate, gaining courage, offered imitations of some leading members of the profession. " Nay, now," says Garrick, " Sir, you must take care of this, for I used to call myself the first at this business." Tate began with an imitation of Foote, and encouraged by the manager's brightening countenance, gave of his best. " Hey, now! Now-what-all," says Garrick (with his usual hesitation and repetition of words). " Why —well, well. Do call upon me again on Monday, at eleven." It was now Wednesday. Tate bounded home and was folded in the embrace of the best of mothers. (She had been born Miss Tate of Carlisle, where her father had been an alderman of substance.) Punctually on Monday, and " spruced out ", Tate again approached Southampton Street, but with an assured gait. Garrick asked kindly after Mrs Wilkinson and then told him that he had, as he had promised, consulted with Lacy. Tate was to be put on the books at thirty shillings a week for the forthcoming season. " I will think of some line of characters for you." Meanwhile the manager's time was short, he must be at Hampton for dinner. Before he flew off, he asked for a repetition of last Saturday's imitations. Tate began with Foote, and passed to Barry and Woffington in *Macbeth*. Garrick laughed, Tate laughed. To the surprise of Tate, their merriment was echoed. " On a sudden a green cloth double door flew open, which I found led to a little breakfast parlour, and discovered a most elegant lady—no less a personage than Mrs Garrick . . . Mrs Garrick apologized for her rudeness and intrusion." The truth was that she had been posted to form a judgement. If it had been unfavourable " Mrs Mouse would not have appeared, but kept snug in her hole." Before they parted, Garrick could not resist a scene in the Polonius vein. In a most impressive speech he spoke wise words to a young gentleman about to come on the stage. Stripped of its beautiful language and gestures, it seemed, when Tate came to write down his lesson, that two things were most important—to keep off the bottle and always to be word-perfect.

He had asked permission to accept an engagement at Maidstone during the summer, until Drury Lane reopened. He was so ingenuous, he never suspected that four elderly tea-drinking actresses there had been asked to report to Drury Lane on his behaviour. This had been rather silly. He could not resist what he called " friends of the frisky cast ". He was Romeo, Macbeth. . . . When, at last, he presented himself at Drury Lane for a rehearsal of *Romeo and Juliet*, he was told by Cross, the prompter, that he was to be a Torch Bearer in the last act and a Waiting Gentleman in every play. Garrick strode up, and seeing his sulky look told him sharply that unless he did as he was told " I shall take your coat off and do the business myself ". After being a Waiting Gentleman in three plays, and twice riding a hobby-horse on the field of battle in *The Rehearsal*, Tate was relieved to hear that Garrick had been talking of him to Foote. " Egad, Foote! there is a young fellow engaged with me who I really think is superior to either of us in mimicry. I used to think myself well at it, but I actually give him the preference. He has tried to resemble me; but that will not do; though Mrs Garrick says she is sure he will be like me! " The result of this was that Foote took the boy over to Ireland for six weeks, with Garrick's permission. On his return Tate called at Drury Lane for his salary, and was told by the sub-treasurer that his name was not yet on the books. When he met Garrick in Bridge Street a few days later, the manager upbraided him for audacity. Tate produced his articles of agreement, dated on the cover, October 24, 1757. Garrick told him to go home to his Mama and ask her to read aloud the contents. " You will there find, that on the inside, it does not commence until September 1758." To Tate's astonishment, the agreement was " really and truly as Garrick had said ". He betook himself sadly to fashionable Bath to fill in the time from another May till September, and to gay Portsmouth, where his mother had friends. Major Strode, Commander of the garrison, and Mrs Strode, got him an engagement at the theatre. As he had now appeared with some success in leading parts, in Ireland and the provinces, he was much dissatisfied when he again presented himself at Drury Lane, to be given nothing better than a small part in *The Rehearsal*, and on the day before the performance to have it taken away and given to what Garrick grimly called " some steady person ". The fact was that he had been at what Garrick called his tricks again. The part had given an opportunity for mimicking Barry.

At this point in his career, unfortunately for him, he met Foote again, and Foote was very ready to listen to complaints of Garrick. Tate thought that Garrick was always on a fidget, eager for attention and adulation. His hesitation, and never giving a direct answer, arose from two causes—affectation, and fear of being led into promises he never meant to perform. He would dash off saying heartily, " I shall see you again on Tuesday then; Mrs Garrick is waiting ". He never walked about the streets with any money in his pockets, so was always borrowing half-crowns. All this

was delightful to the ears of Foote, who loved to tease Garrick.
" Bless me! we have been laughing away our time; it is past three
o'clock. Have you and Mrs Garrick enough for a third, without
infringing on your servants' generosity, for I know they are on board-
wages? Besides, the kitchen-fire may be out if it be one of your
cold-meat days, or if one of Mrs Garrick's fast days." Garrick
would pretend to laugh, but the laugh came from his boots. As
manager he had early realized that Tate Wilkinson, that pie-faced
mother's darling, whose countenance seemed in repose a blank, was
a born mime. He gave the boy his chance to appear with Foote,
in Foote's two-act farce *The Diversions of the Morning*. He called
the pair " my two exotics ". Colonel Caesar of the Guards, with
whom Woffington had long been living, came to say that if young
Wilkinson attempted any such caricatures of this great lady as he
had offered in Dublin and Portsmouth, the manager must expect
to be called out. Garrick not only promised that none should take
place; he expressed a detestation of such things. Tate was not
surprised. It was well known that in his salad days the manager had
" paid his devoirs " to Mrs Woffington.

On the day before the first performance Garrick called in Foote
and Tate, told them of his promise, commanded Tate not to make
any reference to Mrs Woffington and told Foote that he should regard
him as responsible for the younger man. He seemed very uneasy,
and with good reason. During the second act, the audience got out
of hand and repeatedly called for Wilkinson to reappear. His
imitations of the leading lights of Covent Garden soon brought down
to Drury Lane Mr Isaac Sparks, senior, asking to see the managers.
After this, Garrick had to tell Tate that he had entered into another
promise, in that direction. He chose, as his moment for reproving
the young beginner, a noon rehearsal, and, to Tate's great chagrin,
Mrs Clive took part against him, and Mossop " the turkey-cock of the
stage ". Mossop's intervention saved him, for this actor had a
famous pedantic staccato manner of speech. He advanced towards
Tate, with his hand on the hilt of his sword, and breathing hard.
" Mr Wil-kin-son, Sir, I say—(*phew!*)—how dare you, Sir, make free
in a public theatre, or even in a private party, with your superiors?
If you were to take such a liberty with me, Sir, I would draw my
sword and run it through your body, Sir! You should not *live*,
Sir! " He made a splendid exit, and even Garrick could not help
laughing. Tate was disgusted when Foote meekly agreed that the
boy should not be allowed to perform anything except the part of
Bounce; but the audience was on Tate's side. A riot threatened
when it appeared that the young mimic had been muzzled. Garrick

came into the green-room himself to reproach Tate, who, for his part, firmly believed that the people making the disturbance had been " planted " by Garrick and Foote, out of annoyance at Covent Garden's interference. Lights were lowered, but the house continued to shout for Wilkinson. A compromise was hastily agreed upon. Tate must go on to give representations of Foote, and Garrick. The manager and the playwright with their own hands pushed him on. Tate " advanced, without mercy, cried havock and produced Mr Garrick in three characters ". Lear, Biron and Hamlet were his choice, and as the season advanced, he gradually realized that Garrick had failed to appreciate the really excellent caricatures of " his own bad acting " for which he had himself asked. This was sad, for in his heart Tate regarded Garrick as " beyond compare—the most universal great actor the world ever produced on the stage, or probably ever will ". After Christmas Foote took an Edinburgh engagement. At the last moment he realized he needed journey funds. " Damn it! I must solicit that hound Garrick! " He immediately did, and got the reply that the hundred pounds for which he had asked were waiting for him at the theatre. He sent Tate to get the cash, and they had a first-class supper together. As the feast proceeded, it seemed a moot point whether Foote would stay in London and spend the rest of Garrick's money, or continue north in hopes of more. Prudence prevailed, and by way of gratitude, he told the most ludicrous anti-Garrick stories that Tate had ever heard. He said that David's verses were so bad (and he so fond of writing) that if he died first he dreaded the thought of Garrick composing his epitaph. Before they parted, Tate asked Foote to play for him at his benefit, which could not take place until after Foote's return. He was a little surprised that Foote had not volunteered to do this, for he had, after all, been very useful to him, both in Dublin and London. However, Foote said he had always intended to make the offer; it would be trifling trouble and a pleasure to him. Tate went home perfectly easy and happy.

April came, and Foote arrived back in London, but was strangely elusive. When Tate ran him to earth, he was very rude. He finally said he had already done too much for a vain young man. " I left him, most truly with an honest contempt, and said to him, when at the door, ' Farewell, Mr Foote! ' " This was very dramatic, but the fact remained that he had told Garrick that Foote would appear for him, and his last interview with Garrick had not been encouraging. He had gone, as minor members of a company must, on the approach of spring, to ask if, and when, he was to have a benefit. Garrick had been rather snubbing. An actor asking for a " clear " benefit, that is one for himself alone, selected his own programme, and received the balance of the proceeds. But he had to pay the house charges for salaries, lighting, service, etc. Garrick had said that these expenses now really were (" and Mrs Garrick agrees ") enormous.

In the end he had agreed to let Tate play Othello, with the proviso that an experienced partner should perform in the second piece. There was nothing for it but to go to the manager and tell his tale of woe. Tate did so, and as soon as Garrick gathered that he had quarrelled with Foote (which was very soon) he was all benevolence. " He stepped forward, and said ' Well, Tate ' (O, thought I, if it is ' Well Tate ' all will be right), you will now be convinced of your error in offending me, and you will learn in future, I hope, to distinguish between your real friends and your professional ones." He called for wine to be brought in and sent Tate away with a copy of Othello. Tate could not help noticing that, although Mr Garrick asked if he would like a third glass, he had already put back the cork in the bottle, and that the copy of Othello was price 1s. 6d. He gave the Othello, in due time, to his son, as an heirloom. It never struck him that Mr Garrick might have thought two glasses of good wine quite enough for a youth in his teens who had dined too often with Foote and Shuter at the Bedford, Thatched House, etc.

Tate's imitations of " that Foote " at Drury Lane, on his benefit night were brilliant. " I was Mr Foote! " Indeed they were too successful, for they meant another complaint from the Lord Chamberlain's Office. Tate had slipped back one of the scenes from The Author, prohibited after the affair of Mr A'Preece.

16

## 4

Without Woodward, who had written the script as well as playing Harlequin, there could be no pantomime at Drury Lane for Christmas 1758. Garrick decided to appear in a part which had been considered as Woodward's perquisite, Marplot, in The Busy Body. Amongst the plays which he had refused recently, was one which had come to him by way of Johnson. Johnson had praised Cleone by Robert Dodsley, but not very heartily. He thought it had " more blood than brains ". Dodsley was his publisher. Garrick found the tragedy wholly distressing, " cruel, bloody and unnatural ". He sent it back to the author, with regrets. But he had been mistaken about Douglas. He asked for Cleone again. A second reading only confirmed his first opinion. Dodsley took it on to Covent Garden, and it was announced for November 30. Garrick announced The Busy Body for the same night, and Covent Garden postponed Cleone for a fortnight. Eventually both plays were produced on Saturday, December 2.

Next morning Garrick sent Dodsley a friendly line of congratulation, but not exactly apology. *Cleone* had been much applauded, but at Drury Lane, although a very large audience had arrived to see Garrick challenge Woodward, critics seemed to think that Garrick looked too intelligent for Marplot. Dodsley's answer showed that friends who had told Garrick that Dodsley was very angry with him had not exaggerated. His offer to see Dodsley, " and let me know I can support your interest without absolutely giving up my own ", had added fuel to flames. Dodsley wrote that it was now too late for Garrick to redress the injury he had done to his tragedy. " You have taken effectual care to nip its reputation in the bud, by preventing the town, as far as lay in your power, from attending to it." He threw back, in Garrick's face, the offer of a meeting.

Garrick's reply was one of the warmest he ever sent.

Master Robert Dodsley.
When first I read your peevish answer to my well-meant proposal to you, I was much disturbed at it—but when I considered that some minds cannot bear the smallest portion of success, I most sincerely pitied you; and when I found in the same letter, that you were graciously pleased to dismiss me from your acquaintance, I could not but confess so apparent an obligation, and am, with due acknowledgments.
Master Robert Dodsley,<br>Your most obliged<br>David Garrick.

17

Johnson had gone to the first night of *Cleone*. (" Doddy, you know, is my patron, and I would not desert him.") When he told Garrick that his friends Dr Joseph and the Rev. Thomas Warton had been in Town, and had been taken to Covent Garden, Garrick feared they must have been starved with cold in such an empty house. The brothers Warton were, respectively, second master at Winchester College, and Professor of Poetry at Oxford University. It gave David pain that they had been taken to Covent Garden. " David and Doddy have had a new quarrel," chuckled Johnson. But even he thought it remarkable that the author went to his own play every single night to shed tears at the distress of poor Cleone.

Garrick's New Year opened somewhat bleakly. He had thrown his heart into a production of *Antony and Cleopatra*. It had been provided with " a Bacchanalian song, new habits, scenes and decorations ". There was a command performance for the Prince of Wales. Garrick was not much praised as Antony, and after six nights never played the part again. Among his new plays for this

season was one expanded from *La Pupille* of Fagan—a one-act
comedy. He believed that Voltaire and other writers had considered it the most complete *petite pièce* on the French stage. He
had written a good part for himself. Heartly (the Guardian) was an
attractive figure. *The Guardian* was a success, and added to the
permanent list. David Mallet had revised his *Eurydice*, and Garrick
played another new part in that, Periander. The Greek tragedy ran
four nights.

Holland fell ill on the first night of *Antony*, and a beginner had to
be called in. Cross's diary entered him, dispassionately, as " one
Moody, a stroler ". Many years later John Moody told Kemble
that he owed to Holland's sudden failure his introduction into Drury
Lane company. Garrick had given him five guineas for his performance as Thyreus. At the end of January, when houses should
have been full, the news of the death of the Princess of Orange meant
Court mourning, and no plays for nine nights. During the interval
Taswell died. He had not been young, but he had been a good stock
player long before Garrick and Lacy had gone into partnership. He
would be missed. In the height of the benefit season Mossop could
not appear for a week. He had lost his father, in Dublin. He
never came back. In his native town he had succumbed to the offers
of Barry and Woodward. The invaluable Cross borrowed a Mr
Smith from Covent Garden to replace him, and later a Mr Clarke.
When " Gentleman " Palmer took to his bed, a Mr Ridout was
supplied by the rival house. Rich was believed to be nearly eighty.
John Beard, an accomplished vocalist, had first appeared at Drury
Lane in 1749. At the end of this season he married Rich's daughter,
and Cross noted, " Mr Beard is gone to Covent Garden, 'tis said to
be Manager ".

The Garricks went to Hampshire in July. They stayed with
Dr Joseph Warton, author, critic and lover of Shakespeare, who had
so misguidedly attended *Cleone*. In Winchester they just missed
Murphy, who was pursuing the manager with neurotic letters since
*The Orphan of China* had been the success of the season. They ran
into Tate Wilkinson in Portsmouth.

It was on the night of Monday, July 23 (Tate was always keen on
dates), that Mr Kennedy, the elderly manager of the Portsmouth
Theatre, plucked him by the sleeve. " Mind what you do, for Mr
Garrick is in the pit." Tate was Hamlet, and Moody was the first
gravedigger. They had reached the fifth act. As far as Tate could
see, before he made his entrance, there was nobody in the audience in
the least resembling Garrick, nor had any person seen him. He took
the alarm (which he must confess he had felt) for a bad joke, went

out to supper, and stayed late. Next morning a messenger arrived from the Fountain Tavern with Mr Garrick's compliments and an invitation to breakfast. Garrick's sober living and early hours were the horror of his company. Even at Hampton he was up with the lark, as gay as the lark. Tate, who had been thoroughly spoilt, staying in the Strodes' house, enjoying his newspapers and letters in bed, made a hasty toilet and ran to the Fountain. The morning that followed was incredible. Portsmouth in war-time, full of soldiers and sailors, all with money in their pockets, was an invigorating place. The road from Hilsea Barracks to the Harbour was a continued chain of drawbridges. After a most agreeable breakfast, Garrick suggested a turn on the ramparts. When they got back he ordered a bottle of hock to be put in a cool tankard, with herbs. He gave the extreme heat as his excuse for a draught so extraordinary to him before dinner. On the Continent, too (where the war was going better since Prince Ferdinand of Brunswick had taken over command of the allied troops opposed to Marshal de Contade), the weather was very warm. English cavalrymen, perspiring in powder and scarlet, were drawing towards the cherry orchards on the banks of the Weser, on their way to the Battle of Minden. Tate, walking arm in arm with Britain's most famous actor-manager, at an hour when the streets of Portsmouth were crowded, felt as if he was in a dream. The explanation of the Garricks' presence in Portsmouth was quite simple. For years they had promised to pay a week's visit to Dr Garney, an old and intimate friend, a gentleman of eminence, who lived at Wickham. The Garniers were, in fact, of Huguenot origin, like the Garricks, but this was not explained, and from first to last they were, to Tate, the Garneys. Dr Garney had sent his compliments and told Garrick to get his young friend to fix a day, as early in the week as possible, to pay a visit to Wickham, a matter of not more than eight miles. Tate made a longer and much more careful toilet before he set out for Wickham. In his gold-laced Kevenhuller hat, and his best laced suit, he looked splendid. His only doubt, when he arrived in a pastoral landscape, was whether he was not too splendid. Garrick had greeted him like a son, so he asked his opinion. Garrick said that all was well, except that the buckles of his shoes were too large. They looked like a sailor's. But no one could mind looking like an officer of Britain's glorious Fleet, the terror of the French. Dr and Mrs Garney, and their son, and all their friends—for the company was large—were very well-bred. Their house and grounds were a little paradise. Tate saw all at Wickham through rose-coloured spectacles. Garrick himself showed him over the house and took him up to Dr Garney's observatory,

P

skipping ahead like a lad of twenty. Here the view was of Portsmouth and the Fleet, and the Isle of Wight; St Helen's and Southampton beyond. After dinner they played bowls. Tate had arrived before noon; he left after 10 p.m. His cup of joy was full when Garrick announced that twelve of them would be coming in to witness his benefit, and Mrs Garrick insisted that he should drink a cup of tea with them after. Mrs Garrick had received Tate as if he was a beloved relative returned from the East Indies. " She was in truth a most elegant woman—grace was in her step."

On Friday, July 27, all Tate's fears that he was living in a dream returned, for the Garrick party did not arrive in the theatre until the middle of the second act. But supper, afterwards, was wonderful. The Fountain was packed with people who had heard that Garrick was in the town, and also friends of the Garneys, whose acquaintance seemed to be very large. Mrs Garrick politely congratulated Tate on his performance as Cadwallader. Everyone stopped talking to listen. At twelve-thirty Mrs Garrick was for retiring, so her attentive husband accompanied her to her lodging, in the house of one of the Garney's friends, though it was only a few yards down the street and there was a man servant in attendance. Tate had come to supper in a long cloak called by sea-officers a boatcloak. Garrick was so much taken with it, that after borrowing it to escort his wife, he asked Tate to order one for him. It would, he said, on winter nights save him many a sedan-chair for the journey from Southampton Street to the theatre. He had given Tate a copy of *Barbarossa* and told him to be ready to play Bajazet in *Tamerlane*, and also to get perfect in Hastings in *Jane Shore*. He had sent for Moody and engaged him for next season, to appear first as Henry VIII. He asked Tate very pointedly if he ever saw Foote, to which the answer of course was an indignant " No ". The party broke up at 3 a.m. and Tate, feeling that something magnificent was required, " wished him a good morning, and a safe and pleasant journey to his seat at Hampton Court ".

Mr Garrick at breakfast in " the Palais Royale ", Southampton Street, was still just as pleasant as he had been *en vacance* in Portsmouth. November 4 was fixed for Tate's performance in *Tamerlane*, and Garrick rehearsed him in his own dressing-room. Garrick in his dressing-room, attended only by the prompter and two seasoned players, was so Elizabethan in his wit that a young man was shocked. When the great night came, the great man himself came in to see Bajazet dressed. He was at the theatre by five-thirty, showed Tate " the art of properly lining my face with Indian ink ", and watched the application of the necessary red and white, and the yellow ochre. "My Bajazet, upon the word of a gentleman, was better than well received."

Foote was in difficulties. Garrick was still holding him off; Rich would have none of him. Foote advertised comic lectures at the Haymarket. Garrick wanted to hear what was happening, so Tate attended one. Unluckily, when he came running hot-foot to Southampton Street, to report a full house, but an indifferent performance, he burst in upon a stately *tête-à-tête*—Colonel Keppel of the Guards and the manager of Drury Lane, both in full-dress, had just returned from His Majesty's levée at St James's. Garrick was punctilious in going to Court, which was indeed, as a patentee of one of the Royal Theatres, his duty. He had his *chapeau-bras* under his arm. Tate's hat was still on the back of his head. The manager, with a wink and a gesture, drew the attention of a young puppy to a lapse of manners, and Colonel Keppel kindly said, "He was sure it was from a hurry of spirits." Two or three days later Tate was summoned to Southampton Street. Garrick had heard that Foote had got an engagement with Barry and Woodward. He suggested that Tate should go over to Dublin, but not to act for Barry and Woodward. Tate was delighted at the idea. His mother was not so pleased, for besides dreading the thought of the sea passage for him, she would have to look after Tate's sweet monkey again. It was, like its owner, very spirited and a good mimic.

Before they parted, Tate got his three guineas for the boat-cloak in which the manager now often walked "the theatrical deck of his royal man of war". He rather felt that Garrick expected him to say it was a gift, but he stood firm. This was awkward when the night of his departure came, for in his excitement he had locked up all his cash in his boxes, which had gone down to the coach. It was eleven o'clock, but he knocked up Southampton Street. Garrick, in his night-cap, admitted him. Tate asked for fifteen guineas; he got twenty. In Dublin, playing at Smock Alley, in opposition to Foote at Crow Street, he was highly successful. When he got back to London, "my pockets well-lined", he hastened to pay his homage at Drury Lane, and repay the twenty guineas. But it was quite another matter when he called on the Treasurer at the theatre to ask for his miserable salary. Tate held that as Garrick himself had suggested that he should go to Ireland, and had provided him with introductions, he had been on granted furlough. The manager was obdurate. Tate threatened to go to law, though he had suspicions that this would be a hazardous experiment. Garrick gave him his clear benefit, and his engagement was not renewed. He never again appeared at Drury Lane. But he took off Garrick at Covent

Garden, in 1760, when his old master was in a front box. "As to Mr Garrick, I made no scruple. . . . O! thought I, my master, this is my day of triumph, and from that night he never forgave or forgot." Tate proceeded to quarrel with Rich, and went on to act at Portsmouth, Winchester, Bath, Norwich. In the provinces he prospered. He ended life as proprietor and manager of several theatres in the north of England. He had been thought in tragedy to have caught something of the manner of Garrick. As a manager he was exemplary. He became noted in this capacity for a curious manner of speech—a jolting out of disconnected words and phrases. It was never suggested that in this too he was modelling himself on a great master. 18

## 5

In the war, the turn of the tide had come. On Thursday, November 29, 1758, there was no play at Drury Lane. The day had been appointed one of thanksgiving for the Battle of Quebec. Garrick had written a pantomime himself for this Christmas. It was called *Harlequin's Invasion*. Harlequin invaded Parnassus and was defeated by Shakespeare. William Boyce, who had been working for the theatre since 1749, performed his last duty for it, and amongst the songs by Garrick which he set to music was one to become famous. The manager's visit to Portsmouth had borne fruit.

> Hearts of oak are our ships,
> Jolly tars are our men,
> We always are ready,
> Steady, boys, steady!
> We'll fight and we'll conquer
> Again and again.

*Harlequin's Invasion* was also supplied with something new in the way of scenery. French, the principal designer at the Lane, was a good artist, but not original. Garrick had drawn in talent from Italy. Domenico Angelo Malevolti Tremamondo (generally known in London simply as Angelo) was by profession a fencing-master and equestrian teacher. He had first seen "*les tableaux mouvants*" at Venice, at the carnival. They were transparencies, against which figures flitted in silhouette. They had been the work of Canaletto. Garrick described the enchanted wood, through which Harlequin must be pursued, and Angelo instructed French as to a transparent backscene. He then "caused screens to be placed diagonally, which were covered with scarlet, crimson and bright blue moreen, which, having a powerful light behind them, and by turning them towards the scenery, reflected these various colours alternately, with a success that astonished and delighted the audience. Indeed, the whole stage appeared on fire." A night-scene on Ludgate Hill, illuminated for a victory, was also much admired.

Cross's notes were becoming briefer, but not less trenchant. " Miss Pope in *Corinna,* fine." " *High Life Below Stairs*—hissed." This farce had been more than hissed. It had caused a riot in the footmen's gallery. It had been written by the Rev. James Townley, High Master of Merchant Taylors' School, but nothing would persuade London that Garrick had not, at least, lent his pen. It satirized the folly of fashionable folk and their exploitation by their many retainers. Despite its first reception, it had come to stay. " Great alterations in *Oroonoko* ", announced Cross. The alterations were mostly excisions of the low-comedy scenes. Garrick in this play, in which he had first appeared as Aboan in his pupil-days, now performed Oroonoko. " This is a farce of Macklin's writing. It went off very greatly." But two days later *The Tutor,* a play from the Italian, was offered for one night only. " *The Tutor* damned."

The sea-breezes of Hampshire which Murphy had hoped would rouse his Muse from a desponding state had inspired *The Desert Island,* a dramatic poem in three acts, and a comedy, *The Way to Keep Him.* When Garrick said that he could not perform a capital part in both, Murphy flew off in a pet and said he had offered the plays to Mossop for Dublin. He did this twice before Garrick agreed to produce both, but on the same night, which was displeasing to Murphy. When they went into rehearsal, he begged to be excused attendance. The other day, in the bustle and turmoil of the green-room, he had been persuaded to cut a scene which he now saw would have to go back again when the play was printed. But a sudden shortage of funds obliged him to ask for the remainder of his salary in advance. Garrick sent what cash he had by him in Southampton Street. " Mrs Garrick is gone to Hampton and taken the keys with her." Any more needed should follow. In the end a compromise was found. Garrick wrote and spoke a prologue for *The Desert Island,* and played Lovemore in *The Way to Keep Him.* The comedy was gay, and with two more acts, added next season, went on the regular list. He still had Home's third heavy tragedy to bring to birth, and acted as Aemilius, a conscientious consul of the Marcus Brutus type. He had never thought the piece dramatic—but he had been wrong about *Douglas. The Siege of Aquileia* ran eight nights. *The Tender Husband* was revived for O'Brien's benefit, and to oblige an actor of promise and parts, Garrick played, for the first and last time, Sir Harry Gubbin. The season ended, and on April 25 came a sad entry. " Benefit of Mrs Cross (widow of the late

prompter)." William Hopkins, who succeeded Cross, served throughout the remainder of Garrick's management.

The Garricks went up to Lichfield again this summer. When the
theatre re-opened, Drury Lane management had found another
novelty to induce the curious. Thomas Sheridan, who had given up
the command at Smock Alley, had returned to London. He was
weary of the struggle against Barry and Woodward's new theatre,
and the suggestion that he should act with Garrick had come from
him. Garrick had never found him a likable man, but it was to
their mutual interest to come to an understanding. They did not at
first appear together, but Sheridan played several of Garrick's most
famous parts, and as Richard and Hamlet his name filled the house
just as well. This was providential, for when the season was a
month old, all theatres had to close for three weeks. The king, who
had appeared in his usual health on the morning of October 25, when
preparing to go out for his usual seven o'clock constitutional in the
gardens of Kensington Palace, had dropped dead. He had not been
a popular monarch, or a discerning patron of the drama. He had
received an unfavourable impression of Garrick after seeing him as
Richard III, and asked to see more of Taswell, who was playing the
Mayor, and seemed to him a better kind of man. But he had
attended Drury Lane regularly, especially for comedians. Garrick
preserved a silhouette of his late Majesty, inscribed: "The best
likeness of the King that has ever been done." George II had always
displayed a singular aversion from having his portrait taken. The
longest reign yet in English history had begun.

## CHAPTER IX

# THE NEW REIGN

## 1760–1763

### I

GREAT expectations were formed of the new king. He was twenty-two, a bachelor, fair and rosy, blue-eyed, a good height, and not much known. He had been kept in perfect seclusion by his widowed mother and Lord Bute. When his speech for the opening of Parliament was sent to him, he returned it, having added, " Born and educated in this country, I glory in the name of Britain." His delivery of it was good. Old Quin, who had instructed the royal grandchildren for their private theatricals, commented from his retirement, " I knew the boy would do it well, for I taught him." A Coronation, a Royal Wedding and Peace all seemed likely to render next year happy and glorious. Garrick, now that he had Sheridan to fill his house for him, exerted himself in only two new parts this season. He appeared as Mercutio, and convinced his audience that he could do without Woodward. As Oakley, seated with Mrs Oakley (Mrs Pritchard) on a sofa, each partner trying to find out what amours the other intended, he was unforgettable. He had not yet drawn the line at receiving visitors in his dressing-room. As one young aspirant departed from his life, another stole in. Joseph Cradock, who was to rival Tate Wilkinson in Garrick anecdotes, remembered that the first time he ever had the pleasure of being introduced into the presence was in Coronation year, and that Mr

1 Garrick was dressed for the character of Oakley. The Jealous Wife met with greater applause than anything since The Suspicious Husband. A farce called Polly Honeycomb, also by Mr Colman, had been produced two months earlier, and after a bad start had made an excellent recovery. The author had preferred to remain anonymous, and a good many people believed that Garrick had written the play in which he had so congenial a part as Oakley. · After the success of his second comedy, Mr George Colman allowed his name to appear. He was continually in and out of Southampton Street, and collaborated with Garrick and others in a publication called The St James's Chronicle, issued three times a week, in which they had a controlling interest. He was eight and twenty, and had valuable connections. His father had been Envoy to Tuscany, and George had received his christian name as a god-son of his late Majesty. His uncle, Lord

Bath, wanted him to continue practising at the Bar.  Lady Bath
hoped he would take holy orders.  Both wished he would leave off
living with Miss Ford, the actress.  Miss Ford, whose christian
name was Sara, had perhaps been upon the stage.  She certainly
possessed a daughter, Harriet, by Mossop, who soon became a child
performer at Drury Lane.

On November 21 George III made his first appearance at Drury
Lane to witness Garrick as Richard.  As he entered, the whole
audience arose and sang *God Save the King*.  Two nights before
Christmas he came again.  Garrick and Sheridan were both playing
in *King John*.  " A very intimate " but not a tactful acquaintance
told Garrick that His Majesty had been uncommonly pleased with
Sheridan as King John.  When Garrick pressed to know what the
king had thought of his Falconbridge, the word " over-charged " was
mentioned.  Both Davies and Murphy believed that Garrick was
already jealous of Sheridan's successes.  *King John* was given only
once more, amongst the benefits, and Sheridan did not offer to
continue his engagement when the season ended.  But two years
later he was seen at Drury Lane again.  Garrick had accepted a
comedy, *The Discovery*, by Mrs Sheridan, in which he gave the
authoress's husband the leading part.  After this, the Sheridans
went abroad to recruit their health and finances.

The Christmas piece at Drury Lane in the first year of George III
was very well received.  Its title was alluring.  *The Enchanter, or
Love and Magic* by David Garrick.

## 2

If there was one thing that filled the master of Hampton House
with utter misery and self-pity, it was having to bring down to the
country, for reply, letters from members of the profession.  He
headed his sheet of March 13, 1762, addressed to Mrs Palmer with a
quotation.

" *E'en Sunday shines no Sabbath day for me.*"

It was, in fact, a Saturday, but Mrs Palmer had surpassed herself.
The young king, who had soon after his succession issued a proclama-
tion against immorality, and who was disappointed in his efforts to
end the war, had appointed Friday, March 12, as a national day of
fasting and humiliation.  No theatres had been open.  Mrs Palmer
had employed herself writing to her manager.  He opened tragically:

> I flattered myself that I should, yesterday, have been freed from any
> business of the Theatre, on account of the solemnity of the day, and I little
> expected that Mrs Palmer would have broken in upon it with a letter of
> altercation.

Mrs Palmer was the Pritchards' girl, and had made her début in 1756 as Juliet, led on by Mrs Pritchard, drenched in tears, as Lady Capulet. Such theatrical family occasions were relished by audiences, and Garrick had himself played Romeo, from respect to her excellent mother. Nay, he had even made himself a motley to the view, playing Benedick to the Beatrice of this chit. Miss Pritchard had a very pretty face. But a pretty face was by no means everything in the theatre. Never had he forgotten, or forgiven, Mrs Ward, who, when he was expending himself as the gay Lothario, had distracted him, and the audience, by suddenly recollecting to fasten her glove.

The fair Pritchard had, last spring, married one John (known as " Gentleman ") Palmer, a handsome young man, good in small comedy parts. Palmer was conceited, but probably old Pritchard had put her up to writing her presumptuous letter, had she needed encouragement. As far as Garrick could judge—for though long and full of underlinings it lacked clarity—he had been guilty in two respects. Why had he not brought on *The School for Lovers* earlier? Why was her benefit two days later than last year? " Heavy charges! But I trust in my innocence." To indulge her, although the most accomplished performer had not a shadow of right to ask such a question, he would satisfy her curiosity. Mr Whitehead, the author, had particularly desired that his new play should be produced when it was. The managers had never meant it to come on earlier. But he begged that Mrs Palmer might not think this an excuse for the fact that she had not been called on to play Celia. " I never intended that you should, and for one reason, among many, that it would have showed too strongly the similitude between *The Guardian* and *The School for Lovers*." (She had been well cast as the *ingénue*, Lucy, in *The Guardian*. If it came to that, Celia was supposed to be sixteen, and dear Susanna Cibber, who had insisted upon her rights, was fifty-four. This was one of the reasons he would not mention. He did mention that even if he had been foolish enough to offer Celia to Mrs Palmer she should not have accepted something beyond her powers.) As to her benefit, if Mr Palmer thought it worth while to discuss that question, he would be very pleased to see him. " Now I come to the more serious part in your letter, which concerns me only." Mrs Palmer accused him of having professed and shown an esteem for her *last* season. " Yes, Madam, I think I did, and upon an occasion when your filial tenderness got the better of my resentments for a behaviour in your father which few managers would have forgiven." He repeated in his postscript that he would be very ready to see Palmer—who would not at all want to quarrel with him, as he had just been given a very good part in a new play. He had protected himself against an incursion by old Pritchard. He had made a handsome reference to Mrs Pritchard, " who deserves everything we can do for her ". He was himself again; but at the cost of a spoiled morning. [2]

Arthur Murphy, who thought that nobody in this world had any troubles like his, believed, and eventually wrote down, that Garrick in the second year of the new reign had every reason to be complacent in his situation as actor, as manager, as author. (He had to make a reservation about what he called " the disturbance " at *The Chinese Festival*; but that had been an accident.) Nothing, nowadays, ever occurred to give Garrick the smallest discontent. He was the idol of his audiences, an admitted master of dramatic verse. He basked in the sunshine of public admiration, enjoying an endless succession of halcyon days. If he was, at times, molested by enemies, such was the fate of superior merit. Murphy had dined with the Garricks last Christmas Day. There had been one other young Irishman, Edmund Burke, who, like Colman, was supposed to be a lawyer, but was much more interested in literature and the stage. Burke had never before met Johnson.

In fact, the world upon which the author, actor and manager looked forth from his Hampton window, over the lawns towards Bushey Park, on a morning of March 1762, was full of interest, but it was also full of anxieties. As an actor, he had been slightly shaken by Sheridan's success in his theatre. It might be that the public, always demanding novelty, were getting a little too well accustomed to him as Richard, Lear, Hamlet, Macbeth—even as Benedick, Ranger and Don Felix. The only answers to this were to appear more in new parts (which was just what he had been trying to avoid lately), or to cease to appear at all for a little. He longed to go abroad again, but Charles Selwyn wrote from Paris that it would be quite unsafe to come at present. Even French subjects, who had been domiciled in England, were being questioned on their entry, and many had been arrested. Lawrence Sterne had risked it.

January 31, 1762.
Dear Garrick,
   Upon reviewing my finances this morning, with some unforseen expenses, I find I should set out with twenty pounds less than a prudent man ought. Will you lend me twenty pounds? [3]

Sterne had also taken letters from Garrick to Paris friends. The French Fleet had now been driven off the seas, but peace had not yet been declared, and at the close of last year Spain had entered the war, which had meant sending British troops to protect Portugal. Garrick resigned himself to waiting.

On Saturday nights, when he was not playing, this season, his

carriage called constantly at a very small establishment in Poland
Street, off the Oxford Road, to collect a guest who needed comforting.
The poor little Burneys seemed dogged by misfortune. Charles's
health had been so bad that he had been obliged to abandon his
London career and take up the post of organist at Lynn Regis, at an
annual salary of one hundred and twenty pounds. Nine years in
Norfolk had completely restored him, but then his wife had died, of a
consumption. He was left with six children under ten, and a broken
heart. Saturday to Monday at Hampton House by the wise, quiet
river, with " Roscius and Violetta " did much to restore him; but he
was a musician. . . . During this first terrible winter of his bereavement, Garrick also called often to see him on week-days. If he was
told that Mr Burney was out, giving a music lesson, he stayed and
played with the children. At Christmas and on many other occasions
4 all witnessed the Drury Lane performance from the manager's box.
While the children watched the stage, Garrick watched their faces.

He had been seen as Posthumus in a new version of *Cymbeline*
before Christmas, and was continuing to play this. He had been,
and still was, appearing in Whitehead's new comedy. Next week
he would carry all the burden in a little topical one-act piece of which
he was the author. Last winter he had suffered from a persistent
vexatious cold. Dr Barry said he should take more outdoor
exercise, so he was now riding down to Hampton when he could.
Warburton had warned him five years past that he should take more
care of himself. " When you enter into those passions which most
tear and shatter the human frame, you forget you have a body; your
soul comes out, and it is always *dagger out of sheath* with you." This
was absolutely true. On a first night he was still on fire, burning
himself out. He had written a duty letter to Brother Peter a month
ago, heading his sheet, " Drury Lane, quarter past six ". He had
been in his dressing-room, in costume, having spoken the Prologue
" and don't appear again till the beginning of the second act, when
Sir John Dorilant (that's the name) makes his entrance ". All the
thrilling noises of the theatre, packed for a new play by the Poet
Laureate, penetrated, muffled, to the manager's dressing-room,
where, to the anxiety of his staff, he sat, writing as if his life depended
upon it, all about nearly nothing, to dear Lichfield. He said he was
going to play this humbug for nine nights. (It was going to succeed
and he was going to play it for twelve.) He finished, as he had begun,
in haste, " Brother George, backed by the crowing of the prompter,
summons me away. So, my dear brother, I shall give you, in the
5 words of Hamlet, ' Remember me '."

While it was closed, this summer, he was going to improve the

seating accommodation in Drury Lane.  Last year he had lent the
theatre from June till August to an odd pair—Foote and Murphy.
The man with the dancing dogs had got in to the Lord Chamberlain
before them for the Haymarket.  They had nowhere to go.  They
had done quite well.  He had been across to Covent Garden to see
the manager there and study their arrangements.  He had asked
Rich how many people they reckoned they could pack in.  Old Rich,
leering, had softly said that, Ah! to answer that, Mr Garrick would
have to appear for a night.  Covent Garden, always the theatre for
shows, had carried away the palm over the coronation.  Garrick had
always foreseen this, and had hardly attempted to compete.  He
had announced a pageant, the coronation of Anne Boleyn, to be presented at the end of *Henry VIII* and before the afterpiece.  He had
got out the costumes kept in the wardrobe since the last coronation
(that of his present Majesty's grandfather in 1727), and used occasionally since.  The fact that they were neither quite antique nor at all
new would pass unnoticed, because the stage would be in semi-
darkness, until great doors opened, actually on to Drury Lane, to
show a real bonfire burning in the street outside, and Tudor citizens
huzzaaing and drinking porter.  The project was ill-conceived,
because the first date on which it could be shown was the very end of
September.  He kept it on for forty nights, during which the actors
and audience were nearly suffocated by the smoke and frozen by the
raw air.  Rich's show at the end of *Henry V* had quite outshone
Drury Lane's real bonfire.  " Such a profusion of fine cloathes, of
velvet, silk, satin, lace, feathers, jewels etc had not been seen on any
stage."  Bellamy, as Catherine the Fair, passing to her coronation,
attired in the height of fashion and an enormous hoop, had been as
proud as a peacock.  Old Rich had died during the run of his
pageant, and his son-in-law, Beard, was making Covent Garden,
more than ever, notable for its musical entertainments.

Although there had been a queen as well as king to be crowned,
the real coronation had gone off somewhat at half-cock.  The royal
wedding had taken place in the chapel of St James's Palace, at nine
o'clock on the night of the bride's arrival in London, a fine but sultry
night.  The coronation had followed a fortnight later.  At both the
stage-management had been lamentable.  Walpole had noted that
the pallid little queen had advanced to the altar almost throttled by
her finery.  Her endless violet velvet train, lined with crimson,
fastened inefficiently by a bunch of pearls to the shoulder of her gown,
had dragged the bodice down behind, almost to her waist.  The
Lord Chamberlain, the Duke of Devonshire, was already disliked by
the king as " a Whig prince ", but he could hardly be held responsible

for a strike of the workmen putting up the scaffolding for spectators in Westminster Hall, or a chairmen and coachmen's strike. It would have been a tragedy if these had not been settled, for the desire of the populace, of all degrees, to see their new king and queen was almost pathetic in its eagerness. Six days after the bride's arrival in England, on Friday September 14, after the wedding and before the coronation, Messrs Garrick and Lacy waited at Drury Lane with candles, ready to show Their Majesties to the royal box. The play commanded was *The Rehearsal*, and Garrick was in his costume as Bayes. Their time of waiting, which was protracted, was enough to shake the strongest nerves. Rumours floated in that a girl had been crushed to death by the mob, and a man trampled underfoot, so that his condition was despaired of. The house had been packed before the doors opened, for the admission of people who had not reserved seats, and only about a hundred of would-be spectators, who had been standing outside for hours, were able to get in. Some ladies who had rashly tried to fight their way upstairs, had lost their caps and fichus and had their gowns torn. The route, all the way from St James's, was lined by excited subjects waiting to see Their Majesties going to Drury Lane in chairs, followed by their suite in coaches, and escorted by the Horse Guards. Most of the nobility attending would be wearing their gala attire, which hardly anyone had been able to witness at the wedding. At last the strains of *God Save the King* were heard, and the deeply bowing managers saw their new queen. She was no beauty. But she was seventeen, had dignity and was evidently determined to be pleased with everything. Walpole had found her " sensible, cheerful and remarkably genteel ". It was certainly disappointing to find her outright plain, with a broad nose, little eyes and very ordinary curly light hair. Some most dishonest printsellers, to meet the demand, had published an engraving of quite another and very fair lady. However, it was said that nobody had laughed more than the queen when shown the portrait of this ravishing creature.

There were dreadful stories that the king had been in love elsewhere. The scandalous version was that he was already married to a fair Quaker, a linen-draper's daughter or niece, who had borne him a child. A smaller circle discussed another story. There were two high-spirited girls at Holland House—Lady Sarah Lennox, the late Duke of Richmond's daughter, a true beauty, and her cousin, Lady Susan Fox-Strangeways, daughter of the Earl of Ilchester. Garrick knew them both well. To them he was " Mr Garrick, sweet soul ", and " the angel ". They were devoted to the Play, and a handsome junior member of Drury Lane company, William O'Brien, often went to Holland House to help them with their amateur theatricals. During the summer, the young king had often been seen on the Hammersmith road riding past Holland House. He had fallen in love with Lady Sarah, making hay in the park. But Lord Bute and his mother had seen to it that he married a small German princess, who would be docile. Lady Sarah had been a bridesmaid at the wedding, superb in white satin embroidered with silver. "Miss Charlotte Mecklenburgh" looked prosaic, to a nation starving for a little glamour in their royalty, and in an astonishingly short time the world of fashion had made up its mind that the court was not going to be fashionable. A select few of very high degree, invited to the palace by the queen to dance after her command performance at Drury Lane, had been allowed to do so until 1 a.m., but had not been offered any supper. The play chosen by the queen on this occasion had been *Rule a Wife and Have a Wife*. The court was going to be homely. But Their Majesties had attended Drury Lane nearly every week, this season, and the queen was doing her duty. A Prince of Wales was hoped for in August. Garrick also was doing his duty. He had written a loyal one-act " prelude " in which he would appear as an English farmer, come home to his family after witnessing the coronation. *The Farmer's Return* was to hit exactly the right note, and he had to keep it on until the theatre closed in May.

As far as his company went, he had now no cause for complaint. He had got what he had long needed, promising young actresses. Miss Jane Pope, no longer a Lilliputian, and well coached by Clive, was shaping well, especially in light comedy. Miss Bride, who danced and sang well, had created a furore on her début. He had Mrs Yates, who possessed classic beauty and every virtue. He had Mrs Abington, " not handsome, but stylish ". When her fame was established, it was found that she came of an old county family, the Bartons of Norton in Derbyshire. This may have been so, but her father had been a stalwart guardsman who kept a cobbler's stall in Vinegar Yard, and a brother was an ostler, up the Tottenham Court Road. Frances Barton, " Nosegay Fan ", had sold flowers in St James's Park, and sung and recited inside and outside the taverns around the Piazza. She had been assistant to a milliner in Cockspur Street and had learnt French and Italian, and the manners of ladies of birth, certainly with remarkable ease. She had first appeared on the stage during a summer season at the Haymarket, and Lacy, looking out for talent, had seen her acting in a barn theatre at Richmond. She had been engaged at Drury Lane for three years and during them had married James Abington, a trumpeter in the King's service, who had taught her music. That episode had lasted a very short time, and he was never mentioned, though she kept his name. It was generally believed that he turned up now only on pay days, to collect his allowance for keeping away. In Dublin, she had made a sensation. She was equally good in well-bred and soubrette parts. She had become a leader of fashion, and shops displaying articles of dress simply labelled them " Abington ". There was an " Abington cap " and a silk cloak, " a pink cardinal ", as worn by her in *High Life Below Stairs*. After five years Garrick had invited her back to Drury Lane. She was still only eight and twenty, but she was as smart as paint and as hard as nails.

He had got someone else, whom he liked much better, back from Dublin. Tom King had returned in the year after Woodward had left. He not only filled Woodward's place to some degree; he was a genuinely helpful member of a company. He had large, dog-like, chestnut eyes, and was irresistible in comedy, high and low, on the stage and off. William O'Brien was growing in stature. Charles Holland was promising, though he tended to produce Garrick-and-water, and to use a fine manly voice too generously. He was touchy. Last summer he had walked off for Dublin. He had been slighted. But after a winter at Liverpool, he had gladly returned. " Nothing in the theatrical world can *succeed* that *you* have not a hand in . . . What a fortunate escape I had in not going to Ireland! I look upon it as the happiest circumstance in my whole theatrical life." (But he still did not want to be Ferdinand, in *The Tempest*, Young Knowall, or Colonel Hanley.) There were three newcomers arriving from Edinburgh this autumn, recommended by the Edinburgh manager, Jackson. The worst of young married couples was they liked to act together, and both were seldom equally good. The William Palmers might be an exception. The third unknown, who was much older, had been in the Edinburgh management and was an author as well as comedian. He had been born in London, where his distinguished father had designed the Mansion House. If he came to Drury Lane he was going to change his surname " for some capital reasons ". He had been born James Dance. He was going to be James Love.

The enemies to whom Murphy alluded so cheerfully did indeed seem to have been less troublesome than usual, of late. The author-actor-manager had realized early that they were a life-sentence. He tried to practise the wisdom of the serpent combined with the meek-ness of the dove. Dr John Hill had been a nuisance. He delighted in " paper wars ". He had brought Garrick a farce. He enjoyed the patronage of Lord Bute. Garrick had brought on the piece, of which he did not think much, during the benefit season, and as the charity named had been the General Lying-In Hospital, the audience had behaved politely. Hill had then demanded a benefit for himself, and this time *The Rout* had been hissed. He had then written against Drury Lane management in every paper that would print his envenomed paragraphs. Garrick summed him up in a neat couplet:

> For *Farces* and *Physic*, his equal there scarce is.
> His *Farces* are *Physic*, his Physic a Farce is.

Hill had replied with a letter " To David Garrick Esq. The Petition of I—in behalf of herself and her fellows " in which he drew attention to the famous actor's dreadful mispronunciation of his vowels. But Hill was a bully. It was well known that when a fiery Irish gentleman had thrashed him publicly at Ranelagh he had ceased to annoy in that direction. Garrick continued to ridicule him. Three years had now passed, and Dr Hill seemed unlikely to return to the charge. 8

The Reverend Charles Churchill had been more of a problem. In March of last year, a satire called *The Rosciad* had been greeted as better than anything in that line since Pope's *Dunciad*. It was discerningly cruel about nearly every leading performer, except a few Drury Lane actresses, a few of Garrick's journalist friends, and the manager himself. Garrick was absolutely lauded. Internal evidence seemed to point at a trio known to write for him—Bonnel Thornton, Robert Lloyd and John Colman. They hastened to disclaim responsibility, in *The Critical Review*, of which Smollett was editor, whereupon Churchill published an *Apology addressed to the Critical Reviewers*, attacking Smollett and Garrick. He signed it, and Colman and Lloyd realized that he was an old Westminster school-fellow. He was the fat man in a blue coat with brass buttons who often sat in the front row of the pit. He was believed to have recently " got rid of two things he did not like—his gown and his wife ". Garrick had naturally been pleased by the acknowledgment given to him in *The Rosciad*; but he must sympathize with the members of his profession who had been so roughly handled—his " stricken deer ". Johnson believed that Tom Davies had given up acting after reading the description of himself mouthing a tragic line " as curs do a bone ". Garrick had said, after reading the pane- 9 gyrics on his own performances, that he thought, whoever the author was, he was someone hoping for a free pass to Drury Lane. This, of course had been repeated. *The Apology* was bitter reading for him.

> Let the vain tyrant sit amidst his guards,
> His puny green-room wits and venal bards,
> Who meanly tremble at a puppet's frown,
> And for a playhouse freedom, sell their own.
> In spite of new-made laws and new-made kings,
> The free-born muse with lib'ral spirit sings.

It was not nearly as good as Churchill's first poem, but that had come " from no mean hand ". Garrick swallowed his chagrin and decided upon diplomacy. He sent Lloyd a letter in which he said that he regretted he did not know Churchill.

> At the first reading of his " Apology," I was so charmed and raised with the power of his writing that I really forgot that I was delighted when I ought to have been alarmed. . . . All I have to say, or will say, upon the occasion is this;—that if Mr Churchill has attacked his pasteboard majesty of Drury Lane from resentment, I should be sorry for it, though I am conscious it is ill-founded. If he has attacked merely because I am the Punch of the puppet-show, I shall not turn my back upon him and salute him in Punch's fashion, but make myself easy with this thought—that my situation made the attack necessary, and that it would have been a pity that so much strong, high-coloured poetry should have been thrown away, either in justice or in friendship, on so insignificant a person as myself. In his " Rosciad " he raised me too high: in his " Apology " he may have sunk me too low.

The letter was shown to Churchill, a meeting was arranged, and a friendship was formed. He was invited to Southampton Street.

George (now Lord) Lyttelton had dissuaded Garrick from embroiling himself with Dr Alexander Bower. Bower had been a Jesuit priest. He had attracted a good deal of attention as " a distinguished convert from Rome ", with lurid anecdotes of his maltreatment by the Inquisition, etc. He was writing a *History of the Popes* to which Lyttelton had subscribed. But presently odd stories about him began to circulate. He was suspected of being an impostor; he was probably personally disreputable. Amongst the " well-known and admired " people who closed their doors upon him were the Garricks. A pamphlet, exposing him, expanded upon this, though without mentioning the Garricks by name. Bower rushed into print in his defence.

> Now, that foreignors may not think that I dare not show my face at the house of any *real gentleman* or *real lady*, I beg to inform them who this gentleman and lady are. The gentleman then, is Mr Garrick, an actor, who now *acts* upon the stage. The lady is his wife, Mrs Garrick, alias Violetti, who within these few years danced upon the stage. The *lady* (though no *Roscius*) is as " well known and admired " for her *dancing* as the gentleman is for his *acting*, and they are, in that sense, *par nobile*. That I dare not show my face in that house is true; nor dare I show it in any other house, the mistress whereof is a Papist.

Garrick, in his first fury, thought of revenging himself by a farce, in which a wicked old mock convert was gradually displayed in his profligacy. He said he had always thought Bower an even richer character than Molière's Tartuffe. But Lyttelton, while repudiating

Q

Bower, convinced him that such a production would not add to his reputation.

Eva-Maria attended regularly the nearest place of worship of her denomination. The carriage took her, very early on Sunday mornings, to Isleworth. It was not very near, but she was always back in good time to entertain her husband's Sunday company (never more than twelve); or, if they were to be alone, to take away his pen.

A portrait of the famous actor which was to become even more popular than Hogarth's charming conversation group, had attracted much admiration at the Spring Gardens Exhibition this year. *Garrick between Tragedy and Comedy* was the work of an artist who had grown steadily in reputation during the past ten years, and now charged top prices. Joshua Reynolds came from the West Country. He had a scar on his lip, the result of being thrown from his horse over a precipice in Minorca, and was slightly deaf, the result of cold endured while copying the works of Raphael in the Vatican. But he was extremely good company.

There was only one person from the literary world at whom it was believed that Mrs Garrick drew the line, and even he continued to visit Hampton until Garrick was convinced he was malicious, which was not for twenty years. Dr Messenger Monsey, physician to Chelsea Hospital, was shockingly uncouth and rude. But he was a character. All the anecdotes about him were too good to be true. Garrick, quite likely, had first met him as a fellow spectator of a trial at the Old Bailey. This story was that when a little fellow had repeatedly and in vain asked a big one to move up, so that he could see the Bench, the little one had finally whispered, " If I were not a coward, I would give you a blow, even in court." Garrick had noticed Dr Monsey with interest. There were two rather well-worn anecdotes—one about Garrick collecting a mob on Ludgate Hill, for a bet, by doing no more than stare up at the sky, and say, " I never saw two before," and the other about Monsey calling on his way to see Garrick play Lear, and finding his friend in bed, ill, saying he had asked an actor called Marr to play for him. On his return from seeing Marr, Monsey had found Garrick still in bed—but he had really witnessed a performance by Garrick.

Dr Monsey displeased Mrs Garrick by bursting out laughing when she said nobody took her for a foreigner. He corrected her English. " Hey-day! " exclaimed Garrick on their arrival home after a drive, " what, have you two lovers fallen out! " On another occasion Monsey got out of the carriage and walked home, from Turnham Green. He had been so snubbed. But the most popular Mrs Garrick-Monsey tale was that when Monsey had promised to behave properly

# GARRICK between tragedy and comedy.

*By Sir Joshua Reynolds* (58″ × 72″)

In January 1765, Garrick wrote to his brother George, to ask him to send " prints " of every available picture of him by Reynolds, Zoffany, Benjamin Wilson, and Liotard which had been " scraped ". He needed them for farewell gifts in Paris after his Tour of Europe. The sequel was unexpected. In the following year, George Colman was in Paris, and wrote to him, " There hang out here, in every street, pirated prints of Reynolds' picture of you, which are underwritten, ' L'Homme entre le Vice et la Vertu'. "

Exhibited Society of Artists, 1762.
Engraved by Edward Fisher, 1762.

*Reproduced by kind permission of the Lord Rothschild.*

because the Duke of Argyll was coming to sup, with ladies of *ton*, Mrs
Garrick forgot to serve him.   He handed up his plate again and again
11 before bursting out, " Will you help me, you bitch, or not? "

### 3

When the season of 1762–1763 opened, the new seating accommodation at Drury Lane was generally admitted to be an improvement.   Garrick and Lacy's rule of " No guests behind the scenes or
on the stage " had always been retained in theory, but abuse had
crept in, especially on benefit nights.   Mrs Cibber had awoken on her
bier in Capulet's tomb to find herself regarded by as close and interested an audience as the corpse in Rembrandt's masterpiece
*The Doctors*.   Holland, when his hat had flown off, in *Hamlet*,
had found it replaced, but back to front, by a helpful girl at whose
feet it had fallen.   The Battle of Bosworth had frequently taken
place " in less space than is usually allotted for a cock-fight ".
Finally, after a performance of *Harlequin's Invasion*, the prompter's
diary recorded, " Miss Piercy, in running off the Stage, which was
greatly crowded, fell down and broke her arm ".

On benefit nights extra seats had been built out in front of the
stage boxes.   The players who collected the takings on such occasions, had not at first been favourably impressed by Garrick and
Lacy's application of their rule to all performances.   But when they
realized that the auditorium had been so rearranged that an extra
one hundred and fifteen pounds a night might be expected, they
made no objections.

Garrick's programme for the new season proceeded calmly.   He
was not going to appear until the New Year, when he would be
Alonzo in Mallet's *Elvira* on January 19.   On February 3 he would
be a charming formal old gentleman (quite a new line for him) in Mrs
Sheridan's little comedy.   He was going to take a new part in an old
favourite, *The Fair Penitent*, in the middle of March.   O'Brien was
now perfectly competent to play the gay Lothario.   Garrick would be
Sciolto.   As far as he, personally, was concerned, that would be all.
But Shakespeare had not been forgotten.   *The Two Gentlemen of
Verona* would be a novelty at Drury Lane.   He had a very strong
cast.   Holland and O'Brien would be the Two Gentlemen; Miss
Bride, Silvia, Mrs Yates, Julia.   Yates, as Launce, with a comical
dog, would alone be enough to bring people to see the pretty show
which would be brought on three days before Christmas.

He had not foreseen what came to be known as " The Half-Price
Riots ".   For some time he had been anxious to get rid of another
abuse—the tiresome old custom, which prevailed at all theatres, that

persons coming in after the third act of a play should pay half price. There was a tall, pallid Irish gentleman, Mr Thadeus Fitzpatrick, a would-be arbiter of fashion and the play.   He haunted the Bedford, and the Jamaica Taverns.   He had been given a free pass for Drury Lane.   Gradually, either from pique, or desire for self-advertisement, he had begun to attack Garrick.   Amongst other impertinences, he had said, on an evening when Garrick failed to turn up for a meeting of the Shakespeare Club, that they need hardly wait for the most insignificant member of their society.   Garrick, who lived, according to Murphy, " in a whispering gallery ", heard the story.   Fitzpatrick had also published a pamphlet which discussed " the real merit of a certain popular performer ".   Garrick replied in verse to a man who reminded him extremely of that pitiable specimen of humanity, Fribble, from *Miss In Her Teens*.   The poem was called *The Fribbleriad*, and " Fitzgig " was unmistakable.

> The creature's male, say all you can
> It must be something *like* a man.

Churchill, to oblige a friend, added a telling stanza to *The Rosciad*.

At the first five performances of *The Two Gentlemen*, people had paid the full fee for a seat at whatever hour they had arrived. " Fitzpatrick issued posters, drawing the attention of the public to their wrongs, and on the sixth night of the comedy he arose in a box and created a disturbance.   Garrick came forward to address the house, but could not get a hearing."   " The Town ", a band of Fitzpatrick's followers, who had been posted at strategic intervals in the house, began to smash the pit barriers and boxes, and the chandeliers.   The play could not proceed.   The damage was repaired, and next night the curtain rose upon *Elvira*.   When Garrick appeared, " The Town ", headed by their spokesman, shouted " as one voice ", " Will you, or will you not, give admittance for half price, after the third act, except for the first performance of a pantomime? "   Pantomimes were notoriously expensive to produce, but all new productions now cost the management three times what they had in the earlier years of the century.   Garrick, strongly advised by Lacy, bowed to the storm.   But this meekness only roused fresh demands.   Moody, on the previous night, had stopped one of the rioters from setting fire to the scenery.   They now called for him to apologize.   Now Moody had known deep waters.   He was something of a dark horse in the company.   He was said to have been the son of a barber in Cork.   His name had been Cochrane.   He had come to London from Jamaica.   There was a strong belief that he had gone to the West Indies after following the Stuart Prince in 1745.   He could speak with a strong Irish accent, whatever his origin. He apologized to the audience, humorously, " for *displasing* them by saving their lives in putting out the fire ". This show of firmness was greeted with yells of rage and demands that he should apologize on his knees. With the words " I will not, by God ", he walked off, to be received by Garrick in the wings with open arms. The manager was heard to swear that, while he had a guinea, Moody's salary should be paid. But the noise in front was alarmingly reminiscent of *The Chinese Festival* disaster. Garrick went on to agree that Moody should not appear again. The theatre was saved, but at a humiliating cost, and " Fitzgig " went on to play the same game at Covent Garden. Here Beard showed fight, and Covent Garden was accordingly wrecked. There could be no performances for a week. But Beard got a warrant, and brought " Fitzgig " and some of his ringleaders before the Chief Justice. Lord Mansfield, looking his most grim, told " Fitzgig " that had a man been killed in the riots provoked by him and his gang, they would have been answerable with their lives. Materially, Drury Lane came best out of a sorry affair. " Fitzgig " had been much frightened by a visit from Moody, and had agreed to sign a letter of abject apology, after which Moody had triumphantly taken up his duties again. At Covent Garden " The Town " made performances impossible by giggling and hissing until Beard also gave way. He had been enjoying a most successful season. " English Opera " was drawing audiences away from Drury Lane. The drawing-rooms and streets resounded to admirers carolling or whistling popular airs from *Love in a Village*. Miss Constance Brent, a favourite pupil of Dr Arne, had not stayed at Drury Lane. And nobody was singing " Who is Silvia? " *The Two Gentlemen* had run for only seven nights.

Tom Davies believed that once, at this date, Garrick and Mrs Cibber had played to a house where the night's takings were £3 15s. 6d. Drury Lane accounts show that they were never less than one hundred, but it could not be denied that audiences were failing to respond to a mixture with which they were too familiar. Garrick continued, until the season ended, to appear resolutely in all his principal old successes. He did not seem soured, but both Murphy and Davies believed that the affair of the Half Price Riots had sickened him.

The Peace of Paris had been signed at last. Ascot Races opened, and on a June morning, a chariot with outriders wearing the Cavendish colours bowled on to the Heath. The Duke of Devonshire had brought Mr Garrick to observe a Hogarthian scene. The duke was now out of office (and it was said that the king had been very rude to him on the occasion of his dismissal); but he was delighted to entertain at leisure at Chatsworth. It was so many years since the Garricks had been there, and they had always come on from Londesborough: he sent them detailed travelling instructions.

> Remember to come by Derby and Matlock; it is much the best way. If you lie at Derby, you may with great ease be with me by dinner; it is but twenty six miles, and all good road: remember to come over Rowesley Bridge, three miles from Chatsworth, and so through my grounds, which shall be open.

Amongst the company whom they were to find, were two more dukes, Bedford and Newcastle, both old friends, but the only fellow-guest of whom their host held out hopes was another player—old Quin, a most diverting figure, driving himself about the Peak district in a one-horse chaise, under an umbrella, ready for rain or shine. The Duke of Devonshire was grieved to hear that after three July weeks of Derbyshire air, Mrs Garrick had fallen ill again on her return to London. [13]

On September 3, a letter from Mrs Cibber arrived at Southampton Street.

> Dear Sir,
> I was last night favoured with yours, and greatly surprised by the news in it, for though I had read a paragraph in the papers that you intended going abroad, I gave no credit to it. However sorry I am for my own sake, I think you do right, and wish to God I could do the same. My best wishes and compliments wait on you and Mrs Garrick. Mr Sloper and my daughter join in the same. I shall take it as a particular favour if you will let me have a line from you in your travels, and should you or Mrs Garrick have any commands in England that I am capable of executing I shall have great pleasure in obeying them. Health and pleasure attend you both!

Another letter, emanating, it would seem, from a dreadful underworld, also caught Garrick before he set forth.

> My dear Mr Garrick,
> *Half drunk, half* mad, and quite stripped of all my money, I should be much obliged *if you would enclose and send by the bearer five pieces* by way of adding to the favours already received by
> Yours sincerely
> Charles Churchill. [14]

On September 17, William Hopkins made the first note in his diary. "The Theatre Royal Drury Lane opened this year (1763–4) Sepr: 17th. Mr Garrick and his Lady left their house in Southampton Street to make the Tour of Europe." They had been gone forty-eight hours, and were already in France.

## CHAPTER X

# TOUR OF EUROPE

## 1763–1765

### I

LAST time, the Garricks had crossed from Dover to Boulogne, and had at once run into trouble, hiring transport to Paris. This time they were going in their own post-chaise, by Calais. They had a fellow passenger. Eva-Maria had found herself quite unable to part with her little Biddy. This had raised the question of what was to become of David's little Phill. For an elegant woman to view the Pantheon, Colosseum etc. with a King Charles spaniel of the first quality tucked under her arm would be quite charming, but David did not take warmly to the picture of himself attendant upon Phill on a Tour of Europe. He had solved the problem by taking the little dog round to the Burneys, and bestowing him as a visitor. With six children to entertain him, Phill had settled delightfully.

At Calais, they put up at the " Table Royal ", " a good and reasonable house with civil and obliging people ", but David was not able to write this down for several days. He had forgotten to bring a note-book. They had a very pleasant journey without any incidents, and were entering Paris in high spirits on the evening of Monday, September 19, when he discovered that he had lost the Calais custom-house receipt. This meant that they had to be searched *en personne* and that all their luggage had to be taken off the chaise and carried into the St Denis gate customs, for a second investigation. However, the Directeur, M. d'Aguemont, treated them with great civility. Next morning David bought his note-book and began his Journal, " meant to bring to my mind the various things I shall see in my journey into Italy ". He was going to record, principally, his opinions and feelings. " I shall say very little of France, as I have done it well, though slightly, in my first Journal, in 1751. I shall always put down my thoughts, immediately, as I am struck, without the least attention to what has been said by writers of great and little repute. D. Garrick." The second Journal, in fact, was to languish, after a very few pages.

On Tuesday evening he set off for the Comédie Française, which on his entrance seemed dark and dirty. The play was *La Gouvernante* of La Chaussée, and Dumesnil was acting much as she had done when he had last seen her, twelve years past, and indeed much as she had done since she had sprung into celebrity in 1737. There was a Mlle Doligny, " a young beginner, with a pleasing look and sweetness of voice ". The evening was suddenly made memorable by a deputation on behalf of the company of comedians, to offer their compliments to M. Garrick, and the freedom of their house. His arrival in Paris had not been unexpected. As long ago as January, Sterne had written to tell him that at two dinner-parties the leading topic had been hopes of seeing Garrick, now that Peace was declared. He was said to be equally good in tragedy and comedy. Was it possible?

Last time he had come to Paris it had been as a tourist. He had been three and thirty, newly married, and the month had been May. It was now September, and he was forty-six, and famous. He was going to have very little time for sightseeing. There was an additional reason for the invitations which now showered upon him. France was undergoing one of her periodic fits of Anglomania. Even the bookshops were full of the works of Sterne, and of Shakespeare.

The Duke of Bedford, the Ambassador, who had negotiated the Peace of Paris, had gone home on June 8, and his successor, Lord Hertford, was not expected until mid-October. Mr Richard Aldworth Neville, who had come out with the duke as Secretary, and lived in the Embassy, in a suite of three rooms on the first floor, had stayed on to fill in the gap, and had been appointed Minister Plenipotentiary. (As Resident, he would not have been of sufficient rank to obtain a private audience with Louis XV.) He had been at Eton with Lord Rochford, in the House of Commons with Rigby, and in Switzerland with Windham. There was a well-founded rumour that the Minister-Plenipotentiary, in private theatricals at Geneva, had appeared both as Macbeth and in a pantomime. Mr Neville prepared to introduce Britain's first actor to Paris with due éclat. A supper-party on a large scale seemed indicated. He asked the leading lights of the French theatre, and the principal literary figures of the capital, especially those at work on the Encyclopédie, France's most-vaunted collaborative effort of the century. Diderot and D'Alembert, who had not yet quarrelled fatally, were both very witty. Marmontel, lover of Clairon and pupil of Voltaire, must be included, and Grimm, dramatic critic and pupil of Rousseau. . . . The English colony and visiting English, in sufficient numbers, would make the gathering half French, half English.

The evening's entertainment opened guilelessly with conversation " of the belles lettres, in which the merits of several eminent writers

were discussed with equal judgment and candour ". It passed on to
" observations on the action and eloquence of the French and English
theatres ". This was the cue for the company to call upon Clairon,
who arose and declaimed passages from Voltaire and Racine.
Garrick thought that she did this most charmingly, but foresaw that
her performance was a prelude " to set me a' going ". Sure enough,
she proceeded to beg her fellow-actor to imitate her example, in
English. " I was in spirits." He began with " the soliloquy from
*Hamlet* ". He gave the dagger scene from *Macbeth*, Sir John Brute,
falling asleep, drunk, and the curse of Lear, " without words ". He
then told the story of how he had learned to imitate madness, and
represented, in what his audience accepted as " dumb-show ", his
well-known terrible anecdote of the English father who, playing with
his little girl, accidentally drops the child out of the window.

> At that moment, his looks, full of wildness and horror, his voice
> broken with anguish, and his frightful cries, discomposed all spectators.
> Tears ran from all eyes. . . . As soon as the company had recovered from
> their agitation, Mademoiselle Clairon catched Mr Garrick in her arms and
> kissed him; then turning to Mrs Garrick, she apologised for her conduct, by
> saying it was an involuntary mark of her applause.

Garrick responded by a quatrain in French.

> J'ai prédit que Clairon illusterait la scène,
> Et mon espoir n'a point été déçu;
> Elle a couronné Mélpomène
> Mélpomène lui rend ce qu'elle en a reçu.

He afterwards confessed it was not quite impromptu. He had composed it, with the help of his dyer, the moment he arrived in Paris.
All the French guests said, with obvious sincerity, that Garrick's
acting was, to them, a revelation. The English, not to be outdone in
politeness, praised the performance of Mlle Clairon, as the leading
attraction of an outstanding Anglo-French social occasion. In so
erudite a gathering many were aware that M. Garrick, the great
English actor, was in fact only half English. They had to thank the
revocation of the Edict of Nantes for the accident that he came from
Drury Lane, not the Comédie Française. But most people in Paris
were quite ignorant of this, and Garrick himself was remarkably
British abroad. According to the journalist Suard, he regretted that
he did not speak French well enough " to mingle with the actors of
Paris and, without other reward than the pleasure he would have
given, and the success he might have had, to act with them ".

Next morning, Marmontel, one of the least profound of the
authors present, sent Garrick a note to tell him that sleep had not

effaced his memories of last night, and he hoped never would. Garrick wrote to Colman, telling him that he was going to send over Marmontel's letter by the first person he found going to England.   He said he was not going to read any newspapers on this side of the Alps.

The Garricks had been to see Clairon act, soon after their arrival, and the experience had been rather comical, for Eva-Maria had been disinclined to go, and at first David had lauded the actress somewhat unreservedly and scolded his wife for her lack of response.   But presently Eva-Maria had declared that never in her life had she seen such acting.   She had seen her husband's acting for eighteen years, and although he admired Clairon and had prophesied her success, she did not fulfil all his ideals.   In some respects he still gave the palm to Dumesnil, whose terrific tirades were occasionally refreshed now-adays, according to green-room tales, by a swig from a bottle prof-fered by a reliable servitor in the wings.   He had gone to call upon Clairon, urged by Selwyn, and had spent an interesting morning. She had surprised him by telling him that " her appointments were only £250, besides having to find herself in everything ".   He thought of Susannah Cibber " getting as much as £700 besides her benefit, and every article of apparel provided, excepting the mere garniture of her head ".   Clairon had to appear on September 25 in Saurin's *Blanche et Guiscard*, a tragedy founded upon the same story as James Thomson's *Tancred and Sigismunda*, and Garrick, who had played Tancred since 1748, and ever since, had watched her rehearse. It was given out that Clairon had taken lessons from the English actor, and when the play came to performance some spectators thought that she had never acted worse.   The piece ran for only three nights.   Some English thought that its failure was due to the poorness of the French version.   However, the author was well pleased with Clairon's efforts, and sent her a congratulatory verse, and everyone present had enjoyed pointing out Garrick in the audience (" the original Tancred ") and whispering his name.

He had gone to see Préville, France's first comedian, three times. " He has the same looks, in every part."   Préville was a round-faced little fellow, fair, and well-made, " remarkably neat on the stage ", rather sleepy looking.   He probably owed his popularity to the extraordinarily innocent expression which he could assume.   But he seemed to Garrick to understand his profession thoroughly.   Off the stage he was " a man of parts ".   He addressed Garrick with great solemnity, as " Maître ".   He had been well educated, though very unhappy in youth, and could speak English.   Clairon's background too had been sad.   She had been born—some forty years past now— the natural daughter of a sempstress and an army sergeant.   It may

have been from her sire that she had got her courage, which was
remarkable. She was not a beauty, but could put on her beauty as
other women put on a hat. She was low-statured, with too prominent a forehead, hair and brows as dark as charcoal, very large blue
eyes and a tight mouth. She could, like Préville, have been nothing
but French. It would have been interesting to see how these players
would be received in England—even more interesting to see how
Drury Lane company would be judged in Paris. The idea of an
exchange visit of companies was a fascinating subject for conversation with a French journalist, but Garrick could not seriously consider it at present. Paris, although the winter season would not
really set in for another month, was already over-full of engagements
for him. A visiting Englishman, with good connections, need never,
it appeared, dine alone in Paris these days. On Thursdays and
Sundays the Baron and Baroness D'Holbach welcomed guests of
every nation at a magnificent mansion in the Rue St Anne. The
Baron was a Palatinate German of unbridled self-confidence, author
of several works on moral philosophy, a militant atheist and a good
linguist. The Baroness was remarkable for her tact and the height
of her coiffure. Their house was known as the " Café de l'Europe ".
On Wednesdays, Monsieur and Madame Helvetius entertained a
circle, " titré, mitré ou littré ". Mondays were Madame Geoffrin's
nights for artists, and Wednesdays for writers. . . .

But the Garricks had to cross the dreaded Mont Cenis before the
first snows came. They were on their road to Italy. This excuse
was appreciated, and they were allowed to depart, after nearly three
weeks, with many protestations of regret, offers of introductions in
Italy and adjurations to return. They did not plan to pass through
Paris again; but on a Grand Tour, so much was uncertain.

2

At Lyons, where Selwyn had passed them on to his fellow-banker
Camp, they sampled the theatre of a great provincial city. By
October 10 they were well on their road to Turin, at a little place in
High Savoy, lovely but obscure, where the supply of writing-paper
was inadequate. Their journey, so far, had been perfectly successful,
but it had been on a great road, down which, in an unending procession, passed the chaises and berlines of English travellers all
bound for Italy. It was unsafe to leave a bedroom door unlocked,
and advisable to leave a servant in it. Boxes had been cut off the
backs of carriages while waiting outside inns, while the coachman
drowsed on the box. The Garricks had not been robbed yet, except
quite openly, by extortionate innkeepers and postmasters. A

French acquaintance had told David that when an English chaise went by, the natives winked and put their tongues in their cheeks.

On Monday, October 10, his thoughts returned to Drury Lane. An experiment should have been tried there on Saturday night. There was a young man, William Powell, who lived in the same lodgings as Holland. In the evenings he spouted at the Wood Lane Debating Club. By day he worked in the counting-house of Sir Robert Ladbrook, distiller. Holland thought he had talent, and Garrick, after seeing him, had agreed. Powell was going to be brought on, thus early in the season, in a capital part, in a play new to Drury Lane, an adaptation by Colman of Beaumont and Fletcher's *Philaster*. Garrick, who had rehearsed him thoroughly, thought he " will surprise, and I most cordially wish it ". He was a tall, thin, polite young man, not ill-made, but a little round-shouldered, and devoted to a young wife and two little daughters, all also tall, thin and polite.

Oct. 10th, 1763.

My dear George,

We are now got to a small village in Savoy called *Mont Meillan* [sic] and surrounded by mountains, but one of the most delightful spots I ever beheld. We see a most beautiful vale, water'd with a fine river, full of vineyards, grass mounds, and the whole bordered with a most noble range of mountains, in the middle of which you may see clouds, ascending like smoke of [a] chimney. We shall go to dinner between 10 and 11, and indeed we are well prepar'd for it.

I shall put you to the expense of this letter, merely to tell you to direct all my letters now to me at ROME, à Monsieur, Monsieur Garrick, *chez* le Marquis Belloni, à Rome. I hope the last you wrote was to Florence. Pray write to me now and then; my friend Colman and you may take it by turns and then I shall have a succession. I long to hear of your success, and indeed I flatter myself that you will have a good season with few altercations. If you should hear of any person you can trust coming to Florence or Rome, pray send me Churchill's " Ghost " or anything will divert me. Remember me most kindly to him, and tell him that I have had a most warm invitation from Voltaire, whom I shall take in my return, tho' I am rather angry with him for saying that tho' Shakespeare is surprising, there is more *Barbarism* than *Genius* in his works. O, the damned fellow!—but I'll see him. Pray, my best wishes and services to Mr Lacy; if he wants any books or prints from Italy, I will be sure to bring them; my Compts. to Mrs Lacy. You see what pages I have to write on, but 'tis the best we have here, and you must pass it. We are arrived here without the smallest accident, and indeed our tackle seems so good that we expect none. My wife and I are in better health than we have been some time, and when we have passed *Mount Cenis*, we shall be quite at our ease. . . . Pray send me all the news you can cram in a letter, with a dash of Politicks. Pray, take a peep at Hampton and the gardener. I hope he is not too fine a gentleman. If Mr Lacy had paid his interest I shall be oblig'd to him. Pray, let me have that affair quite clear (if you can) to the time I shall return.

I hope, when the catalogue of my books is made, that the rest of them will be put in the closet next to our bedchamber, and that Charles has taken care of Hogarth's pictures; if the sun comes upon them, they will be spoilt. God bless you; love to your children. My wife sends hers to you, Colman etc etc.

Colman got a letter from Turin to announce that the Garricks were now safe in Italy. " We had the finest day imaginable for passing the terrible Mont Cenis. I was highly entertained, indeed, and it was much more inconceivable (I mean the manner of ascending and descending) than it is Dangerous or Disagreeable."

But they would have to stay in Turin for a week, while their carriage was fitted with a new perch. The usual drill was that, for the crossing of the Mont Cenis, a carriage was taken to pieces, and carried over on the backs of mules. Its occupants could either ride a mule to the summit, or be carried over in chairs. The Garrick's *voiturier* had chosen to have their carriage dragged up by twelve men. " It was a great miracle that it was not dash'd into ten thousand pieces." The journey through Savoy and Piedmont was the most romantic and beautiful that could be imagined, but the nastiness of the inns was likewise beyond conception. Eva-Maria had been taken suddenly ill, and frightened everyone, including herself, but had recovered as quickly from an attack probably to be attributed to the nasty inns. Mr George Pitt, the British Envoy, and all the English in Turin, were being particularly kind. Turin was admirably neat and clean. Many of its broad, wide streets were arcaded; its squares were spacious. It seemed to David a city of palaces. In the picture-gallery he was especially struck by a Guido Reni and a Guercino, *David and Goliath*, and *The Prodigal Son's Return*. Although not a feature of the Prodigal was to be seen, it was possible to guess all his story from the poignancy of his attitude.

Nothing since they had crossed the Channel amazed the Garricks more than the manners, both of the audience and actors, in the magnificent Opera House. (The dancing David dismissed as the worst he had ever beheld.) Throughout the performance the spectators talked loudly, and even the players, when on the stage and not otherwise occupied, greeted and conversed with their friends in the audience. He hoped Townley would read aloud to Drury Lane cronies, over a bottle of Dr Schomberg's claret, some of his descriptions of his experiences in Italy.

Milan was made delightful by the kindness of Count Firmian, the Austrian Minister, to whom they had been given letters of intro-duction. They had put up at a famous inn, the " Tre Re ", but the count insisted on their taking dinner with him every day. This

Maecenas was particularly interested in everything English. Their
first meeting had been romantic, for on arrival they had hurried off
at once to see the cathedral, and there they had met the count, who
had at once identified them. David promised to send him, in gratitude for so many hours of personally conducted sight-seeing, pictures
of himself in all his capital parts.

They arrived at Genoa " *La Superba* " on a morning of glorious
sunshine. The month was November, but the city shone as if
roofed with gold or silver, and built on blocks of mother-of-pearl.
" What more I think of it," wrote David in his Journal, " shall be
wrote down when I have examined it." But he never added another
word about Genoa. At Florence they had introductions to another
count, Francesco Algarotti, called by Voltaire " my dear Swan of
Padua ". Unfortunately, the much-travelled poet, philosopher and
writer on art was in very weak health. David recommended to him
a remedy much in vogue in England—tar-water. Hearing that they
planned to take Bologna on their homeward road, the count offered
to give them letters to three most influential people there—General
the Marquis Monvi, the Marquise Scappi and the Cardinal Legate.
He also promised, to await them in Venice, addressed to Mr Murray,
British Minister, two volumes of his published works. David, when
he had read some of these, thought Algarotti's merit as great as his
amiability. But they did not meet again next year, for Algarotti
was on his death-bed. His promised letters, introducing " the
illustrious M. Garrick, the Roscius of the century ", were written
actually on the day that he died.

Colman's father had been Envoy to Tuscany, and Colman had
asked them to look up the house in which he had been born, and,
more important, the register of his birth. Both errands were
successfully performed before they left Florence.

The Garricks entered Rome from the north by the Porta del
Popolo on a December morning. David had hardly been able to
sleep the night before, from excitement. " I scarcely know what
sensation to call it . . . but I felt a strange unusual something at
entering the city where the great Roscius exerted those talents
which rendered him the wonder of his age." He was sadly dashed
by his first sight of the Eternal City. The " Place ", " as they call
it ", was adorned with an obelisk, between four water-spouting lions,
of obvious antiquity, but it was totally dismal, so dirty, discoloured
and ill-looking. " Three crooked streets in front, terminated at this
end with two tolerable churches," seemed to promise nothing but
further disillusionment. Even the Tiber was " a pitiful river ",
muddy, and quite yellow. After dinner, he went out, unwillingly,

to see a little more of Rome, and the moment he entered the Pantheon, " My God! what was my pleasure and surprise! I never felt so much in my life as when I entered that glorious structure. I gasped, but could not speak for some minutes." The Colosseum was incomparably more impressive than he had ever guessed from any pictures, or descriptions. In fact, all " the ruins " were far superior to his expectations, founded on pictures. Rome had captured him. He spent his fortnight there almost entirely in sightseeing, and refused to be lured from the antique even to behold the Pope with his troop of cardinals on two or three ceremonial public occasions. He found time, however, to see something of two young English art students. They were George and Nathaniel Dance, much younger brothers of his Dance at Drury Lane; the one who had changed his name to Love. George was going to be an architect. Nathaniel specialized in very large oil-paintings of classical subjects, and would much like to paint Garrick in character. He must return by Rome. He must spend a month there next time. It was, of all places in the world, " the most worth coming to, and writing about ".

All the long way down to Naples, the rain fell in torrents. Short of being murdered, the Garricks suffered every distress, as ridiculous as it was unexpected. But they laughed off their chapter of accidents as something to make a good story at Hampton, and arrived at last on December 17 at the furthest point of their Tour. Garrick wrote to Colman a week later:

> We are basking in a warm sun, with the Mediterranean at our feet, and Mount Vesuvius in our view. Though it is Christmas, we have green peas every day, and dine with our windows open. We are all at this moment, Biddy not excepted, in the highest spirits, and I am much the better for my expedition.

### 3

William Hopkins, Drury Lane prompter, who was devoted to his absent master, kept a much fuller diary than his predecessor. His note on the first performance of *Philaster* was typical.

> October 8. Mr Powell, a young Gentleman, Clerk to Sir Robert Ladbrook, made his first Appearance in the Character of Philaster. A greater Reception was never shown to anybody. He was so much frightened, he could not speak for some time, and when he did, the Tears ran down his Cheeks. But he soon recovered himself, and went through the Part with a great deal of Nature and Feeling. Continued Claps and Huzzas of Bravo! etc etc. Upon the whole, I think him possessed of every requisite necessary to make him an Ornament to the Stage.
>
> N.B. Mr D. Garrick instructed him in the Part; when I see him in another, shall be able to judge better of his Capabilities.

Miss Pope appeared this Night in the Character of Maria in "The Citizen". By endeavouring to be very fine, she over did it, and it was plain to see she wanted her Master.    5

Other people were writing their opinions of Powell. A fortnight before the Garricks had left London, Horace Walpole had warned Horace Mann to expect, in Florence, "the famous Garrick and his once famous wife. He will make you laugh, as a mimic, and as he knows we are great friends, will affect great partiality for me; but be a little upon your guard, remember he is *an actor*." He followed this up, on October 17 by something even more acid. "Have you got Mr Garrick yet? If you have, you may keep him; there is come forth within these ten days, a young actor who has turned the heads of the whole town."

But he was too late. Sir Horace had already entertained the Garricks, and the visit of the English Roscius to the British Resident's palazzo had been immortalized in a caricature by Mr Patch, the leading English artist settled in Florence.    6

David, in Naples, was pleased to hear that Drury Lane was doing so well without him.

Naples, Jany the 2nd. 1763.

My dear George,

I wrote last week to my friend Colman, and since that I have received his most friendly and agreeable packet. I rejoice most sincerely with him at the success of "The Deuce is in him" and am happy that his benefit turn'd out so well without my assistance.

. . . We have been here a fortnight, and are as well and as jolly as a fine climate, fine things, and fine doings can make us. We dine and sup with Lord Spenser, Lord Exeter, the Minister, Consul etc etc etc almost every day and night. We have balls more than twice a week, and parties innumerable—In short we are very much made of, and I have not once yet, (tho' we have had crosses upon the road), wish'd myself in Southampton Street.

I rejoice much at the success of Powell, I hope his head will not be turned with it, and that he will not cease to labour night and day at his profession. I hope too, and believe, that Mr Lacy has rewarded him accordingly. *You* may answer for *me*; pray let it be done handsomely. He has merit, and a family, and will have occasion for our benevolence. I guess by Colman's letter that your season to the 6th Decr: has been tolerable. I long to know how it goes on, and therefore pray write, as soon as you have received this, and I may receive it before I leave Rome, where we expect to be about the latter end of February. I shall write the next post day (this day se'nnight) to Mr. Burney. . . . I have lost a little Memdm: he gave me about some Musick for him; pray ask him to put it down in your next letter. . . .

Colman will tell you how I have been entertained at Rome, and with what appetite I shall return to it again. The two Dances (Love's brothers) were very kind and obliging to us; they are both very ingenious and agreeable men. The painter is a great genius and will do what he pleases when he goes to London, which will be the next spring; I ought to say *this* spring, for it is absolutely more than spring with us. It is as warm here as it is with you in June; it is too hot, nay, it is sultry. My wife sends her love with mine to you and your babes. Pray write as soon as you receive this. Send me a bit of everything, and remember to date your letter.

Yours ever and ever most affectionately,

P.S. Remember me to Love etc.

What's become of the new pantomine?

He had dated his own letter wrong. It was now 1764. The Minister whom he was meeting nearly every day and night was, to be exact, Envoy Extraordinary. Mr William Hamilton was almost a newcomer, for he had arrived in the middle of November. He had an adoring plain wife, and was a remarkably handsome person, of valuable connections, who hoped to rise in his profession, and did not trouble particularly to disguise the fact that he looked on Naples as a stepping-stone. The Spencers, whose name David had not yet learned to spell correctly, were not new acquaintances. He had known them before Lord Spencer succeeded to his title. Indeed, they had been to Hampton. They were now to become friends for life. They were an outstanding young couple, with, it would seem, everything in the world to make them happy; but quite unspoilt, and both highly intelligent. Poor Lord Spencer was not finding the Neapolitan climate agreeable to his health, which had never been robust. Lord Palmerston (who was a bachelor of four and twenty, with a bad stammer) and Mr William Arden (who had been Lord Spencer's tutor) made merry over his remarkable ability for foreseeing troubles on a Grand Tour.

The Garricks went with the Spencers on Christmas Day to Herculaneum, where " they have dug up every utensil that was in use among the Romans, and have even got a lady's *toilette* entire. The lady herself was found dressing herself, and in the act of sticking a bodkin into her hair ". An expedition was planned for next week " to see the top of Vesuvius. . . . In short, we are encompassed with classical prodigies, and when we shall be able to get out of this enchanting circle, I cannot possibly tell." Inevitably, in a country where they did not speak the language, they were seeing most of the English colony, but as the " enchanting circle " into which they had been swept revolved around Lady Orford, a permanent resident, and the British Envoy, they met leading Neapolitans from the royal family downwards. " I am to have the honour and satisfaction of seeing the King's Italian actors perform before him, in the palace; a most extraordinary favour. They perform extempore, and the nobleman who stands in the place of the Lord Chamberlain, has sent me word that if I will write down any dramatic fable, and give the

R

argument only of the scenes, they shall play it before us in twenty four hours." The San Carlo theatre, filled to the roof, and ablaze with lights, really astonished David, on first coming into it. But it was too large, even for the famous voice of the Gabrielli, who was not to be tempted to London by any amount of English gold. " The situation and climate of this place are most extraordinary, and the people are still more so. They are a new race of beings, and I have the highest entertainment in going amongst them, and observing their characters, from the highest to the lowest."

He did not write to George again until January 31.

We have been here six weeks, and intend to stay till about the end of next month, then we shall return to *Rome* for a month or more. Then we shall set out for *Bologna* on our way to *Venice*, and from there through Germany, on our way to England. This is our intended route, which I will despatch with all convenient speed, but I am afraid I shall not see your fat face, or kiss the brawn of it, till the middle of June. Now I am out of your clutches, I must make a meal, and a good one, in Italy. I shall never return to it again, and therefore I will make good use of my time.

We have been very happy here and have received every mark of favour from all sorts of people. I eat and drink too much and laugh from morning till night. Our mirth has lately been damp'd by my poor wife's keeping her bed, and room, for many days with a most obstinate rheumatism in her hip. She has been blister'd etc. etc. and tho' she is better, yet still continues lame, and weak. However, she hopes to be at a Carnival Masquerade (which begins next Tuesday) in the dress of a lame old woman. I have scolded and phyz'd about it, but if she can wag, she goes.

We are continually with Lady Orford, Lady Spencer, Lord Exeter, Lord Palmerston; and the Nobility of the country, who have descended from their great pride and magnificence to honour us with their smiles. In short, we are in great fashion, and I have forgot England and all my trumpery at Drury Lane.

I am glad you go on so well . . . I can say nothing about Powell's benefit as I am not able to give my opinion at this distance. I fear for his *head*, and of course for his *heart*. If he talks of *consequence*, he is undone. You have said nothing lately of Covent Garden? Do they beat you soundly? . . . Have Lacy and you been content with a hundred quarrels a week? Colman has hurt me with an account of his behaviour to him. I fear he dislikes him as my friend. What a beast if it be so! . . .

I have almost seen every curiosity of this place. I was very near wet to the skin yesterday, in the Elysian fields at Baiae, and therefore did not enjoy Julius Caesar's Palace and Tully's villa so much at my ease as I could wish.

I beg one of you will write, the moment you can after the receipt of this, directed to Barazzi at Rome, as usual, with a whole packet full of news, and the other may write a fortnight after, directed to me *chez M. Udney, Consul de sa Majesté Britannique, à Venise*. I will let you know, either here, or at Rome, where you may write after to me, for your letters will be most agreeable upon the road.

## 4

Three circumstances had made them not so sorry to leave Naples for Rome again. In southern Italy the peasantry always lived upon the borderline of starvation. In the early spring of 1764, horrifying stories of famine in the Campagna Felice penetrated to the English tourists. Men and women, reduced to mere skeletons, were being picked up dead in the squalid quayside alleys of the gay city. There were also riots in the streets, between troops posted outside bakers' shops and long queues of impatient and hungry Neapolitans. Eva-Maria was still not well. But her affliction was called the Neapolitan sciatica. In Rome she would get rid of it. The Garricks' third cause for discomfort was also ever-present, and an hourly annoyance. The servant whom they had engaged in Naples was clearly dishonest. People at home were complaining that they did not hear from David, who was writing regularly. He could only conclude that the rogue who was given his letters for the post, pocketed the money and destroyed his prose. The problem of native staff employed by English on a Grand Tour seemed insoluble, and the English themselves were much to blame for this. The characters whom they engaged vaguely as courier, interpreter and *valet de chambre* (and most shockingly spoiled) soon became, if they were not so already, thoroughly demoralized. But travellers were so dependent upon them that they dared not give them their *congés*. David took his courage in both hands, and dismissed his smooth Neapolitan. He refused to give him a reference with which to impose upon future English. The next thing he heard of the man was from Milan, where he had parted from a Mr Newton, with whom, according to him, he had been travelling not as a servant but as a companion. But Fortune favoured David, and sent him Antonio Carara of Padua, the factotum of whom all tourists dreamed. He spoke and wrote excellent English and French. He stayed with the Garricks until they returned to England, and from Paris wrote continually to David. Jean Monnet, to whom David had recommended him, asked if it was possible that this young man, so gentleman-like (but delighted at the gift of David's old *ratine* suit), was descended from the illustrious Paduan family of whom the head had been poisoned in prison by orders of the Republic. It might have been so, for Padua was much upon the decline. There was grass growing in the streets of the University city which had produced Andrea Palladio. David found the place melancholy.

The Spencers and Arden had come to Rome too. In the gardens of the Villa Medici, on the Pincio, commanding one of the most beautiful prospects in the world, Lady Spencer presented Roscius with a wreath of bays. He replied in verse. But in Rome, he did not spend so much of his time amongst fine people as in Naples. " I *9* am antiquity hunting from morning to night." He did not feel so well as he had done in Naples, and " some disagreeable nervous flutterings " made him as grave as an owl for a few days; but then the rains came, " in pailfulls ", followed by brilliant sun on Tiburtine stone, and he frisked up. In a Roman street on a spring morning he noticed a strange-looking small person, with a head much too large for his body, and bandy legs. " What! let me look at you! Are you the little fellow to whom we gave the prizes at the Society of Arts? " " Yes, sir." Joseph Nollekens was invited to breakfast. He had found a source of income in Rome by buying fragments of antique statues. " After he had dextrously restored them with heads and legs, he stained them with tobacco water." He sold them, at high prices, to English gentlemen on the Grand Tour. David did not buy a Venus for Hampton, but he sat for a bust. It was the first that Nollekens had ever modelled, and David gave him twelve guineas in gold for it, and presented it to Arden. On the death of *10* Arden, his widow gave it to Lord Spencer, and it became one of the treasures of Althorp.

Every travelling English notability must sit to Batoni, who was so popular that he was generally alluded to simply by his first name. " Pompeo " depicted David looking pleasantly shrewd, pointing at a volume open at a page showing human visages displaying various emotions. Lady Spencer, brown-eyed and smiling sweetly, had Vesuvius for background. *11*

The story of Dance's portrait of Garrick as Richard was disappointing. Dance came to England, and, as David prophesied, had a great success. Eva-Maria had been promised the picture, for a hundred guineas, and had cleared a place on the wall ready for it. One day, at their dinner-table, Dance announced that he could sell it for fifty or a hundred guineas more to the immensely wealthy young Welsh baronet, Sir Watkin Williams Wynn. Eva-Maria was struck dumb by such perfidy, but David merely commented, " Well, sir, and you mean to take it? " " I think I shall." " Think no more of the picture," whispered David to Eva-Maria. " In a short time, you shall see a better one there." Next morning he asked his wife to come and look at their new picture. Eva-Maria looked, and saw herself, with David smiling behind her shoulder. Her gift was an elegant mirror, for which her husband had given a hundred and twenty-five guineas. But he forgave Dance, and seven years after David had sat to Nathaniel in Rome, George produced two little pencil sketches of the Garricks at their breakfast table—Eva-Maria, serene, in a fashionable lace cap, David in his country-gentleman's undress, and his own hair, sitting with his arms on the table, looking up, in his characteristic quick way.   He said he considered it the best likeness ever taken of him.   Reynolds was a much more handsome character.   When he heard the young Earl of Carlisle say that he would have liked to possess Zoffany's *Garrick as Abel Drugger*, for which Reynolds had given a hundred guineas, he asked what advance his lordship was prepared to make on that figure.   Lord Carlisle said he would give a hundred and twenty, upon which Reynolds said it

12 was a bargain, providing the last twenty pounds went to Zoffany.

At Drury Lane, on April 7, Hopkins made a sad entry in his diary: " Mr O'Brien this morning being married to Lady Susan Strangeways, after the Play Mr Powell made an Apology that Mr O'Brien had sent Word he was not able to do his part (Lovel), and that Mr. King had undertaken it at very short warning, and hoped for their Indulgence."

Lady Susan Fox-Strangeways, who had attained her twenty-first birthday yesterday, rightly foreseeing that her loving parents would never allow her to marry a player, had decided to elope.   From St James's Street, where she had gone to sit for her portrait by Miss Catherine Read, she had sent her carriage home, telling her servants that she had forgotten the cap in which she must be painted.   She had then hailed a hackney chair and told the men to carry her to St Paul's Church, Covent Garden, where O'Brien was waiting for her. They had driven off from the church for his country lodgings at Dunstable, and she hoped her parents would forgive her.   O'Brien had no means of livelihood except as a player, in which he was earning well.   It was unthinkable to the bride's parents that their son-in-law should continue to exhibit himself publicly at Drury Lane. After much, and dreadful, family conclave (which took many months), it was decided that the young couple had better make a fresh start in the New World—North America.   The Duke of Devon-

13 shire wrote to his old friend on April 17.

You will think me a strange beast not to have returned you my thanks for your former letter sooner.   I am indeed ashamed of myself.   Do not impute it to any want of regard for you, for that is impossible.   [A states-man out of office said that he could send very little news of what was happening in the world, beyond what his friend could read in the news-papers.   Of the world of the theatre he had, of course, heard what everyone had heard.]

I am glad to hear that your administration has gone on so well in your absence.   I have now and then made some inquiries, and have heard it doubted whether there would not be a considerable difference.   A moderate one, perhaps, would not be disagreeable, as it would be flattering.

However, I heard two days ago that you must come over, as one of your chief performers had left you. What a silly thing had Lady Susan Strangeways done. Lord Ilchester thought he had reasoned her out of it, and she had desired him to take her into the country; he is by all accounts most terribly affected by it, and poor Lady Sarah Bunbury as much.

As you have lost your relish for the stage, and *virtu* has taken its place, we shall have you come over a perfect Dilettanti, and I trust we shall have some battles upon the subject.

I am much obliged to you for your offer of purchasing pictures and statues, but I have no money. I should, however, be obliged to you if you would get me all the prints that Bartolozzi has engraved; as you are such a connoisseur, you must meet him. I believe he lives at Rome; I know they are sold there. If you meet with Lord and Lady Spencer again in your travels, I beg you will make my compliments, and assure them of my great regard and esteem for both, and shall be very glad to see them return in perfect health. I shall be impatient till I hear Mrs. Garrick is quite well. **14**

Eva-Maria was much better, and David had not the slightest intention of allowing William O'Brien to spoil his holiday. On the contrary, he was adding a month to his programme. The Duke of York, the king's young bachelor brother, had now arrived in Italy. There were going to be great fêtes for him in the Duchy of Parma. All loyal English were going; the Spencers were going. The Garricks trysted with their friends for a May meeting in Parma, and set off for Leghorn and Bologna. Both of them had now made considerable bulky purchases. At Leghorn, Sir John Dick, Consul, saw to it that cases of Florentine wine, some boxed models of Italian stage-scenery, David's volumes, and Eva-Maria's essences, were shipped in the *Raven* (Captain Alexander Scott) for London. Under Sir John's roof, David frequently met the chaplain to the British Factory, and told him that if ever he wanted to attend a performance at Drury Lane, to drop him a line. Dr Burnaby waited eleven years, and then hit the morning of the day on which Garrick was making his last appearance as Lear. But he got his seat. **15**

The détour to Parma was rewarding. David was asked to a select dinner at the Hotel Pallavicini, to have the honour of meeting the Duke of York, who was an odd-looking young man, so fair that his eyebrows and lashes were almost white. The Duke of Parma was so taken by a performance of the dagger scene that he expressed his admiration of Shakespeare, and Garrick, in fair English, and next morning sent David an invitation to lodge in his palace, and " a very handsome gold box, with some of the finest enamelled painting upon all sides of it, I ever saw ". (Holland, whose temper had not been sweetened by the astounding success of his protégé Powell, was very rude when he was shown David's gifts from foreign princes. " So,

you went about the continent mouthing for snuff-boxes? " But
16 David, who knew what jealousy was, showed no offence.)

The Duke of York was going on to Venice. The Garricks had
intended to end their tour of Italy there, in any case, but now they
could not move. Eva-Maria, whose sailing gait and elegant atti-
tudes had distracted many hearts, was now a heart-breaking spectacle. She could not put on her own shoes. At nights she could not
lie easy in any position. David would gladly have compounded for
her being lame for life if only she could be relieved of what were,
clearly, agonies. On June 6, he wrote to George:

> Here we are still, and indeed very much against my mind; but that
> the Physicians here all advise me to return to Padua in order to try an
> application of the mud of some mineral spring at Abano, near that city,
> which they say is a specific for the Rheumatism and Sciatica. My wife's
> lameness has been rather worse here, perhaps owing to the watery situation
> of the place. But I am much out of spirits about it, and would give the
> world I was at home. . . . We go to Padua in a day or two, and shall see
> what effect the mud will have in three or four days; if a good one, we
> imagine that a fortnight will do, and then we shall set forward for England
> as fast as we can, unless I am prevented by a letter from you at Augsburgh,
> which I hope you have written, and which I shall receive very soon. I have
> prepared a great deal of music for our use. I am about to engage some
> dancers (a man and a woman) and will endeavour to send you over a good
> violin, from Rome, and an excellent one. [He had to cram into a post-
> script his description of Venice en fête.] Last Monday, I saw one of the
> finest sight my eyes ever beheld. It was the Regate, in honour of the
> King's birthday, and appeared to be a dream or a fairy-tale realiz'd. I am
17 grown fat, and sleep half the day in a gondola.

Some of his news from home was sad. The last of the Lichfield
spinster sisters had died. " Lenny " had been laid to rest in the
cathedral, beside her parents and " Jenny ", on May 13. David's
letters no longer ended " love to sisters ". Gibraltar had nearly
killed Captain Peter Garrick. Minorca had been the death of his
soldier son, William. The Garricks were not long lived.

The Spencers and Arden and Lord Palmerston said it was to be
only au revoir, for the Spencers had a pleasant home near London—
Wimbledon Park—as well as their town house; Arden was often
with them, and Lord Palmerston was coming to Hampton as soon as
possible.

On July 12 the Garricks were still at Venice, and getting harassed.
If they made the best speed possible they might reach England a
month before Drury Lane opened, but they must set out soon.
David told Colman much more about Venice. It was an astounding
place. " It glares upon you at first, and enchants you, but living
here a month (like the honeymoon) brings you to a temperate

consideration of things, and you long for *terra firma* liberty again."
He was fagged to death attending scenes which transcended the wonders of the Arabian Nights.   In the comparative cool of the evenings
he walked on the Rialto, which consisted of a single arch, but a very
noble one, of marble.   Its beauty was impaired by two rows of
booths.   He could easily imagine himself going to keep an appointment with Pierre, from *Venice Preserv'd*, but never, strange to say,
with Bassanio or Antonio.   Venetian gentlemen of today looked like
attorneys in a spiritual court.   With a mask stuck in his hat, and a
kind of black mantle, trimmed with lace, on his shoulders, a modern
Venetian considered himself dressed for any assembly.   Masks had
no sinister significance.   They were in general used as an apology for
not being in full dress, which was a thing only seen on a great occasion.
The Garricks were fortunate in having arrived during the Duke of
York's visit, for the native nobility mingled very little with foreigners,
and seldom entertained anyone outside their own families.   The
Cassinos on the Piazza of St Mark were of very bad reputation, but
ladies and gentlemen (in mask and domini) went to them under
starlit and velvet skies to enjoy the music, and order an inexpensive
al fresco repast of coffee, lemonade and fruit.   He had been to the
Courts of Justice, and laughed more than at the Italian Comedy.
Theatres in Venice were curious.   There were plenty of them, and
you paid a small sum for entrance.   If you wanted a seat, a chair was
unlocked, and you paid again.   The back part of the pit was filled by
footmen and gondoliers, all standing.   The nobility and better sort of
citizens owned boxes, which were pitch dark, unless you paid for
candles.   Only the stage was brilliantly lit.   This was very effective.
He was buying more books, and some pictures, but longing to be
on the move.   The rumour in Rome had been that, following the
famine, the plague had spread as far as Trieste, and there was talk
of quarantine in the neighbouring States.   " If so, we shall run the
gauntlet terribly; but we are not dismayed, and must go through
with it."                                                        [18]
   The ordinary populace of Venice were remarkably sober, obliging
to strangers and gentle in manner, after the Neapolitans.   Gambling
in Venice was very high.   David heard with horror that in a single
night, playing with the Marquis Prie and Don Pepy (the Neapolitan
gamester), Lord Ossory had lost four thousand sequins, and the
Honourable Topham Beauclerk, twenty thousand—ten thousand
good English pounds.   The smell of some of the lesser canals was
stupefying.   He felt sad and tired.   " I have no joy now in thinking
on the stage, and shall return (if I must) like a bear to the stake; and
this baiting my good friend, is no joke after forty."   Venice, like

Padua, was suffering from declining trade. But unlike Padua she had unique attractions for foreign tourists.

Extraordinary cures for his wife's sciatica were being pressed upon him by well-meaning foreign friends. Countess Bujovich had told Signor Joseph Baretti of a plaister, made of Venetian soap and the yoke of an egg, applied on paper, which must be blue. Baretti's final suggestion was literally connected with black magic, " Have you forgot the black hen? Do not forget that particularity, and abstain from laughing, you incredulous mortal! " The Garricks had met him first at home four years past, when he had been producing an Italian–English dictionary, to which Johnson had supplied a dedication, and the little Tuscan lexicographer had fallen a victim at first sight to the charms of poor suffering Eva-Maria.

> I wish, with all my heart, it may produce a good effect, as I had really a great value and even affection for your lady, ever since she poured me a dish of tea the first time I ever saw her, in London. I never shall forget that adventure, though she may. She did it in so graceful a manner, I could still paint her in that pretty attitude, had I Reynold's or Guido's powers. Do not interpret this as a bold declaration of love to your best half; for was my love to her of the wicked kind, Faith! husband, a cunning
> 19  Italian would know better than to let thee in the secret.

They left for Abano, at last, on July 13, and while Eva-Maria took her cure, David got to know the antique shops of Padua thoroughly. There was a Jew, called Marchetto, who was still, a year later, sending him messages, of oriental suavity, by Count Marsili of Padua; and a bookseller, Scappino, who forwarded a " small " list of twenty titles, which included a folio with pictures of Palladio's architecture published in Venice in 1561, and a Vita Nuova 20 (Florence, 1547). Abano did seem to benefit Eva-Maria, but David was not sure that her improvement was anything to do with mud-baths. " She underwent, like any of her own papistical martyresses, various violent operations, and was at last cured by an Old Woman's 21 recipe—blush, physic, blush! " She went out for a walk without her stick. She was much better, though still not quite well. She eagerly agreed to start for home.

The passage of the Alps by the Brenner to Innsbruck, and over the mountains of the Tyrol, was renowned as one of the most beautiful spectacles in Europe. For David, it was the worst journey of his life. He had been feeling unusually languid just before he left Venice, and had been low-spirited at Padua, but had attributed these symptoms to late hours, too many banquets and his anxiety over the sufferings of " my poor girl ". The roads were good, but the inns so bad that gentlefolk usually preferred to sleep in their carriages for four or five nights, and go straight through, from one town of size to another, stopping only to change horses.   There came a day when it was clear he could travel no further.   He asked where he was, and was told " Munich, the capital of Bavaria ".   For a week of August 1764 it seemed probable that David Garrick, who had been born in an inn, was to die in one.   " I almost gave up myself for gone."   There had been plague at Trieste. . . .

5

Eva-Maria, a woman for whom nobody had ever anything but praise, showed her mettle during the dark weeks while her husband lay between life and death.   By August 22 she understood that she might, without raising false hopes, write to his family.   Her letter, directed *à* M. George Garrick, Somerset Stable Yard near the Strand, London, Angleterre *par Maastricht*, performed its long journey safely, and nearly two hundred years later, although a little faded, appears as neat, well-expressed, informative and composed as on the day that it was written.

> My dear Geo.,
>         I hope this letter will reach you, before you hear through any other means of my Husband's having been taken ill of a violent bilious fever, the 2nd of this month.   He is, thank God, quite well again, and as all is over, I hope he will be the better for it, as it has scour'd him indeed.   We have been here all this while, and shall be obliged to continue till he has recover'd all his strength to pursue our journey, which will be to some waters to wash ourselves quite clean.
>         I have recovered my natural walk again, and tho' I am not quite free of all pains when any change of weather happens, yet I assure you that during your brother's illness, I forgot entirely I ever ail'd anything; and as the rheumatism was so complaisant as to leave me at that time when I most wish'd to be rid of his company, I shall have no objection to let him sport a little longer with me, when I have only to take care of myself.   How is your health?   We long to hear from you, but if you should have wrote, don't make yourself uneasy.   Letters are seldom lost, and we are all impatient by nature, and won't allow for common accidents which may retard our happiness. . . .

She told George that his brother was wanting to write, but must be persuaded against this " as it would only lead him to enquire into business, which he must as yet avoid ".   She said that by the greatest good luck, Mr Turton, the English physician whom they had met in Venice, had been travelling with them, as far as this place, and though bound for Vienna had absolutely refused to leave them. She did not tell George that Turton had called in three German doctors, and until David reached Paris he never realized that he had been attended by more than one.   She did not mention that an

English clergyman, but of her faith, had also been in constant attendance. There was no British Minister in Munich. Mr Fulke Greville had been appointed, but had not yet arrived. When he did, eighteen months later, he brought a parcel of books for a Munich resident who had cheered the convalescence of a famous man. The happy recipient, who described himself cheerfully as " a Popish priest ", put an inscription in every volume " That Posterity may know that Mr Garrick and T. Kennedy were friends ". Eva-Maria's round, running hand was much easier to read than her husband's sloping scribble. She ended calmly, as she had begun:

> When we shall be able to stir from this place, God only knows; it will take many days to recruit him for his journey; but if you will direct to your brother at the Spa, it may in all probability arrive when we do. My dear Geo., God bless you,
>
> Ever your faithful sister,
> E. Garrick.
>
> Love to the dear little ones.

David's first letter after his illness was performed next day; much too soon. It was very long, and full of concern about the theatre, and minor troubles. He did not like " Colley's girl ", Miss Ford, and feared the wench would harm his friend. At the risk of offending Colman, he meant never to engage her—" an Idiot ". He wished that he could be rid of the manor of Hendon. While lying here he had often thought of Hampton.

> I hope you have had your family there, sent for the cows, had the old mare, rid about, eat the fruit, and got yourself as stout as a Lion again to go through your next campaign. Pray go often to Hampton, and do as if it was your own.

Like Eva-Maria, he repeated the physician's soothing opinion that if he took care his health would be the better hereafter for this " purification ", though, " I have had a most violent bout of it, indeed." He had been dreadfully distressed by an accusation in George's last letter that he loved to hurt his brother. (Contrary to his expectations, the worst quarrels at Drury Lane had been between Lacy and Colman, but George had been drawn in, and both seemed to have set upon him.) He could hardly hold his pen to tell George to write to him directly, *chez* Monsieur Leger Munck at Franckfort, and take care to put his letter in the proper post.

He was much better by the time he replied to Arden, on September 15, but he had had a relapse, and been obliged to lie up for another week. He had always been a great believer in fresh air and exercise. As soon as possible he had ridden out, twice a day. The result had been " a fit of the gravel or stone ". He attributed this to his having lain in bed so long, and he attributed his " most dangerous bilious fever " to " all the combustibles " he had been storing up at Italian dinners.  The word " typhoid " did not enter the English language for another thirty years, and he was to suffer for the rest of his life from what he called " the sequel ".

The party so long detained in Munich set out next day on a short journey to Augsburg, where if all went well Turton would turn off for Ratisbon.  The Garricks would make up their minds, when they saw what letters were waiting for them there, or at Stuttgart, whether to push for Spa or make the best of their way to some French watering place.   " You have read," wrote David, " ' Letters from the Dead to the Living ', and from the living to the dead, but, I believe, never received one before from the half-dead to the living. I am most truly the Knight of the Woeful Countenance, and have lost legs, arms, belly, cheeks, etc, and have scarce anything left but bones, and a pair of dark, lack-lustre eyes, that are retired an inch or more into their sockets, and wonderfully set off the parchment that covers the cheek-bones."  He really thought that instead of returning to Drury Lane, he had better enter himself at Sadler's Wells. " I can thread through the smallest tumbler's hoop."

Fate was not kind to the convalescent.   The great attraction of Spa had been that the Duke of Devonshire, who had been ill at Chatsworth in August, had been ordered there.   But now it appeared that on arrival he had not taken the waters there, and might have gone on to Aix-la-Chapelle.   At Nancy, David made heavy weather of refusing a second invitation from Voltaire to visit him in Switzerland.   " The best of women and wives " kept from him, until he was " better able to struggle with such a heart-breaking loss ", the news that the Duke of Devonshire had died, at Spa, on the night of October 3.   They gave up the idea of a French watering place, and went on by easy stages for Paris.

It was much too late to think of organizing the season of 1764–1765 at Drury Lane, even if David had felt up to such a task.   The theatre had opened two months past.   On November 10, Garrick, who had found a letter from Colman awaiting him, told him that " a fortnight ago, I was not known till I spoke " but that now he was filling out.   (" Eight physicians, my good friend, and still alive! ")

But my nerves, Sir, my nerves, they are agitated at times, and the Duke of Devonshire's death had very nearly cracked them.  He loved me to the greatest confidence, and I deserved it by my gratitude, though not by my merits.  I must not dwell upon this subject, it shakes me from head to foot.  I cannot forget him, and the blow was dreadful to me in my weak condition, as it was unexpected.

The death of Hogarth, of which Colman had told him, had not been totally unexpected, but was a sad blow.   Critics sometimes said that David's verses were not his strong point, but the epitaph which he eventually composed for Hogarth's grave in Chiswick churchyard was to live.

> Farewell, great Painter of Mankind,
>    Who reach'd the noblest point of Art;
> Whose pictur'd Morals charm the Mind,
>    And thro' the Eye correct the Heart!
>
> If Genius fire thee, Reader stay;
>    If Nature touch thee, drop a tear:—
> If neither move thee, turn away,
>    For Hogarth's honour'd dust lies here.

He was distressed by the belief that Hogarth's last months of life had been shadowed by a cruel attack made upon him by Churchill ("The most bloody performance that has been published in my time"), and he heard of Churchill's death with less emotion.   That had taken place at Boulogne, on November 4, and the last words of the satirist had been typical—"What a fool I have been!"   David wrote to George that Wilkes, who had been with him at the end, said that he had left enough money to pay his debts and "some besides for his *wife*, Miss *Carr*, whom he lived with etc.   You'll do what is proper".   Wilkes was unduly optimistic.

## 6

The Garricks settled happily in the Hôtel de Malthe in the Rue St Niçaise.   Their suite was on the first floor, and consisted of a noble ante-chamber, a handsome *salle à manger*, a superb *salon* and an excellent bed-chamber, out of which opened a *boudoir* for Madame and a dressing-room for Monsieur.   A door from the *salon* led down steps into the garden, and an iron gate in the garden directly into the Tuileries.   The Opéra was so near, it was scarcely worth while to get into a carriage.

The Paris doctors prescribed "*l'exercice du cheval, et beaucoup de dissipation*".   David began to pick up quickly, but was disappointed that he grew tired with equal speed.   His letter to Powell had been hanging on his conscience for months.   It must be a very good letter, and Powell was humourless.   The young tragedian had written to him in March, most properly.   He was modest, and grateful to an almost embarrassing degree.   He said that his infant daughters were taught to remember the name of the manager in their daily prayers.   Mr Colman was showing him such friendship as he had never experienced (except from the manager), and Mr

George Garrick, abundant good nature. He hoped, by unwearied diligence, to prevail upon Mr Lacy, too, to become his friend. As yet he could boast of no more than " scarcely common civility behind the curtain ". Lacy was writing that in their year without Garrick they had made a profit of nine thousand pounds. Their Majesties had been to see the new actor as Philaster, and after the performance had sent Lord Huntington to convey their thanks for the entertainment he had given them, and good wishes for his success. Powell was filling the house as well as ever it had been when Garrick played. But from other sources Garrick had heard that Powell was " tearing himself to rags ". William Hopkins's diary continued grimly:

> November 22nd, " Venice Preserv'd ". Mr Powell's first Appearance in Jaffier. He performed the first Part of it with Feeling, but in the fourth Act he was wild, and wanted Power. But was much applauded. January 7th. Zara. Mr Powell played Lusignan with great feeling, but spoke much too low and cryed too much. March 20th. Mr Powell very wild in Alexander, and took his Voice too high.

David achieved his letter to Powell on December 12. He opened with apologies for his unavoidable delay. He proceeded paternally:

> The news of your great success gave me a most sensible pleasure—the continuance of that success will be in your own power; and if you will give an older soldier leave to hint a little advice to you, I will answer for its being sincere at least, which, from a brother actor, is no small merit. The gratitude you have expressed for what little service I did you in the summer before your appearance on the stage, has attached me to you, as a man who shall always have my best wishes for his welfare. I have not always met with gratitude in a playhouse. You have acted a greater variety of characters than I should expect in the first winter, and I have some fears that your good-nature to your brother actors (which is commendable when it is not injurious) drove you into parts too precipitately. However, you succeeded, and it is happy that you had the whole summer to correct the errors of haste, which the public will ever excuse in a young performer, on account of his beauties. But now it is time to make sure of your ground in every step you take. You must therefore give to study, and an accurate consideration of your characters, those hours which young men too frequently give to their friends and flatterers. The common excuse is " they frequent clubs for the sake of their benefit ". But nothing can be more absurd or contemptible. Your benefits will only increase with your fame, and should that ever sink, by your idleness, those friends who have made you idle will be the first to forsake you. When the public has marked you for a favourite (and their favour must be purchased with sweat and labour) you may choose what company you please; and none but the best can be of service to you.
> The famous *Baron*, of France, used to say that " an actor should be nursed in the laps of Queens "; by which he meant that the best accomplishments were necessary to form an actor. Study hard, my friend, for seven

years, and you may play the rest of your life. I would advise you to read, at your leisure, other books besides plays in which you are concerned. Our friend Colman will direct you in these matters, and as he is a good judge of acting, consult him as often as you can about your theatrical affairs. But above all, never let your *Shakespeare* be out of your hands, or your pocket; keep him about you as a charm. The more you read him the more you will like him, and the better you will act him. One thing more, and then I will finish my preaching.

His last word of advice, very tactfully expressed, was against over-acting and playing to the gallery.

A true genius will convert an audience to his manner, rather than be converted by them to what is false and unnatural. Be not too tame, neither. . . . I shall leave the rest to your own genius and the friendship of Colman.

At the British Embassy, Lord Hertford was experiencing all the inevitable difficulties of having succeeded the magnificent Duke of Bedford. He wrote pathetically to his cousin Walpole to say that he believed he had omitted to invite no Englishman of rank or name. Mr Walpole, who was himself intending to visit Paris, suggested that Mr Selwyn, the banker, had been omitted, much to his chagrin. Mr Walpole did not point out that every Englishman coming to Paris, or passing through it, was dependent upon Selwyn. Lord Hertford had been provided as Secretary with Sir Charles Bunbury, a young Suffolk landowner, recently married to the beautiful Lady Sarah Lennox. Both were what Lady Sarah cheerfully described as " horse-mad ". She looked forward to Paris, but seemed doubtful what Sir Charles would find to do there. Sir Charles did not come. An excuse was made that he had to stay to vote in the Commons, and Lord Hertford was allowed to choose his own Secretary. The appointment which resulted was brilliant, although apparently he had never seen his man till he arrived. Mr David Hume, the philosopher from Edinburgh, had adequate French. He was large, lumbering and much shrewder than he looked. He had no social graces, and perfect poise. To see " *le gros David* " at a theatrical entertainment, surrounded by a galaxy of the most elegant women of France, all adoring him, was an unforgettable sight. He showed himself extremely obliging to his namesake from Drury Lane, who in consequence haunted the house of an Ambassador irrevocably summed up by Paris as colourless and stingy. Mr Hume sent a messenger round to the Rue St Niçaise regularly to collect Mr Garrick's letters and packets to go to London by the Embassy bag.

Christmas in Paris was not so agreeable, as far as weather was concerned, as Christmas in Naples, but, as his health improved,

David enjoyed his second winter abroad even more than his first. He saw a very wide section of Parisian society. A carriage took him out to Le Raincy, the country château of the Duke of Orleans, and a prince of the blood watched, over the artist's shoulder, while M. de Carmontelle performed one of his lightning sketches. He found the actor's expression difficult to catch. In the end he presented M. Garrick in a tragic part, interrupted by M. Garrick in a comedy part —two figures, one declaiming nobly, the other, tiny and crumpled, creeping in through the tall folding doors of a French palace. David 27 also dined well above the shop of Leviéz, the print-seller in the Rue de St André des Arcs, who had been ballet-master at Drury Lane and had an English wife, fat, handsome and cross-eyed. He became a familiar figure in the bookshop of M. Pancoucke, whose pretty sister was going to marry Suard. He sat for a head-and-shoulders profile to M. Charles Nicolas Cochin (fils) and was able to assure him that, of all the books which he had carried with him on his Tour, Cochin's three volume *Voyage d'Italie* (lent to him by Dr Burney) had been of the most use. He was being plagued for " prints " of himself as souvenirs, and ordered Cochin's picture to be engraved. Meanwhile, he wrote to George to send him over all that he could lay hands upon that had been " scrap'd " from pictures of him by Reynolds, Zoffany and Wilson, and even McArdell's " scrape " of the Liotard, taken on his first trip to Paris, thirteen years past. The result was unexpected. Next year Colman visited Paris, and lodged with Leviéz. " There hang out here," he reported " in every street, pirated prints of Reynolds's Picture of you (' Garrick between Tragedy and Comedy ') which are underwritten, ' L'Homme entre le Vice et la Vertu '." 28 Garrick also had a portrait of Clairon engraved, above his famous impromptu verse in praise of her. Marmontel, returning thanks for a farewell print of David Garrick, *Acteur Anglais*, said that he had hung in his oratory, side by side, his mistress and Roscius.

Stories of Garrick and Préville became traditional in Paris. As the two actors rode towards the village of Passy one day, Préville suddenly announced, " Now I'm going to be a drunk man." He was as good as his word, and of the villagers who soon surrounded them, the females cried out in terror and the children in mockery. Older people shrugged their shoulders, or pitied the drunkards. When they had got out of Passy, Préville asked softly, " Have I done well, Maître? " " Well, very well indeed," agreed Garrick. " Only you weren't drunk in the legs." Presently Garrick fell off his horse, and lay motionless. Préville dismounted and ran to help him. When he considered that he had won the contest, Garrick opened his eyes and sat up, laughing at the distress of his companion. On another occasion they sat interminably in the diligence going to Versailles. The driver refused to start until he had at least four other passengers. Garrick got out of the vehicle, and changing his gait and voice, hailed the driver before stepping in again. He did this four times, after which the man whipped up his horses and drove off, satisfied that he now had six fares on board.

After his return to England Garrick was in constant communication with his French friends. The letters, usually of great length, formed a third of his filed correspondence. Several valued *Parisiens* came over to London, and Hampton, often at rather short notice. Le Kain was inclined to be huffy when he arrived in March 1765, and David, who was at Bath taking the waters, did not come up to London, over snow-covered roads. Le Kain was found lodgings at Madame Violette's " over against Burlington House ", and George and Colman were called in to take him down to David's house (which he thought was Hampton Court) and show him the garden and Shakespeare's Temple. (Two of the French visitors who were entertained at Hampton preserved tender memories of David's romantic weeping willows, immortalized by Zoffany.) But it is possible that David might have cut short his cure to welcome France's first tragedian, had he not by then heard from Clairon, in her most dramatic vein, of her base betrayal by " the biggest cheat, knave and nastiest rascal in this world ". This was a long, sad story. Just before David had left Paris, a member of the Comédie Française, one Dubois, had disgraced the company by refusing to pay his doctor's bill. Several of the players, led by Clairon and Le Kain, had refused to act until the account was settled. The authorities had proceeded against the rebellious royal actors, and they had all been arrested. Clairon had ridden off to prison with great *éclat*, in the coupé of the Intendant of Paris, but perched on the lap of the Intendant's lady, as the police-inspector insisted on sitting with them. It was believed in Paris that Garrick had sheltered Molé and Le Kain in his lodgings, and they certainly were not picked up until two days after the rest of the rebels. Having made their gesture, and been duly imprisoned for a fortnight, they had then returned to their duty. But Clairon had stuck to her guns, fallen ill and retired to Switzerland, never again to perform in public. Garrick wrote to offer her a gift of five-hundred pounds. This much impressed Voltaire, who had already been wholesomely impressed by Garrick's failure to accept invitations. " Is there, in all France, a Duke or a Marshal generous and honourable enough to do as much? "

Marmontel had ceased to be her lover. Clairon returned to Paris, *faute de mieux*, and David invited her to England. He made an

s

elaborate but unsuccessful effort to send her a pineapple from Hampton. It was collected by the Abbé Bonnet, who could not help being amusing, even in English, and he nursed the unaccommodating parcel as far as Calais, where by mistake it was carried on to St Omer. Bowed with shame, he ordered from London another such rare fruit, for presentation to the invalid actress. In due time David's pineapple turned up, but in lamentable condition.

"One of the things I love best in the world," wrote Clairon, "is my Garrick; certainly I would go to see him, if I was his mistress; but how can I travel without fortune?" She said that Garrick would have to come to Paris, to see her. Her closing sentence declared that she would love both the Garricks for ever, but this was the last of her letters to be filed by David. A life-size *gouache* head-and-shoulders portrait of her decorated the walls of Hampton, but the Garricks never saw her again. It is possible that Eva-Maria bore this with equanimity. The public career of La Clairon was finished, but her *vie passionelle* was not nearly done. In the nick of time came an invitation, to visit his court, from the young Margrave of Anspach. 31

If ever, during the next twelve years (and this happened very often), David found a very long letter signed " Riccoboni " waiting on his desk, he knew that he was going to read something remarkable. The Riccoboni's letters always opened arrestingly. " My ladyship is infuriata! " " *Avez-vous un démon familier?* " She was an ex-actress, and, David thought, a very good novelist, and " a generous creature ". He helped her to get her romances translated into English and published in London. She sat in the Holbachs' salon, in the shadows, a woman of fifty odd, who had been very pretty but was now haggard. She seemed rather silent. This last impression was mistaken. On paper, in a mixture of French and English, she was multiloquent.

> Help! help! murder! dear Theresa, make haste, give me some relief. I am in a fit. I am distracted. Cut off Mr Burke's throat. 32
>
> Mercy on us! forbear, O tyrant! *Mais il n'est pas prudent d'irritater ce méchant diable.* Honest Mr Noise, I implore your pity upon my knees, I crave your pardon! Be merciful, do not cut nothing to the lovely Dick. Faith, his eyes are fine eyes, his smiles are sweet smiles. Well! and what for this? *Venez-ici, répondez à ma question; tenez-vous là, soyez sage . . .* You are hasty Sir. *En parlant de Mr Burke, je dis, " le bel Anglais " ou " mon aimable écolier "; en parlant de Mr Garrick, je dis, "* the dearling of my heart—the charming David, my dear sweet friend."

There were two ameliorating features in the outpourings of Riccoboni. She often addressed a good third of them to Eva-Maria, and, in contrast to her style, her script was disciplined.

The Abbé Morellet, another regular attendant at the Holbachs, taxed David with sitting down, folding his arms and watching like a lynx when his friend was engaged in a disputation with Diderot or Marmontel. David explained that when the Abbé argued, he was interesting " on account of the vehemence and natural freedom of his gestures ". He was going to the Law Courts, also, to observe French gesture, and saw " Gerbier, the French Mansfield " pleading with great warmth and force. " It was a *cause célèbre.*"

Grimm was engaged on very full painstaking descriptions of Garrick. He believed that in Paris, where he had received the most distinguished welcome, Garrick had preferred the society of the Philosophers. (Garrick had written to Colman " We had a fine laugh at Baron d'Holbach's, about the wicked company I keep; I am always with that set.") Riccoboni told him that London was more tolerant than Paris. The character of Ranger would be impermissible on the Paris stage. Grimm found that Garrick's great art was that he abandoned his own personality when acting, and so effectively that you would swear he could change his features. Garrick was of middle stature, small rather than big, graceful and well proportioned, with a witty expression, wonderfully animated eyes and extreme vivacity. He was a great admirer of Shakespeare, and had himself written several plays, but these were said to be mediocre. He went into all sorts of company, mixing with the crowd to study the workings of human nature. He had amassed a considerable fortune, and was said to be fond of money. Grimm doubted if he would long continue to perform. The activity which he put into his rôles must exhaust the strongest constitution, and he did not appear to be robust. He had been brought to the edge of the grave, in the Tyrol, by a malignant fever. Amongst Grimm's observations on Garrick was one wholly untranslatable, " *Il est naturellement singe.*"

## 7

By the end of January, Garrick wrote home that he was fixing his return for the beginning of April—perhaps he might have to add a week for the business of packing up and getting off. He was feeling better and better, but the doctors were at one in advising him against thinking of business. " I have, at present, lost all taste for the stage; it was once my greatest passion, and I laboured for many years like a true lover, but I am grown cold." He might have grown cold, but he was beginning to want to know what people at home were saying about him. He suggested that Colman should insert in *The St James's Chronicle* a paragraph about him supposed to come from a visitor to Paris. " Our little stage hero looks better

than he did etc." Colman over-did this, said that Garrick was woe-
fully missed, both as manager and actor, and, most unhappily,
quoted the very description of himself that Garrick had sent in a
letter to Arden. Now everyone would attribute the paragraph to
him, and he had never (excepting in *The Fribbleriad*, which he always
regretted), " praised myself knowingly ". On March 18 he said he
was sending to Colman " a little parcel, a great secret; it is a fable I
have written, ' The Sick Monkey ', to be published upon my return.
Severe upon myself, I have given some of my friends, whom I love, a
little fillip." He told Colman to cut it about as much as he liked.
*The Sick Monkey*, prefaced by an engraving by Gravelot, was charmingly produced. It bore on its title-page a quotation from a newspaper. " Thursday afternoon, David Garrick Esq. arrived at his
house in Southampton Street." It really was amusing, especially
when it described the poor monkey attended by doctors who, when
all other wisdom failed them, diagnosed " nerves ".

> The moment he gets fame and wealth
> (How ill exchang'd for ease and health!)
> The envious crew set on him.

But he had miscalculated the effect of his " puff oblique ". It
produced none.

The business of packing up took him until the last week of April.
He had many commissions to execute. (Colman wanted silk stockings, which would certainly be seized by the customs.) The most
coveted Paris novelty was something from the royal porcelain manu-
factory. Most people could afford but a single cup and saucer. He
ordered from Sèvres a tea-service for six. The decoration was
lovely—a hop-trellis, the prevailing colours rose-red, pink, sea-green
and blue. There were twenty-two pieces, and they fitted into a case
of kingwood, lined with sea-green silk, edged with gold braid. 34
Monnet was sending after him something for Drury Lane—footlights
from Paris. At present the stage was lighted by six branches of
candles which were let down at the end of every act to be snuffed.
He was going to have oil-lamps with reflectors, both for footlights and
side-lights. He was getting some rich new scenery too, designed by
Boquet, who, according to Monnet, also looked after such " devilish
instruments " as flaming torches and towns on fire. Monnet said
that the licopodium should be dyed red, and Garrick could easily get
it in London; but Garrick found he could not. He had to send to
Germany for the powder to fill Boquet's torches. 35

The round of farewell calls and parties began. Everyone had
appreciated Eva-Maria " *cette belle et grande* lady, *si bien faite, si*

*jolie "*. De La Place considered her one of the most captivating of women, " though entirely devoted to her husband ". As for David, " *Ce Monsieur Garrick, étoit fait pour vivre parmi nous* ". Many au revoirs were said, not farewells. For the Garricks were coming back next year.

Eva-Maria had been able to pack most of her female frippery, but men's suits are bulky. David had to leave no less than four with Monnet, and a pair of pistols, and three plated candlesticks, and a packet of candles, and a sword. . . . Monnet was to prove as invaluable to Eva-Maria as to her husband. As the years slipped past, and they never came back, she received designs for dresses, beautifully drawn and coloured, and for the coiffure, and materials for gowns, and particularly French gauzes and laces. Sometimes they were collected by members of the company, on Paris trips. Grimaldi, the ballet-master of Drury Lane, was to be seen gravely pocketing two important packets—white satin ribbon for Madame Garrick.

They got off at last on April 24 and into London three days later. Lady Sarah Bunbury, on her way out to Paris, met them at Calais, and reported to the poor O'Briens (who were dreadfully home-sick in New York) that Garrick was grown to look very old and thin. She had heard that he had become mightily spoilt by the immense fuss that had been made over him in France. " But that's *entre nous*, for I have no notion of owning it is possible he can be spoiled, to any but best friends."

## CHAPTER XI

## " TIED TO THE STAKE "

### 1765–1769

I

WHILE all the bells of Paris rang for Easter Sunday morning, David had written to ask Colman to tell George to engage two maids—a good cook, and a housemaid. He had asked pathetically that they might have " some character fixed to their tail ". He hated continual domestic changes, and knew from experience that he had put up, before, for the sake of a clean house and a good table, with most undesirable characters. The gardener at Hampton, who had been a good one, had left while they were abroad. It seemed odd that he had not waited to state his grievance. It could only be supposed that he had quarrelled with Charles, major domo at the villa.

One of the first calls he paid on arriving at Southampton Street was to the Burneys, " to see, caress and reclaim " Phill. He found himself taking part in the most unsuccessful recognition scene of his career. The little Burneys were well-mannered children. They said farewell to their darling, without shedding a single tear. His master had been away two years. Phill showed the most dismal reluctance to follow him. A few days later there was rejoicing in Poland Street. Phill was back, in the highest spirits. A polite message said that " the little animal had seemed so moping, so unsettled, and so forlorn, that Mr and Mrs Garrick had not the heart to break his new engagements, and requested his entire acceptance and adoption ". Later, when Phill died, full of years, and was replaced by a greyhound, Mr Garrick still remembered his faithless favourite. " *You* will never take his place, Slabber-chops! " He looked at the fawning newcomer, with immense melancholy. " Soft enough, poor whelp! Like all your race—tenderness without ideas." Frances, " Fanny " Burney, never forgot. *1*

He did not get another spaniel. He got a huge dog, Dragon, an English mastiff. They had been fashionable in the great houses of England since Van Dyck had painted the children of Charles I. Lord Pembroke had one, and Reynolds had painted him with it, and his son and heir. Dragon dwelt at Hampton, but once came up to London to appear upon the stage at Drury Lane.

The manager's return from the Continent had come just at the right time for him to see everyone before the season closed. Rising players often took a summer engagement in the provinces. Powell went to Bristol. There was to be a new theatre opened at Richmond, and King wanted a Garrick prologue for the first night. The manager had no objection to the company making their own arrangements for the holidays, but he was much incensed when Mrs Yates, without the least word to him, went off and was the tragedy queen of Birmingham. He liked also, thus early, to look through what he called his " theatrical stores " for next season. While he had been away, Colman's *Deuce is in Him* had succeeded greatly. Another version of *A Midsummer Night's Dream* had entirely failed. He never seemed to be able to get audiences to like that play as much as he did. Colman, who had spirit, had tried again, putting back all the clowns, and turning the affair into a farce. This had done well, and so had *The Royal Shepherd*, a New English Opera. There had been no other new Shakespearean production, and two classical tragedies, and two light comedies by charming ladies, Mrs Sheridan and Mrs Griffith, would never do for the permanent list. Mrs Griffith was to pester him with plays for the next twelve years. Her letters varied in style from the arch to the waspish, her addresses from Hertingfordbury to Windsor Castle. Her connections were good, and both Drury Lane and Covent Garden succumbed to her pertinacity, sometimes with fair results.

As far as Garrick could see, the very satisfactory financial situation during his absence was chiefly due to a good company and to Colman. The atmosphere between his ' dear Coley ', Brother George and Lacy was thunderous. He wondered if he could get Lacy to retire and sell his share of the patent to Colman. He wondered if he could sell his own share. But by November, a very long letter from Clutterbuck had convinced him that this would not do. Clutterbuck said that he would get much less for his share than he should, unless he continued to act; and that was just what he was hoping not to do. His list for 1765–1766 was not ambitious. *Daphne and Aminot* was classical, but Bickerstaffe had wit. Love (who wanted his salary increased) had written a Pantomime about Harlequin in Rhodes. It would be expensive to mount and he would need help with it. *Falstaff's Wedding*, a continuation of Shakespeare's *Henry IV*, was by William Kenrick, a revolting little man, who quarrelled with everyone. The success of the season should be Colman's new comedy *The Clandestine Marriage*, but already he foresaw difficulties about the casting.

They did not open until mid-September. He had the summer in which to enjoy himself and make up his mind as to his own future. Edmund Burke, who had, most imprudently, moved into a country-

house, Gregories, in Buckinghamshire, and was playing at being a
farmer, wrote charmingly asking him to stay. So did Susanna
Cibber, who doubted if she would be well enough to appear in London
this year. But he did not want to spend his first summer at home in
other people's houses. He accepted his easiest invitation, and midsummer saw him in Essex. Richard Rigby had now proceeded far
with the improvement of his property. Mistley Hall, built of
white Suffolk brick, was most conveniently placed for visitors going
to and from the Continent. The Duke of York had stayed there on
his return from Italy. The view from its drawing-room (which was
decorated with large and very fine Italian landscapes, surrounded by
a black fret, on pink paper) was always romantic and, at high tide,
arresting. It overlooked the park, and beyond a ha-ha, green fields,
sloping down to the flashing estuary of the Stour, full of sails and
birds. The roofs and lights of Harwich were visible in the distance.
Rigby also owned the village and inn, and his whalers, shipbuilding
yards and warehouses, made the harbour busy. There were eleven
guest-rooms at Mistley, several of them suites, and a gravel drive ran
all round the estate, so that Rigby could take replete guests in his
phaeton, to admire his kine, deer, pheasants and hares, without their
having to set foot to ground. He had a kitchen-garden of nine acres,
with cherry-trees, peaches and pineapples, and the finest flower-
garden in England. He was going to have the church, built by his
father, entirely altered by Robert Adam. He had been appointed
Vice-Treasurer for Ireland, last year, at a salary of three thousand
five hundred pounds per annum. His father had sold the family
linen business, and made a fortune in the South Sea Company.
Rigby had been sent on a Grand Tour, but was not very well educated.
He was a jovial, bold, frank, big fellow, and a telling orator. He had
never married; not everyone liked him, but no one had ever been
known to refuse an invitation to Mistley. The Garricks' midsummer
visit became almost an annual event.                              2

There was a young guest at Hampton when they returned in July.
Signor Angelo was visiting his native Turin. As they already had
Brother George's five, one more child made very little difference.
"Little Angelo" was six, and all he could remember of his first stay
at Hampton was the grotto arch, leading under the road to what he
called the summer-house, with a statue of Shakespeare in it. His
chief amusement was throwing his hat at the swallows as they
sped through the black arch towards the blue river. He had vague
memories of two frequent visitors from London "Holland and Powell,
favourite actors of the day". On July 25, from Hampton, the  3
master of the house wrote to M. Le Kain, in Paris:

SHAKESPEARE'S TEMPLE and portraits of Mr and Mrs Garrick resting in the steps of the portico, with a favourite dog in the front ground, and a view of a reach of the river.

*By Johann Zoffany*

Garrick first made the acquaintance of Zoffany when he was engaged in the studio of Benjamin Wilson, painting draperies etc., about 1759. Wilson was exceedingly jealous of Garrick's patronage of his employee, and wrote in complaint: " On coming to town this morning, I could not resist the temptation to inquire after my very worthy brother artist, Zoffani. But, alas! how unlucky, he had left his work and was gone to breakfast, loaded with his pencils etc. in an invisible conveyance. As you will chance to see him before I shall, you will oblige him by desiring him to fulfill his engagements, and act, if he can, like an honest man." Garrick replied that Mr Wilson " need not employ his runners and spies to discover what Zoffani is doing at my house; it will save some expense in feeing them, and save themselves from a ducking if they should be caught near our part of the river ". This picture was bought at the sale at Christie's on the death of Mrs Garrick, for £28 7s. 0d. by Mr Lambton, and descended by inheritance to the present owner.

*Reproduced by kind permission of the Earl of Durham.*

In spite of the fact that I have been received by my fellow-country-
men in the most honourable fashion, I am almost decided to leave the stage,
as an actor, at once, and as manager as soon as I can.   I am very happy
with my wife, my family, and my fortune, and it is not in the power of the
first man in the kingdom to do me the least wrong; but my inclination for
the stage is over, and that's the reason.   When will you come to England
and share my happiness?   I have a very pretty country house, a fairly
well served table, and pretty good wine in my cellars; and more than all
4    that, I have a heart ever warm and open for my friends.

He had not yet made up his mind when the season opened, most
promisingly.   Bickerstaffe's play, which was produced on Tuesday,
October 8, ran for eighteen nights and was only halted by royal
mourning—the death of the " Butcher " Duke of Cumberland.   But
a very grim business was absorbing the manager as that first night
approached.   At the Old Bailey, the son of a member of the profession,
one Robert Turbott, had been convicted of theft and had been condemned to be hanged.   Since Elizabethan days, moralists had been
inveighing against the habit of tavern-keepers, who, to attract the
custom of the nobility and gentry, provided table-ware, which was a
terrible temptation to the penurious.   Robert Turbott, junior, had,
apparently, taken a silver cup.   Garrick got short notice.   At
seven o'clock on Friday night, October 4, he heard that the sentence
was to be carried out next Wednesday.   " A petition signed by a
nobleman only can save him."   Turbott wrote himself, on Monday
7th, from Newgate Cells, to " Most ever good and gracious Sir ", to
thank him for his " kind endeavours and good intention ".   The
news that he was to die had at first overwhelmed him.   But now he
had recovered sufficiently to wish to commend his poor wife to his
friends.

Oh!   I could say a great deal on this head, but that my heart is too
full, and for fear I be too troublesome.   I here return you my last thanks
for all your goodness to me in this world, and am, with due respect, your
5    dying and ever obliged humble servant.

Robert Turbott was reprieved at the last moment, " owing to the
intercession of powerful friends ", but one McKenzie, sentenced with
him, went to Tyburn on the 9th.

The theatres re-opened on the night of November 11, and on the
14th the manager was to be seen, getting into the costume of
Benedick.   His indecision had been solved by a Royal Command,
and he had chosen, for his return, the character in which he had
appeared for the first time after his wedding.   He had written a
prologue for the occasion, and in the last lines compared himself to
an old soldier.

The Chelsea pensioner, who, rich in scars,
Fights o'er in prattle all his former wars,
Tho' past the service, may the young ones teach
To march, present, to fire, and mount the breach.
Should the drum beat to arms, at first he'll grieve
For wooden leg, lost eye, and armless sleeve;
Then cocks his hat, looks fierce, and swells his chest;
" Tis for my King, and Zounds! I'll do my best! "

The house was packed.   He heard for the first time after two
years, London applauding Garrick, a sound as noisy and dear and
unmistakable as that under London Bridge when the tide was coming
in.   He was home again.

2

It was generally agreed that Garrick, that season, played better
than he had ever played before.   After all, Powell was nothing to
him.   How could he be, being but a young man, fresh from a
counting-house, no scholar, and very nervous?   Garrick seemed to
have gained in experience during his two years' absence.   It was not
for nothing that he had gasped with awe in the Pantheon, and with
glee on Naples quaysides, and in the Paris law-courts, and from heat
in a gondola, and on what had nearly been a death-bed in Munich.
He was now so easy, so much the master of his craft that audiences
felt happy the moment he stepped on the stage, or if they were not
intended to be happy, at least that they were in good hands.   He
did not spoil them.   He appeared thrice as Benedick, twice as
Lusignan, Sir John Brute and Lord Chalkstone, and once as Kitely;
ten performances in all.   " My resolution ", he told George, " is to
draw my neck as well as I can, out of the collar, and sit quietly with
my wife and books by my fireside."   But this resolution meant
trouble with Colman.   Lord Ogleby, in *The Clandestine Marriage*,
was, if not written by Garrick, undoubtedly a Garrick part.   He
bore a strong resemblance to Lord Chalkstone in *Lethe*.   One of the
longest angry letters Garrick ever received arrived at Southampton
Street at a bad moment.   Somebody in Bath had told Colman that
Garrick had said, " Colman lays a great stress on his having written
this character on purpose for me.   Suppose it should come out that
*I wrote it*? "   Was Garrick going to claim the authorship of the
whole play, and was he going to persist in refusing to appear in it?
Garrick seized his pen.    " Though I am to obey His Majesty's com-
mands this evening, and my head is full of the character I am to
play, yet I will answer your long letter."   He said that if they were
to vie with one another in repeating stories, three independent witnesses had told him that Colman had said that if Garrick did not

play Ogleby, "There is an end of our friendship!" He regretted that he had to complain, not for the first time, that he had found Colman very peevish recently. Colman himself admitted that it had always been agreed that when the play was printed both their names should appear on the title-page.

He went off to play Sir John Brute, in fine fettle, but conscious that another letter from Colman would arrive to-morrow. Susanna Cibber had come up from Berkshire, by easy stages, to appear as Lady Brute. She had been shocked at his proposal to desert his company, enchanted to hear of his brilliant reappearance. When her old huntsman wound his horn, although she was by no means " in running order, I will certainly hark to Garrick ".

As the world had not stood still while he was abroad, two things which vexed him had come to his notice on his return. Covent Garden had thought of something which ought to have been initiated at Drury Lane—the Theatrical Fund, a voluntary benefit subscription by the company to relieve their poorer fellows in distress and on retirement, and also their widows and children. He at once opened Drury Lane Theatrical Fund, and planned a benefit for it, for the final night of the season. Eventually, his contributions were reckoned at four thousand four hundred pounds, and he paid the expenses of an Act of Parliament, legally establishing the Fund.

A new club which was called just The Club sounded exactly the thing for him. It met for supper and conversation at the Turk's Head, in Gerrard Street, Soho, once a week at seven p.m. The members, who were never to number more than twelve, took the chair in rotation. Conversation was brilliant and went on very late. Half of his best friends seemed to belong—Reynolds, Johnson, Burke, Topham Beauclerk. He said to Reynolds, " I think I shall be of you! " But then came a hitch. It appeared that Reynolds had repeated this to Johnson, who had exploded. " *He'll be of us!* How does he know we will *permit* him? The first Duke in England has no right to hold such language." Nothing happened. Amongst the chosen few was a Mr John Hawkins, a wealthy retired attorney, a Middlesex magistrate. He lived not two miles from Garrick's villa, on Twickenham Common. Mr Hawkins had a sharp little daughter, Letitia Matilda, who, like Fanny Burney, wrote down things later. Garrick often rode over to see her father, on the excuse that he was delivering proofs of Johnson's edition of Shakespeare. It was quite pathetic how soon he began to ask questions about the Paradise from which he was excluded. " Were you at the Club on Monday night? What did you talk of? Was Johnson there? I suppose he said something of Davy?—that Davy was a clever fellow in his way,

full of convivial pleasantry, but no poet, no writer, ha! " Hawkins
could not tell him that he had himself remonstrated with Johnson,
and the answer had been, " He will disturb us, sir, by his buffoonery." 6
Eight years passed before Garrick was regularly proposed, and at
once elected to membership of The Club, but on his death it was
Johnson who moved that, in tribute, this vacancy should not be
filled for a year.

His oldest friend in London was not behaving very kindly to his
Davy at present. The reason could hardly be jealousy, for Johnson's
own worldly position had steadily improved. It was in this year that
Trinity College, Dublin, created him a Doctor of Laws. He already
had his royal pension. His edition of Shakespeare, with notes on
previous editors and on the playwright, was naturally of great
interest to David. All seemed to be going well. Then came a very
stiff " Dear Sir " letter, offering to send any particular plays Mr
Garrick wished to see. George came running to explain what had
upset the Doctor. He believed that David had not been an original
subscriber. David wrote in haste to say that he was sure that he had
been—just before he went abroad. He had put down his own name,
and those of the Duke of Devonshire, and Mr Beighton, the Rector
of Egham. Unluckily, he could not find his memorandum of this.
Johnson's Shakespeare duly appeared, and the name of Garrick was
not to be found in it, from start to finish. When taxed with this, he
said that if he had mentioned Garrick he would have been obliged to
mention others—Mrs Pritchard, Mrs Cibber, nay, even old Cibber;
he too had tinkered with Shakespeare. " But," persisted Boswell,
" has he not brought Shakespeare into notice? " " Sir, to allow
that would be to lampoon the age. Many of Shakespeare's plays
are the worse for being acted; ' Macbeth ', for instance." This
augured ill, and it was soon evident that the Doctor was by no means
blind to the shortcomings of David's idol. *The Two Gentlemen of
Verona*, for instance, got very short shrift. " In this play is a strange
mixture of knowledge and ignorance, of care and negligence." *All's
Well That Ends Well* fared little better. " This play had many
delightful scenes, though not sufficiently probable, and some happy
characters, though not new, nor produced by any deep knowledge of
human nature."

Another thing likely to upset the Doctor was looming. Kenrick,
" the hackney writer ", had published a venomous attack on the
new edition of Shakespeare, and Garrick was producing Kenrick's
*Falstaff's Wedding* in the following April.

But the most probable solution of his old friend's sourness towards Garrick is to be found in his health. This was exactly the

date at which he told Boswell that he was " afflicted with a very severe return of the hypochondriac disorder which was ever lurking about him ". He was fifty-five, and in a deplorable state, " sighing, groaning, talking to himself and restlessly walking from room to room ". " I would consent to have a limb amputated to recover my spirits." All his life he had dreaded losing his reason. He was to live to the age of seventy-five, and was never to do so. David had always been generous to him. He had twice had a benefit night at Drury Lane for a protégée of Johnson with no earthly claim upon the management—old blind Mrs Williams, a minor poetess, a friend of the late Mrs Johnson. Before he went abroad he had left instructions that if Mr Johnson called he was to be given the keys of the library. This was noble, for he knew that Johnson treated books very roughly. Fanny Burney treasured the memory of Roscius on a visit to her father, giving an imitation of himself and Johnson.

" David! Will you lend me your Petrarca? "

" Y-e-s, Sir! "

" David! You sigh? "

" Sir—you shall have it certainly."

On Christmas Day, 1765, sitting in Hampton Church, listening to the sermon, with Dr Garnier beside him, David's thoughts wandered. He told Colman in a letter that afternoon that (" God forgive me!") he had then written, or rather composed, a poem to a most unwelcome Christmas visitor. His new acquaintance was, he was instructed, the gout, and the only thing for it was to go to Bath. But how could he, with only three acts of *The Clandestine Marriage* ready, and the first performance billed for February 20? King was going to be Ogleby. He had been very difficult about this, and at first refused. His interpretation of the part was not at all what Garrick had intended.

On January 23, 1766, Eva-Maria, who had experience, survived what she afterwards described to Joseph Cradock as the most uncomfortable evening in her life. David Hume had arrived from Paris, bringing with him " the celebrated M. de Rousseau ". The press had much sympathy for the persecuted, free-thinking author, and it was surmised that in England " his peaceable and exemplary life will entitle him to protection ". Rousseau arrived in a very strange state of mind, which was to become much more so, followed by a mistress of few attractions and doubtful fidelity, and a dog as wild as himself. (Hume thought it had collie blood. It kept on escaping, and causing its infatuated owner agonies of bereavement and raptures of reunion.) Garrick could not break his rule of never dining before he played, moreover, the night on which he was to install Rousseau in his own front box, opposite to the Royal Box, was that of a command performance. He was himself going to appear in both the main play and after-piece. William Hopkins reported loyally. " Mr Garrick played Lusignan and Lord Chalkstone. It is impossible to express how finely he played both Characters." Hume observed that their Majesties looked more at the manager's box than at the stage. Eva-Maria told Cradock that " the recluse philosopher was so very anxious to display himself that she was obliged to hold him by the skirt of his coat, that he might not fall over, into the pit ". The recluse's costume was arresting. He was attired nowadays in an Armenian dress—a loose *caftan*, with collar and cuffs of fur, and an upstanding fur cap. After the performance he told Garrick, " I have cried all through your Tragedy, and laughed through all your Comedy, without being at all able to understand the language." Eva-Maria's sufferings were not yet at an end. " When the whole was concluded," an elegant supper party was staged at Southampton Street, to which many of the first literary characters of London were invited to meet the famous foreigner. But one of the first literary characters was not present, and was furious. Thomas Percy, a member of The Club, whose recently-published *Reliques of Ancient English Poetry* had charmed London, had sent to Southampton Street after dinner, asking for a seat. Nobody had dared take a note into the manager's dressing-room, at the theatre, when he was just ready to appear. Cradock believed that Percy never forgave the mistake. Rousseau within six months was engaged with Hume in one of the bitterest quarrels in literary history, and Paris friends kept on writing to ask Garrick what had really happened. He did not preserve copies of his replies.    8

The weather was bitterly cold. On January 30, Susanna Cibber died. She was buried in the cloisters of Westminster Abbey on February 6, and Garrick pronounced, " Tragedy is dead on one side." He went on to say that she had troubled him more than any actress; for while he could deal with the noisy complaints of Mrs Pritchard and Clive, Mrs Cibber had such a way with her—she always got her way with him. She left a daughter, named for herself, and people said that it much resembled Garrick. An excellent authority, Lord Rochford, pronounced firmly on this, though much later. " I have never heard it surmised that there was ever any improper intimacy between Garrick and Mrs Cibber. He often went to Woodhay, near Newbury, from which several of his letters were dated— the paternal inheritance of Captain, afterwards Sir Robert Sloper, a General in the Army." Garrick had always been fond of " Mrs Cibber's child, he was much attracted to children ". In fact, Mrs Cibber had borne five. There had been two by her marriage to

Cibber, both of whom had died before she left him. A daughter, born in secrecy in 1739, after her flight with Sloper, had died in her teens. Charles, and Susanna Maria, both born after Garrick's marriage, survived her. And that any child of hers resembled Garrick was not surprising, for Garrick and she had been so alike in build and colouring that it had often been declared they could have passed for brother and sister.

The Clandestine Marriage, " this unhappy comedy, as you very properly call it ", said Colman bitterly, opened with everything against it, but just before the worst late snows in the memory of man descended upon the country. Messrs Garrick and Colman's new piece was at once recognized to have novelty and spirit. King had found, in Ogleby, his greatest part, and Clive, as Mrs Heidelberg, a social climber, was " a host in herself ". The house, which had been the scene of a minor riot before the curtain rose, shook with laughter and surprise as Clive produced what were later to be known as " malapropisms ". Garrick had done his duty—produced both a prologue and epilogue. He set off, over snowy roads, towards Bath. Quin had died there. On January 21, he composed, for his old companion's monument in Bath Abbey, an epitaph which began with a couplet destined to be much quoted:

> That Tongue which set the Table on a roar
> And charm'd the public ear, is heard no more. . . .

Several of the letters which followed him were not of the kind to cheer a man nursing "my gouty leg of the street-post order ". Dear William Windham's beautiful widow had received shocking news from Eton school. Young William, to whom Mr Garrick was guardian, had been a ring-leader in some fighting. Dr Dampier wrote, " In order, therefore, to cover his retreat and to prevent a public expulsion, which would probably be the consequence of his longer stay, I shall *see* him home to you to-morrow morning." Young William's case was disposed of suitably. He was sent to finish his education in a sterner climate—Glasgow.

Paterson, after consultation with Lacy, advised Garrick against letting trouble-makers come between them. He did not really believe it would suit either to part. Brother George's letter for £150 was also endorsed " I complied ".

William O'Brien had sent, from New York, a present of seeds for the garden at Hampton. This was awkward, as the present gardener was not experienced. David wrote that George had better get Dr Beighton to come over from Egham to advise. Poor O'Brien's story sounded so sad.

Dear George,

Though I think you don't deserve it at my hands, yet I must write to you, and beg you will let me have the first opportunity to hear from you, how you do, and how everything goes on among you at old Drury, where I often wish myself, just to take a peep behind the curtain, and have a frisk in the green-room.

O'Brien said that their passage of thirty-four days had been a serious affair, worse than any tempest in the theatre, and he had begun to say his short prayers. Lady Susan had been vastly ill the whole way, but was now quite well again. (She had, in fact, miscarried, and was never to have a child.)

New York is not equal to London, but we shall be very comfortable, I make no doubt—everyone seems extremely disposed to make it as agreeable as possible to us. Everything appears just in the bud—a world in its infancy. . . .

Foote had broken his leg, and had been obliged to undergo an amputation. David wrote very kindly to him too. His postscript apologized, " I write in the bar of a Coffee house and with a Skewer." 11

### 3

When the season of 1765–1766 ended, Colman seemed to be threatening a nervous breakdown. He was sent off to Paris, where Monnet found him lodgings with Leviéz. With him went Miss Ford, and her daughter. Colman had hopes which were disappointed of collecting a debt from a dashing baronet now in Paris. The weather was very bad. " Madame " did not like Paris. Garrick, who had foreseen this, could only express hopes that Miss Harriet would return bringing some French airs and the language to perfection.

Miss Ford's son by Colman, aged three, was received at Hampton. Colman wrote that he hoped " Georgy-Porgy " was being very saucy. Garrick replied that Georgy and he had been very busy in the garden together, and had played nine-pins till he was obliged to declare off. When the Garricks got back from Mistley, Georgy was to come again " to make love to my niece Kitty and a plum pudding ". He could now sing *The Chimney Sweep* to admiration, and had promised that Mrs Garrick should hear " his whole budget of songs and stories ".

Georgy became a constant visitor at Garrick's Villa, and as soon as he could ride, used to accompany the servant carrying letters from his father. " On these occasions, I always, on arriving at Garrick's, ran about his gardens, where he taught me the game of trap-ball, which superseded our favourite nine-pins. He practised, too, a thousand monkey-tricks on me; he was Punch, a Harlequin, a cat in a gutter, then King Lear, with a mad touch at times that almost terrified me. . . ." Georgy ungratefully closed his description by

saying that all this was " very kind and condescending ", but that
Garrick always seemed to him to be playing to please himself, " as
he did in a theatre ". Now Goldsmith " had bonhomie; he played
to amuse the child ". Garrick " diverted and dazzled me, but never
made me love him, and I had always this feeling for him, though I
12 was too young to divine it ". But by the time that Georgy was promoted from nine-pins to trap-ball, his father had a bad conscience
regarding Garrick, and his mother had never had any reason to love
a manager who had failed to employ her, and disapproved of her
influence over his best collaborator. " Little Angelo ", who turned
out a much more reliable man than Georgy Porgy, had kindlier
memories.

Boys were sent to Eton very young. Little Angelo, looking back
sixty years later, believed that it was in 1764 that his mother and
Mrs Garrick had driven over to see that " pet Harry " was comfortably lodged at his dame's. But Eton College register shows that
Harry Angelo came in 1765, aged nine, and he had for companions
two of George Garrick's sons, Carrington, past thirteen, who had been
there five years, and Nathaniel, aged ten. Harry thought it was
two or three years later that Mr Garrick himself arrived, and they
were all sent for to dine at the Old Christopher Inn. Before dinner
they went over Windsor Castle, and Mr Garrick asked the custodian
for a picture of John Lacy, a comedian of the Restoration, which he
wanted to show to Mrs Garrick. His attention was attracted by the
Windsor Beauties, the ladies of the court of Charles II, painted by
Sir Peter Lely, and the affected way in which they held their hands.
Afterwards, he delighted in handing a cup or glass, with fingers dis-
tended *à la Lely*. After dinner, which was very good, he brought out
of his pocket three parts which Lacy had played, and read them
aloud, changing his voice utterly, Harry thought, though Mrs
Garrick said she would have detected her husband's voice in all, with
her eyes shut. When the hour came for their departure, just before
stepping into his coach and four, Mr Garrick gave each boy a golden
guinea, with an admonition " to be good boys and mind our books ".
This was dreadful for Harry. He whispered and stammered,
" Please sir, to excuse me." " Hey, what? " exclaimed Mr Garrick.
" Sir, my father has made me promise not to accept money from any
of his friends." Mr Garrick put back the guinea into his purse, and
instructed his nephews, " Mind, my dear boys, that you do as little
Harry has done; do not break faith with your father." He shook
Harry very warmly by the hand, " I shall remember you for this."

Many happy days followed, at Southampton Street and Garrick's
Villa. Harry remembered Mr Garrick reading Chaucer's *Cock and*

T

*the Fox* to them after supper, and Goldsmith's *Hermit*, after which he would fall asleep in his chair, and Mrs Garrick would drape her lace apron over his visage, and the boys would troop up to bed on tip-toe. 13

Garrick did not keep many of the anonymous letters which came to him, but one received on his return from staying with Rigby was preserved.

Sir,
    Spending the evening very often near where your brother George lives, he is very often the subject of the conversation—that he who has such a family of fine children, should have such a crew of women about his house, besides his Dancer etc. out of doors. His housekeeper takes the state of a Lady upon her, and they say spends more than many of that rank upon herself and family. Her young sister, whom he has had at boarding school, and the Mother, dines at his table. Another sister, who had run away from her husband, lives with the mother. Another Lady, who they say is an officer's wife, one of their relations, is mostly there. Such a sett is enough to ruin any man, besides being making him the laughing stock of all that knows him. It has often been told to him, to no purpose, and had I not seen the title of a pamphlet " The History of the little Groom in the Green near Somerset House with his surprising Seraglio ", I should not have taken this means of acquainting you.
    There is none hates the name of an Informer more than I, but in such a case and being, every word fails. I daresay you will think commendable when upon enquiry you find out so.
                                        Amor Virtutis.
August 26, 1766. To Hampton.
Being an admirer of your great ability made me take this trouble. Him, I never spoke to, so can have no malice. 14

David added this, without comment to an increasing collection. All the children came to Hampton, and George departed for a stay with Brother Peter. David wrote to him on August 30 to tell him that the children were " the delight of the whole neighbourhood ". The Lichfield gardener chosen by Peter had at last arrived, and seemed to be a good-natured, stirring young fellow. A year passed before " Two letters from Bro: George about Money-vile management " were added to the George file. George at his worst could be heart-rending.

Dear Brother,
    I am so ill of a fever and violent Headache that I can not hold my head up. And indeed the thought of troubling you almost distracts me. But I have put off my Trades People so long I am compelled, but with the utmost reluctance, to beg of you to let me have £150. I am surely the most unhappy Man that ever was born, and I am sure, was you to feel but half of what I feel, you would pity.
                            Your very unfortunate Brother,
                                George Garrick. Seven o'clock.
Saturday morning.

But George, at his best, could be dignified. His next effort was written on a Sunday morning:

Dear Brother,
    It is with the greatest reluctance that I make this application to you, for nothing gives me so much uneasiness as to think I am in the least troublesome. My allowance from the theatre is £200, out of which I pay for stamps, engrossments, etc., £50. So that there remains clear £150, which with your kind allowance makes £250. My boys' bare schooling costs me upwards of £120. So that there remains clear £130, out of which I pay for the boys more than £40 for clothes, shirts, etc., etc., which reduces the above to £90. This is what remains to maintain myself and the rest of my family and to find us in clothes and every other necessary. I mention these particulars by way of apology, and that you may in some measure account for this application, and at a time when everything is so very dear with regard to housekeeping.

This time his suggestion was a loan of two hundred pounds. David put with these "my letter to George—not sent". When Paterson, in 1768, suggested that relations with Lacy might be easier if George retired, David replied that if George retreated he would assuredly follow him. Lacy had behaved badly to George. But two years later he wrote a letter to George which he did send. An old clergyman whom he had encountered at His Majesty's levée at St James's had "attacked me as your neighbour in the country". George, it appeared, had for some time been the owner of a country house, a chariot and horses. "Had you been possessed of the fortune of Lord Clive, such a brother as I think I have been to you, should have been, in common civility, at least acquainted with it." In 1774 came what might prove a solution of George's impossible behaviour. He remarried. His second wife was Miss Elizabeth Tetley, and she had a brother, Colonel James Tetley, in the Indian service. Except that a new family began to appear, and his complaints about his health increased, George's letters did not display the slightest improvement. Five months after the birth of his fourth son (little George), came a request of the familiar type. George was a life-sentence. David had always realized this, and he would always be fond of him. George was faithful.

## 4

While Colman was in Paris, Garrick had told him that he heard Beard wanted to sell the Covent Garden patent. " 'Tis true, but mum. We have not yet discovered the purchasers." Colman had said that he had received a mysterious letter from "a person of fashion" apparently offering him a share. Thereafter the subject had been dropped between them. Colman had failed to alter

Wycherley's *Country Wife* for production at Drury Lane, owing to weak health and low spirits, and Garrick had done the job himself. Colman had been well enough, however, to get ready *The Englishman in Paris*, taken from Voltaire's *L'Écossaise*, and these together with *Neck or Nothing*, a farce from the French of Le Sage, and Dryden's *Cymon*, both adapted by Garrick, had been the successes of the season. Garrick had played nineteen times, and thought he had got through this winter much better than last. " Hampton has had a prodigious effect upon me—my cough and hoarseness are fifty per cent better." He went to Bath in March, and it was from Lacy and George that he heard first that Colman, together with two City backers, and (was it to be believed?) Powell, were buying Beard's patent. An agreement with Powell had been signed. In April, Colman arrived at Bath. " We pulled off our hats, but did not smile. Our friends here will stir heaven and earth to bring us together— make the best of it, 'twill be but a darn." He noticed that Colman seemed to have some affair to broach, but could not quite bring it forth. They always got interrupted. They clattered out of the grey streets of Bath together, on horseback, in spring sunshine. They met at supper parties which sat late. Still Colman said nothing. His situation was, indeed, extremely delicate. His mother, who was dying, would leave him six thousand pounds. But his uncle, General Pulteney, from whom he had much greater expectations, had always disapproved of his theatrical tastes. The General was said to have offered him a seat in Parliament and a fine provision if he would quit the theatre and Miss Ford. Miss Ford, with tears in her eyes, had begged Becket, the bookseller, to lend her Coley one thousand pounds. Beard was asking sixty thousand pounds, of which a Mr Harris, a soap manufacturer, and a Mr Rutherford, a wine-merchant, would find half. A friendly nobleman, at the instance of a beautiful mistress, had offered Powell eleven thousand pounds, and more if necessary. Garrick, still in the dark, asked George and Lacy, " Who finds the money? What is the plan? Who are the directors? " If Powell was to be one of them he would rejoice, " for he is finely calculated for management ". Colman had been extremely valuable to him, but was under no legal obligation. Powell would be breaking his articles. " He is a scoundrel." Lacy advised, and Garrick agreed, that they should exact from Powell his due forfeit. Gradually, Garrick knew the facts. Clutterbuck and " Dr Ralpho " Schomberg of Bath, twin-brother of Dr Isaac of London (who had been provided with a life pass for Drury Lane in 1759), had done their best to bring about a reconciliation. Colman brought forth his story. He had been approached first by Powell.

He could not deny that Powell had no business training, and that Messrs Harris and Rutherford had been strangers to him. He did think his situation extremely hazardous. He showed Garrick his latest letter from General Pulteney, stiff but not unkind. He had offered to give up his project of theatrical management if the General would engage to leave him the great Newport estates, which the General's brother, Lord Bath, had failed to do. But the General wished him to give up, also, Miss Ford. Garrick urged him to go and see his uncle, but Colman did not feel up to that. On that note they parted.

On May 5, George received instructions from Bath:

> My wife desires you to write a note, the night you receive this, (Saturday), to our maid at Hampton, Nancy Hetherington, to prepare some mutton, and a pudding with some asparagus, for our dinner on Tuesday, about five o'clock, or rather six. . . .

He had told Lacy that the sale of the other house gave him not the least uneasiness. He calculated his losses and assets. The Yateses were not going to renew their contract. They were going with Colman to Covent Garden. Yates was almost his oldest friend in the theatre, but Mrs Yates had long irked him. Tom King had broken his leg last autumn, and had been off duty for many months. But a lame leg would not be at all inappropriate for such parts as Ogleby, and a "most iniquitous offer" of Powell and Colman to King had been resisted. Clive and Pritchard must soon retire. Mrs Abington was a brilliant but uncertain quantity. Hopkins's diary, when the new season opened, showed that Drury Lane had got new blood. The house had been enlarged to hold three hundred and seventy-seven guineas instead of two hundred and twenty. Barry was returning—after nine years—a great sensation. He was bringing with him Mrs Dancer, whom he was going to marry. Hugh Kelly, the Irish playwright, had said in his satire *Thespis* that she was "a moon-eyed idiot", but she was very lovely. She was twenty-three, a young widow, shortsighted and elegant. The pair were going to be very expensive. Garrick had been obliged to offer them one thousand five hundred pounds for the season. But he had also promising beginners. Hopkins thought that Samuel Reddish, who had never before appeared in London "will be useful". Charles Bannister had a tall figure, a good voice and sang well. Mrs Jefferies was "a smart little figure", Mrs Robert Baddeley, who had joined the company while Garrick was abroad, was Imogen for the first time, "but an indifferent figure in Breeches". People who said that the manager was too available to persons of rank, would have been surprised to see a letter addressed to the Duchess of Portland.

> Madam,
>
> I shall always be happy to obey your Grace's commands, but our company at present is so full, and all the parts disposed of, that I could not, without great injustice to those actors I have already engaged, employ the person you recommended.
>
> I have given Mr Collins the best advice in my power, and apprised him that I shall be ready at the end of the season to examine his qualifications for the stage.
>
> If your Grace will permit me to speak my mind, I think he has the most unpromising aspect for an actor I ever saw—a small pair of unmeaning eyes stuck in a round unthinking face, are not the most desirable requisites for a hero, or a fine gentleman—however, I will give him a tryal, if he is unemployed at that time of the year, and if he can be of service to me or himself, I shall most certainly obey your Grace's commands.
>
> Mrs Garrick presents her respects to your Grace, and thinks herself greatly honoured by your mention of her.
>
> I am, Madam,
>                     Your Grace's most humble and obedient servant,
>                     D. Garrick.
>                     Oct. 29th, 1767.                     16

No Collins is recorded amongst Drury Lane company.

Drury Lane opened on September 12, and Covent Garden on the 14th, and from the start it was war to the knife between them. Johnson had pleaded pressure of work and ill-health as his reason for refusing to write a prologue for Colman's opening. " Covent Garden played against us, unexpected," on the 15th, and thereafter both theatres offered performances every night. A typical Garrick comedy, *A Peep Behind the Curtain*, was a secure favourite. A typical Murphy classical tragedy, *Zenobia*, was applauded. Colman made Shakespeare his prey. He announced a new *Lear*, and *Cymbeline*, both of which were already being played at Drury Lane. A week before Colman produced the first play of Oliver Goldsmith (refused by Garrick after much delay, in the previous year) Hugh Kelly's much-advertised *False Delicacy* drew all London to Drury Lane. Poor Goldsmith's far more valuable *Good Natur'd Man* ran for only ten nights. Lacy, always nervous, had hoped for " an agreement or friendly intercourse " with the new managers, but Garrick had stuck to it, " That would be ruin indeed ". He believed that Colman already repented his bargain, and he was right. Before a season which had been very profitable for both houses closed, tales of deadly quarrels at Covent Garden had reached the clubs and even the press. It must be admitted that Colman was phenomenally unlucky. In October, General Pulteney died, and, as he had warned Colman, had not been " so much his friend " as had always been hoped. As soon as his creditors heard that the General had willed the Newport estate elsewhere they began to look upon Colman with a jaundiced eye. A dispute between the four proprietors passed, from a pamphlet war, to litigation. Powell died suddenly in the summer of 1769, of a cold, caught watching a cricket match at Bristol, and Miss Ford, whom Colman had at last married, two years later, also suddenly. She had, " Georgy " was told, " swallow'd by mistake a wrong medicine ". Colman had an epileptic fit, in the theatre, that winter, but recovered. Garrick and he resumed friendship surprisingly soon, and his old manager gave evidence as to Colman's ability, as a witness in one of his lawsuits; but there was never the old warmth in their meetings or letters. Colman resigned from managership at Covent Garden in 1774, having won his case against his partners, and scored his last great success with a Goldsmith play, *She Stoops to Conquer*. After a period of aimless retirement at Bath, he went on to revive the Haymarket. Garrick produced several minor works from his pen, but he never again brought forth anything to compare with *The Jealous Wife* and *The Clandestine Marriage*. He survived Garrick by fifteen years, but for the last decade of his life, his reason was clouded.

## 5

Rigby had now attained the avowed summit of his ambitions. He was Paymaster to the Forces. A letter in his large energetic hand, accepting congratulations, was dated June 13, 1768.

> Do you imagine my David, that any paltry consideration of office or business shall deprive me of the pleasure of our Mistley party? I should be worth but half the Pay-Office, indeed, if I could sacrifice the rites of Mistley to any earthly consideration. No; they begin the 25th, at dinner, and you and your *Cara Sposa* are expected by her, and your, faithful humble servant,
>
> Richard Rigby.

After Mistley, the Garricks set out upon a long-planned circular tour. Arden, who was now thirty-five, had married, a year past, a young lady of Northampton, aged twenty-four, with a good fortune, but a cast in one eye. He was now the father of an infant William, and appeared settled as Rector of Brampton, where he had a good house for entertaining, and a garden improved by orders of Lord Spencer, who had sent his own gardener from Althorp to superintend alterations at considerable expense. Arden had also recently been appointed a Prebendary of Worcester Cathedral. With such a patron to help him on, so talented a man seemed marked for preferment.  The Garricks had arranged to take him with them from Brampton to Lichfield, but on the day before they were due to leave, Joseph Cradock, who had heard that they were in his neighbourhood, came over, and insisted that they must pause for at least a dinner with him, as their road, by Leicester, ran close to his house.  He was, in fact, what he called " between two houses ", for he was busy demolishing his ancestral home, and building something fit for a prince—an operation which was to lead him into serious financial trouble.  However, he had, in his temporary residence, one large room, and having told the Garricks to expect nothing better than cold meats, was able to furnish up a very fine dish of stewed carp, caught in a small pond on his estate.  After dinner he took Garrick and Arden round Gumley.  Garrick, on seeing the size of the room in which they had dined, had said it was quite large enough for them to give a performance.  Arden as Falstaff, he assured Cradock, excelled even the late Quin.  But when they got back from their walk, they found the hour too far advanced, so they took the road for The Four Cranes at Leicester, where they supped in the Great Room.  Garrick, amongst boon companions, on holiday, in an old inn, in an old town, was " all life and spirits ", and when supper was over a scene from *Henry IV* was undertaken.  Presently, they heard their own laughter echoed.  Garrick strode to a door of the Great Room, which was a little ajar.  It opened upon a bed-chamber, absolutely packed by natives of Leicester, friends of Cradock, who had heard from him that the great actor was in their midst.  " So," cried Garrick, " we have got an audience, I find! "  He very civilly told the gentlemen of Leicester that if they were at all entertained they might leave the door open, and their only regret next morning was that Cradock had not given them longer notice, so that many more might have been present.  Cradock turned home from Leicester, but after their stay at Lichfield, the Garricks went on with Arden to Warwick.  Here arrangements went awry.  They had understood that Lord Warwick expected them to dine.  They were shown all the wonders of the place, and even met their host, but he seemed unconscious of their expectations and presented them merely with a volume containing the history of his family.  Both Garrick and Arden produced verses on the ludicrous occasion, and unfortunately these got into circulation, much to the chagrin of the earl (who had failed to get the message announcing them), and somewhat to their own embarrassment.                                                      18

It was on a July day of 1768 that the Garricks' carriage drew up for the first time at the gates of Althorp.  From the hall quite a false impression might easily be formed of this house.  Like many in the country, it had enormous equestrian and sporting mural paintings, classical busts, and a fine plaster ceiling. But the entrance hall was a piece of patchwork, added in the first quarter of the present century. Nothing had been added since. Althorp had never been ' new-built ' throughout. It had been completed in E shape, before the Spanish Armada sailed, and re-faced after the accession of Charles II, in warm red brick and Weldon stone. The inner courtyard had been covered in, but the form and extent of the original house had been followed, and in the grounds some picturesque relics, that had defied time and chance, were still visible —the moat, the falconry, with faded frescoes on its walls, from which the ladies of a family devoted to the chase had watched field-sports. Anne of Denmark and Henry, Prince of Wales, had come to Althorp to witness a masque by Ben Jonson. When a Lord Arundel of that date had taunted a Lord Spencer, speaking of mediæval days, " In those days your lordship's ancestors were keeping sheep," the reply of the head of a very old land-owning family had been quelling. " When my ancestors were keeping sheep, your lordship's ancestors were plotting treason." John Evelyn had thought the kitchen being in the body of the house, and the chapel too small, were defects. Horace Walpole liked it much, for the number of its por- traits and its old simplicity. He admired the avenues of old oak and ash and elm, bowering over; the diamond-paned casemented win- dows. Except for the stables, which were of large dimensions with a pedimented entry resembling that at St Paul's, Covent Garden, he decided that Althorp was a good, but not a fine, house. But the library on the first floor, in the centre of the north front, was digni- fied, and the long gallery, which looked Elizabethan, until the size of its panels was observed, was romantic. Kings and cardinals, gods and goddesses, Lely beauties, Spencer family portraits, landscapes, Flemish, Dutch, Italian and French, hung, in no particular order, on its walls. Of course it needed renovation. The bedrooms were dotted all over the house, some on the ground floor and some on the first. There were not nearly enough, especially at Christmas, which the family liked to celebrate in the old style. The furniture was more a miscellaneous accretion of many generations, than a collection. There was much dismissed by Walpole as oldish, but there were also Chinese Chippendale pieces, lacquered cabinets, French gilded suites. The result was comfort, and Garrick reading the plays of Shakespeare to the party after dinner, or trying to write a letter with three of the most beautiful young women in Europe trying to prevent him, was never so happy. The atmosphere of the house was essentially that of a home. After their first visit, the Garricks came annually.

Nine years after they had first arrived there, Lady Spencer, disappointed to hear that they could not come for Christmas, as Eva-Maria had not been well, urged them to come as early as possible in the new year.

> She must not ail anything—you, I am sure can neither see, hear nor understand without her. After all, it is comfortable to find that a few people can live a good many years together without wishing one another at the d——. It will to-morrow be one and twenty years since Lord Spencer married me, and I verily believe we have neither of us repented of our lot from that time to this. [19]

### 6

Eva-Maria, who kept a diary, began a new volume on the return from Althorp. It was her tenth, a convenient size to slip into a pocket—four-and-a-quarter inches by six-and-a-quarter—and bound in blue marbled paper. The Duke of Devonshire, having found it impossible, in ten days, to catch either of the Garricks at home, had once declared he thought them " strange rambling people ". Lord Camden, trying to fix a date for a visit, with equal lack of success, had concluded that they were " strangers to the pleasure of one day's solitude ".

Eva-Maria's diary for the last half of 1768 confirms these opinions. [20]

> Tuesday, August 2.  I went to London and brought the children back to Hampton.
> Saturday, 6th.  We set out by ten, arrived by 2 at Greagres (Gregories) at Mr Burkes.
> Monday, 8th.  We went to see Ld. Despencer at West Wickham.
> Tuesday, 9th.  Set out half past six, came to Hampton by ten.
> Wednesday, 11th.  The Prince of Saxe Gotha breakfasted with us.
> Saturday, 13th.  We went to dine with Mr Foot, from thence to London.
> Sunday, 14th.  We returned to Hampton.
> Tuesday, 16th.  We went to London.
> Friday, 19th.  We returned to Hampton.
> Tuesday, 23rd.  My Husband dined at Walton Bridge.  The children came from London.  Bell not very well.
> Thursday, 25th.  We went to Town.

One of the neighbouring houses most often visited by the Garricks was that of the Hawkinses, on Twickenham Common.

Prim little Letitia Hawkins, like Harry Angelo, had the most vivid recollections of Mr Garrick.

> I see him now, in a dark blue coat, the button-holes bound with gold, a small cocked hat, laced with gold, his waistcoat very open, and his countenance never at rest; and, indeed, seldom his person; for in the relaxation of the country he gave way to all his natural volatility, and with my father was perfectly at ease, sometimes sitting on a table, and then, if

he saw my brothers at a distance on the lawn, shooting off like an arrow out
of a bow in a spirited chase of them round the garden

She clearly remembered walking hand in hand with her father
on Twickenham Common, on a very hot afternoon of 1768, and
meeting Mr Garrick, bound for London, on horseback. "He had
been summoned to play before the King of Denmark." She was
round-eyed with concern for him, as he lamented the misery of
being haled up to town in such weather; but after he had cantered
off, in a cloud of dust and importance, her father, from whom she
inherited her primness, assured her that Mr Garrick was really "very
well pleased, and that what he groaned at, as a labour, was an honour
paid to his talents". Mr Hawkins, on an occasion when he deemed
his two sons and his daughter were not treating him with due
respect, took them all to see Garrick as Lear, an experience which
reduced Letitia almost to hysterics.

Garrick's problem, however, was serious. He would have to
re-open the theatre, and most of his principal performers were either
on holiday or occupied with provincial engagements. Mrs Pritchard
had retired in April, after thirty-seven years on the stage, and had
died four months later. He had acted with her in *Macbeth*, for her
benefit, and written her farewell epilogue. He said, and stuck to it,
that he would never again appear as Macbeth. The Lord Chamberlain now wanted him to display himself, to entertain his Danish
Majesty, in half a dozen of his principal parts. On September 8,
Eva-Maria wrote, "My husband played for the King of Denmark".
Drury Lane had been re-opened and special performances "by
particular desire" had been announced. It had meant crawling to
Harry Woodward, for old time's sake, to approach the ineffable
Bellamy. Both were Covent Garden employees. Hopkins was
enthusiastic over "Richard by Mr Garrick for the first time these
six years. Beyond Description fine—his voice clear to the last."
The actor-manager entertained the visiting monarch at Hampton
on Sunday, September 11. Attended by the Danish Ambassador,
Baron Diede, Christian VII, "and all his suite", paced the riverside lawn of Garrick's Villa and were shown Shakespeare's Temple
"my house and garden, the Owner and his Wife". "You would
think me vain," wrote David to Riccoboni; "should I tell you what
he said." The king was tiny, "as diminutive", wrote Horace
Walpole, "as if he came out of a kernel in the Fairy Tales". He
was not ill-looking, though, and had, upon the whole, more royalty
than folly in his air—"white, strutting, prominent eyes, *galant* and
condescending enough. His Court behaves to him with an Eastern
submission." Garrick composed a letter for Bickerstaffe to send to

the king, expressing his pleasure that a play from his pen (*The Padlock*, a comic opera in two parts) should have been the only new piece presented during the stay of his Majesty, who had graciously allowed it to be dedicated to him.   The Danes passed on to Paris, and Riccoboni wrote that everyone there had gone mad over this young king.   Nobody guessed yet that the guests to whom Garrick had played host at Hampton formed almost the complete cast of a tragedy as dark and dreadful as any ever performed at Drury Lane.

Christian VII was indeed a young king.   He was barely nineteen.   He had married, two years past, the Princess Caroline-Matilda, youngest sister of George III.   She had been fifteen, and had wept bitterly at parting from her mama at Harwich.   She had been a posthumous child, and it was believed that her family had somewhat spoiled her.   Like her brother the Duke of York, she was a white rabbit, with hair and eyes so fair as to be almost silver. " *Elle est si blonde,*" complained her Scandinavian bridegroom.   A son and heir had been born in January of the year in which the young king had set off for a continental pleasure tour which was to last for eight months.   The press announced that the special performances at the London theatres were " in honour of the visit and marriage of the King of Denmark ".   Nobody asked in print why the queen had not come too; but there were already whispers that all was not well with this marriage.   Count Holk, Marshal of the Court, included amongst his duties finding mistresses for his master.   Walpole wrote him down " a complete jackanapes . . . about three and twenty, but who will be tumbled down before he is prepared for it ". Dr Struensee, an elegant atheistical physician, of Altona, who accompanied the king as surgeon-in-ordinary, did not apparently engage Garrick's attention, but he had considerable correspondence during the next eighteen months with another member of the Danish royal suite, " my friend Sturtz, at Copenhagen," who wrote and spoke English.

> Since our return, the English language, the English fashions, have a great run . . . There has been spread a report of late that you had a mind to come over and pay a visit to your Danish friends.   Such a trip would be a very meritorious thing.   Kings and Queens would delight at it, and you would for ever be remembered by the bards at the feast of the Shells.

After Christmas 1769, however, no further letters came from Copenhagen.   Events in the royal Danish tragedy had moved with speed.   Within three years, Christian VII had sunk into imbecility, Holk had been dismissed, and Count Struensee, who had risen to supreme power, had been convicted of criminal familiarity with the queen.   He was beheaded, drawn and quartered.   Caroline-Matilda died, an exile in Hanover, in 1775. Her death was attributed to poison, but five of the nine children of " poor Fred " had inherited his lamentable constitution, and died prematurely. In England, the news of Caroline-Matilda's arrest created a passing indignation, and a busybody wrote to Garrick to suggest that *Hamlet*, at present being performed at Drury Lane, should be withdrawn. Garrick replied that it had never entered his head that anyone could suspect him of disloyalty. " The play of ' Hamlet ' was promised the week before last, to the public, and before any news came from Denmark. . . . Would not the stopping of the play have given great offence and occasioned enquiries why it was put off? " He did not find there was " a single circumstance in the play resembling the many stories coming from Denmark, even supposing them all true ". He had sent his brother to the Lord Chamberlain's department, to ask if there would be any impropriety in producing the play, and the answer had come " none at all ".

## 7

On Sunday, October 16, 27, Southampton Street was a house of mourning. Biddy was no more. She had been taken ill on Saturday. " I walk'd out with her," recorded Eva-Maria's Journal. " She could hardly bear it." Biddy died at half-past eleven the same night. *"Hélas!"* The little King Charles had enjoyed a long life, even for a small dog—fifteen years—and her progeny had been numerous. But she had been the first in the Garrick's home. Her mistress had been accustomed to take her in her lap at the theatre. On one occasion Garrick had quitted the box with some murmur of " something wrong on the stage ". A country bumpkin had presently appeared to speak a prologue. Eva-Maria had thought the actor to be a stranger, but Biddy's tail had begun to thump. She had known her master, however disguised.

On October 21, Hopkins entered in his diary, " Mr Barry's first appearance this Season. A Quarrel in the Green-Room between Mrs Barry and Mr Aickin ". Mrs Barry's ethereal airs concealed considerable force of character. Garrick was to become sadly familiar with her " very dangerous cold " caught at rehearsal, and sudden decisions not to attempt parts she had herself chosen. There were two Aickins, Frank and James, brothers, from Dublin. They had graduated as strolling players, and had winning manners. Frank had come to Drury Lane three years past, James, who was the younger but better actor, last season. Frank was a tragedian; James excelled in such parts as a heavy father or worthy steward. Fifteen months after Hopkins's boding entry, Garrick filed " a penetential letter " from one who had not dared approach personally a manager whom he feared had quite withdrawn his favour. Mr Garrick's coldness of deportment was causing Frank the greatest concern.

On the night after Mrs Barry's scene with Frank (behind the scenes), Hopkins announced the first appearance of an actress who was to become important—Miss Elizabeth Younge, as Imogen, " an elegant figure in both Dresses—a very good Voice, but wants Management. A great Deal of acting about her, and would make a great Figure if she had a better Face ". Miss Younge, like Mrs Abington, had been a milliner's assistant, but was a very different type. She was to prove more than a successor to Mrs Pritchard. She had more range. She was equally good in tragedy and comedy. She had soft features, blue eyes, a delicate complexion, and good manners, and was of a commanding stature. It was presently rumoured that the king had admired her because she reminded him of his first love, Lady Sarah Lennox. Her private life was strictly correct. After a successful first season at Drury Lane, during which Garrick brought her on as the heroine in an Eastern tragedy, *Zingis*, by a Captain Dow (on leave from Bengal), she swept out, on a question of terms, and went over to Dublin. But she returned after two years, and when Garrick came to take his farewell of the stage, she was his " Bess " and a mainstay of his company.

Cradock had now married a young lady of good family but a weak constitution, and had a house in Town until Gumley was ready. On the night of October 28, 1768, when he had a party to dine with him at his house in Dean Street, Soho, he was startled by a violent rapping at his doors, and a messenger from Drury Lane. Mr Garrick had suddenly received news of the death of a friend, and wished to speak with him about the particulars. Cradock apologized to his guests and hurried to the threatre, where he found Garrick " quite in an agony ". The piece to be played that night was *The Wonder*, and Garrick was already in his costume as the gay Don Felix. He greeted Cradock with the words, " Can this dreadful news possibly be true—about Arden? " Seeing that Cradock knew nothing, he put a letter in his hand, and begged him to hurry to Spencer House. Cradock read the letter, in the coach, on his short journey westward, but on his return to the theatre had to confess failure. He had not been able to see Lord Spencer, who was very ill, but had sent down word that " we must judge the worst ". The news in the letter had been that, yesterday, Arden had gone out into his garden at Brampton Ash, and there shot himself. By the time that Cradock had performed his mission, the hour for the curtain to rise at Drury

Lane was over-due. The orchestra had continued playing, but the audience was becoming clamorous. Garrick, with tears running down his face, gave the order for the curtain to rise on the comedy, and "absolutely rushed on" to perform his duty. How he got through the part of Felix, Cradock could not imagine. He had to have someone to see him home after the play was over, and when he got there, he took to his bed for a week.

The death of Arden remained a sad mystery. He had been in London, and had dined at Southampton Street, as recently as September 13. Cradock thought he had noticed something odd in his manner, on a recent visit, and wrote of " a lurking melancholy ". James Sharp, writing from Cambridge, three months later, had begun to believe that their friend had sunk into despair " owing to his marrying a woman whom he did not love, and losing one whom he did love, and might (when too late) have had ". Miss Ekins, at whose shrine Arden had worshipped, had married Major Barton, who had been Lord Spencer's " governor " in his school-days. She had been left a widow, suddenly, after Arden had made his *mariage de convenance*.

The Wonder was the play chosen by Clive for her farewell performance at the end of this season. His " Clivy-Pivy " was much touched by Garrick's offer to play " Don Felix ".

> It gives me a double pleasure—the entertainment my friends will receive from your performance, and the being convinced that you have a sort of sneaking kindness for your Pivy. I suppose I shall have you tapping me on the shoulder (as you do to Violante) when I bid you farewell, and desiring one tender look before we part—though perhaps you may recollect, and toss the pancake into the cinders. You see, I never forget any of your good things.

Her country neighbour and constant admirer, Horace Walpole, was writing the epilogue which she was to speak. Naturally, to a fine gentleman so small and frail, Drury Lane's best *soubrette*, loud, noisy and very vulgar (when she chose) had been eternally attractive. But the time had clearly come for her to cease attempting at least youthful parts. There had been a ludicrous occasion, shortly before Mrs Pritchard's retirement. Both the leading ladies of Drury Lane had been so stout that when a letter was dropped on the stage neither could, or would, attempt to pick it up. Clive, attired as a smart chambermaid, had saved the situation by ringing peremptorily for yet another maid, and nobody in the audience had guessed that the effect was unrehearsed.

Garrick had been ill. Arthur Murphy, calling at Southampton Street in March, was glad to be told by an unconsciously comic

servitor, " I think my master is a good deal perter to-day ".   Clive
wrote to thank her manager for coming up from Bath.

> I am *glad* you are well for the sake of my audience, who will have the
> pleasure to see their own Don Felix.   What signifies fifty-two?   They had
> rather see *the* Garrick and *the* Clive, at a hundred and four, than any of the
> moderns.   The ancients you know, have always been admired.   I do assure
> you I am at present in such health and spirits that when I recollect I am an
> old woman, I am astonished.   The dear town are giving me such applause
> every time they see me, that I am in great fear for myself on my benefit
> night. . . . You are very much mistaken if you imagine I shall be sorry to
> hear Mr Clive is well.   I thank God I have no malice or hatred to anybody;
> besides, it is so long ago since I thought he used me ill, that I have quite
> forgot it . . .

This letter was preserved by Garrick, together with that joyously
accepting his offer to play at her benefit, on which he had written
" A love-letter—the first I ever had, from that truly great comedian,
Mrs Clive ".

On the Saturday after Clive's farewell, a letter from another
senior member of his company had to be answered by the manager,
from his country retreat.   Tom King (who had just renewed his
engagement) had, failing to find Brother George, sent a verbal complaint by " Mr Hopkins ".   This called for a rebuke opening in
Olympian style.

> Mr Garrick's compliments to Mr King—Though he is seldom surprised    24
> at what may happen in a theatre . . .

## CHAPTER XII

# STRATFORD-UPON-AVON JUBILEE

## 1769

### I

In the first week of May 1769 a deputation on behalf of the Mayor, Aldermen and Burgesses of the ancient borough of Stratford-upon-Avon waited upon Mr Garrick at 27, Southampton Street. He was formally presented with the Freedom of the borough, enclosed in what he described in his letter of thanks as " an elegant and inestimable box ". The box had been made from a mulberry tree " undoubtedly planted by Shakespeare's own hand ". He had been expecting this recognition of his art for six months, and had bought half a dozen pieces of the mulberry tree seven years before. It had flourished in the gardens of New Place, the handsome house bought by Shakespeare in the days of his prosperity, and in which he had died. It had, apparently, flourished exceedingly. In 1756, the then owner of New Place, deeming it shadowed his windows and gave his house the damps, had sacrilegiously cut it down. He had evidently anticipated local opposition, for the felling had been done by his gardener, under cover of darkness. The result had been painful for him. " Not the going out of the Vestal Fire at old Rome, or the stealing of the Palladium from old Troy, could have astonished Romans and Trojans more than this horrid Deed did the Men, Women and Children at old Stratford." An angry mob had gathered outside New Place. Much alarmed, the barbaric Priest (for he was in Holy Orders) had, after consultation with his friends, fled his house, and eventually, after " skulking from Place to Place ", the town of Stratford. The inhabitants announced a decision never again to suffer any one of his name to dwell amongst them. His name was Gastrell, so the deprivation did not seem likely to affect a large clan, but, by a curious chance, it was familiar to Garrick. The relict of the Reverend Francis Gastrell had, after her husband's death, settled near Lichfield. She had been a Miss Aston, sister-in-law of Gilbert Walmesley. Johnson had taken Boswell to dine at Stowhill, and told him (unfortunately too late for Boswell to make inquiries on the spot) that he believed Gastrell had cut down the tree to vex his neighbours, and that Mrs Gastrell had participated in her husband's guilt. The Gastrells had not profited by their iconoclasm, but somebody else had, considerably. Thomas Sharp,

U

of Stratford, watchmaker, silversmith and carpenter, had bought the timber, and begun to issue souvenirs suited to every purse— standishes, ink-horns, tobacco stoppers, tea-chests. . . . Already, by the time Garrick had made his purchase, it had been thought necessary for a certificate of authenticity to accompany the sale. His pieces had been vouched for by two persons whose names were to become well known to him—William Hunt, attorney, of Stratford, and John Payton, Master of the White Lion Inn. Garrick had paid two guineas, and had the wood made up into a Shakespeare chair, which in suitable weather stood in Shakespeare's Temple on the river-bank at Hampton. The box containing the Freedom had a likeness of Shakespeare carved on one side, and on the other Garrick as Lear. Nothing could have been more flattering. This, indeed, had been the intention of the donors. Stratford had recently embarked upon a new Town Hall. In its north wall there was an empty niche, obviously designed to receive a statue. As the building approached completion, letters from the Middle Temple, signed Francis Wheeler, began to arrive to William Hunt, now Town Clerk of Stratford. Wheeler had taken counsel with George Steevens, the editor of Shakespeare's plays, who knew Mr Garrick well. To assist him in his studies, Mr Garrick had lent Mr Steevens several scarce quartos from his famous library. Mr Steevens, who was a great romancer, with a bitter tongue, but an accepted penalty of London literary life, had hinted that Garrick, who was rich, and vain, might easily be flattered into a present to the Corporation's new building of a very handsome bust, statue or picture of Shakespeare.

To Garrick, Wheeler explained, " The lower part of the building is used as a market-place, and is of great benefit to the poorer sort of people; over it is a handsome assembly room. It would be a reflection on the town of Stratford to have any public building erected there without some ornamental memorial of their immortal townsman."

Thereafter affairs had proceeded smoothly, though not very fast. The Corporation had, by October 1768, passed a resolution that " David Garrick Esq, the greatest theatrical genius of the age, and who has done the highest honours to the memory of the immortal Shakespeare, should be invited to become an honorary burgess ", and Garrick, who had heard of the honour proposed, had asked Wheeler to get the measurements of the niche. " His presents are finishing." His presents, in the end, were an imaginative oil-painting, *Shakespeare in his Study*, performed for him by Benjamin Wilson, and a leaden figure of Shakespeare. The figure was a version of that by Peter Scheemaker from the design of Kent, commissioned in 1741 for the Poets' Corner in Westminster Abbey. Three years ago the sculptor had produced an "improved" copy for Lord Pembroke, at Wilton: the one sent to Stratford resembled this. Still, Garrick was not satisfied. One of Wheeler's letters had mentioned that the Corporation " would be equally pleased to have some picture of yourself ". There was another artist, of growing reputation, whom he would have liked to have seen employed on the Stratford business. Thomas Gainsborough had worked for a short spell in the studio of Hayman, scene-painter at Drury Lane, but had been settled for the past eight years in Bath, depicting fashionable clients, largely come from London for the cure. All that Garrick asked, was for him to produce a composite picture of Garrick and Shakespeare, as like both as could be. This would mean going down to Stratford to look at the memorial half-length figure above the poet's tomb in Holy Trinity Church, and then considering, together with this, the only undoubted picture, the engraving by Martin Droeshout published as frontispiece to the First Folio in 1623. Both were, of course, posthumous, but not, as Shakespeare had died in 1616, hopelessly so. The people who had produced them had seen the man. Throughout the summer of 1768, Garrick looked for a letter in Gainsborough's handwriting, postmarked Stratford. Garrick knew the monument. He had once visited Stratford in company with Charles Macklin, in his salad days. Gainsborough, in lengthy letters regrettably garnished with expletives, had not, by August 1768, yet got down to Stratford. He blamed the weather— continual rains. They damped his genius. However, he had been for days rubbing in and rubbing out designs. His idea was " something a little out of the simple portrait way ". He asked when Garrick would be coming to Bath. Eventually, he evidently had seen his prey, but the result was discouraging. " Shakespeare's bust is a silly smiling thing." The Droeshout engraving pleased him no better. " Damn the original picture of him, with your leave. . . . A stupider face I never beheld. . . . I intend, with your approbation, my dear friend, to take the form, from his pictures and statues, just enough to preserve his likeness past the doubt of all blockheads at first sight, and supply a soul from his works. It is impossible that such a mind and ray of heaven could shine with such a face and pair of eyes as that picture has." He mentioned that he would leave the price to Garrick, and did not care whether he got a farthing. His usual portrait price nowadays was sixty guineas, but Shakespeare would not exactly be sitting to him. At last, Stratford Corporation accounts noted, " Mr Gainsbrough for Mr Garrick's Picture £63 ", and a full length of Garrick, draping himself around something

resembling the Scheemaker Shakespeare bust, in park-like sur-
roundings, was delivered and hung in Stratford's new Town Hall.
Gainsborough, who had himself a spare figure, excelled in elongating
sitters. Eva-Maria, years later, assured friends that Gainsborough's
full-length was in her opinion the best likeness ever taken of " my
Davy ".

By the spring of 1769 the idea of a Shakespeare Jubilee at Stratford had been decided upon. It was no new scheme. It had been
mooted in 1764, the bicentenary of the poet's birth, but Garrick
had been on his Grand Tour then. He was now at the height of his
reputation, but Stratford was a small place, not much visited. Was
his arm long enough and his purse deep enough to send down there
the necessary material from his own theatre, and draw there, from
all over the country, the nobility and gentry whose presence would
make the occasion a social success? He decided that the opportunity was too dazzling to be disregarded. He accepted an invitation to become Steward of a three-day Festival, and began his
*Ode upon dedicating a building to Shakespeare*. Clutterbuck, at his
request, paid Dr Thomas Arne £63 for the music to it. On his last
appearance of the season at Drury Lane, on May 18, the manager
gave his audience a thrilling notification.

> My Eyes, till then, no Sights like this will see,
> Unless we meet at *Shakespeare's Jubilee*!
> On Avon's banks where Flowers eternal blow,
> Like its full stream, our Gratitude shall flow!
> There let us revel, shew our fond Regard.
> On that lov'd Spot, first breath'd our Matchless Bard.
> To Him all Honour, Gratitude is due,
> To Him we owe our All—to *Him* and *You*.

He set out for Stratford, to view the terrain, in early June, put
up for the night at Oxford, and had an agreeable evening discussing
Shakespeare with Thomas Warton, Fellow of Trinity College, and
twice Professor of Poetry. Thomas had in mind his *magnum opus*,
a History of Poetry, and Garrick promised to lend him some early
metrical romances. Both the Warton brothers were tremendous
talkers, and for oddity of manner most people gave the palm to
Thomas, rather than to Joseph, now Headmaster of Winchester
College.

At Stratford the enthusiasm displayed by the Corporation was
touching, but it very soon became evident to the manager of a
theatre that the Jubilee, proposed for August, would have to be
postponed to September. This was risky, for the weather might
have broken; and inconvenient, for Drury Lane season opened on

September 16; but it was quite unavoidable. *The Gentleman's Magazine* published an engraving of " A House in Stratford-upon-Avon in which the famous Shakespear was born ", and a paragraph announcing that over a hundred trees had been felled upon the banks of Avon, by permission of the Duke of Dorset, to enlarge the prospect against the approaching Jubilee. The edifice to be imposed upon a pastoral site near the river was variously described as the Amphitheatre (modelled upon that at Ranelagh of which Lacy had been one of the progenitors), the Rotunda, Shakespeare's Hall and The Great Masquerade Booth. In it were to take place banquets, concerts and balls, and on the level country surrounding it, a Jubilee horse-race. Angelo, senior, was put in charge of the fireworks, and Angelo, junior, was reminded of Marlborough outside Lille or Tournay as he watched his father directing the engineers who were to play off rockets, crackers, catherine wheels and squibs on the banks of the Avon. Lacy, not a man for humour, unbent sufficiently to mention " Our friend Angelo is to make the most *brilliant* figure of the undertaking ". Garrick returned to London, and Jubilee paraphernalia began to descend upon Southampton Street—proofs of tickets, to be signed by George, giving admission to the Oratorio, Ball and Great Booth at the Fireworks, samples of Jubilee ribbon, rainbow-coloured, which one enterprising tradesman was to exhibit in his window with a quotation from Johnson's famous prologue on the opening of Drury Lane Theatre:

> Each change of many colour'd life he drew.

David and Eva-Maria ordered their gala costumes, of material so good that two hundred years have scarcely touched them. David's Steward's suit was plain but magnificent, in the best of taste, and height of fashion, of mole and amber changeable velvet. The long waistcoat had thirteen buttons, and even the coat was lined with ivory taffeta. Eva-Maria's gown was of white corded silk, brocaded with sprays of roses and silver stars, and trimmed with silver lace. It had a tiny waist, and a stay bodice, and very wide skirt, and would, in mercer's parlance, " stand by itself ". David's memoranda began to look harassed. " Boats on the Avon? Lodgings for Lord Spencer and family. *A good bed for Mr Foote.*" At Stratford, the Town Clerk was also getting worried. Mr Gore of Kiddington wanted lodgings for four servants and six horses, at Shottery, outside the town, and, if it was true there was to be a Jubilee Ball, a masquerade costume. Lady Mostyn simply wanted places at all entertainments. Dr Richard Warner had called to say he would be at the Musical Performance. Joseph Cradock believed that, at this point, he had been of great assistance to Garrick. His mother-in-law, at Merevale Hall, only three miles from Stratford, was a power in the land. A call by the Merevale coachman at the White Lion, to engage rooms, seemed to denote that all was not well in Stratford. Cradock, who had always been pleased that he was thought to resemble Garrick in figure, felt that he owed him attention. (He had heard from the lips of the great man himself that the scene of Iago working up Othello to jealousy was the finest in Shakespeare, that the first three acts of *Hamlet* were the finest, and that *Macbeth* was altogether the best tragedy.) Garrick, off-duty in Southampton Street, had put an enthusiastic amateur through his paces. "Let us now try these scenes . . . as easy and natural as possible, I mean, divested of all stage strut and trick. Begin— 'Excellent wench!' " Cradock took a horse and rode in to Stratford, to prospect.

He found everything in the town indeed in a parlous condition. He laughed away fears, soothed the anxious, and had valuable talks with Payton at the White Lion. A gentleman whom he met in the street began by assuring him that there would be no Jubilee this year, and there would be a riot. The boards had not yet arrived for the completion of " what they call the amphitheatre. They are not even yet bargained for at Birmingham." Cradock went down to the river banks and had to confess he was alarmed by the scene. (" Take care," said his comforter, " that you do not cut your shoes from the broken lamps that have just arrived. They were intended for the illumination of this building, but, if ever they left Drury Lane in safety, you see they are here all shivered to pieces.") Cradock shook off this acquaintance, and took counsel with " some steady persons, from London ". They were frankly uneasy. The inhabitants absolutely refused to co-operate. " They looked upon Mr Garrick as a magician who could, and would, raise the Devil. They were confirmed in their Absurdities by the Black looks of those who were employed in the Fireworks." Sanderson and his myrmidons said, " We would do anything in the world to serve our good Master, but he is entirely kept in the dark as to the situation of everything here." At supper Joseph met more local gentry. Some of them were thinking of packing up and leaving their houses until the Jubilee was over. The only deterrent was that, in this case, they must expect on their return to find their houses ransacked by the undesirable characters from London and elsewhere who were going to flood Stratford. The Paytons were good people, but they could not accommodate one twentieth of the old customers who had applied to them for beds and food. Cradock, after miserable brooding, wrote a full account of his experience to Garrick, and returned to Merevale Hall to inform the intending Jubilee party there that he had done his best for them. He had got them bedrooms at the White Lion, and made arrangements with a baker, who had a clean house, for bread from his oven, and that the coach-load of cold provisions which they would be bringing should be stored safely. He foresaw, and the Paytons did not disagree with him, that they might run out of food. Whether Cradock's information was a help or redundant, the result was magical. Amongst the many complaints recorded of the Jubilee, no one ever suggested that the buildings were not ready for the appointed date. They had meant a great deal of labour, and expense, but they were magnificent and completed for September 6.

It was not to be expected that a great number of Drury Lane performers would be present. Many had summer engagements at provincial theatres. Tom King was coming, and Love, and the beautiful Mrs Baddeley, Mrs Yates and the Rosses, from Edinburgh. Old Havard had written charmingly to ask if he might be " a walker in the cavalcade, and hold up the train part of the ceremony ". A leading actor from Covent Garden wanted to come—" Gentleman Smith ". It was believed that he was not getting on very well with Colman. Literary friends and enemies were coming in force— Colman, Kenrick, Murphy, Victor, Bickerstaffe, Kelly, and, of course, Foote. Johnson was not coming. He was happy at Brighthelmstone, staying with Mr Thrale, the brewer, who had a charming and intelligent wife. James Boswell very much regretted his friend's absence. For he was certainly coming. To be going to the Jubilee was fashionable, he was sure. He could not resist telling everyone where he was bound. He was going to appear at the Grand Masquerade Ball as a Corsican chief. He bought, for six shillings, in Cheapside, the last thing he needed to complete his costume, a beautiful staff, with a bird upon the top. He told the mystified master of the shop, " It is a Jubilee staff. That bird is the bird of Avon."

Six principal eye-witnesses wrote down their experiences of Garrick's Shakespeare Jubilee—Boswell, Cradock, Harry Angelo, Murphy, Victor and an anonymous contributor to *The Gentleman's Magazine*. The last two writers displayed pathetic anxiety to
3 represent everything as having been a richly-deserved success.

" Little " Angelo had been hardly able to believe his good fortune when he was told he had been specially invited to attend his parents to Stratford Jubilee. He was going to be Ariel in the procession of Shakespearian characters. He never forgot watching the

grey skies lighten for dawn of Monday, September 4. The Angelos'
chariot came round at five a.m., but they did not reach the famous
Star inn, opposite Queen's College, in Oxford, until long past
dinner hour—eight o'clock. All post-horses had been taken up
days before, by other people bound for Stratford, and the Angelos
had been obliged to go on without changing horses. Harry did not
identify many of the supper party at the Star that night, except
Mr Wilson, whose name he mistakenly imagined was Robert, and
whom he believed to have painted a full-length of Mr Garrick for the
Stratford Town Hall. A tired boy, sent up to bed soon, remembered little of that evening except Mr Wilson's most entertaining
stories about Mr Lacy, which had set the table on a roar, and how
good supper had been. Mrs Garrick had brought a sumptuous display of wall-fruit from Hampton, for their dessert. She had
brought a great deal more sustaining food, and the Angelos, at their
lodgings above a grocer's shop in the market-place, were presently
very grateful for a portion. Next morning the Garricks set off early,
taking Wilson in their carriage, but the Angelos were again delayed.
A message from the stables had told them that one of their horses
was absolutely knocked up by yesterday's effort. The Master of the
Star came to their rescue. His name was Costar, and he was an
old friend of Garrick. He said he knew of a dealer who had a pair of
carriage-horses for sale. They were trotted in, and Angelo, who must
at all costs be at Stratford to superintend his fireworks, bought them
for thirty-two guineas. They proved an extraordinarily good
bargain, and fourteen years later " Angelo and his old grays " were
well known in London.

The Corporation had ordered that the bells should be rung to
announce Mr Garrick's arrival for the Jubilee. The Angelos missed
that triumphal entry owing to their late start, but there was plenty
to admire in the small, obscure town, which was filling fast. Down
at the amphitheatre, Drury Lane carpenters and painters were
hastily putting the finishing touches to the Rotunda. In contrast
to them, many of the normal inhabitants were " either pursuing their
occupations in the old dog-trot way, or staring with wonderful
vacancy of phiz at the preparations ". They speculated much as to
whether the word should be " Jubilo ", " Juvilium " or " Jew Bill ".
A man from Banbury, employed to carry to Stratford a double bass
viol, said it was to be used at " the resurrection of Shakespeare ".
He did not know how to play it, but had no doubt They would show
him. When darkness fell, there were the illuminations to be admired.
The most striking transparencies were in the windows of the new
Town Hall. These represented tragic and comic characters from the

plays of Shakespeare. Those decorating the little old house in which the poet had been born, showed the sun struggling through clouds to enlighten the world. Thomas Becket, from London, had been appointed " Grand Bookseller to the Jubilee ", and honoured with a residence in the Birthplace. The party from Merevale Hall, who arrived about the same time as the Angelos, were not quite so lucky. They were unable to drive up to the doors of the White Lion, owing to a complete traffic block, and when they turned down a neighbouring street, the ladies were afraid to alight, there were so many loose horses in it. Payton himself came to their rescue, and had them privately conveyed into the inn by a back way and up to the only comparatively quiet spot in the hostelry, Mrs Payton's bed-chamber. They had supper on a landing, and did not get to their bedrooms until after midnight. All through that night, James Boswell, who had dined at Oxford and experienced the prevalent trouble in getting transport, was taking up post-chaises from stage to stage, regardless of expense. " The Jubilee begins tomorrow. I have forty miles yet to go. . . . The Jubilee, which makes all my veins glow. . . ." At Woodstock he could not even get a post-chaise, so he rode, for which he was not attired, six miles to the next stage.

The programme for the first day of the Jubilee had been that several pieces of cannon should be let off with dawn, after which singers in masquerade habits with guitars and other instruments of music, should serenade the lodgings of the most important visitors, and burst into a full chorus outside the Birthplace. Printed handbills were distributed, giving information as to details of the three days revelry provided.

Wednesday began with a public breakfast at the new Town Hall. At nine a.m. Garrick, attired as Steward, wearing gauntlet gloves, and carrying a wand of office, made of the mulberry tree, was there soon after eight. Before the company arrived, the Mayor and Corporation made him a speech of welcome, delivered by the Town Clerk, in whose house he was lodging, and he was presented with a medallion of Shakespeare, carved out of a piece of the mulberry tree, and set in gold. He made a suitable reply and " instantly fastened the medal to his breast ". During the breakfast a fife-and-drum band played favourite marches outside. After it, the guests—not so many as had been expected—proceeded to the church, to hear the Oratorio of *Judith* by Dr Arne. Mrs Garrick took in her coach one of Dr Arne's young nieces, and gracefully laid a floral tribute below Shakespeare's monument. A gentleman who did not at all wish to find anything ridiculous in the situation could not help noticing that Shakespeare's bust, smirking out of a perfect thicket of fresh laurels,

reminded him of the heathen god, Pan. Cradock considered that
" the airs were all given in the best style, but the choruses were
almost as meagre as the appearance of the audience; and I felt much
hurt for all that were engaged to perform in it. The company of
any rank had not half arrived." James Boswell arrived, two hours
late, extremely dirty and mud-stained. His first view of the river,
and the house in which Shakespeare had been born, gave him all the
feelings that men of enthusiasm have on seeing remarkable places.
He remembered that Cicero had them, when he walked at Athens.
But he had other feelings. He had composed an Ode which he
hoped to recite at the Masquerade. He had wasted time, trying to
get accommodation at the White Lion until a maid had pointed out
to him old Mrs Harris, who had a house exactly opposite the Birthplace. Mrs Harris had asked a guinea a night, " the stated Jubilee
price for beds ". She had not provided him with facilities for a
wash and brush-up. He caught sight of Garrick, and they waved to
one another. He felt very uncomfortable. The church was filled
with well-dressed people, and he thought they were all whispering
about him. But Mr Garrick shook hands with him heartily, at the
close of the performance, and promised to respect his incognito.
Boswell wanted to be known to nobody until he was in his Corsican
dress. When people asked the Steward of the Jubilee who his
young friend was, Mr Garrick answered, " A clergyman in disguise ".

Outside the church, Foote, in one of his worst moods, was stumping along on his wooden leg. " Murphy, let us take a turn on the
banks of the Avon to try if we can catch some inspiration." Foote
was no sooner seen on the margins of the river than a crowd gathered.
He gave them full measure, and soon peals of laughter were resounding all over the lawn. An immensely stout, very over-dressed gentleman broke through the crowd to converse with the famous comedian.
Foote asked him, presently, " Has the county of Warwick the honour
of giving birth to you, Sir, as well as to Shakespeare? " " No,"
said the uncouth gentleman. " I come out of Essex." " Where,
Sir? " " I come out of Essex." " Out of Essex," repeated Foote.
" And who drove you?" The crowd considered this most delicate
wit.

The season had been uncommonly wet, and the Avon was very
full, but the weather held up for the Steward and company to wend
their way on foot, headed by musicians and singers, from the church
to the Amphitheatre. This enormous wooden structure fulfilled the
highest expectations. It was of the same shape, though not quite
so large, as the Rotunda at Ranelagh, " a truly elegant and tasteful
room, supported by a colonnade of the Corinthian order, distant

about ten feet from the sides ". It was to have been illuminated by a powerful and glorious central chandelier, and *The Gentleman's Magazine* had announced this, with a footnote that it had been " afterwards omitted ". It had been omitted because it had been a casualty on its journey from Drury Lane. No reveller, however, complained of the lighting of Shakespeare's Hall. The dinner (at ten shillings and sixpence a head), served to between six and seven hundred ladies and gentlemen, began badly. There were not enough waiters, and high-born guests were soon helping themselves. But claret and madeira, both good, were in good supply. The Jubilee began to warm up. The band appeared in the gallery, and played glees and catches. The mere sight of the band aroused awful feelings in the bosom of the Steward. Charles Dibdin, who had produced music for several Covent Garden successes, had been engaged to set and re-set some of the songs for the Jubilee. Now Charles Dibdin had been a chorister at Winchester Cathedral, and a protégé of Hoadly *père*; but he was a young man of most unsatisfactory character. He had deserted his wife, when he had spent her dowry, and was now raising a family by Miss Pitt, the *danseuse* from Covent Garden. He was going to desert her too, and start a third family, after which Garrick was to dismiss him, but not yet. He had been so impudent about the Jubilee music that it seemed doubtful whether he would turn up at all. However, he had composed *Let Beauty with the Sun Arise!* as a surprise for Garrick, hurried after him, and got the company to serenade him with it. Garrick's *Warwickshire*, to Dibdin's music, was performed for the first time, and was an immediate success. " For the lad of all lads was a Warwickshire lad! " Mrs Baddeley trilled, " The pride of all Nature was sweet Willy-O ", and Joseph Vernon, Drury Lane's first tenor, with a cup of the tree in his hand, sang " Shakespeare's Mulberry Tree ". The scene looked gay, for many of the guests had obeyed the Steward's injunction to decorate themselves with Jubilee rainbow-coloured cockades, and silver Shakespeare medals, pendant from sky-blue ribbons. Lord Grosvenor proposed a bumper to the Steward, " whose behaviour exhibited the greatest politeness with the truest liveliness and hilarity ", and the Steward proposed a bumper to the Bard, followed by three cheers. *God Save the King* was the signal to disperse.

The first night's ball, which opened only an hour late (at ten o'clock), was brilliant and crowded. During the interval, while the guests had retired to their lodgings to " new dress ", innumerable unseen hands had lit seven hundred wax candles. The writer of a letter to *The Gentleman's Magazine* considered this evening " remarkable chiefly for the most elegant minuet that I ever saw, or shall see, by Mrs Garrick and Mr ——" The partner whose name was withheld had, in fact, been Cradock, who had first tried to get Lord Beauchamp to perform. But that young officer, who regretted that the Militia had not been available to take part, had merely ridden over to wish the Jubilee well. He said he was in boots, had never been to Stratford before, and that if his father learned that he had been long absent from his duties, he would be in trouble.

The ball ended about three, and Thursday dawned. This was to be the big day, the happiest day in the career of Garrick, the day of his Ode. On Wednesday people might be still arriving, and by Friday some of them might be thinking of getting home. It was a sad surprise to wake and find, " a hateful drizzling rain ". Little Angelo, an active boy with nothing to do, sped from place to place, picking up impressions. The pageant on which Garrick had spent largely would have to be abandoned, or at least postponed. For it to be omitted altogether would be a tragedy, for it was the only thing in the programme displaying performers representing (though in dumb show) characters from Shakespeare's plays. Already critics were asking what Dr Arne's *Judith* had to do with Shakespeare. Angelo, senior, was to have been Antony, and Mrs Yates, Cleopatra, fanned by cupids. But it was no day for fans or cupids. Many of the troupe had struggled into their finery, and waited, shivering, for a decision, while Lacy, in a very bad temper, argued noisily with his fellow manager. " Who the devil, Davy, would venture upon the procession under such a lowering aspect? Sir, all the ostrich feathers will be spoiled, and the property will be damnified five thousand pounds! " Garrick was not in spirits. In the Great Room, at the White Lion, where Foote was holding his court, while the rain poured down outside, he had been unwise enough to ask, " Well, Sam, what do you think of all this? " " Think of it? " roared Foote. " Why, as a Christian should do. I think it is God's revenge against vanity."

Cradock did not see much of Garrick that morning, but had frequent conferences with " Mrs Garrick, who indeed was indefatigable. My wife and sister were all astonishment at her skill, and constant exertions in such difficulties as she had to encounter."

Amongst her troubles had been that a local barber " perhaps not quite sober " after last night, had absolutely cut her husband's face, from the corner of the mouth to the chin. Up to the last moment before he had to appear at the Public Breakfast at the Town Hall, Eva-Maria and her friends had been " engaged in applying constant styptics to stop the bleeding ". By eleven o'clock, it was plain that Stratford-upon-Avon was going to experience a very wet day indeed. Even little Angelo realized that he could not fly about, as Ariel with wings, "in this real Tempest". Victor's list of the eminent patrons who were now all arrived, looked rather intimidating than cheering—the Dukes of Dorset and Manchester, Lords Carlisle, Craven, Denbigh, Grosvenor, Hertford, North, Pembroke, Plymouth and Spencer, Sir Watkin Williams Wynn. Most of them had brought their families. Harry Angelo chanced upon an old lady of fashion, looking up at the wet welkin. "What an absurd climate!" commented the imperturbable dowager to the Eton boy.

The Rotunda was packed by mid-day. When Garrick appeared in front of the orchestra, he received a great ovation. People had arrived early in order to get good places for the only entertainment left on the programme, in view of the weather. But the audience was puzzled. There were several points about this most important item of the whole Jubilee that needed explanation. It was called *Ode upon dedicating a Building and erecting a Statue to the Memory of Shakespeare*. The building must be the Town Hall; but the statue was here, in the Amphitheatre Gallery, up behind Mr Garrick. He kept on directing reverential glances at it, for which he was awkwardly situated, as he had been provided with a gilt arm-chair with a high back. Very few present knew that this chair was another of his disappointments. He ought to have had Shakespeare's own chair, in which the Bard had sat when writing most of his inimitable plays. It belonged to Paul Whitehead, the satirist, and Bacon had been quite sure he would lend it. But Mr Whitehead, with a considerable degree of ire, had absolutely refused to trust so valuable a gem to a mountebank.

Garrick had bestowed infinite pains on the Ode. It must communicate to the world his appreciation of Shakespeare. But it must not be too heavy, for it could not be too short. He had thought of something quite new. He was going to declaim to Dr Arne's accompaniment, instead of chanting "in what is called recitative".

The Ode began:

> To what blest genius of the isle
> Shall gratitude her tribute pay,
> Decree the festive day,
> Erect the statue, and devote the pile?

The answer came, after three verses, "Shakespeare! Shakespeare! Shakespeare!" and the chorus took up the idea lustily. An Air followed:

Sweetest bard that ever sung
Nature's glory, Fancy's child;
Never, sure, did witching tongue
Warble forth such wood-notes wild!

Much more verse by Garrick, in patriotic vein, preceded further Airs, as he worked up to his Birth of Falstaff.  His imitation of that character certainly went well, but after it came something of an anti-climax, more declamation about the Sweet Swan, and four more Airs, largely about the Avon.  Outside the rain was coming down in an even downpour, and the lauded silver stream was in fact threatening to become triumphant.  It was quite a relief when the chorus declared for the last time that " His Name and undiminish'd Fame, Shall never, never, pass away ".  Garrick was not nearly done, though.  He was going to make a speech (not forgetting a tribute to Dr Arne, who was being difficult about yesterday's scant attendance at his Oratorio).  At this point a diversion had been planned. " Now, Ladies and Gentlemen, will you be pleased to say anything, for, or against, Shakespeare? "  This was the cue for Tom King to arise amongst the audience, dressed in a foppish blue and silver Macaroni suit, to announce that he had a great deal to say against Shakespeare.  Even Cradock did not realize that King's violent abuse of the Bard was part of the entertainment.  It fell quite flat. Garrick's Address to the Ladies was painstaking.  It mentioned most of Shakespeare's best-known female characters, especially poor Desdemona.  (" She was of Venice too—a warmer Air! ")  At last he announced that Beauty should ever prove the Patroness of Wit. The glad sound of the dinner-bell came none too soon, and the audience, stiff and hungry, adjourned expectantly to feast upon a turtle of a hundred and fifty pounds.  Some people said afterwards that their piece had not been turtle.

The Ode had been received rapturously by a few present.  Lord Grosvenor's veins had swelled.  But persons of discernment here, as elsewhere, had been somewhat glum.  Garrick had sent complimentary copies to Warburton and both the Wartons.  Warburton said (though not to him; in a letter to Archdeacon Hurd of Gloucester), that it was portentous, had only one line of sense in it (" When he calls Shakespeare the God of our idolatory "), and was below any Ode by the late Cibber.  The Warton brothers evidently had correspondence about what on earth they could say, but did not send one another drafts of what they sent to Garrick.  Consequently, Joseph found the Ode had " a great many strokes of poetry ", Thomas, that it contained " many strokes of true poetry ".

It was rather difficult to arrive again at the Amphitheatre, for the Grand Masquerade Ball, because the Avon had now overflowed her banks.  Horses had to wade through the meadow, knee deep, to reach the entrance, which had been hastily planked.  Angelo's fireworks display, advertised for eight o'clock on the far side of the river, had not been cancelled.  It had just failed to take place. " The rockets would not ascend, for fear of catching cold, and the surly crackers went out at a single pop."  The Masquerade Ball was very merry after supper, in spite of gloomy prophecies from without.

Kenrick, as Shakespeare's Ghost, stalked about shivering.  Lord Grosvenor, in an eastern habit, was magnificent.  Mr Boswell, " the well-known friend of Paoli ", as a Corsican patriot, was particularly noticeable.  He was armed to the teeth, with gun, pistol, staff and stiletto, and wore across his grenadier cap the motto " *Viva la Libertà !* "  He produced the poem which he had hoped to read aloud, " but was prevented by the crowd ".  (Afterwards, he had it published.)  There were some cleverly-conceived costumes.  Until the three witches removed their masks, nobody could have guessed that these hid three of the fairest faces in England—those of the Countess of Pembroke, the Honourable Mrs Crewe, and the Honourable Mrs Bouverie.  There were some pretty classical ladies carrying sheaves and bouquets, and an excellent jockey, conjuror, Dutch skipper and Devil.  There was a good deal of duplication—half a dozen sailors, of whom only one could dance a hornpipe, and as many young gentlemen in cap and gown, not one willing to state his name and college.  A London firm of theatrical costumiers had recently provided for a masquerade at Birmingham.  Big prices had been asked, however, for this tumbled trash, at Stratford. When the signal came to unmask, there was not quite the desirable dismay and gaiety.  Half those present had not been able to muster a " Venetian " mask; those that had, seemed rather more austere than usual in them.  Stratford-upon-Avon was not Venice, though it was beginning to bear a resemblance.  The Merevale Hall party left the Amphitheatre and Jubilee for ever, early, but not easily. Their coach wheels were sunk two feet deep in water.

The rain came down in a deluge all Thursday night, and next day at noon was still descending.  There was no hope of the postponed Pageant, but the race for the Jubilee Cup of fifty pounds was attempted, in very soft going.  The card looked well—Lord Grosvenor's colt; Honourable Mr King's; Mr Fettiplace's. . . . In the end, there were five runners, and the winner was a groom called Pratt, who said he knew very little about plays, or Master Shakespeare.  Towards evening the skies cleared, the surviving fireworks

were let off and the last Ball took place.    A great many people, wet
through more than once, and in most uncomfortable lodgings, had
already left for home.    Far more were to find great difficulty in
doing so.    The White Lion was full of grumblers, drinking tea.
James Boswell got away at 5 a.m. on Saturday, after the most uneasy
realization that he was in a little village, in bad weather, and out of
funds.    He found Mr Garrick, and presented him with a copy of
*Verses in the Character of a Corsican*, and an exhausted and bitterly
disappointed man had the kindness to read it aloud, on the spot,
very finely.    Boswell then asked for a loan.    Mr Garrick said
Brother George had taken almost all he had from him.    But, upon
being pressed, he went to Mrs Garrick, and returned with five
guineas.    By Sunday, all that was left of the Jubilee was the
Rotunda, a gaunt, dark shape, looking like the Ark sailing upon the
face of the waters.    Mr Hunt, Town Clerk, wrote apologetically to
Hampton that he expected Mr Garrick would burn every letter with
a Stratford postmark.

2

The Jubilee had been his worst set-back since *The Chinese
Festival*.    Harry Angelo believed that after their return to London,
the managers had wrangled for days over the reckoning.    The press
was being well fed with derisive letters, poems and epigrams.    It
was a shock to Garrick to discover that the source of most of these
was George Steevens, and he never trusted him again.    (" When I
was busying myself about that foolish hobby-horse of mine, the
Jubilee, my good friend Master Steevens was busying himself,
every other day, in abusing me and the design.")    Steevens had
bragged to the *St James's Chronicle* that he was responsible for about
forty skits on Garrick, " With this liberal addition, that it was fun
to vex me."    Foote, at the Haymarket, was being very merry.    He
said he had been urged by puffing to go to a Jubilee, travelling post
without horses, to an obscure borough without representatives, to
celebrate a great poet by an Ode without poetry, music without
melody, dinners without victuals, a masquerade where half the
people were barefaced, a horse-race up to the knees in water, fireworks that did not go off, and a gingerbread amphitheatre that
tumbled to pieces as soon as it was erected.    Lord Stafford prevailed
upon him to give up his most iniquitous scheme for deflating poor
Davy.    Foote had planned to introduce a mock procession led by a
figure dressed to resemble Garrick as Steward, in his velvet suit and
gauntlet gloves, and carrying his magic wand.    Out of the mob, a

ragamuffin was to emerge, quoting the Poet Laureate's well-known couplet:

A Nation's Taste depends on you,
Perhaps, a Nation's Virtue, too.

To this Garrick was to reply by rising on tip-toe, flapping his arms, and crowing " Cock-a-doodle doo! " Lord Stafford asked both actors to dine. Descending from their chariots at the same moment they stood transfixed. " Is it war or peace? " asked Garrick. " Oh! peace, by all means," said Foote.

Colman was going to bring on *Man and Wife, or the Shakespeare's Jubilee*, at Covent Garden, on October 7. " Be patient, my dear Sir," said Garrick to Lacy. " I'll bring out a piece shall indemnify us." The Ode was announced for Drury Lane for September 30, " as it was performed at the Jubilee ". Hopkins was loyal. " Mr Garrick's speaking in this Performance is equal to anything he ever did, and met with as much Applause as his Heart could desire." The music, by Dr Arne, and Messrs Dibdin, Barthelemon and Ailwood, and the songs, by Garrick and Bickerstaffe, went much better at the theatre than in Shakespeare's Hall on the banks of the Avon. The Ode was given four times, and then Garrick was ready with something inspired. *The Jubilee* turned the tables on all who had been laughing at his late disaster, and into it he was able to introduce " the Procession, as it was intended for Stratford on Avon ". *The Jubilee* opened with a dialogue between two old wives in a farmhouse (Goody Benson and Neighbour Jarvis) expressing every apprehension that the people of Stratford had ever voiced at the prospect of a Jubilee. Their terrors lest they should be dealing with the devil were only surpassed by their desire to make money. The noise of cannon firing put them into an agony of terror, a troupe of serenaders entered, and attention was directed to a post-chaise, standing in the courtyard of the White Lion. Moody let down a blind, and put out a white face. He declared in broad Irish that it was extremely hard that people were not allowed to rest in their beds. He was one of those who had not been able to get a lodging, so he had taken up the first floor of this post-chaise. There was another gentleman on the ground floor. He descended, saying that it was no bad thing to be ready dressed, and while he held a conversation with a gaffer (King) who quoted every complaint ever made by Foote in mockery of Garrick's efforts, the White Lion yard sprang to life. There were gentlemen who had got the wrong boots, and taken one another's breakfasts. Ostlers, chambermaids, and waiters ran about the stage in confusion. An order was heard for eight glasses of jelly to be taken up to the little thin

x

gentleman who is with the tall lady in *Love's Labour Lost*, and another
to stop the quarrelling in *Catherine and Petruchio*. A pedlar selling
toys made of the sacred mulberry tree began a brawl with another,
whom he denounced as an imposter. Constables marched on, joy-
bells rang, and while *Sweet Willy-O* was sung, transparencies
parted to display Shakespeare's Hall and the Pageant, at last.
Persons carrying banners bearing the names of the plays represented,
preceded Drury Lane Company in full force. Garrick was Benedick,
Holland, Richard (giving directions for the murder of the little
princes). Cautherly (promoted from Master to Mr) was a young
Hamlet (beckoned by his father's ghost), and Reddish was Lear,
mad. . . . Two magnificent cars bore Mrs Abington as the Comic
Muse and Mrs Barry as the Tragic Muse. A statue of Shakespeare,
resembling that in Westminster Abbey and Stratford Town Hall,
closed the procession. " It was received with bursts of applause.
There never was an Entertainment produced that gave so much
pleasure to all Degrees, Boxes, Pit and Gallery." Garrick had taken
upon himself the charges for the Stratford failure, amounting to
two thousand pounds. The Jubilee ran for ninety-two nights, and
he had been able to use up all the dresses, and most of the songs.
Lacy commented, " Davy is an able projector, Sir, this was a devilish
lucky piece."                                                        5

   But he never again attempted a Shakespeare celebration at
Stratford. In February 1771, a townsman named Eaves sent to
Wheeler a suggestion which Wheeler passed on to Garrick. It was
filed, endorsed "About an annual Stratford Jubilee ". In June of
the same year came the last echo from Stratford, a most extraordinary letter, from a person called Cooper, of Swine Street. He
admitted that although he had been to the same school where
Shakespeare went, he had received a very slender education. He
had something to do with Shakespeare which he would like to sell to
Honoured Sir.

   I have a very hansom remarkable spoted coach-dog, that his spoted
   like a leper, which I add of one Mr Shakespear of Coventry, and of Shakespear's famuley, and for that account I don't set a little store by my dog,
   for I could have parted with him several times, but I ont, without your
   honour will except of him, he shall be at your service.                  6

   The Ode brought Garrick one new friend—a young one. The
Racketts, who lived in King Street, Covent Garden, and at Wandsworth, had a very bright boy, Thomas. At the age of fourteen he
had learned the Ode, complete, and recited it to the author so
admirably that he was sent away happy with " a gilt copy ". Next
year he got a folio Shakespeare, inscribed; *The Fables of La Fontaine*,

in two volumes, illustrated, followed. " Dear Tom " seemed to possess every attractive quality. He could draw; he was a promising musician; he was particularly interested in antiquarian research and natural history. He was very good-looking, and he did not want to go on the stage. Admittance tickets into the boxes at Drury Lane were sent to " Mrs Rackett, who is always most welcome to her most obliged D. G." Thomas Rackett, senior, lent Mr Garrick (who had left his black horse with his soldier nephew, at Chichester) a horse which pleased him well. All the Racketts came to Hampton, with the Tattersalls. James Tattersall was Rector of the church at the top of Southampton Street, St Paul's, Covent Garden.

### 3

While he was still appearing nightly in *The Jubilee*, Garrick found himself called upon to give evidence at the Old Bailey.

Joseph Baretti, walking down Haymarket on October 6, after dark, had found himself accosted and presently pestered and insulted by a woman of the town. He had given her what he described as a blow on the hand, whereupon she had called out loudly. Three men had arrived on the scene and set upon Baretti. A few moments later, a native of Turin had found himself very disagreeably situated. The watch had come up, and he was panting in the centre of a large and hostile mob, with a gory knife in his hand and a dead Englishman at his feet. The man proved to be Welsh, and still alive, but he died of his wounds in the Middlesex Hospital. Next morning Baretti was brought before Sir John Fielding, and committed for trial at the Old Bailey for the murder of Evan Morgan. The names of the friends who offered to give evidence as to his good character were a delight to the press—Sir Joshua Reynolds, Dr Samuel Johnson, Dr Samuel Hallifax (Professor of Arabic in the University of Cambridge), the Honourable Topham Beauclerk, Mr William Fitzherbert (Member of Parliament for Derby), Dr Oliver Goldsmith, Mr Edmund Burke, Mr Garrick. " Never did such a constellation of genius enlighten the awful Session House."

Goldsmith had been one of the first to hear of Baretti's plight, and he had truly played the Good Samaritan to a fellow-author in distress who had never been particularly amiable to him. He had insisted on going with Baretti in the coach to Newgate. He had " opened his purse and would have given every shilling to him it contained ".

In Newgate, the highly-strung Italian went to pieces quickly. Johnson and Burke went to see him there. He grasped them by

their hands, and said, " What can I fear that hold such hands? "
They thought his predicament very ugly.   Reynolds and Garrick
went to see Lord Mansfield about his bail.   Garrick, who was thinking
of nothing but Newgate and Tyburn, was chilled to find that the
great lawyer, who prided himself on his interest in the drama,
thought the moment suitable to discuss with him a passage from
*Othello*, Scene III, Act V, " Put out the light ".

The Sessions were due to begin on the 18th.   During the interval,
Baretti's friends met frequently, to discuss his defence.   The result
was that Garrick somewhat altered his opinion of Goldsmith, with
whom his relations, for many years, had not been happy.   Garrick
had refused Goldsmith's first play, and Goldsmith had retaliated by
a pamphlet attacking Drury Lane management.   Soon after, Goldsmith had wanted to apply for the secretaryship of the Society of
Arts, and when he had called upon Garrick to ask for his vote, it
had been refused.   Many years had then passed before Reynolds
had pressed upon Garrick Goldsmith's *Good Natur'd Man*, and after
tiresome delays Garrick had refused that too.   Goldsmith had taken
it on to Colman, at Covent Garden.

Not all the meetings between the friends of Baretti, while his
fate hung in the balance, were of a business nature.   Boswell gave
a dinner-party at his lodgings in Old Bond Street on October 18
at which the guests were Sir Joshua, Murphy, Bickerstaffe, Davies,
Goldsmith, Garrick and Johnson.   Garrick's attentions to his old
master were noted by their host with delight.   " Garrick played
round him with a fond vivacity, taking hold of the breasts of his
coat, and looking up in his face with a lively archness, complimented
him on his good health which he then seemed to enjoy; while the
sage, shaking his head, beheld him with a gentle complacency."
One guest was late, and while they waited, Goldsmith absorbed the
conversation.   He had come in a new suit and seemed to be
" seriously vain " of his appearance, which could never be anything
but slightly comical, as he was a little Irish elf, with an over-
large round head, a pallid complexion, marred by the small-pox
and large, wondering, round, child-like eyes.   His *naïveté* had
seemed rather to increase with his success.   " It is amazing," commented Johnson, " how little Goldsmith knows.   He seldom comes
where he is not more ignorant than any."   " Yet ", suggested
Reynolds gently, " there is no man whose company is more liked."
At Boswell's party he was at his most ridiculous.   " Let me tell you,
when my tailor brought round my bloom-coloured coat, he said
' Sir, I have a favour to beg of you.   When anybody asks you who
made your clothes, be pleased to mention John Filby, at the Harrow,

Water-Lane.'" Garrick tried to divert him. "Nay, you will always *look* like a gentleman; but I am talking of being *well* or *ill drest.*" Johnson unkindly suggested that Filby had known that the strange colour would attract crowds to gaze at it, and see how well a coat could be made, " even of so absurd a colour ".

After dinner, there was brilliant conversation on the merits of Pope, Dryden, Congreve and Shakespeare. Johnson, trailing his coat, thought a passage in *The Mourning Bride* finer than anything Shakespeare had ever written. Garrick leapt to the defence of his idol with " tragick eagerness ". Later, he had to defend a lady too. The elegant Mrs Montagu had written an Essay on Shakespeare. Reynolds, always the peacemaker, said he thought the essay did her honour, Johnson said, " It does *her* honour, but it would do nobody else honour." He blandly admitted that he had not read it. " But when I come to take up the end of a web, and find it pack-thread, I do not expect by looking further, to find embroidery." Garrick thought that she had been the only person to show how Voltaire had been mistaken in his criticism of Shakespeare. " Sir," said Johnson, " nobody else has thought it worth while."

The trial of Baretti came on on the 20th. He refused the privilege of a jury composed half of foreigners. It soon came out under cross-examination that the two men who had attacked him, in company with the deceased Morgan, had been associates of that character in previous acts of violence, and were connected with the two women of the town called as witnesses. The second man contradicted the first in important facts, and the second woman abused the first. A witness from the Middlesex certainly had thought that Morgan had seemed to think himself wounded without sufficient provocation. Baretti's defence was surprisingly clear and collected. He said that he had been " shoved at " and hit repeatedly by the three men. The suddenness of their onslaught had intimidated him. He was short-sighted, and in the dark, and when he had started to run for refuge, had been hard pressed, repeatedly struck and pursued by the populace. He had drawn out his fruit knife (" an instrument which foreigners generally carry about with them "), and warned his assailants to keep off. He had scarcely known what he had done when he had stabbed Morgan. The surgeon who had attended the dying man confirmed his evidence, and " a gentlewoman who accidentally beheld the whole fray ".

Dr Samuel Johnson spoke slowly in a deliberate distinct manner which was very impressive. Mr Garrick was polished and business-like. He had himself, when travelling abroad, carried such a knife as Signor Baretti had employed. In foreign inns, forks only were

provided. " I never knew a man of more active benevolence."
Questioned again as to Baretti's character, he enlarged upon this,
" He is a man of great probity and morals." The jury disappeared
for a very short while. Baretti was reprimanded but acquitted.
Sir Joshua got him a post as secretary for foreign correspondence
at the Royal Academy, and Johnson prevailed upon the Thrales to
accept him as tutor in their family. He soon regained his spirits,
and the Thrales found him a perfect nuisance. 8

## CHAPTER XIII

ADELPHI

1770–1776

I

As long ago as the summer of 1768, John Paterson, calling at the theatre to get some seats, had met George Garrick and asked searchingly after David. " From some oracular answers to some of my inquiries, I had reason to suspect that all is not well in Denmark. Some dark hints of your being disgusted, and resolved to quit the stage, have alarmed me." David was not to quit the stage yet, but he had been considering it ever since he returned from his Grand Tour, and he was beginning to make his preparations. The first of these was a move from Southampton Street.

In 1769, the brothers Adam had begun to build, above a system of subterranean vaults on the slope between the Strand and the Thames, a series of classical streets and riverside terraces—the Adelphi, directly inspired by the palace of Diocletian on the Bay of Spalato. Adelphi Terrace was the centre-piece of their design. They had to reclaim land from the Thames, and the Corporation of London, who declared that they possessed legal rights to the bed and soil of the river, opposed them for two years. After obtaining a Bill for this, they had to proceed with a second bill sanctioning the disposal of the property by lottery. Lord Mansfield, for whom they had designed Ken Wood, near Hampstead, was interested. People were beginning to put their names down for houses. Number 5, later to be re-numbered 4, was allotted on plans to David Garrick Esq. He would have as nearest neighbour Dr Turton, physician to Lord Mansfield's family, and the man who had attended him in his dangerous illness at Munich. There were several reasons for a move from Southampton Street. The old house had been very convenient for the theatre, but he would not be much further in the Adelphi, and he would be much quieter. Also, he was not in such close attendance, as far as acting went. There was a sentimental reason. The area for which the brothers Adam had got a ninety-nine-years lease, covered Durham Yard, where Garrick and Co. had set up their wine-business, and had their vaults, and office, in 1739. The new houses, which were to be of surpassing elegance would, like Garrick's Villa at Hampton, command a superb view of the Thames. The terrace began to arise. It might be ready for occupation about the spring of 1772.

After the resounding success of *The Jubilee*, Drury Lane seemed securely settled for a period of fine weather. This was to be the case, but first there was to be one more storm, reminiscent of the bad old days. Hugh Kelly's *A Word to the Wise* was produced on March 3, 1770. Kelly was unpopular, both in the political world, where he was regarded as a Government hireling, and in the theatrical world, as the author of *Thespis*, in which he had attacked leading members of Drury Lane Company. Wilkes turned up with a party ready to damn the piece. Kelly had expected opposition and prepared for it. There was hissing from the moment the curtain rose. Mr Garrick was called for, " No Play " etc. called out. The actors struggled through that night, but on Monday Garrick had to appear on the apron stage again. He offered the audience several other plays, but " Mr Kelly's party would have none but *A word to the Wise*, and the other Party would not consent ". At last, the manager even offered to play himself; but it was no use. After three hours he had to order the curtain down. Kelly's friends were threatening to break up the theatre, and even he could not control them. A compromise was finally arranged. Money for to-night's cancelled performance would be returned, but to-morrow Kelly's *False Delicacy*, always popular, should be given, for his benefit. Tuesday was a humiliating experience, for the audience was so noisy that the performers could hardly make themselves heard, but it proved the end of the trouble. Kelly published *A Word to the Wise* by subscription, at a crown a copy, and sold enough to compensate him for his loss owing to its withdrawal. It had been rather a good play, " one of his most judicious compositions ", said Davies. Kelly took his next piece, a tragedy, to Colman at Drury Lane. He was a little figure of fun, very stout and ostentatious, with a wife much too good for him. He had some business sense. Davies thought that prosperity had improved him.

The press had hardly recovered from the riot at Drury Lane when something better was supplied to them. " Saturday, March 17th, a duel was fought in Hyde Park between George Garrick Esq, and Mr Baddeley, both of Drury Lane Theatre, when the former, having received the other's fire, discharged his pistol into the air, which produced a reconciliation." The reconciliation did not extend to Mrs Baddeley. In August, David wrote to George, " Did you not tell Mrs Baddeley of the Case her sweet husband is preparing? Will *she* testify the truth against his falsehoods? " He wrote from Hampton, and ended his letter on a happier note: " The children,

with the great child (my wife) at their head, are all dancing and
making such a noise, I can no more." Baddeley had, according to
rumour, begun his connection with the theatre by being Foote's
cook. He had travelled on the Continent, as valet to a gentleman on
a Grand Tour, for three years, and picked up languages. He was
good in low comedy parts, particularly as foreign servants. He was
to be remembered for ever at Drury Lane, for when he died he left
his cottage at Molesey as a home for four pensioners of the theatrical
fund, and the interest on one hundred pounds to provide Drury Lane
company with wine and a cake in the green-room on Twelfth Night.
Mrs Baddeley, too, was destined to be remembered. She had so
much charmed the king and queen by her performance as Fanny in
*The Clandestine Marriage* that they had ordered Zoffany to paint a
conversation piece of her in the part, attended by King as Lord
Ogleby. Her end was tragic. Baddeley was twelve years her senior.
She had been a girl of eighteen when he had eloped with her. Disgusted by her persistent infidelities and extravagance, he separated
from her. She died suddenly in Edinburgh, where she had fled to
escape her creditors. She was barely thirty, but for the past three
years had been hopelessly addicted to laudanum.

The Garricks made social appearances. A masked ball was given
by the gentlemen of the Tuesday Night's Club, at Almacks. The
Duke of Gloucester was Edward IV, and Miss Monckton, the heiress,
a Sultana, wearing thirty thousand pounds' worth of jewellery. The
mob held up torches to the windows of the carriages, and called
upon the occupants to unmask. The Garricks' costumes were
modest. David was a Macaroni doctor, Eva-Maria an Italian
peasant.

His French friends had for some time been begging him to pay
them another visit. Monnet had suggested that he should plan a
trip for this summer. The Dauphin was to be married to an
Austrian Archduchess, hereafter to be known as Marie-Antoinette.
Monseigneur was a lumbering, awkward orphan boy, not yet sixteen,
and his bride, a year younger, was not as yet more sophisticated.
The fêtes being prepared for Paris in May were to be something
memorable. But Garrick had lost his chance of seeing Paris under
particularly favourable conditions. Lord Rochford, who had been
Ambassador there for two years, had now come home. In vain
Monnet wrote, promising the Garricks a suite of apartments
decorated in sky-blue, with garlands of flowers, cupids and the
divine Bacchus on the walls—nine rooms, with all household conveniences, cooking, linen, silver, crockery, etc. Garrick was going
to make holiday at Hampton, at Mistley and St Osyth.

Everyone who had been to Paris recently said that, beneath a veneer of gaiety and luxury, the condition of the country was deplorable. The Princes of the Blood and the nobility lacked spirit, the administration was glaringly corrupt; the populace cursed the aging king and his new mistress, and starved. It presently appeared to Horace Walpole that Madame du Barri had her uses. He believed France was " approaching by fast strides to some great crisis ". She was approaching, but not fast. David Garrick was not to live to see revolution in France. He appeared at Drury Lane for the first time, this autumn, rather late, not till mid-October. Although he had spent the summer so quietly he had been obliged to hurry to Bath in September, for a cure. He played little that winter, though always to good houses. In November he wrote to Riccoboni, " I hate the thought of War, and I dread it." Walpole did not seriously think that France was ready for a war. She had her own troubles and " Our Navy never was so formidable, and in such brilliant order ". Lord Howe " no trifler " had been appointed Commander-in-Chief in the Mediterranean. Nor could Walpole conceive that England, which was in the north of Europe, and Spain, which was in the south, were going to fight about the Falkland Isles, " a morsel of rock which lies somewhere at the very bottom of America ".

In December, Lady Spencer, writing from Althorp (to regret that Lord Spencer could not ask the Bishop of St Asaph to provide for Mrs Garrick's friend Mr Lloyd, as he had already asked the Bishop so much), added to her letter a characteristically charming postscript. " As I am in an old house, in an old park, in the country, I flatter myself it is allowable to send you and Mrs Garrick all the old-fashioned good wishes of the season." Good wishes were needed by Garrick, for early in the New Year he was laid up with the gout. He sat, like an old gentleman, with his leg in its flannel boot on its stool. He arose, to play Leon, in Hopkins's opinion, never so finely. Walpole said of this season that England had five winters after Christmas. Torrents of snow were still sweeping the country in March. But bad weather was always the manager's friend. Drury Lane company played to full houses, and by April the talk of war had blown over. " Spain has sent us word she is disarming," wrote Walpole. " So are we. Who would have expected that a street-walker at Paris would have prevented a general conflagration? " [2] Madame du Barri was generally credited with having engineered the fall of the Duc de Choiseul.

Garrick had lost his best gardening friend, a character so saintly, so simple, he might have been the original of *The Vicar of Wakefield*.

# MR AND MRS GARRICK taking tea upon the lawn of their villa at Hampton.

*By Johann Zoffany*

This picture was bought at the sale at Christie's in 1823, by Mr Lambton, for £49 7s. 0d. and has descended by inheritance to the present owner. The catalogue identifies the figure to whom Garrick is offering a cup of tea as "Mr George Garrick, angling" and the large clergyman as "Mr Bowden".

*Reproduced by kind permission of the Earl of Durham.*

Garrick had exerted himself much to get a more suitable parish than Egham for the Rev. Thomas Beighton, who at an advanced age was, in winter, having to swim his horse through floods, five or six miles, to perform his duties. The good man's stipend had been about thirty pounds per annum—hardly enough on which to keep a curate, although he had confessed he needed one. He had refused Garrick's offer of a loan " till something might happen ". But he had said that if he could have fifty pounds for a curate, and fifty more to keep up his garden, he could think of no happiness beyond. Garrick had tried General Fitzwilliams, and the Duchess of Portland— awkward, as he had just refused her Mr Collins for Drury Lane—and finally Lady Camden, with success. Beighton had enjoyed his preferment less than three years. The ex-Lord Chancellor wrote feelingly that Beighton had been, as far as he could judge, one of the best men that ever Christianity produced, and one whom we must never hope to see again, unless we go to Heaven. Beighton had left his two patrons as executors, and his library was being divided into three portions, one for each of them, and one for Becket, the book- seller. Garrick tried, unavailingly, to prevent Becket from
3 dispersing his share.

Drury Lane was producing new plays by new authors. *Almida* by the Signora Celesia (a daughter of Mallet, who had married a Genoese patrician) had meant a great deal of foreign correspondence: only Mrs Barry's performance kept it running for ten nights. With *The West Indian* a week later came an undoubted success. " It will have a great Run," prophesied Hopkins after the first night. Richard Cumberland had first been brought to the manager by Lord Halifax, who had walked across from Bushey Park to Hampton on a morning call, bringing with him a personable young man, who had written a play, a son of the Archdeacon of Northampton, a Fellow of Trinity College, Cambridge, and his lordship's own private secre- tary at the Board of Trade. Cumberland never forgot the horrors of that interview, for whereas his noble patron had not the slightest doubt that he was doing Garrick a favour, and that anything recommended by him was as good as in rehearsal, the budding dramatist saw soon " my cause was desperate ", and standing there miserably silent, it did occur to him that perhaps he had been unwise, both in his choice of a hero and in the subject of his tragedy. *The Banishment of Cicero* was returned after " a day or two of what might scarce be called suspense ", and Cumberland believed that Lord Halifax was so surprised and huffed that he did not again notice Garrick for some time.

Some ten years later, Colman produced at Covent Garden

Cumberland's first musical comedy, and *The Brothers*, a straight comedy. The author was in a dark back seat of a box at the first night of *The Brothers*, with a good view of Garrick, who was in a box opposite. He noticed Garrick's start when Mrs Yates, speaking the epilogue, alluded to Reynolds's canvas of " th' immortal actor " standing between Tragedy and Comedy. Fitzherbert, who was also in the house, came across to say that Garrick had been surprised by the unexpected compliment from an author with whom he had supposed he did not stand upon the best of terms. Cumberland was now rising forty, and a married man, but Garrick's memory was long. Fitzherbert arranged a meeting. Cumberland thereafter went to Southampton Street frequently, and sometimes accompanied his host down to Hampton. An effort to interest Garrick in an artist friend was a failure. George Romney was at this time wretchedly lodged in Newport Street, and his studio was a scene of chaos, full of half-finished portraits. He was so dilatory that by the time he had advanced at last upon an order " many casualties and revolutions had taken place amongst the families for which they were destined ". Sitters had died off, wives had run away and ladies who had been less than wives had been dismissed. Garrick's " lynx eye " was fatally attracted by an enormous canvas of a family who looked as if they had never thought or moved. He began to mimic the pater-familias in a red waistcoat. " Upon my word, Sir, this is a very regular well-ordered family, and that is a very bright well-rubbed mahogany table, at which that motherly good lady is sitting. . . ." While he rattled on, Romney turned that picture to the wall and produced his portrait of Cumberland. This, Garrick thought, was very like, especially the coat, which Cumberland was at the moment wearing. " But you must give him something to do; put a pen in his hand, a paper on his table, and make him a poet. If you can once set him down well to his writing, who knows but in time he may write something in your praise? " These words, Cumberland solemnly remembered as prophetic; but Garrick never sat to Cumberland's " second Correggio ".

Fitzherbert said that one had to be a little careful whom one asked to meet Garrick. Once, at his own country house, where the company had been perhaps a little unappreciative, he had missed Garrick after they had risen from the table. He had found him in the back-yard, imitating a turkey-cock, to the delight of one of the servants, a little black boy, who was capering with joy. " Massa Garrick do so make me laugh! I shall die with laughing! " Garrick was good at birds, and when the little Cumberlands came to Hampton could charm a circle of them about him while he acted turkey-cocks, peacocks and water-wagtails.  There were six little Cumberlands, all under six, and even Foote, who had been heard to say that he venerated Herod, could not have complained of their manners. They had been trained—four boys and two girls—to stand like soldiers to be reviewed, and, like the troops, dismissed at a word. A look from their excellent mother was enough to warn them they must not exhaust Mr Garrick.  Whatever George Colman, junior, might say, children did like him.  Mrs Montagu reported that when she had told her little nephew that he must dine upstairs today, because she had " a tableful " coming.  " With all my heart," quoth the little man.  " I do not desire to dine at table unless when Mr Garrick comes."

The Cumberlands went off for Ireland, and the dramatist wrote *The West Indian* in a little closet with no view but a turf-stack, at the back of the palace of the Bishop of Clontarf (for by Lord Halifax's interest the Archdeacon had been promoted).  Garrick took to the piece instantly.  The author had thought of Barry for the Irish major, but Garrick believed that Moody, though not nearly so well known, would be the ideal O'Flaherty.  He gave Cumberland hints as they clattered down to Hampton together in his coach and four. " I want something more to be announced of your West Indian before you bring him on the stage. . . ."  Cumberland asked how this could be done.  " Why, that is your look out, my friend, not mine. . . . But if neither your merchant nor your clerk can do it, why send in the servants, and let them talk about him.  Never let me see a hero step upon the stage without his trumpeters of some sort or other."

At the first night the Cumberlands sat with the Garricks in the manager's box.  Garrick seemed " much agitated ".  He said that the house, particularly the pit, was more hostile than he had ever seen it.  But as soon as the audience discovered that Belcour, the West Indian (King), was a hero of the Ranger type, the clamour turned into applause.  The new comedy contained every popular ingredient—a missing heir, missing jewels, a comic Irish major (Moody), a duel, and a persecuted but lively heiress (Mrs Abington, at her best).  Cumberland modestly described his play as " a lucky hit ".  Personally, he thought *The Fashionable Lovers*, produced the next year, preferable.  But Hopkins knew better.  " Very well received, and great Applause—but it will not be so profitable as ' The West Indian '."  Garrick told Cumberland that he was much too sensitive to criticism, " the man without a skin ".  Cumberland, for his part, thought that Garrick's " brilliant vivacity " was clouded too often suddenly " by little flying stories. . . . Certainly there

were too many babblers who had access to his ear." A long period of
collaboration followed. It was almost like having Colman back
again—but not quite. Colman had been gay. Poor Cumberland
had, said Garrick exasperatedly to Reynolds, " a dish-clout face.
. . . His plays would never do if I did not cook them up." Cumberland altered *Timon of Athens* for production. *The Note of Hand, or
A Trip to Newmarket* was put on the regular list. *The Cholerick
Man* was his last effort under Garrick's management. Hopkins
thought it much inferior to its predecessors, but it was applauded.
Public taste, however, was beginning to find the comedies of a
middle-aged man a little old-fashioned—sentimental. His tragedies
had never been his strong point. A new and brilliant star had arisen
in the theatrical firmament—young Richard Sheridan, who was a
wit. Good stories were told of the rival dramatists. Cumberland
had been seen in a box at the first night of *The School for Scandal*
reproving his children for laughing at the piece. Sheridan's comment was, " He ought to have laughed at my comedy, for I laughed
heartily at his tragedy." Cumberland denied the story categorically.
He had been at Bath on that first night, and for many nights before
and after. The anecdote was generally accepted as, at least, *ben
trovato*, and everyone recognized Cumberland as Sir Fretful Plagiary,
the poetaster, when Sheridan brought on *The Critic*. Looking
back, in retirement, proud of having been Britain's most prolific
dramatist, Cumberland thought that those who had acclaimed
Garrick as the best actor in the world took too narrow a view.
Garrick had been much better than that—truly estimable as a man.
" I have been more gratified by the emanations of his heart than by
the sallies of his fancies and imagination."

2

On Sunday evening, May 8, 1771 (Fanny wrote it down in her
diary), visitors were announced at tea-time to the Burneys—Mr
and Mrs Garrick, the Misses Garrick. George's children were growing up; indeed, it was to be hoped that Carrington, now nineteen,
would cease growing, for he was already six foot four. He was
going to Cambridge, and into the Church. David, aged seventeen,
was with his regiment—the Royals. Only Nathaniel still remained
at Eton, and he was leaving this year. Eva-Maria still talked of
taking " the children " in the coach to Acton to their grandfather
Carrington, but they were children no more. The Misses Garrick
were Arabella, " Bell ", and Catherine, " Kate " or " Kitty ", and
their uncle was going to send them to Paris to be polished, at a most
select *pension* kept by Madame Descombes, where the Honourable

Misses Pratt, Lord Camden's three daughters, had been most delightfully polished. Two of the Burney daughters had been to school in Paris. The young ladies should meet. Charles Burney had now taken his degree as a Doctor of Music at Oxford, and had married again—a handsome lady, who liked managing people. Mr Stephen Allen had been a leading wine-merchant of Lynn Regis, and had left his widow very well provided for, but the Rev. Thomas King, the author of *The Rites and Ceremonies of the Greek Church*, had lost her fortune in an unlucky speculation. Everyone was very sorry for him (the Burneys, as a family, had heavenly dispositions), and thankful that the portions of her three children had not been affected; but the fact remained that Fanny and Charlotte, the two Burneys who had not yet been to school in Paris, would now never go. All that Mrs Burney had left was her house at Lynn Regis, to which she frequently went, or sent the children, for health. Moreover, Dr Burney, when he had returned in January from a seven months' tour abroad (upon rewarding research for his *History of Music*), had found that his wife, with her usual skill, had moved her family, and his, from Poland Street, to a large house in Queen Square, Bloomsbury. It had a beautiful unobstructed prospect of the verdant heights of Hampstead and Highgate, and Garrick said that it was so nearly out of town that to arrive at it on foot had almost the refreshment of a country walk. To-day's call, however, was clearly one of more formality. Fanny gathered impressions of her guests.

> Mr Garrick, who has lately been ill, is delightfully recovered, looks as handsome as ever I saw him, is in charming spirits, and was all animation and good humour. Mrs Garrick is the most attentively polite and perfectly well-bred woman in the world; her speech is all softness; her manners, all elegance; her smiles, all sweetness. There is something so peculiarly graceful in her motion, and pleasing in her address, that the most trifling words have weight and power, when spoken by her, to oblige, and even delight.

Fanny, who was nineteen, took a seat beside the younger Miss Garrick, and engaged her in conversation. She thought that Miss Bell Garrick resembled her aunt; softness, modesty and silence characterized her. Miss Kitty was a regular Garrick, a lively brunette, and very conversable. " Her face is the most expressive I ever saw."

It was a sad set-down for Fanny when another " rat-tap-tap " at the doors was heard, and Dr King was announced; for he was a great talker, and proceeded to engross Mr Garrick, and, what was worse, without giving Mr Garrick a chance to open his mouth.

Another caller arrived, Dr Bever, a civil, heavy-headed man of the Law. He listened well, but when Mr Garrick suddenly turned to him for an opinion (upon a legal point, too) he became so confused, his voice failed him. Mrs Garrick, with much kindness, taking her hand while she spoke to her, engaged the downcast Fanny's attention, and presently her spirits recovered. Mr Garrick moved to them, and inquired particularly after absent friends—her brother, James, sent to sea at ten, " Little Charles " (" Cherrynose " to Mr Garrick), now at the Charterhouse. But Fanny was so shy she could scarcely meet the actor's gaze. " I never saw in my life such brilliant, piercing eyes as his are. In looking at him, when I have chanced to meet them, I have really not been able to bear their lustre."       5

Dr Burney intended, this summer, to study German, in preparation for another foreign tour. He was going to Vienna, Dresden, Berlin, Hamburg and Bremen. The Garricks were going to see more of their own country. Their programme opened with visits to General Conway, at Park Place, near Henley-on-Thames, and to Lord Pembroke at Wilton. They were going to Cornwall, where Lord Mount Edgcumbe, a respectable amateur actor and musician, had an ancestral home set in one of the most picturesque situations in the kingdom. Garrick's description of " this Paradise of the West " called forth a set of verses from old Lord Chatham, retired in dignity to the peace of Burton Pynsent, Dorset.

> Leave, Garrick, the rich landscape, proudly gay.
> Docks, forts and navies brightn'ing all the bay.
> To my plain roof repair. . . .       6

Burton Pynsent had not been " re-built ", but Hagley, which Lord Lyttelton had long wished to display to them, was one of the wonders of Britain. They found a large party assembled there, but their host was rather a pathetic figure nowadays. His wife had left him, and his son was already notorious as a ne'er-do-well. He still pinned hopes on his son's marrying. Hagley had cost him four times what had been estimated. It possessed every fashionable ornament —a hermitage, grotto, Greek temple, ruined castle, cascade. There were seats at every strategic point overlooking the rolling, wooded Worcestershire landscape, ten miles south-west of the increasing city of Birmingham. In the saloon, the owner had hung his own portrait, by Benjamin West; Pope occupied the chimney-piece in the library. Poor Lyttelton was, in fact, a frustrated man, disappointed as politician and author, as well as in his private life. His appearance, too, contrasted strangely with the splendour with which he had surrounded himself. Enemies said that his long, scraggy neck resembled that of an old hen. He had always been thin and lanky, with meagre features and a rasping voice, in which he held forth painfully. Curiously enough, he was amused by Eva-Maria's pronunciation, and hereafter always affectionately alluded to her as " Pid-pad ".

At Gloucester Warburton awaited them in what he described as " my superb palace ". John Hoadly, writing on September 1, hoped they were returned safe and sound " to *dear home*—as every Miss is taught to say, when she has been with Mama a whole summer a-watering ". He asked for news of " your winter operations ". Garrick's first production for the new season had been suggested to him by the success of *The Jubilee*. It was another and better pageant, *The Institution of the Garter*. Hopkins, after a much-applauded first night, only hoped it might " answer the expence ". It had run as first piece for four nights when the outside staff of the theatre were observed, after noon on the short November day, pasting new bills over those advertising for that evening *Every Man* with Mr Garrick as Kiteley. His illness had not been, as the press announced next day, sudden. He had been in increasing pain for a fortnight. While he was still indisposed, he received a letter in a feigned hand, signed " Junius ".

Letters so signed had been appearing for the past three years in *The Public Advertiser*, of which Henry Woodfall, printer and journalist, was publisher. They were addressed mostly to political characters, but remarkable for their devastating, and generally well-informed, personal attacks. They had caused an immense sensation, and much nervousness and many bad guesses as to their authorship. Amongst over forty people suspected of being the dreaded Junius, were Burke, Wilkes, Lord Chatham, the Duke of Portland, Horace Walpole and Lord Lyttelton, all friends or acquaintances of Garrick. In December 1769 had come the most sensational of the series, addressed to the king. Junius certainly had power. Woodfall had been prosecuted by the Crown for libel after that, but the verdict of " printing and publishing only " had been tantamount to an acquittal. Junius had then announced his intention of destroying Lord Chief Justice Mansfield, contriving the fall of the Duke of Grafton, and bringing back Lord Chatham into power.

There was a family of German origin, by the name of Ramus, who occupied various posts in the Royal Household. Garrick was in constant correspondence with one Nicholas Ramus, about attendances of the royal family at Drury Lane, their choice of dates and plays etc. He often saw Ramus, and when the manager was not at

Y

Southampton Street, Mrs Garrick received or gave messages. Early in October, Garrick had received a letter from Woodfall, which told him, amongst other things, that " Junius would write no more ". Some days later, he happened to be writing to Ramus, who was at Richmond Lodge, and passed on the information as likely to be extremely welcome to His Majesty, who had been bitterly affronted by the attack upon him. The letter signed Junius received by Garrick on Sunday, November 10, was indeed a horror.

> I am very exactly informed of your practices, and of the information you so busily send to Richmond, and with what triumph and exultation it was received. I knew every particular of it the *next day*. *Now, mark me, vagabond!* Keep to your pantomimes, or be assured you shall hear of it. Meddle no more, thou busy informer! It is in my power to make you curse the hour in which you dared to interfere with
>
> JUNIUS

Ten days passed before Garrick had composed a reply, addressed to Woodfall. He complained that he was surprised that a gentleman of such talents as the celebrated Junius had descended to scurrility.

> In one particular I will be acknowledged his superior, for, however easy and justifiable such a return may be, I will make use of no foul language; my vindication wants neither violence or abuse to support it; it would be as unmanly to give injurious names to one who *will not*, as to him who *cannot*, resent it.

He pointed out discrepancies in Junius's accusation. If it was a fact that Junius had heard of his " supposed crime " on the day after it was committed, why had nearly a month passed before he took any action? Woodfall's news had not been sent under any promise of secrecy. He had passed it on to many people, and until he had received Junius's attack he had not heard any result, anywhere.

> I beg you will assure Junius that I have as proper an abhorrence of an informer as he can have, that I have been honoured with the confidence of men of all parties, and I defy my greatest enemy to produce a single instance of any one repenting of such confidence. I have always declared that, were I by any accident to discover Junius, no consideration should prevail upon me to reveal a secret productive of so much mischief; nor can his undeserved treatment of me make me alter my sentiments.
>
> One thing more I must observe; that Junius has given credit to an *informer*, in prejudice of him who was never in the least suspected of being a spy before; had any of our judges condemned the lowest culprit on such evidence, without hearing the person accused, and other witnesses, the nation would have rung with the injustice. I shall say no more, but I beg you will tell all you know of this matter, and be assured that I am, with great regard for Junius's talents, but without the least fear of his threatenings.

It was not, perhaps, a very good letter, but it was the best he could do. He took over Hamlet from young Cautherly, who had hitherto been playing it this season, and was received with all the usual enthusiasm. Weeks passed; he appeared in what John Hoadly called " all your great parts ". Gradually it appeared that he was to hear no more from Junius. And within two months the news which he had sent to the king became a fact. After a last, very inferior, attack on Lord Mansfield, Junius did write no more.

### 3

To keep an appointment with the manager of Drury Lane in his new house was a daunting experience for anyone nervous or young. After tussling through the hurly-burly of the Strand, to arrive at the Adelphi, rising serenely on the banks of the river, its classical façade flooded with spring sunlight, was something like coming into port after storm. Everything about the house, within and without, seemed dramatically hushed. Garrick in the Adelphi was better guarded than he had been in Southampton Street. Robert Adam's plans had included accommodation for a housekeeper, butler and footman. The Garricks had made two alterations. The dining-room, on the ground floor, was the front room; the library came behind. These they had transposed. On the first floor, the drawing-room was already commodious enough. They had taken the adjoining back drawing-room as their bedroom. If the manager was at home, therefore, a visitor might be shown straight in to Mr Garrick, sitting amongst his bookcases and pictures, at his walnut-tree desk, rather a small figure in so large a library, slightly like the spider in the centre of his web, but as soon as he looked up, unmistakably Roscius. The windows were shaded by crimson damask festoon curtains and green Venetian sunblinds, and by them stood a reflecting telescope on a stand. The view of the river and bridges, (like himself always on the go), was an eternal pageant. If he happened to be above, it was necessary to follow Thomas up and around a staircase with massive wrought-iron balustrading worthy of a palace, carpeted in the best crimson Wilton. There was absolutely nothing in that dignified pillared hall except six mahogany chairs, a clock in a japanned case, an immense brass-mounted hanging lantern and sixteen precautionary Russia-duck fire-bags. The move to the Adelphi began on February 28, 1772, with the departure of the pictures. Garrick was a familiar figure in the auction-rooms of Mr Christie of Pall Mall, who never tired of telling how, in his early career, when he had suffered a large loss, a friend had taken him out to dine at Hampton, and after the friend had paced the garden with Garrick awhile, the actor had called his unknown guest into his library. " What is this story I hear from Mr Wallis? If five thousand pounds will extricate you, come here with him any day you please, and you shall have it."

Garrick had also received many oil-paintings, some of high repute, as gifts from admirers. Richard Cumberland wanted the Andrea del Sarto given to him by Lord Baltimore, although he believed it to be a copy.

After the oil-paintings went the sketches and engravings—a pair of French theatrical scenes, Foote as Major Sturgeon, Garrick as Lear, Ben Jonson by Vertue, a monkey and fruit in crayons, the Holy Family after Caracci, by Bloemart. . . . Soon there was furniture moving in six directions. A quantity used in London for twenty-six years, and well worn, was to go down to the Hampton Villa, and some things from there were to come up direct to the Adelphi, accompanied by some given by Lord Pembroke. There was a motley collection that would be needed at the Adelphi but must first be repaired. Everything else from Southampton Street would be going to the Adelphi, but the new house was much larger, and classical. The Garricks had bought for their new house furniture conceived by the architect as part of his composition. The dining-room was pure Adam, with a new mahogany dining-table, with circular ends and spare leaves, and pedestals, and twelve chairs to match, with red morocco seats. The dining-room was severely simple, and its predominant colour was red. Illumination was provided by Derbyshire spar vases, mounted in ormulu, holding candlebranches. They would have to get some new table silver to match—candlesticks with rams' masks, and laurel swags. The drawing-room was green. The chairs, bergères and sofa, japanned green and yellow, were upholstered in the same silk damask used for the curtains. The ceiling was by Zucchi—Venus adorned by the Graces, in a pink and blue cloud-land. The marble chimney-piece had cost above three hundred pounds, and four very large pier-glasses, in frames of burnished gold, more than that. There were twenty-two horseloads of new furniture brought up from the premises of Messrs Chippendale Haig, in St Martin's Lane, to the Adelphi. The wall-papers began to go up—China papers imported by the East India Company. On March 11 the first beds were taken down, and four days later, Garrick, who must write a letter, had trouble to muster, in the old house, a chair, ink and paper. The guest-rooms in the Adelphi were ready—surely the best in London. As the owners had chosen the back drawing-room as their bedroom (which meant having a very rich marble chimney-piece as constant companion), the guests on the next floor got the view. They also got an unusual number of bookcases, and even nests of bookshelves, and the backgammon board; but the curtains to windows and four-posters were of gay flowered or striped cotton, to match the sofa and japanned chairs.

At last the move was accomplished; they sent out cards, and their friends began to arrive, to admire. Dr and the Misses Burney came on April 30. Fanny was charmed by " the Adelphi Buildings, a sweet situation ". Eva-Maria received them with the politeness and sweetness of manner inseparable from her. David was in his high-comedy vein. Fanny had to explain, haltingly, why no answer had been sent to the card of invitation. Papa had not let her reply. He had pointed out that Mr Garrick had scribbled on the bottom of the card that no excuse would be taken. David pondered this. " Why, ay! I could not take an excuse. But *if* he had neither come or sent me a card . . . ! " He threw himself into the attitude of one *en garde*. Fanny hastened to cry, " O! he certainly would have done one or the other." David relaxed. " If he had *not*— why then we two must have fought. I think you have pretty convenient fields near your house? "

A month later Fanny realized a long-cherished ambition; she saw Garrick as Richard. Everyone agreed that he excelled in conveying terror and horror. " Garrick was sublimely horrible! Good Heavens—how he made me shudder whenever he appeared. It is inconceivable how terribly great he is in this character. I will never see him again so disfigured; he seemed so truly the monster he performed, that I felt myself glow with indignation every time I saw him. The applause he met with exceeds all belief of the absent. I thought at the end that they would have torn the house down; our seats shook under us."

Not all Garrick's friends approved of his move. Cradock regretted Southampton Street. It had been cosy, warm and sheltered. He found the situation of the Adelphi bleak. In his opinion, David's health was declining. He had been twice ill suddenly this season, completely incapacitated by what he airily described as " a fit of the stone ", and he had not recovered fast, though it must be admitted that his claim that as soon as he was well he was quite well, and in highest spirits, could not be denied. Dr Beattie, in Aberdeen, heard with reserve that his friend believed his late attacks to have been the last struggles of a disorder on the point of yielding to the power of medicine. Other friends disapproved of his change of residence for other reasons. He was thought to have been tempted by the view of the river, and a little

external display on the part of the architect.   But within, there was
only one room which could truly be called fine—the front drawing-
room, and in it, on fine days, the green Venetian blinds were a
necessity, from sunrise to sunset.   All the rooms behind were black
holes, gloomy dungeons, without enough light, at any hour in any
season, to display his collection of pictures.   One passed from being
fried to being frozen.   Johnson was possessively benevolent.   He
said that Garrick now lived rather as a prince, than as an actor.
He was only surprised that those who criticized him for avarice did
not now accuse him of living beyond his station.   He never would
allow that Garrick assumed the airs of a great man.

> Sir, it is wonderful how *little* Garrick assumes.   Garrick did not *find*,
> but *made* his way to the tables, the levées and almost the bedchambers of
> the great. . . .  Here is a man who has advanced the dignity of his pro-
> fession.   Garrick has made the player a higher character. . . .  If all this
> had happened to me, I should have had a couple of fellows with long poles
> walking before me to knock down everybody that stood in the way.   Con-
> sider, if all this had happened to Cibber or Quin, they'd have jumped over
> the moon.

He smiled, and ended, " Yet Garricks speaks to *us*."                  11
To Mr John Cleland, who was annoyed that his *Vespasian* had not
been accepted, David explained himself at some length, on May 24.
" Your observation upon my Marquises, Counts etc., and my *indis-
pensible* business, appears to carry an edge with it;—but if you mean
that I pretended that I had business when I had it not, or if you
suspect me of being fond of worthless titles, you wrong me.   I would
no more avoid the company of a man because he was a Marquis, than
I would keep him company if he were a fool or scoundrel."
Chippendale Haig's men were still employed at the Adelphi
when the Garricks left London in mid-July.   One of the last items
on their account testified to Eva-Maria's warm heart.   " A poor
boy " who had broken a hand organ had brought it to be repaired at
St Martin's Lane " by Mrs Garrick's orders ".
Their summer tour this year was again extended.   They were
guests of the Duke of Richmond at Goodwood, and the Governor of
the Isle of Wight.   Hans Stanley put his yacht at their service.
The weather this August was perfect, but Garrick was having to
emulate the Spartan boy.
Isaac " Nyky " Bickerstaffe had for the past four years been
increasingly useful to him at the theatre.   He was talented, hard-
working, had a true vein of pleasant comedy, and had given the
English stage at both the royal houses many fresh agreeable pieces.
When he wanted to borrow fifty pounds from his manager, he did so

in light verse. His manners were good and he moved in the best society. At the age of eleven he had been a page to Lord Chesterfield, then Lord Lieutenant of Ireland. There was something wrong about his leaving the marines. He had not resigned his commission; he had been dismissed the service. As soon as the summer season of 1772 closed, he left the country, in disguise, and under an assumed name. It was generally accepted in literary circles that he had done so only just in time to escape arrest. Thrale, the brewer, broached the subject with Johnson. He understood that Bickerstaffe had long been " a suspected man ". But Johnson did not wish to discuss sodomy. " By those who look close to the ground, dirt will be seen. I hope I see things from a greater distance." It was a disagreeable surprise for Garrick to lose so suddenly, and under such circumstances, one of his leading writers, but the sequel was worse. William Kenrick, who had long nourished grudges against Drury Lane, published at once a satire, *Love in the Suds, a Town Ecologue. Being the Lamentation of Roscius for the loss of his Nyky.* It was prefaced by a most impudent letter, boldly signed " W.K." While he was on holiday, Garrick received sympathetic messages from many indignant colleagues. Moody said it wounded him to the heart that " that execrable fiend K——" should have the power to disturb the tranquillity of his most honoured friend. But when he considered the horrid attack, he could not wonder. He hoped that Garrick, on going to law, would punish Kenrick as he deserved, and make him an example for the tribe of scoundrels of his type. Thomas Fitzmaurice, from the Isle of Wight, hoped that on his return to London, Garrick would find himself protected " from further attacks of the shocking fiend who plagued you, and us, here ". Garrick put away in his desk a letter in French, from St Malo dated June 22. He wrote on it, " From that poor wretch Bickerstaffe. I could not answer it." The writer, who implored secrecy as to his whereabouts, seemed in mortal terror. In England, at this date, the penalty for his offence was death.

Garrick was going to law, but that would take time, and meanwhile Kenrick was jubilant at the sensation he had caused. His libel, with additions, continued to be re-published. He swaggered about, armed, and saying that Garrick was afraid to meet him. He had offered the manager satisfaction, but as a married man and a father, he had been obliged to ask that Garrick would agree that if Kenrick fell in the combat, half Garrick's fortune should be settled on the Kenrick family. Garrick returned to his desk, also, a letter " Not sent to that scoundrel Dr Kenrick. It was judged best not

to answer any more of Dr Kenrick's notes: he had behaved so un-
worthily." " I would have honoured you by giving you the satisfaction of a gentleman, *if you could*, as Shakespeare says, *have
screwed your courage to the sticking place*, to have taken it. What
single instance of my neglect or injustice to you can you produce?
You say that the comedy ought to have been acted four years ago.
Gentlemen of your cast should have better memories. The first
offer of your comedy was in March 1770, and if you would have put
it in my hands (for I have not yet seen a line of it), provided it had
been approved, it had been played last season." His postscript
was not so mild. " May every enemy I have, whether open or
secret, behave as you have done! There can be but one answer
given to your falsehood and malignity, which may be as *speedy* as
you please: I will take care that it is explicit." Amongst the
anonymous letters which he had received was one offering details as
to Kenrick's career. He had been a Government spy in France,
until Mr Pitt threw him out. Garrick did not fall into that trap.
He believed the letter to come from Kenrick himself.

At the end of five months, Kenrick agreed to publish a letter of
apology. It appeared in the press on November 26, and Garrick
professed himself satisfied. To have gone into court would have
meant that a very much larger public would have heard Kenrick's
accusations. Kenrick's reputation was foul, and his own was
excellent. The worry of those five months, during which every day
might, and many did, bring him another move from Kenrick, had
made him ill. When it was all over, and he was utterly discredited,
Kenrick coolly told Thomas Evans, the publisher, that he had always
known his accusations against Garrick were false. He " did it to
plague the fellow ". Garrick had indeed been troubled, and his
illness had not been the gravel, or the stone, or the gout. He had
been suffering from such headaches as he had never known. They
lasted for days. In the following February, when Dibdin's *The
Wedding Ring* was produced, there was an uproar at Drury Lane.
The audience had got a notion that this was " one of Mr Bickerstaffe's Productions ". Garrick came on to assure them that it was
not, but the noise continued until Dibdin arrived to announce himself the author. After that the piece went on with applause. Three
seasons later, when Bickerstaffe's *Love in a Village* was revived,
nobody objected. Memories were short, and no biographer who
had known Garrick thought it worth while to mention something
purely libellous. The year of his move to the Adelphi had not been
a lucky one; and his ill-luck was to hold out to the very end.    *12*

Hopkins's entries became sombre. " Two young Gentlewomen

appeared in the Characters of Polly and Lucy ", (*The Beggar's Opera* brought out by Dr Arne). " Miss Weller's figure was very well for Polly; but she is a piece of still life, sings out of Tune and will never make an Actress." Miss Mansell, in *The West Indian*, fared worse. " A slattern Figure, rather clumsy—a coarse Voice, and no Simplicity." The manager's *Irish Widow* succeeded, though Mrs Barry did not answer his expectations; Miss Jaratt, who made her début in *Miss in her Teens*, met with applause. She had a small, pretty figure. " I have no great Opinion of her," noted Hopkins, and was right. There was much hissing at *The Rose* by Dr Arne. The manager had always been against its being performed. On November 8 came another and greater disappointment. The O'Briens were back from America. Everyone agreed that they had been sent there at quite the wrong time. England was drifting fast towards the loss of America. O'Brien and Lady Susan were as charming as ever, though both had grown stout. In any case, there was no question of his returning to the stage as an actor. He had, however, written a play. The plot of *The Duel* was taken from a popular French comedy, *Le Philosophe sans le Savoir*. Garrick did his very best for his former leading young actor. The first night came on when he was still distracted by Kenrick's persecution. He was feeling so ill he could hardly hold up his head. He had written a sprightly prologue:

> A book is never lik'd till first we're told
> Who is the Author, whether Young or Old.
> A virgin Bard untried this night appears. . . .

It was quite hopeless. From the first it appeared that there was " a party in the house against the author ". In fact, there were two. O'Brien was not much liked by members of his profession, whom he had deserted so abruptly for a lady of quality. His relations-in-law had received even his wife with hauteur, and the fashionable world was therefore giving the couple the cold shoulder. Poor Lady Susan and her author-husband, sitting with Mrs Garrick in her box, witnessed a complete failure. From the second act onwards, the hissing was incessant. The audience would not allow an announcement of any further performance.

Throughout his dark hours this autumn, Garrick had been at work altering *Hamlet*. This came on ten days later. " I think it a very fine Alteration," wrote Hopkins. Few people agreed with him, and Garrick himself told a friend, on the eve of his retirement, that he thought his alteration in *Hamlet* had been the most imprudent thing he ever did in his life. " But I had sworn I would not leave the stage till I had rescued that noble play from all the rubbish of the fifth act. I have brought it forth without the gravediggers' trick and the fencing match." He had also cut out the fates of Rosen- 14 crantz and Guildenstern, and poor Ophelia. Hamlet, after slaying Polonius, had a duel with the King, whom he despatched, whereupon Laertes attacked him. Hamlet, mortally wounded, died slowly, exhorting Horatio in high-flown phrases not to slay Laertes. The Queen was not poisoned. She was led out, mad from remorse. Garrick claimed, " The alteration was received with general approbation, beyond my warmest expectations," but Murphy believed that he was not, upon reflection, so proud of it. He never published his revision, and the prompter's copy at Drury Lane was not available for examination by outsiders. The caricaturists seized the occasion to fall upon him.

> Behold the Muses Roscius sue in vain.
> Taylors and Carpenters usurp their Reign.

Garrick was depicted trampling on the works of Ben Jonson and Shakespeare, to the cry of " Processions for ever ".

On January 12, 1773, he told Arthur Murphy, " I am too much indisposed to write long letters, and too old, and too happy, to love altercation." 1773 was a blessedly uneventful year. Of course, the company and authors continued to behave characteristically. Cautherly, who had been giving himself airs about accepting what he deemed inferior parts, received a snub. " You talked to my brother of being *just to yourself*—a foolish conceited phrase; you had better take care to be just to other people, and do your duty." Mr William Woodfall, the printer's much younger brother, had heard that he was being criticized in Drury Lane green-room for partiality in the paper war between Macklin, Reddish and " Gentleman " Smith. Eva-Maria wrote firmly on David's reply, " The answer to that puppy Woodfall, by my husband ", and on Woodfall's apology to " the most capable actor this, or any country ever produced ", " Puppy Woodfall's answer again to my husband's letter."                                                                         15

The Garricks' summer visits included Mistley, Bowood, Camden Place near Chislehurst, and, in the end of August, Althorp. Cradock met them by chance, on their homeward journey, at Dunstable, resting their horses, and went on in their coach to St Albans, where they all drank tea together. Hearing that they had never visited the old Abbey church, he insisted that they must, and they were both greatly struck by the beauty of the interior. The clerk who showed them the Duke of Gloucester's glorious chantry tomb, entreated

them to examine the vault beneath, in which the remains of good
Duke Humphry (according to Shakespeare foully murdered by
Cardinal Beaufort) had been deposited. Garrick, delighted,
recollected the scene at once.

> Stand back! thou manifest conspirator,
> What! am I dared and bearded to my face?
> Draw, men, for all this privileged place;
> Blue coats to tawny coats! Priest, beware your beard;
> I mean to tug it, and to cuff you soundly.

Eva-Maria had to remind him that he also was in a privileged
place. The great actor's splendid voice raised tremendous echoes
in the sacred edifice. Cradock, outside, exhorted him to revive all
the *Henry VI* series and make them into a single tragedy. He could
be Cardinal Beaufort. But Garrick said soberly that he had
absolutely pledged himself never to appear in a new character, not
even one taken from Shakespeare.

He had been staying with Lord Camden, Lord Shelburne, Lord
Spencer, and was going to the Duke of Portland at Oatlands to meet
Lord Lincoln. Cradock had heard—some years past, for poor Arden
had made the inquiry—that members of his profession, from
jealousy, took rather a mean revenge when Garrick was staying at
great houses. Little dirty notes would be sent to await his arrival,
addressed " Mr David Garrick, player ". Arden had asked if any
had been sent to Gumley, and said that Garrick knew from whom
they came. He had seemed much annoyed.

Garrick regretted that he had not been able to go to the Isle of
Wight again. He had recently met, at the table of Angelo, an
artist who was to become his best scenic designer. Philip de
Loutherbourg, who had been born in Fulda, but was of Polish
descent, had gained high repute in Paris with his pastoral and wildly
romantic landscapes. He was painstaking over his models and had
new ideas about stage illumination. He produced the scenery and
effects for two productions at Drury Lane this winter. Garrick was
reviving *Alfred*. A play about the founder of Britain's Navy seemed
appropriate in the year of the Grand Naval Review at Portsmouth.
Loutherbourg's scenery was " an exact representation " and raised
so much enthusiasm that it was shown again as an addition to the
*The Fair Quaker of Deal*. His second effort was for Garrick's
*Christmas Tale*, brought on in Christmas week. It had been written
in a hurry, but the effects included the burning of a fairy palace.
Horace Walpole was sour about Garrick's part, but, like everyone
else, enchanted by Loutherbourg. " Mr Garrick has been wonderfully jealous of the King's going twice to Covent Garden, and, to

lure him back, has crammed the town's maw with shows of the Portsmouth Review, and interlarded every play with the most fulsome loyalties . . ." But he had to admit that Loutherbourg's scenery, especially for the *Christmas Tale*, was most beautiful.

This was the winter in which Garrick, at last, was admitted a member of The Club. When his name came up for election Goldsmith seconded it with enthusiasm. David, as a new boy, behaved discreetly. He did not, as Johnson had once predicted, annoy the company with his buffoonery, or seek to dominate it. He appeared simply as a private gentleman, interested in the arts, a rôle in which he gave much satisfaction, and he came to enjoy his evenings at The Club as much as he had ever hoped. Johnson, who had been known to say that Davy's talk was a dish of all sorts but with no solid meat in it, was now heard to admit, " He is the first man in the world for sprightly conversation." Goldsmith seemed to have become more noisy and talkative than ever. At the St James's coffee-house one evening, when he had been outrageously laughable, Garrick said that nobody could possibly draw the character of Oliver Goldsmith until he was under ground, for what anyone would say after an hour's reading of his works would inevitably be reversed after an hour of his chat. The company began to write epitaphs for one another—a dangerous game. Garrick's for Goldsmith was brief.

> Here lies Nolly Goldsmith, for shortness call'd Noll
> Who wrote like an angel, but talk'd like poor Poll!

Goldsmith's sense of humour did not extend to appreciating this when he was shown it at the next meeting. He said he would retaliate, and hurried off in a pet. His " Retaliation " became famous.

> Here lies David Garrick, describe me who can,
> An abridgement of all that was pleasant in man;
> As an actor, confess'd without rival to shine;
> As a wit, if not first, in the very first line;
> Yet, with talents like these, and an excellent heart,
> The man had his failings. A dupe to his art,
> Like an ill-judging beauty, his colours he spread,
> And beplastered with rouge, his own natural red.
> On the stage he was natural, simple, affecting;
> 'Twas only that when he was off, he was acting.
> With no reason on earth to go out of his way,
> He turn'd and he varied, full ten times a day.
> Though secure of our hearts, though confoundedly sick
> If they were not his own by finessing or trick,
> He cast off his friends as a huntsman his pack,
> For he knew when he pleased he could whistle them back.

Of praise a mere glutton, he swallowed what came,
And the puff of a dunce, he mistook it for fame,
Till, his relish grown callous, almost to disease,
Who pepper'd the highest, was surest to please.
But, let us be candid, and speak out our mind,
If dunces applauded, he paid them in kind.
Ye Kenricks, ye Kellys, and Woodfalls so grave,
What a commerce was yours, while you got and you gave!
How did Grub Street re-echo the shouts which you raised,
While he was be-Roscius'd and you were be-praised.
But peace to his spirit, wherever it flies,
To act as an angel, and mix with the skies;
Those poets who owe their best fame to his skill,
Shall still be his flatterers, go where he will;
Old Shakespeare receive him, with praise and with love,
And Beaumonts and Bens be his Kellys above.

Garrick wrote a reply, but while it was still being passed from hand to hand in manuscript, came the news that Goldsmith had died. Amongst the childish facets of his character had been that he could not resist gambling. Garrick had drawn attention to this. It came as a shock to some at The Club to learn that Goldsmith had died in misery and embarrassed circumstances. Johnson believed that his fever had been increased by worry about a debt. Burke burst into tears; Reynolds painted no more that day. Garrick surprised the Burneys, when Goldsmith's work and character were being praised, a few days later, by mentioning " what no one else in his presence could have hinted at, the poem of ' Retaliation ' ". He said he had brought it upon himself. He had been elected to another club that winter, Topham Beauclerk had put him up for Brooks's.

17

### 4

The New Year of 1774 opened with floods following snow. Clive wrote from her picturesque riverside cottage at Twickenham, " I might date this letter from the Ark; we are so surrounded by water that it is impossible for any carriage to come to me, or for me to stir out; so that at present my heavenly place is a little devilish." Garrick was " untuned by a violent cold and hoarseness ". In March came a death which was to mean much more work for the manager, at a time when he was not feeling up to it. He had not always agreed with Lacy, who had been a difficult man, but Lacy's son, young Willoughby, was a very bad successor as co-patentee. And he wanted to act. To add to Garrick's troubles, Brother George was taken ill. He was sent off for Bath, as soon as he was able to travel, and Cumberland, who had been told to look after him, thought that, on his arrival, he looked like a dying man. But the

Bath waters produced an astounding effect. David had asked George to report on a young actor, Henderson, whom they had refused, once or twice, for Drury Lane. David had given Henderson a letter to the Bath manager and advised him to perfect his art in the provinces. The beginner had written with very proper gratitude. He was now apparently enthralling Bath. He was so like Garrick. " He must be your bastard ", wrote Gainsborough. He was certainly not that, but it seemed possible that he presented the first serious rival to Garrick since Barry. So far, he had succeeded best in tragedy. It was observed in London that Garrick appeared this season " as seldom as possible in the laborious parts of tragedy ". He played Archer, Ranger, Benedick, Don Felix, always with Mrs Abington as his heroine. This was bad for her. Nobody would have guessed from their polished performances that the manager and his leading lady were often hardly upon speaking terms, off the stage. He must get Mrs Yates back. Mrs Yates, from Edinburgh, sent him a letter in which the iron hand was concealed in the velvet glove.

> On considering every circumstance in my situation here, and my novelty, to say nothing of my beauty, I think I cannot in conscience take less than £700 a year for my salary. For my clothes (as I love to be well dressed, and the characters I appear in require it), I expect £200. As to benefit, you shall settle that yourself; but as I have an infinity of *Scotch pride*, had rather not take one, though I am sure of losing by it. Dickey, who considers only the main chance, is of a different opinion; but I am clear the worst advice a woman can possibly follow is that of her husband, and I had much rather you should determine that point for me. ¹⁸

Dickey was getting very elderly, but Mary Ann's return to Drury Lane after eight years should draw audiences. She agreed to receive seven hundred and fifty pounds per annum salary, plus fifty pounds annually for two years, and a benefit on the usual terms. If Dickey cared to come for the second year of her contract, said Garrick, he would have twelve shillings a week and a benefit. The Yateses came, and Mrs Abington sharpened her claws. It was said afterwards that three actresses had driven Garrick from the stage— Mrs Abington, Mrs Yates and Miss Younge.

Garrick was interested in two weddings in high life which took place this summer. Both were to turn out sadly. Lord Stanley had at last persuaded the Duke of Hamilton's sister to accept him. She was a little blonde creature, so infantile that nobody ever spoke of her except as Lady Betty. She would have preferred her cousin, the Duke of Dorset, but he had not offered. General John Burgoyne, the bridegroom's uncle, wrote a masque, *The Maid of the Oaks*,

which was performed in honour of Lady Betty at The Oaks, Lord
Stanley's country house near Epsom. Garrick assisted, and produced it, with additions, and scenery by Loutherbourg, in the
following November, at Drury Lane. "A general relish was very
discernible."

Lord and Lady Spencer's eldest daughter, Lady Georgiana, was
married in June, five days before her seventeenth birthday, to the
Duke of Devonshire, "the first match in England". The young
duke was twenty-five, and the orphan child of the Garricks' old
friends the fourth duke and Lady Charlotte Boyle. He was a disappointing result of an ideally happy marriage. He was backward,
stiff and heavy. Lady Georgiana was, if not regularly beautiful, so
attractive that it was later said that the word charming might have
been invented to describe her. Even Horace Walpole thought she
was "a lovely girl, natural, and full of grace". This wedding meant
that after twenty years, Chatsworth was to have a duchess, and that
next summer the Garricks were to receive an invitation to re-visit
scenes of which they had the happiest memories.

They spent nearly the whole summer of 1774 "between London
and Hampton". Garrick had been so pleased with Adam's work at
the Adelphi that he had ordered a classic façade for his villa, and was
to order one for his theatre. The alteration to the villa was completed by August, when, undeterred by his experience of English
summer weather at Stratford-upon-Avon, he bravely planned "a
splendid entertainment or Fête Champêtre at his gardens at Hampton". It was, though nobody noticed this, a belated celebration
of an anniversary which had taken place in May. The Garricks had
now been married twenty-five years.

Up to the last moment he was kept on tenterhooks. The
summer had been very wet. On Tuesday 16th rain fell all day. On
Wednesday and Thursday there were flying clouds and fair intervals.
Friday 19th dawned in thick fog. At ten o'clock this lifted, and
brilliant sunshine settled upon the scene. The night was balmy. An
Italian expert, Signor Torre, conducted the fireworks in the gardens;
illuminated by six thousand lamps. "Shakespeare's Temple and a
Forge of Vulcan made a splendid appearance." The Hampton fête
was remembered as brilliant, in every sense, both by invited and un-
invited guests, for it drew large crowds on both the Surrey and
Middlesex banks of the river. After it was all over David got rather a
grim note from his dear Clivey-Pivey, who would prefer to visit him
on an evening when there were not squibs, crackers, rockets etc.,
to which he humbly replied that but for the gout he would have
been at her feet three days ago. He would be with her today, at six.

5

The Burneys had moved again. There had been some mistake
about the title-deeds of the big new house in Queen Square which
Mrs Burney had so skilfully taken for them.  But, with her usual
firmness, she had transplanted them back to the centre of Town, to a
most picturesque dwelling hallowed by historic associations.  36, St
Martin's Street had been built by Sir Isaac Newton.  His observatory still surmounted the roof.  Dr Burney's first care was to repair
this eyrie at large cost, and it had become Fanny's favourite secret
scribbling place.  It had old-fashioned glass windows all round,
overlooking all London.  She wrote down that the new house was
smaller than the one in Queen Square.  It had a confined air, and
the immediate neighbourhood was shabby, dirty, ill built and
vulgarly peopled.  Mr Garrick's first visit to it was "indeed
matinal".  He arrived at 8 a.m. and terrified the innocent maid
washing the front steps, who did not know whether or not to admit a
strange gentleman in an old coat and terribly old wig, who seemed to
have no doubts as to his welcome.  He pushed past her, and ran
upstairs, to tell the family how prodigiously he loved their new cross
maid, who did not know the great Roscius.  " ' Child! ' " says I.
" ' You don't guess whom you have the happiness to see!  Do you
know, I am one of the first geniuses of the age?  You would *faint
away* upon the spot if you could only imagine who I am! ' "  Dr
Burney, though immersed in his books and papers, was engaged
with the hairdresser.  Susanna was reading a newspaper to her papa,
Charlotte was making his tea, and Fanny was sorting his books for
to-day's work.  Mr Garrick threw himself plump into a chair well-
cushioned with pamphlets, and told the doctor not to apologize for
a little confusion.  He always came early, and the reason seemed
that he was in top spirits at the hour when most people, especially of
his profession, were not at their best.  He liked an early walk.  He
had once come to Queen Square before eight o'clock and found
nobody down.  " I shall tell Mrs Garrick that I found the Doctor
reading Petrarch, in flannels, like a *young man*—but where, says I,
were the young ladies? where do you think were *my* favourites?
why in bed! "  When little Charlotte had appeared, he had caught
her up in his arms, and run with her out of the house, saying he was
stealing his own Reynolds' Comedy.  " How many pities he has not
children," wrote Fanny, " for he is extremely, nay passionately,
fond of them."  But she was tormenting herself by a theory as to
why he had come so early to St Martin's Street.  It was in the
working quarter of the town, not a genteel quarter.  Mr Garrick

was now so well known that he could not take a step at an hour
when the narrow streets down here were filled by "his gallery
admirers", without being recognized and stared at, if not pursued
and hailed. "Look! Garrick!" "There's Mr Garrick." "Mr
Garrick excuse me . . ." "Mr Garrick, I have long hoped . . ."
A crowd would grow up around him as he waited at the dirty cross-
ings. . . . He did not say a word about quitting the stage on this
May morning; indeed, he turned Dr Burney's apartment into a stage.
First he put on his stupid air, making his expressive eyes look like
what one of his actors had described as "two coddled gooseberries".
He appeared immersed in wonder at the skill of the hairdresser who
was decorating his friend's head. The man, who was very conscious
of the celebrated Garrick, betook himself with redoubled vigour, and
flurried importance, to his frizzing, curling, powdering and pasting.
In vain Dr Burney tried to entertain his guest. Abel Drugger had
taken possession of Garrick's form. He stared at the *friseur* so
idiotically, and finally so close, that the man could not bear it. He
finished his business hurriedly and prepared to retreat. But Garrick
would not let him escape. He lifted his own wretched scratch wig
from his head, and perching it high in the air upon a finger and
thumb, squeaked out dolorously, "Pray now, Sir, do you think,
Sir, you could touch up this here old bob a little bit, Sir?" The
man, perceiving that Mr Garrick would be acting, grinned broadly,
scampered out of the room, and almost before he had closed the door
behind him, burst into an uncontrollable horse-laugh. Mr Garrick,
well satisfied, next turned his attention to his friend's library. Dr
Burney had far too many books for his new premises. Mr Garrick
was suddenly a smart, conceited, underling auctioneer. "A penny
a piece! a penny a piece! a-going! Going! a-going! a-going! each
worth a pound not to say a hundred—a rare bargain, gem'men and
ladies! down with your copper!" He was a raree showman next,
blowing the trumpet of fame (his cane) in praise of Dr Burney's
forthcoming volume. "The only true History! No counterfeit!
but all alive!"

They asked him to come into the parlour, to breakfast, but he
had the Rev. Francis Twiss and Mr James Boswell, great travellers
both, coming to eat at the Adelphi. He gave them imitations of
these gentlemen, and then of Dr Arne, and finally of Dr Johnson,
whom everyone in this room loved. It was quite uncanny; when
he was Johnson, he seemed actually to grow in stature. When
he said, "Davy has some convivial pleasantry about him, but 'tis
a futile fellow", he seemed to *be* Johnson. But he was most
like, arising in front of an imaginary punchbowl, squeezing a lemon
z

into it, and calling out in broadest Lincolnshire, "Who's for poonsh?"

Next time he visited the Burneys, he was even better. He was Sir Jeremy Hillsborough, baronet, dressed for the part, and with a toothache, which explained a red handkerchief above a mouth which might have betrayed him. When they heard Sir Jeremy announced, (a gentleman whom they held in dislike), both Dr Burney and Mr Twining exclaimed, "No! no!" They were expecting Mr Garrick, by appointment. But they were too late. The servant had let in Sir Jeremy. The baronet was at his worst. He silently took the chair of honour by the fire, and seated himself, nodding at them in so hostile a fashion that they wondered if he had at last taken leave of his understanding. They were entirely surprised when Sir Jeremy suddenly started up, threw off his slouched hat and old surtout, flung his handkerchief in the fire, and displayed to view, lustrous with vivacity, the sparkling eyes and laughing countenance of Garrick, the inimitable imitator. [19]

## 6

Letitia Hawkins too was growing up, and confessed to feeling a iittle jealousy of the beautiful Garrick nieces. She had also developed a social sense. "At Hampton, and its neighbourhood, Mr and Mrs Garrick took the rank of the *noblesse*;—his highly-finished manners, and his lady's elegance of taste, making their house and themselves very attractive. Yet I do not recollect that there was in them any of that calculated display now much too common. I never heard noble visitors named, or any affected intimacies with great people brought forward." She well remembered an August day when her father found the Garricks in their garden, eating figs. Garrick complained of the wasps, and said that he had heard lately of a man who had died from swallowing one. Hawkins too had heard the story, from the apothecary who had attended the victim. "I believe it," said Garrick, "and have been persuading this lady"— indicating his wife. "But I cannot convince her, though she can believe the story of Saint Ursula and the eleven thousand virgins." Hawkins had been very much surprised the first time he had realized that Mrs Garrick was a Catholic, and born at Vienna. Letitia never forgot her graceful sailing gait when the party, as was common after a dinner at the Hawkins's, paced along a broad terrace at the back of their house. She never would allow that Garrick was vain, or that he should be called "Mr" Garrick. "He was Garrick, and Garrick only." She supposed that "nobody of his profession ever attained a higher degree of respectability". [20]

## CHAPTER XIV

# " FAREWELL! REMEMBER ME! "

## 1776–1779

### I

On a mid-January day of 1776, when snow lay in the streets of London, a young teacher on holiday wrote to one of her sisters in Bristol:

> Let the Muses shed tears, for Garrick has this day sold the patent of Drury Lane Theatre, and will never act again after this winter. *Sic transit gloria mundi!* He retires with all his blushing honours thick about him, his laurels as green as in their early spring. Who shall supply his loss to the stage? Who shall now hold the master-key of the human heart? Who direct the passions with more than magic power? Who purify the stage: and who, in short, shall direct and nurse my dramatic muse?

Miss Hannah More's information was quite correct, except that Garrick was to continue playing until the end of the season, June 10. His sale of the patent and his retirement from the stage were announced in the press on March 7. He had disposed of his share to Mr Richard Brinsley Sheridan, Mr Thomas Linley and Dr James Ford. Everyone knew that " Mr Sheridan, jun: " as such old stagers as Tom King called him, was the son of Thomas Sheridan. He was twenty-five, author of *The Rivals*, *The Duenna* and other Covent Garden successes. He did not act, but had political aspirations. Mr Linley the musician, famous for his productions of the works of Handel, was his father-in-law. Dr Ford was a fashionable accoucheur, physician-extraordinary to Queen Charlotte. Clutterbuck hoped that perhaps he represented the solid financial background of the alliance. Kitty Clive thought she should have died with laughing when she saw a man-midwife amongst the strange jumble of people published by the newspapers in their first guesses as to Davy's successors. She had some opinion of Mr Sheridan; everybody said he was very sensible. Her letter of mingled condolence and congratulation was in her best style, and David wrote on it, " My Pivy excellent! "

> Is it really true that you have put an end to the glory of Drury Lane Theatre? *If it is so*, let me congratulate my dear Mr and Mrs Garrick on their approaching happiness. . . . In the height of public admiration for you, when you were never mentioned with any other appellation but the Garrick, the charming man, the fine fellow, the delightful creature, both by

men and ladies; when they were admiring everything you did, and everything you scribbled, at this very time, *I, the Pivy*, was a living witness
that they did not know, nor could they be sensible of, half your perfections.
I have seen you, with your magical hammer in your hand, *endeavouring* to
beat your ideas into the heads of creatures who had none of their own.   I
have seen you, with lamb-like patience, endeavouring to make them
comprehend you; and I have seen you when that could not be done.   I
have seen your lamb turned into a lion.   By this, your great labour and
pains, the public was entertained; *they* thought they all acted very fine—
They did not see you pull the wires. . . . While I was under your control,
I did not say half the fine things I thought of you, because it looked like
flattery, and you know your Pivy was always proud; besides, I thought
you did not like me then; but *now* I am sure you do, which makes me send
you this letter.

Garrick had notified Colman, before he accepted any other offer,
but Colman had recently taken over the Haymarket, and did not
want to have Willoughby Lacy as co-patentee.   Garrick had mentioned to Colman, at the end of last year, that he expected to get
thirty-five thousand pounds for his share.   Sheridan and Linley had
each found ten thousand pounds.   Dr Ford, who already held a
mortgage on the theatre, would invest a further fifteen thousand
pounds, and Sheridan was making arrangements to raise the last ten
thousand pounds, on loans and mortgages.   They were receiving a
theatre which had been splendidly redecorated, without and within,
as recently as four months ago, by what Hopkins called " the
Adams's ".   The entrances to the front and side boxes in Bridge
Street had been enlarged, which had meant taking in part of the old
Rose tavern.   The grand entrance had six Ionic pillars above a
balcony and colonnade.   The royal arms were in the centre of the
pediment, and on either side, above, a lively-looking lion and uni-
corn.   These were surmounted by " a suit of ancient armour,
resembling the trophies raised by a conqueror on slaying the leader
of an army, such as were described by Virgil ".   Not everyone
appreciated this ornament and there were some ribald jests about
the retiring manager's discarded armour.

His list of productions for the past two seasons showed that he
had been casting his net wide.   Talented amateurs had brought
him varied fare.   *The Rival Candidates*, a comic opera by the Rev.
Henry Bate, had been very well received.   *Braganza*, by Robert
Jephson, once a captain of infantry, had been preceded by so much
advertisement that something as good as Otway, if not Shakespeare,
had been expected.   It had not been nearly as good as that, but the
acting of Mrs Yates as a Portuguese duchess, and Loutherbourg's
scenery, had carried it along.

Mrs Hannah Cowley, the lady of an East India Company officer, had once told her husband, on returning from the theatre, that she could have written something better herself. In her *Runaway* she had been much indebted to Garrick, for assistance, and she was pronounced a promising writer for the stage. This prophecy was to be fulfilled, with her *Belle's Stratagem*, but not until after Garrick's retirement. Mrs Charlotte Lennox, daughter of a Lieutenant-Governor of New York, had been one of Johnson's recommendations. She was in reduced circumstances, but had an indefatigable pen. Her alteration of *Eastward Hoe!* ran only nine nights. Cumberland and Dibdin had supplied ballad farces and comedies. General Burgoyne and Colonel Dow had not been so successful as in their previous works.

Garrick himself had been very active. He had presented Tom King, for his benefit night, with an old two-act play *Bon Ton or High Life above Stairs*, which fully deserved to be got out of the desk and on to the stage. *The Meeting of the Company, or Bayes's Art of Acting*, could have been written, thought Hopkins, by nobody but Mr Garrick. " It is full of fine Satyr, and a most excellent Lesson to all Performers. It was received with great and general applause, and will be profitable to the Proprietors." He added a financial note.

1774–1775

| | | |
|---|---|---|
| Total Receipts | £33,614 | 15s. 10d. |
| Total Payments | £29,719 | 1s. 11d. |
| Total Profits | £3,897 | 4s. 1d. |

The salaries that season had been ninety-four pounds seven shillings and eight pence per day. Drury Lane Pay Roll showed that by December 16, one thousand, seven hundred and seventy five salaries had risen to one hundred and five pounds three shillings. The profits for the season of 1769–1770 had amounted to nine thousand four hundred and sixty-three pounds, but that had been the year in which *The Jubilee* had run for ninety-three nights. In the year of Garrick's retirement, he noted that he was getting eight hundred pounds for acting and five hundred pounds for management.

He had always been fond of the idea of May Day, an old English Festival. At Hampton he liked to celebrate it by a little feast for the village children. He sat in state in Shakespeare's Temple, and as each child came up, he asked its name, which he wrote down, and then gave every one a piece of plum cake and a shilling. Some of his more sophisticated friends did not approve, for a churchwarden, of Mr Garrick's Old Women's Race.

His musical one-act comedy, *May-Day, or the Little Gipsey*, had been written in order to introduce what Hopkins called " Miss Abrams, a Jew Girl, upon the Stage. She is very young and small, has a very sweet Voice and a fine Shake, but not Power enough yet." Some of her songs had, like herself, an early-morning freshness.

> Hail Spring! whose charms make nature gay,
>   O breathe some charm on me,
>   That I may bless this joyful day,
>   Inspir'd by Love and thee!

At the very end of last year, on December 29, Portia had been played for the first time by a new-comer to the company simply announced as " a Young Lady ". Mrs Sarah Siddons was given her own name when she appeared as the heroine in Ben Jonson's *Epicoene, or the Silent Woman*. She was seen in five more parts, all comedy except Lady Anne to Garrick's Richard. The manager was observed to be most fatherly towards her. At rehearsal he led her to a seat beside his own.

She came of a very large theatrical family. Her grandfather had played with Betterton, her old father had been manager of a touring company, and her young husband was on the stage. She was twenty, tall and of statuesque beauty. She was " Garrick's Venus " in a revival of *The Jubilee*; and when Mrs Yates and Miss Younge, whom she thought would like to poison her, pushed in front of her in the procession, Garrick himself led her down to the front again. Her memories of him were not very grateful. " The fulsome adulation that courted Garrick behind the scenes cannot be imagined." She remembered being shown by him where to stand, as Lady Anne, so that he could keep his full face to the audience; and that his look of reproach to her in this character had so much upset her that she had not been able to do herself justice. When the season ended he promised to recommend her to Sheridan, but no further engagement at Drury Lane had followed. Hopkins made no comment on her. Eleven years later, his daughter Priscilla married her brother. John Hopkins ended life as the father-in-law of the great Kemble. [2]

On the night of Mrs Siddons's first appearance as Portia, Garrick had written to Colman that he was calling in another opinion. He was going to be overhauled by Percivall Pott in a few days time. Pott came, and did not forbid Adams's solvent. He had long known it. It was Perry's really. Garrick longed for a cure, not a remedy. Last November, after six hours in the theatre, he had found himself, after dinner, good for nothing except falling asleep in his great chair. It was so quiet up in the Adelphi, with the traffic of the Strand out of sight and out of mind. Still, in the mornings especially, he often felt his old self. " Gout, stone and sore throat! yet I am in spirits! "

Miss Hannah More thought him in high good humour and inexpressibly agreeable on the evening when she heard from his own lips of his retirement. She did not know the Garricks very well as yet. She was one of five sisters, and they kept a little school, which was flourishing. Her father had also been a teacher, but her mother had been the daughter of a Gloucestershire farmer, and Hannah's appearance suggested country similes—a robin red-breast, a rosy apple. She had blunt short features, curly hair, large brown eyes and, although past thirty now, did not look her age. She had been engaged to be married once, years ago, to Mr Turner, who had a very fine house, Belmont, on the hill above Flax Bourton, six miles out of Bristol. But Mr Turner, who had been twenty years her senior, had not, in the end, been able to face matrimony. She had surmounted a humiliating experience with fortitude, and now she was happier than she had ever been in her life, for she had taken two poems to Mr Cadell, the publisher, who had given her forty guineas for them, and she was going to write a play for Drury Lane. About two years ago, she and her two sisters had visited London, and she had seen Garrick in *Lear*. She had written a letter about it to a friend, who was a good friend, and an invitation to the Adelphi had followed. She had also longed to see Dr Johnson, and Miss Reynolds had managed that. Soon she had met the sublime Edmund Burke, and all the ladies of the blue-stocking circle, headed by "a certain Mrs Montagu, a name not totally obscure". Her first visit to London had been such a success that she had repeated it next winter. Dr Johnson had told her, to her face, that she laid on her flattery too thick, she choked him with it; but it was perfectly genuine. Mr Garrick was much more polite. He sat down beside her, and when he had satisfied her curiosity on one subject, he asked, all vitality, "Now, madam, what next?" She could hardly believe her ears when it was suggested that the Misses More should spend a Friday to Monday at Hampton, "the Temple of taste, nature and Garrick."

"I have at last slipt my theatrical shell," wrote Garrick to Colman, "and shall be as fine and free a gentleman as you would wish to see upon the North or South Parade, at Bath." Before he got there he had one more bad week at the theatre. The Rev. Henry Bate, whose *Blackamoor Wash'd White* was produced on February 1, was a most extraordinary character. He had the promise of one of Lyttelton's livings, but was very unsuited for holy orders. He had fought one or two duels, and edited *The Morning Post* and been committed to jail for twelve months for a libel on the Duke of Richmond. He was known as "the Fighting Parson", and had plenty of enemies. On the first night of *The Blackamoor* there was much hissing, and on the fall of the curtain cries of " No more ". Next time there was hissing from the beginning of the second act. Poor King went in front on the third night, begging to know the pleasure of the audience. Hopkins thought the House would have been pulled to pieces. Old Woodfall (not Puppy) wrote to complain that he had been very nearly murdered by some of the author's party. There was nothing for it but to get the manager to come up from Hampton, on a Monday, which was not his habit. Even he had difficulty in getting a hearing. He told the audience, " His theatrical Life would be very short and he should be glad to end it in Peace." A man in the pit called out, " If you have a mind to die in peace, don't let *The Blackamoor* be played again ", whereupon the uproar redoubled. A gentleman in the boxes called out, " For Shame! hear Mr Garrick speak." Another gentleman, who had, most improperly, persuaded the box-keeper to admit him behind the scenes, because he thought he could prevent disturbance from spreading there, believed he had prevented murder, though at risk of his own life. He had been cut in the hand, wresting a knife from " an ill-looking and desperate scoundrel " who was pursuing an actor with the cry " I will cut his liver out ". There was nothing for it but to withdraw a promising piece.

The Misses More went to Hampton, and Miss Martha wrote to Bristol that from dinner to midnight Mr Garrick had entertained them in a manner infinitely agreeable. He told the elder school-mistress how he longed to study the more important duties of life, and that when he retired his habits should be so regular that they should be a credit to himself and an example to others. Next time they came, Miss Hannah was to bring her writing. The sisters found out that the Garricks' dual birthday was approaching, and Hannah wrote a sonnet for the occasion, " addressed to the River Thames and written in the Temple at Hampton ". She said she had been suffering from the headache, or it would have been better. She was lucky that she had not suffered from the pneumonia, as the date was mid-February. She took the sonnet round to the Adelphi, where they dined snugly, in the library, on the eve of the birthday. She was having a *petite assemblée* at her own lodgings after dinner, to which she had invited the Garricks; and Eva-Maria tried to press upon her delicacies from her own kitchen. " But as I hate admixtures of finery and meanness, I refused everything except a little cream and a few sorts of cakes." The Misses More's tea-party was brilliant. Hannah could hardly believe her ears when Mr Garrick took up the *Monthly Review* and read aloud with all his pathos and grace, " Sir Eldred and the Bower," by Miss Hannah More. She cried like a child. " Mrs Garrick twinkled as well as I . . ." " Garrick was the very soul of the company, and I never saw Johnson in such perfect humour." After Mrs Boscawen, Miss Reynolds, Dean Tucker etc. had withdrawn, Johnson and Garrick began " a close encounter, telling old stories, ' e'en from their boyish days ' at Lichfield. We all stood around them, above an hour, laughing in defiance of every rule of decorum and Chesterfield. I believe we should not have thought of sitting down, or parting, had not an impertinent watchman been saucily vociferous."

Before the Garricks went there was " a little private whisper " that Hannah must dine with them again to-morrow, to assist at the birthday.

Nobody would have guessed from his serene social exterior that Garrick was being plagued, to the end of his theatrical life, by Dr Arne, Mr Kelly, Mrs Yates and Mrs Abington. The musician, he disposed of easily—

> Dear Sir,
> I have read your play and rode your horse, and do not approve of either. . . . (Designed for Dr Arne, who sold me a horse, a very dull one, and sent me a comic opera, ditto.)

Hugh Kelly had a disarming manner of re-entering the lists.

> My Dear Sir,
> Do not be frightened when you see my name; for this is not a letter of importunity but of apology. Foolish I am, but ingratitude is not among my vices. . . .

He did want something, though—an interview.

Mrs Yates went back fourteen years in her catalogue of complaint —to the season in which she had given up the part of Almeria, with Mr Garrick's consent. She still thought it—" a part unworthy of a capital actress . . . But if my playing it a few nights will oblige you, I am ready to do it. I cannot help concluding with a few lines from your favourite author:

> Oh! 'tis excellent
> To have a giant's strength etc.

His collection of notes from Mrs Abington was his masterpiece. He kept them all, and he kept copies of his replies. This was very necessary in dealing with somebody so tricky.

> Mr Garrick behaves with so much unprovoked incivility to Mrs Abington that she is at a loss how to account for it, and her health and spirits are so much hurt by it that she is not able to say *what* or *when* she can play. If he had been pleased to give her a day's notice, she could have

played her part in " The West Indian ", but it was not possible for her, at three o'clock to read her part, get her clothes ready and find a hairdresser all by six o'clock.

(She had known of Reddish's illness as soon as he had, which was between twelve and one, and he had been obliged to crawl to Colman for a loan of Mrs Mattocks from Covent Garden.)

Sir,
        The servant has brought me word that Mr Garrick is very angry at my not attending rehearsal this morning.   I do not believe him.

    Mrs Abington has kept her room with a fever for some days past, or she would have complained to Mr Garrick of a letter she has received from Mr Hopkins, dictated in the spirit of incivility and misrepresentation. . . .

    Sir, I am very much indisposed, and desire to be excused when I tell you I cannot act tomorrow night.   If the consideration of the salary I receive is a reason for my being called out to play to empty benches, I must beg leave to decline receiving any more pay at your office.

During the quarrel about her forthcoming benefit at the end of this season she had, without notifying him, put the matter in the hands of her solicitor.  This was splendid.  He replied to Mr Lodge that he thought Mrs Abington did him rather a favour than an incivility, and passed the correspondence to his solicitor, who took counsel's opinion.   Albany Wallis of Norfolk Street, Strand, was a very old friend as well as a very good man at his business.   The result was that Mrs Abington thankfully accepted Mr Garrick's very obliging offer to play at her benefit, in May (the quarrel had been about two March dates), as it had been for some time her fixed determination to quit the stage at the end of the present season, and never to return to it.   (" The above is a true copy of the letter, examined word by word, of that worst of bad women, Mrs Abington, to ask my playing for her benefit—and why? ")   However, she said that Mr Lodge had told her so, and when May 7 arrived, Mr Garrick, as Archer (his last appearance in the part), filled Drury Lane, and on May 8 of the next year Mrs Abington as Lady Teazle, in Mr Sheridan's new play, entered upon the most spectacular success of her career.                                                                    6

While he was still seeing Wallis about Mrs Abington, something dreadful happened.   On March 29 Wallis's son, " a most hopeful youth at Westminster School ", was accidentally drowned.   Garrick spent the week-end trying to comfort an almost distracted man.   By an unlucky coincidence, both the Garricks' houses had spectacular views of the Thames.   Wallis was a big, heavy-looking fellow even when depicted by Reynolds.

Dr Burney thought Garrick was getting to look much older.

Johnson pronounced with authority. "Why sir, you are not to wonder at that. No man's face has had more wear and tear." Tate Wilkinson thought Garrick was lucky in that his features did not become pinched, although he had lost so much weight. Reynolds had painted a conversation group of the Garricks in their garden, three seasons past, which had been exhibited at the Royal Academy. It was not his happiest effort, as Garrick in his best velvet suit, with a book in his hand, appeared to be reading his lady (also much dressed) to sleep; but it seemed a prediction of peaceful days to come. As spring of 1776 advanced Garrick's letters grew jubilant.

"I shall shake off my chains, and no culprit in a jail delivery will be happier. I really feel the joy I used to do when I was a boy, at a breaking up." But before that day came he had to face his farewell performances. He told Cradock that he would like to leave the stage in the same character in which he had made his first great success, at Goodman's Fields. But there was a serious consideration. "I can play Richard; but I dread the fight and the fall. I am afterwards in agonies." He ordered one new costume only, for Richard to wear as King and on Bosworth Field, and announced, "I shall play Lear in my new Richard dress." Cradock laughed. "Pray, where's the impropriety? What costume is better, pray, on any authority?" Cradock begged him not to give his enemies such an opportunity of accusing him of historical inaccuracy. Garrick said he was determined, and ordered only a new wig for Lear—grey locks.

Steevens wanted him to give "the genuine text of Lear" ("Cordelia dead in his arms, "Howl! howl! etc."), but he said that this would mean un-learning, and re-learning, and he would be agitated, and might make mistakes. The fact was, that it was years since he had learned anything new, and except for such things as epilogues and prologues, which he had written himself, his memory was not what it had been. Cradock told Steevens not to plague him any more about Shakespeare's original texts. "Johnson had never interfered about the matter."

As the date of the final performances approached, it became clear that the ordeal was going to be much worse than anyone had expected. Theatrical parties were coming over from Dublin, and down from Edinburgh. A fashionable French contingent headed by Madame Necker was coming from Paris. All these visitors would have to be entertained at the Adelphi or Hampton. It seemed an unsuitable moment for the Garricks to add a permanent resident to their household, but the elder Miss More must return to their school and the younger Miss More said that when Garrick quitted the stage she would be very well contented to relinquish plays also. She must see him take his leave in at least half a dozen of his characters.

She wrote archly to Bristol when preparing for another Thames-side country visit:

When I come back from Hampton, I shall change my lodgings; not that I have any objection to these, but those I have taken are much more airy, large and elegant. Besides the use, when I please, of the whole house, I shall have a bed-chamber and a dressing room for my own particular company; the master and mistress are themselves well-behaved sensible people and keep good company; besides, they are fond of books and can read, and have a shelf of books which they will lend me. The situation is pleasant and healthy—the centre house in the Adelphi.

Mrs Garrick took Miss Hannah More to the trial for bigamy of the Duchess of Kingston—London's best show that April, outside the theatre. She offered to take her to the Pantheon, but Miss Hannah More could not get the better of her repugnance to those sort of places. At great evenings at the Adelphi she met Lady Chatham and her daughters, and Lord Dudley, and Mr Rigby, and Lord and Lady Camden and their daughters. She would have taken Lord Camden for an old physician, but upon closer inspection thought there was something of genius about his nose. At Hampton she met " our noble neighbours, the Pembrokes ", and found the countess a pretty woman, and my lord a good-humoured lively chatty man. On a spring evening she was taken to dine at Sir Joshua's house on Richmond Hill overlooking another famous view of the Thames. Hannah was in Paradise. Whenever she pleased, she might join " the most polished and delightful society in the world. Our break-fasts are little literary societies. There is generally company at meals, as they think it saves time, by avoiding the necessity of seeing people at other seasons. Mr Garrick sets the highest value upon his *time* of anybody I ever knew. From dinner to tea we laugh, chat and talk nonsense: the rest of his time is generally devoted to study."

He needed a little time for study. Between April 11 and June 1 he was going to appear in eleven characters, and give nineteen performances. He was going to appear twice as Benedick, Don Felix, Ranger, Hamlet, and three times as Richard and as Lear—with the new dress and wig. He was going to get rid of most of his light comedy parts as early as possible, but continue alternating between tragedy and comedy to the very end, building up to a grand finale with Richard and Lear. But for the very last night, which would be overcharged with tragedy anyway, he had decided upon a comedy. It would be much best, and easiest, to bow himself

# GARRICK as Abel Drugger in Act 2, Scene VI of Ben Jonson's "The Alchymist".

*By Johann Zoffany*

Garrick first appeared in this part on March 21, 1743, and played it for the last time on April 11, 1776, in his farewell season. "Last night I played Abel Drugger for the last time. I thought the audience were cracked, and they almost turned my brain." Dr Johnson related that a Lichfield tradesman, who was urged by Peter Garrick to witness a performance by his famous brother, when in London, reported on his return: "Well, by God! Mr Garrick, though he is your brother, he is one of the shabbiest, meanest, most pitiful hounds I ever saw in the whole course of my life." Detail, engraved from a conversation piece, which includes the figures of Burton as Subtle and Palmer as Face, by John Dixon, 1771. There are versions of the picture in the Garrick Club and Lord Durham's collection.

*Reproduced by kind permission of the Trustees, the Victoria and Albert Museum, from the engraving in the Enthoven Theatre Collection.*

out, as politely as possible, with a smile, if possible, as the gay and polished Don Felix.

At Hampton, in early May, Hannah noted the lilacs and syringas were at their best. At the Adelphi she helped to entertain the first of the visitors from Paris. " On Wednesday we had a very large party to dinner, consisting chiefly of French persons of distinction and talents, who are come over to take a last look at the beams of the great dramatic sun, before he sets. We have had *beaux esprits, femmes sçavantes*, academicians etc. and no English person except Mr Gibbon, the Garricks and myself. We had not one English sentence the whole day."

Hannah witnessed Garrick as Abel, on April 11, as Benedick on the 16th, as Kiteley on the 25th, Hamlet on the 27th and Sir John Brute on the 30th. She had been most unfavourably impressed, on arriving in town, by the amazing new coiffures of London ladies. They had copied them from the ladies of Paris, who had copied them from the extravagances of their young queen. Heads were now worn, powdered, two feet high; on them were complete cornucopias and market-gardens, and starting out behind, from a silly little cap, four or five ostrich plumes. Garrick, when playing Sir John Brute disguised as a lady, now wore a modern headdress that set the house roaring. It had pendant carrots over either ear. At *Hamlet* Hannah found herself not only in the best seat, but with the best company in the house, " for I sat in the orchestra, in which were a number of my acquaintances (and these not vulgar names) ". The names included Edmund Burke, Mr Sheridan and Dr Warton. As to Garrick's Hamlet, she simply pitied those who had never seen it. Posterity would never be able to form the slightest idea of his pretensions. Had she not seen him a few days before as Abel, she would have thought it impossible for the same man to have played two such different parts with such superlative and finished excellence. " When I see him play any part for the last time, I can only compare my mixed sensations of pain and pleasure to what I suppose I should feel if a friend were to die and leave me a rich legacy. There is a certain sentiment of gratification and delight in the acquisition; but as you are beginning to indulge it, it is all of a sudden checked by recollecting on what terms you possess it, and that you are purchasing your pleasure at the costly price of losing him to whom you owe it. He is one of those summer suns, which shine brightest at their setting." She felt as if she had been " assisting at the funeral obsequies of these individual characters ".

She had written this to the Rev. James Stonhouse, whom the Garricks knew. Mr Stonhouse had been a successful physician for many years, but had heard a Call.   (David had once told him that, in his new part, he displayed faults of manner.)   Hannah showed her letter to Eva-Maria, who was so much touched and penetrated that she insisted on having a copy.   On May 17, having witnessed Garrick as Leon and Don Felix, Hannah went home.   She had been in London for six months and with the Garricks for the last three. Their introduction of her " to the greatly-endowed " was remarked as having been " sudden and general ".   Only Mrs Kitty Clive, a much older friend, had taken one of her full-blooded violent dislikes for what she called " the purring Miss Moors ".   She could not understand why her poor Davy and Violetta had taken them up, and rightly foresaw in Hannah, an increasingly frequent guest.   It apparently never occurred to her that Hannah was about the age to have been their daughter, and that after the next few weeks of exceedingly high tension were over, they would be needing a daughter.

### 2

Letters as well as guests arrived in large numbers at the theatre, the Adelphi, and Hampton, in May and June; but supported by Dr Pott, Dr Cadogan and Dr Schomberg, Garrick appeared in such health and spirits that everyone who met him deplored anew his retirement.   He scribbled on the back of letters.   " Just going to perform Benedick for the last time."   " Mr, Mrs and Miss Pott to me, upon leaving the stage."   Friends did not scruple to trouble him.   The Duke of Portland wanted a box below-stairs for *Macbeth* if it was true he was going to appear in that character.   (It was quite untrue.)   Miss Cadogan's young friend, Miss Pine, had been chiefly induced to visit London " to see the man you adore ".   Mrs Pine's request was modest—" any obscure corner, in box, pit or gallery where her child might only once behold Garrick in safety! "   If a seat could not be promised she must give up the whole scheme, " for I will not venture her in a crowd ".   Lady Colebrooke was reasonable.   She wanted a side box, or eight places in front boxes for Garrick's last appearance, as she was desirous that her children might be present at a scene of which they could talk fifty years after she was departed this life.   Sir Grey Cooper, a particular friend, said he accepted a row of seats without complaint, but he had heard that a certain Monsieur Necker and a certain Dean of Derry had secured boxes for every farewell performance.   Garrick wrote back at once to say that the Dean of Derry had not got a single seat through him. If bribery and corruption had crept behind the scenes, he was sorry. He pleaded guilty to " Madame Necker ".   " I received many favours from her in France." Governor Johnstone of West Florida was simply going to send his servant at five o'clock to see if places could still be had. If there were, he would be joyful, if not, resigned. He got in to *Hamlet* after a struggle, and, much pleased, asked for three places for *The Suspicious Husband* next night. By June 9, Lady Simpson was lachrymose. Her man had been sent almost every day to the theatre, in her name, but he could never get a place.

The scenes outside the theatre were a show in themselves. A clergyman from America, called Curwen, wrote sadly that after being thumped, squeezed and nearly suffocated in his efforts to see Garrick as Archer he had been obliged to retire baffled. Three days later, supported by a major of the British army and another friend, he had tried again. It was the night on which Their Majesties came to see the last of Richard—June 5. Next day there was no play, " Mr Garrick being exhausted with Fatigue ". On Saturday, 7th, he said a farewell to Lear made memorable by a scene behind the scenes. Miss Younge, who had been as tiresome as possible for several seasons, suddenly saw herself as Garrick's spiritual daughter. She fell upon her knees, attired as Cordelia, " Sir, if you would indeed give me your blessing! " Lear rose to the occasion.

His grand finale was arranged to fall upon a Monday, so that it should have been preceded by a day of rest. On June 10, doors were opened an hour and a half before the rise of the curtain at six-thirty. Garrick was giving the profits to the Theatrical Fund. He had written an appropriate prologue:

> A vet'ran see, whose last act on the stage
> Intreats your smiles for sickness and for age.
> Their cause I plead, plead it with heart and mind;
> A fellow feeling makes one wond'rous kind!

He was going to make a private presentation to his oldest friend in the company.

> Dear King,
> 
> Accept a small token of our long and constant attachment to each other.
> 
> I flatter myself that this sword, as it is a theatrical one, will not cut love between us; and that it will not be less valuable for having dangled at my side some parts of the last winter.
> 
> May health, success and reputation still continue to attend you.
> 
> Farewell! Remember me!

Eva-Maria was being cared for by the Angelos in the manager's box. Looking back, Garrick himself thought that he had played Don Felix with as much, if not more, spirit, as ever in his life.

Yet, when I came to take the last farewell . . . I not only lost almost the use of my voice, but of my limbs too; it was . . . *a most awful moment.* You would not, [he told Madame Necker,] have hought an English audience void of feeling if you had then seen and heard them.

After the curtain fell on the last scene of *The Wonder*, there was a strangely funereal effect. The claps sounded like muffled drums. An expectant hush fell upon an audience most uncomfortably crowded, before the curtain rose again upon an empty stage. The wings were observed to be packed with groups of players, their faces all turned one way, as Garrick came on, and walked down to the front slowly. He had prepared something brief, quiet and suitable.

Ladies and Gentlemen,
    It has been customary with persons under my circumstances to address you in a final epilogue. I had the same intention, and turned my thoughts that way; but indeed I found myself *then* as incapable of writing such an epilogue as I should be *now* of speaking it.
    The jingle of rhyme, and the language of fiction, would but ill suit my present feelings. This is to me a very awful moment. It is no less than parting for ever with those from whom I have received the greatest kindness and favours, and upon the spot where that kindness and those favours were enjoyed.
    Whatever may be the changes of my future life, the deepest impression of your kindness will always remain here [putting his hand on his breast] fixed and unalterable.
    I will very readily agree to my successors having more skill and ability for their station than I have; but I defy them all to take more sincere and more uninterrupted pains for your favour, or to be more truly sensible of it, than your humble servant.

This is what he had prepared, but in fact when he got to the first " kindness " his voice failed him. He pulled himself together, and finished brokenly, but nobody heard much more. He made his bow, and began to retire, slowly, as he had advanced. His look was thought to hold something of agony. As he passed from sight, the audience broke into shouts of applause with which were mingled loud cries of woe. The words, " Farewell! Farewell! " mingled with sounds of bitter lamentation. An after-piece, Dibdin's *Waterman* had been advertised. Nobody wanted it. Garrick was gone. He had broken his wand. There was not a dry eye in Drury Lane.

Mrs Angelo and Eva-Maria, who had held up so far, were sobbing in one another's arms. Angelo told them that anyone would have supposed they were following Garrick to the grave. The case was just the reverse. His labours ended, he was going to live happily ever after.

Hopkins wrote his last entry:

> Mr Garrick has quitted the Stage with the greatest Éclat that anyone
> could wish or desire, but not more than his Deserts. I can only say "*I ne'er*
> 10 *shall look upon his Like again.*"

### 3

Rigby, who could not really understand anyone relinquishing
anything, wrote somewhat doubtfully:

> I do not know, nor you neither, till you have tried it, how you will
> relish an idle life, who have always been used to a most active one. If
> your quitting the stage will contribute to your health, that is the first
> consideration. Amusement is the next, and that people do not always
> find as they grow older.

But his David had no fear of idleness. Before he had made his
final bow, people living far afield had written to say that now he
could visit them. He was pressed to come to Fermanagh and North
Wales. He replied with caution to Sir James Caldwell. It had long
been his wish to re-visit a kingdom where he had been honoured
with every mark and regard of kindness; but he had not only his own
wishes to consider. " As I have not left Mrs Garrick one day since
we were married, near twenty-eight years, I cannot now leave her;
and she is so sick and distressed by the sea that I have not the
resolution to follow my inclination, on account of her fear." However, he held out hopes that when he had settled his affairs, which
were at the moment in some confusion, and prevailed upon a fearful
lady to cross a very small branch of the sea, he might present himself at Castle Caldwell. To Sir Watkin Williams Wynn, he promised
11 " next year ".

He spent the holiday season of 1776 rather quietly. He went on
what he called " rambles ", to the Henry Bunburys at Barton, in
Suffolk, and Rigby at Mistley. He went to Wilton for the second
year running. (Last year, the diversion there had been the cutting
of silhouettes. That labelled " Mr Garrick " looked rather old.)
Towards the end of August, the figure of Roscius was to be seen
silhouetted against a dramatic background. He had discovered a
marine resort very congenial to members of his profession. Brighthelmstone was as yet a very small place, but the Garricks liked it so
well that they considered taking a lodging there next summer. Lady
Bathurst wrote most obligingly to say that Mrs Garrick had only to
say what kind of a house they wanted, and she would take care of the
pots and pans. She was convinced that nothing was so salutary as
the sea-air, and that a peep of this fine ocean was one of the few
things of which one never tired. In October they went to Althorp.

A A

On a late February morning of 1777, a chariot breasted the hill in Windsor town, and clattered in over the cobbles of the castle court-yard. Mr and Mrs Garrick had been summoned by Their Majesties. The retired patentee was going to give a reading from his works to the assembled royal family. He had wintered pretty well. November to January were always his bad months, and gout had afflicted him as usual, but nothing worse. He had, so far, no lack of occupation. He was writing an epilogue for Colman and a prologue for Sheridan. He had been often to Drury Lane since the new season opened to observe and advise. There was a young Mrs Robinson whose pathos reminded him of Mrs Cibber. He had intended her for Cordelia, but she had run off and made an unsuccessful marriage. He now suggested her to Sheridan as Juliet, and was rehearsing her himself, playing her Romeo, a part he had long discarded. Newcomers to the company believed that in his youth there had been an expression " as gay as Garrick ". Nowadays they said " as deep as Garrick ".

He had taken great pains over his performance for Windsor. His Majesty was not a Shakespeare enthusiast. The royal children now numbered eleven. The Prince of Wales was fifteen. Children always liked his bird imitations. He had decided upon a reading of *Lethe* with which everyone present would be familiar. It was always popular, and gave opportunity for change of voice and guise; and he had added one more comic character. He had also written for the occasion, a little fable, in the style of La Fontaine—*The Blackbird and the Royal Eagle*. It opened gaily, with a parliament of birds, all of which he would imitate—the lively blackbird, the thrilling nightingale, the raucous crow and magpie. Then, the blackbird began to notice that he was not as young as he had been. His fine glossy plumage was dull; there was grey amongst his feathers; his eye had lost its lustre and, worst of all, he began to be lame. This determined him to give up his mimicry, to retire to a single snug bush. But the royal eagle, having heard of his talents, sent for him to court, and told him to sing. This call overturned all his prudent resolutions. He found his strength returned, his feathers black again, his eye as quick as ever. He was his old self again.

Exactly what happened on that winter morning at Windsor was a little difficult to discover. Walpole, who had neither gone to see any of Garrick's farewell performances nor even mentioned them in his frequent news-letters from London, excelled himself in satire about a scene at which he had not been present. " He had solicited King George to solicit him to read a play. The piece was quite new, *Lethe* which their Majesties have not seen above ten times every year for the last ten years. . . . The piece was introduced by a prologue *en fable*; a Blackbird, grown grey-haired, as blackbirds are wont to do, had retired from the world but was called out again by the Eagle. Mr Hare asked Garrick, if his Majesty looked very like an Eagle? The audience was composed of King, Queen, Princess Royal, Duchess of Argyll, Lady Egremont, Lady Charlotte Finch; the Prince of Wales was not present, and all went off perfectly ill, with no exclamations of applause, and two or three formal compliments at the end. Bayes is dying of chagrin, and swears he will write no more."

The story was discussed at Mrs Montagu's tea-table, where the company included the Burneys, the Sewards from Lichfield and Johnson. Johnson was humourous. " The call of an eagle never yet had much tendency to restore the voice of a blackbird. The eagle may entertain the blackbird; but the entertainment always ends in a feast for the eagle."

" They say," cried Mrs Thrale, " that Garrick was extremely hurt at the coolness of the King's applause, and did not find his reception such as he had expected."

" He has been so long accustomed," said Mr Seward, " to the thundering applause of the Theatre that a mere ' Very well ' must necessarily disappoint him."

" Sir," said Dr Johnson, " he should not, in a Royal apartment, expect the hallooing and clamour of the One Shilling Gallery. The King, I doubt not, gave him as much applause as was rationally his due."

Whatever his disappointment, (" it was as if they had thrown a wet blanket over me "), Garrick did not cease to refer to his summons, and when he read his fable, at the Adelphi, to Miss Hannah More, on 12 her next visit, she found it lively, entertaining and affecting. He had written to tell her of a tribute of which he was very proud which had taken place a few weeks later. He often used to drop in at the House of Commons to listen to a debate. When two members fell into such an altercation that the House was cleared of strangers, a country member, Squire Baldwin, Member for Shropshire, looked up and saw one figure still in the gallery. An old actor was spellbound, watching gentlemen quarrelling. But when Mr Baldwin drew the Speaker's attention to the fact, the feeling of the House was instantly against him. A general groan went up. Burke sprang to his feet and asked why they should exclude a man to whom they were all obliged, the great master of eloquence, in whose school they had all learned the art of speaking and the very elements of rhetorick. He was warmly seconded by Fox and Townshend. There was very nearly a motion that Mr Garrick be given an exclusive privilege to be present whenever he pleased.   Baldwin was celebrated as the 13 dullest man in the House and generally held to be a trimmer.   He complained noisily that Garrick " gloried in his situation ".   Garrick, in reply, wrote a set of verses, not for publication:

> Squire Baldwin rose, with deep intent,
> And notified to Parliament
> That I, it was a shame and sin,
> When others were shut out, got in.
> Asserting in his wise oration
> I gloried in my situation.
> I own my features might betray
> Peculiar joy I felt that day . . .
> But if, Squire Baldwin, you were hurt
> To see me, as you thought, so pert,
> You might have punished my transgression
> And damped the ardour of expression.
> A brute there is, whose voice confounds
> And frights all others with strange sounds,
> Had you your matchless pow'rs displaying,
> Like him, Squire Baldwin, set a-braying,
> I should have lost all exultation,
> Nor gloried in my situation.

There was another rumour connected with his Windsor audience, but it came from France.   " I do most sincerely rejoice to find," wrote his old friend Mrs Pye, from Paris, in April, " that you are not sunk into *Sir David*; for, as I said before, titles can add nothing to fame like yours.   Indeed, I should never have supposed it to be a matter of your own seeking, for it has ever been remarked, to your honour, that you have never employed your ample fortune to excite envy and make fools stare, but in the rational and sober enjoyment of life."   It could not be said that the arts had not been honoured 14 recently.   The President of the Royal Academy had become Sir Joshua.   But, although Garrick claimed in his Baldwin poem that he had friends in both parties, Whigs and Tories, it was perfectly well known that some characters who were anathema to Windsor were his closest friends.   Wilkes (" Jack Cade ") had been to dine at Hampton.   He supplied Burke with funds.

He was enjoying life in one way usual with most retired actors. He was constantly seen at the theatre.   At the first night of *The School for Scandal* he was observed applauding, in the highest spirits, a comedy as successful as any that had ever been produced under his management.   He had left Drury Lane running on an even keel.   A complimentary croaker said to him, " This is but a single play.   The Atlas that propped the stage has left his station."   " Has he?" asked Garrick. "If that be the case, he has found another Hercules to support the office."

The Burney children saw him at the Haymarket Theatre, alone, on a fine June day. The piece was *The Merchant of Venice*. He did not see them immediately, for although he looked about him with his opera-glass in every direction, they were exactly behind him. At last, in the middle of one of Henderson's declamations, one of the box-keepers let a door slam. The ex-manager turned right round sharply and discovered his young friends. At once, he was all fatherly attention, shook hands all round, and asked, "You arn't alone?" "Oh no! sir, we have a lady with us." "Well, but what have you done this long while? I'm so glad to see you." "And we're so proud to be acknowledged," piped Sukey. Fanny had never felt so consequential. He was merry, too; presently, there was a Lilliputian dance by about a dozen children, "Come," said he, "shall you and I make one among 'em? Come! If you will, I will . . . I only wait for you." "I fancy," ventured Fanny, "we should look like Patagonians among them." "Oh!" says he, "I should be a *fatta*gonian."

At the end of the second act, a gentleman came scrambling over two boxes to ask, "What he thought of the imitation?" "Imitation, sir?" "Ay, sir, this imitation of Shylock." "Oh, sir, I am no judge." How quick, how comical and how reasonable, thought Fanny; for everyone said that Henderson imitated Garrick, and ill-natured people said that the retired actor was jealous of the new star. Fanny nearly jumped into the pit, for joy, when Mr Garrick said, on parting, with "one of the gruffest of his lion looks", that he was 15 coming to see her father to-morrow.

He did not go to Bath this spring, and Hannah, who had built much on hopes of his making an expedition from Bath to Bristol, had been terribly disappointed. She decided to come to London, but there again fate seemed against her. "A very particular friend who lives near Portman Square, with whom I was engaged to spend the Spring" was not able to have her. She had got the painters in. Hannah set off, with dignity, for a tour of Norfolk and Suffolk, where she had relations. Garrick held her in high esteem, but she was now writing her play for Drury Lane. It was twelfth-century, called simply *Percy*, and was supposed to happen soon after the battle of Chevy Chase. "No offence to history if I have been guilty of a few anachronisms." She had sent him the first two acts, and begged him not to spare the rod. He would rather see the rest before he saw Hannah again, for he knew from experience how a sucking dove might be turned into a roaring lioness when her play was not

suitable for performance.   He had replied, " Mrs Garrick is studying
your two acts," a sound dreadful to the ears of experienced authors.
But Hannah was naïve.   It was part of her charm.   She honestly
thought that she had only to send her play to Mr Garrick.   But he
was no longer the manager of Drury Lane.   She sent him an Ode
written to his house-dog, Dragon, and a jar of codlings done in
Indian pickle for Eva-Maria, but no more *Percy*.   From what he
had seen, it did appear possible that he might be able to place it at
Covent Garden.   He had read aloud the existing portion to the
family at Althorp, and the reception there had been favourable.
He sent her warmest thanks for the Ode.   " Good, and very good—
partial and very partial."   He had given her one of his nicknames.
She was " Nine ", the embodiment of the nine muses.   She asked if
he would write an epilogue for *Percy*.   This was easy.   " Write you
an epilogue! give you a pinch of snuff! "   If she would send him a
line, to the Adelphi, telling him which character was to speak the
epilogue and what kind of a character, he would do his best on his
return.   For he was at the moment setting out to go by launch up
the Thames, with a party of ladies and gentlemen, for at least a
week.   Such expeditions were the latest fashion.   The Duchess of
Devonshire had set it.   If he should happen to be drowned before he
had written her epilogue he hoped she would excuse him and write
his epitaph.   The provisions had gone on board, his wife called.
He wrote " upon a full gallop ".   Upon second thoughts, he considered, though he could not say so, that what she needed first was a
prologue.   Epilogues to plays which did not succeed were sometimes
not heard.   He sent her a prologue, and she was all gratitude.   She
had now reached her fifth act, for which she trembled, but which she
was afraid would not make anyone else tremble.   " Let your fifth
act be worthy of you," wrote Garrick, " and tear the heart to pieces,
or woe betide you! "

Lord Sandwich was living this summer at Lord Halifax's house
on Hampton Green, and there arrived to stay with him in very hot
weather, Admiral Sir Edward Hughes, from the East Indies station.
On his homeward cruise, the Admiral had captured, off Ascension
Island, one of the finest turtles ever seen.   He had brought it with
him, and his own cook to dress it for the table.   Lord Sandwich
said to Cradock, who was also staying, " You are intimate with Mr
Garrick.   Could you, without impropriety, inform him of particulars,
apologizing for the short notice? "   Cradock wrote a note and sent
it over to Garrick's Villa, betimes.   In the stable-yard there, the
only soul to be seen was an old coachman, examining the wheels of a
carriage.   " When can Mr Garrick be seen? " asked Cradock's

servant, for the hour was very early. "Now," replied the figure, "give me the note"; and while Cradock's servant watched, aghast, a countenance which had resembled that of Abel Drugger, changed to that of a country gentleman *en déshabille*, considering a dinner invitation. On getting back to Hampton Green, the poor man made a clean breast of the affair, but added that he hoped he might be excused waiting at the dinner-party. He was so miserable, he could not appear in the parlour, if his life was at stake. Cradock said it could not be helped, and he would make apologies. He did so, as soon as Garrick arrived, and a look of quiet satisfaction and great kindliness stole over the features of Roscius retired. He asked Cradock to tell his man that Mr Garrick's coachman was a much better-looking fellow than his master. "By the mistake he has paid me a compliment."

The turtle-party, which was rather numerous, went off to admiration, and after coffee, when Lord Sandwich happened to mention Lord Onslow, the Speaker, Garrick recounted an anecdote of his earliest days upon the stage. The Speaker never went to the play, so he had asked a friend to bring the young actor to his house, to give a specimen of his performance. Garrick, much elated, had asked if he might recite a soliloquy from *Macbeth*, and the Speaker had bowed gravely. Garrick guessed that Macbeth and Macheath were alike indifferent to him. He did his best with "Is this a dagger?", but in a dramatic pause, suddenly the silence was broken by the old lord asking of the gentleman who sat next to him, "Pray, sir, was you at the turnpike meeting at Epsom on Thursday last?"

"My dear Sir!" said Lord Sandwich, "you have hit the old Speaker exactly." Cradock thought he had never seen Garrick
17 more entertaining than he was that night.

He was a little out of spirits after attending the annual dinner of the Theatrical Fund. It had been insufferably dull, and there had been two persons there who should not have been allowed. (One had disgracefully broken his contract with a manager on receiving a more inviting advantageous invitation, and the other had been in the courts with "a degrading plea".) He did not think, although he had the seat of honour at the head of the table, that his reception had been what he had reason to expect. Even King had been cold and short. He had dressed himself out as fine as possible, in honour to the day and the Committee. But he had
18 been worried. . . .

Letitia Matilda Hawkins knew what had disturbed him so greatly that midsummer. He had arrived to call upon her father, on a private matter, most violently agitated. Never had she seen a man whose attitude expressed more complete dejection. The matter on which he needed advice was delicate, and terrible. He had just heard, by chance, that there was a wicked report abroad that he and Mrs Garrick lived so ill together, they were about to separate. And this was not the worst. The reason affirmed was his persistent infidelity to her. He grew vigorous as he complained of the injustice done to him, and the danger of Mrs Garrick being made uneasy. Letitia Matilda watched round-eyed, as one who had been a great lover, in his unhallowed youth, confessed that then he had been guilty of much irregularity. His expression changed magically as he passed on to the hour of his marriage, since when his affection had never swerved from one whose attaching powers and valuable qualities he could never hope in words to do justice. The serious part of his complaint being over, he dashed off into imaginings of the story spreading in the Hampton district. " It was a most perfect piece of acting, as to every imitable particular, even to the click of encouragement." He was a gentleman bearing the ill news from village to village, setting his horse off again at the gallop directly he had disburdened his mind of the saucy scandal.

Whatever advice the lawyer gave, by the time that Garrick wrote to Hannah again he had decided to do the sensible thing, which was to continue to live happily with his wife and allude to the story as a joke. " To our very great surprise, a great friend of ours came from London, and to his greater surprise, found us laughing over our tea under our walnut-tree. He took me aside, and told me it was all over the town, from Hyde Park Corner to Whitechapel dunghill that I had parted from Mrs Garrick. You may easily imagine that this was a great matter of mirth to us. We imagined somebody had had a mind to joke with our friend, but upon inquiry we found that such a report had been spread; but to comfort your heart, be assured that we are still as much united as ever, and are both so well that there is a prospect of dragging on our clogs for some years to come." He was writing from Rigby's, in his dressing-room, where the view from the windows was fine—" no less than fifty vessels under sail, and one, half an hour ago, saluted us with thirteen guns." [19]

A new arrival was installed at the Adelphi and Hampton, Mrs Garrick's niece, her sister's daughter, from Vienna, Miss Betty Fürst. She was there when Hannah arrived at Hampton in September, having completed *Percy*. To her surprise, on calling at the Adelphi on her arrival in London, Hannah had found a coach waiting to carry her to Hampton. Upon her arrival she was immediately (in spite of the presence of Miss Fürst) " put in possession of my old [20] chamber . . . We have had a great deal of company here, lords, ladies, wits, critics and the poets. Last Saturday, we had a very agreeable day. Our party consisted of about twelve, for these dear people understand society too well ever to have very large parties." Garrick had written to a business correspondent on August 23 that he had been very much indisposed, but Hannah noticed nothing wrong with him. At a party at which the company included his old friend Windham's son, Sheridan, and Lord Palmerston, he surpassed himself, especially in telling his famous story of Jack Pocklington— an interview between himself and a theatrical candidate with an impediment in his speech. Sunday was most agreeable. Hannah did not approve of the Hampton parson. He was worldly. His sermons were polished, but when they were over, there was nothing with which to wrestle in reverie. "After supper, on Sunday, Garrick read to us out of *Paradise Lost* that fine part on diseases and old age. Dr Cadogan and his agreeable daughter have spent a day and night here. The Doctor gave me some lectures on anatomy." Dr Cadogan, described by Garrick to Miss Cadogan as "your anti-Shakespeare father", was a person of massive kindly features, and a valuable addition to her acquaintances, but better was to come. "We go on Friday, into Hampshire, to Mr Wilmot's." Farnborough Place swallowed the Garricks, Miss Fürst and Miss More easily. "The Wilmots live in the greatest magnificence, but what is a much better thing, they live also rationally and sensibly." The Wilmots were *nouveaux riches*, but of good family. Mr Henry Wilmot had made a large fortune as a lawyer. The amenities of Farnborough Place included a conservatory, filled with balsams and geraniums, which Garrick mentioned nostalgically and tactfully in his letter of thanks, after the visit. Indeed, he was all tact, as a guest. Hannah was so grateful to him on the Sunday evening. "There was talk of music. Sacred music was the ostensible thing, but before I had time to feel uneasy, Garrick turned round and said, ' Nine, you are a Sunday woman; retire to your room. I will recall you when the music is over.' "

After Farnborough, Hannah went home and the Garricks set off North. They had intended to go to Sir Watkin Williams Wynn earlier, but now they must take Lichfield on their way. A niece was to be married; the first wedding in the second generation. Merrial Docksey was to settle in her own countryside; Mr James Patton was of Lichfield.

North Wales, in early October, and perfect weather, was a revelation to Garrick, "a most divine country", and nothing could be more agreeable than Sir Watkin's hospitality. When the baronet

21

had been fresh from school on his Grand Tour, Antonio Carara had
compared sadly the open-handed magnificence of Sir Watkin with
the cold and careful demeanour of the young Duke of Devonshire.
Sir Watkin, now married, and a father, still liked to give very large
parties—indeed the taste was to increase—but he was no mere man
of fashion.   He revelled for the enjoyment of his tenants and neighbours.   His private theatre sounded much grander than it was.   He
had beautiful headings designed for his playbills—Falstaff etc. surrounding a bust of Shakespeare.   He had got his scene-painter—
Mr Fosbroke—from Drury Lane, and his wardrobe book showed
over a hundred items.   A large new kitchen had been built at
Wynnstay for his coming of age.   For the last seven years it had
been used for theatricals, particularly at Christmas.   (Georgy
Colman, who had taken part, said that the company off the stage was
far superior to any regulars on it, but no London manager would
have offered the best a good salary.)   The stage was lit from above,
there was a pit only, no boxes or gallery, and the amateurs behaved
like amateurs, nearly knocking one another down in their entrances
and exits.   Sir Watkin himself was good.   He had been a little
disappointed that Garrick had sent a message that he would prefer
to remain a spectator; but to have got him so far at all was creating
a sensation.   On September 26 David wrote to Peter to arrange
their homeward journey.

> We shall certainly be at Birmingham on Saturday evening, the 5th of
> October, and shall stay the next day till about twelve, so we may have a
> good deal of gabble.   I hope you will bring Cousin Bailey, with you, and
> let us have a snug party. . . . These Welsh scenes are quite new to us,
> and very well worth everybody's curiosity.   At Shrewsbury the town was
> in an alarm at my coming and the " Raven " inn was beseiged.   I little
> expected so much honour from Salopian swains and Welch mountaineers.
> Their observations upon my person, age etc. you shall have at Birmingham.

His next letter showed that the style in which Roscius-retired
travelled was comfortable.

> I beg you'll bespeak beds sufficient for us all.   There will be two
> wanted for you and Cousin Dick, one for me and my wife, and one for
> Fosbroke, and my wife's niece.   I have six horses, for which I must have a
> good stable, and four men servants.

Sir Watkin had told him that it was a good inn, and he wished
Peter would order a large joint of meat for the servants, some fish
(if any was to be had) and some chickens boiled or roasted, and
whatever else Peter and cousin liked, to be ready 7 p.m. or sooner.   22

4

Hannah's play was produced by Mr Harris at Covent Garden on Wednesday, December 10, and her letter home, written the same evening, displayed strong emotion.

*Mr Garrick's study, Adelphi, ten at night.*

He himself puts the pen into my hand and bids me say that all is just as it should be. Nothing was ever more warmly received. I went with Mr and Mrs Garrick; sat in Mr Harris's box, in a snug dark corner, and behaved very well, that is, very quietly. The prologue and epilogue were received with bursts of applause; so indeed was the whole; as much beyond my expectation as my deserts! Mr Garrick's kindness has been unceasing.

(He had, in fact, been even kinder than she knew, for in a letter to the elder Rackett, on Monday, he had doubted if he would be able to get up to London at all this week. He had been " almost dead with my cold ".)

She was " the celebrated Hannah More ", Mr Garrick himself said so. He had always been sanguine, but she had been very low. The news from America had been so bad. She had thought that if the people of a disgraced, undone nation had the least spark of virtue left, nobody would think of going to the theatre. *Percy* had been running three nights when the House of Commons, in session, learned of the surrender of General Burgoyne's starving force of five thousand, at Saratoga, to an American army of twenty thousand. The prospect was grim. France would no longer hesitate to conclude a treaty with the revolted colonies, and must be expected to attack the wounded lion. The blow to British pride which spoiled Christmas week 1777 was to be met with courage. So many new regiments were to be raised (many by leading noblemen and cities at their own expense) that England would resemble one huge camp this summer. *Percy* continued to run. Hannah had taken lodgings for herself, when Mr Garrick had said that she ought to come up to London for her first night. But she had arrived with " a great cold " and had soon been swept off to Hampton, to her own comfortable room, promised by Eva-Maria, " a good fire, and all the lozenges and all the wheys in the world ". She was getting almost as many letters as Mr Garrick. Dr Percy came to bring the compliments of the Duke of Northumberland and Lord Percy. She felt quite sad for Mr John Home when he was shown into the Adelphi drawing-room, and Mr Garrick, taking her by the hand, begged leave to introduce the *Percy* to the *Douglas*. Mr Home's *Alfred* had run only three nights. He nobly said that he had not hurt Miss More much. The sisters came up from Bristol, and Hannah returned to her lodgings. She was receiving five invitations a night to dine out, but when Eva-Maria came in one morning to call, she found her in bed. Mrs Garrick wanted to go herself to fetch a physician—the great Dr Cadogan. At six the same evening a coach halted in Gerrard Street, Soho, and out of it stepped Mr Garrick, on his way to dine at The Club, in the same street. He brought with him a minced chicken, in a stew-pan, hot, a canister of Mrs Garrick's best tea and a pot of cream. " Were there ever such people? " When *Percy* ended its respectable run of twenty-three nights, Hannah went on to Hampton to go to bed there. Dr Cadogan and Mrs Garrick had battled an hour about whether she could leave her room; for she had been laid up for a whole month. She did not go home till April, by which time Mr Garrick had been so good as to lay out her author's profits, of more than four hundred pounds, on the best security, in the five per cents. 23

Drury Lane finances were causing him anxiety. There had been a players' strike at the opening of the 1776–1777 season led by Sheridan, who had discovered that Willoughby Lacy had negotiated the sale of his share of the patent to a Captain Thomson and Mr Langford. When Sheridan had announced that he would have nothing more to do with the management, these gentlemen had withdrawn. *The School for Scandal* was to bring the patentees twenty-one thousand pounds in its first three seasons, but stories of Sheridan's negligence and inattention were becoming widespread. The young manager would lounge into the green-room to hear the reading of a new play by Cumberland, yawn through a couple of acts, and say, in excuse, that he had not been to bed for two nights. He did not know all his company by sight. " Everyone is raving against Mr Sheridan for his supineness," wrote Clive, in March 1778. " There was never such a contrast as Garrick and Sheridan. What! have you given him up, that he creeps so? "

Garrick was far from having given him up. Sheridan came to Hampton with his beautiful wraith-like wife, whom Hannah More had not expected to like, but found that she must. He was always amiable. But he wanted to have sole control of Drury Lane, and he was going to get it. Garrick held a mortgage on Lacy's share, which was, however, secured on the whole four shares. In January, last year, he had endorsed " Bond from Lacy, Sheridan, Linley and Ford to David Garrick, in the penalty of forty-four thousand pounds for payment of twenty-two thousand pounds interest." " 'Tis a thumper! " It looked well on paper, but the interest was not being paid. In November, while he was staying at Althorp, en route for Lord Ossory's at Ampthill, he had heard from Albany Wallis that a

Mr Bateman of Maiden Lane had applied for an account of the mortgage, saying that he had authority to settle Mr Lacy's debts. A statement had been forwarded, but by March nothing further had happened. Lacy, when approached, gave explanations, which were not satisfactory. He said that as he had not found any hidden treasure, and his share of the profits last season had been but five hundred pounds, Garrick must see that he was quite unable, at present, to pay the interest on the mortgage, which amounted to two thousand two hundred pounds per annum. Bateman's inquiry had been occasioned by a question about a debt of his late father. There were increasingly heated meetings, with and without Albany Wallis, Bateman and a Mr Sainsbury, a kinsman of Lacy. Lacy wrote that he supposed Mr Garrick would have taken measures for the security and support of a theatre in which he and the late Mr Lacy had been so long connected, rather than distress his son and successor. But no oppression should overcome him. Garrick replied that as Lacy had said that he had received an offer for the mortgage, he would be glad for him to accept it. But he would not be accused of unkindness, and would wait until Lacy had settled matters with his partners. The next move was a sudden notification, in May, on behalf of all the patentees that it would not be in their power, in the future, to pay the interest on Lacy's mortgage until the debts and expenses of the threatre were discharged. This was intolerable, and Garrick sent them notice of foreclosure, and to Lacy a line of reproach. Lacy answered that the letter had been sent off without his knowledge or consent. There was no reason to suppose that the dividend would not be paid. He could only add that while he retained any share in Drury Lane he would never give his consent to the interest on the mortgage being paid except as had been originally agreed. Garrick wrote a despairing note on this, " I sent an answer by my brother George, that he might depend upon my not distressing him. Before George saw him, Mr Lacy had bargained to sell his share to Mr Sheridan, at an enormous price."

Lacy vanished from the dispute to play Hamlet in Cork, but Sheridan's father-in-law, Linley, entered the lists, on a new issue. He had mistakenly assumed that an article reflecting on the management's ingratitude had been written by Garrick, and he had produced an injudicious reply. He had to apologize. By August, Garrick's relations with the patentees had become so strained that he addressed them finally and collectively:

Gentlemen,
     The rudeness of your letters, which is always the sign of a bad cause, I shall pass over with the greatest contempt. But as you have

proposed to my friend, Mr Wallis, and my brother, an arbitration, I cannot, as an honest man, refuse to meet you upon any ground.

He therefore desired that in future they would communicate with him on business, only through Wallis.  The interest on the mortgage appeared, but it could not be said that his mind was at ease as to the future.                                                                                          24

He wrote to Hannah that his theatrical curiosity diminished daily, and his vanity as an author was quite extinct, but when a young son of one of his old players called upon him, he heard Mr Jack Bannister recite and promised a prologue for him to speak at his father's benefit at the Haymarket.  Charles Burney had declared, years ago, that when Garrick acted, even his coat-tails seemed animated. Master Bannister, after seeing *Lear,* had thought that even the mad king's stick acted.  Jack was a good mimic, with an excellent memory.  His account of his most awful interview with Roscius became a piece of theatrical history.

One morning I was shown into his dressing-room, where he was before his glass, preparing to shave; a white night-cap covered his forehead; his chin and cheeks were enveloped in soap-suds; a razor cloth was placed upon his left shoulder; and he turned and smoothed his shining blade with as much dexterity as if he had been bred a barber at the Horse-Guards . . .

"Eh! well-what! young man.  So you are still for the stage?  Well— how—what character do you—should you like to—eh? "

" I should like to attempt Hamlet, sir."

" Eh! what?  Hamlet the Dane! Zounds! that's a bold—have you studied the part? "

" I have, sir."

" Well, don't mind my shaving—speak the speech—the speech to the ghost—I can hear you—never mind my shaving."

After a few hums and haws, and a disposing of my hair so that it might stand on end " like quills upon the fretful porcupine ", I supposed my father's ghost before me, armed " Cap-a-pie " and off I started.

"*Angels, and ministers of grace, defend us!* ' He wiped the razor— " *Bring with thee airs from heaven, or blasts from hell* "— (he shaved on) " *Be thou a spirit of health, or goblin damn'd*—" (he strapped the razor) " *Thou com'st in such a questionable shape That I will speak to thee!*—" (he took himself by the nose) " *I'll call thee Hamlet.  King, father, royal Dane—O, answer me!  Let me not burst in ignorance.*"

He lathered on.  I concluded, but still continued my attitude, expecting prodigious praise; when, to my eternal mortification, he turned quick upon me, brandishing the razor, and, thrusting his half-shaved face close to mine, he made such horrible mouths at me that I thought he was seized with insanity, and I was more frightened of him than my father's ghost. He exclaimed in a tone of ridicule, " *Angels, and minister of grace, defend us!* Yaw, waw, waw, waw! "  The abashed Prince Hamlet became sheepish, and looked more like a clown than the Grave-digger.  He finished shaving, put on his wig, and with a smile of good-nature took me by the hand, and said, "Come, young gentleman—eh! let's see now what we can do." He spoke the speech; and how he spoke it, those who have heard him can never forget.

Bannister paid many more visits, and in the autumn Garrick rehearsed him and Mrs Robinson in *Zaphna*. His kindness produced another of the pin-pricks to which he was becoming accustomed from Drury Lane. Old Tom Sheridan, always a difficult man, had been engaged by his son to superintend rehearsals. The arrangement had soon broken down; some people said on the question of salary. But he continued to haunt the theatre possessively, and stir up trouble. Garrick passed off the awkward incident as lightly as possible.

*Pray, assure your father that I meant not to interfere in his department. I imagined (foolishly indeed) my a tending Bannister's rehearsal of the part I once played, and which your father never saw, might have assisted the cause without giving the least offence. I love my ease too well to be thought an interloper, and I should not have been impertinent enough to have attended any rehearsal, had not you, Sir, in a very particular manner desired me. However, upon no consideration will I ever interfere again in this business, nor be liable to receive such a message as was brought to me this evening by young Bannister.*

You must not imagine that I wrote this in a pet. Let me assure you, upon my honour, that I am in perfect peace with you all, and wish you from my heart all that yours can wish.

### 5

On two occasions in the spring of 1778, Roscius was to be seen setting off for a wedding, his white favour in his hat, his countenance all benevolence, although, as he wrote ruefully to Hannah, "I am to pay the piper." Kitty Clive, after a little natural acidity about his generosity to Miss More, in dandling and nursing her play, passed on with a full heart, and complete absence of tact, to something upon which she could send nothing but congratulations—"the noblest action of your life, your generosity to your nephew David. All the world is repeating your praises; those people who always envied you, and wished to detract from you (always declaring that you loved money too much ever to part with it) now they will feel *foolish* and look contemptible. All I can say is, *I wish that Heaven had made me such an uncle*. I know the young lady, am acquainted with her, she is extremely agreeable, with a temper as sweet as her voice; and she sings like an angel."

The announcements looked well in *The Gentleman's Magazine.*

David Garrick Esquire, junior, to Miss Hart of Brentford.
Captain Shaw of the Surry Militia, to Miss Garrick, the niece of David Garrick Esquire.

Bell's marriage, of course, in the year 1778, had much the most prestige, for her bridegroom wore a scarlet coat. The career of David Garrick, junior, had been a cause of anxiety to his namesake. Uncle David had got him, by means of Governor Johnstone, an appointment in the East India Company. Grandfather Carrington had opposed sending the lad so far, so he had been put in the army. Uncle David had approached Lord Pembroke, and Grandfather Carrington had bought him his commission. Two years ago, much against Lord Pembroke's advice, and having reached the rank of Captain, young David had sent in his papers, on account of " a very dangerous state of health ". Now he regretted this, felt better, and forwarded the suggestion that his uncle should help him to get back into the army again—buy him another commission. He said that his grandfather approved the idea. David, senior's, reply to " Mr Carrington's evasive letter about David " was firm. Old Nathan was by no means as senile as his signature suggested. He said that young David and Nathan, junior, had cost him seven thousand pounds, but that he had never considered he had taken them out of the hands of their father and uncle. David, senior, answered that he hoped he had done his duty in providing wholly for three of Mr Carrington's grandchildren. Except for paying some of their bills, he had not understood that two more were to be directed to him. (On second thoughts, he took out the bit about having paid young Nathan's debts, and said he would be willing to provide for four out of six of his brother's children.) The sad truth seemed to be that young David was fairly happy doing nothing at all—not even thinking. So was young Nathan. Their uncle, who had worked hard all his life, thought that to see " two brothers strutting about the circle of non-existence, may be very convenient, but not very spirited ". As usual, his bark was worse than his bite. He wrote a fairly enthusiastic character of his nephew to Lord Buckingham, who might take him on his staff to Ireland. But Lord Buckingham replied, reasonably, that he had already too many applications, and would be expected to give preference to Irish candidates. David and Nathan did credit to their good education. Both married heiresses, though in Nathan's case this happy solution was not achieved until after his uncle's death. The bounty to David, junior, alluded to by Clive, included the purchase of a house for the young couple, and so close to Garrick's Villa as to be visible from the Temple Lawn. When little Emma Garrick died in infancy, Eva-Maria mourned as if the child had been her own. Bell's happy match was a cause of unclouded satisfaction to her uncle. If she had never married, he might have been haunted by remorseful visitings. For he had nipped her first romance in the bud. The finishing school of Madame Descombes had been so aristocratic that when Louis XV died all the pupils had to go into court mourning. It was therefore a blow to her uncle to receive news from Madame Descombes that his niece had been carrying on a secret amour with a man old enough to be her father, whom she had, literally, picked up in the street. Worse must be admitted. M. de Molière, an officer in the Légion de Corse, had conducted his campaign from close quarters. He had actually taken a garret in the same house in the Rue Verte, Faubourg St Honoré, in which Madame Descombes kept her select *pension*. Madame was desired to set out for London instantly, bringing Bell and Kate, and while a voluble French lady told her tale of woe in the Adelphi, her pupils trembled in their father's house. (George could take no part. He was having one of his attacks—brought on by worry.) On hearing that they had offended their aunt and uncle by failing to appear, Bell wrote a most humble letter, signed " Your truly miserable but dutiful niece A. Garrick ". David asked for her story. Madame had brought with her an intercepted letter from de Molière addressed to Miss Garrick. It was a proposal in form. Madame had said that he had been showing letters from Bell and had said that the girl was violently in love with him. " Is he not near fifty and very plain? " David needed to know where his niece had made the acquaintance. Was it in society? Was he the person she had once mentioned as having known a friend of her uncle who had been upon a water-party from Hampton? Was it true that she would be unhappy without him? Bell's answer, in the most beautiful tiny Italian hand, was reassuring. " Was he everything that is amiable, and had a sceptre to offer me, and to crown all, *your* encouragement, I would not accept of him." The story she unfolded was certainly highly romantic. She would try to tell it clearly, but the effort she had made to forget the wretch might render it impossible for her to be as exact as she would wish. She had met him on the stairs of the *pension*, never anywhere else, except once, most unluckily, after she had seen him in his true colours. That had been in the public walks, and she had taken no notice of him. She had never met him at any place unknown to Madame, as Madame seemed to fear. She had never been in a room with him in her life. " He passed in the house for an

B B

officer who, having had an affair of honour, and having wounded his antagonist, was obliged to conceal himself. His person is not bad; he is tall and well made, and tho' you cannot absolutely call him ugly, can have no pretensions to beauty. I should give him about five or six and thirty years. As his door was generally open, he saw me go upstairs one morning and he gave me a letter, which, in my fright, I took, and put in my pocket." The contents of the letter had been thrilling. He was in the house because he had fallen in love with her. But Bell had acted, she hoped, properly. When she had next seen him she had run past fast, throwing his letter back to him. Two or three days later he had given her another. It told her his name and his regiment (which last she had forgotten), and offered full information for her guardians. He wanted to get leave and go over to England to see them. She had answered that her father and step-mother were coming over to fetch her home in about eight months. She had urged him to leave his garret " most humiliating for a gentleman ", and leave her in peace. Any further letters must have been intercepted by Madame.

David was satisfied. He had made his inquiries in Paris, and an acquaintance of Monnet, a M. Lancastre, who had written from an address in the Boulevard du Temple, had received a quietus for M. de Molière, " The proposal is as romantic as it is ruinous." M. de Molière, who declared that his first attempt should be to obtain the consent of her relatives, had endeavoured to gain the affection of a young English girl at school, without the least knowledge of her family or Madame Descombes. Was this the conduct of a man of honour and character? His colonel had spoken well of him, but his colonel had wisely hinted at the necessity of fortune's aiding the advance of a soldier, and M. Lancastre, on hearing that Miss Garrick's dependence was upon an uncle who had been the sole architect of his fortune, had taken the liberty of observing that " in that case he might be tenacious of the building ". David's last word was, he hoped, explicit. " As my consent is in a manner asked, I never *will* or *can* give it upon this occasion." Monnet had promised, if he could, to get back the letters. He thought de Molière's conduct " idiotic " and advised David to forget all about it. So he would, but his letter of forgiveness, and warning, to Bell, must be in his best tragic vein. She was a very pretty, innocent, perfectly truthful, simple young creature, with a rich, childless old uncle. 26

## 6

In the evening hours of a late July day of 1778 an empty carriage drove as quietly as possible out of the stableyard of Garrick's Villa.

Dr Percivall Pott lived in the heart of London, Lincoln's Inn Fields. But Dr Cadogan, the kindest of men, had a house at Hurlingham. Eva-Maria had acted on her own responsibility, and before dark the most outspoken of physicians was at the bedside of a personal friend who was somewhat surprised to see him. The patient had to write afterwards, in apology, to Miss Cadogan, to say that Mrs Garrick had been in a panic, and that nothing but her great fears could excuse her. He was up, and coming to London, and the Cadogans might expect, in a few days, to be visited by " Banquo's ghost, in his pale brown horror ". But Eva-Maria had been frightened by the sight of a man in agony, and this attack was not so lightly regarded by Pott, when he took charge. David still persisted in describing his complaint as " bilious ", and resented extremely being treated as an invalid for more than a month of an Elysian summer. It made him feel worse. He wrote to Craddock on September 14, from the Adelphi, to regret that he could not attend the first night of *The Czar*.

> I am like a state-prisoner, debarred the use of pen, ink and paper. I am going into Hampshire, for change of air, and thence, if I recover but slowly, to Bath; so that my stay there, or absence from town, will prevent for some time my even seeing a theatre.
>
> Indeed, Sir, I am growing unfit for anything, but sitting in a great chair, or walking (or rather, at present, creeping) about my garden. The least business agitates me, and my friends of the faculty have ordered me abstinence from all theatrical matters.
>
> I have not seen Sheridan but once, since the death of poor Linley, but he called yesterday, and I was out to take the air. I had promised to write him a little trifle for his opening but found myself so unfit for scribbling that, for the first time, I gave up the business, and was brought in (like the tars that are admitted into Greenwich Hospital) *disabled*.
>
> As I can only pray for you, be assured you shall have my prayers for your success. Should I be in town and able to attend the theatre, I will certainly be there.

27

His tour into Hampshire sounded a bold undertaking for an invalid. He never could resist a pageant, and intended taking " a peep at the Camp " on his way to three country houses. Most luckily, Lord Palmerston, to whom the Garricks had never yet been, wrote to ask them to take Broadlands first. For, when the appointed day came, Garrick was wrestling with a second " trembling cold fit ". However, he put off his start for a mere four days; and now he would be able to see an even better spectacle than he had expected, at the Camp. His Majesty was leaving London on September 28 to review all the troops stationed near Winchester. The Garricks found at Broadlands " a good host, a sweet place, and a warm

welcome ". The west front of the handsome, solid house overlooked stretches of the Test, the merriest of English rivers, with
banks haunted by so many and diverse wild-fowl that the vistas
laid out by " Capability " Brown were at once the gayest and most
soothing imaginable. Palmerston had lost his wife in child-bed,
ten years ago, and had not yet re-married. His taste for pictures
had developed on several further continental tours since the Garricks
had first met him, at Naples, and his collection was fine. Garrick
thought the company assembled witty, without malignity, and yet
neither satiating nor prudish. He wrote to Hannah:

> My dear Nine,
>     I have been half-dead, and thought I should have never seen you
> more. I took care of your property, and have shown my love to you by a
> trifling legacy—but that is at present deferred. . . .

It was deferred because he was " again growing fat, and over-
flowing with spirits "; but he had seen Albany Wallis before he left
London, and on Thursday, September 24, asked his host to witness
his Will, which he had brought with him. Lord Palmerston, and
two members of his house-party (of whom the gentleman was a
connection of Lady Spencer, and the lady a great crony of John
Hoadly), obliged him in the library. Four days later, Eva-Maria,
who had brought a new diary for their tour, entered:

> We went to dine with Dr Warton at Winchester; saw the illumina-
> tions.

After the king had seen the Camp, the whole royal party were
going to pay a visit to the cathedral, and at the College were to be
received *ad Portas*, with a Latin declamation, delivered by the senior
scholar.

Joseph Warton was, to put it mildly, the least practical of men.
John Hoadly, who had been Master of St Cross, so knew, had drawn
so dark a picture of the squalor in which his neighbour the Headmaster of Winchester abode, that no thinking person would willingly
expose himself to it. Hoadly's most trenchant criticisms had been
made while Warton was a resentful widower. He had re-married,
and added to the number of what Hoadly fiercely called " his good-
for-nothing sons ". Sir Joshua was to be a fellow guest. . . . The
Garricks had decided to stay at Wickham, and make expeditions to
Winchester.

On September 28 Winchester *en fête* presented a perfect Georgian
crowd-scene, calling for the pencil of the departed Hogarth. Floods
of early autumn sun poured down upon a famous city of narrow
streets and ancient buildings, and a landscape particularly suited

for a martial display on a large scale. The troops assembled on the Downs, one mile north east of the town, included the militia of West Kent, Gloucestershire, Lancashire, Staffordshire, Yorkshire and Wiltshire. Their Majesties, who had set out from Windsor about one o'clock, arrived at Eastgate House, rented by Mr Henry Penton, Member of Parliament for the city, about five. The villages along their route had been decorated with loyal messages, flowery garlands and greenery. Bells pealed, and large crowds cheered vociferously. The Mayor and Bailiffs waited upon them with an address, followed by the Dean, with the Warden and fellows, and the two masters of the College. As the date was the very end of September, it was possible to admire the illuminations in the town at a comparatively early hour. The College had surpassed itself in loyal attention. The treasured sixteenth-century painting of the Trusty Servant in the lobby outside the kitchen, had undergone an alteration in honour of the royal visit. He had been put into Windsor uniform.

Next morning, the Grand Review started at 9 a.m., and as the king passed by, he heard a spectator who had " casually alighted ", imploring, " A horse! a horse! " " That must be Garrick," said His Majesty. " See if he's on the ground." A very large number of people, including a sweet girl, a friend of the Misses More, watched Roscius being brought up to receive the compliment that his delivery of Shakespeare could never pass unnoticed. After the Review, royalty adjourned to dine in two of the many tents adorning the martial scene, but the Garricks returned to Wickham for a stay of two nights. Here David was, most disappointingly, taken ill, but the attack was slight, and passed in a couple of hours. On October 2 (the house-party from Park Place, West Wickham having preceded them by a day), the Garricks moved on to Paulton's, Hans Stanley's house. Garrick was very ill all that night, and had to stay in bed for two days, feverish. But on the 6th the indefatigable travellers were off again. They breakfasted with Dr Warton, and got to the Wilmots, at Farnborough Place, for dinner. They dined next day with Mr Lester, at Hall Grove, Bagshot, and arrived home at Hampton by seven. It was October 10.

Eva-Maria's diary carried on serenely. They spent a night with the Racketts, at Wandsworth. George and his clergyman son dined and went with them to the play. They sent the coach to bring all the George Garricks to tea. Guests were entertained at the Adelphi —M. Letexier, the French actor, Mr Vandergucht, at whose sale of pictures David had bought two Poussins. Callers included Lady Spencer and the Duchess of Devonshire, Mrs Home, Mrs Vesey, the Duchess of Portland. David rode out on a horse lent by Mr Rackett.

He furbished up a prologue for *The Invasion*, and staying on late at Drury Lane after the audience had left one night, to see the effect of the scenery for a topical piece, *The Camp*, caught a very severe cold. (Loutherbourg was amongst the staff who had not stayed at Drury Lane under the new management, and Sheridan had needed an expert opinion.)

Towards the end of November came a letter in a feigned hand, but of a sickeningly familiar type:

> Plume yourself, Sir, on being sufficiently important to engage so amply even the generous *severity* of *Curtius*. The public have hitherto seen you only in the polished mirror of a parasite's adulation. The exact reflection will astonish. Garrick's nature must be humbled to the dust.

It had always been his experience that answering such people reasonably produced the desired result. He replied to Curtius (who offered to send him copies of three letters to be published) with indeed astonishing mildness. Only his final paragraph showed spirit, " I will likewise assure you, that the *horrid timidity* you accuse me of will not be the least alarmed, though the pen of Curtius was to drop its gall to-morrow." His tormentor replied, after five weeks, that when he had leisure, he would re-devote himself to Roscius. 29

As the winter drew on, Garrick appeared more often at The Club. Eva-Maria, on nights when he dined out, sent a coach to fetch Miss Cadogan, to bear her company at the Adelphi, bidding her friend to bring her sewing. On December 12, Eva-Maria had drama to report—" Poor Isaac fell under the coach," and next day came startling news that Bell was brought to bed of a son. She had believed that she was to become a mother in the coach, on her way back from seeing her doctor in Guildford. But after a whole night of labour she had produced a seven-months child. Captain Brydges Schaw excelled himself in attentions. He asked her uncle to attend the christening, and name the day, and child. He had just attained his majority, and his colonel, Lord Onslow, would be the other sponsor. On December 16 David dined with Rigby, and went to 30 Westminster Play. On the 30th the Garricks set off for New Year at Althorp. Lady Spencer had written to say that the ladies of the house-party were all ordering from a certain mercer in the City a scarlet-and-white silk, so that they would appear in a sort of uniform. She offered, as usual, that the Garricks should break their journey, if they wished, at Lord Spencer's St Albans house. David knew it well. It was, like their Wimbledon house, full of memories of the builder, Sarah, Duchess of Marlborough; and above a mantelpiece hung a very flattering portrait of that redoubtable lady. The house-keeper at Holywell, if she got a line by post the night before, would have all ready for them, beds aired and dinner waiting. The Garricks chose to dine only, and travel through the night—sixty-six miles—sixteen hours. An actor-manager had always seen to it that his horses were young and his coach was well built. He was accustomed to sleep in it, and could always do so, except over roads which were, like himself, too old. They left the Adelphi at 9.45 a.m. and were at St Albans by 1.30. Mrs Maitland, "a civil prating dame" devoted to her employers, saw them off again at 3.15. They were at Dunstable by 9 p.m., Newport Pagnell before 11. Eva-Maria wrote it all down, though the journey was as familiar as the kind house to which they were going.

It grieved Garrick much that tongues were so busy with the young Duchess of Devonshire. Jealousy was doubtless the reason, for her only faults seemed to be those natural to youth and in-experience. Natural was the word for her. He had often used it to endorse letters from her mother. "Lady Spencer always natural!", "Lady Spencer's letter from Althorp. Nature for ever!"

Of course, as the duchess was not breeding, and was sad about it, she was searching a little wildly for gaiety. He had himself sent her a copy of verses, "Sonnet, left on the Duchess of Devonshire's breakfast-table, in consequence of calling on her Grace at noon, and finding she had not left her Chamber." He had taken what measures he could to stop talk about her high play. He had written on his return from his first visit to Chatsworth, to one of the biggest talkers in London, the editor of the old *Morning Post*.

Her Grace of Devonshire is a most inchanting Exquisite beautiful young Creature. Were I five and twenty, I would go mad about her. As I am past five and fifty, I would only suffer Martyrdom for her. She is no Gamester, my friend, nor was there ever any gaming at Chatsworth.

That had been three years ago. . . . It seemed that she was now playing high. . . . Her mother had another constant cause for anxiety—Lord Spencer's health. After two operations he was increasingly deaf. He had silver ear-trumpets, specially designed. The Spencers had to go abroad for his cure at Spa every season now.

After a breakfast at their last halt on the road, the Garricks' coach turned in at the gates of Althorp at 2.30 a.m. The invalid had stood the journey well, and was in the best of spirits next day. They were indeed wise to have travelled without a break. That New Year's Eve was to make history. "31st of this month," wrote Eva-Maria, "was the greatest high wind that was ever felt." Next morning tales of disaster came in to the press from all over England. A friend took the trouble to go down to the Adelphi and take a look at Adam's proud structure, so new, so lofty. He could assure David that not a brick or tile was missing from Number 5. But the howling winds had surpassed anything produced at Drury Lane for Lear.

The Garricks had arrived in the small hours of Thursday. On Sunday morning, Eva-Maria's diary began to take a serious turn. " My husband was still not well enough to dine at table." The Spencers' local physician was summoned. Dr William Kerr of Northampton diagnosed shingles, a malady by no means uncommon, but attended by much inconvenience, and denoting a low state of the constitution. His prescriptions were followed, and did much service. On Saturday David went downstairs before and after dinner for an hour. Next day he was not so well. Eva-Maria alone passed down the dark oak great staircase to dine. That night his pain became great, and familiar, but in the other—right-hand—side, and worse than ever before. He was clearly very ill, and would be better under his own roof than in a house full of a large gay party.

Becket, to whom he had written, since he was taken ill, wished that he was back in his own great chair, in the Adelphi. But even if he had been well enough to travel, there was now a disobliging circumstance. A hard frost had set in on New Year's Day. Every variety of bad winter weather followed, including fog. On the 13th, at last, came a moist day, a gentle thaw. The Garricks set out for home next day, in sunshine, but a snowstorm. It was the worst journey of their lives. They left Althorp at 11 and were at Dunstable in five hours, but after dark. David had " his pain all the way " and took remedies when they halted, for the night, and on the road. Laudanum seemed to help him. They got in to the Adelphi at 4 p.m. on Friday, 15th.

He had known he would feel better when he was home. He rose next morning, and when Mr Lawrence, his apothecary, arrived, he found him up and shaving. John O'Keefe, the Dublin playwright, saw Roscius for the last time " walking very quick (his way) " up and down the Adelphi terrace. But next morning Dr Cadogan, summoned by Lawrence, told the patient, with his usual frankness, that " his disorder was so uncertain in its progress that if he had any worldly affairs to settle it would be prudent to despatch them ". The reply was resolute, " Nothing of that sort lay on his mind, and he was not afraid to die."

News of his illness had penetrated to many quarters. Amongst the pile of letters awaiting him had been one from Curtius. Nothing would be passed to the press until Curtius had heard again from Mr Garrick, " or at least until he understands that gentleman is in a state of body to *answer* public charges ". That letter was laid aside, never to be answered by Garrick.

Johnson, although fed by Mrs Thrale with gloomy bulletins, muttered that Davy was not as ill as folk said. Dr Heberden was called in, and advised no more physic, but to continue the hot baths. Dr Warren followed. Gradually, every eminent member of the profession in town was voluntarily at the bedside of Roscius, who was sinking into a coma. He looked at them, uncomprehending, and quoted a couplet from *The Fair Penitent*:

> Another, and another still succeeds;
> And the last fool is welcome as the former.

He knew Schomberg, and taking him by the hand, said with a smile, " Though last, not least in love."

His last appearance was tragic. Mr Rackett had called, and Eva-Maria asked him to stay and dine with her. While they were talking, suddenly the invalid appeared, wrapped in a rich dressing-gown such as he had worn when playing Lusignan, the old king of Jerusalem. He sat down, and stayed for about an hour, but without uttering a word. After he had risen, and gone back to his chamber, Rackett waited to dine alone with Eva-Maria. He thought it might help her, for she seemed absolutely ill after her nights of watching.

There were intervals in which the sinking man recognized people. He said to the servant who brought him his medicine, " Well, Tom, I shall do very well yet, and make amends to you for all this trouble." Lawrence listened while he alluded with clarity to a great grief. " He did not regret his being childless; for he knew the quickness of his feeling was so great that, in case it had been his misfortune to have had disobedient children, he could not have supported such an affliction."

The Spencers had returned to London, and Eva-Maria's journal noted, " Lady Spencer came ", every day. On Thursday, January 20, a moist, foggy morning, she made her last entry as a wife.

" At a quarter before eight, my Husband sighed, and Died without one uneasy moment, the Lord be Praised."

On February 1 she wrote, " My Dear Husband was Buryed at Westminster Abbey ", and on February 3, " I came home in the evening. Lay in the dear bed in which my Dear husband dyed."

32

# EPILOGUE

By ten o'clock on the morning of Monday, February 1, 1779, streets all along the route from Adelphi Terrace to Westminster Abbey were filling fast, and by quarter past one, when the *cortège* set out, even house-tops were thronged, and there were so many spectators in carriages that a complete traffic block resulted. Big crowds had been foreseen, and a detachment of military cavalry cleared a passage, and was ready to keep order, but it was remarked that the onlookers who had gathered to see Garrick take his last journey gave, by their mournful silence and good behaviour, the most evident demonstration of their woe.

The day was very fine and mild. The tolling of the bells of St Martin's and the Abbey " smote upon the very soul " of Hannah More, cowering in a hackney-coach with Miss Cadogan. There were multitudes striving for admittance at the cloister entrance, and she supposed that no man in England had ever had so many particular friends.

It was the most magnificent funeral that London had ever witnessed. The head of the procession arrived outside the Abbey after about an hour, but another hour passed before fifty mourning coaches had discharged their distinguished occupants, and the Dean and Chapter advanced to meet the coffin, to the strains of Purcell's anthem. The list of pall-bearers looked impressive; all were in fact close friends—Lord Camden, Earl of Ossory, Right Hon. Richard Rigby, Hon. Hans Stanley, Duke of Devonshire, Earl Spencer, Viscount Palmerston, Sir Watkin Williams Wynn, John Paterson Esq., Albany Wallis Esq. Sheridan, with two attendants bearing up his black velvet train, was chief mourner. From Drury Lane had come the Treasurer, Housekeeper, Book-keeper and Carpenter, and a dozen " gentlemen of the theatre ", including King, Smith, Moody, Palmer, Baddeley and an Aickin. Covent Garden list of twelve also showed an Aicken. There were six coaches filled with Gentlemen of the Literary Club, and eleven simply styled " intimate friends ". Garrick's family was represented by three nephews, and one niece's husband. The Bishop of Rochester read the service, in a very low voice. As the coffin was lowered under the pavement of Poets' Corner, at the foot of Shakespeare's monument, the sobs of Burke broke the silence, and Cumberland noticed " old Samuel Johnson " bathed in tears. All the long way to the Abbey he had talked of his lost friend, to Dr Percy, Mr Dunning and the Dean of Ferns. A few days later he left at the Adelphi a stately card presenting " respectful condolences to Mrs Garrick and wishes that any endeavour of his could enable her to support a loss which the world cannot repair ". His best tribute to his old pupil was to appear in his next published work. " I am disappointed by that stroke of death which has eclipsed the gaiety of nations, and impoverished the public stock of harmless pleasure."

Sheridan produced a Monody, spoken by Mrs Yates at Drury Lane, which opened promisingly:

> If dying excellence deserves a tear,
> If fond remembrance still is cherished here . . .

It was left to Henderson to break into an Impromptu, ridiculing the pompous funeral, which he identified as a second Drury Lane *Jubilee*. His lines were in execrable taste, but he certainly was unlucky in that, by the time they appeared, George, whom he had represented being sent at the run by Roscius to ransack the theatrical costumiers for blacks, " moth and all " and even darker blues, had also died. George had always been regarded by the company as a slightly comic character. His panting inquiry, " Is David needing me? " was too well known. When it was learned that he had followed his famous brother, two days after the Westminster Abbey ceremony, Cumberland suggested, not unsympathetically, " David needed him ". Accounts of George's funeral, at Hendon, said that Mr Peter Garrick, the last surviving brother of the family, had died on his road from Lichfield. But Peter, who had had a stroke, survived for another fifteen years.

The Angelos had taken the widow to their house while the undertakers came in, and the Adelphi was hung with black for the lying-in-state which preceded the funeral. Hannah More, who had come up from Bristol voluntarily, arrived at the Cadogans to hear that Mrs Garrick was at that moment quitting the house of mourning. They eventually met at the Racketts. " She ran into my arms, and we both remained silent for some minutes; at last she whispered ' I have this moment embraced his coffin, and you come next '." She soon recovered herself to add with great composure that she had desired to die, but that as it was not the will of God, she was convinced that she was not to be quite miserable. Astonishing strength had been given to her body, and grace to her heart.

There was a painful incident when the carriage bringing Mrs Garrick and Hannah arrived at Hampton. The dog, Dragon, ran

up to meet his master.   Eva-Maria went to her own room and shut
herself up for half an hour.   When Hannah expressed her surprise
at her self command, she replied, " Groans and complaints are very
well for those who are to mourn but a little while; but a sorrow
which is to last for life will not be violent and romantic."   It was to
last for forty-three years.                                                                    *1*

Hannah stayed with her until June, and Kitty Clive, who had
sent a truly beautiful letter of appreciation of her old manager,
commented with asperity that Miss More was being very careful of
Mrs Garrick.   But Clive was not to be baffled.   She wrote to Mrs
Rackett, also a much older friend, and asked her to discover if her
letter had penetrated.   She sent a copy.                                          *2*

Hannah had always particularly approved that at Garrick's
table she had never, but once, met " a person of his own profession ".
This must have meant considerable planning, for he liked nothing
more than entertaining his company, especially the beginners.
Hannah had brought up with her to London her second play, four
acts of which Garrick had seen.   Mr. Harris, at Covent Garden,
insisted on bringing it out at once.   *Fatal Falsehood* was received
with great applause but did not run.   This was the end of her career
as a playwright.   But she was to have great success with her
Tracts.

Garrick had died, announced *The Gentleman's Magazine*, " immensely rich ".   He had left a fortune calculated at nearly one
hundred thousand pounds.   He had appointed as executors Lord
Camden, Rigby, Paterson and Albany Wallis, all men of business.
But when Johnson went down to Lichfield, three years later, he
reported that the legatees had not yet received anything; and
Ireland, the undertaker, whose name had appeared in very large
type on the elegant invitation cards for the funeral, sent out by the
executors, went bankrupt while awaiting settlement of his bill of
one thousand five hundred pounds.   Cradock believed that shortly
before his death, Garrick had lost a large sum in a West Indies
investment.   Joseph Farington, R.A., who heard the gossip of the
artistic world, had something surprising to add in December 1793.
" Garrick made a will very much exceeding his real fortune.   In
estimating the value of some of his property he added all he might
have laid out upon it to the first expense, and reckoned the whole
together.   His property might be about £50,000, and he reckoned it
at more than £100,000."                                                                    *3*

Lady Sarah Lennox felt deep sympathy for Mrs Garrick, not
only because she believed her to have been in love with her husband.
By the terms of the will, two-thirds of her income must be appro-

priated to keeping up the houses at the Adelphi and Hampton, both of which were " so compleat that she has not a chair or table to amuse herself with altering ". The two houses, with all their contents, had been left to the widow for life and a legacy of six thousand pounds. Only an annuity of one thousand five hundred pounds was to be continued if she remarried. It was the Testator's request and desire that she should continue to live in England, and if she should reside abroad, or in Scotland or Ireland, she forfeited all except an annuity of one thousand pounds per annum. After her death Roubillac's statue of Shakespeare was to go to the British Museum, to which also he bequeathed his large collection of old English plays. He gave the houses in Drury Lane which he had bought for the fund for decayed actors of that theatre, back to that fund. Nephews and nieces were remembered very amply. David, junior, was given five thousand pounds, and the house at Hampton which he was occupying, and the Reverend Carrington six thousand pounds and all books, except those up to the value of one hundred pounds which the widow might choose. Arabella Shaw and Catherine Garrick also received six thousand pounds apiece, and Elizabeth Fürst, Mrs Garrick's niece, one thousand pounds. In the older generation, brother Peter and sister Merriel each got three thousand pounds, and poor George ten thousand pounds.

When a year had passed and nothing had been done about a monument to Garrick in Westminster Abbey, there was criticism of the widow. Albany Wallis eventually provided one. It was understood that Mrs Garrick had made herself responsible for one at Lich-
4 field, on which was to be engraved Johnson's famous tribute. When Sir Joshua died, thirteen years after Garrick, leaving a fortune certainly exceeding one hundred and forty thousand pounds, his niece, his principal heiress, held out firmly against erecting a monument which should, she was advised, be the result of a national subscription. Kent's Shakespeare monument at the base of which Garrick had been laid, had been the result of coffee-house and general subscriptions in 1740.

Lady Sarah had prophesied that she foresaw no future for
5 Garrick's widow except " to vegetate ", and Hannah More's descriptions of visits to her during the next two years fully bore this out. In January 1780, arriving to spend the anniversary of " the fatal twentieth ", she found her friend " more of a recluse than ever, and with quite a horror at the thought of mixing in the world again. . . . I fancy, indeed, she will never go much into it. Her garden and her family amuse her; but the idea of company is death to her. . . . We dress like a couple of Scaramouches, dispute like a couple of Jesuits,

eat like a couple of aldermen, and read as much as any two doctors of either university."

Yet, Mrs Garrick always seemed cheerful, especially in company. She spent so very few hours in her bed that Hannah, who was not strong, could not imagine how she could be so active, both in mind and body. She had flashes of her old gaiety. "Mrs Garrick gave me an elegant cap, and put it on herself, so that I was sure of being smart." With the spring the ladies walked out four or five miles to the neighbouring villages and had the coach back.

Hannah paid calls on all the élite of London, "for Mrs Garrick and for myself". The gentlemen of the Museum came to remove poor Mr Garrick's legacy of the old plays and curious black-letter books. Hannah, who was not a scholar, decided that "though they were not things to be read, and are only valuable to antiquaries for their age and scarcity", yet she could hardly see them carried off without a pang. Eva-Maria had found herself quite unable to part with the library, left to Carrington. She offered to buy it from him, and he accepted. She would leave to his son, the Greek and Latin classics, and the Italian books.

Her year of mourning being "out" she sent out her cards of thanks for condolences. There were about seven hundred; Hannah doubted if she would ever let six hundred of the recipients into her house again. 1781 opened as sadly. "As to poor Mrs Garrick, she keeps herself as secret as a piece of smuggled goods, and neither stirs herself out, or lets anybody in. The calm of Hampton is such fixed repose that an old woman crying fish, or the postman ringing at the door, is an event which excites attention." Soon it was even more quiet. Hampton was in a snow-scene. The greenhouse, full of beautiful blossoms and oranges, looked like some region of enchantment. The ladies devoted themselves to "reading over all the private letters of the dear deceased master of this melancholy mansion". "Poor Mrs G" said that she intended always to spend the anniversaries of her wedding and her loss with her husband's tomb, in the Abbey.

With the second spring, however, she showed signs of life. She accepted an invitation to dine with Bishop Shipley, to meet a small and very choice party. Her fellow guests were the Spencers and their son and his bride, Sir Joshua, Bennet Langton, Gibbon, Dr Johnson (an agreeable surprise for Hannah) and Boswell. To Hannah's disgust, Mr Boswell, when he reappeared at the tea-table after dinner, was disordered with wine, "and addressed me in a manner which drew from me a sharp rebuke, for which I fancy he will not easily forgive me ". Johnson came to call at the Adelphi next morning, and when Garrick's widow told him that she always felt more at her ease with persons who had suffered the same loss as herself, he replied " that was a comfort she could seldom have, considering the superiority of his merit and the cordiality of their union ". On April 20 Boswell had one of the happiest days of his life. He was asked to dine by Mrs Garrick. " The company was Miss Hannah More who lived with her, and whom she called her Chaplain, Mrs Boscawen, Mrs Elizabeth Carter, Sir Joshua Reynolds, Dr Burney, Dr Johnson, and myself. We found ourselves very elegantly entertained at her house in the Adelphi where I have passed many a pleasing hour with him ' who gladdened life '. She looked well, talked of her husband with complacency, and while she cast her eyes on his portrait which hung over the chimney-piece, said that ' death was now the most agreeable object to her ' ". For his part, Boswell found " the very semblance of David Garrick was cheering ". " We were all in fine spirits; and I whispered to Mrs Boscawen, ' I believe this is as much as can be made of life '." Johnson refused, but Dr Burney and Sir Joshua cordially partook with Boswell of a vaunted Lichfield ale. Boswell found, when faced with the task of recalling the conversation of a day which he remembered most fondly, that he had not recorded much. He left with Johnson, and they stopped a little while by the rails of the Adelphi, looking on the river, and thinking of the two friends who had lived in the buildings behind them—Topham Beauclerk and Garrick. " Ay sir," said Johnson tenderly, " and two such friends as cannot be supplied."

Horace Walpole met Mrs Garrick next year in the Blue-Stocking section of society. She looked serene and well, was well dressed, spoke very little and was paid great attention by all present. Particular attentions, with a view to marriage, were being paid to her, this season, and she twice refused Lord Monboddo, a Scottish judge, two or three years her late husband's senior, a widower, with two daughters. Lord Monboddo was temperate in his habits, but eccentric. He always rode down from Scotland, on horseback, accompanied by a single groom, because the ancients had not commonly used so effeminate an engine as a carriage. Sir William Pepys was sadly struck when Mrs Garrick took him to the stables at Hampton to see " the dear horse " and to ask his opinion. Ought she to get it a companion? But she remained single.

As the novelty of her reappearances wore off, stories of Garrick's widow grew rarer. Horace Walpole called at the Hampton villa one day in 1795, and was quite surprised to be let in. Mrs Garrick told him that she had with her " a hundred head of nieces ", and he did indeed find her parlour crowded. There was a stout dame who addressed her repeatedly, with great unction, as aunt. (This must have been Merrial Paton, née Docksey.)

A profuse source of information failed, as the years passed. Mrs Garrick, a continental by birth, and a Catholic, liked to go to her Mass in London at the church in Golden Square, early on Sunday mornings, and after that, enjoy seeing her friends. Sunday was for her the gayest day in the week. Hannah's Sunday had always been strictly observed, and by 1787 she had found that she could not, as a Christian, enter a playhouse. She refused to witness Mrs Siddons in a revival of *Percy*. Mrs Garrick had begun to go to the play again regularly. Her figure in her own box at Drury Lane was a familiar sight on all important occasions, and she was most kindly received. She presented Kean with a malacca cane, which had belonged to Roscius. She approved his Richard, but her criticism of his performance in one of Garrick's most famous comedy parts became a favourite anecdote in the green-room.

Dear Sir,
    You cannot act Abel Drugger,
                                        Yours M. Garrick.

Madam,
    I know it,
                                        Yours E. Kean.

The Garricks had early realized that their nephews were no eagles. David, junior, was a pleasant companion and neighbour. He died, prematurely, in 1795, leaving no issue, and his young widow remarried and left Hampton. The Rev. Carrington Garrick of Hendon, had predeceased him by six years, " a martyr " according to Cradock to " a too free use of the bottle ". He had married a parishioner, and left an infant son. But there was nobody of the name left in Lichfield, except old Peter, within two years of the death of David Garrick. Peter, a bachelor to the last, and living on alone in the old family house, ended as a source of nothing but anxiety. He had become childish. After his death, his sister, Mrs Docksey, who had been named heiress in an earlier will, to a fortune believed to amount to thirty thousand pounds, contested successfully a will drawn up by an attorney called Panting, in favour of the apothecary who had attended the late Mr Peter Garrick. He had also been called Panting, and proved to be the brother of Mr Peter Garrick's attorney.

In 1807 Mrs Garrick's advisers instituted legal proceedings in

Chancery, relating to her late husband's estate. She claimed, under the residuary clause in his will, a share of the sum to be divided amongst his next of kin. Her claim was rejected, and within the next eight years she had distributed amongst her Viennese relations, as much as twelve thousand pounds.

There was a popular story that when Queen Charlotte called at Hampton she found Mrs Garrick peeling onions. She had only one maid now. Her Majesty had asked for an apron, and soon there was a fine flow of German to be heard in Mrs Garrick's kitchen. Her carriage—very shabby now—was often to be seen entering the Royal Parks, for which she had a plaque of admittance. King George IV and his successor both paid their respects at Garrick's Villa. Kensington Gardens was one of her favourite expeditions.

In the year of Queen Victoria's birth, the fashionable caricaturist Cruikshank published a likeness of an immensely old lady, inscribed " Mrs Garrick, taken September 1820, Aetat 97 ". The figure represented, wearing an enormous black bonnet, and bearing a large flat black muff, had nut-cracker features, but eyes still sparkling with intelligence. She was kindly remembered by Dean Stanley in his *Westminster Memorials* as " a little bowed-down old woman, who went about leaning on a gold-headed cane, dressed in deep widow's mourning, and always talking of her dear Davy ".

Mr. Smith of the British Museum had a pleasant morning in August 1821 with her in the Print Room when she came to examine and comment upon the collection of playbills and engravings relating to her husband left to the Museum by Dr Burney. Smith went to the Adelphi on hearing of her sudden passing on October 16 of the following year, to inquire if the day had been fixed for the funeral. From the staff, he picked up all the gossip. Mr Elliston had been redecorating Drury Lane and had invited her to come on the night of the 16th for a private view of the improvements. She had ordered her maids to lay out two or three gowns in the front drawing-room, overlooking the river, so that she could ponder upon them while taking her tea in her arm-chair. " I was informed that one of these attentive women had incurred her mistress's displeasure by kindly pouring out a cup of tea, and handing it to her in her chair. ' Put it down, you hussey, do you think I cannot help myself? ' She took it herself, and a short time after she had put it to her lips, died." Smith was asked, " Would you like to see her? She is in her coffin? " He very much wanted to make a sketch of her, and have it etched, so he accepted with alacrity. He was ushered into the back-room on the first floor. " Pray, do tell me," he asked one of the maids, " why is the coffin covered with sheets? "

" They are their wedding sheets, in which both Mr and Mrs Garrick wished to have died."                9

2

On April 15, 1830, a correspondent signing himself " Vindicator " sent an indignant letter to the Editor of *The Times*.  He wished to correct statements in an article which had appeared in yesterday's issue, giving an unamiable view of the late Mrs Garrick.  It was not true that at the time of her death she had been living at Hampton in unimaginable squalor, in a single attic, attended by one under-paid local woman.  She did keep only one maid at the villa, and had left her one thousand pounds in her will; but she had there also, two gardeners, and at the Adelphi two maids, a footman and a coachman.  The furniture at the villa might well have been old, but hardly to be described as " unworthy of a common tavern of the present day."  Her husband had chosen and delighted in it.  It was not true that a dish of tea was the usual extent of her hospitality, and that although she had continually complained about the in-adequacy of her income, she had left nearly seventy thousand pounds.  She had entertained friends at the Adelphi to the last, and had not left even a tenth part of that sum.  " She was frugal, she was just, she was kind-hearted, and lived and died a pattern to wives, an ornament to her sex; and long will her memory be cherished by those who had the happiness to know her."

The Reverend Thomas Rackett, Rector of Spettisbury, Dorset, one of her executors, had, at the age of fifteen recited the Jubilee Ode to its author.  He had known Garrick.  Yet, when Smith of the British Museum paid a visit to Hampton in the previous year, Mrs Garrick's solicitor, and his wife, who were now occupying the villa, had mentioned that they had arrived only just in time to keep the roof from falling in. . . . Albany Wallis had been a sad man, with a boding countenance.  Drury Lane finances had been in a chaotic state under Sheridan's management.  Garrick's wife had never been encouraged to interest herself in her husband's larger financial operations.  It seems very possible that from the moment of his death she had believed herself to be trembling on the brink of ruin, and this was not an obsession likely to diminish with increasing years.

Smith was uncommonly lucky in his visit to Hampton.  He had ventured to pull the bell at Garrick's Villa, just to ask if he might see the Temple, which had once contained the statue of Shakespeare now in his Museum.  He not only saw everything in the house; a tremendous storm was coming up; he got his dinner.  The Carrs and

Smiths (for Mrs Smith had come too) pattered upstairs and down, while thunder cracked and lightning flashed. The place was a perfect Garrick Museum. " This is the drawing-room, the decorated paper is just as it was in Mr Garrick's time. . . . Now you shall see our best bed-room. . . . We will now go to Mr and Mrs Garrick's bed-room." On one side of the dining-room chimney piece hung a half-length of a serenely smiling girl, holding a mask in her right hand—Mrs. Garrick, before her marriage. " That mulberry-tree was a sucker from Shakespeare's tree at Stratford; that tulip-tree was one of her planting, and so was the cedar." " Your grounds are beautiful," observed Mrs Smith. But torrential rain was now lashing the windows. It was impossible to see the Temple in such a storm. After dinner they returned to the bow-room and were told that they were sitting on the very sofa, with the very cover, frequently used by Dr Johnson. " Now," said Mrs Carr, " I will show you my Garrick jewels." The first treasure produced was a miniature, set in brilliants. Smith would not have recognized it, though he knew, of course, whom it must represent. For, when he was nine, his father had taken him to a performance of *The Alchymist*, and it was often his delight to startle all occupants of a stage-coach into respectful exclamations of " Indeed, sir! " when he casually
10 mentioned that he had once seen Garrick.

# NOTES

## CHAPTER I

### " FIRST THE INFANT "

1. *The London Gazette*, No. 5514. Tuesday February 19–Saturday February 23, 1717.

2. Charles Mathews (1776–1835), actor, who claimed to have been dandled by Garrick as a child, was struck by the picturesqueness of the Angel when staying in Hereford, and remarked in histrionic style, " Altogether Mr. Garrick *ought* to have been born here ". " To be sure he ought, sir," replied the attendant waiter. " I am glad to hear you say that. It was too bad of his father to go to Hereford when his wife was so near her time; but we claim him, for all that."

3. The author wishes to thank Mr J. F. W. Sherwood, City Librarian and Curator, Hereford, for information and a photograph of an old engraving of the Angel Inn. The Angel, after a devastating fire, ceased to function as an inn towards the close of the eighteenth century, but visitors to Hereford were shown a jeweller's shop and an oak room as the birthplace of Garrick. To-day a plaque on the present Raven Hotel states that Garrick was born on this spot.

4. The dates of David Garrick's birth and baptism have been very generally mis-stated. Until 1752, when the Gregorian Calendar was established in England and Scotland, years began on March 25. Garrick was born on February 19, 1717, according to modern reckoning, but 1716 according to the practice followed at the date of his birth. He himself wrote down February 19, 1716, when sending a list of the family's birthdays to his father. His first biographers, Thomas Davies and Arthur Murphy, gave February 20 for his baptism and All Souls Church. James Boaden pointed out Murphy's error, but gave February 20, 1716, as date of birth. Percy Fitzgerald gave February 19, 1716. Of later biographers, Joseph Knight and Adolphus Ward and Robert Carruthers realized the problem, and gave 1716/17, but Frank Hedgcock, writing in 1912, still gave 1716. Margaret Barton in 1948 got it right. (*Memoirs of the Life of David Garrick*, Thomas Davies, 2 vols., 1780; *The Life of David Garrick, Esq.*, Arthur Murphy, 2 vols., 1801; *The Private Correspondence of David Garrick*, edited James Boaden, 2 vols., 1831; Forster Collection, Victoria and Albert Museum; *The Life of David Garrick*, Percy Fitzgerald, 1899 edition; *David Garrick*, Joseph Knight, 1894; *David Garrick and His French Friends*, Frank Hedgcock, 1912; *Garrick*, Margaret Barton, 1948—hereafter cited as Davis, Murphy, Forster, Boaden, Fitzgerald, Knight, Hedgcock, Barton.) Quotations from the Forster Collection printed by Boaden are cited as " Forster, Boaden ". Those which do not appear in Boaden as " Forster, Garrick ".

5. Henri IV, by the Edict of Nantes in 1598, granted the Protestants of France free exercise of their religion, and the rights and privileges of which they had been deprived after the Massacre of St Bartholomew's day; but he was unable or unwilling to repress occasional outbursts of persecution, and

since they were still excluded from all public offices they turned their talents principally to commerce. They were industrious and enterprising, gained a high reputation for honesty, and became a wealthy and flourishing part of the population. In 1685, the year of Peter Garric's flight, Louis XIV, encouraged by some of his advisers, particularly his confessor and Madame de Maintenon, decided to resort to violence to compel the Huguenots to abjure their faith. He had been persuaded that so meritorious an action would enhance his glory and atone for his iniquities. Bodily ills and the fear of approaching death drove him to ferocity. The Huguenots saw their places of worship razed to the ground, their pastors put to ignominious death, their children seized and their possessions confiscated. Attempts to leave the country were punished with torture, transportation, the galleys or death. The Garrics' experiences were not unusual. The family of the Chevalier de Champagne, who, like the Courtaulds, came from the Saintonge, escaped in relays, in small vessels, hidden in wine-casks in the hold, and were not discovered, although one of the ships was searched while lying at anchor off the French coast.

*Protestant exiles from France in the reign of Louis XIV; or the Huguenot refugees and their descendants in Great Britain and Ireland*, Rev. David Agnew, London 1871, Vol. II, 125, 167–70, 230, 312; hereafter cited as Agnew.

6. The Journal of the first David Garric (*sic*) is a single MS. sheet, written closely on both sides, in the collection of MSS. bequeathed to the Corporation of King's Heralds' and Pursuivants of Arms by James Pulman, Clarenceux King of Arms, under a codicil to his will, dated March 29, 1858 (Pulman 63, V. ff 412–425). The owner added several Garrick pedigrees and odd notes about the family, but no details about the ancestors of David Garrick I. The Journal is printed by Agnew, 284–285.

7. Peter Fermignac believed this child, whose name occurs at a place where the manuscript is torn, to have been another Stephen, but the record of his baptism at L'Eglise de Londres, Threadneedle St. shows that he was Jean. *Publications of the Huguenot Society of London* XVI. 93.

8. Letter addressed to Christopher, First Viscount Hatton (1611–1704). Addit. MSS. B.M. 29,548,596.

9. The author wishes to thank Mr W. Verco, Rouge Croix Pursuivant, for information about Garrick's coat of arms. It does not appear from records at the Heralds' College that Garrick registered officially any account of his family genealogy, or established his right to arms. The arms of which there are large coloured sketches in Colonel Solly's collection of Garrick relics are:

(1) Per pale or and azure, on the dexter a tower gules and on the sinister on a mount vert a sea horse argent mane, fins and tail of the first of a chief gold three mullets of the second. Crest—a mullet or, (2) As before, impaling a stag gules, rampant, on a field or.

These arms do not appear on Garrick's silver in Colonel Solly's collection, but are on the pewter, possessed by the Stratford-upon-Avon Memorial Theatre Museum.

10. Captain Peter Garrick's military career is somewhat difficult to trace. He was on half-pay 1718, probably on the disbandment of Tyrrell's Dragoons. On the augmentation of a company to Kirke's Regiment of Foot (later the 2nd Queen's) in 1726, he was promoted Captain. He does not appear to have held a commission in any other regiments than Bradshaigh's Foot, Tyrrell's Dragoons and Kirke's.

11. David Garrick's letters to his father are in volume XXXVII of the Garrick Correspondence, Forster Collection, Victoria and Albert Museum, 1–18, and are here reproduced without alteration except of punctuation and spelling of proper names in which the writer was inconsistent. Boaden printed none of this series. Forster himself in the second (1877) edition of his *Life and Times of Oliver Goldsmith*, quoted (226–227) from several. Knight quoted more profusely, and Fitzgerald, as Hedgcock points out, quotes inaccurately. Professor David Mason Little printed all, with notes, for the first time, in 1930.

12. Samuel Johnson suffered in infancy from infected eyes and a tubercular infection of the lymphatic glands of the neck, then called scrofula or the King's Evil. He told Mrs Thrale, in later life, of his having been taken at the age of thirty months, by his mother, to London, to be " touched " by Queen Anne, and retaining a sort of confused recollection of " a lady in diamonds and a long black hood ". An attack of smallpox marked him further, and his latest biographer, Professor J. S. Clifford, considers it difficult to judge how much of his facial disfigurement was the result of scrofula and how much from other causes. *The Young Samuel Johnson*, Professor J. S. Clifford, 1955 (hereafter cited as Clifford), provides, particularly in chapters two, six and nine, information invaluable to biographers of Garrick; for the lexicographer and actor were less than nine years apart in age, and resided in youth in the same town. There is a map of Lichfield in Johnson's (and Garrick's) time as end papers in the book.

13. The Bishop's Palace, Lichfield, is the subject of an illustrated article in *Country Life* for December 30, 1954. Professor Clifford (Clifford, 8) identifies the north withdrawing-room as the room in which *The Recruiting Officer* was produced. The Palace is now occupied by St Chad's Cathedral School.

14. Davies, I, 6, 7.

15. Mrs Garrick's note accompanying David's second letter to his father, is endorsed " Copy ". It is written in the same sooty ink used for erasures of some proper names in other letters of this series, and there is a note " torn here " between the words " tender " and " Dear Soul ". It is folio 3 in volume XXXVII of the Garrick Correspondence, Forster Collection.

16. Dr Robert James (1705–1776), a native of Staffordshire, after practising in Sheffield, Lichfield and Birmingham, went to London and became famous as the inventor of a pill and powder called by his name, for which he took out a patent in 1745. Dr James's Powder makes many appearances in eighteenth-century letters and memoirs. Chronic invalids and even officers on active service dosed themselves ruthlessly with it, often to the annoyance of their regular medical attendants.

17. Fitzgerald, 18. The person to whom Garrick told this story was the Reverend Perceval Stockdale, several of whose letters appear in the Garrick Correspondence, Forster Collection. The date of Captain Garrick's return was late 1735 or early 1736, not 1737, as stated by Davies.

18. Davies, I. 8. An engraving of Edial Hall, from a drawing by Pye, is reproduced by Clifford. A. L. Reade (*Johnsonian Gleanings*, Part VI, Chapters IV and VI, 1933, hereafter cited as *Gleanings*) proves that Johnson's Academy, partly demolished in 1809, survives as Edial Hall Farm.

19. *Boswell's Life of Johnson*, 2 vols., O.U.P. 1924, Vol. I, 69; hereafter cited as Boswell.

20. Garrick's story of this incident was repeated by Sir John Hawkins, Mrs Piozzi and Boswell. (*The Life of Samuel Johnson*, John Hawkins, 1887,

439; hereafter cited as John Hawkins; *Thraliana, the Diary of Mrs H. L. Thrale (later Mrs Piozzi)*, ed. K. Balderston, 2 vols., 1942, 189; hereafter cited as *Thraliana*.)

21. Boswell, I, 67.

22. *Literary and Miscellaneous Memoirs*, Joseph Cradock, 4 vols., 1828, IV. 244; hereafter cited as Cradock. Clifford, 156.

23. Gilbert Walmesley's two letters, endorsed " Mr. Walmesley's letters about me and Mr. Johnson" are in volume XXXVII of the Garrick Correspondence, Forster Collection, the last in the volume. They were printed by Boaden, and have often been reproduced, in part and in full. The originals were given to Garrick by Alderman Newling, a nephew by marriage of Colson, who had previously sent them for publication to *The Gentleman's Magazine*, apparently to Garrick's annoyance. See also Boaden I. 334.

24. Boswell, I. 69.

## CHAPTER II
### SALAD DAYS

1. Davies, I. 7.
2. Ibid., 13.
3. *Gleanings*, VI. 62.
4. *The Gentleman's Magazine*, 1779, 117. *Genuine Biographical Anecdotes of Mr Garrick*. The information about Captain (Brevet-Major) Garrick's sale of his commission was given to the anonymous writer of the *Anecdotes* by a gentleman from Sheffield, signing himself E.G., who, fourteen years before, had heard the details from " a gentlewoman whose intelligence might be relied upon ". Boaden (*Biographical Memoir* IV, V) agrees that Captain Garrick very likely held the brevet rank of major " but having gone on full-pay without giving any difference and being considered as exchanging with a view merely to *realise*; the permission to sell, though sometimes granted, was refused, and the expected resource to the family fell to the ground." Boaden goes on to state, incorrectly, that Mrs Garrick died within a twelve-month of her husband.
5. *Gleanings*, VI. 62.
6. Professor Clifford disposes of the theory that Nathaniel Johnson committed suicide, by pointing out that he was buried in consecrated ground.
7. Hawkins, 43.
8. Boswell, I. 70; Fitzgerald, 23–24 n.
9. *Historical Antiquities of Rochester*, T. Fisher, 1772. Forster, Boaden, I. 334. *The Gentleman's Magazine*, 1779, 489.
10. Boswell, I. 76, 670.
11. Fitzgerald, 25.
12. *David Garrick and his Circle*, Mrs Clement Parsons, 1906, 36; hereafter cited as Parsons.
13. *Annals of Covent Garden*, E. Beresford Chancellor, 1930, 36–38, 71, 206; hereafter cited as Chancellor. The earliest surviving nobleman's house in Covent Garden square is familiar from engravings of *Morning* in Hogarth's series *The Four Times of the Day*, but the plate being reversed, the house appears on the wrong side of the church. Button's coffee-house had collapsed before Garrick arrived in London. The account quoted comes from

John Macky's *Journey Through England*, 1714, frequently re-published. Macky was himself a secret agent, he died in Rotterdam in 1726, but " Gentleman Jemmy " did not go to the gallows till 1750.

14. A playbill of a performance of *Lethe* by Giffard's company, produced at Ipswich on July 21, 1741, shows that " Ventre-Bleu " (obviously " the Frenchman ") was played by the author himself, " Mr Lydall ". Samuel Johnson's preface is to be found in the manuscript collection called *Garrick's Poems* belonging to Colonel Solly. For information about porcelain figures of Garrick, see articles in *Theatre Notebook* (Bulletin of the Society for Theatre Research), Vol. XI, Nos. 2 & 4, by Martin Holmes, Raymond Mander and Joe Mitchenson. The figures of Garrick were made at the Chelsea-Derby factory.

15. *Hogarth's Progress*, Peter Quennell, 1956, 189–190. The original of " Strolling actresses dressing in a barn " (Horace Walpole's favourite Hogarth) was destroyed, but it had been engraved.

16. *Memoirs of Charles Macklin*, William Cooke, 1804, 92–94; hereafter cited as Cooke. *Charles Macklin*, E. A. Parry, 1891, 64–65. *Memoirs of the Life of Charles Macklin, Esq.*, J. T. Kirkman, 2 vols., 1799, 254–264; hereafter cited as Kirkman.

17. Forster, Garrick, XXVII. 10–16. This series has never been printed in full. Forster in his *Life and Times of Oliver Goldsmith* (1877 edition), 233–241, prints copious extracts. Barton, Appendix 1, 299, reproduces a facsimile of the first sheet of the letter of November 24. Professor Little published four, with notes.

18. Richard Glover (1712–1785) published in 1735 *Leonidas*, an epic poem in blank verse and nine books, commended by Lord Lyttelton and Fielding.

19. Davies, I. 38; Cooke, 98.

20. Tate Wilkinson thought Dance's portrait of Garrick as Richard (bought by Sir Watkin Williams Wynn) a much better likeness—" My old master; just as I had seen him ".

21. Davies, I. 39–43; Murphy, I. 23–26; Fitzgerald, 40–43.

22. The Reverend Thomas Newton (1704–1782) was the son of a Lichfield brandy-and-cider merchant. He was when he began to write to Garrick, Reader at the Grosvenor Chapel in South Audley Street. He became Bishop of Bristol in 1761.

23. Cooke, 100, 163; Davies, I. 45–46. Murphy makes the actress who attacked Cibber, Woffington. Both may have done so.

24. Ibid., 45; Murphy, I. 32.

25. The authority for this story is Cooke, Macklin's biographer. Fitzgerald (55 n.) points out that Garrick's name appears in the playbills for every night of the fortnight during which the play was put off, but is inclined to believe that the story must have had some foundation in fact, and incomprehensibly suggests that it may have been Giffard who was wounded. Garrick was unwell around December 7 and 22. On the first occasion he reports " a cold and looseness " to his brother, on the second Mr Newton regrets to hear he has a cold. In April he speaks of better health; but none of these fit for the date of the supposed duel—February.

26. Fitzgerald, 51.

27. Boswell, I. 569, 115; Fitzgerald, 49 n.

28. Forster, Boaden, I. 5–6.

29. Davies, I. 27–30.

30. The parts played by Garrick at Goodman's Fields in his first London season included Richard III, Clodio in *Love Makes a Man*, Chamont in *The Orphan*, Jack Smatter in *Pamela*, Sharp in *The Lying Valet*, Lothario in *The Fair Penitent*, Ghost in *Hamlet*, Fondlewife in *The Old Bachelor*, Costar Pearmain and Captain Brazen in *The Recruiting Officer*, Aboan in *Oroonoko*, Witwou'd in *The Way of the World*, Master Johnny in *The Schoolboy*, Lear, Foppington in *The Careless Husband*, Captain Duretête in *The Inconstant*, Pierre in *Venice Preserv'd* and perhaps three parts in *Lethe*. Colonel Solly's collection includes a manuscript booklet (neat copper-plate, with dates), in a paper cover, *Characters played by David Garrick Esq. at the Theatre in Goodman's Fields*. Garrick evidently had two copies made, as he lent one to his nephew Carrington.

## CHAPTER III

### WOFFINGTON

1. *Memoirs of Charles Lee Lewes*, 4 vols., 1805, II. 4; hereafter cited as Lewes. Article by Joseph Knight in the *Dictionary of National Biography*. *Lovely Peggy*, J. C. Lucey, 1952, 19–32; hereafter cited as Lucey. Knight and Lucey both suggest 1714 as Woffington's probable date of birth. The tablet to her memory erected by her sister and brother-in-law in the parish church at Teddington, where she had a country house for many years, gives "Margaret Woffington, spinster, born October 18, 1720." In her marriage certificate, Mary Woffington was stated to be "the daughter of Arthur Woffington Esquire".

2. Murphy, I. 36. Tate Wilkinson (I. 34) attributes the remark to Clive.

3. *The History of the Theatres of London and Dublin*, Benjamin Victor, 2 vols., 1761, I. 190; hereafter cited as Victor.

4. Ibid., I. 15–16.

5. Forster, Boaden, I. 12–14.

6. Victor, I. 94.

7. Davies, I. 139–140. See also *The Early Life and Diaries of William Windham*, R. W. Ketton-Cremer, 77; hereafter cited as Ketton-Cremer.

8. The MS. of *To Sylvia* was bought by Mr J. H. Leigh at Sotheby's 1899. Fitzgerald, 30–31, quotes four verses.

9. "To Mrs Woffington", June 1745. Fitzgerald, 83–84.

10. "To have recalled to his mind the time of his early passion (and I have never heard of more than one) would have been, I suppose, to have forfeited his friendship for ever. He was a great instance of the entire change of conduct which so many plead as impossible." *Anecdotes*, Letitia Matilda Hawkins, 1822; hereafter cited as Letitia Hawkins.

11. Cooke, 116–118.

12. Ibid., 144–147; Kirkman, I. 117.

13. Boswell, II. 200.

14. Cooke, I. 119.

15. Kirkman, I. 271 *et seq.*; Fitzgerald, 64; Murphy, I. 42.

16. Cooke, 110–111.

17. Ibid., Kirkman, I. 274; Davies, I. 65.

18. Cooke, I. 134; Davies, I. 68.

19. Kirkman (I. 274–291) criticizes Garrick for coming to his agreement with Fleetwood without seeing Macklin first, and considers his actions calculated " for aggrandisement of himself and friends ".　Murphy (I. 57–69 and II Appendix IV) claims that he saw all " the documents and curious papers " connected with the dispute, and that Macklin said he refused an offer of £200 from Fleetwood to ensure that the company would perform at reduced salaries. Fleetwood denied making this offer.　Davies admits that " the trouble and anxiety which Garrick brought upon himself during this disagreeable contest, proceeded from a conduct which, in a greater or less degree, pursued him through life; the precipitancy of his temper often hurried him into engagements which he either could or would not, and indeed sometimes ought not, to fulfil ".

20. *Life of Sir Charles Hanbury-Williams*, Earl of Ilchester and Mrs Langford-Brooke, 1929, 78; hereafter cited as Hanbury-Williams.

21. *Autobiography and Correspondence of Mary Granville, Mrs Delany*, ed. Lady Llanover, 1861–1862, 6 vols., VI. 63.

22. Hanbury-Williams, 80.

23. Murphy, I. 172.

24. Lucey, 124–125, 228, 241–244.　Margaret Woffington's villa at Teddington, at which Garrick performed in private theatricals, was, by tradition, Teddington Place House, re-named in 1851 Udney Hall, and now demolished.　" Hon. Mr Cholmondeley about the loan of £400.　Done.　September 25, 1777."　Forster, Boaden, II. 274.

25. Forster, Boaden, I. 15, 19–21, 30–32.

26. Murphy, I. 105.

27. Forster, Boaden, I. 33.

28. Ibid., 35–36.

29. Cooke, I. 120–212.

30. *Memoirs of Tate Wilkinson*, 4 vols., 1790, I. 33, 118–119; hereafter cited as Tate Wilkinson.

31. This portrait is now in the National Portrait Gallery.　The story that after their triumvirate experiment at 6, Bow Street failed Woffington and Garrick " kept house together " seems to lack foundation and originates from Cooke (I. 111–119); but it has been repeated by nearly every author who was not a contemporary.　Knight (57) states that they lived together at an unascertained address in Southampton Street.　This may be a confusion with Garrick's later house at 27, Southampton Street.　Cooke follows his Woffington anecdote with a later one when Garrick was in Southampton Street.

32. Victor, I. 67–68; Fitzgerald, 79–80, 111–112; Davies, I. 81–82.

33. Davies, I. 84.　Amongst the MSS. at Felbrigg is a *petite pièce* of Garrick's salad days, left by him with Windham, 1746; a vague parody of the quarrel scene between Brutus and Cassius in *Julius Caesar*. Ketton-Cremer, 42.

34. Mrs Cibber's letters of this date, to Garrick, were kept by him, and printed by Boaden, I. 33 *et seq*.　But Boaden has misdated those pp. 445–450.

35. *Proceedings of the Huguenot Society*, II. 453.

36. Horace Walpole was sarcastic about the scheme of raising new regiments, and declared that not six of the fifteen proposed by the Duke of Bedford were ever raised.　Lord Granby of " The Leicester Blues " took his regiment into action in March 1746, at Strathbogie.　After long clamour for discharge, it was disbanded on the following Christmas Day.

37. Forster, Garrick, XXXV. 25.　No previous biographer seems to have detected this letter, not printed by Boaden.

## CHAPTER IV

### Roscius

1. *Autobiography of the Reverend Dr Alexander Carlyle, Minister of Inveresk*, 1860, 182–185, 344; hereafter cited as Carlyle.
2. Davies, I. 85.
3. Forster, Boaden, I. 38–39.
4. Davies, I. 86–87.
5. *An apology for the life of George Anne Bellamy*, 6 vols., 1785, I. 55, 101, 120–124; VI. 15; hereafter cited as Bellamy.
6. Carlyle, 190–191.
7. Forster, Boaden, I. 42–43.
8. *Unpublished Correspondence of David Garrick*, ed. Professor G. F. Baker, 1907, 32–35; hereafter cited as Baker.
9. Fitzgerald (102–103) was told this story by a lady who had it from Mr Rossan, the visitor to London charged with the message to Mrs Garrick. The date is fixed by the poem, printed by Bishop Forbes in his collection of Jacobite manuscripts, *The Lyon in Mourning*, 3 vols., 1896, I. 241, *Ode upon a young lady that died on seeing her lover, Mr Dawson, executed on the 30th of July, 1746*, and by reports in contemporary newspapers and magazines. The fate of Young Wilding was sad. His sentence was altered to transportation, and he went to the North American colonies, but was killed in a skirmish with Red Indians.
10. Davies, I. 310–311.
11. Ibid., 96–98.
12. *Memoirs of Richard Cumberland*, 1806, 59–60; hereafter cited as Cumberland.
13. Forster, Boaden, I. 44.
14. Davies, I. 101–102; Parsons, 130–131.
15. Davies, I. 101–102.
16. Forster, Boaden, I. 47.
17. Ibid., I. xvii.
18. Ibid., I. xix. 50–53, 205; Forster, Garrick, XXVI. 5; Fitzgerald, 110–113. See also *The History of the English Stage*, Fitzgerald, 11, 149 *et seq.*; Davies, I. 103–104, 107; Victor, I. 62–84; Murphy I. 129–132; Bellamy, VI. 98–100. An engraved portrait of Lacy appears in *The European Magazine*, July 1, 1802.
19. Forster, Garrick, XVII. 47.
20. Wren's arches still stand, and " The Crypt " was used as an air-raid shelter when Drury Lane was occupied by ENSA during the Second World War.
21. Parsons, 131.
22. Davies, I. 111–112.
23. Forster, Garrick, XVII. I. E.O. was an early form of roulette but without a zero. The circular table, about four feet in diameter, had a counter round the outside edge, on which stakes were placed, the letters E & O for Even and Odd being marked all round it.
24. Davies, I. 103–104; Tate Wilkinson, I. 22.

25. Clifford, 296.

26. Forster, Garrick, XVII. 49.

27. *A manuscript account book of Drury Lane Theatre for 1746–48*, and *More concerning a manuscript account book of Drury Lane Theatre*, articles by E. B. Chancellor in *The Connoiseur*, July and October 1926.

28. Forster, Boaden, I. xxii.

29. *The Letters of Horace Walpole*, ed. Mrs Paget Toynbee, 1903, 16. vols., II. 382; hereafter cited as Walpole. Amongst the miscellanea which passed to the Rev. Thomas Rackett, now preserved in the Solly collection, is an unexplained trifle of this date—a playing card, the ace of diamonds, decorated with a little sketch of a stuffed chair, and inscribed " E. Violette delineavit, November 14, 1748." Garrick was playing Richard that night.

30. Boswell (I. 132–135) has got this story wrong in detail. Cradock (I. 240–241) explains that Garrick played Demetrius to please Johnson. See also Davies I. 119–120. Percivall Pott also attained immortality by sustaining the fracture known by his name.

31. Walpole, II. 155–156, 160–161.

32. *Notes & Queries*, March 31, 1877, " Where was Garrick married? " quotes *The General Advertiser*, June 23, 1749, which states that Garrick was married by Francklin " at his chapel, Russell Street, Bloomsbury." The licence was issued for a chapel, and Walpole also says that Garrick was married " first at a Protestant and then at a Roman Catholic Chapel ". Francklin officiated at different dates at two proprietory chapels. He was at the one in Great Queen Street, which is in the parish of St Giles's, 1761–1784. The *Notes & Queries* letter says that " Lady Rachel Russell (d. 1723) gave a piece of land in Queen Street, Bloomsbury, between Hart Street and Little Russell Street, for the purpose of erecting a chapel and school house. Queen Street is now Museum Street, and on the site of the chapel, the parochial charity school—the second house from Hart Street ".


CHAPTER V

27, SOUTHAMPTON STREET

1. *London Marriage Licences, 1521–1869*, J. L. Chester, 1887, under date.

2. Review of Fitzgerald's *Life of Garrick* by Sir T. Martin, *Quarterly Magazine*, July 1868, 23. Professor G. P. Baker prints in full the *Quadrupite Marriage Agreement*, in his collection of sixty-six unpublished Garrick letters. See also Walpole, II. 392.

3. Knight (126) notes in a contemporary satire against the Jesuits written and published in France a statement that " my Lord Burlington had given his natural daughter, Violette ", in defiance of " a certain Majesty " to " the little Garrick, with a considerable pension charged upon the poor Kingdom of Ireland ".

4. Murphy, I. 171–172; Lee Lewes, II. 66–68; Forster, Boaden, I. xv–xvii.

5. *A book for a rainy day: recollections of sixty-six years* (1766–1833), J. T. Smith, 1845, 287; hereafter cited as J. T. Smith.

6. Fitzgerald, 100–102, 122–127. Sir Charles Wyndham and Miss Mary Moore appeared in *David Garrick* by T. W. Robertson, in 1886, at the Criterion

Theatre, and the title part became one of Wyndham's best known characters. In January 1888 he gave the play in German (his own translation) before royal audiences in Berlin, and at a command performance St Petersburg.

7. *Household Words*, a weekly journal conducted by Charles Dickens, August 1857, 166–168.

8. Pulman MS. Heralds' College, 63, V. 412–425. Philpot, xlii.

9. Walpole, II. 197–198.

10. Varying versions of these stanzas appear in *The Gentleman's Magazine*, *London Magazine*, 1749, and Forster Garrick MS. 146, xvii.

11. The author wishes to thank the Rev. G. C. Taylor, Rector of St Giles's in the Fields, for showing her the register of Garrick's marriage. This appears under date, June 22, 1749—" David Garrick of St. Paul's, Covent Garden, to Eva Maria Violette, of St. James's West ". St James's West was St James's, Piccadilly; Burlington House stood in that parish.

12. Parsons, 143.

13. Fitzgerald, 125. *The Gentleman's Magazine*, May 1755, 230, gives the final verse.

14. There are illustrated articles on Chiswick House in *Country Life*, CLIII. 130 and 160, by H. Avery Tipping, and LX. 308 and LXVI. 181, by Christopher Hussey. Colin Campbell was, apparently, Lord Burlington's original adviser for his improvements, planned 1727 and completed 1736; but he died 1729.

15. Baker, 5–7, 15–22. Letter to Peter Garrick quoted by kind permission of the Trustees, the London Museum.

16. Cradock, IV. 251.

17. 27, Southampton Street still stands, essentially unchanged. It is now appropriately occupied as business premises by Messrs French, publishers of plays. The author wishes to thank Mr Elsbury for showing her the premises.

18. Lee Lewes, II. 89–91.

19. *Drury Lane Calendar*, 1747–1776; Professor D. MacMillan, 1938; hereafter cited as *Drury Lane Calendar*.

20. Ibid., 14.

21. Forster, Boaden, I. 54–56.

22. Bellamy, I. 185; II. 57–59, 87–94, 106–111.

23. Ibid., II. 114; Murphy, I. 188–194; Davies, I. 124–129; Cooke, 161, 205.

24. Murphy, I. 198.

25. Walpole, III. 44.

26. Forster, Garrick, XVII. 1–3; Little, 34–35. Nathaniel Carrington, King's Messenger, had the Jacobite Lord Kilmarnock as his lodger while that ill-fated nobleman was awaiting trial. Kilmarnock gave his host a ring, set with a diamond, which descended in the family of Elizabeth Carrington and George Garrick to Dorothea Solly, daughter of Thomas Rackett, executor to Mrs Garrick. Solly Collection.

## CHAPTER VI

### HAPPY DAYS

1. *The Diary of David Garrick, being a record of his memorable trip to Paris in 1751*, edited from the original MS. R. C. Alexander, Oxford University Press, New York, 1928. The story of this manuscript is interesting. The flyleaf bears the inscription *Hill collection*. Dr John Hill, writer of many letters to Garrick, predeceased the actor by four years. The little volume was sold first at Sotheby's in 1899; and at Maggs's in 1915, to Mr Mossmore Kendall of New York City. Its existence was unknown to Knight, who devotes a single paragraph to Garrick's first French trip. Fitzgerald says: " This first French visit appears to have had no special glories or interest ", and " This journal has been lost ". Hedgcock (10, 111–113, 415) in 1911 produced from the Bibliothèque de l'Arsénal (Archives de la Bastille) the information that the Paris police had been looking for Garrick, and Collé's mention of having met him, but was reduced to very unhappy guesses as to what other people he met. Miss Margaret Barton, by 1948, had seen the diary and quoted from it. Knight and Fitzgerald mentioned two outside anecdotes of very doubtful authenticity, one that Garrick had been presented to Louis XV, and the other that, having made himself up to resemble a certain Sir George Lewis, who had been murdered in the Forest of Bondy, he had been so successful as to wring a confession of guilt from the suspected murderer (Knight, 137; Fitzgerald, 142).

2. Garrick's young admirer Cradock, who also visited Paris before the Revolution, saw every one of the principal sights recorded in the diary and expanded upon some.

3. Liotard's portrait of Garrick (the best documented of Garrick pictures, as every sitting is entered in Garrick's diary) is one of the least inspired. It is reproduced by Hedgcock as the frontispiece in *David Garrick and his French Friends*. Liotard represents the actor as a most commonplace young man with a smirk.

4. *Drury Lane Calendar* shows that Leviéz, " ballet-master ", continued in Garrick's employment until May 1762. Dévisse, who is noted on his first appearance in November 1750, as " from Paris ", and had his first benefit in April 1751, appears again on the benefit list in March 1752 and never again.

5. Forster, Garrick, XXVII 28. Garrick did not refer to these Lichfield acquaintances by initials only, but the remainder of their names have been scored out in the same sooty ink employed by whatever member of the Garrick home circle censored other of David's letters.

6. Murphy, I. 205–208, 221–223; Davies, I. 158–162; Bellamy, II. 130. David Ross went on to Covent Garden in 1757, and stayed there ten years; he then attempted to establish a theatre in his native Edinburgh. This effort was disastrous and he returned to dwindle, though not in figure, at Drury Lane. A broken leg sent him off the stage at the age of fifty, and growing intemperance kept him off it. He became known as unreliable.

Henry Mossop went back to Dublin after eight years at Drury Lane, and took Smock Alley Theatre in competition to Barry at Crow Street. Barry was actually arrested for debt on the stage, so for a brief period Mossop governed both theatres; but what money he had left after incessant litigation he lost at the gaming-table. After confinement in the King's Bench he suffered a nervous breakdown, from which he never fully recovered. He developed marked *folie de grandeur*, and refused to apply to Garrick for employment, saying that Garrick knew he was in London, and any application should come from him. All chances of his being engaged again at Drury Lane were demolished by the publication in 1772 of a pamphlet, *Letter to David Garrick on his conduct*, written for Mossop by one of his less well advised friends. He died in 1774 in extreme poverty. Garrick, who had lent him money, volunteered to pay for his funeral, but an uncle, a bencher of the Inner Temple, refused the offer.

7. Davies (II. 474–476), who prints the letters from Stone and Garrick, says they were all written in 1748; but *Henry VIII* was not produced until April 10, 1752.

8. *The Genuine Works of William Hogarth* (Nicholas and Steevens, I. 1808, 210–213) prints Hoadly's letter, dated April 21, 1757, so it would appear that the picture was not completed for five years.

9. Boswell, I. 166. Hawkins, *Johnson*, 433.

10. Forster, Garrick, XVII. 22–24.

11. Murphy, I. 224–241. Davies, I. 166–174. Bellamy, II. 131–136.

12. Forster, Garrick, XVII. 26.

13. *History and Topography of Hampton on Thames*, H. Ripley, 1885 hereafter cited as Ripley, 13. Hampton House, now known as Garrick's Villa, still stands, now subdivided into flats. The author desires to thank Mr T. V. Roberts, Borough Librarian, Twickenham, for kind assistance, and Mrs Vernon Gatti for showing her Garrick's Villa.

14. Of the two-volume collection of *The Private Correspondence of David Garrick* printed by Boaden, only the first fifty-five pages are of a date before Garrick bought his country house.

15. Forster, Boaden, I. 59–60.

16. Bellamy's private character deteriorated after she left Drury Lane. She states that she was married to an actor called Digges, but he proved to be already married. She describes herself at the age of thirty as " a little dirty creature, bent nearly double, enfeebled by fatigue ". Her Memoirs include an illustration of a half-hearted attempt to commit herself to the river at Westminster Bridge. At a benefit given for her at Drury Lane in 1785 she could take no part and only mumble a few words of gratitude. She died three years later, pursued by her creditors, and in and out of prison to the last. Her sons by Metham and Calcraft, after several bad starts, did well in the army, and East India Company. Woodward died in her arms, having tried ineffectually to provide for her in his will.

17. Murphy, I. 247.

18. Ibid., 248–249.

## CHAPTER VII

### DANGER

1. Forster, Boaden, II. 379–421; Hedgcock, 116–149.

2. *Journal Étranger*, December 1755, 223. "Lettre écrite de Londres . . . au sujet de ballets de Sieur Noverre." Murphy, I. 276–282. Murphy was present on November 8, but his account contains inaccuracies. He believed the play which preceded the ballet to have been *Richard III*, and says that the repairs after the fracas of the 18th took five or six days. *Drury Lane Calendar* accounts show that the house never closed. Tate Wilkinson (IV. 214–216) (who reproduces the play bill for November 8, I. 73) is the only person to give the account of Garrick's courageous appeal to his audience on November 21, though Murphy was, as Fitzgerald points out (162) a member of the company, and Davies's wife was performing in the second piece that night. Victor (II. 131–135) states, as do Davies, Murphy and Tate Wilkinson, that war had already been declared. Davies (I. 178–183) says that Garrick " thought his life was in danger from the ungovernable rage of the people who threatened to demolish his house ". See also: *Life and Works of the Chevalier Noverre*, C. E. Noverre, 1882. The author was Jean-Georges Noverre's great-grandson. Jean-Georges Noverre fled to England, with some of his company, on the outbreak of the French Revolution, in which he lost the savings of fifty years. His London productions were received with enthusiasm, but he did not succeed in re-establishing his health or fortune. He returned to France in 1800, and died in reduced circumstances, aged eighty-two.

3. Forster, Garrick, XLVIII. 9; Forster, Boaden, I. 60–62. The poem on Biddy is in a bound volume of manuscript poems in the Solly Collection.

4. Cradock, IV. 248.

5. Rev. W. Warburton to Mr Garrick, May 4, 1756; Forster, Boaden, I. 64; Duke of Devonshire to Mr Garrick, April 17, 1756; Forster, Garrick, XLVIII. 11.

6. Forster, Boaden, I. 65–73, 83–84, 89, 91, 100–114, 116, 119, 121, 128–130; Murphy, I. 330–341.

7. Forster, Garrick, XXVII. 38.

8. After Garrick's death, the manor was left in trust for his nephew, Carrington, and after he died, in 1787, it passed to James Bond, who already owned much of the copyhold. Brian Scotney, who bought it in 1822, added to the façade of Hendon Hall a solid red-brick early Georgian house, the portico from Wanstead House, Essex, which was demolished in 1823. Hendon Hall was again sold in 1897, together with many Garrick relics, although it does not appear that Garrick ever lived there. In 1947 Major Norman Brett-James arrived too late to stop the demolition of an octagonal temple, in classic style, with glass paintings, busts and statues; but two obelisks of stone, inscribed with tributes to Garrick and Shakespeare, were preserved. Garrick's property extended across the present Watford By-Pass, north-east of Manor Hall Avenue, and Major Brett-James failed, in spite of devoted efforts, to save another Garrick memorial, a brick pylon, forty feet high, faced with cement, and decorated with four life-sized, but now headless, figures representing Tragedy, Comedy, History and Shakespeare.

*The Story of Hendon Manor and Parish*, Norman Brett-James, 1931, 89. *Transactions of the London and Middlesex Archaeological Society*, Vol. X, Part 1, 55–58. The author wishes to thank Major Brett-James, President of the Mill Hill and Hendon Historical Society, for information. Hendon Hall is now the Hendon Hall Hotel, Parson Street, Hendon. See also Forster, Boaden, I. 63, 205–207.

In 1794, when there was a shortage of small change, which the Mint did little to remedy, companies, tradesmen, etc., began to issue tokens. Hendon produced a large copper coin, value one halfpenny, bearing on the obverse a likeness of the parish church, and on the reverse a bust, " David Garrick, Esq." *Copper Coinage*. D. Batty, 1868, I. 131.


## CHAPTER VIII

### GARRICK'S VILLA


1. It is not easy to discover at what dates Robert Adam made the various alterations at Hampton House. He may have met Garrick before going to Italy, 1754–1758. Horace Walpole mentions that Garrick is building the Temple in August 1755, and Garrick in a letter to Brother Peter, July 1757, is " over head and ears in dirt and mortar ". The Orangery was completed before 1758, and further rebuilding took place in 1772–1774. *The Architecture of Robert and James Adam*, A. E. Bolton, 2 vols., 1922, I. 27–35. A plan of the elevation of the south front and ground floor exists in the invaluable illustrated brochure of the sale at Hampton House, June 11, 1823, and Colonel Solly possesses an undated unsigned pencil sketch of, apparently, a proposed elevation of the south front and first floor.

2. Carlyle, 342–345.

3. The relics from the Shakespeare Temple here described are in the Solly Collection. The Roubillac statue is in the British Museum, and the Temple itself still *in situ*, is the property of Hampton Urban District Council. The lead tank has been placed in the hall of the villa.

4. J. T. Smith, 289.

5. Boswell, II. 512.

6. Forster, Boaden, II. 346–348.

7. Walpole, III. 329.

8. Tate Wilkinson, II. 24–25.

9. Ripley, 17. Garrick's bedroom furniture came with the Forster Collection to the Victoria and Albert Museum. Lord Fairhaven possesses a dressing-table. Chippendale's bill is in the Solly Collection.

10. Forster, Garrick, XXVII. 36.

11. Davies (I. 192–196) and Tate Wilkinson (II. 52–54) do not agree as to the Lord Chamberlain's actions over *The Author*. Wilkinson states that the farce was to be revived, with a new scene, in which he was to act, for the first time, in the season of 1757–1758, for Foote's benefit, near Christmas, and that the Lord Chamberlain then objected. *Drury Lane Calendar* shows that it had been played ten times since October, and was played four times early in 1758. After February 1, 1758, it was laid aside for twelve years.

12. *The Correspondence of Gray, Walpole, West and Ashton*, ed. Mrs Paget Toynbee, 1915, II. 172–173.

D D

13. Forster, Garrick, XXVII. 36.

14. Murphy, I. 325–326; Tate Wilkinson, II. 3–4; Davies, I. 257–262.

15. Victor, I. 11–43.

16. Tate Wilkinson, I. 11–43; II. 52–54, 75–78, 80–90.

17. Forster, Boaden, I. 79–80.

18. Tate Wilkinson, II. 101–111, 124–125, 130–144, 210–214; II. 26–27, 47.

19. *Reminiscences of Henry Angelo*, 2 vols., 1828. I. 9–10, 13–15; hereafter cited as Angelo.

20. Forster, Boaden, I. 100–102, 104, 106–109, 111–115.


CHAPTER IX

THE NEW REIGN

1. Cradock, I. 193.

2. Forster, Garrick, I. 108.

3. Ibid., XXVI., Additional.

4. *Memoirs of Dr. Burney, by his daughter, Madame D'Arblay*, 3 vols., 1832, I. 166–167; hereafter cited as Charles Burney.

5. Forster, Garrick, XXVII. 40.

6. *The Life and Letters of Lady Sarah Lennox*, ed. Countess of Ilchester and Lord Stavordale, 2 vols. 1902, I. 26–28, 47–51, 133–145; hereafter cited as Lennox.

7. Forster, Boaden, I. 124, 142.

8. Dr John Hill turned his attention to the publication, in twenty-six volumes, of his *magnum opus, The Vegetable System*, dedicated to Lord Bute. This won him, from the King of Sweden, a decoration, the Order of St Vasa. He thereafter styled himself Sir John. He died of gout (for which disease he had claimed to have a complete herbal cure) in 1775.

9. Davies, I. 313 *et seq.* Murphy says that *The Rout* was performed for the benefit of the Marine Society. *Drury Lane Calendar* shows that it was for the General Lying-In Hospital. Davies displays reserve and dignity in his account of the attacks on himself in *The Rosciad*.

10. Davies, I. 271 *et seq.*; Forster, Boaden, I. 123; Fitzgerald, 235–237.

11. Fitzgerald, 217–219; Forster, Boaden, II. 288–289.

12. Davies, II. 1–26; Murphy, I. 370–381; Fitzgerald, 242–245.

13. Forster, Boaden, I. 161.

14. Ibid., I. 167, 201; II. 338; Forster, Garrick, XX. 31.


CHAPTER X

TOUR OF EUROPE

1. Fitzgerald, 142, 283. Fitzgerald announces in a footnote that Garrick's first travel diary has been lost. But he had evidently seen it. When Hedgcock applied to him for information as to the second, his reply was, " Mr. Fitzgerald himself has forgotten where the documents came from " (Hedgcock 156). Hedgcock mentions a contemporary French anecdote.

Members of the Comédie Française, having discovered the hour of Garrick's arrival in Paris, arranged with his postilion that his carriage should break down outside the inn nearest to the St Denis barrier. He was entertained by them, at the inn, where they had assumed the disguise of a wedding party. After he had been well plied with wine, Garrick turned the tables on them by arising from his pretended intoxication and paying compliments, by name, to every member of the company. He had read so much about them that he had no difficulty in recognizing them. If this story is founded on fact, it is surprising that Fitzgerald did not, apparently, find it in the Journal.

2. In Dr Joan Evans's article "The Embassy of the Duke of Bedford to Paris, 1762–1763" (*Archaeological Journal*, CXIII), the British Embassy, the Hotel de Grinberghen, is fully described. But as accounts show that the duke removed even his kitchen equipment before departing, and hired a *batterie de cuisine* and crockery for his last days in Paris, it seems unlikely that Neville was still living in the house, which had been rented from the Duc de Chaulnes. All Garrick's biographers assume that Neville's party took place in 1764, on Garrick's return to Paris, but it was clearly on his 1763 visit, as Neville left Paris early in November of that year, and Garrick's letter to Colman mentioning it is dated October 8, 1763. *Memoirs of the Colman family*, Richard Brinsley Peake, 2 vols., 1841, I. 83; hereafter cited as Colman. Davies II. 81–83. Murphy, II. 16. Hedgcock, 219–220. Fitzgerald, 285–286. *Correspondance par Grimm, Diderot Raynal, Meister etc.*, 1876, VI. 286; hereafter cited as Grimm.

3. Forster, Garrick, XVII. 7; Hedgcock, 302; Little, 43–44. The letter of October 18 to Colman passed from one of Sir Henry Irving's *Garrick Memorial* volumes to the Pierpont Morgan Library.

4. Fitzgerald, 287–288; Colman, I. 89–91.

5. *Drury Lane Calendar*, 97–98.

6. Walpole, V. 368, 378. Thomas Patch's caricature is an exhibit of the Royal Albert Memorial Museum, Exeter.

7. Forster, Garrick, XVII. 5–9; Colman, I. 90.

8. Forster, Garrick, XXVI. 395 *et seq.*; Forster, Boaden, II. 526, 534.

9. Solly Collection.

10. *Nollekens and his Times*, J. T. Smith, 1829, 2 vols., I. 6–7, 9; hereafter cited as Nollekens. Colman, I. 100.

11. This portrait is now an exhibit of the Ashmolean Museum. The suit worn by Garrick is an exhibit of the London Museum. The portrait of Lady Spencer is at Althorp.

12. Nollekens, I. 148–149. Various versions exist of the sum paid to Zoffany.

13. *Drury Lane Calendar*, 106; Lennox, I. 136–137.

14. Forster, Boaden, I. 171.

15. Cradock, IV. 243.

16. Murphy (II. 18) says that the box displayed on this occasion came from the Duke of Wurtemburg. The Duke of Parma's box was painted in enamels, after Teniers.

17. Forster, Garrick, XVII. 11; Forster, Boaden, I. 237.

18. Colman, I. 100, 110–112.

19. Forster, Boaden, I. 172–173.

20. Ibid., 181.

21. Baker, 117.

22. Forster, Garrick, XVII. 11; Forster, Boaden, I. 237.

23. Forster, Boaden, I. 176; Colman, I. 25–26. The Duke of Devonshire had what Horace Walpole described as " a fit " at Chatsworth, in August, " very slight, much less than the former, and certainly nervous, by all the symptoms. . . . The Duke perceived it coming and directed what to have done, and it was over in four minutes." So, although his death was a surprise to Garrick, it had been foreseen by the duke, who left all his affairs in remarkable order. Walpole, VI. 99, 102, 109, 111, 122–123, 126–127, 130. Lord Palmerston reported that " by all accounts " his death had been hastened by the palsy.

24. Forster, Boaden, II. 218.

25. Ibid., I. 177–178.

26. Colman, I. 137, 143.

27. Carmontelle's sketch of the tragic and comic Garrick is reproduced by Hedgcock, 78. On the back of the original, in the Musée Condé, are notes by Gruyer, biographer of Carmontelle.

28. Colman, I. 182. Forster, Boaden, I. 232; II. 426, 437. The Rev. William Cole (*Journal of my Journey to Paris*, ed. F. G. Stokes, 1931) often visited Léviez, calls him Livier, and says he had lived in London for twenty years, and returned to France 1762.

29. Grimm, VI. 320.

30. Baker, 81. It seems that either Mrs Garrick's mother or sister-in-law was in London.

31. Boaden, I. 196; II. 428, 432, 460–461, 463. The portrait of Clairon is in the Solly Collection.

32. This Burke was Richard, brother to Edmund.

33. Grimm, VI. 318–322; Boaden, II. 432–636; Hedgcock, 214–402.

34. This service was bought by the Baroness Burdett-Coutts at the sale of Mrs Garrick's effects in 1822, and appeared again at Sotheby's May 21, 1957.

35. Forster, Boaden, II. 441, 500; 36. Lennox, I. 163.

# CHAPTER XI

## " TIED TO THE STAKE "

1. Charles Burney, I. 168, 353.

2. *Our Story, The History of Three Parishes, Lawford, Manningtree, Mistley,* publ. Manningtree Branch Workers' Educational Association, 1954. *A Frenchman in England,* 1784, F. de la Rochefoucauld, ed. J. Marchant, trans. S. C. Roberts, 1833, 163–170.

3. Angelo, II. 92.

4. Hedgcock, 249.

5. *The Gentleman's Magazine,* 1765, 489; Forster, Boaden, I. 202.

6. Boswell (I. 321) denies Mrs Piozzi's story that Johnson threatened to blackball Garrick if his name was put up for The Club. Forster, *Life and Times of Oliver Goldsmith,* 2 vols., 1877, I. 310 *et. seq.*; hereafter cited as Forster, Goldsmith. Hawkins, 427.

7. Boswell, I. 393, 322–333, 331; Forster, Goldsmith, I. 402; Charles Burney, I. 353.

8. *St James's Chronicle*, January 1766. Cradock, I. 205–206.

9. *An Account of the Life of Mrs Susanna Maria Cibber*, Anon. 1887; Davies, II. 106–111; Murphy, II. 35; Cradock, I. 206; Solly Collection (Lord Rochford's letter).

10. *The Windham Papers*, edited Earl of Rosebery, 2 vols, 1913; I. 9.

11. Forster, Boaden, I. 190; Colman, I. 181. Forster, Goldsmith, I. 354 n; Forster, Garrick, XXVI. 177.

12. Colman, I. 182–183; Forster, Garrick, XVI. 8, 12, 14; Little, 48–50.

13. Angelo, I. 8, 38, 40.

14. Forster, Garrick, XVII. 45.

15. Ibid., 28, 39, 153; Forster, Boaden, I. 263–264, 311, 411.

16. Two copies of this letter exist, one being probably Garrick's draft. One is in the Garrick Club, the other in the library at Welbeck, and printed by Little (54–55).

17. Colman, I. 184–190; *George Colman, the Elder*, E. R. Page, 1935, 136–147; Forster, Boaden, I. 254–256; Fitzgerald, 315–318; Forster, Goldsmith, II. 42–44.

18. Cradock, I. 193–196; IV. 237–239.

19. Boaden, II. 192–193, 195, 197; Little, 82. *Country Life*, Vols. XLIX. 714, 764; and L.14 (articles by the Earl Spencer). The author wishes to thank Lord Spencer for kindly giving her information, at Althorp.

20. Solly Collection. (Mrs Garrick's Diary.) Little, 58.

21. Letitia Hawkins, 21; John Hawkins, 427; Forster, Boaden, I. 356–361, II. 359–361; Baker, 53; Walpole, VII. 213–221.

22. Letitia Hawkins, 321; Nollekens, I. 151.

23. Cradock, IV. 239–241; Forster, Boaden, I. 333.

24. Forster, Boaden, I. 320, 338, 341, 343.

## CHAPTER XII

### STRATFORD-UPON-AVON JUBILEE

1. Forster, Boaden, I. 311, 323, 328, 345. Horace Walpole identified the buildings in the background as those at Prior Park, Widcombe, four miles outside Bath, residence of Garrick's friend Warburton, who had married the niece of the late owner, Ralph Allen. Later writers thought they represented Lord Pembroke's well-known Palladian bridge and summer-house at Wilton. Both Gainsborough's and Wilson's pictures, painted for Garrick's Shakespeare Jubilee, perished in the fire in 1946 at Stratford.

2. Solly Collection.

3. *London Magazine*, September 1769, 497–498; *Boswell in Search of a Wife*, ed. F. Brady and F. Pottle, 1957, 219, 295, 297–303; Cradock, I. xvii, II. 211–219, IV. 133; Angelo, I. 44–52; Murphy II. 66–72; Victor, III. 200–232; *The Gentleman's Magazine*, 1769, 344, 364, 375, 421, 446, 458.

4. Shakespeare's Chair is now in the collection of Lord Fairhaven. It bears on its back the letter of John Bacon of Fryern House, Barnet, describing his humiliating effort to arrange a loan of it for Garrick from Whitehead. On Whitehead's death Bacon bought it. It is illustrated in *History of Furniture*, F. Litchfield, 1892–1907, 88, 89.

5. Davies, I. 217–245, 270–272; Forster, Boaden, I. 145, 328, 345, 350–353, 363–365, 368–369, 414, 424. The Ode and songs for the Jubilee are printed in Garrick's Works, I. 53–57, 71, II. 426–434. A half-length portrait of Garrick as Steward by Vandergucht, is in Lord Spencer's Collection, at Althorp, and an engraving of Garrick reciting his Ode in the Enthoven Theatre Collection at the Victoria and Albert Museum. The Folger Shakespeare Library, Washington, possesses a manuscript copy of *The Jubilee* as performed at Drury Lane.

6. Forster, Boaden, II. 362.

7. Solly Collection.

8. Forster, Goldsmith, II. 162–163; Boswell, I. 389–396; Davies, II. 169; *The Gentleman's Magazine*, 1769, 508; Parsons, 264.


## CHAPTER XIII

### ADELPHI

1. Forster, Boaden, I. 411.

2. Walpole, VII. 28, 393.

3. Forster, Boaden, I. 190, 263, 409.

4. Cumberland, 154, 198, 202, 205, 215–219, 244–245, 254–255, 265–266.

5. *The Early Diary of Frances Burney*, edited A. E. Ellis, 2 vols., 1907 edition, I. 117–120; hereafter cited as Fanny Burney.

6. Lord Chatham's invitation, with Garrick's reply, also in verse, appear in Garrick's *Collected Poetical Works*, II. 525–526.

7. Forster, Boaden, I. 443–444. The identity of Junius was not disclosed in his lifetime, and the result of later research proved something of an anticlimax. He appeared, most probably, but not certainly, to have been Sir Philip Francis (1740–1818) a brilliant but disappointed Civil Servant.

8. Murphy, II. 195. *Memorials of Christie's*, W. Roberts, 2 vols., 1897, I. IX. 4, 108. The Andrea del Sarto, Madonna and Child attended by three angels, given to Garrick by Lord Baltimore, was bought by Prince Leopold for 255 guineas at the sale of Garrick's pictures at Christie's in 1823. It was then stated to have been acquired by Lord Baltimore in Rome, but his letter to Garrick, dated *Venice, 1770* (of which there is a copy in the Solly Collection), says that he had bought it in Paris, ten years earlier. See also Cumberland, 218.

9. There are three full descriptions of Garrick's establishment at Adelphi Terrace. The Victoria and Albert Museum possess, and published in 1920, *Accounts of Chippendale Haig and Co., for the Furnishing of David Garrick's House in the Adelphi*. The auctioneer's catalogue for the sale of the house, on the death of Mrs Garrick, dated 1823, contains a reproduction of Adam's design for the façade, a plan of the ground floor, and a description of the rooms, including measurements. The furniture, sold three weeks later, on the premises, is described in detail in the catalogue of Messrs Burrell. Garrick's silver, in the Solly Collection, bears the maker's marks of James Young, Orlando Jackson and John Carter, and date marks 1774–1775. See also *The Architecture of Robert and James Adam*, A. E. Bolton, 2 vols., 1922, II. 28–29, 35. Garrick's house was demolished when Adelphi Terrace was taken down in 1936.

10. Cradock (I. 97; II. 250) says that when Garrick was upon a visit to him, he was much struck by the comment of a fellow-guest that a local grasier, whom they observed riding by, had been thought to be dying of the stone, but had been miraculously cured by Adam's solvent. Garrick's physician, Dr Brocklesby, was displeased by Cradock's interference, and said that whoever had recommended such a remedy to his patient would be the death of him. Garrick replied, " I have taken all your medicines, and from this solvent only, I think I feel some relief, and I had rather die than suffer as I do."

11. Fanny Burney, II. 158; Boswell, II. 199–200.

12. Forster, Boaden, I. 472–477, 480; II. 340–341. Kenrick died in 1779. He had long been dependent upon a bottle at his elbow to assist him as he wrote. His last shot at Garrick, a letter to the press in 1773, criticizing Drury Lane management, attracted little notice. One more letter from Bickerstaffe, signed with initials, exists in Garrick's collection of private correspondence. It is dated 1777, and is mainly concerned with a complaint that Garrick had joined with the enemies who attacked him in the press. He asks for assistance, and it seems probable that he got it. He appears to have lingered on, in exile, " despised of all orders of people " until at least 1812.

13. O'Brien produced one more play, *Cross Purposes*, for Colman at Covent Garden. The persistent amiability of the couple eventually wore down Lady Susan's family, and employment in England was provided for O'Brien. He became Commissioner for San Domingo and Receiver-General of Taxes for Dorset. They settled at Stinsford House, near Dorchester. O'Brien died in 1815, and Lady Susan in 1827, in her eighty-fourth year.

14. Forster, Boaden, II. 126.

15. Ibid., I. 578, 584–585.

16. Cradock, I. 198; IV. 251.

17. Cumberland (271) and Cradock (I. 229–230) were both present at the St James's coffee-house when Garrick produced his extempore-distich, but their accounts differ in detail. Cradock says that Garrick had arrived late, full-dressed, saying he had been detained at the House of Lords, and would have been later, had not Lord Camden brought him here in his carriage. " Johnson said nothing, but looked a volume." Forster, Goldsmith, 410, quotes Garrick's *Reply* to the *Retaliation* and a second epitaph, published in *The Public Ledger* over Garrick's initials. See also Charles Burney, I. 358–360; Fitzgerald, 440.

18. Forster, Boaden, I. 623.

19. Fanny Burney, I. 150, 221; II. 28, 30–31; Charles Burney, I. 288–290, 344–357; Boswell, I. 671.

20. Letitia Hawkins, 23, 28.

## CHAPTER XIV

### " FAREWELL! REMEMBER ME ! "

1. Forster, Boaden, II. 126, 128–129.

2. *Drury Lane Calendar*, 179; Drury Lane Theatre Royal Pay List, December 1775; Solly collection; *The Kembles*, Fitzgerald, 2 vols., 1871, I. 60–65.

3. *Memoirs of Mrs Hannah More*, William Roberts, 4 vols. 1835, I. 63–64; hereafter cited as Hannah More.

4. Forster, Boaden, II. 133–137, 178; *Drury Lane Calendar*, 193–194.

5. Hannah More, I. 68–70, 73.

6. Forster, Boaden, II. 24–32, 102–106, 108–112, 142.

7. Cradock, IV. 249–250.

8. Garrick appeared as Abel Drugger April 11; Benedick April 16 and May 9; Kitely April 25; Hamlet April 27 and May 30; Sir John Brute April 30; Leon May 2; Archer May 7; Lear May 13 and 21, June 8; Ranger May 23 and June 1; Richard May 27, June 3 and 5; Don Felix May 16 and June 10. He had said his farewell as Lusignan earlier in the season on March 7.

9. Hannah More, I. 73–75, 80–90.

10. Davies, II. 348–349; Murphy, II. 134–139. Fitzgerald, 428–432; *Drury Lane Calendar*, 199; Angelo I. 37; Forster, Boaden, II. 149–153, 158–159.

11. Forster, Boaden, II. 125, 150.

12. Walpole, X. 21, 16. Fanny Burney, II. 156–157; Hannah More, I. 91–98.

13. Davies, II. 358–362; Hannah More, I. 118.

14. Forster, Boaden, II. 219.

15. Fanny Burney, II. 277–279.

16. Hannah More, I. 107, 114, 221, 254–256, 262, 287; Fanny Burney, II. 164, 204. The editor of Hannah More's letters has got the years 1776–1777 inextricably mixed, but the correct order can be settled by checking the More–Garrick correspondence with the Forster, Garrick MS. and in some cases Fanny Burney's early diary.

17. Cradock, IV. 235–237. Cradock says that Halifax told him he " had never met Garrick above once in company " which would put the date before 1767, when invitations from him to dine at Admiralty House appear in Garrick's correspondence. But Admiral Hughes did not strike his flag until 1777. Halifax had a reason for wishing the invitation to the Turtle party to be sent *via* Cradock. At his country house the establishment was presided over by Miss Ray, the unfortunate actress who was shot dead by an infatuated clergyman outside Covent Garden Theatre two years later. Cradock says that Garrick had never met Miss Ray before, and was much pleased by her behaviour and attention to him.

18. Forster, Boaden, II. 237.

19. Letitia Hawkins, 25–27. Hannah More, I. 117.

20. Miss Betty Fürst arrived in England in April 1777, and stayed until August. Fanny Burney and Hannah More must have met her frequently. Neither comments on her. Eva-Maria's Journal is enlightening. By the May after Garrick's death she had resolved to part with a girl who was "ill-humoured", and sent her a letter announcing this. The Mores and Racketts kept her until Wallis could make arrangements for her return to Vienna. Eva-Maria sent her a very handsome gift upon her marriage.

21. Hannah More, I. 111–113; Forster, Boaden, II. 358.

22. Forster, Garrick, II. 716; Colman II. 24–25.

23. Hannah More, I. 121, 140.

24. Forster, Boaden, II. 180–182, 291–294, 303–304, 309–310.

25. *Memoirs of John Bannister*, J. Adolphus, 2 vols., 1839, I. 21–24; Forster, Boaden, II. 357.

26. Forster, Garrick, XVII. 89–92; Forster, Boaden, II. 194, 295; Baker, 50. David Garrick and Nathaniel strongly resembled their uncle in appearance. In 1803, when travelling in Wales, Nathaniel was arrested under the belief that he was Buonaparte, but allowed to return to England by way of Tenby, under a pass from the Mayor of Haverfordwest (Fanny Burney, I. 11 n). The house given to David by his uncle was afterwards known as The Cedars. He died in 1795 after a long illness and Hannah More wrote a laudatory epitaph for the tablet above his grave in Hampton Old Church. Bell's suitor, de Molière, became a lieutenant at the Invalides, and died in 1793, when his widow and three children applied unsuccessfully to the Military Committee for a pension. Forster, Garrick, XVII. 60–72; Little, 70; Hedgcock, 385–390.

27. Baker, 65; Cradock, III. 79.

28. Hannah More, I. 115. *Annals of Winchester College*, T. F. Kirby, 1892, 412–414. *The Gentleman's Magazine*, 1778.

29. Forster, Boaden, II. 318–319, 321, 327, 330.

30. Forster, Garrick, XVII. 107–115.

31. Solly Collection (Letter to the Rev. H. Bate, September 15, 1775); Forster, Boaden, II. 179, 317, 326.

32. The immediate cause of Garrick's death was uraemia. It appears from details of the autopsy, communicated to Murphy (II. 332–336) by Dr Fearon of the Adelphi, that Garrick possessed only one kidney. The condition found was one of pyonephrosis. Davies, II. 366–371; *Recollections of John O'Keefe*, 1826, I. 387.

## EPILOGUE

1. *The Gentleman's Magazine*, 1779, 98. Cumberland, 463; Davies, II. 372, 485–491; Murphy, II. 150, 151; Hannah More, I. 147–149, 156–159. Hannah More gives a long description of Garrick's last days, as recounted to her by Mrs Garrick; it does not agree in detail with Mrs Garrick's diary, and is tinged throughout by Hannah's own emotions.

2. Solly Collection.

3. *The Farington Diary*, ed. J. Greig, 8 vols., 1922, I. 24. The Solly Collection includes a note of payment in December 1770 by Garrick, *via* Messrs. Panchard of Paris, of 1,200 livres to the French East India Company, "Mrs Garrick's annuity ".

4. Murphy (II. 492–502) publishes Garrick's will in full, and states that the first sculptor employed by Wallis for Garrick's monument went bankrupt. Wallis went on to Henry Webber, " who finished the business in an elegant style. The whole, including the former disbursements, amounted to the sum of £1,000 " (II. 151). Murphy prints the inscription by Samuel Jackson Pratt in his Appendix II. XXII.

5. Lennox, I. 294.

6. Hannah More, I. 167, 170–176, 253; IV. 168. The sale of Garrick's library is described in *The Gentleman's Magazine*, 1823, pp. 253, 451. Drayton's *Polyolbion*, given to Garrick by the Duke of Devonshire in 1760,

contained the signature of Killigrew as a previous owner. Boswell, II.
403–404; Horace Walpole, XII. 360; XV. 357.

7. Fitzgerald, 467; Letitia Hawkins, 43 n. The cane presented by Mrs
Garrick to Kean is an exhibit of the Shakespeare Memorial Theatre, and was
later used by Sir Henry Irving in *The Lyons Mail*. A large brass-bound
chest, in which Garrick kept his theatrical wardrobe, was used by the Kemble
family, Macready and Sir Herbert Beerbohm Tree, whose grandson, Mr David
Parsons, now possesses it.

8. Fitzgerald, 433, 467. Obituary of Mrs Garrick by George Beltz, *The
Gentleman's Magazine*, 1822, 468–470.

9. J. T. Smith, 236–242. The Garrick Club possesses an engraved plaque
admitting Mrs Garrick's carriage to the Royal Park, and a copy of the Cruikshank engraving of her in 1820. Hannah More wrote in 1813 that she had
not seen or heard of Mrs Garrick for some years. She wrote on October 21,
1822 (IV. 168), " I was much affected yesterday with a report of my ancient
and valued friend Mrs. Garrick! She was in her hundredth year! I spent
above twenty winters under her roof, and gratefully remember not only their
personal kindness, but my first introduction through them, into a society
remarkable for rank, literature and talents. Whatever was most distinguished in either, was to be found at their table. He was the very soul of
conversation."

10. J. T. Smith, 67; Ripley, 77–80.

# INDEX

# INDEX

E E